DISCRETE MATHEMATICAL STRUCTURES

AUTHOR (S)

Dr. Narendra S Chaudhari
Professor, Dept. of CSE, IIT Indore

Mrs. Sharmila S P
Assistant Professor, Dept. of ISE, SIT, Tumakuru

REVIEWER

Dr. Rama
Professor, Dept. of Mathematics, IIT, Madras

All India Council for Technical Education
Nelson Mandela Marg, Vasant Kunj,
New Delhi, India

ISBN: 978-93-5538-522-2

Book Code: UG431EN

Discrete Mathematical Structures

by Dr. Narendra S. Chaudhari and
Mrs. Sharmila S P

First Edition: 2026

Originally Published by:
All India Council for Technical Education, Ministry of Education, GOI

Exclusively Published & Distributed by:
Khanna Book Publishing Co. (P) Ltd.
4C/4344, Ansari Road, Daryaganj,
New Delhi (INDIA)

Visit us at: **www.khannabooks.com**
Write us at: **contact@khannabooks.com**

To view complete list of books, Please scan the QR Code:

Printed in Bharat.

प्रो. टी. जी. सीताराम
अध्यक्ष
Prof. T. G. Sitharam
Chairman

अखिल भारतीय तकनीकी शिक्षा परिषद्
(भारत सरकार का एक सांविधिक निकाय)
(शिक्षा मंत्रालय, भारत सरकार)
नेल्सन मंडेला मार्ग, वसंत कुंज, नई दिल्ली–110070
दूरभाष : 011–26131498
ई–मेल : chairman@aicte-india.org

ALL INDIA COUNCIL FOR TECHNICAL EDUCATION
(A STATUTORY BODY OF THE GOVT. OF INDIA)
(Ministry of Education, Govt. of India)
Nelson Mandela Marg, Vasant Kunj, New Delhi-110070
Phone : 011-26131498
E-mail : chairman@aicte-india.org

FOREWORD

Engineers are the backbone of any modern society. They are the ones responsible for the marvels as well as the improved quality of life across the world. Engineers have driven humanity towards greater heights in a more evolved and unprecedented manner.

The All India Council for Technical Education (AICTE), have spared no efforts towards the strengthening of the technical education in the country. AICTE is always committed towards promoting quality Technical Education to make India a modern developed nation emphasizing on the overall welfare of mankind.

An array of initiatives has been taken by AICTE in last decade which have been accelerated now by the National Education Policy (NEP) 2020. The implementation of NEP under the visionary leadership of Hon'ble Prime Minister of India envisages the provision for education in regional languages to all, thereby ensuring that every graduate becomes competent enough and is in a position to contribute towards the national growth and development through innovation & entrepreneurship.

One of the spheres where AICTE had been relentlessly working since past couple of years is providing high quality original technical contents at Under Graduate & Diploma level prepared and translated by eminent educators in various Indian languages to its aspirants. For students pursuing 2nd year of their Engineering education, AICTE has identified 87 books, which shall be translated into 12 Indian languages - Hindi, Tamil, Gujarati, Odia, Bengali, Kannada, Urdu, Punjabi, Telugu, Marathi, Assamese & Malayalam. In addition to the English medium, books in different Indian Languages are going to support the students to understand the concepts in their respective mother tongue.

On behalf of AICTE, I express sincere gratitude to all distinguished authors, reviewers and translators from the renowned institutions of high repute for their admirable contribution in a record span of time.

AICTE is confident that these outcomes based original contents shall help aspirants to master the subject with comprehension and greater ease.

(Prof. T. G. Sitharam)

Acknowledgement

The authors are grateful to the authorities of AICTE, particularly Prof. Anil D. Sahasrabudhe, Chairman; Prof. M. P. Poonia, Vice-Chairman; Prof. Rajive Kumar, Member-Secretary and Dr Amit Kumar Srivastava, Director, Faculty Development Cell for their planning to publish the books on **Discrete Mathematical Structures**. We sincerely acknowledge the valuable contributions of the reviewer of the book Prof. R. P. Dahiya, Adjunct Professor, NSUT; former Professor, IIT Delhi, former Director, MNIT and former Vice-Chancellor, CDL University and DCR University of Science and Technology for making it students' friendly and giving a better shape in an artistic manner.

For deciding the level of the delivery suitable to the students within the country at large, the authors were benefitted by the discussions with many senior faculty members in various technical universities in the country. A few of these are: (i) Chattisgarh Swami Vivekanand Technical University, Bhilai, Chattisgarh, (ii) Rajiv Gandhi Technological University (RGPV), Bhopal, Madhya Pradesh, (iii) Jawaharlal Nehru Technological University (JNTU), Hyderabad, (iv) Rajasthan Technical University, Kota, Rajasthan, (v) Anna University, Tirunelveli campus, Tamil Nadu.

This book is an outcome of various suggestions of AICTE members, experts and authors who shared their opinion and thought to further develop the engineering education in our country. Acknowledgements are due to the contributors and different workers in this field whose published books, review articles, papers, photographs, footnotes, references and other valuable information enriched us at the time of writing the book.

Dr. Narendra S Chaudhari

Mrs. Sharmila S P

Preface

The book titled "Discrete Mathematical Structures" is an outcome of our experience of teaching this course at IIT Indore, Institute of Engineering and Technology (IET), DAVV, Indore, and interactions with students, faculty members in engineering colleges in the country. One purpose of writing this book is to distinguish discrete mathematics from the continuous mathematics such as calculus, analytical geometry and abstract mathematics such as topology and functional analysis. The book exposes many important topics for which large body of knowledge is available; however, we have preferred to dwell them at expository level and with rapid pace of coverage

The book is primarily targeted for applications of discrete structures in engineering with special focus on recently growing tremendous applications in Computer Science and Engineering. Our aim is to introduce mathematical rigor that can be appreciated by second year engineering student, and ignite his/her interest in further pursual of the applications of discrete structures for solving engineering problems that he/she would encounter in subsequent years of the study as well as in the professional life. Keeping in mind this purpose, we have preferred to use semi-rigorous treatment of the subject, that can be appreciated by the present generation of engineering students within the country. At some places, to ignite the minds, we have provided supplementary information. We have also included the topics recommended by AICTE, in systematic and orderly manner throughout the book. Efforts have been made to explain the fundamental concepts of the subject in the simplest possible way.

During the process of preparation of the manuscript, we have considered the various standard text books and accordingly we have developed sections like critical questions, solved and supplementary problems etc. While preparing the different sections emphasis has also been laid on definitions, lemmas and theorems and also some formulae for a quick revision of the basic principles. The book covers all types of medium and advanced level problems and these have been presented in logical and systematic manner. The gradations of those problems have been tested over many years of teaching to a wide variety of students.

We sincerely hope that the book will inspire the students to learn and discuss the ideas behind basic principles of discrete structures and will surely contribute to the development of a solid foundation of the subject. We would be thankful to all beneficial comments and suggestions which will contribute to the improvement of the future editions of the book. It gives us immense pleasure to place this book in the hands of the teachers and students. It was indeed a big pleasure to work on different aspects covering in the book.

Dr. Narendra S Chaudhari

Mrs. Sharmila S P

Outcome Based Education

For the implementation of an outcome based education the first requirement is to develop an outcome based curriculum and incorporate an outcome based assessment in the education system. By going through outcome based assessments evaluators will be able to evaluate whether the students have achieved the outlined standard, specific and measurable outcomes. With the proper incorporation of outcome based education there will be a definite commitment to achieve a minimum standard for all learners without giving up at any level. At the end of the programme running with the aid of outcome based education, a student will be able to arrive at the following outcomes:

PO1. Engineering knowledge: Apply the knowledge of mathematics, science, engineering fundamentals, and an engineering specialization to the solution of complex engineering problems.

PO2. Problem analysis: Identify, formulate, review research literature, and analyze complex engineering problems reaching substantiated conclusions using first principles of mathematics, natural sciences, and engineering sciences.

PO3. Design / development of solutions: Design solutions for complex engineering problems and design system components or processes that meet the specified needs with appropriate consideration for the public health and safety, and the cultural, societal, and environmental considerations.

PO4. Conduct investigations of complex problems: Use research-based knowledge and research methods including design of experiments, analysis and interpretation of data, and synthesis of the information to provide valid conclusions.

PO5. Modern tool usage: Create, select, and apply appropriate techniques, resources, and modern engineering and IT tools including prediction and modeling to complex engineering activities with an understanding of the limitations.

PO6. The engineer and society: Apply reasoning informed by the contextual knowledge to assess societal, health, safety, legal and cultural issues and the consequent responsibilities relevant to the professional engineering practice.

PO7. Environment and sustainability: Understand the impact of the professional engineering solutions in societal and environmental contexts, and demonstrate the knowledge of, and need for sustainable development.

PO8. Ethics: Apply ethical principles and commit to professional ethics and responsibilities and norms of the engineering practice.

PO9. Individual and team work: Function effectively as an individual, and as a member or leader in diverse teams, and in multidisciplinary settings.

PO10. Communication: Communicate effectively on complex engineering activities with the engineering community and with society at large, such as, being able to comprehend and write effective reports and design documentation, make effective presentations, and give and receive clear instructions.

PO11. Project management and finance: Demonstrate knowledge and understanding of the engineering and management principles and apply these to one's own work, as a member and leader in a team, to manage projects and in multidisciplinary environments.

PO12. Life-long learning: Recognize the need for, and have the preparation and ability to engage in independent and life-long learning in the broadest context of technological change.

Course Outcomes

Essential CO's: After completion of the course the students will be able to:

CO-1: Understand Examples in Computer Science through Mathematical Terminology and Notation.
CO-2: Construct Direct, Indirect Proofs of basic theorems.
CO-3: Understand the differences between a Mathematical Proof, a Heuristic, and a Conjecture.
CO-4: Learn how to divide a Problem, or a Proof, into smaller cases.
CO-5: Formulate Mathematical Claims and be able to construct Counterexamples.
CO-6: Apply the knowledge of Mathematics to solve real-world problems.

Desirable CO's: After completion of the course the students should attempt to:

CO-7: Identify formal algebraic structures in computer science.
CO-8: Work with probability and statistics in rigorous ways.
CO-9: Use this course topics to design, and rigorously analyse, real world algorithms.

Course Outcomes	**Expected Mapping with Programme Outcomes** *(1- Weak Correlation; 2- Medium correlation; 3- Strong Correlation)*											
	PO-1	PO-2	PO-3	PO-4	PO-5	PO-6	PO-7	PO-8	PO-9	PO-10	PO-11	PO-12
CO-1	3	-	-	-	-	-	-	-	-	-	-	-
CO-2	3	3	-	-	-	-	-	-	-	-	-	-
CO-3	-	-	-	2	-	-	-	-	-	-	-	-
CO-4	-	-	-	-	3	-	-	-	-	-	-	-
CO-5	-	-	3	-	-	-	-	-	-	-	-	-
CO-6	-	2	-	2	-	-	-	-	-	-	-	-
CO-7	2	2	3	-	-	-	-	-	-	-	-	-
CO-8	-	-	-	2	-	-	-	-	-	-	-	-
CO-9	-	3	-	-	-	-	-	-	-	-	-	-

Guidelines for Teachers

To implement Outcome Based Education (OBE) knowledge level and skill set of the students should be enhanced. Teachers should take a major responsibility for the proper implementation of OBE. Some of the responsibilities (not limited to) for the teachers in OBE system may be as follows:

- Within reasonable constraint, they should manoeuvre time to the best advantage of all students.
- They should assess the students only upon certain defined criterion without considering any other potential ineligibility to discriminate them.
- They should try to grow the learning abilities of the students to a certain level before they leave the institute.
- They should try to ensure that all the students are equipped with the quality knowledge as well as competence after they finish their education.
- They should always encourage the students to develop their ultimate performance capabilities.
- They should facilitate and encourage group work and team work to consolidate newer approach.
- They should follow Blooms taxonomy in every part of the assessment.

Bloom's Taxonomy

Level	Teacher should Check	Student should be able to	Possible Mode of Assessment
Create	Students ability to create	Design or Create	Mini project
Evaluate	Students ability to justify	Argue or Defend	Assignment
Analyse	Students ability to distinguish	Differentiate or Distinguish	Project/Lab Methodology
Apply	Students ability to use information	Operate or Demonstrate	Technical Presentation/ Demonstration
Understand	Students ability to explain the ideas	Explain or Classify	Presentation/Seminar
Remember	Students ability to recall (or remember)	Define or Recall	Quiz

Guidelines for Students

Students should take equal responsibility for implementing the OBE. Some of the responsibilities (not limited to) for the students in OBE system are as follows:

- Students should be well aware of each UO before the start of a unit in each and every course.
- Students should be well aware of each CO before the start of the course.
- Students should be well aware of each PO before the start of the programme.
- Students should think critically and reasonably with proper reflection and action.
- Learning of the students should be connected and integrated with practical and real life consequences.
- Students should be well aware of their competency at every level of OBE.

List of Figures

Figure	*Page No.*
UNIT-1	
Figure 2.1. Left Associative Evaluation Tree for (a+b+c)	
Figure 2.2. Right Associative Evaluation Tree for (a+b+c)	
UNIT-2	
Figure 2a First Example Image	
Figure 2b Second Example Image	
Figure 1.1 Venn Diagram for the subset relationship $Z^+ \subseteq Z$	154
Figure 1.2 Venn Diagram for the subset relationship $N \not\subset Z^+$	155
Figure 1.3 Venn Diagram for the subset relationships	155
Figure 1.4 Venn Diagram for set union $A \cup B$	164
Figure 1.5 Venn Diagram for set intersection $A \cap B$	167
Figure 1.6 Venn Diagram for set complement Compl(A)	169
Figure 1.7 Venn Diagram for set difference $A - B$	170
Figure 2.1: Cartesian Product of two sets as two-dimensional array	178
Figure 2.2: Cartesian Product R×R	179
Figure 2.3: Cartesian Product N×N	179
Figure 2.4: Cartesian Product R×N	179
Figure 2.5. Labeled digraph representation of a binary relation.	193
Figure 2.6. Digraph representation of a binary relation.	193
Figure 2.7: Matrix representation of subset relation	196
Figure 2.8: Labeled digraph for the relation $\subseteq$.	196
Figure 2.9: Hasse Diagram representation of labeled digraph for the relation $\subseteq$.	197
Figure 2.10: Hasse Diagram for poset in Example 2.34	198
Figure 2.11: Hasse Diagram for poset in Example 2.36	198
Figure 2.12: Hasse diagram for poset in Example 2.40	200
Figure 2.13: 0-1 Matrix representation for relation in Example 2.44	205
Figure 2.14: Rearranged 0-1 Matrix representation for relation in Example 2.44	206
Figure 3.1: Block diagram representation of a (real valued) function of a real variable	*209*
Figure 3.2: A graph of function sin x.	*210*
Figure 3.3: Block diagram representation of an arbitrary function.	*210*
Figure 3.4: Block diagram representation of a *Rank* function	*211*
Figure 3.5: Block diagram representation of a function $f: A \rightarrow B$.	*212*
Figure 3.6: Arrow diagram for f: $\{a, b, c\} \rightarrow \{1,2,3\}$ in Example 3.2.	*214*
Figure 3.7: Graph of a function f: {a, b, c} □ {1,2,3} in Example 3.2	*215*
Figure 3.8: Arrow diagram for an *assignment rule1*	*216*
Figure 3.9: Arrow diagram for an *assignment rule2*	*216*
Figure 3.10: Arrow diagram for an *assignment rule3*	*216*
Figure 3.11: Arrow diagram for a typical one-to-one function.	*220*
Figure 3.12: Arrow diagram for a typical onto function	*220*
Figure 3.13: Arrow diagram for a typical bijective (one-to-one onto function).	*221*
Figure 3.15 Representation of function composition f o g	*224*
Figure 3.15 Representation of function composition *g* **o** *f*	*225*
Figure 4.1: Bronze monument	*227*
Figure 4.2: George Cantor	*227*
Figure 4.3: Diagrammatic representation to list all integers	*232*
Figure 4.4: Enumeration (one-way infinite list) for all integers	*233*
Figure 4.5: One enumeration scheme for rationals	*235*
Figure 4.6: One enumeration (listing) of all positive rational numbers	*235*
Figure 4.7: Other way of enumeration of points in two-dimensional arrangement	*236*
Figure 4.8: All real numbers (Fractions) in interval from 0 upto 1 enlisted	*238*
Figure 4.9: Diagonalization technique to construct number *b*	*239*
UNIT-5	
Figure 5.1 : Set of students who have taken Spanish, French and Russian	*338*
Figure 5.2: pigeons in 9 pigeonholes	*339*

UNIT-6	
Figure 6.1: Evaluation tree for 29+57	354
Figure 6.2: Evaluation tree for (29+57)+91	354
Figure 6.3: Evaluation tree for 57+91.	355
Figure 6.4: Evaluation tree for 29+(57+91).	355
Figure 6.5: Evaluation tree for 2^3	357
Figure 6.6: Evaluation tree for $(2^3)^5$.	357
Figure 6.7: Evaluation tree for 3^5	358
Figure 6.8: Evaluation tree for (2^{3^5}).	358
Figure 6.9: The function $2^n : \mathbb{N} \rightarrow \mathbb{Z}^+$	361
Figure 6.10: Behaviour of log function	366
Figure 6.11: $S^1 \equiv$ set of complex numbers with absolute value 1	367
Figure 6.12: pictorial illustration of the function $f(r \times e^{i\theta})$	368
Figure 6.13: pictorial illustration of upper triangular matrix.	371
Figure 6.14: Multiplication table for the set $\mathbb{Z}_8 = \{0, 1, 2, \ldots, 7\}$	375

CONTENTS

Foreword	*iii*
Acknowledgement	*v*
Preface	*vii*
Outcome Based Education	*viii*
Course Outcomes	*ix*
Guidelines for Teachers	*x*
Guidelines for Students	*x*
List of figures	*xi*

Unit 1: Logic	***1-139***
Unit specifics	*1*
Rationale	**2**
Pre-requisites	*2*
Unit outcomes	*2*
Part-1 Propositional Logic	***4-30***
1.1 Propositions	***6***
1.2 Compound Propositions	*7*
1.2.1 Negation	*8*
1.2.2 Disjunction	*9*
1.2.3 Conjunction	*10*
1.2.4 Truth table for Compound Proposition	*11*
1.3 Equivalence	*12*
1.4 Tautology, Contradiction and Contingency	*14*
1.5 Laws of Logic	*14*
1.6 Conditional	*16*
1.6.1 Non-commutativity of Conditional and Converse Error	*18*
1.6.2 Conditional in terms of Disjunction	*19*
1.6.3 Contrapositive of Conditional	*20*
1.6.4 Inverse of Conditional and Inverse Error	*21*
1.6.5 Conditional and Common Phrases	*22*
1.6.6 Other Common Phrases: Unless, Else, Otherwise	*25*
1.6.7 Biconditional and Equivalence	*26*
Part-1 Summary	*27*
Exercises	*27*
Part-2 Arguments and Inference Rules	***31-84***
2.1 Two useful rules	***31***
2.1.1 Replacement Rule	*31*
2.1.2 Tautology Generation Rule (TGR)	*33*
2.2 Propositional Expressions and their Evaluation	*34*
2.2.1 Review of Arithmetic Expressions	*34*
2.2.2 Propositional Expressions	*37*
2.3 Arguments and Argument forms	*38*
2.4 Valid and Invalid Argument forms	*39*

2.5 Implication	*46*
2.6 Inference Rules	*50*
2.6.1 Modus Ponens	*51*
2.6.2 Law of Syllogism	*55*
2.6.3 Modus Tollens	*59*
2.6.4 Rule of Conjunction	*63*
2.6.5 Disjunctive Syllogism	*64*
2.6.6 Conjunctive Simplification	*65*
2.6.7 Disjunctive Amplification	*66*
2.6.8 Proof by Contradiction	*68*
2.6.9 Other inference Rules	*69*
2.6.10 Summary Table : Inference Rules	*76*
2.7 Proofs using Inference Rules	*77*
Exercises	*80*
Part-3 Predicate Logic	***85-124***
3.1 Predicates	*85*
3.1.1 Notations	*87*
3.1.2 Instantiation	*88*
3.2 Predicate Logic	*90*
3.2.1 Compound Predicates	*90*
3.2.2 Quantification	*92*
3.2.3 Modeling using one-place Predicates	*96*
3.2.4 Note on "Interpretation" of formula in predicate logic	*100*
3.3 Equivalent Formulae (Predicate Logic):Part I	*101*
3.3.1 Negated Quantifiers	*101*
3.3.2 Interchanging Quantifiers of the same type	*104*
3.4 Modeling using two place predicates	*104*
3.4.1 Modeling Using the Quantifiers of different types	*105*
3.4.2 Expansion of $\forall x\ \exists y\ B(x, y)$	*105*
3.4.3 Expansion of $\exists x\ \forall y\ B(x, y)$	*107*
3.4.4 Interchanging Quantifiers of different types	*108*
3.4.5 Expansion of $\exists y\ \forall x\ B(x, y)$	*109*
3.5 Equivalent Formulae (Predicate Logic):Part II	*113*
3.5.1 Distributing $\exists$ *Quantifier*	*113*
3.5.2 Distributing $\forall$ *Quantifier*	*114*
3.5.3 Equivalences from Equivalent Propositions	*114*
3.6 Inference Rules and Proofs (in Predicate Logic)	*117*
3.6.1 Universal Instantiation	*118*
3.6.2 Universal Generalization	*119*
3.6.3 Existential Instantiation	*120*
3.6.4 Existential Generalization	*120*
Exercises	*122*
Part-4 Semantic Entailment, Proof Systems, Consistency and Completeness	***125-139***
4.1 Pragmatics and Semantics	*125*
4.2 Well Formed Formulae(WFF) in Predicate Logic	*127*
4.3 WFF in Predicate Logic, Semantic Entailment, Proof Systems	*129*
4.4 Soundness, Consistency and Completeness	*130*
Unit Summary	*135*
Exercises	*136*

Laboratory Work	*137*
Know More	*138*
References and Suggested Readings	*138*
Dynamic QR Code for Further Reading	*139*
Unit 2: Sets, Relations and Functions	***141-259***
Unit specifics	*141*
Rationale	*141*
Pre-requisites	*143*
Unit outcomes	*143*
Part-1 Sets	***144-176***
1.1 Set: Definition and Basic Concepts	*144*
1.1.1 Universal Set and Definition of set	*144*
1.1.2 Describing sets as a list	*144*
1.1.3 Equality of sets	*147*
1.1.4 Describing sets by properties (one-place predicates)	*149*
1.1.5 Some well-known sets	*152*
1.2 Subset Relationship – A special Operation on sets	*153*
1.2.1 Subset as a relationship amongst two sets	*153*
1.2.2 Venn Diagram for subset relation	*154*
1.2.3 Membership Table	*156*
1.2.4 Power Set	*158*
1.2.5 Establishing Set Equality Using Subset Method	*160*
1.3 Set Operations – Union, Intersection, Complement and Set Difference	*162*
1.3.1 Union of two sets	*163*
1.3.2 Intersection of two sets	*166*
1.3.3 Complement of a set	*168*
1.3.4 Set Difference	*169*
1.4 Counting elements in Union of Finite Sets	*170*
1.5 Set Equivalences and their Proofs	*174*
Part-2 Binary Relations	***177-208***
2.1 Cartesian Product of Sets	*177*
2.2 Binary Relations	*180*
2.3 Basic Properties of Binary Relations	*182*
2.3.1 Reflexivity	*182*
2.3.2 Symmetry	*183*
2.3.3 Antisymmetry	*185*
2.3.4 Transitivity	*188*
2.4 Representation of Binary Relations	*191*
2.4.1 Binary relation as a two-place predicate	*191*
2.4.2 Binary Relation as a set	*191*
2.4.3 Binary Relation as a 0-1 Matrix	*192*
2.4.2 Binary Relation as a directed Graph	*192*
2.5 Partial Orderings	*194*
2.5.1 Definition of Partial Order	*194*
2.5.2 Hasse Diagrams	*195*
2.5.3 Minimal and Least Elements	*197*
2.5.4 Maximal and Greatest Elements	*199*
2.5.5 Poset, Linearly ordered set and Well ordered set	*200*

2.6 Equivalences	201
2.6.1 Definition of Equivalence Relation	201
2.6.2 Definition of Partition of a set	204
2.6.3 Theorems relating Equivalences and Partitions	204
Part-3 Functions	**209-225**
3.1 Functions	209
3.1.1 Notion of Abstract Function	210
3.2 Image and Range	213
3.3 Arrow Diagram, Pre-Image set	213
3.4 Graph Representation of Function	215
3.5 Examples of Non-Functions	215
3.6 Some Useful Functions	217
3.7 Bijective Functions	219
3.7.1 One-to-one Functions: Injections	219
3.7.2 Onto Functions: Surjections	220
3.8 Inverse Functions	221
3.9 Composite Functions	223
Part-4 Uncountability and Limits to Counting	**227-259**
4.1 Countable and Uncountable Sets	227
4.2 Cantor's Diagonal Argument	237
4.3 Power set Theorem	240
4.4 Limits of Computing	242
Unit Summary	244
Exercises	247
Laboratory Work	256
References and Suggested Readings	258
Dynamic QR Code for Further Reading	259
Unit 3: Proof Strategies	**261-303**
Unit specifics	261
Rationale	261
Pre-requisites	262
Unit outcomes	262
3.1 Introduction to Proof Methods and Strategies	263
3.2 Terminology	268
3.3 Direct Proof (Forward Proof)	270
3.4 Recasting the statements as conditions for Proof	271
3.5 Indirect Proof (Contrapositive Proof)	272
3.6 Proof by Contradiction	273
3.7 Numbers: Some Definitions	278
3.8 Proof by Necessity and Sufficiency	291
3.8.1 Necessity	291
3.8.2 Sufficiency	292
3.8.3 Necessity and Sufficiency	292
3.8.4 Examples	292
3.9 Disproof by a Counter Example	293
3.10 Proof by Exhaustive Cases	296
3.11 More Terminology	297

3.12 Principle of Mathematical Induction	*298*
Unit summary	*300*
Exercises	*301*
Supplementary Reading and Additional Material	*302*
Know more	*302*
References and suggested readings	*302*
Dynamic QR Code for Further Reading	*303*
Unit 4: Modular Arithmetic	***305-329***
Unit specifics	*305*
Rationale	*305*
Pre-requisites	*306*
Unit outcomes	*306*
4.1 Modular Arithmetic	*307*
4.1.1 Properties of Congruences	*308*
4.1.2 Modular Arithmetic Operations	*308*
4.1.3 Properties of Modular Arithmetic	*310*
4.2 Divisibility	*312*
4.2.1 Division Algorithm	*312*
4.2.2 Primes	*313*
4.2.3 Fundamental Theorem of Arithmetic	*315*
4.2.4 Congruence Relation	*315*
4.2.5 Theorem on Congruences	*316*
4.2.6 Congruences of Sums and Products	*316*
4.2.7 Arithmetic modulo m	*316*
4.3 Coprimality and Euler's Totient Function	*317*
4.3.1 Properties of Euler's Totient Function	*318*
4.3.2 Application in Euler's Theorem	*319*
4.4 GCD and Extended Euclidean Algorithm	*321*
4.4.1 GCD	*321*
4.4.2 Applications of GCD	*322*
4.4.3 Extended Euclidean Algorithm	*323*
4.4.4 Solving Linear Diophantine Equations	*323*
4.5 Chinese Remainder Theorem	*325*
Unit summary	*328*
Exercises	*328*
References and suggested readings	*329*
Dynamic QR Code for Further Reading	*329*
Unit 5: Combinatorics	***331-349***
Unit specifics	*331*
Rationale	*331*
Pre-requisites	*332*
Unit outcomes	*332*
5.1 Permutations	*333*
5.2 Combinations	*334*
5.3 Inclusion Exclusion Principle	*336*
5.4 Pigeon hole Principle	*339*
5.5 Generating Functions	*341*
5.6 Recurrence Relation	*344*

Unit summary	*346*
Exercises	*347*
Practicals	*348*
Know more	*348*
References and suggested readings	*348*
Dynamic QR Code for Further Reading	*349*
Unit 6: Some Algebraic Structures	*351-422*
Unit specifics	*351*
Rationale	*351*
Pre-requisites	*352*
Unit outcomes	*352*
6.1 Semigroup	*353*
6.2 Homomorphism	*359*
6.3 Isomorphism	*363*
6.4 Group	*369*
6.5 Abelian Group	*374*
6.6 Permutation Group and Cayley Theorem	*376*
6.6.1. Cauchy notation for representing Permutation	*379*
6.6.2 Cycle notation for representing Permutation	*379*
6.6.3 Reading the symbol of permutation	*381*
6.7 Subgroup	*390*
6.8 Isomorphic Structures	*392*
6.8.1 Revisit to Homomorphic Structures	*392*
6.8.2 Definition of Isomorphic Structures	*392*
6.9 Sketch of the Proof of Cayley's Theorem	*393*
6.10 Cosets and Normal Subgroups	*395*
6.11 Lagrange's Theorem	*398*
6.12 Corollaries (and Consequences) of Lagrange's Theorem	*400*
6.13 Euler Theorem	*402*
6.14 Fermat's Little Theorem	*407*
6.15 Rings, Fields and Finite Fields	*412*
Unit summary	*416*
Exercises	*418*
Know more	*420*
References and suggested readings	*421*
Dynamic QR Code for Further Reading	*422*
Unit 7: Graphs	***423-475***
Unit specifics	*423*
Rationale	*423*
Pre-requisites	*424*
Unit outcomes	*424*
7.1 Fundamentals of Graphs	*425*
7.1.1 What is a Graph?	*425*
7.1.2 Graph Terminology	*425*
7.2 Connected Components	*432*
7.2.1 One Connected Component	*433*
7.2.2 More than One Connected Component	*433*
7.3 Path, Cycle and Trees	*434*

7.3.1 Walk	*434*
7.3.2 Trail	*435*
7.3.3 Circuit	*435*
7.3.4 Path	*436*
7.3.5 Cycle	*436*
7.3.6 Types of graphs	*437*
7.3.7 Trees	*447*
7.4 Euler and Hamilton Paths	*449*
7.4.1 Euler Paths	*449*
7.4.2 Euler Circuit Theorem	*450*
7.4.3 Hamilton Path	*451*
7.4.4 Hamilton Circuit	*451*
7.4.5 Dirac's Theorem	*452*
7.4.6 Ore's Theorem	*452*
7.5 Graph Coloring	*453*
7.5.1 Vertex Coloring	*454*
7.5.2 Region Coloring	*454*
7.5.3 Edge Coloring	*454*
7.5.4 Chromatic Number	*455*
7.6 Graph Planarity	*456*
7.7 Matching	*461*
7.7.1 Maximal Matching	*463*
7.7.2 Maximum Matching	*463*
7.7.3 Perfect Matching	*464*
7.7.4 Bipartite Matching	*467*
Unit Summary	*467*
Exercises	*467*
Know more	*474*
References and suggested readings	*475*
Dynamic QR Code for Further Reading	*475*
Unit 8: Discrete Probability	*477-503*
Unit specifics	*477*
Rationale	*477*
Pre-requisites	*478*
Unit outcomes	*478*
8.1 Discrete Sample Space	*479*
8.1.1 Terminology	*479*
8.1.2 Set operations on Events	*480*
8.1.3 Types of Events	*482*
8.1.4 Rules of Probability	*482*
8.1.5 Conditional Probability	*482*
8.2 Random Variables and Probability Distribution	*484*
8.2.1 PMF and PDF	*487*
8.3 Mean of a Random Variable	*489*
8.4 Variance of a Random Variable	*491*
8.5 Bernoulli Trials	*492*
8.6 Conditional Probability and Dependence	*494*
Unit Summary	*497*
Exercises	*500*
Know more	*500*

References and suggested readings	*502*
Dynamic QR Code for Further Reading	*503*
CO-PO Attainment Table	504
INDEX	505-508

1 Logic (Propositional Logic, Predicate Logic)

UNIT SPECIFICS

We cover the following subtopics in this module:

PART-1: Propositional Logic

- *Representation of logic with propositions;*
- *Compound propositions*
- *Equivalence Laws in Propositional logic*
- *Tautology, Contradiction and Contingency*

Part-2: Arguments and Inference Rules in Propositional Logic

- *Propositional Expressions and their evaluation*
- *Arguments and Argument Forms: Validity and Invalidity*
- *Inference rules*
- *Proofs using Inference rules in Propositional Logic*

Part-3: Predicate Logic

- *Predicate: Notations and instantiation*
- *Quantification*
- *Equivalent Formulae- Modelling*
- *Inference rules in Predicate Logic*
- *Proofs using Inference rules in Predicate Logic*

Part-4: Semantic Entailment, Proof Systems, Consistency, Completeness

- *Pragmatics and Semantics*
- *Well Formed Formula (WFF) in Predicate Logic*
- *Knowledge Base (KB) and Semantic Entailment*
- *Proof Systems*
- *Soundness, Consistency and Completeness*

Introduction: Logic

Today's developments in computer science heavily rely on logic. It is desired to have an explicit training on logic for a better/ matured understanding of both software as well as hardware. Further. logic and its familiarity is a pre-requisite for studying core areas of computer science such as Databases, Compilers, Algorithms and Complexity, Computing models like various automata,

Cryptography and security, and so on. Propositional Logic is used in Artificial Intelligence for planning, problem solving, intelligent control and decision making. Predicate logic is more powerful than propositional logic and extensively used in Databases, Artificial Intelligence etc.

RATIONALE

Why do you learn Propositional and Predicate Logic?

Propositional logic deals with a collection of declarative statements which have a true or false truth value, Predicate logic is an expression consisting of variables with a specified domain. It consists of objects, properties of objects, the relations amongst the objects, and functions between the objects. Understanding the concepts of basic logic would help you to appreciate formal treatment as needed to prove the correctness of computer programs and establish proper functioning of computing systems. Logic also studies how information can be captured in sentences, how one statement is related to the other, and how we draw logical conclusions from such body of knowledge.

Why is study of logic important to computer science?

Logic is the science of reasoning. Logics are used to design the digital circuits; knowledge representation is based on logical formalisms. It has many practical applications in computer science like design of computing machines, artificial intelligence, definition of data structures for programming languages etc. Propositional Logic is concerned with statements to which the truth values, "true" and "false", can be assigned. Though it has certain limitations like, we cannot use propositional logic to establish the truth of a proposition that isn't given as a premise, or which can't be inferred by the laws of inference. In particular, we cannot use propositional logic to reason about propositions that obey laws (such as arithmetic laws) beyond the logical inference system.

PRE-REQUISITES

Mathematics at school level (till Class X)

UNIT OUTCOMES

List of outcomes of this unit is as follows:

U1-O1: Understand propositions and compound propositions

U1-O2: Apply Laws of propositions and simplify expressions

U1-O3: Prove tautology, contradiction and contingency

U1-O4: Apply inference rules to evaluate any given propositional expressions

U1-O5: Apply quantification to generate equivalent formulae

U1-O6: Apply inference rules and proofs for predicate logic

Unit-1 Outcomes	EXPECTED MAPPING WITH COURSE OUTCOMES (1- Weak Correlation; 2- Medium correlation; 3- Strong Correlation)								
	CO-1	CO-2	CO-3	CO-4	CO-5	CO-6	CO-7	CO-8	CO-9
U1-O1	3	-	-	2	1	1	-	-	-
U1-O2	2	-	2	-	-	2	-	-	-
U1-O3	1	2	3	-	1	-	-	-	-
U1-O4	-	-	2	-	-	-	-	-	-
U1-O5	3	-	-	2	1	3	-	-	1
U1-O6	-	-	2	-	-	2	-	-	2

PART - 1

Propositional Logic

Amit has just finished the morning session of lectures in computer science, and it is the time for lunch. In canteen, he meets a new friend Chetana. Amit asks Chetana whether she is from school of Biological Sciences. Chetana does not give a straight answer, but she says:

> "If I am a student in School of Biological Sciences, I am not a student in School of Computer Science. I am student in School of Computer Science, or I am not a student in School of Biological Sciences."

Did Chetana give answer to Amit's question? Can Amit conclude that Chetana is a student in the School of Biological Sciences?

To give an "acceptable" justification of the conclusion in such arguments, Amit needs to *analyze* Chetana's statements further. Is there a systematic method to perform this analysis? The analysis involves throwing away irrelevant details, and concentrating on the bare minimum essential "contents" of the argument needed to establish the "justification". This process is also called as an *abstraction*. The verb *abstract* (from which the abstraction is derived) does not mean that it is difficult, or unrelated to the objects or things we consider. Rather, it means the discussion on which we wish to concentrate is not tied to one particular situation; here, it is one particular argument – consisting of one particular set of statement(s) – like the one we have given in the opening of this part of the module on logic. Thus, the process of abstraction empowers us to guarantee that the results of our study are applicable to a variety of different arguments.

The skills picked up by Amit for doing such an analysis has surprisingly many applications for writing correct programs, software testing, as well as for design of "awesome" computer systems and robots to perform "all pervasive" tasks, possessing *thinking* capabilities. As an engineer, in Amit's professional life, Amit would be expected to solve the practical problems for which solutions do not yet exist. Amit's solution would necessarily involve modelling, designing the solution schemes to "make" specific technologies (like software testing systems, mobile communications, signal processing, neural networks, etc.) work for the problem. However, Amit's skills for proving that: (i) his solution would work correctly, and (ii) his solution is optimal in the sense that he has been able to "use minimal resources" to solve the problem, is what would distinguish him as a professional engineer.

We normally attribute the notion of abstraction to Greek philosophers. However, we can trace the use of abstraction to as early as the dawn of human civilization. When people from different places traded their goods, they needed some common basis for the exchange of their goods. They abstracted the common property of diverse goods in terms of the *value* of goods. They used this *value* of the goods (say cattle, metal, food, etc.) in their exchange of goods. India has long history of economic development much earlier, about two-and-half millennia B.C., and the concept of *value* of the goods was well-understood. Vedic texts have references to *nishika*, *suvarna*, *shatamana*, and *pada*. Harappans (civilization matured around 2600 B.C.) used metals like silver of fixed weight for trade and mercantile activities. In eighth century B.C., Chinese represented this value of goods in terms of the governmental inscriptions; the next stage of abstraction was to replace it with paper money, and Chinese government issued paper money in the twelfth century. Europe issued paper money at least four centuries later.

Humans have probably recognized the notion of arguments very early, even in the Stone Age. Historically, our understanding of the world has made advancements whenever our *common sense* is challenged. To challenge common sense, we need the process of concentrating on important aspects, and throwing away irrelevant details; in other words, we need abstraction. Further, we need to use the correct patterns of reasoning. We attribute the discovery of the acceptable (or "correct") patterns of reasoning is mainly attributed to Greek philosopher Aristotle (around 350 B.C.). As the legend goes, Aristotle's disciple travelled with Alexander to India and took back the concept of Logic. All Western Logic is 2-state based (True or False) but Ancient Indian Logic was more nuanced. Rigveda (dated about six to eight millennia back) mentions about *nasadiya sutra*s, (there is no '*sat* – existence of it' and no '*asat* – non existence of it', there is also *transcendental* existence, *etc.*) where logic originates (Reference: "*Was Ancient India's Logic System more advanced?*" lecture on youtube by Prof Subhash Kak - link: https://www.youtube.com/watch?v=dGuhdstugMs). Aristotle adopted the Indian system, and we know it today in the form as the western world acknowledges it. Aristotle once said that common sense is neither common nor sense.

The importance of human ability to prove that the reasoning is *correct* has now given rise to full-fledged subject of Logics. Most commonly used logics as applied in today's computer science are: (i) Propositional logic, and, (ii) Predicate logic, which we shall introduce in this course. Besides these logics, other logics that find applications in computer science are: fuzzy logic (*e.g*, Fuzzy controllers in washing machines), modal logic, non-monotonic logic (Artificial Intelligence), temporal logic (Databases – for ensuring logical consistency and correctness of transactions using timestamps), *etc*. In addition to these logics, theoreticians have also developed a variety of other logics based on more abstract concepts in topology and functional analysis.

We shall introduce propositional logic in this module. It is also known as Boolean Logic. Historically, we note that John Boole was an English shoe-maker in 18th-century. John never went to any school, but he loved to think. He read Greek classics during his spare-time, and to do this he studied Greek language on his own. John's son George (1815-1864) was a prodigy. George learned math on his own.

In 1854, he published his famous contribution *Investigation in the Laws of Thought on which are founded the Mathematical Theories on Logic and Probabilities* (London, 1854). This famous work explores the idea of substituting symbols for sentences, and studies the resulting forms. We call it as *Boolean logic*: logic of today's computers.

George Boole

George married to Mary Everest in 1855. At the age of 49, George died due to pneumonia. George is survived by his 32-year-old wife, Mary, and five daughters. Mary had no income and had to look after her five daughters. Mary had to sell George's gold medal to buy harmonium for her daughters. Mary Boole's grandson Sir Geoffrey Ingram Taylor (G.I. Taylor), a Cambridge mathematician, was given the very same gold medal that his grandmother had sold – for his fine work about fundamentals in mathematics, which forms the basis of today's diverse engineering topics like fluid flow, turbulence, applied mechanics, the action of micro-organisms, or stability theory.

1.1 Propositions

Definition 1.1: *Proposition*: A proposition is a declarative statement, which is either true or false but not both.

Example 1.1: Some examples of the propositions are:

(i) Anuhya is a student in School of Biological Sciences.
(ii) Suvarna is a student in School of Computer Science.
(iii) Tomorrow is Anand's birthday.

(iv) $2+3 = 4$.
(v) $4+5 < 25$.

Note that the proposition "2+3 =4" is a proposition (it would be false, *i.e.*, it would have false truth value, but that does not disqualify it to be a proposition).

□

A few examples of statements which are not propositions are given below.

Example 1.2: Some examples of the statements that are not propositions are:

(i) $x+3 = 4$.
(ii) $x + y < 25$.
(iii) This statement is false.

For the Example 1.2 (i), "x" refers to some element; unless it is assigned a 'value', we cannot determine whether "$x+3 = 4$" is true or false. You may say that the Example 1.2 (iii) looks fine to be a proposition. However, consider the following two cases:

Case (i): Let us assume that "This statement is false" is true. This forces the statement's truth-value to be false. So, we cannot assign the truth-value "true" to it.

As (the only) other alternative,

Case (ii): Let us assume that "This statement is false" is false. This forces the statement's truth-value to be true. So, we cannot assign the truth-value "false" to it.

Thus, we cannot assign any of the truth-values "true" or "false" to this statement. So, the statement in Example 1.2 (iii) is not a proposition.

□

In the propositional logic, the only property of interest to us about the statement is its truth-valuc: "truc" or "false". Common conventions for representing these truth-values are: "T", "F", or even as "1", "0" respectively. Further, since we are not interested in other details about the proposition except the fact that it is either "T", or "F", in our study of logic, there is no need to keep repeating the complete proposition like "Chetana is a student in School of Biological Sciences.". Hence, we represent it by some (short) symbol, say p. Here, p is a propositional variable, a statement variable or a Boolean variable, denoting the statement "Chetana is a student in School of Biological Sciences". By saying that p is a Boolean variable, we emphasize the aspect that the variable p can have only values "T", "F" (or 0, 1). The propositions are conventionally denoted by symbols p, q, r, etc.

1.2 Compound Propositions

Let us recall the statement Chetana has made: "Chetana is a student in School of Computer Science or Chetana is not a student in School of Biological Sciences."

Within Chetana's statement, we identify two propositions:

p: Chetana is a student of School of Computer Science.

q: Chetana is not a student of School of Biological Sciences.

Each of the above propositions (p, q) can have truth-values {T, F}. Using these propositions, we obtain the representation of the proposition "Chetana is a student in School of Computer Science or Chetana is not a student in School of Biological Sciences." as: p OR q. Here OR is an operator similar to the operation of addition on numbers; however, here we do not consider numbers, but propositions. This operator operates on two propositions p, q to give new proposition, say p OR q, which we may denote it by r. The proposition r is called as *compound proposition*, because has been expressed further in terms of two propositions p, q. In modelling the statements, the propositions (like p, q) which are not broken down further in terms or other propositions are called as atomic propositions, which the proposition r is compound proposition as would be represented as p OR q, where p, q are atomic propositions. In propositional logic, we identify a few operations that are frequently needed for modelling the statements. They are: a unary operation NOT, and two binary operations OR, and AND. The meaning of these operations is neatly expressed by the truth values the resulting compound statement has when the constituent propositions have different combinations of truth values. In other words, it is truth table which defines the meaning of these operators.

1.2.1 Negation

If p is a statement variable, the negation of p is denoted by $\sim p$, (the symbol "~" literally reads as "tilde") read as "**not** p", and is translated as "It is not the case that p." The negation of p has opposite truth-values from p. Thus, if p is false, $\sim p$ is true; if if p is true, $\sim p$ is false. We summarize this in the form of truth table below.

Truth Table for $\sim p$
(with Truth values F, T)

p	$\sim p$
F	T
T	F

Truth Table for $\sim p$
(with Truth values 0, 1)

p	$\sim p$
0	1
1	0

Example 1.3: Let p be the atomic proposition, say, "It rains.". In terms of this proposition, we model the following statements as a compound proposition $\sim p$:

(i) It is not the case that it rains.

(ii) It does not rain.

(iii) The sky is clear.

□

We note that, to be a negation, the negated proposition must be false in all possible circumstances under which the first (atomic) proposition is true and vice versa.

Other frequently used symbols used for negation are: $\neg p$, or $\overline{p}$.

1.2.2 Disjunction

If p and q are statement variables, the disjunction of p and q, denoted by $p \vee q$, (the symbol "$\vee$" literally reads as "wedge", and can conveniently be remembered as modification of union $\cup$ symbol) read as "p **or** q ", and is translated as "p or q." We summarize truth-values for this disjunction operator in the form of truth table below.

Truth Table for $p \vee q$
(with Truth values F, T)

p	q	$p \vee q$
F	F	F
F	T	T
T	F	T
T	T	T

Truth Table for $p \vee q$
(with Truth values 0, 1)

P	q	$p \vee q$
0	0	0
0	1	1
1	0	1
1	1	1

Example 1.4: Model the following statement as a compound proposition:

(i) You help me in my homework or I play football.

(ii) You help me in my homework, otherwise I play football.

(iii) Chetana is a student in School of Computer Science or Chetana is not a student in School of Biological Sciences.

Solution: For (i) and (ii), we identify two atomic propositions:

p: You help me in my homework, and,

q: I play football.

In terms of these, we model both the propositions (i) and (ii) as: $p \vee q$.
For (iii), we identify the following two atomic propositions:

r : Chetana is a student in School of Computer Science, and,

s : Chetana is a student in School of Biological Sciences.

Using the above atomic propositions, the given proposition is modeled as $r \vee \sim s$.

□

Note: In formula "$r \vee \sim s$", we assume that the negation is applied first. We may explicitly represent this "order of evaluation" by fully bracketing this expression as : $(r \vee (\sim s))$. In technical terms, we express this as: "$\sim$ takes precedence over the operator $\vee$". Other common symbols used for disjunction are: $p + q$, p **or** q.

1.2.3 Conjunction

If p and q are statement variables, the conjunction of p and q, denoted by $p \wedge q$, (symbol "$\wedge$" can conveniently be remembered as modification of intersection $\cap$ symbol) read as "p **and** q ", and is translated as "p and q." We summarize truth-values for this disjunction operator in the form of truth table below.

Truth Table for $p \wedge q$ (with Truth values F, T)

p	q	$p \wedge q$
F	F	F
F	T	F
T	F	F
T	T	T

Truth Table for $p \wedge q$ (with Truth values 0, 1)

p	q	$p \wedge q$
0	0	0
0	1	0
1	0	0
1	1	1

Other frequently used symbols used for conjunction are: $p.q$, p **and** q, or just pq (here, the operator is omitted, but the context makes it clear that the conjunction operator is present in two adjacent propositions.)

Example 1.5: Model the following statements as a compound proposition:

(i) It rains and your sister has not loaned you the umbrella.

(ii) Although it rains, your sister has not loaned you the umbrella.

(iii) It rains but your sister has not loaned you the umbrella.
(iv) It rains whereas your sister has not loaned you the umbrella.

Solution: We identify two atomic propositions:

p: It rains, and,

q: Your sister has not loaned you an umbrella.

All the above statements represent the meaning that they are true only when each constituent atomic proposition is true. Under this assumption, all the above four statements are represented by the compound formula: $p \wedge q$.

□

1.2.4 Truth Table for Compound Propositions

In our previous discussion, negation is the (only) operator that is not a connective; it affects single statements only, and does not join statements into compounds. The conjunction and disjunction are commonly used connectives to obtain the compound statements. In general, a formula in propositional logic (which represents a compound proposition, and is also called as a Boolean formula), like the familiar arithmetic expression, may contain many occurrences of the constituent operations ~, ∨, ∧. We construct the truth-table by progressively appending the columns for the sub-expressions needed in expression evaluation process to the right in the truth table. Note that, to evaluate the operator, we need the truth values of its operand(s). This requires us to pre-determine the order of operators when the expression is evaluated. For the sake of simplicity, we rely on the analogy with the evaluation of familiar arithmetic expressions for determining this order. In case of ambiguity, the order of application of the operators can be represented by fully bracketing the expression; the other equivalent way is to express it in terms of *evaluation tree*. Note that, we need to appreciate hierarchical structure that we call it as *tree* (to be more precise, rooted *tree*) by formally defining it. In such a definition, we need to formally identify and specify the operations that we need to perform on such a structure. We shall study such "tree" structure in Module 6: Graphs.

Example 1.6: Construct a truth table for the compound proposition $(\sim p \vee \sim q) \wedge r$.

Solution: We first identify the atomic propositions; they are p, q, r. These atomic propositions are assigned as the leftmost (first) three columns in the truth table. Assign the truth values to these columns, with the rightmost column having fastest change of truth values, and subsequent left columns having progressively slower change of truth values. Next, identify the order in which the sub-expressions in this compound expression are evaluated. For this expression, we identify this order as (i) $\sim p$, (ii) $\sim q$, (iii) $(\sim p \vee \sim q)$, and finally, (iv) $(\sim p \vee \sim q) \wedge r$. We need one column of truth table for each of these sub-expressions; they are progressively added as the right columns. For filling the truth values in the recently added column, if it involves application of binary operator (to sub-expressions whose truth values are evaluated earlier), we need to refer to earlier two columns (for unary operator, we need to refer to only one column). The resulting truth table is given below.

Truth Table for the formula $(\sim p \vee \sim q) \wedge r$

p	q	r	$\sim p$	$\sim q$	$\sim p \vee \sim q$	$(\sim p \vee \sim q) \wedge r$
F	F	F	T	T	T	F
F	F	T	T	T	T	T
F	T	F	T	F	T	F
F	T	T	T	F	T	T
T	F	F	F	T	T	F
T	F	T	F	T	T	T
T	T	F	F	F	F	F
T	T	T	F	F	F	F

□

In modeling the statements of Chetana, we need the connective to represent "*if..then..*". We call this connective as *conditional*. The *conditional* can be expressed as an *equivalent* compound proposition involving the negation and disjunction; we postpone the discussion about this connective. However, this necessitates the notion of *equivalence* of the compound formulae in propositional logic.

1.3 EQUIVALENCE

Definition 1.2: *Equivalent Propositions*: Two compound propositions involving the same set of atomic propositions are (logically) equivalent they have identical truth values for every set of truth values of the constituent atomic propositions.

By definition, the equivalent propositions have, as their constituents, the same set of atomic propositions. Since the initial columns representing the atomic propositions in their truth tables are same for both, we can combine their truth tables. In such a combined truth table, the column below the (compound) proposition represents its *semantics* (meaning). Thus, in terms of truth table, we say that two propositions are logically equivalent if and only if they have the same column of truth values in the truth table.

Example 1.7: Using the truth table method, prove that the compound propositions (i) $(\sim p \vee \sim q)$, and (ii) $\sim(p \wedge q)$, are (logically) equivalent.

Solution: Within the truth table, we compare the columns for the compound propositions (i) and (ii), and check whether they are identical. To do this, we introduce the last column labeled as (i) ≡ (ii), with value in its row as "T" if the truth values of (i) and (ii) (in the corresponding row) are same, and "F" if the truth values of (i) and (ii) (in the corresponding row) are different.

Truth Table for: (i) $(\sim p \vee \sim q)$, and (ii) $\sim(p \wedge q)$.

				(i)		(ii)	*Equivalence*
p	q	$\sim p$	$\sim q$	$\sim p \vee \sim q$	$(p \wedge q)$	$\sim(p \wedge q)$	(i) ≡ (ii)
F	F	T	T	T	F	T	T
F	T	T	F	T	F	T	T
T	F	F	T	T	F	T	T
T	T	F	F	F	T	F	T

□

In the solution of Example 1.7, we made use of the binary logical operator "≡". We call this operator as "(logical) equivalence" operator; its formal definition is given in the following truth table.

Truth Table for $p \equiv q$
(with Truth values F, T)

p	q	$p \equiv q$

Truth Table for $p \equiv q$
(with Truth values 0, 1)

p	q	$p \equiv q$

F	F	T
F	T	F
T	F	F
T	T	T

0	0	1
0	1	0
1	0	0
1	1	1

1.4 TAUTOLOGY, CONTRADICTION, AND CONTINGENCY

After defining ≡ as a logical operator, we note that the expression (i) ≡ (ii) in the solution of Example 1.7 is actually a compound proposition $(\sim p\vee\sim q)\equiv\sim(p\wedge q)$. In the solution process of Example 1.7, we emphasized on checking that the column denoting this expression $(\sim p\vee\sim q)\equiv\sim(p\wedge q)$ contains all its entries as T's in the truth table. In logic, such compound propositions with their column consisting of all T's are called as *Tautologies*. Their negation would have its column in the truth table with all entries as F's, and they are called as *Contradictions*. While tautologies and contradictions have found important applications in proving whether our arguments are logically sound, we note that there are expressions like the compound proposition $(\sim p\vee\sim q)\wedge r$ of Example 1.6, which are neither tautologies nor contradictions. Such compound propositions are called as *Contingencies*, or contingent propositions. For contingent propositions, there exists some assignment of the truth values of the atomic propositions for which it is true.

The assignment of truth values to atomic propositions is also called as an *interpretation*. For contingencies, there exists some assignment of truth values to the atomic propositions (i.e., there exists some interpretation) for which the proposition evaluates to the truth value *false*; also there exists some (other) assignment of truth values to the atomic propositions (i.e., there exists some (other) interpretation) for which the proposition evaluates to the truth value *true*.

In other words, contingencies are true for some interpretations while contingencies are false for some (other) interpretations. Tautologies are true for all interpretations. Contradictions are false for all interpretations.

1.5 LAWS OF LOGIC

In arguments, we should avoid contradictions, and should make use of tautologies. Unfortunately, there are too many (in fact, infinitely many) tautologies and the same number of contradictions (the negation of a tautology is a contradiction). The truth table method for verifying whether a given formula is a tautology has very limited utility; it does not give us any insight into our approach of *discovering* a correct pattern or reasoning for solving a problem. This necessitates us to further study a set of basic tautologies from which we can *generate* all tautologies. Our approach here is to gain some insight into commonly used reasoning, as formulated by George Boole. However, we note that economy (minimality) of concepts for generating infinitely many possible tautologies requires us to know the formal Axiom systems; some of these Axiom systems are Frege-Lukasiewicz Axiom System, Hilbert-Ackermann Axiom System, etc. Some aspects such a study are covered in the later part of standard computer science curricula in courses related to Formal Languages, Automata and Computability; these topics are beyond the scope of our present discussion. This study has deep consequences for developing niche technologies of reasoning in artificial intelligence, programming paradigms in logic programming, knowledge extraction in web services, design of software and hardware testing schemes, etc.

George Boole gave us the collection of some "useful" tautologies, which we use in our common reasoning; this collection helps us to logically infer the infinitely many tautologies. We give this set of tautologies as "Laws of Logic" in the table below. Each of these laws of logic can be established using the truth table method illustrated in Example 1.7, and this left as an exercise.

Laws of Logic

Double Negation	$\sim(\sim p) \equiv p$	Commutative Laws	$p \wedge q \equiv q \wedge p$ $p \vee q \equiv q \vee p$
De Morgan's Laws	$\sim(p \wedge q) \equiv \sim p \vee \sim q$ $\sim(p \vee q) \equiv \sim p \wedge \sim q$	Associative Laws	$(p \wedge q) \wedge r \equiv p \wedge (q \wedge r)$ $(p \vee q) \vee r \equiv p \vee (q \vee r)$
Idempotent Laws	$p \wedge p \equiv p$ $p \vee p \equiv p$	Distributive Laws	$p \wedge (q \vee r) \equiv (p \wedge q) \vee (p \wedge r)$ $p \vee (q \wedge r) \equiv (p \vee q) \wedge (p \vee r)$
Identity Laws	$p \wedge T \equiv p$ $p \vee F \equiv p$	Absorption Laws	$p \wedge (p \vee q) \equiv p$ $p \vee (p \wedge q) \equiv p$

Inverse Laws	$p \wedge (\sim p) \equiv F$ $p \vee (\sim p) \equiv T$	Domination Laws	$p \wedge F \equiv F$ $p \vee T \equiv T$

1.6 CONDITIONAL

We now come back to modeling Chetana's first statement in the framework of propositional logic:

> "If I am a student in School of Biological Sciences, I am not a student in School of Computer Science."

We may identify the following two atomic propositions:

p : Chetana is a student in School of Biological Sciences, and,

q : Chetana is not a student in School of Computer Science.

We introduce a binary operator *conditional* ($\rightarrow$) for modelling sentences of the form: if p then q, denoted symbolically as $p \rightarrow q$. The truth table definition of this binary operator $\rightarrow$ is given below.

Truth Table for $p \rightarrow q$ (with Truth values F, T)

p	q	$p \rightarrow q$
F	F	T
F	T	T
T	F	F
T	T	T

Truth Table for $p \rightarrow q$ (with Truth values 0, 1)

P	q	$p \rightarrow q$
0	0	1
0	1	1
1	0	0
1	1	1

In the conditional $p \rightarrow q$, p is also called as antecedent (or premise, or, hypothesis), and q is called as consequent (or conclusion). The conditional is false only in one condition (interpretation); it is: when the antecedent (hypothesis) is true and consequent (conclusion) is false. We explain this meaning of the conditional through one more example below.

Example 1.8: Your mother has instructed you the following: "If it rains (today), then (you should) carry an umbrella (today)." In which of the following cases you violate the mother's instruction?

Case (a): It does not rain, and you do not carry an umbrella.
Case (b): It does not rain, but you carry an umbrella.
Case (c): It rains, but you do not carry an umbrella.
Case (d): It rains and you carry an umbrella.

Solution:
We identify two atomic propositions:
p: It rains (today), and,
q: You should carry an umbrella (today).

We model the mother's instruction as a compound proposition $p \rightarrow q$. With this modeling, we identify *cases (a), (b), (c), (d)* as precisely corresponding to rows with the four truth-value assignments to variables (p,q) as = (F,F), (F, T), (T, F), and (T,T). These are also precisely the rows in truth-table definition of $p \rightarrow q$. From this, we conclude that mother's instruction is violated only in *case (c)*: It rains, but you do not carry an umbrella.

From the truth table of conditional, we conclude that the conditional is true when the antecedent is false. When the antecedent is false, to determine the truth value of the conditional, we need not know the truth value of the consequent. We say that the conditional is *vacuously true* when the antecedent is false. The following truth-table illustrates the vacuous truth of the conditional.

Vacuous Truth of $p \rightarrow q$
(with Truth values F, T)

p	q	$p \rightarrow q$
F	-	**T**
T	F	F
T	T	T

⇔

Vacuous Truth of $p \rightarrow q$
(with Truth values 0, 1)

P	q	$p \rightarrow q$
0	-	**1**
1	0	0
1	1	1

1.6.1 *Non-commutativity of Conditional and Converse Error*

When we change the *order* of the two operands in binary operators $\vee$, $\wedge$, we get the logically equivalent (propositional) formulae. In fact, we have, two laws of logic stated in section 1.5: (i) $p \wedge q \equiv q \wedge p$, and (ii) $p \vee q \equiv q \vee p$. These laws guarantee us the commutativity of the operators $\wedge$, $\vee$. The commutativity of these operators allows us to conclude that the order of the operands is not important when we model the sentences using these operators.

Example 1.9: In the conditional $p \rightarrow q$, when we change the order of its operands, we get other conditional $q \rightarrow p$. To settle the question whether the expressions (i) $(p \rightarrow q)$, and (ii) $(q \rightarrow p)$, are equivalent, using method similar to Example 1.7, we construct the truth-table below.

Truth Table for examining equivalence of (i) $(p \rightarrow q)$, and (ii) $(q \rightarrow p)$.

p	q	(i) $(p \rightarrow q)$	(ii) $(q \rightarrow p)$	*Equivalence?* (i) ≡? (ii)
F	F	T	T	T
F	T	T	F	F
T	F	F	T	F
T	T	T	T	T

Since the last column is not a tautology (does not contain all T's), the expressions (i) $(p \rightarrow q)$, and (ii) $(q \rightarrow p)$ are not logically equivalent. In other words, the operator $\rightarrow$ is non-commutative.

□

The non-commutativity of the conditional is important in the modeling of sentences. The converse of the mother's instruction "If it rains, then you carry an umbrella" is "If you carry an umbrella, then it rains", and you would certainly agree that this is not equivalent to the earlier mother's instruction.

Definition 1.3: *Converse*: The converse of the conditional $(p \rightarrow q)$ is defined as another conditional $(q \rightarrow p)$.

Although we proved in Example 1.9 that the converse is not equivalent to the conditional, in the flow of conversation, we sometimes erroneously try to conclude the converse on the basis of the conditional alone. This logical fallacy deserves a special mention, and it is known as a *Converse Error*. We illustrate this error in one example below.

Example 1.10: Consider the following conversation:

Subhash: "If I work hard, then I do well in my studies."

Sneha: "Ahhh..., based on Subhash's information, I conclude that if Subhash does well in his studies, then Subhash has worked hard."

In the above, Sneha has committed *converse error*, and her conclusion is wrong!

□

1.6.2 Conditional in terms of Disjunction

The conditional operator can be expressed in terms or disjunction and negation.

Example 1.11: Consider the expressions (i) $(p \rightarrow q)$, and (ii) $(\sim p \vee q)$. Prove that they are equivalent.

Solution: Using the method similar to Example 1.7, we construct the truth-table below.

Truth Table for examining equivalence of (i) $(p \rightarrow q)$, and (ii) $(\sim p \vee q)$.

p	q	(i) $(p \rightarrow q)$	$\sim p$	(ii) $(\sim p \vee q)$	*Equivalence?* (i) ≡ (ii)
F	F	T	T	T	T
F	T	T	T	T	T
T	F	F	F	F	T
T	T	T	F	T	T

Since the last column is a tautology (contains all T's), the expressions (i) $(p \rightarrow q)$, and (ii) $(\sim p \vee q)$ are logically equivalent.

□

1.6.3 Contrapositive of Conditional

Definition 1.4: *Contrapositive*: The contrapositive of the conditional ($p \to q$) is defined as another conditional ($\sim q \to \sim p$).

Example 1.12: Consider the expressions (i) ($p \to q$), and (ii) ($\sim q \to \sim p$). Prove that they are equivalent.

Solution: Using the method similar to Example 1.7, we construct the truth-table below.

Truth Table for examining equivalence of (i) ($p \to q$), and (ii) ($\sim q \to \sim p$).

p	q	(i) $(p \to q)$	$\sim q$	$\sim p$	(ii) $(\sim q \to \sim p)$	*Equivalence?* (i) ≡ (ii)
F	F	T	T	T	T	T
F	T	T	F	T	T	T
T	F	F	T	F	F	T
T	T	T	F	F	T	T

Since the last column is a tautology (contains all T's), the expressions (i) ($p \to q$), and (ii) ($\sim q \to \sim p$) are logically equivalent.

□

We summarize the results in section 1.6.2 and 1.6.3 to add the following row in the table of Laws of Logic:

Conditional	$p \to q \equiv \sim p \vee q$	Contrapositive of conditional	$p \to q \equiv \sim q \to \sim p$

As a corollary, for the result in Example 1.11, we note that the binary operation disjunction ∨ can be expressed in terms of the binary operation → (and unary operation ~). Explicitly, we have the following logical equivalences:

(i) $(p \vee q) \equiv (\sim p \to q)$, and,

(ii) $(p \vee q) \equiv (\sim q \to p)$.

1.6.4 *Inverse of Conditional and Inverse Error*

Definition 1.5: *Inverse*: The converse of the conditional ($p \rightarrow q$) is defined as another conditional ($\sim p \rightarrow \sim q$).

Example 1.13: To settle the question whether the expressions (i) ($p \rightarrow q$), and (ii) ($\sim p \rightarrow \sim q$), are equivalent, using method similar to Example 1.7, we construct the truth-table below.

Truth Table for examining equivalence of (i) ($p \rightarrow q$), and (ii) ($\sim p \rightarrow \sim q$).

p	q	(i) ($p\rightarrow q$)	$\sim p$	$\sim q$	(ii) ($\sim p\rightarrow\sim q$)	*Equivalence?* (i) ≡? (ii)
F	F	T	T	T	T	T
F	T	T	T	F	F	F
T	F	F	F	T	T	F
T	T	T	F	F	T	T

Since the last column is not a tautology (does not contain all T's), the expressions (i) ($p \rightarrow q$), and (ii) ($\sim p \rightarrow \sim q$) are not logically equivalent.

□

In other words, the conditional is not logically equivalent to its inverse. Many times, in the flow of conversation, we sometimes erroneously try to conclude the inverse on the basis of the conditional alone. This logical fallacy deserves a special mention, and it is known as an *Inverse Error*. We illustrate this error in one example below.

Example 1.14: Let us assume that CS 203: Data Structures and Algorithms is prerequisite for courses CS 204: Design and Analysis of Algorithms as well as for CS 207: Database and Information Systems.

Consider the following conversation:

Subhash: "If you want to take the course CS 207: Database and Information Systems, then you must take CS 203: Data Structures and Algorithms."

Sneha: "Ahhh…, based on Subhash's information, I conclude that if I do not want to take the course CS 207: Database and Information Systems, then I need not take CS 203: Data Structures and Algorithms."

In the above, Sneha has committed *inverse error*, and her conclusion is wrong! Consider the scenario that Sneha needs to take CS 204: Design and Analysis of Algorithms. With the above inverse error, when Sneha decides not to take CS 203: Data Structures and Algorithms, Sneha would not be able to take CS 204: Design and Analysis of Algorithms as well.

□

1.6.5 Conditional and Common Phrases

The conditional is an important construct for identifying the logical structure of the argument. The simplest translation of the construct $p \rightarrow q$ is the compound statement form "If p then q" (Remember the modeling in Example 1.8, Mother's instruction). In this translation, we called p as antecedent (premise), and q as consequent (conclusion). In identifying the logical structure of the sentences, it is often a challenge to identify the consequent. At times consequent is stated in the beginning, and there may not be explicit words to signal that it is a consequent. Consider the example below.

Example 1.15: Express the following statements as formulae in propositional logic:

(a) You may pass the exam if you are hard-working.
(b) You may pass the exam as you are hard-working.
(c) The passport processing time is three working days if all the information provided meets Passport Authority's (PA's) requirements.

Solution: In all the above statements, conclusion is stated first and the antecedent (premise on which conclusion is based) is stated later. The start of the consequent is not signalled by any word; however, the beginning of the premise is signalled by the word "…*if*.." in (a), (c), and by the word "…*as*.." in (b). Thus, for (a) as well as (b), we identify the following two atomic propositions:

p: You may pass the exam, and,

q: You are hard-working.

With these atomic propositions, the statement in both (a) and (b) is: $q \rightarrow p$.

Similarly, for (c), we identify the following two atomic propositions:

p: The passport processing time is three working days, and,

q: All the information provided meets Passoport Authority's (PA's) requirements. With these atomic propositions, the statement in (c) is: $q \rightarrow p$.

□

The above example illustrated the situation in which conclusion is stated in the beginning without any explicit signaling keyword suggesting its presence. However, the start of the premise, or antecedent is explicitly signaled by the presence of keyword "...*if*...", "...*as*..". A few phrases commonly used to explicitly signal the premise are:

(i) if, (ii) as, (iii) because, (iv) "... (it) is a necessary (condition) that...", (v) since, (vi) "...is necessary for...", (vii) " whenever ...",

The example 1.16 given below illustrates the situation in which there is no explicit signaling keyword suggesting the start of premise. Since there is no explicit signaling keyword suggesting the beginning of premise, for the purpose of clarity, we need the keyword to explicitly signal the start of the conclusion. In common language, in the place of the keyword "...*then*..." which explicitly signals the start of conclusion, we use many other words. A few such words are:

(i) then, (ii) therefore, (iii) only if ...,
(iv) "... (it) is sufficient (condition) that...", (v) consequently,
(vi) thus, (vii) so, (vii) accordingly,
(viii) as a result, (ix) it follows that, (x) "... is sufficient for...",
(xi) hence.

A few common examples of the usage of these phrases that are logically equivalent to "If p then q" are:

1) p only if q	2) q if p
3) p is sufficient condition for q	4) For q, it is sufficient that p
5) Whenever p, q	6) q whenever p
7) For p, it is necessary that q	8) q is necessary for p
9) Because p, it follows that q	*10)* q because p
11) p, as a result q	12) q, as p

13) As p, q	14) p, so q
15) Since p, q	16) q, since p
17) p, hence q	18) p, accordingly q

Example 1.16: Model the following statements as formulae in propositional logic:

(a) Mr. Mohapatra possesses a doctoral degree in Software Engineering from the University, and he has 5 years of software development experience, therefore is a good software developer.
(b) It follows that Mr. Mohapatra a good software developer; he possesses doctoral degree in Software Engineering from the University, and he has 5 years of software development experience.
(c) You can authorize a proxy to collect a passport on your behalf only if you have submitted your passport application in person.

Solution: In all the above statements, these are no signalling word(s) used for identifying the premise's beginning. In (a) and (c), the premise is stated first; hence we need to search for explicit phrase for locating the start of the conclusion. In (a), the start of the consequent is signalled by the word "*...therefore..*", and in (c) the start of the consequent is signalled by the word "...only if...". In the statement (b), the consequent is stated first, and there is explicit phrase "*It follows that ..*" which signals the beginning of the consequent. There is no explicit word or phrase which signals the beginning or the antecedent in statement (b). Thus, for (a) and (b), we identify the following two atomic propositions:

p: Mr. Mohaptra possesses a doctoral degree in Software Engineering from the university,

q: Mr. Mohapatra has 5 years of software development experience, and,

r: Mr. Mohapatra is a good software developer.

In (a) and (b), the (atomic) proposition r is consequent, and $(p \wedge q)$ is antecedent. Thus, both (a) and (b) can be modeled as a formula: $(p \wedge q) \rightarrow r$.

Similarly, for (c), we identify the following two atomic propositions:

s: You can authorize a proxy to collect a passport on your behalf, and,

t: You have submitted your passport application in person.

With these atomic propositions, the statement in (c) is modeled as: $s \rightarrow t$.

□

1.6.6 *Other Common Phrases: Unless, Else, Otherwise*

The connective "..unless.." signals the start of the negated premise (negated antecedent). Hence, we define: " p unless q" ≡ "p if $\sim q$"≡ $\sim q \rightarrow p$.

Example 1.17: Model the following statement as formulae in propositional logic:

"You cannot go to sleep unless you have said goodnight to your mother."

Solution: We first identify the following two atomic propositions:

p: You can go to sleep, and,

q: You have said goodnight to your mother.

Next, we rewrite the given sentence,

"You cannot go to sleep *unless* you have said goodnight to your mother."

by replacing the phrase "... *unless* ..." by "... *if* ... *not* ..." as follows:

"You cannot go to sleep *if* you have *not* said goodnight to your mother."

Using the atomic propositions p, q, we model it as: $(\sim q\rightarrow \sim p)$.

We note that it is also logically equivalent to its contrapositive: $p \rightarrow q$.

□

The connective "... else ..." signals the start of the consequent of the negated premise (often stated earlier). Hence, we define: "p else q" ≡ $\sim p\rightarrow q$.

Example 1.18: Model the following statement as formulae in propositional logic:

"You help me in my homework, else I play football."

Solution: We first identify the following two atomic propositions:

p: You help me in my homework, and,

q: I play football.

Next, we rewrite the given sentence,

"You help me in my homework, *else* I play football."

by replacing the phrase "... *else* ..." by introducing its negated premise as "... *if* ... *not* ..." as follows:

"*If* You do *not* help me in my homework *then I* play football."

Using the atomic propositions p, q, we model it as: $(\sim p\rightarrow q)$.

□

The connective "... otherwise ..." signals the start of the consequent of the negated premise (often stated earlier) (n exactly the same way with the connective "... else ...") Hence, we define: "p otherwise q" $\equiv \sim p \rightarrow q$.

Example 1.19: Model the following statement as formulae in propositional logic:
"You help me in my homework, otherwise I play football."

Solution: We first identify the following two atomic propositions:
p: You help me in my homework, and,
q: I play football.
Next, we rewrite the given sentence,
"You help me in my homework, *otherwise* I play football."
by replacing the phrase "... *otherwise* ..." by introducing its negated premise as "... *if* ... *not* ..." as follows:
"*If* You do *not* help me in my homework *then I* play football."
Using the atomic propositions p, q, we model it as: $(\sim p \rightarrow q)$.

□

1.6.7 Biconditional and Equivalence

We define the propositional operator biconditional, represented by the symbol $\leftrightarrow$, as follows:
$p \leftrightarrow q \equiv (p \rightarrow q) \wedge (q \rightarrow p)$.
With this definition, the truth table for $\leftrightarrow$ is given below.

Truth Table for $p \leftrightarrow q$ (with Truth values F, T)

p	q	$p \rightarrow q$	$q \rightarrow p$	$p \rightarrow q) \wedge (q \rightarrow p)$
F	F	T	T	T
F	T	T	F	F
T	F	F	T	F
T	T	T	T	T

Comparing this truth-table for the biconditional with the truth-table of the logical equivalence operator $\equiv$ introduced earlier in section 1.3, we note that this is not really a new operator. Thus, biconditional and (logical) equivalence are the same.

In sentences, the following phrases can be used to identify the presence of this operator: (i) "… if and only if .." (also abbreviated as "… iff …"), (ii) "… is necessary and sufficient condition for …", (iii) "… is (logically) equivalent (to) …".

PART-1 SUMMARY

In this part, we introduced basic concepts in propositional logic. The purpose of formulating the sentences as formulae in propositional logic is to allow us to concentrate on the aspects hidden in these sentences which are important for logical reasoning. To achieve this goal, in section 1.2, we introduced important logical operators: Negation (NOT, ~), Disjunction (OR,∨), Conjunction (AND, ∧). In section 1.3, we introduced the notion of logical equivalence of propositional logic formulae. The formulae in propositional logic can be classified into one of the following three categories: (i) Tautology, (ii) Contradiction, and (iii) Contingency. We introduced these categories in section 1.4. In section 1.5, we gave commonly used laws of logic. In section 1.6, we introduced commonly used operator "If…then.." (CONDITIONAL) and seen various examples which illustrate formulation of many situations in sentences using this operator.

At this stage, we briefly note that the tautologies (which are negations of contradictions, hence the contradictions as well) play an important role in revealing the logical validity of an argument. The notion of argument and the determination of logical validity of an argument using commonly used rules of inference is our topic for discussion in the next part of this module.

EXERCISES (FOR PART 1)

1.1 Give the truth-table definition for the operation $\sim(p \equiv q)$. This operation is also called as "exclusive-or" operation, and is denoted by ⊕. Thus, $p \oplus q$ is $\sim(p \equiv q)$. An important property of the operator ⊕ is as follows. Given one operand, say q, we easily get back the other operand (i.e., p) by performing the same operation ⊕ with the known operand q. Specifically, using truth table, prove: $(p \oplus q) \oplus q \equiv p$. Similarly, we have: $(p \oplus q) \oplus p \equiv q$. Comment on the application of these results for devising a simple coding-decoding scheme (say for a simple cryptographic system, or a toy game).

1.2 The truth table for one *unary* operation ~ (NOT) is given in section 1.2.1. Prove that there are exactly four unary operations on propositions. Give the truth-table definitions of these four different *unary* operations. From your definitions of these four unary operations, comment on why NOT is of special interest in logic.

1.3 The truth-table definitions of two *binary* operations $\vee$ (OR), $\wedge$ (AND) are given in sections 1.2.2 and 1.2.3. This question explores different binary operations.

(a) Prove that we there are exactly 16 different *binary* operations on propositions. Give truth-table definitions of these 16 operations. How many of these operations have been assigned the names in this chapter? How many of these operations are commutative?

(b) A propositional operation is *functionally complete* (or, just *complete*) iff every formula in propositional logic can be expressed in terms of the equivalent formula involving only the (single) operation. Prove that, out of 16 different binary operations on propositions, there are exactly two of the operations which are functionally complete. Give their truth table and state their popular name(s).

1.4 In section 1.2.4, we constructed the truth-table by progressively appending the columns for the sub-expressions needed in the evaluation of the expression. This is common convention for construction of truth-table. In this construction, we needed 7 columns. In the formula $(\sim p \vee \sim q) \wedge r$, the total number of operators and propositional variable is also 7. There is one way of construction of the truth table in which the order of the operators and variables is retained. In this construction, one column is assigned to each operator as well as propositional variable. No column is assigned to brackets. Thus, for the example 1.6, we construct the truth table as follows:

Other Truth Table Construction for the formula $(\sim p \vee \sim q) \wedge r$

($\sim$	p	$\vee$	$\sim$	q)	$\wedge$	r
T	F	T	T	F	F	F
T	F	T	T	F	T	T

T	F	T	F	T	F	F
T	F	T	F	T	T	T
F	T	T	T	F	F	F
F	T	T	T	F	T	T
F	T	F	F	T	F	F
F	T	F	F	T	F	T

(a) In the above construction, specify the order in which you need to fill up the columns.

(b) Give a rule to determine the column number (or the column label) which represents the column corresponding to the final expression of the given formula $(\sim p \vee \sim q) \wedge r$.

1.5 In section 1.6.2, conditional is expressed in terms of exactly one application of binary operator disjunction, and one application of unary operator negation. In this problem, we explore the issue or representing the negation of conditional (i.e., $\sim(p \to q)$).

(a) Express $\sim(p \to q)$ in terms of exactly one application of the binary operator conjunction, and one application of unary operator negation.

(b) Is it possible to express the negation of conditional (i.e., $\sim(p \to q)$) in terms of the basic set of connectives $\{\sim, \vee\}$? If yes, comment on minimum number of negations needed.

1.6 (a) In section 1.6.6, we defined "p unless q" ≡ "p if $\sim q$". Treat unless as new binary operator, say ⊗. Give the truth-table definition of $p \otimes q$. Prove that the operator ⊗ is commutative. In the propositional logic framework, for modeling the sentences in involving the connective "… unless …", what does the commutativity of mean?

(b) Further, in section 1.6.6, we also defined "p else q" ≡ "$\sim p \to q$". Treat unless as new binary operator, say θ. Give the truth-table definition of $p \theta q$. Prove that the operator θ is commutative. In the propositional logic framework, for modelling the sentences in involving the connective "… else …", what does the commutativity of mean?

1.7 Model the following statements as formulae in propositional logic:

(a) Workmen are eligible for compensation if they are injured in the course of their work.

(b) Mr. Jain is a good software developer, as he possesses doctoral degree in Software Engineering from the university, and has five years of software development experience.

(c) Fix my bath tub, or I do not owe you the rent.

(d) You help me in my homework problems, otherwise I play football.

(e) You help me in my homework problems, unless I play football.

(f) You help me in my homework problems, unless otherwise I play football.

(g) Nishita is allowed on Ram's motorcycle only if Nishita wears the helmet.

(h) Practicing Mr. Sharma's daily exercises is a sufficient condition for Mr. Sharma not to get a second stroke.

(i) A man should look for what is, and not for what he thinks should be. (Quote by Albert Einstein)

(j) Human beings want to be good, but not too good, and not all the time. (Quote by George Orwell)

(k) Happy families are all alike, but each unhappy family is unhappy in its own way. (Quote by Leo Tolstoy, The first sentence in the novel *Anna Karenina*)

(l) The confined space can be certified same for entry only if:
- the oxygen level is within 19.5% to 23.5%;
- the flammable gas level is less than 10% of the lower explosive limit;
- the toxic level does not exceed the permissible exposure level; and,
- steps have been taken to prevent ingress of dangerous substance.

PART 2

Arguments and Inference Rules (in Propositional Logic)

In our daily life, we use arguments. The argument consists of hypotheses (or premises), and the conclusion. The correctness of such an argument is important to us as it forms the basis of all our human activity. This notion of argument is not a quarrel, or a dispute, and warrants careful study of reasoning. In such reasoning, we use one or more statements as evidence (support, or grounds); these statements form premises. From the premises, the argument proceeds to draw the conclusion. Studying argument is important because we assume that the argument establishes the truth of their conclusions. The study of logic is the accumulated wisdom, a body of knowledge, about the result of study of such arguments. Typical argument has certain assumptions, known as premises. The argument also has structure, or form, and this argument structure must be logically acceptable. Logic is study of such acceptable argument structures (also called as argument forms). Such acceptable argument form is expressed as inference rules. In our study of logics, we are interested in "form" of an argument (also referred to as "argument form") rather than individual argument. Using this "form" of an argument through which we would establish the validity (or invalidity) of argument; hence the logics that we study are called as "formal" logics. We begin our journey to appreciate the concepts needed to describe the inference rules.

2.1 TWO USEFUL RULES

In section 1.5, we gave laws of logic. We use these laws of logic to simplify the formulae in propositional logic using substitution of logically equivalent formula. Formally, we state this rule below.

2.1.1. Replacement Rule (RR)

Replacement Rule (RR): (Useful for Simplifying a formula $\mathcal{F}$ in propositional logic): Suppose that the sub-formula $\mathcal{G}$ is a part of formula $\mathcal{F}$. Let $\mathcal{G} \equiv \mathcal{H}$ ($\mathcal{G}$ is logically equivalent to $\mathcal{H}$). Then in formula $\mathcal{F}$, an occurrence of $\mathcal{G}$ can be replaced by $\mathcal{H}$, and the resulting formula is logically equivalent to $\mathcal{F}$.

Example 2.1: Let $\mathcal{F}$: $((p\to q)\to r)\wedge(s\vee(p\to q))$. Within $\mathcal{F}$, we identify a sub-formula $\mathcal{G}$: $(p\to q)$. This sub-formula $\mathcal{G}$ is logically equivalent to another formula $\mathcal{H}$: $(\sim p\vee q)$. We may replace the second occurrence of $(p\to q)$ in $\mathcal{F}$ to obtain:

$\mathcal{F}$: $((p\to q)\to r)\wedge(s\vee(p\to q))$

$\equiv((p\to q)\to r)\wedge(s\vee(\sim p\vee q))$ … RR (replace second occurrence of $(p\to q)$ by $(\sim p\vee q)$).

□

Example 2.2: Let $\mathcal{F}$: $(((p\wedge q)\to r)\wedge(p\to q))\to(p\to r)$. Simplify the formula $\mathcal{F}$.

Solution: To apply the laws of logic, we first replace $\to$ by its logically equivalent formula expressed in terms of $\sim$, and $\vee$. Within $\mathcal{F}$, we identify a sub-formula $\mathcal{G}$: $((p\wedge q)\to r)$. This sub-formula $\mathcal{G}$ is logically equivalent to another formula $\mathcal{H}$: $(\sim(p\wedge q)\vee r)$. We continue the simplification, with the steps given below.

$\mathcal{F}$: $((p\wedge q)\to r)\wedge(p\to q))\to(p\to r)$

$\equiv((\sim(p\wedge q)\vee r)\wedge(p\to q))\to(p\to r)$ … RR (replace $((p\wedge q)\to r)$ by $(\sim(p\wedge q)\vee r)$)

$\equiv((\sim(p\wedge q)\vee r)\wedge(\sim p\vee q))\to(p\to r)$ … RR (replace $(p\to q)$ by $\sim(p\vee q)$)

$\equiv(\sim((\sim(p\wedge q)\vee r)\wedge(\sim p\vee q))\vee(p\to r))$ … RR (express ("$\to$" in terms of "$\sim$, $\vee$")

$\equiv(\sim((\sim(p\wedge q)\vee r)\wedge(\sim p\vee q))\vee(\sim p\vee r))$ … RR (replace $(p\to r)$ by $\sim(p\vee r)$)

$\equiv(\sim(((\sim p\vee\sim q)\vee r)\wedge(\sim p\vee q))\vee(\sim p\vee r))$ …DeMorgan's law (replace $\sim(p\wedge q)$ by $(\sim p\vee\sim q)$

$\equiv((\sim((\sim p\vee\sim q)\vee r)\vee\sim(\sim p\vee q))\vee(\sim p\vee r))$…DeMorgan's law (replace $\sim(((\sim p\vee\sim q)\vee r)\wedge(\sim p\vee q))$ by $(\sim((\sim p\vee\sim q)\vee r)\vee\sim(\sim p\vee q)))$)

$\equiv((\sim(\sim p\vee\sim q)\wedge\sim r)\vee\sim(\sim p\vee q))\vee(\sim p\vee r))$…DeMorgan's law (replace $\sim((\sim p\vee\sim q)\vee r)$ by $(\sim(\sim p\vee\sim q)\wedge\sim r)$)

$\equiv(((p\wedge q)\wedge\sim r)\vee\sim(\sim p\vee q))\vee(\sim p\vee r))$ …DeMorgan's law (replace $\sim(\sim p\vee\sim q)$ by $(p\wedge q)$)

$\equiv(((p\wedge q)\wedge\sim r)\vee(p\wedge\sim q))\vee(\sim p\vee r))$ … DeMorgan's law (replace $\sim(\sim p\vee q)$ by $(p\wedge\sim q)$)

$\equiv((p\wedge(q\wedge\sim r))\vee(p\wedge\sim q))\vee(\sim p\vee r))$ …Associativity (replace $((p\wedge q)\wedge\sim r)$ by $(p\wedge(q\wedge\sim r))$)

$\equiv((p\wedge((q\wedge\sim r)\vee\sim q))\vee(\sim p\vee r))$ …Distributivity of $\wedge$ over $\vee$ (in reverse) (replace $((p\wedge(q\wedge\sim r))\vee(p\wedge\sim q))$ by $(p\wedge((q\wedge\sim r)\vee\sim q))$)

$\equiv ((p\wedge((q\vee\sim q)\wedge(\sim r\vee\sim q)))\vee(\sim p\vee r))$ ...Distribute $\vee$ over $\wedge$ (replace $(q\wedge\sim r)\vee\sim q$ by $(q\vee\sim q)\wedge(\sim r\vee\sim q)$)

$\equiv ((p\wedge(T\wedge(\sim r\vee\sim q)))\vee(\sim p\vee r))$ ...Inverse law (replace $(q\wedge\sim q)$ by T)

$\equiv ((p\wedge((\sim r\vee\sim q)))\vee(\sim p\vee r))$ ...Identity law (replace $T\wedge(\sim r\vee\sim q)$ by $(\sim r\vee\sim q)$)

$\equiv (((p\wedge((\sim r\vee\sim q)))\vee\sim p)\vee r))$ ...Associativity of $\vee$ (replace $(p\wedge((\sim r\vee\sim q)))\vee(\sim p\vee r)$ by $((p\wedge((\sim r\vee\sim q)))\vee\sim p)\vee r)$)

$\equiv ((((p\vee\sim p)\wedge((\sim r\vee\sim q)\vee\sim p))\vee r))$ ... ...Distribute $\vee$ over $\wedge$ (replace $(p\wedge((\sim r\vee\sim q)))\vee\sim p)$ by $((p\vee\sim p)\wedge((\sim r\vee\sim q)\vee\sim p))$)

$\equiv (((T\wedge((\sim r\vee\sim q)\vee\sim p))\vee r))$ ... Inverse Law (replace $(p\wedge\sim p)$ by T)

$\equiv (((((\sim r\vee\sim q)\vee\sim p))\vee r))$...Identity law(replace $T\wedge((\sim r\vee\sim q)\vee\sim p)$ by $((\sim r\vee\sim q)\vee\sim p)$)

$\equiv [\{(\sim r\vee\sim q)\vee\sim p\}\vee r]$ ...modification (for clarity) of Brackets

$\equiv [(\sim r\vee\sim q)\vee\{\sim p\vee r\}]$ ...Associativity of $\vee$ (replace $\{(\sim r\vee\sim q)\vee\sim p\}\vee r$ by $(\sim r\vee\sim q)\vee\{\sim p\vee r\}$)

$\equiv [(\sim r\vee\sim q)\vee\{r\vee\sim p\}]$ ...Commutativity of $\vee$ (replace $\sim p\vee r$ by $r\vee\sim p$)

$\equiv [(\sim q\vee\sim r)\vee\{r\vee\sim p\}]$ ...Commutativity of $\vee$ (replace $\sim r\vee\sim q$ by $\sim q\vee\sim r$)

$\equiv [(\sim q\vee\{\sim r\vee r\})\vee\sim p]$ ...Associativity of $\vee$ (repeated application – all steps not shown)

$\equiv [(\sim q\vee T)\vee\sim p]$ ...Inverse Law of $\vee$ (replace $r\vee\sim r$ by T)

$\equiv [T\vee\sim p]$ ... Identity Law of $\vee$ (replace $(\sim q\vee T)$ by T)

$\equiv T$ ...Identity Law of $\vee$ (replace $(T\vee\sim q)$ by T)

The above simplification reveals that, the given expression is a tautology.

□

The laws of logic given in section 1.5 (of part 1) are a useful set of tautologies. The solution of above example 2.2 also illustrates tediousness of the application of laws of logic for the simplification.

In section 1.5 (of part 1), we gave a few tautologies. However, using any known tautology, we can generate other tautology by replacing every occurrence of a propositional variable, say p, by a formula (say $\mathcal{G}_p$). Formally, we state this "tautology generator rule" below.

2.1.2. Tautology Generation Rule (TGR)

Tautology Generator Rule (TGR): Suppose that we have a formula $\mathcal{F}$ in propositional logic, which is a tautology. Suppose that a propositional variable p occurs in the formula $\mathcal{F}$. Further, assume that $\mathcal{G}_p$ is any formula in propositional logic (note that $\mathcal{G}_p$ is generally not a tautology). Let $\mathcal{F}_G$ be the formula obtained from $\mathcal{F}$ by replacing all occurrences of p in $\mathcal{G}$. Then $\mathcal{F}_G$ is also a tautology.

Example 2.3: Let $\mathcal{F}$: $\sim(p\wedge q)\leftrightarrow(\sim p\vee\sim q)$. Within $\mathcal{F}$, we have a propositional variable q. Let $\mathcal{G}_q = (r\wedge s)$. From F, by replacing all occurrences of q, we obtain another formula $\mathcal{F}_G = \sim(p\wedge(r\wedge s))\leftrightarrow(\sim p\vee\sim(r\wedge s))$. Then, TGR guarantees us that $\mathcal{F}_G$ is also a tautology.

□

As we shall see in this part, tautologies are important for valid arguments. TGR allows us to generate additional (in fact, *infinitely many*) tautologies from the known tautologies; indirectly, TGR allows us to generate (additional) valid arguments from the known valid arguments.

2.2 Propositional Expressions and Their Evaluation

In Example 2.2, we saw a propositional expression. It is similar to familiar arithmetic expression to the extent that it also involves variables, but they are now statement variables (atomic propositions). The expression (also called as a formula) is in general a representation of a compound sentence.

2.2.1. Review of Arithmetic Expressions

A typical (and familiar) recursive definition of an arithmetic formula (also known as arithmetic expression) involving the arithmetic operators $-_u$ (unary minus, also represented by just negation sign: $-$), $+$, $-$, $*$, $/$, and $\uparrow$ (exponentiation) is given below.

Definition 2.1: Simple variable symbols like a, b, are arithmetic formulae. Additionally, if x and y are arithmetic formulae, then the following is also an arithmetic formula:

(ii)(x)
(ii) $-_u x$ (also represented as: $-x$)
(ii)$x+y$
(ii)$x-y$
(ii)$x*y$
(ii)x/y
(ii)$x\uparrow y$

Further, nothing is an arithmetic formula unless its being so follows from (a), …, (g) above.

Example 2.4: Let a, b, and c be (arithmetic, say integer) variables. Then the following are arithmetic formulae:

(i) $a + b$
(ii) $a + b + c$
(iii) $(a + b) + c$
(iv) $a + (b + c)$
(v) $-_{u}a + b * c$
(vi) $(a + b) * c$
(vii) $a + (b * c)$
(viii) $a \uparrow b \uparrow c$
(ix) $a/b*c$
(x) $a+b-c$

We leave it to the reader to work out which sequence of applications of the steps in the recursive definition 2.1 yields the above arithmetic formulae. We however note that, the sequence of this application can be represented in the form of expression evaluation trees. In Example 2.4 above, for the expression (ii), we note that there are two expression evaluation trees. These two trees are shown in Figure 2.1 and Figure 2.2.

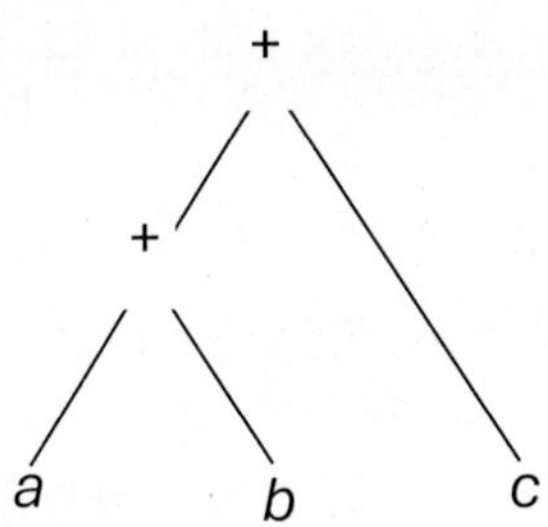

Figure 2.1. Left Associative Evaluation Tree for $(a+b+c)$

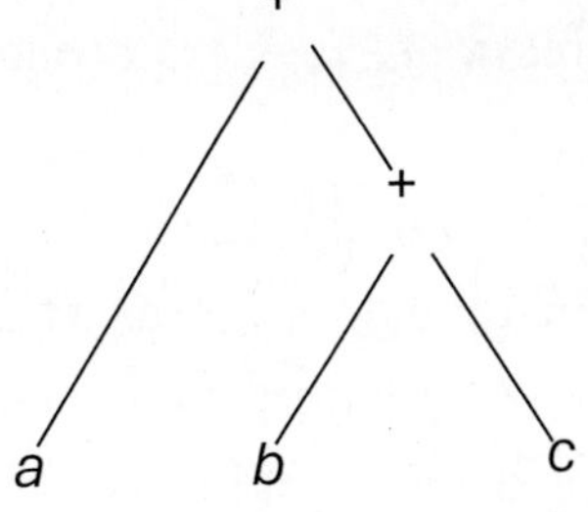

Figure 2.2. Right Associative Evaluation Tree for $(a+b+c)$

We note that the intermediate results in these evaluation trees are different. Since the evaluation process proceeds by evaluating the intermediate results, and then combine them to obtain the final result, these two evaluations are different evaluations (from the point of view of the evaluator – this job may be carried out by the computer, or other machine). Thus, the process or evaluation for expression as decided by the evaluator needs to decide about one of these two possible choices. Whenever the evaluator is faced with such a situation in which he has more than one choice, we say that he is faced with ambiguous situation, or the expression is ambiguous. The evaluator must choose one of these two evaluations for obtaining the result. This is called as *ambiguity resolution*. Incidentally, we note that *ambiguity resolution* can be done by adding more parentheses. Indeed, a sequence of matched parentheses is used quite frequently in computer science, and we study the structure of sequence of matched parentheses in courses on Data Structures, Automata Theory, as well as Algorithms. Our convention is to avoid additional parentheses for the sake of brevity, thereby resulting us to permit ambiguity.

We identify two different cases for ambiguity the resolution.

Case (a): The first situation is when we need to resolve the ambiguity of two occurrences of the same operator. This is the case for the expressions (ii), and (viii) in Example 2.4 above.

Case (b): The second situation is when we need to resolve the ambiguity of two occurrences or the two different operators. This is the case for the expression (v), (ix), and (x) in Example 2.4 above.

The ambiguity resolution for Case (a) is by specifying the *associativity* of the operator. For arithmetic expressions, +, –, *, / are left associative, and the exponentiation operator ↑ is right associative.

The ambiguity resolution for Case (b) is by specifying the *precedence* relationship amongst the pair of operators. This relationship is also specified by first listing the operators which have highest precedence, next the set of operators which have precedence at the next level, and so on. For arithmetic expressions, the operator ↑ has highest precedence; the operator $-_u$ has second highest precedence; the operators multiplication and division (*, /) are at the next level, and the operators addition and subtraction (+, -) are at the lowest level. The operators, namely, multiplication and division (*, /) are at the same level of precedence; they are also said to have co-equal precedence. In expression (ix) of Example 2.4 above, the ambiguity of the expression cannot be resolved as it involves two operators which are co-equal. In such a case, we say that we have a structural (*syntax*) error. Similarly, expression (x) of Example 2.4 results in syntax error (why?).

2.2.2. *Propositional Expressions*

For the construction of a compound sentence, we usually identify the operators ~, ∨, ∧, →, and sometimes ↔. With this observation, we formally define the structure of a propositional formula (or, propositional expression, which itself is also *a proposition*, so we call it as a proposition as well) recursively as follows:

Definition 2.2: Atomic (simple) propositions, denoted by symbols like p, q, are propositional expressions. Additionally, if x and y are propositions, then the following is also a proposition:

(a) (x)
(b) $\sim x$
(c) $x \vee y$
(d) $x \wedge y$
(e) $x \rightarrow y$
(f) $x \leftrightarrow y$

Further, nothing is a proposition unless its being so follows from (a), …, (f) above.

Example 2.5: Let p, q, and r be propositions. Then the following are propositions:

(i) $p \vee q$
(ii) $p \vee q \vee r$
(iii) $(p \vee q) \vee r$
(iv) $p \vee (q \vee r)$
(v) $p \vee q \wedge r$
(vi) $(p \vee q) \wedge r$
(vii) $p \vee (q \wedge r)$
(viii) $p \rightarrow q \rightarrow r$

We now give our convention about the ambiguity resolution below. Note that these rules may differ slightly in different books. While reading the different sources, you need to look for the details.

Ambiguity Resolution:

Case (a): (*Associativity*) The binary operators ∨, ∧ are left associative, and the binary operators →, ↔ are right associative.

Case (b): (*Precedence*) The unary operator ~ has highest precedence. At the next precedence level, the binary operators ∨, ∧ . (Note that we assume that these operators are co-equal; some authors assume that ∧ has higher precedence level than $\vee$). At the lowest precedence level, we have two binary operators $\rightarrow$, $\leftrightarrow$.

2.3 Arguments and Argument Forms

Argument is a sequence of propositions, ending in another proposition called as conclusion. We often specify an occurrence of the conclusion by adding the special symbol $\therefore$ (to express this symbol in words, we replace it by "Therefore").

Example 2.6: The following is an argument:

Subhash is in the tutorial room or he is in the canteen.
Subhash is not in the tutorial room.
$\therefore$ Subhash is in the canteen.

The logical form of the above argument can be extracted by assigning propositional variables to concrete propositions. To do this, let:

p: Subhash is in the tutorial room.

q: Subhash is in the canteen.

Using the above abstract propositions p, q, form of the argument (also called as the argument form) in Example 2.6 is:

$p \vee q$
$\sim p$
$\therefore q$

In the above argument form, we have two premises $P_1 = p \vee q$, and $P_2 = \sim p$. We also denote the conclusion $C = q$. In terms of these premises, the argument form is represented as a conditional: $(P_1 \wedge P_2) \rightarrow C$. In terms of statement variables, this argument form $\mathscr{A}$ is: $((p \vee q) \wedge (\sim p)) \rightarrow q$. We also use the notation $\mathscr{A}(p,q)$ to emphasize that the argument form $\mathscr{A}$ involves two (atomic) statement variables p, q.

The structure of general argument form involving of m premises $P_1, P_2, \ldots, P_m$, and conclusion C is as follows:

$$(P_1 \wedge P_2 \wedge \ldots \wedge P_m) \rightarrow C \qquad \ldots(2.1)$$

2.4 VALID AND INVALID ARGUMENT FORMS

Definition 2.3: An argument form, say $\mathscr{A}$, consisting of m premises $P_1, P_2, \ldots, P_m$, and conclusion C, (and consisting of n statement variables $p_1, p_2, \ldots, p_n$) is valid if and only if, whenever the premises $P_1, P_2, \ldots, P_m$, are true, the conclusion C is also true.

Using the truth table method, to check the validity of the argument form, we have the following steps:

(1) Construct the truth table consisting of (i) the statement variables $p_1, p_2, \ldots, p_n$, (ii) all premises $P_1, P_2, \ldots, P_m$, and, (iii) the conclusion C, as columns in the truth table.

(2) Find the rows in which all premises are true (these rows are called as critical rows).

(3) If in each critical row, conclusion C is true, then the argument form is valid. If there is a critical row in which conclusion is false, then the argument form is invalid.

Example 2.7: Consider the following argument form:

$p \wedge q$

$p \rightarrow q$

$\therefore\ q$

Is the above argument form valid?

Solution: Let us explore the validity problem by the truth-table method. We identify the premises P_1: $p \wedge q$, P_2: $p \rightarrow q$. We first identify the statement variables involved as p, q. Using these as atomic variables, we construct truth table with P_1, and P_2 as its columns.

p	q	P_1: $(p \wedge q)$	P_2: $(p \rightarrow q)$	*Critical Rows*
F	F	F	T	(not critical)
F	T	F	T	(not critical)
T	F	F	F	(not critical)
T	T	T	T	✓

The conclusion C: q. After identifying all critical rows, we find the truth-value of Conclusion in all the critical rows. We get the following truth-table.

		P1:	P2:	*Critical Rows*	C:
p	q	$(p \wedge q)$	$(p \rightarrow q)$		q
F	F	F	T	(not critical)	..
F	T	F	T	(not critical)	..
T	F	F	F	(not critical)	..
T	T	T	T	✓	T

Next, create a new column in which we state the answer to the question: "Is the conclusion C = T (True) in the (concerned) critical row? The answer (Yes/No) is entered in the respective critical row.

		P1:	P2:	*Critical Rows*	C:	In this critical row:
p	q	$(p \wedge q)$	$(p \rightarrow q)$		q	C = T?
F	F	F	T	(not critical)	..	..
F	T	F	T	(not critical)	..	..
T	F	F	F	(not critical)	..	..
T	T	T	T	✓	T	Yes

Since we have all "Yes" in the column titled "In this critical row: C = T?", the argument form is valid.

□

If there is a critical row, for which, in the column titled "In this critical row: C = T?" we have the answer as "No", then the argument form is invalid. This point is illustrated in the following example.

Example 2.8: Consider the following argument form:

$p \vee q$

$p \rightarrow q$

$\therefore p$

Is the above argument form valid?

Solution: Let us explore the validity problem by the truth-table method. We identify the premises P_1: $p \vee q$, P_2: $p \rightarrow q$. We first identify the statement variables involved as p, q. Using these as atomic variables, we construct truth table with P_1, and P_2 as its columns.

p	q	P_1: $(p \vee q)$	P_2: $(p \rightarrow q)$	*Critical Rows*
F	F	F	T	(not critical)
F	T	T	T	✓
T	F	T	F	(not critical)
T	T	T	T	✓

The conclusion C: p. After identifying all critical rows, we find the truth-value of Conclusion in all the critical rows. We get the following truth-table.

p	q	P_1: $(p \vee q)$	P_2: $(p \rightarrow q)$	*Critical Rows*	C: p
F	F	F	T	(not critical)	..
F	T	T	T	✓	F
T	F	T	F	(not critical)	..
T	T	T	T	✓	T

Next, create a new column in which we state the answer to the question: "Is the conclusion C = T (True) in the (concerned) critical row? The answer (Yes/No) is entered in the respective critical row.

p	q	P_1: $(p \vee q)$	P_2: $(p \rightarrow q)$	*Critical Rows*	C: q	In this critical row: C = T?
F	F	F	T	(not critical)	..	..
F	T	T	T	✓	F	No
T	F	T	F	(not critical)	..	..
T	T	T	T	✓	T	Yes

Since we have one row with "No" answer in the column titled "In this critical row: C = T?", the argument form is invalid.

□

The critical row with the "No" answer in the column titled "In this critical row: C = T?" gives us a counter-example (the specific interpretation, i.e., the specific assignment of truth values to the statement variables p, q) which invalidates the argument form.

Thus, to invalidate the argument form, it suffices to specify the counter-example of truth-value assignments p = T, q = T. Next, we verify that, with these truth-value assignments, both the premises P_1: $p \vee q$, P_2: $p \rightarrow q$ are T, but the conclusion C: p is F. Hence the argument form is invalid.

This method, in which we specify just one assignment of truth-values to all statement variables, verify that all premises are true under this assignment, and conclusion is false, is also referred to as "proof of invalidity of argument form using a counter-example". This one case provides a counter-example for the argument form, and hence the case shows that the argument is invalid.

<u>Example 2.9</u>: Consider the following argument form:

p

$p \vee q$

$q \rightarrow (r \rightarrow s)$

$t \rightarrow r$

$\therefore\ \sim s \rightarrow \sim t$

Is the above argument form valid?

<u>Solution</u>: There are five statement variables, p, q, r, s, and t in this argument form, and hence, the truth-table method would need $2^5 = 32$ rows. This makes the applicability of truth-table method inconvenient.

Suspecting that this argument form may be invalid, we try to prove its invalidity by discovering a suitable counterexample.

We first identify the following premises P_1, P_2, P_3, P_4 and the conclusion C, as follows:

$P_1 : p$

$P_2 : p \vee q$

$P_3 : q \rightarrow (r \rightarrow s)$

$P_4 : t \rightarrow r$

$C : \sim s \rightarrow \sim t$

To construct the counter-example, we attempt to obtain the assignment of truth values to the variables p, q, r, s, and t which would satisfy the following two conditions:

- conclusion C is false, and ...(2.2)
- all premises P_1, P_2, P_3, P_4, are true. ...(2.3)

Due to condition (2.2), conclusion C is false; so $\sim s \rightarrow \sim t$ is false. Hence, $\sim(\sim s \rightarrow \sim t)$ is true. Since $\sim s \rightarrow \sim t \equiv s \vee \sim t$, this means, $\sim(s \vee \sim t)$ is true. Since $\sim(s \vee \sim t) \equiv \sim s \wedge t$ (De Morgan's Law), $\sim s \wedge t$ is true. This means, the truth-value of t must be T, and the truth-value to $\sim s$ also must be T. In other words, the truth-value of s must be F. This, just by condition (1), we are able to determine the truth values of two variables s, t as s = F, and t = T.

Now, let us consider the premise P_4: $t \rightarrow r$. Since the truth value of t = T, in order that P_4 to be T, the truth value of the statement variable r must be T. Thus, we get truth-value of additional variable r = T.

With the truth-values r = T, and s = F, we have $(r \rightarrow s)$ = F. Hence, the premise P_3 : $q \rightarrow (r \rightarrow s)$ gets converted to P_3 : $q \rightarrow$F. Next, the premise P_3 : $q \rightarrow$F is true for discovering our counter-example. This fixes the truth-value of statement variable q to be F.

Let us quickly take a stock of all truth-value assignments we have done till now. We have: Thus, the truth values s = F, t = T, r = T, and q = F. We need to take care of the premises P_2 and P_1.

With these truth-value assignments, the premise P_2 : $p \vee F \equiv p$. The premise P_2 is true with the truth-value assignment p = T. With this, we have fixed truth-values of all variables as: p = T, q = F, r = T, s = F, and t = T. We still have to verify that with these truth-value assignments, premise P_1 is true. The premise P_1 : p = T, so we succeeded in constructing a counter-example, which gives us the assignment of truth values p = T, q = F, r = T, s = F, and t = T, with which all the premises are true, and conclusion is false. Hence, the argument form is invalid.

□

Example 2.10: Consider the following argument form:

$\sim p$

$p \vee q$

$q \rightarrow (r \rightarrow s)$

$t \rightarrow r$

$\therefore \ \sim s \rightarrow \sim t$

Is the above argument form valid?

Solution: One way to prove that this argument form is valid is to construct a truth-table; find out all critical rows, and show that, for all critical rows, the conclusion has the entry T. However, we already commented earlier that there are five statement variables, p, q, r, s, and t in this argument form, and hence, the truth-table method would need $2^5 = 32$ rows.

Many of you would have started suspecting that, after all, we do not seem to construct such truth-tables. We have developed some methods to *logically derive* the conclusion by applying some small number of rules on the premises.

Further, many of you would suspect as to why from the premises? Indeed, by essentially reversing the solution process of Example 2.7, we expect that, we should be able to "logically derive" the conclusion from the premises.

We first identify the following premises P_1, P_2, P_3, P_4 and the conclusion C, as follows:

$P_1 : \sim p$

$P_2 : p \vee q$

$P_3 : q \rightarrow (r \rightarrow s)$

$P_4 : t \rightarrow r$

$C : \sim s \rightarrow \sim t$

In the critical rows, all the premises are true. In particular, premise P_1 is true, i.e., $\sim p = T$; this gives us truth-value of variable $p = F$. Next, consider P_2: $p \vee q = F \vee q \equiv q$. Thus, to make premise P_2 to be true (in the presence of premise P_1 is true, i.e., $p = F$), we need the truth-value of variable $q = T$. The premise $P_3 : q \rightarrow (r \rightarrow s)$. Since $q = T$ (which is antecedent part of conditional), to make premise P_3 true, the consequent $(r \rightarrow s)$ must be T. Thus, the conditional $(r \rightarrow s)$ is T. Let us denote $(r \rightarrow s)$ by the modified premise, say P_3'. The premise $P_4 : (t \rightarrow r)$ gives us another conditional. Thus, we may reframe the given argument to the following argument form:

P_3' : $(r \rightarrow s)$

P_4 : $t \rightarrow r$

C : $\sim s \rightarrow \sim t$

If the above argument form is valid, then the original argument form is valid. Investigating the validity of this argument form is relatively easy, as it involves only three variables r, s, and t (instead of earlier five variables: note that we got rid of two variables, namely p, q as well as first two premises for the above example). We may use the truth-table method to determine the critical rows, and discover the validity by checking whether conclusion has the entry T in all these critical rows. To establish this, we construct the following truth-table:

			P_3':	P_4:	*Critical Rows*			C:	In this critical row:
R	*s*	*t*	$(r \rightarrow s)$	$t \rightarrow r$		$\sim s$	$\sim t$	$\sim s \rightarrow \sim t$	C = T?
F	F	F	T	T	✓	T	T	T	Yes
F	F	T	T	F	(not critical)	T	F	F	..
F	T	F	T	T	✓	F	T	T	Yes
F	T	T	T	F	(not critical)	F	F	T	..
T	F	F	F	T	(not critical)	T	T	T	..
T	F	T	F	T	(not critical)	T	F	F	..
T	T	F	T	T	✓	F	T	T	Yes
T	T	T	T	T	✓	F	F	T	Yes

Since we have all "Yes" in the column titled "In this critical row: C = T?", the argument form is valid. Therefore, it follows that the original argument form consisting of five statement variables p, q, r, s, and t and four premises P_1, P_2, P_3, P_4 is valid.

□

To formalize and state clearly the arguments such as given in solution of Example 2.8, we need the notion of implication, and inference rules. We introduce these topics in the next few sections.

2.5 IMPLICATION

In section 2.2, we stated the structure of general argument form involving of *m* premises $P_1, P_2, \ldots, P_m$, and conclusion C is as follows:

$$(P_1 \wedge P_2 \wedge \ldots \wedge P_m) \rightarrow C \quad \ldots (2.1)$$

In section 2.4, we defined the above argument form to be valid if and only if the formula (2.1) is a tautology. In formula (2.1), the conditional operator is the last operator in the expression evaluation process (hence it is the last column in our truth-table construction of a formula (2.1)).

Definition 2.4: *Logical Implication*: If the conditional "→" in the argument form (2.1) above evaluates to T in all rows in the truth-table (i.e., in all possible cases), then we also say that this conditional is a logical implication.

Note that the logical implication is a convenient terminology we introduce to establish the language for speaking about the valid argument forms. The notion of logical implication involves two concepts:

(i) a conditional "→" in the argument form (2.1), and,
(ii) the argument form (2.1) is a tautology.

After establishing that formula (2.1) is a tautology, we say that the premises $P_1, P_2, \ldots, P_m$, imply (or, logically imply) the conclusion C. Since we speak about the implication very frequently in the proofs, we introduce special notation for the logical implication as "⇒" (to be read as "implies"). Thus, we denote the valid argument form using this notation as follows:

$$(P_1 \wedge P_2 \wedge \ldots \wedge P_m) \Rightarrow C. \quad \ldots (2.4)$$

Note: The symbol " ⇐" is sometimes used to denote the phrase "is implied by". Thus, conclusion C is implied by $(P_1 \wedge P_2 \wedge \ldots \wedge P_m)$ is symbolically denoted by:

$$C \Leftarrow (P_1 \wedge P_2 \wedge \ldots \wedge P_m). \quad \ldots (2.5)$$

Further, the symbol ⇔ is used to denote "implies and is implied by".

Example 2.11: In Example 2.2, we simplified the following formula

$$\mathcal{F} : (((p \wedge q) \rightarrow r) \wedge (p \rightarrow q)) \rightarrow (p \rightarrow r)$$

to prove that it is a tautology. Rewrite formula $\mathcal{F}$ using the logical implication.

Solution: The conditional within the above formula $\mathcal{F}$ which would be evaluated in the end is a conditional $\rightarrow$ before $(p\rightarrow r)$. Hence, we identify the part $(p\rightarrow r)$ as a conclusion part of the argument form, and the part $(((p\wedge q)\rightarrow r)\wedge(p\rightarrow q))$ as a premise. Since there is a conditional in the tautology as represented by the formula F, we also say that the premise $(((p\wedge q)\rightarrow r)\wedge(p\rightarrow q))$ implies (the conclusion) $(p\rightarrow r)$. Symbolically, we write:

$$(((p\wedge q)\rightarrow r)\wedge(p\rightarrow q))\Rightarrow(p\rightarrow r)$$

□

Example 2.12: In Example 2.6, we established the validity of the following argument form:

$p\vee q$

$\sim p$

$\therefore\ q$

Express the above valid argument form as an implication.

Solution: We identify the premises P_1: $p\vee q$, P_2: $\sim q$. The conclusion C: q. Hence the implication has the form $(P_1\wedge P_2)\Rightarrow C$. Substituting P_1, P_2, and C, we have:

$$(\,(p\vee q)\wedge(\sim p)\,)\Rightarrow q.$$

□

Example 2.13: In Example 2.7, we established the validity of the following argument form:

$p\wedge q$

$p\rightarrow q$

$\therefore\ p$

Express the above valid argument form as an implication.

Solution: We identify the premises P_1: $p\wedge q$, P_2: $p\rightarrow q$. The conclusion C: p. Hence the implication has the form $(P_1\wedge P_2)\Rightarrow C$. Substituting P_1, P_2, and C, we have:

$$(\,(p\wedge q)\wedge(p\rightarrow q)\,)\Rightarrow p.$$

□

Example 2.14. In the solution process of Example 2.10, we established, using the truth-table method, validity of the following argument form:

$r \rightarrow s$

$t \rightarrow r$

$C : \sim s \rightarrow \sim t$

Express the above valid argument form as an implication.

Solution: We identify the premises P_1: $r \rightarrow s$, P_2: $t \rightarrow r$. The conclusion C: $\sim s \rightarrow \sim t$. Hence the implication has the form $(P_1 \wedge P_2) \Rightarrow C$. Substituting P_1, P_2, and C, we have:

$$((r \rightarrow s) \wedge (t \rightarrow r)) \Rightarrow (\sim s \rightarrow \sim t).$$

□

Example 2.15. In the Example 2.10, we established the validity of the following argument form:

$P_1 : \sim p$

$P_2 : p \vee q$

$P_3 : q \rightarrow (r \rightarrow s)$

$P_4 : t \rightarrow r$

$C : \sim s \rightarrow \sim t$

Express the above valid argument form as an implication.

Solution: We identify the premises $P_1 : \sim p$, $P_2 : p \vee q$, P_3: $q \rightarrow (r \rightarrow s)$, P_4: $t \rightarrow r$. The conclusion C: $\sim s \rightarrow \sim t$. Hence the implication has the form $(P_1 \wedge P_2 \wedge P_3 \wedge P_4) \Rightarrow C$. Substituting P_1, P_2, P_3, P_4, and C, we have:

$$((\sim p) \wedge (p \vee q) \wedge (q \rightarrow (r \rightarrow s)) \wedge (t \rightarrow r)) \Rightarrow (\sim s \rightarrow \sim t).$$

□

To emphasize that the premises P_1, P_2, …, P_m, do not imply the conclusion C, we use the special notation for the logical non-implication as "$\sim\Rightarrow$". Thus, we denote non-validity of the argument form using this notation as follows:

$$(P_1 \wedge P_2 \wedge \ldots \wedge P_m) \sim\Rightarrow C. \quad \ldots (2.6)$$

Example 2.16: In Example 2.8, we established the non-validity of the following argument form:

$$p \vee q$$
$$p \to q$$
$$\therefore\ p$$

Express the above non-valid argument form as a non-implication.

Solution: We identify the premises P_1: $p \vee q$, P_2: $p \to q$. The conclusion C: p. Hence the implication has the form $(P_1 \wedge P_2) \Rightarrow C$. Substituting P_1, P_2, and C, we have:

$$(\,(p \vee q) \wedge (p \to q)\,) \sim\Rightarrow p.$$

□

Example 2.17. In the Example 2.9, we established the non-validity of the following argument form:

$P_1 : p$

$P_2 : p \vee q$

$P_3 : q \to (r \to s)$

$P_4 : t \to r$

$C : \sim s \to \sim t$

Express the above non-valid argument form as a non-implication.

Solution: We identify the premises $P_1 : p$, $P_2 : p \vee q$, P_3: $q \to (r \to s)$, P_4: $t \to r$. The conclusion C: $\sim s \to \sim t$. Hence the non-implication has the form $(P_1 \wedge P_2 \wedge P_3 \wedge P_4) \sim\Rightarrow C$. Substituting P_1, P_2, P_3, P_4, and C, we have:

$$(\,(p) \wedge (p \vee q) \wedge (q \to (r \to s)) \wedge (t \to r)\,) \sim\Rightarrow (\sim s \to \sim t).$$

□

To establish the validity of an argument form, we need to establish the tautology. To do this, the solution process of Example 2.10 did rely, at least partly, on truth-table method. In Example 2.34 (below), we describe a scenario which involves 9 statement variables. We note that the scenario in Example 2.34 is simplified one, and many scenarios may involve as many as 50 (or even 500) statement variables. Even with 9 variables of Example 2.34, the truth-table method with its $2^9 = 512$ rows results in very large truth-table, which we would not like to construct. Rather, we would look for some alternate ways to establish the validity.

If the argument form has 50 statement variables, the truth-table would need 2^{50} = 1000,0000 G ($\approx 10^{15}$) rows in a truth-table. Such a computation is still well beyond the capabilities of today's powerful computers. When the numbers of statement variables grow from 50 to 500, the truth-table method requires 2^{500} ($\approx 10^{150}$) rows in the truth table. It is widely believed that there aren't a googol ($\approx 1\text{x}10^{100}$) atoms in the universe. It is not unthinkable to construct an argument involving 500 atomic statements. For such an argument involving 500 statement variables, it is impossible to prove its validity by truth-table method even if we can deploy one atom in the universe for representing one row of this truth table. This renders the applicability of truth-table method very limited, and we must look for alternate (hopefully, reflecting more *human-like* thinking of the use of correct patterns of reasoning) methods for establishing the validity of argument. Indeed, evolving such an efficient method is the central problem in computer science, having immediate far-reaching practical implications in the areas like Artificial Intelligence and Machine Learning (AIML), Data Sciences, Data Analytics, etc.

We have also noted earlier that the explanation of the first part of solution process for the solution of Example 2.8 in which we got rid of premises P_1 and P_2 is not very systematic. Hence our formalization should give us rules which we can apply in such cases. In our arguments usually expressed in the language, we use some common *rules of inference*, and these rules should help us to formalize the solution process of Example 2.10. This leads us to study commonly used *rules of inference*. We give them in the next section.

2.6 INFERENCE RULES

Inference rules (IRs) are used to validate or invalidate the argument logically without taking a resort to the truth-table method. We now give 12 commonly used rules of inference. Since all these 12 rules of inference involve at most four statement variables, the validity of these rules can easily be proved by truth-table method (for four variables, truth-table would consist of 16 rows, which is manageable). We do not establish the validity here, and it is left as an easy exercise to the reader.

2.6.1. *Modus Ponens (MP)*

This rule is also called as the rule of detachment, as it allows us to remove the antecedent part of conditional, and infer the conclusion part of conditional. Its form is given below.

$$\begin{array}{l} p \\ p \rightarrow q \\ \hline \therefore\ q \end{array}$$

To establish the validity of MP, we need to prove that the following formula in propositional logic is a tautology:

$$(p \wedge (p \rightarrow q)) \rightarrow q$$

This can easily be established using the truth-table method, and we leave it to the reader to complete this proof.

Example 2.18. Establish the validity of the following argument:

Pradeep has not paid the rent for last 12 months for the apartment. If Pradeep has not paid the rent for 12 months for the apartment, then Pradeep has to vacate the apartment. Therefore, Pradeep has to vacate the apartment.

Solution: We identify the following statement variables:

p: Pradeep has not paid the rent for last 12 months for the apartment.

q: Pradeep has to vacate the apartment.

With this choice, the above argument has the following structure (form):

$$\begin{array}{l} p \\ p \rightarrow q \\ \hline \therefore\ q \end{array}$$

This is exactly the form of Modus Ponens (MP), which is one of the rules of inference. Hence, the argument is valid.

□

We represent a logical argument by writing the statements on separate lines. For the statements which logically follow from the earlier statements, we give a justification of the known rule of inference. Thus, we also write the above argument form as:

(1) p ... Premise 1
(2) $p \rightarrow q$ ... Premise 2
(3) q ... MP on (1),(2)

Notation: The information "MP on (1), (2)" in the third line indicates the following. This current line (line (3)) is a Conclusion of the sub-argument, whose form is Modus Ponens (MP), with MP's premises present in the lines (1), (2). For brevity, sometimes we may omit the word "on" and write this information as "MP, (1), (2)".

The following example illustrates the convenient use of the above proof structure.

Example 2.19. Identify the structure of the following argument, and establish its logical validity:

If Sneha is participating in tennis tournaments, then she is not participating in chess tournaments. If Sneha is not participating in chess tournaments, then she is not eligible for the travel grant in the chess players' category. Sneha is participating in tennis tournaments. Therefore, Sneha is not eligible for the travel grant in the chess players' category.

Solution: We identify the following statement variables:

p: Sneha is participating in tennis tournaments.
q: Sneha is not participating in chess tournaments.
r: Sneha is not eligible for the travel grant in the chess players' category.

With this choice, the above argument has the following structure (form):

$p \rightarrow q$
$q \rightarrow r$
p

$\therefore\ r$

This form is not in the exact form of Modus Ponens (MP). However, the repeated application of MP within the proof can be used to establish the validity of this form as follows.

We represent a logical argument by writing the statements on separate lines. For the statements which logically follow from the earlier statements, we give a justification of the known rule of inference. Thus, we also write the above argument form as:

(1) $p \to q$ ... Premise 1
(2) $q \to r$ ... Premise 2
(3) p ... Premise 3
(4) q ... MP on (3), (1)
(5) r ... MP on (4), (2), (also, Conclusion.)

This forms a valid proof.

□

Note that, this proof has been written using the repeated application of MP. Later, in section 2.5.2, we shall see other rule of inference, called Logical Syllogism (LS), which can also be used to establish validity.

2.6.1.1. Caution on application of MP

In the flow of conversation, we may come across the argument given below:

> If Nischit's program is correct, then Nischit would complete the assignment in two hours. Nischit has completed the assignment in two hours. Therefore Nischit's program is correct.

Further, someone may argue that the validity of this argument follows from Modus Ponens (MP). However, this is not so. You may like to refer to section 1.6.1: Noncommutativity of Conditional, and review the Example 1.10, in which we pointed out error in Sneha's argument, which we referred to as "Converse Error" in section 1.6.1. To further emphasize this erroneous application, we need to uncover the structure of the argument as explained above.

Example 2.20. Identify the structure of the following argument, and establish its logical invalidity:

> If Nischit's program is correct, then Nischit would complete the assignment in two hours. Nischit has completed the assignment in two hours. Therefore Nischit's program is correct.

Solution: We identify the following statement variables:

p: Nischit's program is correct.

q: Nischit would complete the assignment in two hours.

With this choice, the above argument has the following structure (form):

$$p \to q$$
$$q$$

$$\therefore\ p$$

This is *not* the form of Modus Ponens (MP), and it turns out that this argument form is invalid. To establish the invalidity of this argument form, we use the method exactly similar to Example 2.8. For the sake of completeness and to emphasize the method for establishing the non-validity, we repeat it below.

Let us explore the validity problem by the truth-table method. We identify the premises P_1: $p \to q$, P_2: q. We first identify the statement variables involved as p, q. Using these as atomic variables, we construct truth table with P_1, and P_2 as its columns.

p	P_2: q	P_1: $(p \to q)$	*Critical Rows*
F	F	T	(not critical)
F	T	T	✓
T	F	F	(not critical)
T	T	T	✓

The conclusion C: p. After identifying all critical rows, we find the truth-value of Conclusion in all the critical rows. We get the following truth-table.

p	P_2: q	P_1: $(p \to q)$	*Critical Rows*	C: p
F	F	T	(not critical)	..
F	T	T	✓	F
T	F	F	(not critical)	..
T	T	T	✓	T

Next, create a new column in which we state the answer to the question: "Is the conclusion C = T (True) in the (concerned) critical row? The answer (Yes/No) is entered in the respective critical row.

	P2:	P1:	*Critical Rows*	C:	In this critical row:
p	q	$(p \rightarrow q)$		p	C = T?
F	F	T	(not critical)	..	..
F	T	T	✓	F	No
T	F	F	(not critical)	..	..
T	T	T	✓	T	Yes

Since we have one row with "No" answer in the column titled "In this critical row: C = T?", the argument form is invalid.

It is important to translate the above formal proof back to the English language sentence(s) to assure the reader what invalidates the argument. The critical row which invalidates the argument form gives us truth assignments p=F, q=T, in which both the premises are true, but the conclusion is false. Translating back this interpretation which invalidates the argument form to the sentences in the given argument, we have the scenario:

$\sim p$: It is not the case that Nischit's program is correct.
q: Nischit would complete the assignment in two hours.

In the above scenario, both the premises are true, but the conclusion is false. So this scenario invalidates the argument.

□

2.6.2. Law of Syllogism (LS)

This rule is also called as the rule of transitive reasoning. Its form is given below.

$p \rightarrow q$

$q \rightarrow r$

$\therefore\ p \rightarrow r$

To establish the validity of LS, we need to prove that the following formula in propositional logic is a tautology:

$$((p \rightarrow q) \wedge (q \rightarrow r)) \rightarrow (p \rightarrow r)$$

This can easily be established using the truth-table method, and we leave it to the reader to complete this proof.

Example 2.21. Identify the structure of the following argument, and establish its logical validity:

If 35244 is divisible by 396, then it is divisible by 66. If 35244 is divisible by 66, then it is divisible by 3. Therefore, if 35244 is divisible by 396, then it is divisible by 3.

Solution: We identify the following statement variables:

p: (The number) 35244 is divisible by 396.

q: It (the number 35244) is divisible 66.

r: It (the number 35244) is divisible 3.

With this choice, the above argument has the following structure (form):

$p \rightarrow q$

$q \rightarrow r$

$\therefore\ p \rightarrow r$

This is exactly the form of LS. Hence, due to the structure of the argument (as LS), it is valid.

□

Example 2.22: Let us visit the scenario in the beginning of Part 1 of this module. Chetana has made the following statements:

"If I am a student in School of Biological Sciences, I am not a student in School of Computer Science. I am student in School of Computer Science or I am not a student in School of Biological Sciences."

Can Amit conclude that Chetana is a student in the School of Biological Sciences?

Solution: Let us identify the following statement variables in the statements of Chetana:

p: Chetana is a student in School of Biological Sciences.

q: Chetana is a student in School of Computer Science.

We take the Chetana's statements as premises, and carry out the analysis as follows.

(1) $p \rightarrow \sim q$ ... Premise 1

(2) $q \vee \sim p$ ... Premise 2

(3) $\sim q \rightarrow \sim p$ ...Equivalence on (2): Law of Logic (introducing $\rightarrow$ to replace $\vee$)

(4) $p \rightarrow \sim p$ ... LS, (1), (3)

(5) $\sim p \vee \sim p$ ... Equivalence on (4): Law of Logic (introducing $\vee$ to replace $\rightarrow$)

(6) $\sim p$ ... Idempotent law on (5)

Hence, Chetana is not a student in School of Biological Sciences.

While the tools introduced till now enabled us to conclude that Chetana is not a student in School of Biological Sciences, you may argue that this is not the humanly justification, or "natural deduction". While we do not intend to introduce the work of logic done in such area of natural deduction (well-known approach being Gentzen's natural deduction system; readable information in Wikipedia at link: https://en.wikipedia.org/wiki/Natural_deduction) and other axiomatic approaches (e.g., Frege-Lukasiewicz System, Hilbert-Ackermann System, etc.), we shall revisit this problem when we introduce the inference rule of Proof by Contradiction (PC) later in section 2.5.8.

Example 2.23. (Example 2.19 revisited) Identify the structure of the following argument, and establish its logical validity:

> If Smita is participating in tennis tournaments, then she is not participating in chess tournaments. If Smita is not participating in chess tournaments, then she is not eligible for the travel grant in the chess players' category. Smita is participating in tennis tournaments. Therefore, Smita is not eligible for the travel grant in the chess players' category.

Solution: We identify the following statement variables:

p: Smita is participating in tennis tournaments.

q: Smita is not participating in chess tournaments.

r: Smita is not eligible for the travel grant in the chess players' category.

With this choice, the above argument has the following structure (form):

$p \rightarrow q$

$q \rightarrow r$

p

$\therefore\ r$

This form is neither the exact form of Law of Syllogism (LS), nor Modus Ponens (MP). However, using these two rules of inference, we can establish the validity of this form as follows.

We represent a logical argument by writing the statements on separate lines. For the statements which logically follow from the earlier statements, we give a justification of the known rule of inference. Thus, we also write the above argument form as:

(1) $p \to q$ ... Premise 1

(2) $q \to r$ ... Premise 2

(3) p ... Premise 3

(4) $p \to r$ ... LS on (2), (3)

(5) r ... MP on (3), (4) (also, Conclusion.)

This forms a valid proof.

□

Note that, the alternate proof can also be written using the repeated application of MP as was done in Example 2.19 earlier. While the above solution illustrates that LS may not be needed as separate rule of inference (as proof can be constructed in terms of repeated application of MP), we also note that, for situations like the ones in Example 2.21 and Example 2.22, LS is a convenient rule of inference. In the Exercise 2.1, we shall probe this question further about the rewriting arguments with conditional in the conclusion further, whether, even in situations like Example 2.21, we need not use LS, and we can only apply MP to derive the conclusion. This is mainly because we can antecedent of the *conditional conclusion* can be taken as additional premise (which we call A_p in exercise 2.1), and the argument form can be re-cast in the new (but equivalent to the original) form which has only consequent of the *conditional conclusion* is made the conclusion (of this re-formulated new argument form). For the situations like Example 2.22, construction of proofs which do not use LS requires us to explore its alternative proof structure as we shall discuss later in Example 2.29.

2.6.3. *Modus Tollens (MT)*

This rule is another form of Modus Ponens, or another form of the rule of detachment. This allows us to remove the consequent part of conditional, and infer the negation of the antecedent part of the conditional. Its form is given below.

$\sim q$
$p \rightarrow q$

$\therefore \sim p$

To establish the validity of MT, we need to prove that the following formula in propositional logic is a tautology:

$$((\sim q \wedge (p \rightarrow q)) \rightarrow (\sim p)$$

This can easily be established using the truth-table method, and we leave it to the reader to complete this proof.

Example 2.24. Establish the validity of the following argument:

> If Smita is not participating in chess tournaments, then she is not eligible for the travel grant in the chess players' category. Smita is eligible for the travel grant in the chess players' category. Therefore, Smita is participating in chess tournaments.

Solution: We identify the following statement variables:

p: Smita is not participating in chess tournaments.

q: She (Smita) is not eligible for the travel grant in the chess players' category.

With this choice, the above argument has the following structure (form):

$p \rightarrow q$
$\sim q$

$\therefore \sim p$

This is exactly the form of Modus Tollens (MT), which is one of the rules of inference. Hence the argument is valid.

□

Alternate proof of the validity of the argument form of Example 2.21 is as follows:

(1) $p \rightarrow q$ ... Premise 1
(2) $\sim q$ ... Premise 2
(3) $\sim q \rightarrow \sim p$... RR :(replace ($p \rightarrow q$) by its logical equivalent contra-positive ($\sim q \rightarrow \sim p$))
(4) $\sim p$ ... MP on (2), (3) (also, Conclusion.)

This is an alternate valid proof, which does not make use of Modus Tollens (MT), but it makes use of MP, and the fact that the conditional ($p \rightarrow q$) is logically equivalent to its contra-positive ($\sim q \rightarrow \sim p$). Thus, in the light of laws of logic, MT can always be expressed a replacement of the conditional by its contra-positive, followed by one application of Modus Ponens (MP). This also indicates the power of MP for proofs.

2.6.3.1. Caution on the application of MT

Recall our earlier conversation that we introduced in section 1.6.2.

> Subhash: "If you want to take the course CS 207: Database and Information Systems, then you must take CS 203: Data Structures and Algorithms."
>
> Sneha: "Ahhh..., based on Subhash's information, I conclude that if I do not want to take the course CS 207: Database and Information Systems, then I need not take CS 203: Data Structures and Algorithms."

In the above, someone may (erroneously) argue that the validity of this argument follows from Modus Tollens (MT). However, this is not so. You may like to refer to section 1.6.2: Inverse of Conditional, and review the Example 1.10, in which we pointed out "Inverse Error" in the above argument in section 1.6.2. To further emphasize this erroneous application, we need to uncover the structure of the above argument. We do the same in the following example.

Example 2.25. Identify the structure of the following argument, and establish its logical invalidity:

> If Sneha wants to take the course CS 207: Database and Information Systems, then Sneha must take CS 203: Data Structures and Algorithms. Sneha does not want to take the course CS 207: Database and Information Systems. Therefore, Sneha need not take CS 203: Data Structures and Algorithms.

Solution: We identify the following propositional (statement) variables:

p: Sneha wants to take the course CS 207: Database and Information Systems.
q: Sneha must take CS 203: Data Structures and Algorithms.

Notes: $\sim p$: Sneha does not want to take the course CS 207: Database and Information Systems.
$\sim q$: Sneha does not need to take CS 203: Data Structures and Algorithms.

With this choice, the above argument has the following structure (form):

$$p \to q$$
$$\sim p$$

$$\therefore \sim q$$

This is *not* the form of Modus Tollens (MT). Note that, in MT, we must have negation of *consequent* as an additional premise. In the above form, we have negation of antecedent as an additional premise. It turns out that this argument form is invalid. To establish the invalidity of this argument form, we use the method exactly similar to Example 2.8. For the sake of completeness and to emphasize the method for establishing the non-validity, we repeat it below.
Let us explore the validity problem by the truth-table method. We identify the premises P_1: $p \to q$, P_2: $\sim p$. We first identify the statement variables involved as *p*, *q*. Using these as atomic variables, we construct truth table with P_1, and P_2 as its columns.

p	*q*	P_1: $(p \to q)$	P_2: $\sim p$	*Critical Rows*
F	F	T	T	✓
F	T	T	T	✓
T	F	F	F	(not critical)
T	T	T	F	(not critical)

The conclusion C: $\sim q$. After identifying all critical rows, we find the truth-value of Conclusion in all the critical rows. We get the following truth-table.

p	q	P_1: $(p \to q)$	P_2: $\sim p$	*Critical Rows*	C: $\sim q$
F	F	T	T	✓	T
F	T	T	T	✓	F
T	F	F	F	(not critical)	..
T	T	T	F	(not critical)	..

Next, create a new column in which we state the answer to the question: "Is the conclusion C = T (True) in the (concerned) critical row? The answer (Yes/No) is entered in the respective critical row.

p	P_2: q	P_1: $(p \to q)$	P_2: $\sim p$	*Critical Rows*	C: $\sim q$	In this critical row: C = T?
F	F	T	T	✓	T	Yes
F	T	T	T	✓	F	No
T	F	F	F	(not critical)	..	..
T	T	T	F	(not critical)	..	..

Since we have one row with "No" answer in the column titled "In this critical row: C = T?", the argument form is invalid.

□

It is important to translate the above formal proof back to the English language sentence(s) to assure the reader what invalidates the argument. The critical row which does not invalidate the argument form gives us truth assignments p=F, q=F, in which both the premises are true, and the conclusion is also true. Translating back this interpretation which invalidates the argument form to the sentences in the given argument, we have the scenario:

$\sim p$: Sneha does not want to take the course CS 207: Database and Information Systems.

$\sim q$: Sneha does not need to take CS 203: Data Structures and Algorithms.

In the above scenario (interpretation), both the premises are true, and the conclusion is also true. However, this interpretation does not establish the validity of the argument. For example, imagine a situation that CS 203 is prerequisite for another course say CS 204: Design and Analysis of Algorithms, and maybe for CS 303: Artificial Intelligence and Machine Learning (AIML) as well. Sneha may want to take one of these courses, say CS 303: Artificial Intelligence and Machine Learning. However, under the above scenario, she would not be able to take CS 303. Thus, there exists at least one scenario that invalidates the argument. To make sure that there is no such scenario (interpretation) that invalidates the argument, for our analysis using truth-table, we have to exhaust all critical rows in the truth table and make sure that, in all critical rows, the conclusion of our argument form is true.

In automated reasoning as needed for areas of AIML, our argument form may involve few thousands, and even millions of propositional variables. In such practical situations, generating all critical rows leads to excessive computations, and writing efficient programs to quickly discover a critical row that invalidates argument form (involving few millions of propositional variables) remains a central problem in Computer Science and Engineering till date. We shall revisit importance as well as the gravity of such efficient solution as central computational problem in more details in the course on Theory of Computation/Automata Theory. While more discussion is beyond the scope our present discussion, interested reader may explore further from Wikipedia the Boolean Satisfiability (SAT) problem, popularly known as SAT.

2.6.4. Rule of Conjunction (RC)

This rule allows us to infer the conjunction of two premises. Its form is given below.

p

q

$\therefore\ p \wedge q$

To establish the validity of RC, we need to prove that the following formula in propositional logic is a tautology:

$$(p \wedge q) \rightarrow (p \wedge q)$$

This can easily be established using the truth-table method. In fact, it is easy to see that both the antecedent and the consequent of the conditional are equivalent. So, one way implication is definitely true. Although RC may look to be too trivial in this sense, we state it as it is a convenient rule of inference while writing proofs in sequential (step-by-step) fashion.

Example 2.26. Establish the validity of the following argument:

The Yoga day celebration was held on time. The T-shirt of the institute was distributed during the Yoga day celebration. Therefore, the Yoga day celebration was held on time and the T-shirt of the institute was distributed during the Yoga day celebration.

.

Solution: We identify the following statement variables:
p: The Yoga day celebration was held on time.
q: The T-shirt of the institute was distributed during the Yoga day celebration.

With this choice, the above argument has the following structure (form):

p
q

$\therefore\ p \wedge q$

This is exactly the form of Rule of Conjunction (RC), which is one of the rules of inference. Hence the argument is valid.

□

2.6.5. Disjunctive Syllogism (DS)

This rule applies when we have one premise as the disjunction of two statement variables, and other premise as negation of one of the constituent statement variables of the disjunction of the first premise. From these premises, this rule allows us to infer the second statement variable. Its form is given below.

$p \vee q$
$\sim p$
$\therefore\ q$

To establish the validity of RC, we need to prove that the following formula in propositional logic is a tautology:
$((p \vee q) \wedge (\sim p)) \rightarrow (q)$
This can be established using the truth-table method. In fact, by the logical equivalence of the conditional (the conditional as expressed in terms of one negation, and one disjunction operation), we obtain:

$(p \vee q) \equiv (\sim p \rightarrow q)$
Hence, the DS is can be written in its equivalent form:

$\sim p \rightarrow q$
$\sim p$

$\therefore \quad q$

Replacing $\sim p$ by other variable, say r, this form is easily recognizable as a Modus Ponens (MP). Thus, RC is another form of MP.

Example 2.27. Establish the validity of the following argument:
There is an undeclared variable in the program or there is a syntax error. There is no undeclared variable. Therefore, there is a syntax error.

Solution: We identify the following statement variables:
p: There is an undeclared variable in the program.
q: There is a syntax error.
With this choice, the above argument has the following structure (form):

$p \vee q$
$\sim p$

$\therefore \quad q$

This is exactly the form of Disjunctive Syllogism (DS), which is one of the rules of inference. Hence the argument is valid.

□

2.6.6. *Conjunctive Simplification (CS)*

From the conjunction, this rule allows us to infer one part. Its form is given below.

$p \wedge q$

$\therefore p$

As an independent rule of inference, this rule (as well as next rule, Disjunctive Amplification – DA) We state this rule CS (as well as DA) as a separate inference rules, because, while constructing the proofs, these rules are useful.

To establish the validity of CS, we need to prove that the following formula in propositional logic is a tautology:

$$(p \wedge q) \rightarrow (p)$$

This can easily be established using the truth-table method.

Example 2.28. Establish the validity of the following argument:

> The Yoga day celebration was held on time and the T-Shirt of the institute was distributed during the Yoga day celebration. Therefore, the Yoga day celebration was held on time.

Solution: We identify the following statement variables:

p: The Yoga day celebration was held on time.

q: The T-Shirt of the institute was distributed during the Yoga day celebration.

With this choice, the above argument has the following structure (form):

$p \wedge q$

$\therefore\ p$

This is exactly the form of Conjunctive Simplification (CS), which is one of the rules of inference. Hence the argument is valid.

□

2.6.7. Disjunctive Amplification (DA)

This rule allows us to *add* (or, amplify, with disjunction operation) any other formula in propositional logic. Its form is given below.

p

$\therefore\ p \vee q$

To establish the validity of DA, we need to prove that the following formula in propositional logic is a tautology:

$$(p) \rightarrow (p \vee q)$$

This can be established using truth-table method, and we leave it to the reader to complete this proof.

Example 2.29. Establish the validity of the following argument:

There is an undeclared variable in the program. Therefore, there is an undeclared variable in the program or there is a syntax error.

Solution: We identify the following propositional (statement) variables:

p: There is an undeclared variable in the program.

q: There is a syntax error.

With this choice, the above argument has the following structure (form):

$$
\begin{array}{ll}
 & p \\
 & \text{--------} \\
\therefore & p \vee q
\end{array}
$$

This is exactly the form of Disjunctive Amplification (DA), which is one of the rules of inference. Hence the argument is valid.

□

By the logical equivalence of the conditional (the conditional as expressed in terms of negation and disjunction operation), we obtain:

$(p \vee q) \equiv (\sim p \rightarrow q)$

Hence, the DA is can be written in its equivalent form:

$$
\begin{array}{ll}
 & p \\
 & \text{--------} \\
\therefore & \sim p \rightarrow q
\end{array}
$$

Example 2.30. Establish the validity of the following argument:

Aditi attends the lecture. Therefore, if Aditi does not attend the lecture, Aditi is in the hostel.

Solution: We identify the following propositional (statement) variables:

p: Aditi attends the lecture.

q: Aditi is in the hostel.

With this choice, the above argument has the following structure (form):

p

$\therefore\ \sim p \rightarrow q$

This is exactly Disjunctive Amplification (DA) written in its equivalent form, which is one of the rules of inference. Hence the argument is valid.

□

2.6.8. Proof by Contradiction (PC)

Suppose that p is a statement which we wish to prove. With the assumption of $(\sim p)$ being true (i.e., p is false), if we are able to establish the contradiction (F), then, using this rule of inference, we conclude that p is true.
Formally, we state this inference rule as follows:

$\sim p \rightarrow$ F

$\therefore\ p$

To establish the validity of PC, we need to prove that the following formula in propositional logic is a tautology:

$$(\sim p \rightarrow \mathrm{F}) \rightarrow (p) \qquad \ldots (2.7)$$

This can be established using truth-table method, and we leave it to the reader to complete this proof.

As promised earlier in section 2.5.2, we revisit Example 2.22 to see how proof by contradiction (PC) can *naturally* help Amit to conclude that Chetana is not the student of School of Biological Sciences. The following solution approach uses some aspects of Gentzen's *natural* deduction system (which we do not cover in detail).

Example 2.31: (Example 2.22 revisited). Chetana has made the following statements:

> "If I am a student in School of Biological Sciences, I am not a student in School of Computer Science. I am student in School of Computer Science or I am not a student in School of Biological Sciences."

Can Amit conclude that Chetana is a student in the School of Biological Sciences?

Solution: Let us identify the following statement variables in the statements of Chetana:
p: Chetana is a student in School of Biological Sciences.

q: Chetana is a student in School of Computer Science.
In our analysis, we take the Chetana's statements as premises.

(1) $p \rightarrow \sim q$ ... Premise 1

(2) $q \vee \sim p$ ... Premise 2

With the above two premises, let us assume that Amit wants to conclude p. This is Amit's additional premise, say premise (3.1). Due to Amit's additional premise, Amit's scenario is affected by it, and hence the additional steps Amit infers due to this scenario are given additional indentation to indicate "inner" nesting level. We continue the analysis, numbering the steps as 3.1, 3.2, ... etc. Note that, the consequents which have made use of premise (3.1) have "inner" nesting level. With the usual *nesting rules* of block structuring, all premises which are at the outer level are available for use within the inner nesting level (Chetana's statements are premises to Amit).

(1) $p \rightarrow \sim q$ ... Premise 1

(2) $q \vee \sim p$ ... Premise 2

(3.1) p ... Amit's Additional Premise

(3.2) $\sim q$ ... MP, (3.1), (1)

(3.3) $\sim p$ ... DS, (3.2), (2)

(3.4) $p \wedge \sim p$ ... RC (3.1), (3.3)

(3.5) F ... Inverse Law on (3.4)

(3) $p \rightarrow F$ ... Result of inner nested analysis steps (3.1) ... (3.5)

(4) $\sim p$ ... by PC

Thus, using Proof by Contradiction (PC), Amit has proved that Chetana is not a student in School of Biological Sciences.

□

2.6.9. Other Inference Rules

For the sake of completeness, we now state the other commonly used inference rules.

2.6.9.1. Proof by Cases (PCS)

This rule applies when we have both the premises as the conditional, whose consequent is same. Due to this inference rule, we infer that the antecedents of common consequent can be collected together by taking their disjunction as a common antecedent. Its form is given below.

$p \rightarrow r$

$q \rightarrow r$

$\therefore\ (p \vee q) \rightarrow r$

To establish the validity of PCS, we need to prove that the following formula in propositional logic is a tautology:

$((p \rightarrow r) \wedge (q \rightarrow r)) \rightarrow ((p \vee q) \rightarrow r)$

This can be established using the truth-table method.

Example 2.32. Establish the validity of the following argument:

If the number x is positive (i.e., $x > 0$), then x^2 is positive. If the number x is negative then x^2 is positive. Therefore, if the number x is positive or (the number x is) negative, then x^2 is positive.

Solution: We identify the following statement variables:

p: The number x is positive.

q: The number x is negative.

r: (The number) x^2 is positive.

With this choice, the above argument has the following structure (form):

$p \rightarrow r$

$q \rightarrow r$

$\therefore\ (p \vee q) \rightarrow r$

This is exactly the form of PCS, which is one of the rules of inference. Hence the argument is valid.

□

Observing that the number zero is neither positive or negative, there is a subtler point to be noted in the above example. In particular, we note that q: The number x is negative, *is not* the negation of the statement p: The number x is positive. Note that the negation of q: The number x is negative, which we denote by $\sim q$, is true for all non-negative numbers, *i.e.*, numbers which are positive, and including *zero*.

Hence the alternate appropriate representation of "the number x is positive or (the number x is) negative" is "the number x is non-zero". Using this, we could have re-written the argument in Example 2.32 as follows:

> If the number x is positive, then x^2 is positive. If the number x is negative then x^2 is positive. Therefore, if the number x is non-zero, then x^2 is positive.

Example 2.33 (Example 2.22 and 2.31 revisited): Let us visit the scenario in the beginning of Part 1 of this module. Chetana has made the following statements:

> "If I am a student in School of Biological Sciences, I am not a student in School of Computer Science. I am student in School of Computer Science or I am not a student in School of Biological Sciences."

Can Amit conclude that Chetana is a student in the School of Biological Sciences?

Solution: Let us identify the following statement variables in the statements of Chetana:

p: Chetana is a student in School of Biological Sciences.

q: Chetana is a student in School of Computer Science.

We take the Chetana's statements as premises, and carry out the analysis as follows.

(1) $p \rightarrow \sim q$ ... Premise 1

(2) $q \vee \sim p$ ... Premise 2

(3) $\sim q \rightarrow \sim p$ ...Equivalence on (2): Law of Logic (introducing $\rightarrow$ to replace $\vee$)

(4) $q \rightarrow \sim p$ ...Equivalence on (1): Conditional in (1) replaced by its contrapositive

(5) $(\sim q \vee q) \rightarrow \sim p$ ... PCS on (3), (4)

(6) $(\mathrm{T}) \rightarrow \sim p$ ... inverse law to substitute the antecedent of conditional in (5), namely, $\sim q \vee q$, with its equivalence as T (Tautology)

(7) $\mathrm{F} \vee \sim p$ ...Equivalence on (6): Law of Logic (replace $\rightarrow$ by introducing $\vee$)

(8) $\sim p$ ... identity law for $\vee$ on (7)

Therefore, Amit can *infer* (*i.e.*, conclude) that Chetana is not student in school of Biological sciences. As per the above proof as given in Example 2.33 above, it is only logical *inference*, and *not* logical *equivalence*, because, in the above proof, we used *inference rule* named PCS in step (5), and steps (6), (7) and eventually step (8) depend on this application of "inference rule", which is not "(equivalence) law of logic". □

Please note the difference between the above proof in Example 2.22, as well as Example 2.31, where we "proved" that the propositions are logically equivalent to $\sim p$.

As an exercise, starting with the simple proposition (fact) that

> "Chetana is not student in School of Biological sciences."

which Laws of Logic were applied by Chetana to get the following set of propositions (that are logically equivalent to the above)?

> "If I am a student in School of Biological Sciences, I am not a student in School of Computer Science. I am student in School of Computer Science or I am not a student in School of Biological Sciences."

Sometimes this inference rule is also stated by "pushing up" the *antecedent* of conclusion conditional to make it as additional premise (refer to Exercise 2.1, which enables us to do this). Thus, modified PCS, which we call M-PCS, is as follows:

$p \vee q$
$p \rightarrow r$
$q \rightarrow r$

$\therefore\ r$

Example 2.34: (Example 2.22, Example 2.31, and Example 2.33 revisited). Chetana has made the following statements:

> "If I am a student in School of Biological Sciences, I am not a student in School of Computer Science. I am student in School of Computer Science or I am not a student in School of Biological Sciences."

Can Amit conclude that Chetana is a student in the School of Biological Sciences?

Solution: Let us identify the following statement variables in the statements of Chetana:
p: Chetana is a student in School of Biological Sciences.
q: Chetana is a student in School of Computer Science.
In our analysis, we take the Chetana's statements as premises.

(1) $p \rightarrow \sim q$ ... Premise 1
(2) $q \vee \sim p$ ... Premise 2
(3) $q \rightarrow \sim p$ ... Law of Logic on (1) : contrapositive equiv. to conditional
(4) $\sim q \rightarrow \sim p$ ... Equivalence Law of Logic on (2) : replace $\vee$ by $\rightarrow$
(5) T ... Tautology can be used as "additional premise"
(6) $q \vee \sim q$ ... Substitute T in (5) by Inverse Law for $\vee$
(7) $\sim p$ ... M-PCS on (6), (3), (4)

Thus, using the Modified Proof by Cases (M-PCS) inference rule, Amit can *infer* (*i.e.*, can conclude) that Chetana is not a student in School of Biological Sciences.

□

2.6.9.2. Conditional Proof (CP)

The form of Conditional Proof (CP) is given below.

$p \wedge q$
$\rightarrow (q \rightarrow r)$

$\therefore\ r$

To establish the validity of CP, we need to prove that the following formula in propositional logic is a tautology:

$$((p \wedge q) \wedge (p \rightarrow (q \rightarrow r))) \rightarrow (r)$$

This can be established using the truth-table method.

2.6.9.3. *Constructive Dilemma (CD)*

The form of Constructive Dilemma (CD) is given below.

$p \rightarrow r$
$q \rightarrow s$
$p \vee q$

$\therefore\ r \vee s$

To establish the validity of CD, we need to prove that the following formula in propositional logic is a tautology:

$((p \rightarrow r) \wedge ((q \rightarrow s) \wedge (p \vee q)) \rightarrow (r \vee s)$

This can be established using the truth-table method.

Example 2.35: (Example 2.22, Example 2.31, Example 2.33 and Example 2.34 revisited). Chetana has made the following statements:

> "If I am a student in School of Biological Sciences, I am not a student in School of Computer Science. I am student in School of Computer Science, or I am not a student in School of Biological Sciences."

Can Amit conclude that Chetana is a student in the School of Biological Sciences?

Solution: Let us identify the following statement variables in the statements of Chetana:
p: Chetana is a student in School of Biological Sciences.
q: Chetana is a student in School of Computer Science.
In our analysis, we take the Chetana's statements as premises.

(1) $p \rightarrow \sim q$ … Premise 1
(2) $q \vee \sim p$ … Premise 2
(3) $q \rightarrow \sim p$ … Law of Logic on (1) : contrapositive equiv. to conditional
(4) $\sim q \rightarrow \sim p$ … Equivalence Law of Logic on (2) : replace $\vee$ by $\rightarrow$
(5) T … Tautology can be used as "additional premise"

(6) $q \vee \sim q$ ... Substitute T in (5) by Inverse Law for $\vee$

(7) $\sim p$ ... Constructive Dilemma (CD) on (6), (3), and (4)

Thus, using the Constructive Dilemma (CD) as inference rule, Amit can *infer* (*i.e.*, can conclude) that Chetana is not a student in School of Biological Sciences.

□

2.6.9.4. Destructive Dilemma (DD)

The form of Destructive Dilemma (DD) is given below.

$p \rightarrow r$

$q \rightarrow s$

$\sim r \vee \sim s$

----------=-

$\therefore \sim p \vee \sim q$

To establish the validity of DD, we need to prove that the following formula in propositional logic is a tautology:

$((p \rightarrow r) \wedge ((q \rightarrow s) \wedge (\sim r \vee \sim s)) \rightarrow (\sim p \vee \sim q)$

This can be established using the truth-table method.

Example 2.36: (Example 2.22, Example 2.31, Example 2.33 Example 2.34 and Example 2.35 revisited). Chetana has made the following statements:

> "If I am a student in School of Biological Sciences, I am not a student in School of Computer Science. I am student in School of Computer Science, or I am not a student in School of Biological Sciences."

Can Amit conclude that Chetana is a student in the School of Biological Sciences?

Solution: Let us identify the following statement variables in the statements of Chetana:
p: Chetana is a student in School of Biological Sciences.
q: Chetana is a student in School of Computer Science.

In our analysis, we take the Chetana's statements as premises.

(1) $p \to \sim q$ ... Premise 1
(2) $q \vee \sim p$ ... Premise 2
(3) $\sim p \vee q$ ... commutativity of $\vee$ on (2)
(4) $p \to q$ ... Equivalence Law of Logic on (3) : replace $\vee$ by $\to$
(5) T ... Tautology can be used as "additional premise"
(6) $(\sim q) \vee \sim (\sim q)$ ... Substitute T in (5) by Inverse Law for $\vee$
(7) $(\sim p) \vee (\sim p)$ ... Destructive Dilemma (DD) on (1), (4), and (6)
(8) $\sim p$ ... Idempotent Law for $\vee$ on (7) (and brackets removed)

Thus, using the Destructive Dilemma (DD) as inference rule, Amit can *infer* (*i.e.*, can conclude) that Chetana is not a student in School of Biological Sciences.

□

2.6.10. *Summary Table: Inference Rules*

For ready reference, in the following table, we summarize the inference rules. This table can be used as a reference while constructing formal proofs.

Inference Rules in Logic

Rule of Conjunction (RC)	$\begin{array}{c} p \\ q \\ \hline p \wedge q \end{array}$	Disjunctive Syllogism (DS)	$\begin{array}{c} p \vee q \\ \sim p \\ \hline q \end{array}$	Law of Syllogism (LS)	$\begin{array}{c} p \to q \\ q \to r \\ \hline p \to r \end{array}$
Conjunctive Simplification (CS)	$\begin{array}{c} p \wedge q \\ \hline p \end{array}$	Disjunctive Amplification (DA)	$\begin{array}{c} p \\ \hline p \vee q \end{array}$	Proof by Contradiction (PC)	$\begin{array}{c} \sim p \to F \\ \hline p \end{array}$
Modus Ponens (MP)	$\begin{array}{c} p \to q \\ p \\ \hline q \end{array}$	Modus Tollens (MT)	$\begin{array}{c} p \to q \\ \sim q \\ \hline \sim p \end{array}$	Conditional Proof (CP)	$\begin{array}{c} p \wedge q \\ p \to (q \to r) \\ \hline r \end{array}$

Constructive Dilemma (CD)	$p \to r$ $q \to s$ $p \vee q$ ――― $r \vee s$	Destructive Dilemma (DD)	$p \to r$ $q \to s$ $\sim r \vee \sim s$ ――― $\sim p \vee \sim q$	Proof by cases (PCS)	$p \to r$ $q \to r$ ――― $(p \vee q) \to r$

2.7 Proofs Using Inference Rules

For modelling a given argument in the domain of propositional logic, we first extract its argument form. Next, to prove the validity of the argument, we establish the validity of this extracted argument form by writing down its proof. For us, the proof consists of a sequence of steps, each of which is numbered, where each step can be derived by exactly one application of the law of logic, or exactly one inference rule.

Example 2.37: Consider the following scenario:

Suppose that Ram is in hurry to reach the office, and discovers that he is not able to locate his spectacles. Ram tries hard to recollect where the spectacles could be. In the process recollection, Ram discovers that the following facts:

(1) If Ram was reading the novel in the bedroom, then the spectacles are on the bed table.
(2) If Ram was reading the newspaper in the living room, then the spectacles are on the coffee table.
(3) If Ram was reading the newspaper in the kitchen, then the spectacles are on the kitchen table.
(4) Ram was reading the newspaper in the living room, or he was reading the newspaper in the kitchen.
(5) If the spectacles are on the kitchen table, then Ram would notice the spectacles at the breakfast today.
(6) If Ram took the medicine yesterday night, and the spectacles are on the bed table, then Ram would have noticed the spectacles on the bed table yesterday night.
(7) Ram took the medicine yesterday night.
(8) Ram did not notice the spectacles on the bed table yesterday night.
(9) If Ram was not reading the novel in the bedroom, then he was reading the newspaper in the living room.

From the above facts, can Ram (logically) infer where the spectacles are?

Solution: We identify the following statement variables:

p: Ram was reading the novel in the bedroom.

q: The spectacles are on the bed table.

r: Ram was reading the newspaper in the living room.

s: The spectacles are on the coffee table.

t:. Ram was reading the newspaper in the kitchen.

u: The spectacles are on the kitchen table.

v: Ram would notice the spectacles at the breakfast today.

w: Ram took the medicine yesterday night.

x: Ram would notice the spectacles on the bed table yesterday night.

With this choice, the above argument has the following structure (form):

(1) $p \rightarrow q$ ... Premise 1

(2) $r \rightarrow s$ ... Premise 2

(3) $t \rightarrow u$ ... Premise 3

(4) $r \vee t$ ... Premise 4

(5) $u \rightarrow v$ ... Premise 5

(6) $(w \wedge q) \rightarrow x$ ... Premise 6

(7) w ... Premise 7

(8) $\sim x$ ... Premise 8

(9) $\sim p \rightarrow r$ ... Premise 9

The analysis which Ram can carry out is given below.

(10) $\sim(w \wedge q)$ ... MT, (8), (6)

(11) $\sim w \vee \sim q$ ... De Morgan's law on (10)

(12) $\sim q$ ... DS, (11), (7)

(13) $\sim p$ ... MT, (1), (12)

(14) r ... MP, (13), (9)

(15) s ... MP, (14), (2)

Thus, s is true, *i.e.*, Spectacles are on the coffee table. Using the available information, Ram can infer the location of the spectacles as being on the coffee table.

□

For this inference, Ram did not make use of the information in premises (3), (4), (5). In typical proofs, we find that we may not really need all the information available as premises to complete the proof. What is needed and what is not needed is an important issue in the proof construction, and this freedom is one of the reasons why proofs are difficult to construct. Additional information available in the form of premises may actually make the process of inferring the conclusion difficult as we may get distracted due to this *information overloading*.

Chetana avoided passing direct information (which may be considered as a fact, or as data) to Amit. Would you say that try to distract Amit by *information overlading*?

We note that *proof* is a representation of the reasoning process of an individual by which he has concluded the conclusion (of the argument). The acceptable form of representation of a proof is its writing in sequential (step-by-step) fashion, giving the additional justification of each step clearly. This requirement of clarity needs the discipline of exactly one law of logic, or inference rule to be followed in one step.

The proof in formal logic needs to be carried out to the extent of details exposes certain lines of reasoning to the scrutiny by others. For Amit-Chetana's opening example of Part 1 of Module on Logic, we gave various ways of expressing the reasoning (Example 2.22, Example 2.31, Example 2.33 to 36) by which Amit infers that Chetana is not a student in school of Biological Sciences. Through these different ways of reasoning, we already introduced three different ways of constructing the proofs. Proof construction can be very complicated. To gain further insight in the proof construction process, in Module threee, we shall continue our discussion of proof techniques.

□

EXERCISES

2.1. In section 2.5.2, we stated the Logical Syllogism (LS) as inference rule. In LS, we have the argument with the following structure (form):

$p \to q$

$q \to r$

$\therefore\ p \to r$

Let us rewrite the above argument labelling the premises within the same. (We keep the conditional structure of the conclusion intact).

P_1: $p \to q$

P_2: $q \to r$

$\therefore\ p \to r$

Let us denote the conjunction of premises P_1 and P_2 by J_P. Note that J_P itself is a (compound) proposition, say s. Using the above notation, we reformulate the structure of the above argument form as follows:

J_p: s

$\therefore\ p \to r$

In order to prove the validity of the above argument form, we establish the validity of the following formula in the propositional logic:

$s \to (p \to r)$

(i) Prove that, the formula $s \to (p \to r)$ is logically equivalent to the formula $(s \wedge p) \to r$, *i.e.*,

$$s \to (p \to r) \Leftrightarrow (s \wedge p) \to r \qquad (2.8)$$

(ii) Due to the logical equivalence proved in part (i), the job of proving the formula $s \to (p \to r)$ to be a is a tautology is equivalent to that of proving the formula $(s \wedge p) \to r$ is a tautology. Identifying two premises within this conditional as J_P : s and A_p: p, this means, we need to prove the validity of the following argument form:

J_P: s

A_p: p

$\therefore\ r$

This means, when we have the conclusion in the form of a conditional, we can take the premise for this conclusion conditional as additional premise (A_p), (along with the original (joint, *i.e.*, conjuncted) premises J_p) and formulate a new argument form whose validity needs to be established. Due to the presence of the additional premise, often proving the validity of this modified argument form is easier.

(iii) Replacing J_P by its original constituents ($P_1 \wedge P_2$), the above form is:

P_1: $p \rightarrow q$

P_2: $q \rightarrow r$

A_p: p

$\therefore\ r$

Thus, the LS can be re-cast in its new form as proving the validity of the above argument form. Note that we have already met this argument form in Example 2.17, as well as Example 2.21 (Selena in tournaments). As shown in the solution of Example 2.17, it is easy to prove the validity of this argument form by using two applications of Modus Ponens (MP). This observation, that conditional conclusion's antecedent, when appended with the premises, obviates the need for applying LS (and we can use repeated applications of our basic rule of inference MP), can be used at advantage in proofs.

Give additional suitable example(s) to illustrate that, proofs using LS can be expressed solely in terms of (repeated applications of) MP. Formulate the general (necessary and sufficient) properties of such proofs, and give an algorithm to test whether the proof possesses the property you have formulated.

2.2. (Resolution principle – in propositional logic) In section 2.5.2, we stated the Logical Syllogism (LS) as inference rule. In previous exercise, we reformulated LS as:

J_p: s

$\therefore\ p \to r$

Thus, we can write the form as:

J_p: $(p \to q) \land (q \to r)$

$\therefore\ p \to r$

Using the Law of Logic to replace the conditional $\to$ in terms of $\lor$, we obtain:

$(\sim p \lor q) \land (\sim q \lor r)$

$\therefore\ \sim p \lor r$

Replacing $\sim p$ by x, r by y and q by z, we write the above argument as:

$(x \lor z) \land (\sim z \lor y)$

$\therefore\ x \lor y$

Further, commutativity allows us to replace $(x \lor z)$ by its equivalent formula $(z \lor x)$. The above argument form gives us the following conditional:

$$((z \lor x) \land (\sim z \lor y)) \to (x \lor y) \qquad \ldots (2.9)$$

Prove that (2.9) is a tautology.

2.3. Formulate the following arguments as formal arguments in (propositional logic). Using your formulation of formal arguments, establish the validity of the argument, or give a counter-example to show that the argument is invalid.

(a) If you gamble, then you are a lazy person. You are not a lazy person. Therefore, you do not gamble.

(b) If it rains, then the ground is wet. It does not rain. Therefore, the ground is not wet.

(c) If you are eligible for the admission to the undergraduate program in the university, then you must have an age below 25 years. If your age is not below 25 years, then you do not qualify for the scholarship. Therefore, if you qualify for the scholarship, then you are eligible for the admission to the undergraduate program in the university.

(d) If computers can think, they must first have a mind. But we know that computers do not have a mind. Therefore, computers cannot think.

2.4. Consider the following scenario:

(i) If Shivani goes to the party, then Dhruv and Amit go to the party.

(ii) If Dhruv goes to the party then Ram does not go to the party.

(iii) If Ram does not go to the party, then Amit does not go to the party.

I want to go to the party if Amit goes to the party. Give propositional logic formulation of the scenario, and show how this formulation can be used to determine the question: Should I go to the party?

2.5. In Example 2.34, we commented about "information overload" as follows: "For this inference, Ram did not make use of the information in premises (3), (4), (5). In typical proofs, we find that we may not really need all the information available as premises to complete the proof. What is needed and what is not needed is an important issue in the proof construction, and this freedom is one of the reasons why proofs are difficult to construct."

(a) In Example 2.34, we considered 9 facts, which formed the premises for our analysis. To these 9 facts, add some more facts (which can be formulated as formulae in propositional logic), so that the scenario does not allow Ram to logically infer the location of the spectacles.

(b) Give the algorithm to analyse when the premises consisting of formulae in the propositional logic form a situation you have been asked to create in (a).

(c) Briefly comment on the possible use of (a) and (b) above for automated reasoning.

2.6. In section 2.6.9.1, we formulated the following exercise.

Starting with the simple proposition (fact) that

"Chetana is not student in School of Biological sciences."

which Laws of Logic were applied by Chetana to get the following set of propositions (that are logically equivalent to the above)?

"If I am a student in School of Biological Sciences, I am not a student in School of Computer Science. I am student in School of Computer Science or I am not a student in School of Biological Sciences."

Complete this exercise by showing all steps involved clearly.

2.7. (Question for open discussion, not directly in the scope of what we covered till now.) Comment on the "logic" in the following argument:

> Medical doctors can refer to books on medicine for prescribing the medication to patient. Judges can refer to law books for giving judgement. Therefore, students should be allowed to refer to their study books in their examinations.

□

PART 3

Predicate Logic

3.1 PREDICATES

Let us consider modelling of which students in your university are also the students of the course CS 201. In propositional logic, we are forced to consider the statements like the following:

a) Aayush is a student of the course CS 201.
b) Aditi is a student of the course CS 201.
c) Ami is a student of the course CS 201.
d) Ankur is a student of the course CS 201.
e) Draupadi is a student of the course CS 201.
f) Devendra is a student of the course CS 201.
g) Jambuvant is a student of the course CS 201.
h) Ritika is a student of the course CS 201.

…

…

We note that each of the sentences above can be assigned a truth value T, or F. Assuming that there are 225000 students in your university, listing down the 225000 students' names results in 225000 propositions. Propositional logic needs every proposition to be assigned separate propositional (statement) variable. The formulation of a meaningful argument in terms of these 225000 statement variables is unwieldy and establishing the validity of an argument using truth-table method having 2^{225000} rows is an impossible task.

To develop a formal framework for reasoning in such cases, we look for what is the next best thing we can do. In propositional logic, we considered complete sentences which can be assigned truth-value T or F. The above collection of sentences gives us clue about what is common between them and what part is variable. The common part is the common property "… is a student of the course CS 201.", and the variable part is the name of student in your university. We note that the grammatical structure of a sentence is specified by the grammar rule: "a sentence is a subject followed by a predicate." The common part is precisely the predicate part. Allowing the variable part

to be substituted by a variable, say x, the collection of these statements can be specified by the common property, say P(x), as:
P(x): x is a student of the course CS 201.

So we got rid of the problem of keeping track of 225000 statement variables (at least for the time being). We also call P(x) as open statement, because it is *open* for the value of its subject. We note that, for modelling any scenario with a predicate, we must specify the collection from which the variable x assumes its value. This forms the *domain of discourse*, also called as *universe of discourse*, or just *universe*, for the variable x. In the absence of *Universe*, the predicate cannot be assigned any truth-value, and cannot be used for the reasoning.

Let us consider another example. In Part 1, for the Example 1.2 (i), "x" refers to some element; unless it is assigned a 'value', we cannot determine whether "$x + 3 = 4$" is true or false. If we assign a specific value to x, say $x = 1$, then the statement is true (T). For other value, say $x = 2$, the statement is false (F). Thus, the truth of falsity of the open statement depends on what value the variable x is assigned to. We call such statements as open statements, or predicates. For modelling using open statements, in addition to the open statement, we need to clearly specify the allowable choices of values which can be assigned to the variable x. The collection of values which the variable x can take is called as *Domain of discourse*, or *Universe of Discourse*, or sometimes just *Universe*, denoted by $\mathcal{U}$. We also call the open statement "$x + 3 = 4$" as one-place predicate, as it has one free variable, and denote it by the symbol P(.), or P(x).

In Example 1.2 (ii), we have other open statement "$x + y < 25$", which is another open statement. This open statement involves two free variables x, and y. The variable x may take values from one universe, say $\mathcal{U}_x$, and the variable y may take values from other universe, say $\mathcal{U}_y$. The universes $\mathcal{U}_x$ and $\mathcal{U}_y$ may in general be different (although usually they may be same, say integers, for the open statement "$x + y < 25$"). We call such statements as two-place predicates, as they have two free variables, both of which need to be assigned a value to make it a proposition. We denote two-place predicated by the symbol P(.,.) or P(x, y).

<u>Definition 3.1</u>. Open Statement (Predicate): A declarative sentence is an open statement (also called as predicate) if:

(1) the sentence contains one or more variables,
(2) the sentence is not a proposition (it cannot be assigned a truth value); however,
(3) the sentence become a proposition when the variables are replaced by certain allowable choices (from their respective Universes of Discourse).

In definition 3.1 above, we note that, in the absence of the universes of discourse, the predicate looses its context that we are referring to.

3.1.1. Notations

(i) We use the Script Capital letters like $\mathcal{U}$ to denote the universe.

(ii) We use the lowercase letters *x*, *y*, *z*, ... to denote the variables. Note that the variable *x* denotes an arbitrary value of the universe. These variables may assume values from their respective universes which must be clearly specified.

(iii) We use the Capital letters like P(.), Q(.) to denote *one-place* (also called as one-argument) predicates. Similarly, *two-place* (also called as two-argument) predicates also have the names like P(.,.), Q(.,.), etc.

(iv) Sometimes, we also need to represent specific values from the universe $\mathcal{U}$. Such values are called as constants, and we use the lowercase letters *a*,*b*,*c*, ... to denote them.

Example 3.1: Let $\mathcal{U}$ = all students in your university. Some of the university students included in $\mathcal{U}$ are: Aayush, Ami, Draupadi, Ankur, Jambuwant, Devendra. The following are predicates:

(a) G(x) = x is a graduate student.
(b) U(x) = x is an undergraduate student.
(c) S(x) = x is a student in the School of Computer Science and Engineering (SCE)
(d) C(x) = x is a Computer Science (CS) student.
(e) E(x) = x is a Computer Engineering (CE) student.
(f) M(x) = x is a Mechanical and Aerospace Engineering (MAE) student.

Additional Notation: When we discover that the capital letters are not enough for modelling predicates for the situation within the problem, we may use appropriate string of CAPITAL letters to denote a predicate. Thus, we may also re-write the predicates in Example 3.1 above as follows:

Example 3.2: Let $\mathcal{U}$ = all students in your university. Some of the university students included in $\mathcal{U}$ are: Aayush, Ami, Draupadi, Ankur, Jambuwant, Devendra. The following are predicates:

(i) GRAD(x) = x is a graduate student.
(ii) UG(x) = x is an undergraduate student.

(iii) SCE(x) = x is a student in the School of Computer Engineering (SCE).
(iv) CS(x) = x is a Computer Science student.
(v) CE(x) = x is a Computer Engineering student.
(vi) MAE(x) = x is a Mechanical and Aerospace Engineering student.

Example 3.3: Let $\mathscr{U}$ = all living beings. The following are predicates:

(a) A(x) = x is an animal.
(b) P(x) = x is a plant.
(c) B(x) = x is a bacterium.
(d) V(x) = x is a virus.

The above examples involve predicates with one free variable (also called as one-place predicates). The following example illustrates two-place predicates.

Example 3.4: Let $\mathscr{U}$ = all students in your university. Some of the university students included in $\mathscr{U}$ are: Aayush, Ami, Draupadi, Ankur, Jambuwant, Devendra. The following are predicates:

(a) H(x, y) = x's hostel is the same as y's hostel.
(b) T(x, y) = x's height is more than (or equal to) y's height.
(c) B(x, y) = x's birthday is within 7 days after y's birthday.
(d) L(x, y) = x likes y.
(e) R(x, y) = x relies on y.

3.1.2. Instantiation

Note that the predicate like P(x) is has no truth value by itself; it is neither T (true) nor F (false) depending on what value is assigned to the variable x. We note that the predicate always involves one (or more) variable(s) due to its definition.

Definition 3.2: (*Free* Variable) We also call the variables in predicates (open statements) as free variables, as they are *free to take any arbitrary value* from their respective universe of discourse.

We note further that, when we assign a specific value a to the variable x, the predicate P(x) is either true (T) or false (F). This process of assigning the variable x a value a is given a formal name.

Definition 3.3: (*Instantiation* of a Variable) When we assign a specific value, say a, to a free variable, we say that we have instantiated the free variable. After instantiation, a variable is no more free to take any arbitrary value, but is assigned a specific value a from the universe of discourse.

In other words, the variable x is instantiated to (the instance) a. Due to this assignment; we also say that the variable x is *bound* (to the constant a) because it looses its freedom due to this assignment. Symbolically, we also write:

$$\mathrm{P}(a) = \mathrm{P}(x)|_{x:=a} \quad \ldots (3.1)$$

Let us explain the notation in the context of Example 3.2.

Example 3.5: In Example 3.2, we had $\mathcal{U}$ = all university students. Some of the university students included in $\mathcal{U}$ are: Aayush, Aditi, Ami, Draupadi, Ankur, Jambuwant, Devendra. Let us instantiate the predicate in Example 3.2(a) by x = Jambuwant. We use the following notation:

$\mathrm{GRAD(Jambuwant)} = \mathrm{GRAD}(x)\ )|_{x:=\mathrm{Jambuwant}}$

This also denotes "Jambuwant is a graduate student." This is a proposition, as, depending whether Jambuwant is a graduate student or not, its truth-value is either T (true) or F (false).

□

Example 3.6: In Example 3.4, we had $\mathcal{U}$ = all students in your university. Some of the university students included in $\mathcal{U}$ are: Aayush, Aditi, Ami, Draupadi, Ankur, Jambuwant, Devendra. Let us instantiate the predicate in Example 3.4(a) by x = Jambuwant, retaining the variable y. We use the following notation:

$$\mathrm{H(Jambuwant}, y) = \mathrm{H}(x, y)\ )|_{x:=\mathrm{Jambuwant}}$$

This also denotes "Jambuwant's hostel is the same as y's hostel." This is not a proposition, but it can be viewed as a predicate with one free variable (which is y), or one-place predicate. To obtain the proposition which can be assigned the truth-value either T (true) or F (false), we need to additionally instantiate the variable y, which is *free* variable in this one-place predicate H(Jambuwant, y).

□

Example 3.7: In Example 3.4, we had $\mathcal{U}$ = all students in your university. Some of the university students included in $\mathcal{U}$ are: Aayush, Aditi, Ami, Draupadi, Ankur, Jambuwant, Devendra. Let us instantiate the predicate in Example 3.4(a) by x = Jambuwant, y = Aayush. We use the following notation:

H(Francis, Aayush) = $H(x, y)\,)|_{x:=\text{Jambuwant},\, y:=\text{Aayush}}$

This also denotes "Jambuwant's hostel is the same as Aayush's hostel." This is a proposition, as, depending whether Jambuwant and Aayush stay in the same hostel, its truth-value is either T (true) or F (false).

□

Example 3.8: In Example 3.4, we had $\mathcal{U}$ = all students in your university. Some of the university students included in $\mathcal{U}$ are: Aayush, Ami, Draupadi, Ankur, Jambuwant, Devendra. Let us instantiate the predicate in Example 3.4(c) by x = Ami, y = Devendra. We use the following notation:

B(Ami, Devendra) = $B(x, y)\,)|_{x:=\text{Ami},\, y:=\text{Devendra}}$

This also denotes "Ami's birthday is within 7 days after Devendra's birthday." This is a proposition, as, depending whether Ami's birthday and Devendra's birthday, its truth-value is either T (true) or F (false).

□

From Examples 3.5, 3.6, 3.7 and 3.8, we note the following:

Observation 3.1: After instantiating all variables in a predicate, we obtain a proposition.

However, as illustrated in Example 3.6, we also note that, if we instantiate some variables in a predicate, and it still has some other variables as free, then such an instantiation results in another predicate (involving less number of free variables).

3.2 Predicate Logic

3.2.1. "Compound" Predicates

In section 3.1.2, we saw how instantiation of all variables in a predicate result in a proposition. Once we have the proposition, we can utilize the machinery of propositional logic, including the standard operators propositional logic, namely ~, ∨, ∧, →, ↔ available to us to obtain more complex formulae (or, expressions).

We wish to examine the possibility of obtaining complex predicates using these connectives in propositional logic. To examine whether application of these connectives to predicates makes sense, we first note the important property of these connectives for propositions. The result of applying these connectives on propositions is itself a (more complex) proposition. This closure is important, as it allows us to construct complex propositional expressions involving these connectives, starting from the atomic propositions.

In the same vein, the result of applying these connectives to predicates would be useful for us to construct more complex predicate expressions if the result of the application of propositional connectives ~, ∨, ∧, →, ↔ gives us a (more complex, compound) predicate. To examine whether this is the case, let us consider the following example.

Example 3.9: Let us see a few examples of the application of these connectives in propositional logic to predicates, and see whether it makes sense.

We note that:

(a) SCE(x)∧GRAD(x) denotes the following compound open statement (predicate): x is a student in the School of Computer Engineering **and** x is a graduate student. We may like to use other name, say SCE-GRAD for the combined predicate. Thus, SCE-GRAD(x) = SCE(x)∧GRAD(x).

(b) CS(x)→SCE(x) denotes the following compound predicate: **If** x is a Computer Science student, **then** x is a student in the School of Computer Engineering.

(c) MAE(x)∨SCE(y) is a compound open statement involving two free variables, i.e., it is a two-place predicate. It denotes: x is a student in the School of Mechanical and Aerospace Engineering, **or** y is a student in the School of Computer Science and Engineering.

(d) CS(x)∨CE(x) denotes the compound open statement (predicate): x is a computer science student **or** x is a computer engineering student. Alternately, we can also say that CS(x)∨CE(x) denotes: x is a computer (science or engineering) student.

(e) CS(x)∨CE(x)↔SCE(x) denotes the compound open statement: x is a computer (science or engineering) student **if and only if** (**iff**) x is a student in the School of Computer Engineering.

(f) L(x, y) ∧ ~L(y, x) denotes the compound open statement (predicate): x likes y **and** y does **not** like x.

□

The above example leads us to the following observation.

Observation 3.2: The standard operators $\sim$, $\vee$, $\wedge$, $\rightarrow$, $\leftrightarrow$ on propositions, can be used for predicates as well.

3.2.2. Quantification

Based on the application of two binary operators $\vee$, $\wedge$ for all elements in the universe of discourse, we introduce two quantifiers. The quantifier associated with $\vee$ is called as "existential" quantifier, and the quantifier associated with $\wedge$ is called as "universal" quantifier. We also informally associate "somebody" with the existentially quantified variable, and "everybody" with the universally quantified variable. We shall introduce these concepts in this section.

3.2.2.1. Universal Quantification

Consider the modelling of the following rule:

> "A student of Computer Science is a student in the school of Computer Engineering."

This rule involves "a typical" student, which can be identified as a variable, varying over the (often implicitly stated, but clear from the context) universe of discourse, say, all students in your university. Since the useful (valid) rule should evaluate to True for all students in the universe, we may also re-phrase it as follows:

> "Every student of Computer Science is a student in the school of Computer Engineering."

To formulate this rule in the formal framework, we identify the (implicitly understood) variable denoting the "typical student" by a variable *x*, and we obtain the following equivalent statement:

> "For every *x*, if *x* is a student of Computer Science, then *x* is a student in the school of Computer Engineering."

This statement can be assigned a truth-value (i.e., it is either true or false). We are able to assign the truth-value because the occurrence of a free variable *x* is constrained by the phrase "For every *x*", which precedes the compound predicate $CS(x) \rightarrow SCE(x)$ in the above (Example 3.9(b)). In the formalism of predicate logic, we have a special symbol $\forall$ do denote the phrase "For every". Thus, symbolically, we represent the above statement as:

$$\forall x\, [CS(x) \rightarrow SCE(x)] \qquad \ldots (3.2)$$

This statement can also be expressed as: "All computer science students are students in the School of Computer Engineering."
In computer science, we usually have finite number of elements in our universe. Let assume that the universal set $\mathcal{U}$ has M elements, and they are denoted by $a_1, a_2, \ldots, a_M$. We use the symbol $\forall x\ [P(x)]$ to denote the following equivalent formula in propositional logic:

$$\forall x\, [P(x)] \equiv P(a_1) \wedge P(a_2) \wedge \ldots \wedge P(a_M) \qquad \ldots (3.3)$$

$$\equiv \bigwedge_{i=1}^{M} [P(a_i)] \qquad \ldots (3.4)$$

Note that the above formula consists of conjunction of propositions, and hence it results in a proposition, which has a truth-value either T or F.

We also say that the universal quantification $\forall x$ binds all the occurrences of the (free) variable x that are within its scope (marked by the square brackets [...]).

3.2.2.2. Existential Quantification

Consider the modeling of the following statement:

"There is a graduate student in the school of Computer Engineering."

Note that this is a statement, because it can be assigned a truth value "True" or "False". This statement involves "a typical" student, which can be identified as a variable, varying over the (often implicitly stated, but clear from the context) universe of discourse, say, all students in your university. However, the statement is "True" when there is at least one student in the universe, who satisfies the two conditions, viz., he is a graduate student, and he is a student of Computer Engineering. In predicate logic formalism, these two conditions are modelled as two separate predicates. evaluate to True for all students in the universe, we may also re-phrase it as follows:

"There exists a student, who (possesses the property that he/she) is a graduate student, and is a student in the school of Computer Engineering."

To formulate this rule in the formal framework, we identify the (implicitly understood) variable denoting the "typical student" by a variable *x*, and we obtain the following equivalent statement:

> "There exists *x*, (such that) *x* is a graduate student **and** *x* is a student in the School of Computer Engineering."

This statement can be assigned a truth-value (i.e., it is either true or false). We are able to assign the truth-value because the occurrence of a free variable *x* is constrained by the phrase "There exists *x*", which precedes the compound predicate $\mathrm{GRAD}(x) \wedge \mathrm{SCE}(x)$ in the above (Example 3.9(a)). In the formalism of predicate logic, we have a special symbol $\exists$ to denote the phrase "There exists". Thus, symbolically, we represent the above statement as:

$$\exists x\,[\mathrm{GRAD}(x) \wedge \mathrm{SCE}(x)] \qquad \ldots (3.5)$$

This statement can also be expressed as: "There is a graduate student in the School of Computer Engineering."

Let assume that the universal set $\mathfrak{U}$ has M elements, and they are denoted by $a_1, a_2, \ldots, a_M$. We use the symbol $\exists x\,[\mathrm{P}(x)]$ to denote the following equivalent formula in propositional logic:

$$\exists x\,[\mathrm{P}(x)] \equiv \mathrm{P}(a_1) \vee \mathrm{P}(a_2) \vee \ldots \vee \mathrm{P}(a_M) \qquad \ldots (3.6)$$

$$\equiv \bigvee_{i=1}^{M} [\mathrm{P}(a_i)] \qquad \ldots (3.7)$$

Note that the above formula consists of disjunction of propositions, and hence it results in a proposition, which has a truth-value either T or F.

We also say that the existential quantification $\exists x$ binds all the occurrences of the (free) variable x that are within its scope (marked by the square brackets [...]).

3.2.2.3. *Scope and Binding*

In section 3.1.3, we saw one method that results in the loss of freedom of a free variable; it was due to instantiating it to some constant value in the universe of discourse. In the above two sections, we saw another method that would make the free variable loose its freedom to take any arbitrary value from the universe of discourse. It is due to its presence in the scope of some quantifier that binds its occurrence. This is an important part in predicate logic, and hence, we summarize the observation about the scope of a quantifier and its resulting binding below.

Definition 3.3. *Scope and Binding*: We specify the scope of a given quantifier ϑ (= $\forall$, or $\exists$) for a variable x, denoted by ϑx, by the square brackets [...] (or round brackets (...) when no confusion arises). The quantifier ϑx binds all the free occurrences of a variable x which are within its scope.

Further, suppose there are other free variables, say y, z, which are within the scope of the quantification ϑx. Then the resulting formula is a predicate involving these free variables. This resulting formula, being an open statement, cannot be assigned a truth value. Following the standard notation in the literature, we omit the square brackets "[...]" when the scope of the quantifier is clear.

3.2.2.4. *Additional Quantifications: A note*

We defined predicate as a generalization of proposition for a suitable universe of discourse $\mathcal{U}$ for its subject. To obtain a proposition from predicate, in section 3.1.3, we have seen a basic mechanism of instantiation of a variable by assigning a value in the universe $\mathcal{U}$. Existential quantification captured other way of obtaining a proposition from the predicate by $\vee$ (OR)-ing over all values in the universe. Similarly the universal quantification captured yet another way of obtaining a proposition from the predicate by $\wedge$ (AND)-ing over all values in the universe.
The existential quantification results in resulting value T if there are one or more values in the universe result in instantiated predicate being true (T). To this extent, the existential quantification helps us to exclude the possibility of zero elements in the

universe result in the instantiated predicate being true (T). However, it does not tell us other (additional) *count*.

In general, quantifiers can be interpreted to signify the *quantity* (in terms of *how many* distinct elements of the universe result in the instantiated predicate being true (T)). However, following standard predicate logic framework, besides our two basic quantifiers (one based on $\vee$, other based on $\wedge$), we do not assume that our predicate logic framework has additional quantifiers. This simplification, however, poses us a challenge to model the sentences requiring the exact count. This issue, however, is not the main focus of our discussion, so we illustrate this aspect in a few exercises.

3.2.3. Modeling using one-place Predicates

In modelling statements involving one-place predicates P(x), it is useful to know when the quantified formulae $\forall x$ [P(x)] , $\forall x$ [~(P(x))], $\exists x$ [P(x)] , $\exists x$ [~(P(x))] are true, and when they are false. We summarize these conditions in the following table.

Quantified Formula	When the formula is True	When the formula is False
$\forall x$ [P(x)]	For every value v in the universe $\mathcal{U}$ the proposition P(a) is true.	There is at least one value v in the universe $\mathcal{U}$ for which the proposition P(a) is false.
$\forall x$ [~(P(x))]	For every value v in the universe $\mathcal{U}$ the proposition P(a) is false.	There is at least one value v in the universe $\mathcal{U}$ for which the proposition P(a) is true.
$\exists x$ [P(x)]	There is at least one value v in the universe $\mathcal{U}$ for which the proposition P(a) is true.	For every value v in the universe $\mathcal{U}$ the proposition P(a) is false.
$\exists x$ [~(P(x))]	There is at least one value v in the universe $\mathcal{U}$ for which the proposition P(a) is false.	For every value v in the universe $\mathcal{U}$ the proposition P(a) is true.

We notice the similarity of interpretations in this table. For example, the second row, middle column entry representing when the quantified formula $\forall x$ [P(x)] is true is exactly the same as the last row, last column entry denoting when the quantified formula $\exists x$ [~(P(x))] is false; similarly, the second row, last column entry for the quantified formula $\forall x$ [P(x)] is false is exactly the same as the last row, middle column entry representing when the quantified formula $\exists x$ [~(P(x))] is true. Similarly, the fourth row, middle column entry representing when the quantified formula $\exists x$ [P(x)] is true is exactly the same as the third row, last column entry denoting when the quantified formula $\forall x$ [~(P(x))] is false; similarly, the fourth row, last column entry for the quantified formula $\exists x$ [P(x)] is false is exactly the same as the third row, middle column entry representing when the quantified formula $\forall x$ [~(P(x))] is true. This similarity is not accidental, and is indeed stated as an equivalence rule of negation of quantified statements in section 3.2.1 below.

Let us assume that we have the following predicates:

(a) CS(x) = x is a CS (Computer Science) student.
(b) SCE(x) = x is an SCE student (is a student in the School of Computer Engineering (SCE)).

Taking the negation of the above predicates, we may also note:

(a) NON-CS(x) = ~CS(x) = x is not a CS (Computer Science) student.
(b) NON-SCE(x) =~SCE(x) = x is not an SCE student (is not a student in the School of Computer Engineering (SCE)).

Let us now consider the following example.

Example 3.10: Let us see a few examples of the modelling of the following sentences in English language using the predicates:

(a) CS(x) = x is a CS (Computer Science) student.
(b) SCE(x) = x is an SCE student (is a student in the School of Computer Engineering (SCE)).

Express the following English sentences as formula(e) in Predicate logic:

(i) Some CS student is an SCE student.
(ii) No CS student is an SCE student.
(iii) All CS students are SCE students.
(iv) Not all CS students are SCE students.
(v) Every CS student is an SCE student.
(vi) There is a non-SCE CS student.
(vii) No CS student is a non-SCE student.
(viii) All CS students are non-SCE students.
(ix) Not all CS students are non-SCE students.

Solution:

(i) Some CS student is an SCE student. : $\exists x$ [CS(x)$\wedge$ SCE(x)]

(ii) No CS student is an SCE student. : $\forall x\ [CS(x) \rightarrow \sim SCE(x)]$
(iii) All CS students are SCE students. : $\forall x\ [CS(x) \rightarrow SCE(x)]$
(iv) Not all CS students are SCE students. : $\exists x\ [CS(x) \wedge \sim SCE(x)]$
(v) Every CS student is an SCE student. : $\forall x\ [CS(x) \rightarrow SCE(x)]$
(vi) There is a non-SCE CS student. : $\exists x\ [CS(x) \wedge \sim SCE(x)]$
(vii) No CS student is a non-SCE student. : $\forall x\ [CS(x) \rightarrow SCE(x)]$
(viii) All CS students are non-SCE students. : $\forall x\ [CS(x) \rightarrow \sim SCE(x)]$
(ix) Not all CS students are non-SCE students. : $\exists x\ [CS(x) \wedge SCE(x)]$

□

In the above formalism, we note the following observation:

Observation 3.3: (Quantifier Modelling using one-place predicates)

(1) The universal quantifier $\forall$ quantifies the conditional $\rightarrow$.
(2) The existential quantifier $\exists$ quantifies the conjunction $\wedge$.

To justify why this is so, let us consider the statement:

(ii)Some CS student is an SCE student.

We have formulated as follows:

(i) Some CS student is an SCE student. : $\exists x\ [CS(x) \wedge SCE(x)]$

Someone may argue that the answer could also be formulated as follows:

Some CS student is an SCE student. : $\exists x\ [CS(x) \rightarrow SCE(x)]$

However, in this formulation, which involves conditional, we note that the conditional is True (T) even if there are no CS students while our formulation as given in solution is false in such a case. We may note that, in your university/institute, before July 1960, there are possibly no CS students. So, before July 1960, both the following formulae would be " True":

(a) $\exists x\ [CS(x) \rightarrow SCE(x)]$
(b) $\exists x\ [CS(x) \rightarrow MAE(x)]$

We argue that, due to the statement "Some CS student is an SCE student.", the formula like (b) above should not be true for the case when there is no CS student, as the English language formulation of (b) above also would read "Some student is an MAE student.", and it would be True before July 2004.

Let us now consider the statement:

(ii) No CS student is an SCE student.

We have formulated as follows:

(ii) No CS student is an SCE student. : $\forall x\,[CS(x) \rightarrow \sim SCE(x)]$

Someone may argue that the answer could also be formulated as follows:

- No CS student is an SCE student. : $\sim\exists x\,[CS(x) \wedge SCE(x)]$

Note that this formulation is fine, because, in the framework of predicate logic, it happens to be (logically) equivalent to our formulation. In other words, the following formula in predicate logic is in fact a tautology:

$\{\forall x\,[CS(x) \rightarrow \sim SCE(x)]\} \leftrightarrow \{\sim\exists x\,[CS(x) \wedge SCE(x)]\}$

We shall briefly cover this issue of which formulae in predicate logic are equivalent in section 3.3.

Let us now consider the following example.

<u>Example 3.11</u>: Express the following English sentence as formula in Predicate logic:

(a) It is not the case that not every theory has no limits.

<u>Solution</u>: Since we are not given the predicates, our first job is to identify the predicates. Let Model the following statement in the framework of predicate logic:

(i) $T(x) = x$ is a theory.

(ii) $L(x) = x$ has limits.

We did not specify the universe of discourse here, and we noted in our formulation of the concept of predicates that, without the universe of discourse, we shall not allow the specification of a predicate. So, we specify the universe of discourse as the set of all possible theories.

Let us first concentrate on the "inner" statement: "Every theory has no limits." Recognizing it as similar to Example 10 – case (v), we formulate it as:

$\forall x\,[T(x) \rightarrow \sim L(x)]$

Note that this is a formula in predicate logic involving no free variables; hence it is a proposition – it can be assigned a truth-value T or F. Thus, we may denote it by statement variable p.

Now, let us come back to our original statement: "It is not the case that not every theory has no limits.". However, we substitute the statement variable p for "Every theory has no limits.". Thus, the original statement becomes:

" It is not the case that not p. ", which can be modeled as: " It is not the case that $\sim p$.

Recognizing one more negation, we have: $\sim\sim p$. Since $\sim\sim p \equiv p$ using Double negation (Law of Logic), we have the formulation of the original statement in predicate logic as follows:

$\forall x\, [T(x) \rightarrow \sim L(x)]$

□

3.2.4. Note on "Interpretation" of Formula in Predicate Logic

We note that the formulae in predicate logic with no free variables are propositions; hence they have truth value either true or false, and it does not depend on variable involved. This truth value may, however, reflect the nature of universe. We illustrate this point by considering commonly occurring case in typical university, namely, we assume that no student is common between the School of Computer Engineering (SCE) and Mechanical and Aerospace Engineering (MAE).

With the above restriction in our universe, we consider the following example cases.

Example Case 1: Consider a formulation:

Every CS student is an SCE student: $\forall x\, [CS(x) \rightarrow SCE(x)]$

the formulation of "Every CS student is an SCE student" involved a conditional. we know that the conditional is True (T) when there are no CS students. In your university, there is good possibility that, before July 1964, there were no CS students. So, before July 1964, both the following formulae would be " True":

i. $\forall x\, [CS(x) \rightarrow SCE(x)]$
ii. $\forall x\, [CS(x) \rightarrow MAE(x)]$

This means, there exists interpretation(s) of predicate logic formulae when both statements above, *i.e.*,

i. "every CS student is student in School of Computer Engineering"
as well as,

ii. "every CS student is student in Mechanical and Aerospace Engineering" both are true for some interpretation(s).

Example Case 2: Now, consider the following two statements:

1. $\exists x\ [\mathrm{CS}(x) \wedge \mathrm{SCE}(x)]$
2. $\exists x\ [\mathrm{CS}(x) \wedge \mathrm{MAE}(x)]$

We observe now that, there are no interpretation(s) of predicate logic formulae when both the statements above are true.

We would mainly be interested properties that are not dependent on interpretations (*i.e.*, do not depend on the meaning that we assign to the predicates), but dependent only on the quantifiers and structure of predicate logic formulae. Such properties would be very useful for us to develop concept of "logical inference" as we did for propositional logic by developing "inference rules (IR)". In the next few sections, we introduce inference rules for predicate logic.

3.3 Equivalent Formulae (Predicate Logic): Part I

For propositional logic, we are able to give proofs of all laws of logic because we have developed a truth-table method for proving equivalences in prepositional logic. We do not intend to develop the formal set-up to define the notion of equivalent formulae in the predicate logic. Due to this limitation, we shall not be able to give "proof" of these equivalences. However, the study of some useful equivalent formulae in predicate logic is useful even for modeling sentences in the framework of predicate logic; so we shall state a few useful equivalences in this section.

3.3.1. Negated Quantifiers

In Section 1.4, we introduced De-Morgan's laws $\sim(p\wedge q) \equiv \sim p\vee\sim q$. Instead of calling the statement variables as p, q, let us call them as p_1, p_2. Thus, the De-Morgan's law for $\wedge$ takes the form: $\sim(p_1\wedge p_2) \equiv \sim p_1\vee\sim p_2$.

Using the notation similar to (3.4), we can write this De-Morgan's law as follows:

$$\sim\{ \bigwedge_{i=1}^{2} p_i\} \equiv \bigvee_{i=1}^{2} \sim p_i \qquad \ldots (3.10)$$

Example 3.12: Let us consider the result of negating the formula: $p_1 \wedge p_2 \wedge p_3$.
We have: $\sim\{ p_1 \wedge p_2 \wedge p_3\}$

$\equiv \sim\{ (p_1 \wedge p_2) \wedge p_3\}$ ... Associativity of $\wedge$

$\equiv \sim(p_1 \wedge p_2) \vee \sim p_3$ ... De Morgan's law

$\equiv (\sim p_1 \vee \sim p_2) \vee \sim p_3$ ... De Morgan's law

$\equiv \sim p_1 \vee \sim p_2 \vee \sim p_3$ ... Associativity of $\vee$

Thus, using the notation similar to (3.4), we have proved the following:

$$\sim\{ \bigwedge_{i=1}^{3} p_i\} \equiv \bigvee_{i=1}^{3} \sim p_i \quad \text{... (3.11)}$$

□

Example 3.12 demonstrated that the range of index i can be extended from values 1,2 to 1,2,3. We wish to know whether it can be extended up to any arbitrary but finite positive integer M. This in fact can be done, but we do not have sufficient tools to complete such a proof at this stage. We shall postpone this proof (which essentially uses steps similar to the ones in Example 1.11) till we have discussed Principle of Mathematical Induction (P-MI) in upcoming part of module on proof strategies. In the following, we state (without proof) the following logical equivalence for propositions can be proved:

$$\sim\{ \bigwedge_{i=1}^{M} p_i\} \equiv \bigvee_{i=1}^{M} \sim p_i \quad \text{... (3.12)}$$

In the framework of Predicates, since our universe of discourse is in general allowed to contain even infinitely many elements, the *challenge* is allow M to have an arbitrary infinite value, and prove (3.12) with such a value of M. However, we do not intend to deal with such cases involving infinitely many values in the universe (at least for the time being), and hence we shall restrict our discussion to M being finite but arbitrarily large. Using (the intuitive) meaning of the operators $\forall$, and $\exists$ as explained in (3.4)-(3.7), in the following theorem, we state the following logical equivalences for negation of quantifiers:

Theorem 3.4: *Negating* the Quantifier: For any arbitrary formula $\mathcal{F}$ in predicate logic (which would in general have the free occurrences of variable x, and additionally may involve other free variables), we have the following logical equivalences:

$$\sim\{\forall x\, [\mathcal{F}]\ \} \equiv \exists x\, [\sim(\mathcal{F})] \quad \text{... (3.13)}$$

$\sim\{\exists x\,[\mathcal{F}]\} \equiv \forall x\,[\sim(\mathcal{F})]$ ... (3.14)

Example 3.13: (Example 3.10(ii)revisited:) In Example 3.10 (ii), we wanted to express the sentence "No CS student is an SCE student."
We have formulated as follows:

(ii) No CS student is an SCE student. : $\forall x\,[CS(x) \rightarrow \sim SCE(x)]$ ... (3.15)

We also gave its logically equivalent formulation (without equivalence proof) as follows:

- No CS student is an SCE student. : $\sim\exists x\,[CS(x) \wedge SCE(x)]$ ... (3.16)

We now show that (3.15) is equivalent to (3.16). The steps are given below.

$\forall x\,[CS(x) \rightarrow \sim SCE(x)]$
$\equiv \underline{\sim\sim\forall x[CS(x) \rightarrow \sim SCE(x)]}$ ... Double Negation
$\equiv \sim\exists x[\sim(CS(x) \rightarrow \sim SCE(x))]$ ... Using (3.13), Negation Equivalence for $\forall$
$\equiv \sim\exists x[\sim(\underline{\sim CS(x) \vee \sim SCE(x)})]$ ... Introduction of $\vee$ to replace $\rightarrow$
$\equiv \sim\exists x[(\underline{\sim\sim CS(x)} \wedge \sim\sim SCE(x))]$ ... De Morgan's law on $\vee$
$\equiv \sim\exists x[(CS(x) \wedge \underline{\sim\sim SCE(x)})]$ ... Double Negation
$\equiv \sim\exists x[(CS(x) \wedge SCE(x))]$ ... Double Negation (This is exactly (3.16)).

To obtain logical equivalence proof of (3.16) from (3.15), we can simply reverse the steps in the above equivalence proof. Alternately, starting with (3.16), we can directly show that it is equivalent to (3.15). The steps are given below.

$\sim\exists x\,[CS(x) \wedge SCE(x)]$
$\equiv \forall x\,[\sim(\underline{CS(x) \wedge SCE(x)})]$ ... Using (3.14), Negation Equivalence for $\exists$
$\equiv \forall x\,[\sim CS(x) \vee \sim SCE(x))]$ ... De Morgan's law on $\wedge$
$\equiv \forall x\,[CS(x) \rightarrow \sim SCE(x))]$ ... Intro. of $\rightarrow$ to replace $\vee$ (This is exactly (3.15)).

□

3.3.2. *Interchanging Quantifiers of the same Type*

Suppose we have two occurrences of the universal quantifier, next to the other. Then, we can replace their order. The same is true for the existential quantifier.

Theorem 3.5: Interchanging the Quantifiers of *the same type*: For any arbitrary formula $\mathcal{F}$ in predicate logic (which would in general have the free occurrences of variables x and y), we have:

$$\forall x \forall y\, [\mathcal{F}] \equiv \forall y \forall x\, [\mathcal{F}] \quad \ldots (3.17)$$

$$\exists x \exists y\, [\mathcal{F}] \equiv \exists y \exists x\, [\mathcal{F}] \quad \ldots (3.18)$$

Notation 3.3: Due to the (3.17) and (3.18) above, when we have two or more occurrences of the same quantifier, we sometimes combine the variables of the same quantifier, and specify the quantified variables after the quantifier symbol; thus, we also use the following notation to denote (3.17) and (3.18) above:

$$\forall x \forall y\, [\mathcal{F}] \equiv \forall y \forall x\, [\mathcal{F}] \equiv \forall x,y\, [\mathcal{F}] \equiv \forall xy\, [\mathcal{F}]$$

$$\exists x \exists y\, [\mathcal{F}] \equiv \exists y \exists x\, [\mathcal{F}] \equiv \exists x,y\, [\mathcal{F}] \equiv \exists xy\, [\mathcal{F}]$$

3.4 Modeling Using Two Place Predicates

Two-place predicates involve two (free) variables. To bind the two occurrences of these two free variables involve their quantification. We have introduced two quantifiers. Each of the free variable can be bound by each of these quantifiers in two ways; since there are two free variables, this gives us four ways by which both the free variables can be bound. Out of these four ways, two of them involve the quantifiers of the same type. This means, either both the free variables are universally bound, or both the free variables are existentially bound. In either of this case, as we have seen in section 3.3.2, interchanging the quantifier order does not matter.

In this section, we are primarily interested in the remaining two situations. In these situations, we have two quantifiers of different types.

3.4.1. *Modeling Using the Quantifiers of different types*

In Example 3.4, we had the universe of discourse $\mathcal{U}$ = all students in your university. We also considered the following two-place predicate:

(c) $B(x, y) = x$'s birthday is within 7 days after y's birthday.

We note that both the variables have the same universe of discourse $\mathcal{U}$. In other words, suppose the universe of discourse for x is denoted by $\mathcal{U}_x$, and the universe of discourse for y is denoted by $\mathcal{U}_y$. For this example, we have $\mathcal{U}_x=\mathcal{U}_y=\mathcal{U}=$ all students in your university. We shall use this predicate to illustrate the modelling.

Example 3.14: Express the following sentences are formulae in predicate logic: Let us consider the following formulae in predicate logic:

(a) Everyone's birthday is within seven days after someone's birthday.
(b) Someone's birthday is within seven days after everyone's birthday.

Solution: One possible formulation as sentences is given below.

a) Everyone's birthday is within seven days after someone's birthday. :
   $\forall x \exists y\, B(x, y)$.
b) Someone's birthday is within seven days after everyone's birthday. :
   $\exists x \forall y\, B(x, y)$.

□

In situations like (a), (b) above, the inner quantifier is first applied, and it quantifies the concerned variable. This meaning of the formulae (a) and (b) above is important in interpreting formulae involving multiple quantifiers. Hence, we explain this meaning in the following subsections.

3.4.2. *Expansion of*: $\forall x\, \exists y\, B(x, y)$

Notationally, the formula $\forall x \exists y\, B(x, y)$ denotes the formula $\forall x\, [\, \exists y\, [B(x, y)]\,]$. Hence, we first focus our attention on the formula: $\exists y[B(x, y)]$. With $\mathcal{U}_y=\{\text{Ami, Daksh, Raghav}\}$, and using (3.6) we can expand $\exists y[B(x, y)]$ to represent the following:

$\exists y\,[B(x, y)] \equiv B(x, \text{Ami}) \vee B(x, \text{Daksh}) \vee B(x, \text{Raghav})$ ... (3.19)

Note that (3.19) is a predicate involving only one variable x. Hence, to simplify the matters, we may denote it by $P(x)$. Thus, we have:

$P(x) \equiv B(x, \text{Ami}) \vee B(x, \text{Daksh}) \vee B(x, \text{Raghav})$ ... (3.20)

Next, we have focus our attention on universal quantification of variable x, i.e., $\forall x[P(x)]$. Using (3.3), we expand $\forall x[P(x)]$ as follows:

$\forall x\,[P(x)] \equiv P(\text{Ami}) \wedge P(\text{Daksh}) \wedge P(\text{Raghav})$ ... (3.21)

Substituting back the definition of $P(x)$ from (3.21) in the above, we have:

$$\begin{aligned}
&\forall x \exists y\, B(x, y) \equiv \\
&\quad [\,B(\text{Ami}, \text{Ami}) \vee B(\text{Ami}, \text{Daksh}) \vee B(\text{Ami}, \text{Raghav})\,] && \{ = P(\text{Ami}) \} \\
&\wedge [\,B(\text{Daksh}, \text{Ami}) \vee B(\text{Daksh}, \text{Daksh}) \vee B(\text{Daksh}, \text{Raghav})\,] && \{ = P(\text{Daksh}) \} \\
&\wedge [\,B(\text{Raghav}, \text{Ami}) \vee B(\text{Raghav}, \text{Daksh}) \vee B(\text{Raghav}, \text{Raghav})\,] && \{ = P(\text{Raghav}) \}
\end{aligned}$$
... (3.22)

□

To illustrate the meaning of this formula further, we now consider the familiar set of integers Z. This set consists of numbers {..., -2, -1, 0, 1, 2, ... } and it is infinite. We may assume that our universe of discourse $\mathcal{U}_x = \mathcal{U}_y = \mathcal{U} = Z$ = all integers.

<u>Example 3.15</u>: Express the following property:

> "For every integer x, there is another integer y, such that y is greater than x."

as a formula in predicate logic.

<u>Solution</u>: Using the universe of discourse $\mathcal{U}_x = \mathcal{U}_y = Z$, we define the predicate $G(y, x) \equiv y > x$ to denote an open (consisting of free variables x, y) statement " y is greater than x.". In terms of this predicate, the formula to denote the given sentence is:

$\forall x \exists y\, G(y, x)$ ... (3.23)

□

From our earlier knowledge about the integers, we note that (3.23) is a true statement. (Is the formula (3.23) true for the universe of discourse ia N, the set of natural numbers, i.e., the numbers {0, 1, 2, …}?)

Now, we wish to come back to solution of Example 3.14 (b), and explain the expansion of the formula: $\exists x \forall y$ B(x, y).

3.4.3. Expansion of : $\exists x\ \forall y\ B(x, y)$

Notationally, the formula $\exists x \forall y$ B(x, y) denotes the formula $\exists x$ [$\forall y$ [B(x, y)]]. Hence, we first focus our attention on the formula: $\forall y$[B(x, y)]. With $\mathcal{U}_y$={Ami, Daksh, Raghav}, and using (3.3) we can expand $\forall y$[B(x, y)] to represent the following:

$$\forall y\ [B(x, y)] \equiv B(x, \text{Ami}) \land B(x, \text{Daksh}) \land B(x, \text{Raghav}) \qquad \dots (3.24)$$

Note that (3.24) is a predicate involving only one variable x. Hence, to simplify the matters, we may denote it by Q(x). Thus, we have:

$$Q(x) \equiv B(x, \text{Ami}) \land B(x, \text{Daksh}) \land B(x, \text{Raghav}) \qquad \dots (3.25)$$

Next, we have focus our attention on existential quantification of variable x, i.e., $\exists x$[Q(x)]. Using (3.23), we expand $\exists x$[Q(x)] as follows:

$$\exists x[Q(x)] \equiv Q(\text{Ami}) \lor Q(\text{Daksh}) \lor Q(\text{Raghav}) \qquad \dots (3.26)$$

Substituting back the definition of Q(x) from (3.25) in the above, we have:

$$\begin{aligned} \exists x\ \forall y\ B(x, y) \equiv & \\ & [\ B(\text{Ami}, \text{Ami}) \land B(\text{Ami}, \text{Daksh}) \land B(\text{Ami}, \text{Raghav})\ ] && \{= Q(\text{Ami})\} \\ \lor & [\ B(\text{Daksh}, \text{Ami}) \land B(\text{Daksh}, \text{Daksh}) \land B(\text{Daksh}, \text{Raghav})\ ] && \{= Q(\text{Daksh})\} \\ \lor & [\ B(\text{Raghav}, \text{Ami}) \land B(\text{Raghav}, \text{Daksh}) \land B(\text{Raghav}, \text{Raghav})\ ] && \{= Q(\text{Raghav})\} \\ & && \dots (3.27) \end{aligned}$$

Comparing (3.22) with (3.27), we observe that these two formulae are evaluated to be true in different situations (i.e., they model different scenarios).

Example 3.16: In the universe of discourse $\mathcal{U}_x = \mathcal{U}_y$ = Z (integers), we define the predicate G(y, x) ≡ y > x to denote an open (consisting of free variables x, y) statement " y is greater than x.". In terms of this predicate, consider the following the formula in the predicate logic:

$$\exists x \forall y\ G(y, x) \qquad \ldots (3.28)$$

Express this formula in predicate logic in terms of equivalent English statement it represents. Briefly comment on whether this statement is true.

Solution: The formula $\exists x \forall y$ G(y, x) can be translated as the following statement:

"There is *(i.e.,* there exists) an integer x, such that every integer y is greater than x."

□

From our knowledge of integers, we note that the formula (3.28) is not true (for our chosen universe of integers). (Is the formula (3.28) true for the universe of discourse N, the set of natural numbers, i.e., the numbers {0, 1, 2, …}? Indeed, the well-ordering principle as briefly introduced in Module 2 part 2, subsection 2.5.5 would throw some more light on this change of order of quantifiers.

3.4.4. Interchanging Quantifiers of different types

When we interchange the two quantifiers of different types, the resulting propositions are not equivalent. This also gives rise to the ambiguity for modeling English language sentences requiring two-place predicates, with both the (free) variables quantified with different quantifiers. Hence, we do not wish to get into the in-depth investigation of this issue of modeling of such English sentences in the framework of predicate logic. However, we aim to give an exposition of the issues involved in such a modeling. Using the notations and concepts in this section, together with your intuitive meaning of the statement, you should be able to model such statements. In this section, we highlight the fact that interchanging the order of quantifiers of different types results in non-equivalent propositions. We illustrate this point through example(s).

We now wish to see the effect of interchange of the quantifiers; for the formula $\forall x \exists y$ B(x, y), we already examined the expansion in section 3.4.2. Let us now interchange the quantification order, keeping the quantifications of variables x, and y same (i.e., x remains universally quantified, an y remains existentially quantified). This interchange results in the formula: $\exists y \forall x$ B(x, y).

3.4.5. Expansion of : $\exists y \forall x$ B(x, y)

Notationally, the formula $\exists y \forall x$ B(x, y) denotes the formula $\exists y$ [$\forall x$ [B(x, y)]]. Hence, we first focus our attention on the formula: $\forall x$ [B(x, y)]. With $\mathcal{U}_y$={Ami, Daksh, Raghav}, and using (3.3) we can expand $\forall x$ [B(x, y)] to represent the following:

$\forall x$ [B(x, y)] $\equiv$ B(Ami, y)$\wedge$B(Daksh, x) $\wedge$B(Raghav, y) … (3.29)

Note that (3.30) is a predicate involving only one variable y. Hence, to simplify the matters, we may denote it by R(y). Thus, we have:

R(y) $\equiv$ B(Ami, y)$\wedge$B(Daksh, x) $\wedge$B(Raghav, y) … (3.30)

Next, we focus our attention on existential quantification of variable y, i.e., $\exists y$[R(y)]. Using (3.31), we expand $\exists y$[Q(y)] as follows:

$\exists y$[Q(y)] $\equiv$ R(Ami)$\vee$R(Daksh)$\vee$R(Raghav) … (3.31)

Substituting back the definition of Q(y) from (3.31) in the above, we have:

$\exists y \forall x$ B(x, y) $\equiv$
[B(Ami, Ami)$\wedge$B(Daksh, Ami) $\wedge$B(Raghav, Ami)] { = R(Ami) }
$\vee$ [B(Ami,Daksh,)$\wedge$B(Daksh, Daksh)$\wedge$B(Raghav, Daksh)] { = R(Daksh)}
$\vee$ [B(Ami,Raghav,)$\wedge$B(Daksh,Raghav,)$\wedge$B(Raghav, Raghav)]{= R(Raghav)}
… (3.32)

From the expansions in (3.22), and (3.32), we note the following:

Observation 3.5: Interchanging the quantifiers of different types results in non-equivalent formulae (in predicate logic).

Example 3.16: In the universe of discourse $\mathcal{U}_x = \mathcal{U}_y$ = Z(integers), we define the predicate $G(y, x) \equiv y > x$ to denote an open (consisting of free variables x, y) statement " y is greater than x.". In terms of this predicate, consider the following the formula in the predicate logic:

$$\exists y \forall x\, G(y, x) \qquad \ldots (3.33)$$

Express this formula in predicate logic in terms of equivalent English statement it represents. Briefly comment on whether this statement is true.

Solution: The formula $\exists y \forall x\, G(y, x)$ can be translated as the following statement:

"There is (i.e., there exists) an integer y, such that it is greater than every integer x." ... (3.34)

□

From our knowledge of integers, we note that the formula (3.34) is not true (for our chosen universe of integers). (Is the formula (3.34) true for the universe of discourse N, the set of natural numbers, i.e., the numbers {0, 1, 2, ...}?)

Comparing (3.34) with (3.23), we observe that these two formulae are evaluated to be true in different situations (i.e., they model different scenarios).

We have seen the formula: $\exists x\ \forall y\ B(x, y)$ and its expansion in section 3.4.3. When we change the order of quantifiers in this formula, we get another formula $\exists x\ \forall y\ B(x, y)$. We leave it to you to complete the expansion of this formula, and leave the formulation of its meaning to the reader. You may, however, notice how difficult (and at times, even ambiguous) to express the precise meaning in an English statement, without taking a recourse to the notation of predicate logic. This illustrates the need for predicate logic for unambiguous and precise communication.

Example 3.17: Consider the following formulae about two-dimensional arrary, A (also called as a matrix), in Predicate logic:

i. $\forall$ row x, $\exists$ column y, such that $A[x, y] = 1$.

Verify that the following table satisfies the proposition (i)

1					
	1	1		1	
		1			
		1		1	
			1		
		1			

ii. $\exists$ column y, $\forall$ row x, such that $A[x, y] = 1$.
Verify that the following table satisfies the proposition (ii)

1		1			
	1	1		1	
		1			
		1		1	
		1	1		1
		1			

iii. $\exists$ row x, $\forall$ column y, such that $A[x, y] = 1$.
Verify that the following table satisfies the proposition (iii)

1					
1	1	1	1	1	1

		1			
				1	
		1	1		1
		1			

iv. $\forall$ column y, $\exists$ row x, such that $A[x, y] = 1$.
Verify that the following table satisfies the proposition (iv)

1					
	1	1		1	
		1			
				1	1
			1		

Observe that, in two of the above four cases, we have a row / column consisting of all ones. What is common in these two cases (when we have a row /column consisting of all ones)?

□

3.5 EQUIVALENT FORMULAE (PREDICATE LOGIC): PART II

Based on the discussion in section 3.2.2 where we have also given the motivation of definition of quantifiers, we have the following theorems. The proofs of these theorems can be given using the techniques to be discussed in the section 3.6. We shall omit the proofs of these theorems here, and leave these proofs as exercises to be completed by the reader.

3.5.1. Distributing ∃ Quantifier

Theorem 3.6: (Distributing ∃ over ∨) We have the following logical equivalence:

$$\exists x\, [P(x) \vee Q(x)] \equiv (\, \exists x\, [P(x)]\,) \vee (\, \exists x\, [Q(x)]\,) \qquad \ldots (3.35)$$

However, we note that the following is only one way implication when we have the situation for distributing the ∃ over ∧, as indicated in the following theorem below:

Theorem 3.7: (Distributing ∃ over ∧) We have the following logical implication:

$$\exists x\, [P(x) \wedge Q(x)] \Rightarrow (\, \exists x\, [P(x)]\,) \wedge (\, \exists x\, [Q(x)]\,) \qquad \ldots (3.36)$$

Note that the converse of 3.36 above is not a valid conditional, i.e., the following conditional is not an implication:

$$\{\, (\, \exists x\, [P(x)]\,) \wedge (\, \exists x\, [Q(x)]\,)\, \} \rightarrow \{\, \exists x\, [P(x) \wedge Q(x)]\, \} \qquad \ldots (3.37)$$

Theorem 3.8: (Distributing ∃ over →) We have the following logical implication:

$$\exists x\, [P(x) \rightarrow Q(x)] \equiv (\, \forall x\, [P(x)]\,) \rightarrow (\forall x\, [Q(x)]\,) \qquad \ldots (3.38)$$

Note the change of the quantifier to ∀ in the right hand side of (3.39) above.

3.5.2. *Distributing ∀ Quantifier*

Theorem 3.9: (Distributing ∀ over ∧) We have the following logical equivalence:

$$\forall x\,[\mathrm{P}(x) \wedge \mathrm{Q}(x)] \equiv (\forall x\,[\mathrm{P}(x)]\,) \wedge (\forall x\,[\mathrm{Q}(x)]\,) \qquad \ldots (3.39)$$

However, we note that the following is only one way implication when we have the situation for distributing the ∀ over ∨, as indicated in the following theorem below:

Theorem 3.10: (Distributing ∀ over ∨) We have the following logical implication:

$$\{(\,\forall x[\mathrm{P}(x)]\,) \vee (\forall x[\mathrm{Q}(x)]\,)\,\} \Rightarrow \{\forall x\,[\mathrm{P}(x) \vee \mathrm{Q}(x)]\,\} \qquad \ldots (3.40)$$

Note that the converse of 3.40 above is not a valid conditional, i.e., the following conditional is not an implication:

$$\{\forall x\,[\mathrm{P}(x) \vee \mathrm{Q}(x)]\,\} \rightarrow \{(\,\forall x[\mathrm{P}(x)]\,) \vee (\forall x[\mathrm{Q}(x)]\,)\,\} \qquad \ldots (3.41)$$

Example 3.18: A common example to illustrate the non-validity of (3.41) above is: every even or odd natural number is a natural number, but every (natural) number is not even number or every (natural) number is not odd number.

□

3.5.3. *Equivalences from Equivalent Propositions*

Let us start with some formula in propositional logic, say

$(\mathcal{F}_1)$ $(p \vee (q \wedge \sim r) \rightarrow \sim q$ ... (3.42)

Let us choose some formulae in predicate logic, say

(P_1) $\mathrm{MAE}(x) \vee \mathrm{SCE}(y)$

(P_2) LIKES (z, w)

(P_3) $\forall x\,[\mathrm{T}(x) \rightarrow \sim \mathrm{L}(x)]$

Although the predicates like MAE(x), LIKES(x,y) are not propositions and they cannot be assigned truth-values, they can definitely be assigned truth values after instantiating all variables. To this extent, it is possible for us to consider it as a symbolic proposition (you may like to think of it as a proposition, indexed by the indices, e.g., MAE_x, or,

$\text{LIKES}_{x,y}$ where indices are values from the universe of discourse). Thus, we may replace the statement variables p, q, and r in (3.42) by:

p is replaced by $\text{MAE}(x) \vee \text{SCE}(y)$,

q by LIKES (z, w), and,

r by $\forall x\, [\text{T}(x) \rightarrow {\sim}\text{L}(x)]$,

and substitute *all* occurrences of these statement variables in propositional formula ($\mathcal{F}_1$) to obtain a formula in predicate logic as:

$$(\mathcal{F}_1\text{'})(\text{MAE}(x) \vee \text{SCE}(y) \vee (\text{LIKES}(z,w) \wedge {\sim}\forall x[\text{T}(x) \rightarrow {\sim}\text{L}(x)]) \rightarrow {\sim}\text{LIKES}(z,w) \ldots (3.43)$$

Although the formula ($\mathcal{F}_1$') looks very complex, structurally it can also be represented by a formula ($\mathcal{F}_1$) in (3.43) above. In simplifying and obtaining the equivalent formulae in predicate logic, this is a very useful concept; hence we summarize it in the following definition.

Definition 3.4: (*Instance* of propositional Formula) If a formula $\mathcal{P}$ in predicate logic is obtained from a formula $\mathcal{F}$ of propositional logic by replacing all occurrences of one or more statement variables by the *arbitrary* formulae in predicate logic, then we define the formula $\mathcal{P}$ to be an instance of $\mathcal{F}$.

Example 3.19: The formula ($\mathcal{F}_1$'), which is a formula in predicate logic and given in (3.43) above, is an instance of the formula ($\mathcal{F}_1$) in propositional logic, which is given in (3.42).

For such instances, it is necessary to specify the replacements; we (re-) state them. All occurrences of statement variables p, q, and r in (3.42) are replaced as follows:

p is replaced by $\text{MAE}(x) \vee \text{SCE}(y)$,

q by LIKES (z, w), and,

r by $\forall x\, [\text{T}(x) \rightarrow {\sim}\text{L}(x)]$.

□

Although the predicates like MAE(x), LIKES(x,y) are not propositions and they cannot be assigned truth-values, they can definitely be assigned truth values after instantiating all variables.

The usefulness of the above concept is due to the following theorem:

Theorem 3.11: Suppose that we have a formula $\mathcal{F}$' in predicate logic which is an instance of a tautology (or, Law of Logic in Propositional Logic, covered in sections 1.5 and 1.6 in part 1). Then, the formula $\mathcal{F}$' is also a tautology.

In such a formula $\mathcal{F}$', we note that, it may have free variables. Also, it is *not* required for the all occurrences of all variables in such formula $\mathcal{F}$' to be bound. In other words, the above theorem gives us a very powerful tool. It allows us to generate (infinitely many) predicate logic formulae that are tautologies; it is interesting to note that these *tautologies will in general have* even the *free variables*.

Example 3.20: Let us start with the following tautology in propositional logic:

$$(\mathcal{F}_2)\ (p\wedge(\sim p\vee q))\rightarrow q \qquad \ldots (3.44)$$

Let us choose some formulae in predicate logic, to replace propositions p, q as:
($\mathcal{P}_1$) GRAD(x)$\wedge$MAE(y) replaces p
($\mathcal{P}_2$) CS(z) replaces q
With the above replacement, we get the following formula in the predicate logic:

$$(\mathcal{F}_2')\ (\text{GRAD}(x)\wedge\text{MAE}(y)\wedge(\ \sim(\text{GRAD}(x)\wedge\text{MAE}(y))\vee\text{CS}(z)\ ))\rightarrow\text{CS}(z) \ \ldots (3.45)$$

The above formula in predicate logic has three free variables: x, y, z, and it is open statement (predicate). However, it is also a Tautology, in the sense that its truth-value is always T.

□

As per our formulation and notations as discussed in section 3.1, we cannot assign any truth-value to the open statement, and in general it's truth-value should depend on the values assigned to the variables x, y, z, from their respective universes. We have already noted that the formula ($\mathcal{F}_2$') is an open statement, or predicate, involving free variables. What Theorem 3.11 tells us is, in spite of any arbitrary assignment of values (from any arbitrary universes of our choice) to these free variables x, y, z, the formula ($\mathcal{F}_2$') will always have the truth-value T.

As a useful tool for problem solving, we note the following variant of the above theorem.

Theorem 3.12: Two formulae in predicate logic are (logically) equivalent *iff* they are the instances of two equivalent propositional formulae, where both the instances involves the *same replacement* of the concerned statement variables.

Theorem 3.12 gives us an effective tool to generate infinitely many logical equivalence formulae in predicate logic.
As emphasized in Examples 3.18, and 3.19 above, it is important to specify the replacements; further, we repeat that *all occurrences* of the statement variable must be replaced by the same replaced formula in predicate logic.

3.6 Inference Rules and Proofs (In Predicate Logic)

Theorem 3.12 above gives us an interesting tool: Predicate logic formulae which are instances of propositional formulae involved in an inference rule in propositional involving the same replacement of the concerned statement variables are also inference rules in predicate logic. This allows us to generate infinitely many inference rules.

The quantified statements are important formulations in predicate logic,. For the formal reasoning in predicate logic, besides the "in-built" propositional logic inference rules, like the ones illustrated in the example above, we need some rules which allow us to do formal reasoning with quantifiers.
Let us explain the situation where we need some rules which make use of properties of quantifiers.

Example 3.21: Consider the following argument:

> "A student of Computer Science is a student in the school of Computer Engineering. Jambuwant is not a student in the school of Computer Engineering. Therefore Jambuwant in not a Computer Science student"

In section 3.2.2.1, we formulated the first premise in this argument. Using the formulation in section 3.2.2.1, we can express the above argument as:

i. $\forall x\ [CS(x) \rightarrow SCE(x)]$
ii. ~SCE(Jambuwant)

$\therefore$ ~CS(Jambuwant)

To establish the validity of the above argument, we need to show that whenever the premises are true, the conclusion is also true. We do this in two steps. The first step involves inferring the other propositions which are true from the given premises. The second step involves the application of laws of logic and the inference rules in propositional logic, which we have covered in module two. Some arguments (for example, consider the Examples 3.22, 23 below) have the quantified conclusion. For such examples, we need the additional (third) step. For logically inferring such conclusions involving quantifiers, we need inference rules to introduce the quantifiers. For performing step one, we need some inference rules by which we can get rid of quantifiers. Specifically, we have two such rules: Universal Instantiation (UI), and Existential Instantiation (EI). For performing step three, we need some inference rules which allow us to introduce the quantifiers. Specifically, we have two such rules: Universal Generalization (UG), and Existential Generalization (EG).

3.6.1. Universal Instantiation (UI)

This rule states that, if $\forall x\ [P(x)]$ is true, then $P(a)$ is true for every a in the universe of discourse. We also say that the instantiated constant a is "arbitrary".

$\forall x\ [P(x)]$

$\therefore P(a) \quad (a \text{ arbitrary})$

Let us illustrate the application of this rule through its application to Example 20 above.

Example 3.22: (Validity of Argument in Example 21 using UI)
Establish the validity of the following argument:

(i) $\forall x\ [CS(x) \rightarrow SCE(x)]$
(ii) ~SCE(Justin)

$\therefore$ ~CS(Justin)

Solution: To establish the validity of the above argument, we give the following proof:

(1) $\forall x$ [CS(x)→SCE(x)] ... Premise 1
(2) ~SCE(Jambuwant) ... Premise 2
(3) CS(Jambuwant)→SCE(Jambuwant)...UI,(1) (with x = Jambuwant)
(4) ~CS(Jambuwant) ... MT, (2), (3) (Also, a conclusion.)

□

3.6.2. Universal Generalization (UG)

When we have the universally quantified statement as a conclusion, we need the inference rules which enable us to introduce (back) the universal quantifier. Note that, the "arbitrary" elements can only be bound by the universal quantifier in this inference rule. We introduce this rule below.

P(a) (a is arbitrary)

∴ $\forall x$ [P(x)]

We illustrate the use of this rule in the following example.

Example 3.23: (Validity of Argument using UI, EI, and UG)
Express the following argument in the predicate logic formalism, and prove its validity:

"All gamblers are bound for ruin. No one bound for ruin is happy. Therefore, no gamblers are happy."

Solution: Let $\mathscr{U}$ = all persons in the world. With this universe of discourse, we use the following predicates:

(i) L(x) = x is a gambler.
(ii) R(x) = x is us bound for ruin.
(iii) H(x) = x is happy.

Using the above, and formulations in Example 3.10, the argument is as follows:

(i) $\forall x\,[L(x) \rightarrow R(x)]$
(ii) $\forall x[R(x) \rightarrow \sim H(x)]$

$\therefore$ $\forall x[L(x) \rightarrow \sim H(x)]$

To establish the validity of the above argument, we give the following proof:

(1) $\forall x\,[L(x) \rightarrow R(x)]$ … Premise 1
(2) $\forall x[R(x) \rightarrow \sim H(x)]$ … Premise 2
(3) $L(a) \rightarrow R(a)$ … UI, (1) (with $x = a$, a arbitrary)
(4) $R(a) \rightarrow \sim H(a)$ … UI, (2) (with $x = a$, a arbitrary)
(5) $L(a) \rightarrow \sim H(a)$ … LS, (3), (4) (a arbitrary)
(6) $\forall x[L(x) \rightarrow \sim H(x)]$ … UG, (5) (Also, a conclusion.)

□

3.6.3. Existential Instantiation (EI)

This rule states that, if $\exists x\,[P(x)]$ is true, then $P(a)$ is true for some a in the universe of discourse. We also say that the instantiated constant "a" is "non-arbitrary"; sometimes we also say that the element "a" is "specific" one satisfying the property P(.). Further, to keep track of such specific elements, rather than using the symbol "a", we prefer to use "s".

$\exists x\,[\,P(x)]$

$\therefore$ $P(s)$ (s non-arbitrary)

3.6.4. Existential Generalization (EG)

When we have the quantified statements as a conclusion, we need the inference rules which enable us to introduce (back) the quantifiers. Note that, the "non-arbitrary" elements can only be bound by the existential quantifier. We introduce this rule below.

This rule states that, if $P(a)$ is true for some a in the universe of discourse, then $\exists x [P(x)]$ is true. Note that the constant "a" need not be arbitrary (i.e., it can be some specific element satisfying the property P(.)).

> $P(s)$ (s non-arbitrary)
>
> --------
>
> $\therefore \exists x [P(x)]$

Example 3.24: (Validity of Argument using UI, EI, and EG)

Express the following argument in the predicate logic formalism, and prove its validity:

> All Computer Engineering students are the students in the School of Computer Engineering. Some Computer Engineering students are graduate students. Therefore, some students in the School of Computer Engineering are graduate students.

Solution: Let $\mathcal{U}$ = all students in your university. With this universe of discourse, we use the following predicates:

(i) $CE(x) = x$ is a Computer Engineering student.
(ii) $SCE(x) = x$ is a student in the School of Computer Engineering (SCE).
(iii) $GRAD(x) = x$ is a graduate student.

Using the above, the argument is as follows:

(i) $\forall x [CE(x) \rightarrow SCE(x)]$
(ii) $\exists x [CE(x) \wedge GRAD(x)]$

$\therefore \quad \exists x [SCE(x) \wedge GRAD(x)]$

To establish the validity of the above argument, we give the following proof:

(1) $\forall x [CE(x) \rightarrow SCE(x)]$ ... Premise 1
(2) $\exists x [CE(x) \wedge GRAD(x)$ ... Premise 2
(3) $CE(s) \wedge GRAD(s)$ ... EI, (2) (with $x = s$, s non- arbitrary)

(4) $CE(s) \rightarrow SCE(s)$ ... UI, (1) (with $x = s$)
(5) $CE(s)$ ... CS, (3)
(6) $GRAD(s)$ ... CS, (3)
(7) $SCE(s)$ ... MP, (5), (4)
(8) $SCE(s) \wedge GRAD(s)$ ... RC, (7), (6)
(9) $\exists x\, [SCE(x) \wedge GRAD(x)]$ ... EG, (8) (Also, a conclusion.)

□

EXERCISES:

3.1. Model the following statements, using one-place predicates, as formulae in predicate logic:
  (i) Amit goes for swimming everyday.
  (ii) Some persons think of no one but themselves.
  (iii) All Amit's children are shy and stupid.
  (iv) Nobody likes to fall sick.
  (v) All men are mortal.
  (vi) Some men live in the village.

3.2. Model the following statements using two-place predicates, as formulae in predicate logic:
  (i) Everybody likes somebody.
  (ii) Somebody likes everybody.

3.3. Consider the following predicates:
  (i) $T(x)$: x is greater than ten.
  (ii) $E(x)$: x is an even number.
  (iii) $N(x)$: x is negative.

Assume that we have different universes of discourses:

I. $\mathcal{U}_1 = \mathbb{Z}$, the set of integers, i.e., {…, -2,-1,0,1,2,…};
II. $\mathcal{U}_2 = \mathbb{N}$, the set of natural numbers, i.e., {,0,1,2,…};
III. $\mathcal{U}_3 = \mathbb{Z}^-$, the set of negative integers, i.e., {…, -2,-1 }.

Determine the truth values of the following formulae for each of the above universes $\mathcal{U}_1$, $\mathcal{U}_2$, $\mathcal{U}_3$.

(a) $\exists x\, [\, T(x)\,]$
(b) $\forall x\, [\, N(x)\,]$

(c) $\exists x\,[\,\sim N(x)\,]$
(d) $\forall x\,[\,E(x) \wedge T(x)]$.

3.4. Consider the following formula in predicate logic:

$$\forall x \in [0, \pi),\ \sin x \geq \frac{x}{2}.$$

State whether this formula is true, false, or neither. Briefly give a reason for your answer.

3.5. Let the two place predicate $R(x,y) \equiv x$ relies on y. Express the following formulae in predicate logic as statements in English language:

a) $\forall x\,\exists y\,R(x,y)$
b) $\exists x\,\forall y\,R(x,y)$
c) $\exists y\,\forall x\,R(x,y)$
d) $\forall y\,\exists x\,R(x,y)$
e) $\forall x\,\forall y\,R(x,y)$
f) $\exists x\,\exists y\,R(x,y)$

3.6. Let $P(x,y,z)$ be the statement "$xyz = 1$", where $x,y,z \in \mathbb{R}^+$ (Note: $\mathbb{R}^+$ denotes the set of the positive real numbers). State whether the following formulae in predicate logic are true, false, or neither. Briefly explain your answer.

(a) $\forall x \forall y \forall z P(x,y,z)$
(b) $\exists x \exists y \exists z P(x,y,z)$
(c) $\forall x \forall y \exists z P(x,y,z)$
(d) $\exists z \forall x \forall y P(x,y,z)$

3.7. Let $C(x,y)$ mean that student x is enrolled in the class y, where the universe of discourse (say $\mathcal{U}_x$) for x consists of all students in the School of Computer Engineering (SCE) and the universe of discourse (say $\mathcal{U}_y$) for y is the set of all courses offered by the School of Computer Engineering (SCE). Express each of these statements by a simple English sentence.

(a) $\exists x\, C(x, \text{CS 201})$
(b) $\exists y\, C(\text{Mary}, y)$
(c) $\exists x\, (C(x, \text{SC109}) \wedge C(x, \text{CS 201}))$
(d) $\exists x\, \exists y\, \forall z\, ((x \neq y) \wedge (C(x,z) \rightarrow C(y,z)))$
(e) $\exists x\, \exists y\, \forall z\, ((x \neq y) \wedge (C(x,z) \leftrightarrow C(y,z)))$

3.8. Let $M(x,y)$ be "x has sent an email" and $T(x,y)$ be "x has telephoned y", where the universe of discourse $\mathscr{U}$ = all students in your university. Ram and Mamata are two students in the tutorial batch T_1 of the course CS 201. Using these predicates, model the following scenarios in the formalism of Predicate logic.

(a) Ram has not sent an email to Mamata, unless Mamata has telephoned Ram.
(b) There are at least two students in the tutorial batch T_1 of the course CS 201, such that one student has sent the other email and the second student has telephoned the first student.
(c) There are exactly two students in your university who have telephoned all other students in the tutorial batch T_1 of the course CS 201.

3.9. Formulate the following arguments as formal arguments in predicate logic. Using your formulation of formal arguments, establish the validity of the argument, or give a counterexample to show that the argument is invalid.

(a) All humans are Mortal. All Gods are immortal. Mr. Amit is a human. Therefore, Amit is not a God.
(b) Everyone shouts or cries. Not everyone cries. Hence, some people shout and don't cry.
(c) All problems are difficult and frustrating. Some problems are challenging. Therefore some problems are challenging and frustrating.
(d) All animals with scales are dragons. Some animals which are not dragons have sharp claws. So there are animals without scales which have sharp claws.

PART 4

Semantic Entailment, Proof Systems, Consistency and Completeness

4.1 PRAGMATICS AND SEMANTICS

In part 2, we introduced the notion of *implication*. Our notion of implication is based on the structure of sentences that use the connectives in propositional logic. Once we have represented the statement in an abstract way as a propositional symbol, say p, (or, q, etc.), for its interpretation, in earlier parts, we assumed that such a propositional symbol possesses two truth values, namely T or F.

However, unlike the above, in our course of conversation using natural language(s), even in the text that we encounter in media (like print media, social media, etc.), we consider the context in which the statement exists, and such a context refers to pragmatics. The same statement would convey different meanings, and its truth value may vary when they are in different contexts. Consider the following example to illustrate this point.

Example 4.1: Consider the statement "It rained here today". The truth value of this statement depends on the context about what place "here" represents as well as which date "today" represents.

Definition 4.1: *Pragmatics* is the study of how context contributes to the meaning of a statement.

In the field of Artificial Intelligence (AI), we study formal models (and their conversion to computational models) to deal with pragmatics. However, it is beyond our present scope of discussion, and we limit ourselves to the domain of logic. In logic, we are not interested in such aspects of a statement. Hence, we started our journey in logic by giving a definition of "proposition" (as in Definition 1.1).

In our study of logic, in earlier parts, we have already covered (albeit not in strict formal way) the "meaning" of the formulae in propositional logic as well as predicate logic. In the context of logic, we clarify this aspect by giving the following definition of semantics.

Definition 4.2: *Semantics* (in logic): In logic, semantics is the method/approach to determine that aspect of meaning of expression (in propositional logic, and/or predicate logic) in which logicians would be interested.

We recursively defined the *structure* of formulae in propositional logic as given in Definition 2.2. The formulae conforming to such structure are also termed as "Well-Formed Formulae" (WFF) in propositional logic.

Example 4.2: For propositional logic, we studied the truth table method for a WFF in propositional logic. In developing truth table, we assigned two truth values, namely T or F to each atomic propositional variable involved in WFF. We used the term "interpretation" for the same. This "interpretation" is *semantics*. We also saw that we need to uncover the structure of WFF for determining the sequence (order) in which we need to create the columns, so that the final resulting column represents a given WFF in propositional logic.

In part three, we studied Predicate Logic. We developed the formulae in predicate logic in intuitive and informal way. In the next subsection, we formally state the structure of WFF in predicate logic.

4.2 WELL FORMED FORMULA (WFF) IN PREDICATE LOGIC

Formulae in predicate logic should help us in formulating the interesting inferences. The structure of the formulae in predicate logic, that we have informally introduced in part three, is given below in the form of construction rules for WFFs.

Definition 4.3: Some rules for construction of WFF in predicate logic

1. *True* and *False* are WFFs.
2. A predicate name followed by a list of variables forming its arguments, such as $P(x_1, ..., x_n)$, where P is a predicate name of a n-place predicate, (for two place predicate in our example, $x_1 ..., x_n$ are variables, is a WFF and it is also called an atomic formula. Thus, an atomic formula is a specific predicate followed by its arguments as variables.
3. Each propositional constant (*i.e.* specific proposition), and each propositional variable (*i.e.* a variable representing propositions) are WFFs.
4. If *A, B,* and *C* are WFFs, then so are:
   (a) $(\neg A)$,
   (b) $(A \wedge B)$,
   (c) $(A \vee B)$,
   (d) $(A \rightarrow B)$, and,
   (e) $(A \leftrightarrow B)$.
5. If x is a variable (representing objects of the universe of discourse), and A is a WFF, then so are $(\forall x)A$ and $(\exists x)A$. The brackets may be omitted, and we may write these formulae as $\forall xA$ and $\exists xA$. To emphasize that the scope of these quantifiers is limited to the WFF A, we may also write $\forall x(A)$ and $\exists x(A)$.

Example 4.3: Some WFFs in predicate logic are given below.

(i) The sentence "Ujjain is capital of Madhya Pradesh." represents specific proposition, *i.e.*, it is propositional constant. Hence it is WFF by rule 3 above. We noted in part 1 that we prefer to denote such specific proposition by propositional constant, say p.

(ii) Let x be a variable and let CSE(.) be a predicate that stands for the property ". is student in School of Computer Science and Engineering (CSE) department.". Then CSE(x) is WFF by rule 2 above. This WFF denotes "x is student in School of Computer Science and Engineering (CSE) department.".

(iii) Consider the WFF MAE(x) to denote "x is student in School of Mechanical and Aerospace Engineering (MAE) department.". Noting that CSE(x) as well as MAE(x) both are WFF, using rule 4(c), we have CSE(x) ⋁MAE(x) WFF.

(iv) Applying the universal quantification on the WFF CSE(x) ⋁MAE(x), we obtain another WFF as ($\forall x$) (CSE(x) ⋁MAE(x)) . Note that we bracketed the WFF CSE(x) ⋁MAE(x) with extra brackets to convert it as (CSE(x) ⋁MAE(x)) so that the scope of ($\forall x$) quantification is the whole of WFF CSE(x) ⋁MAE(x). This also indicates that in ($\forall x$) (CSE(x) ⋁MAE(x)) there are no free variables; both occurrences of x within the expression (CSE(x) ⋁MAE(x)) are bound by the quantifier ($\forall x$), and hence ($\forall x$) (CSE(x) ⋁MAE(x)) reduces to proposition, which would evaluate to either true (T) or false (F).

(v) ($\forall x$) CSE(x) ⋁ MAE(x) is considered as shorter version to denote the bracketed WFF ($\forall x$) (CSE(x)) ⋁ MAE(x). Note that, the WFF ($\forall x$) (CSE(x)) ⋁ MAE(x) is still a predicate with one free variable, because, in this expression, the occurrence of x in MAE(x) is not within the scope of quantifier ($\forall x$), and hence it is free.

In the formation of WFF as per definition 4.3, we note that, we allow the use of functions returning values in domain of discourse as arguments of predicates. For example, consider the predicate $\exists y \forall x$ G(y, x) that we saw in part 3, example 3.16, and we noted that this predicate has all occurrences of variables bound. It can be read as:

> "There is *(i.e.*, there exists) an integer x, such that every integer y is greater than x."

Now, consider the modified scenario, where we want to model the following.

> "There is *(i.e.*, there exists) an integer x, such that every factorial(y) is greater than x."

We note that factorial(y) is a function defined on the set of natural numbers, and it produces (returns) a natural number. Use of such functions are permitted in the formation of WFF as arguments. They are also called as function constants.

4.3 WFF in Predicate Logic, Semantic Entailment, and Proof Systems

We have already noted the interpretation of formulae in propositional logic in part 2 where we defined the propositional expressions, and their evaluation. We noted that truth table is a tool that captures assignment of truth values to all atomic propositions in the expression involved in propositional logic. A row in such a truth table is one possible assignment of truth values to atomic propositions involved and is an interpretation for a formula in propositional logic. Under such an interpretation, a given formula in propositional logic may evaluate to true or to false. We were particularly interested in formulae in propositional logic whose truth value do not depend on the interpretation (i.e., these formulae can be reduced to either tautologies or to contradictions).

When we deal with formulae in predicate logic, we need more terminology, and we have given it in the remaining part of this section.

Definition 4.4: (*Interpretation*: *Denotation and Semantics*) An interpretation of a WFF in predicate logic identifies the domain of discourse for all domains involved in the predicate symbols. This domain of discourse specifies the range of quantifiers. Subsequently, the interpretation assigns a meaning, also called as denotation, to each non-logical symbol (such as: predicate, function, or constant). It also determines a domain of discourse that specifies the range of the quantifiers.

We note that denotation and semantics is extensively used in the process of creation of knowledge base (*KB*) in expert systems in Artificial Intelligence (as well as in advanced databases). The denotations are typically captured in *ontology*, that is part of creation of knowledge base. We shall leave these topics to be covered in other computer science and engineering courses, and hence we leave these topics to be studied in such courses.

Definition 4.5: (*Knowledge Base - KB*) Expert system designer, specializing in creation of facts and rules reflecting the aspect of some scenario (*e.g.*, modelling of operations involved in factory automation, news analysis, opinion surveys and dynamics, *etc.*) creates knowledge base consisting of formulae in predicate logic that are assumed to be true. Such formulae are also called as axioms in a given knowledge base.

The knowledge base (*KB*) created by knowledge engineer is queried to find out whether some proposition is logical consequence of the facts and rules stored in knowledge base.

Definition 4.6: (*Logical Entailment,* also called as *Semantic Entailment* and denoted by symbol ⊨) Given a knowledge base *KB*, and statement, say *s*, we say that KB *entails* *s* whenever *s* is a logical consequence of *KB*; it is symbolically denoted by KB⊨ *s*.

Definition 4.7: (*Model*) The semantic entailment assumes that all facts and rules in KB are true. When such assumption is true, it is also referred to as a *model* of *KB*.

Definition 4.8: (*Ontology*): *KB* is created in the form of symbols and these symbols are stored in memory of computer. Thus the facts as well as rules are represented as symbols form KB. Knowledge engineer stores the meaning that he assigns to these symbols at separate place, and such a mapping is an *ontology*.

Computing power of computers is utilised for symbolic manipulation for determining the logical entailment *KB*⊨ *s*. In this process, computer does not worry about the meaning assigned to the symbols involved in KB as well as in "*s*".

Definition 4.9: (Proof Systems): Proof systems as studied in logic allow us to automate the logical entailment *KB*⊨ *s* in symbolic way (separating ontologies from the symbolic manipulations).

Any proof system essentially involves deployment of machinery of logic in the form of equivalences, inference rules (with substitution rules) that we discussed in the earlier parts of this module. Efficient algorithms for such deployment as used by present day computers, however, are beyond the scope of our present course. Also formal discussion about proof systems as studied in subsequent courses on logic is beyond our present scope.

4.4 Soundness, Consistency and Completeness

To have proper (and non-confusing) perspective of soundness and consistency require more formal treatment of logics, and the definitions as available in Wikipedia and other sources assume the familiarity with advanced logic course(s). Hence, our discussion about these terms is necessarily elementary and sketchy.

Definition 4.10: (*Soundness*) Soundness is a semantic property that concerns how we interpret the formulas, function symbols, and predicate symbols into mathematical objects and statements. Soundness refers to the property of proof system (inferences in logic) where it is not possible in a proof system to prove something that is "wrong" semantically (*i.e.*, when *interpreted* with any possible interpretation).

Definition 4.11: (*Consistency*) Consistency is concerned with the collection of facts and rules in *KB*/axioms/propositions; two or more propositions are logically consistent if it is possible for them to all be true at the same time.

Greek mathematician Euclid of Alexandria, around 300 BC gave five postulates in his famous work "Elements" for formulating theorems in Geometry. The theorems that can be derived from these five postulates are known as theorems in Euclidean geometry. The fifth postulate, known as *parallel postulate*, became famous as its negation together with other four postulates did not result in contradiction (*i.e.*, the fifth postulate is not logical consequence of the first four postulates). Fifth postulate together with first four postulates formed *consistent* body of knowledge, known as Euclidean Geometry. Negation of fifth postulate together with first four postulates formed *another consistent* body of knowledge, known as non-Euclidean Geometry. Study of *consistency* historically played very important role in our understanding of applications of geometry.

We shall look at another example of consistency in the section 4.3 of Module on Sets, Relations, and Functions. This another example is the *continuum hypothesis*, that states, "*There is no set A with* $\aleph_0 <$ cardinality(A) $< \boldsymbol{c}$" ($\boldsymbol{c}$ denotes the cardinality of $\mathbb{R}$).

Note: In case you are not familiar with the notations and concepts like:

(i) cardinality of infinite set,
(ii) what we mean by "<" when we want to compare sizes of infinite sets,
(iii) $\aleph_0$ (read as "aleph-zero"),

etc.,

kindly browse through part two of Module on Sets, Relations and Functions, where we have developed the understanding of these concepts and symbols in its last part, namely part 4 dealing with Countability and Computability.

Consider the knowledge base, say, KB_M consisting of the standard (and established) axioms of number system forming the basis of mathematics. The continuum hypothesis is consistent with KB_M. Paul Cohen's pioneering contribution in 1963 established that, the negation of continuum hypothesis is also consistent in KB_M.

Definition 4.12: (*Inconsistency*) Inconsistency is concerned with the collection of propositions; two or more propositions are logically inconsistent if it is not possible for them to all be true at the same time.

Definition 4.12: (*Independence*) A proposition *p* is independent with respect a given knowledge base *KB*, if and only if:

(i) *p* is consistent with *KB,* and,
(ii) ~*p* is consistent with *KB*.

Historically, study of independence played great role in advancement of mathematics and its applications. We give two important examples below.

1. Russian mathematician Nikolai Lobachevsky, in 1829, proved the *independence* of parallel postulate for Euclidean geometry. Similar result seems to have been obtained by the Hungarian mathematician János Bolyai (1802-1860) in around 1820-1823, but published only in 1831. This led to non-Euclidean Geometries, and Einstein applied them in explaining physical phenomena including relativity.

2. Paul Cohen's pioneering contribution in 1963 established that *continuum hypothesis* is independent of KB_M.

From the practical point of view for constructing his knowledge base the knowledge engineer look for independent propositions and expands his/her knowledge base by either adding independent proposition (or its negation as is relevant for reflecting the reality in his model).

In systems like KB_M, we can prove (using proof system) many interesting theorems.

At the *International Congress for Mathematicians*, a meeting held in Paris in 1900 (this event is held once in every four years; the list of previous such events held is on website https://www.mathunion.org/icm/past-icms; it was held in 2010, only once, in India at Hyderabad and the event was inaugurated by Honb'le President of India), David Hilbert proposed a list of twenty-three unsolved problems in mathematics, that need to be addressed in the upcoming next century. For the second problem in this list, Hilbert addressed as follows.

> "But above all I wish to designate the following as the most important among the numerous questions which can be asked with regard to the axioms (of arithmetic): to prove that they are not contradictory, that is, that a finite number of logical steps based upon them can never lead to contradictory results."

In other words, Hilbert set out to advocate a program to formulate set of (finitely many) axioms for arithmetic that were consistent. He insisted that all mathematical statements should be written in a precise formal language and manipulated according to well-defined rules (proof system). He insisted that all "theorems" (*i.e.* true statements) in mathematics should be valid and their validity proof can be constructed in finitely many steps in such a proof system. His plan was, mathematicians should formulate such a proof system, which has a few (finite) rules that apply on finite number of axioms.

David Hilbert was proponent of Formalist school. He proposed that proving all (thereby he meant the *completeness*) theorems in classical mathematics involve manipulation of symbols (not necessarily meaning assigned, and hence meaningless) according to certain rules, and consistency of such a system reduces to preventing certain combination of symbols. According to the formulation as conceptualized by David Hilbert, consistency is a syntactic property and its concern is which formal proofs can be constructed in the proof system. When Hilbert conceptualised that all theorems can be proved in finitely many steps by a proof system, he believed that such a formal proof system would be complete, and his plan was to create such a complete and consistent formal proof system.

Definition 4.12: (*Completeness* of a proof system) Completeness means all valid (*i.e.* true) formulae can be proven by a proof system.

Some axiom systems have the property that each formula in such a formal system either follows from them or its negation does. An example is the formulae that we defined in part two in propositional logic - every quantifier-free formula is either true or false.

David Hilbert considered that the most important work for advancing mathematical knowledge is to prove that all theorems classical mathematics can be proved in consistent system (using finitely many non-contradictory axioms). Till 1920's, many mathematicians joined Hilbert's plan of formulating complete and consistent system for proving all theorems in mathematics (and arithmetic). Many interesting partial results were obtained to support Hilbert's plan during that period, thereby spreading the belief that Hilbert's plan would mature and succeed shortly, if not in few years, at most in few decades.

Then came sudden shock, when on Sunday, 07th September, 1030, at the Conference on Epistemology of the Exact Sciences at Konigsberg, Germany, Austrian mathematician Kurt Gödel, who was 24-year old at that time, announced that there is a statement that is true but not provable in a formal system of mathematics.

In 1931, Kurt Gödel proved that no consistent formal system of mathematics can prove its own consistency. He showed that Peano's axioms for numbers that form basis for arithmetic (and its supersets) are not complete (as long as they're consistent). This incompleteness result meant that there would be statements in mathematics which cannot be proved (indeed we still have conjectures like twin prime conjecture, Goldbach's conjecture states that every even number greater than 4 is the sum of two odd primes, etc. for which no proof has been discovered till now) and hence Hilbert's plan needs to be abandoned.

Definition 4.12: (*Incompleteness* of a proof system) Sufficiently expressive proof system (that allows reasonably rich modelling) which is also consistent is incomplete.

Kurt Gödel's proof relies on the argument that any sufficiently rich proof system would allow self-referentiality. In other words, in such a system, one can express statement equivalent to $\{S \mid S \notin S\}$, and it is not provable.

Let us restate the concepts that we reviewed in this section.

Soundness guarantees that it is not possible to prove something that possesses wrong meaning. *Completeness* guarantees that, in a given proof system, all true (*i.e.*, valid) theorems can be proved. In both cases, we refer to some fixed system of rules for proof.

When all provable arguments are valid, a logic is said to be *consistent*. In other words, if a WFF can be derived from a given set of premises, then the corresponding argument is valid. *Completeness* expresses the relationship between provability and validity in the other direction, i.e. all valid arguments can be proven. *Consistency* of the axioms (facts) means that these facts contain no internal contradictions, whereas *completeness* refers to situations where given axioms entail all valid statements in a given context (of axioms).

Completeness deals with the adequacy of a formal system that is employed both in proof theory. In proof theory, a formal system is said to be *complete* iff every formulae in the system is such that either it or its negation is provable in the system.

In 1931, Kurt Gödel proved his famous *incompleteness t*heorem, which states that for any sufficiently strong and consistent axiomatic system, there exist statements which can neither be proved nor disproved within the system.

UNIT Summary

Study of logic has important place in computer science. In this module, we introduced propositional logic as well as predicate logic. We covered equivalence laws, inference rules, and method of writing proofs systematically, in step by step fashion, stating the rule to be applied at each step.

We briefly reviewed the concept of pragmatics and semantics. We noted that, in intelligent systems, a knowledge base designer models a specific world relevant to the domain of interest. The designer uses symbols in logic to model the structure of the world of interest, and this forms Knowledge Base (*KB*) (You may like to think about how *KB* is different than a database (*DB*)). The scenario of world he has intended to model can be obtained from *KB* (*KB* is symbolic representation, devoid of meaning) by assigning the intended interpretation to *KB*. This interpretation requires assigning meaning to symbols as per the chosen domain of interpretation.

The symbols in *KB* can be manipulated by proof systems in logic. The design of inference engine of *KB* requires understanding of proof systems, and its computationally efficient and fast implementation(s). Knowledge engineer creates facts and rules that represent his intended model of reality. Knowledge engineer designs appropriate queries and uses computing power of computers to manipulate symbols in accordance with the underlying proof system to discover the validity of query. Proof systems help us to automate the process of logical entailment from *KB*. When the system computes a logical consequence from a knowledge base, the designer interprets this logical consequence with respect to the intended interpretation.

A designer should communicate the meaning to other designers and users so that they can also interpret the answer with respect to the meaning of the symbols. This necessitates the use of ontologies for knowledge base.

We reviewed the following technical terms:

(i) soundness,
(ii) consistency,
(iii) completeness, and,
(iv) independence of axioms (propositions)

in the context of logic and proof systems. We stated Paul Cohen's famous result that continuum hypothesis is independent in mathematics.

We briefly stated Kurt Gödel's famous incompleteness theorem, that states, "any sufficiently expressive logic system is either incomplete or inconsistent". Although strictly formal proof is not within the scope of our present discussion, we gave intuitive foundation for such a proof. Because of incompleteness, we have to live with unproven conjectures in mathematics, and even in number theory. We note that it may not be possible for us to discover the "proofs" for some of these unproven conjectures. This puzzled scenario keeps mathematics and indeed any formal system interesting.

In the domain of computing, developing intelligent systems and advancements in the areas like Artificial Intelligence remain exciting topics.

EXERCISE

1. Provide an example of two statements that are semantically entailed.
2. Determine whether the following statement is semantically entailed: "All cats are mammals" entails "Some mammals are cats." Justify your answer.
3. Explain the difference between semantic entailment and syntactic entailment.
4. Give an example of two logically equivalent statements and explain how their truth values are related
5. Prove semantically whether "All men are mortal" entails "Socrates is mortal."
6. Give an example of two statements that are not semantically entailed and explain why.
7. Consider the statements: $P \rightarrow Q$ and $Q \rightarrow R$. Determine whether they entail the statement $P \rightarrow R$, and justify your answer.
8. Construct a formal proof using natural deduction to show that $P \wedge (Q \vee R)$ entails $(P \wedge Q) \vee (P \wedge R)$.
9. Explain why the modus ponens rule is sound in predicate logic, providing a formal justification.
10. Provide an example of a proof system that uses axioms and rules of inference in predicate logic and demonstrate how it works with a specific proof.
11. Determine whether the following set of statements is consistent: $\{P \wedge Q, \neg P \rightarrow Q\}$. Justify your answer.
12. Prove that a set of statements is inconsistent if and only if it entails a contradiction.
13. Discuss the consequences of a theory being inconsistent.
14. Consider the set of statements: $\{P \wedge Q, \neg P \wedge \neg Q\}$. Determine whether the set is consistent, and if so, provide a model that satisfies both statements.
15. Prove that a consistent set of statements in predicate logic cannot entail both a statement and its negation.
16. Give an example of an inconsistent set of statements and discuss its implications in logical reasoning.

17. Discuss how Gödel's completeness theorem ensures that every valid statement in predicate logic is provable.
18. Prove or disprove the completeness of a given proof system in predicate logic with a specific example.
19. Explain an application of completeness in the context of automated theorem proving or artificial intelligence.
20. Consider a scenario where a medical diagnosis system uses predicate logic to infer diseases from symptoms. Explain how semantic entailment is applied in this system.
21. Describe how proof systems are utilized in software verification to ensure the correctness of computer programs.
22. Discuss an application of consistency and completeness in the design and analysis of cryptographic protocols.

LABORATORY WORK

The full form of Prolog is "Programming in Logic". As a computer science student, it is important to know what this domain of programming is. Further, programming in Prolog gives insights about how the inference engine (and thereby one practical deployment of formal proof system) of Prolog works. SWI-Prolog is free software available from the web page listed below. The online reference manual is also provided.

- SWI-Prolog Homepage http://www.swi-prolog.org/
- SWI-Prolog Reference Manual https://www.swi-prolog.org/download/stable/doc/SWI-Prolog-8.2.1.pdf
- Online Prolog (swi) compiler and IDE - Ideone.com https://ideone.com › prolog-swi

The following are few more learning resources related to Prolog.

- Ulle Endriss, Introduction to Prolog programming (64 pages); available at http://www.cse.lehigh.edu/~heflin/courses/endriss-prolog.pdf

  Download and go through the materials in these notes.
- Go through Programming in Prolog videos (seven part series) by Ryan Schachte (available on youtube; link given below) https://www.youtube.com/watch?v=gJOZZvYijqk&list=RDCMUC0ckjBtm9SBV7JAjbELiBqQ&index=1

Complete the exercises in Ule Endriss' 64 page notes (point no 1 in the resources above).

KNOW MORE

1. Apostolos Doxiadis, and Christos Papadimitriou, *Logicomix: An Epic Search For Truth*, Bloomsbury Publishing, New York (2015).

2. **Alfred North Whitehead, and Bertrand Russell, *Principia Mathematica: Volume 1* and *Volume 2*, Second Edition, The Syndics of the Cambridge University Press 1927 Bentley House, London, U.K. (reprinted 1963). Volume 1: 671 pages; Volume 2: 742 pages. (downloading links:**
   https://www.uhu.es/francisco.moreno/gii_mac/docs/Principia_Mathematica_vol1.pdf,
   https://www.uhu.es/francisco.moreno/gii_mac/docs/Principia_Mathematica_vol2.pdf)

REFERENCES AND SUGGESTED READINGS

1. Irving M. Kopi, *Introduction to Logic*, Pearson new international Edition (with Carl Cohen, Victor Rodych) 15th Edition (Special Indian Edition), ISBN 9780367376239 Routledge Publishing, 688 pages, (2021).

2. Patrick Suppes, *Introduction to Logic*, Affiliated East-West Press (Indian Edition, Rs 195/-) ISBN: 9788176710183, 9788176710183, 312 pages, Originally published by D Van Nostrand Company, Princeton, New Jersey, (1957). (Downloading link: http://web.mit.edu/gleitz/www/Introduction%20to%20Logic%20-%20P.%20Suppes%20(1957)%20WW.pdf)

Dynamic QR Code for Further Reading

2 Sets, Relations and Functions

UNIT SPECIFICS

In this module, we discuss the following aspects:

- *Sets as a basic abstraction tool.*
- *Sets: operations*
- *Laws of sets*
- *Binary Relations: Equivalences and partial orderings*
- *Functions: Composition and inverse*
- *Bijections*
- *Size of sets: Countable and uncountable sets*
- *Cantor's Diagonal Argument*
- *The Power Set Theorem*
- *Limits of Computation*

RATIONALE

Introduction: Sets as a basic abstraction tool

Consider the following images. The image in Figure1 gives us recollection some famous temple. (can you recollect it?) You immediately seem to throw away details like it is collection of rocks, there is iron door, there are steep stairs, etc., and you concentrate on (seemingly) important characteristic of the complete structure. This process of throwing away details and concentrating on important characteristic (that you perceive) is referred to as abstraction. Mathematical notion of "Set" invokes human ability for abstraction. Abstraction (from the Latin abs, meaning away from and tra here , meaning to draw) is the process of taking away or removing characteristics from something in order to reduce it to a set of essential characteristics. (Question: Is the human ability of abstraction an innate ability?)

Figure 2a. First Example Image

Figure 2b Second Example Image

The image in Figure 2 immediately attracts attention to collection of parrots sitting on the wall. We have ability to throw away details like backside of apartments, wall on which parrots are sitting and the picture drawn on wall, some plants (banana leaves, guava tree leaves, etc.) in background, and using our ability for abstraction, we concentrate on collection of parrots, which mathematically is referred to as "Set". So, "Set" is collection of precise, unambiguous, distinct (these three properties are also referred to as "well-defined" objects of our intuition or of our thought, and set involves the notion of abstraction in the sense of our ability to perceive "oneness" of all objects in the collection (under consideration). In our example, although we have large number of parrots, we have ability to put them together to create (mentally) new (and it is only one) object which is collection, or "Set" of parrots!

Why do we study set theory?

Set theory uses human capability of abstraction to conceptualize and recognize "togetherness" of collection of objects and perceiving this collection as different than any object included in the collection. Interestingly, sets together with logic allow us to construct mathematical structures as well as computing software. We can construct natural numbers, real numbers, computer programs, software systems using sets as basic tool of abstraction.

Why is set theory important to computer science?

Set Theory is a useful tool for formalizing, justifying and computing objects. Set theory, together with formal logic is basis for evolving the notion of computation. This is, and will continue to be, the source of the basic ideas of computer science, from theory to practice. In today's applications of computer science understanding sets is essential to grasp the functionality on techniques in artificial intelligence and machine learning (AI and ML). As computer science has influenced many of its constructs and ideas from set theory. Understanding of set theory promotes the ability to think abstractly. It will provide you with the basis for building a solid understanding and analysis of basic ideas in computer science.

Collection, group, bunch, class, set, are synonyms denoting the same thing – a collection of objects. A mathematical concept called as Set captures this meaning. The set consists of elements. For the discussion of our sets, we rely on our intuitive understanding of a set; in particular, we assume that the element of a set is different from the set.

PRE-REQUISITES

Mathematics at school level (till) Class X

UNIT OUTCOMES

List of outcomes of this unit is as follows:

U2-O1: Describe sets using list and property.

U2-O2: Apply Laws of sets and simplify set expressions.

U2-O3: Use Partial orderings and equivalences for modelling.

U2-O4: Modelling practical scenarios using functions.

U2-O5: Expressing computation using composition of functions.

U2-O6: Classify sets with different sizes (especially infinite sets), explore limits of computation.

Unit-2 Outcomes	EXPECTED MAPPING WITH COURSE OUTCOMES (1- Weak Correlation; 2- Medium correlation; 3- Strong Correlation)								
	CO-1	CO-2	CO-3	CO-4	CO-5	CO-6	CO-7	CO-8	CO-9
U2-O1	3	2	1	2	1	2	1	-	1
U2-O2	3	3	2	2	1	1	-	-	1
U2-O3	1	2	2	-	1	2	2	-	2
U2-O4	2	2	2	1	-	1	2	-	1
U2-O5	1	1	1	-	1	2	-	-	2
U2-O6	1	-	-	-	2	2	2	-	2

PART 1

Sets

1.1 SET: DEFINITION AND BASIC CONCEPTS

1.1.1 Universal Set, and Definition of a Set

When define set, we assume that we have a universe of discourse from which the elements of set(s) are drawn (Later, in the section on Power Set Theorem, we shall challenge this assumption, point out the limitations of this approach, and briefly comment on how modern look of Set fixes this issue). This universe of discourse is also a collection of elements; in other words, it is also a set. In the study of sets, we give special name to this set – we call it a *universal set*, usually denoted by symbol $\mathcal{U}_u$, or (when there is no conflict of notation) just by *U*.

Definition 1.1: A *set* is a collection of objects. The objects, which are members of the set, are also referred to as *elements* of the set.

1.1.2 Describing Sets as a List

Notation 1.1: We use the small alphabet symbols *a*, *b*, *c*, …, to denote elements of the universal set U. The capital alphabet symbols *A*, *B*, *C*, …, are used to denote the sets.

Notation 1.2: We use the small alphabet symbols *a*, *b*, *c*, …, to denote elements of the universal set U. The capital alphabet symbols *A*, *B*, *C*, …, are used to denote the sets.
Example 1.1: A set A consisting of three elements *a*, *b*, *c*, is symbolically represented by $\{a,b,c\}$.

In general, we have,

Notation 1.3: The set whose elements are from the list of objects $x_1, x_2, \ldots, x_n$ is denoted by

$$\{ x_1, x_2, \ldots, x_n \} \qquad \ldots (1.1)$$

The $\in$ operation: The basic operation in set theory is "belonging to" (denoted by '$\in$') operation.

In addition to the basic concepts in logic, the notion of set uses the only concept of an element belonging to a set. Let x denote a typical element of a set S. We represent this by saying that the element x belongs to a set S, and denote it as

$$x \in S \qquad \text{... (1.2)}$$

The belongs to (also called as "is member of") operation is true when x is an element of S. The operation x $\in$ S is false when x is not an element of S. We define $\notin$ as the negation of the $\in$ operation. Thus,

$$x \notin S \equiv \sim (x \in S) \qquad \text{... (1.3)}$$

The operation $\notin$ is read as does not belong to, or "is not a member of".

Thus, "$x \in$ S" is a statement, or a proposition, which is either true or false. In sets we find it very convenient to use another operation $\notin$. The statement x $\notin$ S" is also a statement, or a proposition, which is either true or false.

Table 1.1 gives symbols of logic that we covered earlier in Module 1 on Logic.

Sl.No.	Symbol	Usage	Meaning	Formal name of Symbol (Module 2)
1)	~	$\sim (x \in S)$	➢ It is not the case that $(x \in S)$, that is, ➢ Negation of $(x \in S)$	Negation

2)	$\equiv$	$x \notin S \equiv \sim (x \in S)$	➢ $x \notin S$ is defined as $\sim (x \in S)$, that is, ➢ $x \notin S$ is (logically) equivalent to $\sim(x \in S)$	logical equivalence
3)	$\rightarrow$	$x{\in}A \rightarrow x{\in}B$	➢ If $x{\in}A$ then $x{\in}B$, that is, ➢ $x{\in}B$ if $x{\in}A$, that is, ➢ $x{\in}A$ only if $x{\in}B$	Conditional
4)	$\leftarrow$	$x{\in}A \leftarrow x{\in}B$	➢ If $x{\in}B$, then $x{\in}A$, that is, ➢ $x{\in}A$ if $x{\in}B$, that is, ➢ $x{\in}B$ only if $x{\in}A$	Reverse conditional
5)	$\leftrightarrow$	$x{\in}A \leftrightarrow x{\in}B$	$x{\in}B$ if and only if $x{\in}A$, that is, $x{\in}B$ iff $x{\in}A$	Biconditional
6)	$\wedge$	$x{\in}A \wedge x{\notin}B$	It is the case that $x{\in}A$ and $x{\notin}B$	Conjunction (also called as "and")
7)	$\vee$	$(x{\in}A) \vee (x{\in}B)$	It is the case that $x{\in}A$ or $x{\in}B$	Disjunction (also called as "or")
8)	$\Rightarrow$	$x{\in}A \Rightarrow x{\in}B$	➢ $x{\in}A$ implies that $x{\in}B$, that is, ➢ it is always the case that, whenever $x{\in}A$, then $x{\in}B$ is true.	Logical Implication
9)	$\forall$	$\forall x\ (\text{Dog}(x))$	➢ Everyone is dog, that is, ➢ For every element x in the universe, the property Dog(x) holds.	For every (quantifier, it is followed by variable, which is quantified universally): Universal Quantifier
10)	$\exists$	$\exists x\ (\text{Cat}(x))$	➢ There is a cat, that	There exists (quantifier,

			is, ➢ There exists an element x in the universe for which the property Cat(x) holds.	that is followed by variable, which is quantified existentially): Existential Quantifier

Table 1.1: Some important notations for logic used in this module

We note that "$x \in S$" is a proposition, *i.e.* a statement that is either true or false. In sets, we find it very convenient to use another operation $\notin$. The statement $x \notin S$" is also a proposition, which is nothing but a a statement that is either true or false.

1.1.3 Equality of Sets

We may denote the collection of students, Ram, Arjun, Seeta, using the notation in (1.1) by the following.

$$A = \{\text{Ram, Arjun, Seeta}\} \qquad \dots (1.4)$$

Assume that we have another collection of the students Seeta, Ram, Arjun and Ram. Since "Seeta, Ram, Arjun and Ram" forms a list of all elements in the set, say B, we may denote B by the following.

$$B = \{\text{Seeta, Ram, Arjun, Ram}\} \qquad \dots (1.5)$$

In B, we observe that we have two occurrences of Ram (assuming they represent the same student Ram). In a set as a collection, we do not distinguish two (or more) occurrences of the same Ram. Thus, for the study of collections, which is called as the study of sets, we observe the following.

Observation 1.1: Multiple (more than one) occurrences of elements are considered as exactly one occurrence in a set.

Due to this observation, for defining a set, many authors disallow multiple occurrence(s) of the same element while constructing the set from the list of elements to be enclosed in braces.

We observe that the only important consideration for the set construction is whether an element belongs to a given set or not. For example, in (1.4), the element "Seeta" comes as a third element in the list, while in (1.5), the element "Seeta" is the first element. The position of an element in the set also does not matter. Thus, in our study of sets, we observe the following.

Observation 1.2: There is no particular order of arrangement of the elements in a set.

Based on these two observations, we say that the set B as defined in (1.5) is the same as the set A as defined in (1.4). In other words, we say that two sets A and B are equal, and denote it by the following.

$$A = B \qquad \ldots (1.6)$$

We observe that the statement "A=B" is true if the two sets A, as well as B, are equal in the sense of observations 1.1 and 1.2. We now give the formal definition of the set equality.

Definition 1.2: (Set Equality) We define the two sets A and B to be equal iff the elements belonging to both the sets is exactly the same.

In other words, if an element x belongs to the set A, then the element x belongs to the set B, and vice versa. Note that this description is in two parts: (i) if an element x belongs to the set A, then the element x belongs to the set B, and, (ii) if an element x belongs to the set B, then the element x belongs to the set A. We shall study (in section 1.2) these parts in set equality by defining a subset relationship.

The negation of set equality operation = is denoted by $\neq$. Thus, we have the following definition.

Definition 1.3: (Set Non-equality) We define the two sets A and B to be not equal, denoted by $A \neq B$ iff the statement "$A = B$" is false. In other words,

$$A \neq B \equiv \sim (A = B) \qquad \ldots (1.7)$$

Example 1.2: Consider the set A = {Ram, Arjun, Seeta} given in (1.4) above and the other set C = {Seeta, Ram}. The set A is not equal to the set C, because there is one element (in our example, Arjun) that is in set A, but not in set C; hence these two sets represent different collections (sets). In the above example, the expression $\sim (A = C)$ is true, hence using above definition, we also denote it by $A \neq B$.

1.1.4 *Describing Sets by Properties (One-Place Predicates)*

The sets containing finite number of elements can always be defined completely by listing all its distinct elements and enclosing the list in braces "{, }" (following the notation 1.3). Let us now consider a few examples.

Example 1.3: Describe a set of all characters in a word "WELCOME".

Solution: The set U consists of the set of all possible characters, say A, B, …, Z. The required set, say set S, consists of the characters: W, E, L, C, O, M, and E. We note that there are two occurrences of the character E in the list; we delete the second (which is the second) occurrence of the character E. Thus, we obtain, the required set S = {W, E, L, C, O, M}.

Sometimes the list of elements is long; so we use an informal notation of introducing three ellipsis, …, to denote the sequence of elements which is clear from the context (often from the elements occurring before there three ellipsis). We illustrate this feature in the following example.

Example 1.4: The set $A = \{1, 2, 3, 4, 5, 6, 7, 8, 9, 10, 11, 12\}$ is also denoted (informally) by $\{1, 2, \ldots, 12\}$.

We also describe a set by stating the common property possessed by every element in a set. We describe the notation for this purpose below.

Notation 1.4: Let $\mathcal{P}(x)$ be a one-place predicate defined over the universe of discourse $\mathcal{U}$. We take the universal set $U = \mathcal{U}$. The predicate $\mathcal{P}(x)$ is true for some elements in U, while it is false for the other elements in U. The collection of all elements in U for which the predicate $\mathcal{P}(x)$ evaluates to be true defines a set, say S. We describe S in the property form as follows.

$$S = \{x \in U \mid \mathcal{P}(x)\} \qquad \ldots (1.8)$$

The following example illustrates the above notation.

Example 1.5.: Consider the set S = collection (set) of computer science students in your institute/university. This description of a set has the following features: There is an explicitly stated universal set U = set of all students in your institute/university, which is also the universe of discourse $\mathcal{U}$.

There is a description of a property, "CS(x) ≡ x is a computer science student", which evaluates to *True*, for all elements within the set.

Hence, using this property $\mathrm{CS}(x)$, and the universe U, and using the notation 1.4, we describe the set S as follows.

$$S = \{x \in U \mid \mathrm{CS}(x)\} \quad \ldots (1.9)$$

□

We note that there are some properties which cannot be satisfied by any element in the universe U. Let $\mathrm{N}(x)$ be such a property, which is false for all elements in the universe U. Using the Notation 1.4, we can construct the following set:

$$A = \{x \in U \mid \mathrm{CS}(x)\} \quad \ldots (1.10)$$

What does the set in (1.10) represent? There are no elements in the set A. Further, it does not depend on the choice of universal set U. Hence, this set is given a special name; it is called as a null set, and the standard notation for denoting this set is the Greek symbol Φ (read as "phy").

Definition 1.4: (Null set) The set which contains no elements is a special set; it is called as a Null set.

Notation 1.5: The null set is denoted by Φ.

The set Φ has interesting properties. Since no element belongs to the set Φ, we say that an arbitrary element $x \notin \Phi$, and there is no $x \in \Phi$. One interesting property of Φ is given below.

Observation 1.3: (Theorem 1.11) $\Phi \subseteq A$, for any arbitrary set A.

Describing sets by properties gives us a variety of ways to describe a set over the same universe of discourse. Due to such a diversity way by which sets can be described, the question arises about whether apparently different properties denote the same set. In order to settle this issue, we need to develop tools to analyze the notion of set equality, that we introduced in (1.6) (and its negation in (1.7)); for this analysis, we need techniques which allow us to develop insights and give a formal proof of set equality or otherwise. To achieve this, we need to define an operation $\subseteq$, which is read as "is subset of" (or, "is contained in") over two sets.

1.1.5 Some well-known sets

Sets with finite number of elements are finite sets. Sets containing infinite number of elements are infinite sets. At this stage, we rely on intuitive notion of finite number and infinite number, but towards the end of this module, we would give an approach to be somewhat more rigorous about defining these notions; as a reader, please be patient about understanding our exposition. There is a unique set containing zero elements, and we denote it by Φ (Definition 1.4). Some well-known infinite sets are used very frequently; so we give them specific name. We give such sets in the notation below.

Notation 1.6: Some Infinite Sets.

(i) $\mathbb{N} = \{0, 1, 2, \ldots\}$ = the set of natural numbers,

(ii) $\mathbb{Z} = \{\ldots, -2, -1, 0, 1, 2, \ldots\}$ = the set of integers (you may like to remember the word *Z* integers),

(iii) $\mathbb{Z}^{+} = \{1, 2, \ldots\}$ = the set of positive integers (i.e., natural numbers except *zero*),

(iv) $\mathbb{Z}^{-} = \{-1, -2, \ldots\}$ = the set of (strictly) negative integers,

(v) $\mathbb{Q}$ = the set of rational numbers, the numbers which can be expressed in the form p/q, where p is an integer, and q is a positive integer,

(vi) $\mathbb{R}$ = the set of real numbers, the numbers which are associated with every point on the straight line, commonly known as a real line.

We note that it is possible to be somewhat more rigorous to define the above sets, using the set theory as foundation. Indeed, it is one of the important intellectual pursuits to give somewhat more rigorous basis to the above (intuitive) approach and has interesting and deep consequences. While we would give one such approach for defining Natural Numbers in our section of Countable and Uncountable sets, similar discussion for other sets is out of scope of our present course on Discrete Mathematics. However, we note that such an approach has resulted in the study of mathematical structures that would introduce in Module dealing with Algebraic Structures.

1.2 Subset Relationship – A Special Operation on Sets

1.2.1 Subset as a relationship amongst two sets

In section 1.1.5, we briefly stated that determination of the equality of two sets often involves an operation $\subseteq$, called as "is subset of" or "is contained in" operation defined on sets. Using the quantifier $\forall$, we now give our formal definition of a subset relationship.

Definition 1.5: Let A and B be two sets over the universal set U. We define:

$$A \subseteq B \equiv \forall x\ (x \in A \rightarrow x \in B) \qquad \ldots (1.11)$$

Note that the definition involves the quantified statement, hence it is a proposition. Since it is a proposition, it can be assigned the truth values "T", or "F". The operation "is subset of " is a binary operation, i.e., operation defined over two sets. This operation results in a value "True", or "False", depending on whether the two operands of this operation (i.e., two sets) satisfy the relation of "is subset of". Since this operation results in the two values "T", or "F", it is a proposition. We also use the term "subset relation(ship)" as two sets are related by this relationship iff the application of this operation results in the "T" value.

The negation of the operation $\subseteq$ is called is "is not a subset of" or "is not contained in". We denote this operation by $\not\subset$.

Definition 1.6: Let A and B be two sets over the universal set U. We define:

$$A \not\subset B \equiv \sim (A \subseteq B) \qquad \ldots (1.12)$$

Using (1.10), and the negation of a universal quantification, we have,

$$A \not\subset B \equiv \exists x\, (x \in A \wedge x \notin B) \qquad \ldots (1.13)$$

Example 1.6: Using the notation for set of integers, set of positive integers, and set of natural numbers, we have the following subset relationship.

(i) $\mathbb{Z}^+ \subseteq \mathbb{Z}$,

(ii) $\mathbb{N} \subseteq \mathbb{Z}$,

(iii) $\mathbb{Z}^+ \subseteq \mathbb{N}$,

(iv) $\mathbb{N} \not\subset \mathbb{Z}^+$.

1.2.2 Venn Diagram for subset relation

Venn diagram forms a useful tool for displaying the sets diagrammatically. In a Venn diagram, the atomic sets are represented by ovals; they are drawn in such a way that their overlapping portions represent "interesting" properties visually. In Venn diagram, we always represent the universal set as a rectangle covering all ovals. We give the use of Venn diagram for illustrating the subset relationship $\mathbb{Z}^+ \subseteq \mathbb{Z}$ in Example 1.5 (i).

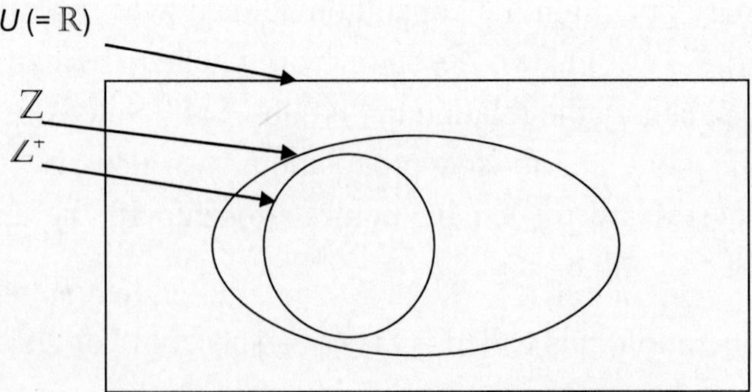

Figure 1.1 Venn Diagram for the subset relationship $\mathbb{Z}^+ \subseteq \mathbb{Z}$

We now give the use of Venn diagram for illustrating the subset relationships ($\mathbb{Z}^+ \subseteq \mathbb{N}$) $\wedge$ ($\mathbb{N} \not\subset \mathbb{Z}^+$) in Example 1.6 (iii) and (iv).

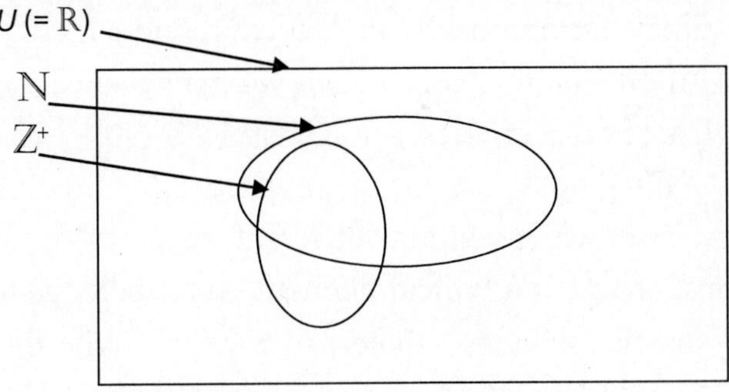

Figure 1.2 Venn Diagram for the subset relationship $\mathbb{N} \not\subset \mathbb{Z}^+$

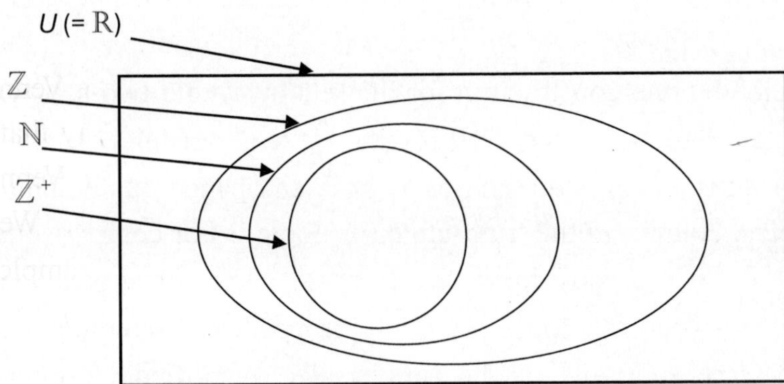

Figure 1.3 Venn Diagram for the subset relationships ($\mathbb{Z}^+ \subseteq \mathbb{Z}$)$\wedge$ ($\mathbb{N} \subseteq \mathbb{Z}$)$\wedge$ ($\mathbb{Z}^+ \subseteq \mathbb{N}$)$\wedge$($\mathbb{N} \not\subset \mathbb{Z}^+$)

Combining the Venn diagrams in Figure 1.1 as well as Figure 1.2, we have the following Venn diagram (in Figure 1.3) for illustrating the subset relationships ($\mathbb{Z}^+ \subseteq \mathbb{Z}$)$\wedge$ ($\mathbb{N} \subseteq \mathbb{Z}$)$\wedge$ ($\mathbb{Z}^+ \subseteq \mathbb{N}$)$\wedge$($\mathbb{N} \not\subset \mathbb{Z}^+$) in Examples 1.5 (i), (ii), (iii) and (iv).

1.2.3 Membership Table

For analyzing (and even for representing the semantics, or meaning) of the formula involving sets, we can adopt an approach. In the expression involving the sets (set expression), we first identify the atomic sets, which we may also call as set variables. It is useful to identify the list of set variables, and construct a table similar to *truth-table (discussed in Module 1 dealing with Logic)*; however, the construction starts with the listing of set variables, and we construct different rows with different possible membership combinations. Thus, if a typical element, say x belongs to the set variable A, then in the column (labeled) A, in the concerned row, we write the symbol $\in$. If a typical element, say x does not belong to the set variable A, then in the column (labeled) A, in the concerned row, we write the symbol $\notin$. Some authors continue to write the truth value T if $x \in A$, and F if $x \notin A$; with such a convention, all columns in membership table look very similar to the columns in truth-table. However, to distinguish a set from a proposition, we shall write the symbols $\in$, $\notin$ in our table. We call such a table as *Membership table.*

We now illustrate the membership table construction for the sets involving two sets A, and B, for the relationship $A \subseteq B$. Note that, since $A \subseteq B$ is either True (T) or false (F), the column below the expression $A \subseteq B$ contains the entries T, or F, and hence this column looks very similar to the typical column in the truth-table (in Logic). For comparison, we also give the truth-table for the propositional operator $\rightarrow$. This illustrates the similarity of the meaning of the subset relationship and the propositional operator $\rightarrow$. Also, note the definition of $A \subseteq B$ in terms of the (universally quantified) formula involving the propositional operator $\rightarrow$. We note that the propositional operator $\rightarrow$ has been discussed and introduced in Module 1 on Logic.

Definition 1.7: Membership table of the relationship $A \subseteq B$.

A	B	$A \subseteq B$
$\notin$	$\notin$	T
$\notin$	$\in$	T

Truth Table for $p \rightarrow q$ *(discussed in Module 1)*
(with Truth values F, T)

p	q	$p \rightarrow q$
F	F	T
F	T	T

∈	∉	F
∈	∈	T

T	F	F
T	T	T

□

We observe that the conditional operator $\rightarrow$ is non-commutative (part 2: section 2.6 of Module on Logic). Like the non-commutativity of conditional, we have the following observation.

Observation 1.4: The relationship $A \subseteq B$ is non-commutative, *i.e.*, in general, $A \subseteq B$ is not logically equivalent to $B \subseteq A$.

Notation 1.7: The relationship $B \subseteq A$ is also denoted by $A \supseteq B$, and it is read as, "A is a superset of B", or "A contains B".

Definition 1.8: Membership table of the relationship $A \supseteq B$.

A	B	$A \supseteq B$
∉	∉	T
∉	∈	F
∈	∉	T
∈	∈	T

Truth Table for $p \leftarrow q$ (with Truth values F, T)

p	q	$p \leftarrow q$
F	F	T
F	T	F
T	F	T
T	T	T

We note that $A \supseteq B \equiv A$ CONTAINS B finds applications in modeling queries in databases using languages like SQL. We shall see this modeling in the course Database Systems.

Example 1.7: We illustrated the relationship ($\mathbb{Z}^+ \subseteq \mathbb{Z}$) in Venn diagram in Figure 1.3. Let us now illustrate the same relationship ($\mathbb{Z}^+ \subseteq \mathbb{Z}$) by constructing the membership table for the same.

$\mathbb{Z}^+$	$\mathbb{Z}$	$\mathbb{Z}^+ \subseteq \mathbb{Z}$
∉	∉	T

$\notin$	$\in$	T
$\in$	$\notin$	F
$\in$	$\in$	T

□

Example 1.8: We illustrated the relationship ($N \not\subset Z^+$) in Venn diagram in Figure 1.2. Let us now illustrate the same relationship $\sim(N \subseteq Z^+)$ by constructing the membership table for the same.

Z^+	N	$N \subseteq Z^+$	$\sim(N \subseteq Z^+)$
$\notin$	$\notin$	T	F
$\notin$	$\in$	F	T
$\in$	$\notin$	T	F
$\in$	$\in$	T	F

□

Note that, in Figure 1.2, the four rows of the above membership table correspond to four regions (identify which are these four regions). The Venn diagram is drawn in such as way that it allows us to visually distinguish the regions corresponding to the rows with truth value "T" from the regions with the truth value "F".

1.2.4 Power Set

In the previous section, we defined the concept of the subset of a set. Note that the subset (containing at least one element) itself is a set, and it is different from all the elements in *U*. Thus, as a (non-empty) subset, we do generate a new object that cannot be in the universal set *U* (with which we started the construction of a subset).

Our study of a subset of a given set, say *S*, empowers us with an interesting tool to generate different sets from a given set *S*. We can think of collecting all the subsets together to form a new collection. Note that, the universal set *U* from which the set *S* derives its elements is not the universal set for defining the set consisting of such a collection. This necessitates us to define the collection of all subsets of a given set.

Definition 1.9: The collection of all subsets of a given set S is defined as a power set of S.

Notation 1.8: We denote the power set by the symbol $\mathbf{P}(S)$, or sometimes by the symbol 2^S.

It is worth repeating that, many elements of the $\mathbf{P}(S)$ are not drawn from the universal set U. In order that the Definition 1.9 is meaningful, we need other universal set whose elements form the sets like $\mathbf{P}(S)$.

We further note that, when the number of elements in the set S is finite, the number of elements in the power set of S is also finite.

Notation 1.9: (Cardinality of a set) We use the symbol $|S|$ to denote the number of elements in the (finite) set S.

Theorem 1.12: For a finite set S, $|\mathbf{P}(S)| = 2^{|S|}$.

We use this theorem to systematically construct the power set of a finite set S.

Example 1.9: Let $S = \{a, b, c\}$. Construct the power set of S.

Solution: The $\mathbf{P}(S)$ consists of $2^3 = 8$ elements. We list the sets with 0 elements, sets with one element (called as *singleton* set), sets with two elements, and a set with three elements, in this order. it is $\{ \Phi, \{a\}, \{b\}, \{c\}, \{a, b\}, \{a, c\}, \{b, c\}, \{a, b, c\} \}$.

□

1.2.5 Establishing Set Equality Using Subset Method

We defined the set equality in Definition 1.2, and we also saw two important properties of equal sets in Observations 1.1, and 1.2. In section 1.2, we saw the definition of a subset relationship ($\subseteq$) in terms of the propositional operator $\rightarrow$.We also defined the superset relationship ($\supseteq$) in terms of the propositional operator $\leftarrow$. In Module 1 dealing with logic, we have defined equivalence of two propositions (in general, compound propositional expressions) in terms of the biconditional operator $\leftrightarrow$, which is and ($\wedge$) of two binary operators $\rightarrow$, and $\leftarrow$. In a similar way, it is possible to define the set equality in terms of the two relationships $\subseteq$ and $\supseteq$.

<u>Theorem 1.13</u>: The two sets A, B are equal iff $(A \subseteq B) \wedge (A \supseteq B)$.

We now state the useful strategies for proving the subset ($\subseteq$), not the subset ($\not\subset$), and equality (=) in the following table.

Statement	The strategy to prove it
$A \subseteq B$	For arbitrary (every, $\forall$) $x \in A$, show that $x \in B$. (See the definition of subset in (1.10)).
$A \not\subset B$	Find (there exists some, $\exists$) an element $x \in A$, such that (and, $\wedge$) $x \notin B$. (See the definition of "not a subset" in (1.12)).
$A=B$	<u>Part I</u>: (Show $A \subseteq B$) For arbitrary $x \in A$, show that $x \in B$. <u>Part II</u>: (Show $B \subseteq A$) For arbitrary $x \in B$, show that $x \in A$.

<u>Example 1.10</u>: (Set Equality Proof: $A=B$) Consider the following sets:

$A = \{n \in \mathbb{N} \mid n \text{ is a prime number between 42 and 50}\}$,

$B = \{ n \in \mathbb{N} \mid n = 4k + 3,\ k \in \{10, 11\} \}$.

Prove that these two sets are equal.

Solution:

Part I: ($A \subseteq B$ Proof) For arbitrary $x \in A$, show that $x \in B$.

Since $x \in A$, $x \in \mathbb{N}$ and x is a prime number between 42 and 50. With our knowledge of primes, two cases arise. Case 1: x = 43, and Case 2: x = 47. We examine both these cases separately as given below.

Case 1: x = 43. We can write x = 4*10 + 3, which is of the form $4k+3$ with k =10. Hence $x \in$B.

Case 2: x = 47. We can write x = 4*11 + 3, which is of the form $4k+3$ with k =11. Hence $x \in B$.

Hence, for arbitrary $x \in A$, it follows that $x \in B$.

Part II: ($B \subseteq A$ Proof) For arbitrary $x \in B$, show that $x \in A$.

Since $x \in$B, $x \in \mathbb{N}$, two cases arise. Case 1: x = 4*10 + 3, which is of the form $4k+3$ with k =10. Hence, x = 43. Case 2: x = 4*11 + 3, which is of the form $4k+3$ with k =11. Hence, x = 47. We examine both these cases separately as given below.

$x \in$A, $x \in \mathbb{N}$ and x is a prime number between 42 and 50. With our knowledge of primes, two cases arise. Case 1: x = 43, and Case 2: x = 47. We examine both these cases separately as given below.

Case 1: x = 43. We note that 43 is prime number between 42 and 50. Hence, in this case, x is a prime number between 42 and 50. Hence, $x \in A$.

Case 2: x = 47. We note that 47 is prime number between 42 and 50. Hence, in this case, x is a prime number between 42 and 50. Hence, $x \in A$.

Hence, for arbitrary $x \in B$, it follows that $x \in A$.

Due to Part I, ($A \subseteq B$), and due to part II, ($B \subseteq A$). Thus, $(A \subseteq B) \wedge (B \subseteq A) \equiv (A = B)$.

□

Example 1.11: (Set non-equality Proof: using Proof of $A \not\subseteq B$) Consider the following sets:

$A = \{n \in \mathbb{N} \mid n = 3k + 1,\ k \in \mathbb{N}\}$,

$B = \{ n \in \mathbb{N} \mid n = 4k + 1,\ k \in \mathbb{N} \}$.

Prove that these two sets *A*, *B* are not equal.

Solution: To prove that the sets *A*, *B* are not equal, we need to prove that $\sim[(A \subseteq B) \wedge (B \subseteq A)]$

is true for all possible membership combinations. In other words, we need to prove that $[(\sim(A \subseteq B) \vee \sim (B \subseteq A)]$ is true for all possible membership combinations. Using the definition of $\not\subset$, this means, we need to prove that $[\ (A \not\subset B) \vee (B \not\subset A)]$ is true. This is $\vee$ of two clauses, viz., $(A \not\subset B)$, and $(B \not\subset A)$. This is true if we prove even one clause is True. So let us choose to prove $(A \not\subset B)$.

$(A \not\subset B) \equiv \exists x\ (x \in A \wedge x \notin B)$ …(definition of a $\not\subset$, as given in (1.12))

So to prove $(A \not\subset B)$, we need to find out some element of *A*, which is not in the set *B*. Using $k = 1$ in the description of set A, we get the number $4 \in A$. Next, we note that set $B = \{1, 5, 9, \dots \}$; so $4 \notin B$. So one element which invalidates the set equality $A = B$ is 4.

□

In the above proof for establishing set non-equality, we choose to show $(A \not\subset B)$. You may like to choose $(B \not\subset A)$, and find out a suitable *x*. In this example, it is possible to show that both the clauses $(A \not\subset B)$ and $(B \not\subset A)$ are true. Finally, we note that the sets are not equal even if you are able to show at least one of these clauses is true.

1.3 SET OPERATIONS – UNION, INTERSECTION, COMPLEMENT, SET DIFFERENCE

In section 1.1.5 (and in equation (1.8)) we saw that a set can be defined in terms of of a one-place predicate. With two sets, we have two one-place predicates defining the two concerned sets. Just as we can apply propositional operations $\vee$, $\wedge$, $\sim$, on predicates to get other predicate, we can apply the set operations $\cup$, $\cap$, and complement (which we define in terms of set difference with respect to the universal set *U*) operations on sets to *get other set*. The operations $\cup$, $\cap$, and set complement (or set difference (denoted by –)) are important operations to construct complicated sets.

As opposed to the $\subseteq$ operation of section 1.2, these operations result in other set. In this section, we give the definitions of these set operations in terms of the defining predicates of their constituent sets.

1.3.1 Union of two sets

Definition 1.10: The union of two sets A and B (over the universal set U) is the set of all elements that are either in A or in B or in both A and B.

Notation 1.10: The union of two sets A and B is denoted by the symbol $A \cup B$.

$$A \cup B = \{ x \in U \mid (x \in A) \vee (x \in B) \} \qquad \ldots (1.14)$$

1.3.1.1 Membership Table of Union Operation

The membership table for $A \cup B = \{ x \in U \mid (x \in A) \vee (x \in B) \}$ is given below. Note that, since $A \cup B$ is a set, the entries in the membership table are the membership symbol (either $\in$, or $\notin$, depending whether an arbitrary element x is within $A \cup B$, or not.)

Membership Table for $A \cup B$

A	B	$A \cup B$
$\notin$	$\notin$	$\notin$
$\notin$	$\in$	$\in$
$\in$	$\notin$	$\in$
$\in$	$\in$	$\in$

In Figure 1.4 below, we give the Venn diagram representation of the set union operation.

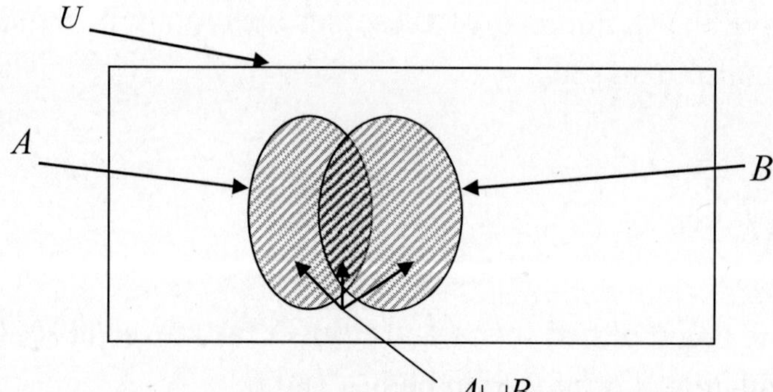

Figure 1.4 Venn Diagram for set union $A \cup B$

Example 1.12: Properties of the set union $A \cup B$.

The set union operation, as defined in (4.12), and whose membership table is given above, satisfies the following properties:

(i) $A \cup B = B \cup A$ ... (Commutativity of $\cup$)

(ii) $A \cup (B \cup C) = (A \cup B) \cup C$ ... (Associativity of $\cup$)

(iii) $\mathrm{A} \cup \mathrm{A} = \mathrm{A}$ ... (Idempotentness of $\cup$)

(iv) $A \cup \Phi = A$ ... (Identity Law of $\cup$)

(v) $\mathrm{A} \subseteq B \leftrightarrow A \cup B = B$

The proof of these properties follows from the membership table, and it is left as an exercise to the reader.

□

Examining the similarities of the above set properties with the laws of logic (equalities in propositional logic, seen in section 1.5 of Chapter 1), we note that the null set Φ has a role identical to the truth-value False ("F"). Further, we note that, the column for the set Φ in the membership table contains the entries $\notin$ in the rows. (That is, for the column for the set Φ in the membership table, the entry $\in$ is not permitted for any row of the membership table).

Due to the associativity of the set union operation (Example 1.11 (ii) above), we can take union of many sets (say, $A_1, A_2, \ldots, A_M$) and represent the same by the following symbol:

$$\equiv \bigcup_{i=1}^{M} [A_i] \qquad \ldots (1.15)$$

Example 1.13: English words as a Union.

Let A_i denote the set of all i-letter words in English language. We note that there are finitely many such i-letter words (can you count how many are there?). Suppose our artificial language does not permit size of each word to be more than 30. Then, we may represent the set of all permitted words as:

$$\equiv \bigcup_{i=1}^{30} [A_i] \qquad \ldots (1.16)$$

□

We note that we need to take the infinite unions infinite (while the formulation of the notion of "infinite" would be done later in this module, at this stage, we rely on our intuition for understanding the same) if we do not restrict the length of the words in our language (in such a case, we may replace the parameter M in (1.15) by $\propto$; more appropriately, we may express the same thing by stating that the variable $i \in \mathbb{Z}^+$ which is given in the Example 1.13 below.)

Example 1.14: Infinite Union of Finite Sets.

Let A_i denote the set $\{-i, i\}$, where $i \in \mathbb{Z}^+$. Here, each set A_i has the size 2 ($|A_i| = 2$). However, there are infinitely many elements in the set $\mathbb{Z}^+$. We can take the would be made union of these finite sets to obtain the following set:

$$\equiv \bigcup_{i \in Z^+} [A_i] \qquad \ldots (1.17)$$

We note that this is precisely the set $\mathbb{Z}^- \cup \mathbb{Z}^+$ (it is a set of all natural numbers, except 0).

□

1.3.2 Intersection of two sets

Definition 1.11: The intersection of two sets *A* and *B* (over the universal set *U*) is the set of all elements that are in both *A* and *B*.

Notation 1.11: The intersection of two sets A and B is denoted by the symbol A∩B.

$$A \cap B = \{ x \in U \mid (x \in A) \wedge (x \in B) \} \quad \text{... (1.18)}$$

1.3.2.1 Membership Table of Intersection Operation

The membership table for $A \cap B = \{ x \in U \mid (x \in A) \wedge (x \in B) \}$ is given below. Note that, since $A \cup B$ is a set, the entries in the membership table are the membership symbol (either $\in$, or $\notin$, depending whether an arbitrary element *x* is within $A \cup B$, or not.)

Membership Table for $A \cap B$

A	B	$A \cap B$
$\notin$	$\notin$	$\notin$
$\notin$	$\in$	$\notin$
$\in$	$\notin$	$\notin$
$\in$	$\in$	$\in$

In Figure 1.5 below, we give the Venn diagram representation of the set intersection operation.

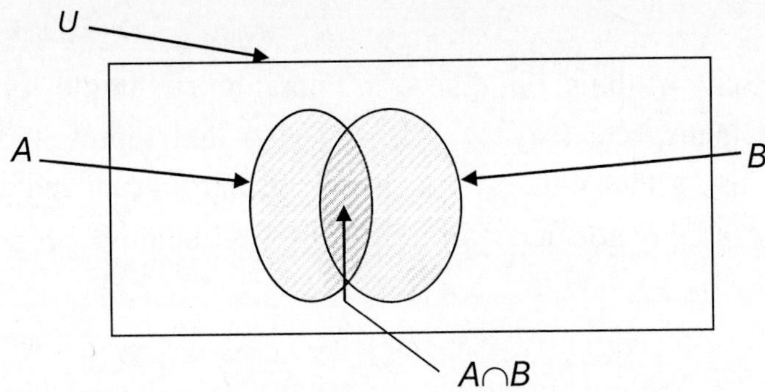

Figure 1.5 Venn Diagram for set intersection $A \cap B$

Example 1.15: Properties of the set intersection $A \cap B$.

The set intersection operation, as defined in (1.13), and whose membership table is given above, satisfies the following properties:

(i) $A \cap B = B \cap A$ ... (Commutativity of $\cap$)

(ii) $A \cap (B \cap C) = (A \cap B) \cap C$ ... (Associativity of $\cap$)

(iii) $A \cap A = A$ ... (Idempotentness of $\cap$)

(iv) $A \cap U = A$ ... (Identity Law of $\cap$)

(v) $A \supseteq B \leftrightarrow A \cap B = B$

The proof of these properties follows from the membership table, and it is left as an exercise to the reader.

□

We observe the similarities of the above set properties with the laws of logic (equalities in propositional logic, would be covered in Module on Logic), we note that the universal set U has a role identical to the truth-value True ("T"). Further, we note that, the column for the set U in the membership table contains the entries $\in$ in the rows. (That is, for the column for the set U in the membership table, the entry $\notin$ is not permitted for any row of the membership table).

Definition 1.12: (Disjoint sets) If $A \cap B = \Phi$, we say that two sets are disjoint.

Due to the associativity of the set intersection operation (Example 1.15 (ii) above), we can take union of many sets (say, A_1, A_2, …, A_M) and represent the same by the following symbol (using the notation similar to the one introduced earlier, where we introduced the existential quantifier ∀ in terms of the associative propositional operator ∧):

$$\equiv \bigcap_{i=1}^{M} [A_i] \qquad \text{… (1.19)}$$

<u>Example 1.16</u>: Infinite intersection of Sets.

Let A_i ($i \in \mathbb{Z}^+$) denote the set = $\{ x \in \mathbb{Z} \mid i \in \mathbb{Z}^+, -i \le x \le i \}$. Then, we have:

$$\equiv \bigcap_{i \in Z^+} [A_i] = \{-1, 0, +1\}.$$

□

1.3.3 Complement of a set

The complement of a set is other set.

<u>Definition 1.13</u>: The complement of set *A* (over the universal set *U*) is the set of all elements which are not in *A*.

<u>Notation 1.12</u>: The complement of set *A* is denoted by the symbol $\bar{A}$, or Compl(*A*), or sometimes even by ~*A* .

$$\text{Compl}(A) = \bar{A} = x \in U \mid (x \notin A) \} \qquad \text{… (1.20)}$$

1.3.3.1 Membership Table of Complement Operation

The membership table for Compl(A) = $\overline{A}$ ={ $x \in U \mid (x \notin A)$ }is given below. Note that, since Compl(*A*) = $\overline{A}$ is a set, the entries in the membership table are the membership symbol (either ∈, or ∉, depending whether an arbitrary element *x* is within Compl(*A*) or not.)

Membership Table for Compl(A)) = $\overline{A}$

A	Compl(A)
$\notin$	$\in$
$\in$	$\notin$

In Figure 1.6 below, we give the Venn diagram representation of the set complement operation.

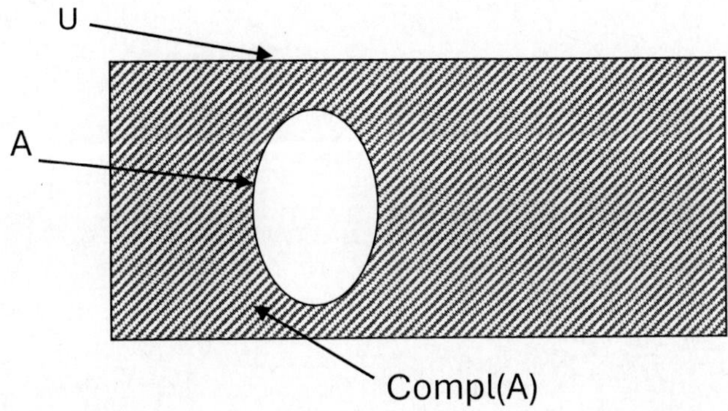

Figure 1.6 Venn Diagram for set complement Compl(A)

1.3.4 Set Difference

The difference of two sets A, B, is denoted by $A–B$, and it is a set whose definition as follows.

Definition 1.14: The set difference $A–B$, of two sets A, B is the set of all elements which are in A, but not in B.

Notation 1.13: The difference of two sets A, B, is denoted by $A–B$. We define the set difference as follows.

$$A-B = \{\, x \in U \mid (x \in A) \wedge (x \notin B) \,\} \quad \ldots (1.21)$$

From the definition of Compl(B) (expression (1.20)), and the set intersection (expression (1.18)), we have the following theorem.

Theorem 1.14: $A–B = A \cap \overline{B}$.

We note that the operation $A-B \equiv A$ EXCEPT B finds applications in expressing database queries in languages like SQL.

1.3.4.1 Membership Table for Set Difference Operation

The membership table for $A-B = \{ x \in U \mid (x \in A) \wedge (x \notin B) \}$ is given below. Note that, since $A-B$ is a set, the entries in the membership table are the membership symbol (either $\in$, or $\notin$, depending whether an arbitrary element x is within A-B or not.)

Membership Table for A-B

A	B	$A-B$
$\notin$	$\notin$	$\notin$
$\notin$	$\in$	$\notin$
$\in$	$\notin$	$\in$
$\in$	$\in$	$\notin$

In Figure 1.7 below, we give the Venn diagram representation of the set difference operation.

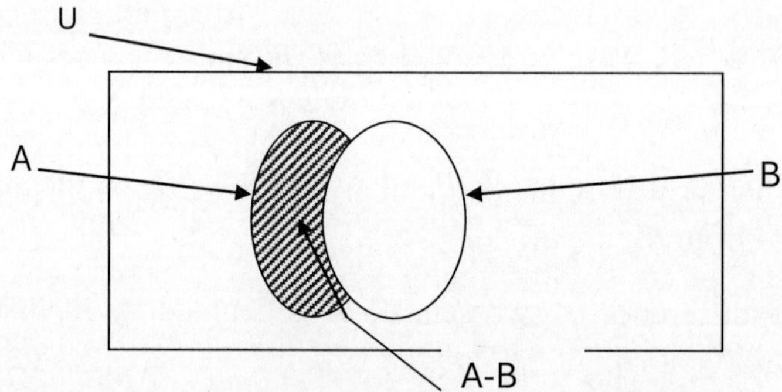

Figure 1.7 Venn Diagram for set difference $A-B$

1.4 COUNTING ELEMENTS IN UNION OF FINITE SETS

The union of two sets which have infinitely many elements (we rely on our intuitive notion of "infinitely many" at this stage; later in this module, we shall give some formulations for the same) would have infinitely many elements, and this situation is not of interest to us in this section.

To formulate the concept of Finite Set using the approach in Set Theory, we need the notions of Cartesian Product of sets, Relations, Functions and we shall do the same later in parts of this module. At this stage, however, we rely on intuition about the concept of Finite Set, and note that the count of the number of elements in a Finite Set is denoted by a natural number.

To illustrate this point, let us consider the following sets:

(a) $A = \{1, 2, 3, 4, 5\}$,
(b) $B = \{a, b, c, d, e, g\}$, and,
(c) $C = \{\text{men living presently in different cities India}\}$

We observe that *A* contains 5 elements and *B* contains 6 elements.

How many elements does *C* contain? We do not know the number of elements in *C*, but it is some natural number somewhere in the range of few tens of millions to about a thousand million. By number of elements of a set *S*, we mean the number of distinct elements of the set and we denote it by n(*S*). If n(*S*) is a natural number, then *S* is finite set. We now state the following theorem.

Theorem 1.14: Let *A* and *B* be finite sets. If $A \cap B = \Phi$, then

(a) $$\mathrm{n}(A \cup B) = \mathrm{n}(A) + \mathrm{n}(B) \quad \text{... (1.22)}$$

In general, if *A* and *B* are finite sets, then

(b) $$\mathrm{n}(A \cup B) = \mathrm{n}(A) + \mathrm{n}(B) - \mathrm{n}(A \cap B) \quad \text{... (1.23)}$$

Proof: (a) The elements in $A \cup B$ are either in *A* or in *B* but not in both as $A \cap B = \Phi$. So, (1.22) follows immediately.

For part (b), to proceed further, we require the following Lemma:

Lemma 1.15: Let A and B be arbitrary (finite) sets. Then,

$$n(A) = n(A - B) + n(A \cap B) \quad \dots (1.24)$$

Proof : Left as exercise (can be worked out from Venn Diagram).

□

Substituting B for A, and A for B, Lemma 1.15 states:

$$n(B) = n(B - A) + n(A \cap B) \quad \dots (1.25)$$

Now, we come back to work out the proof of part (b) of Theorem 1.14.

Proof (Part (b) of Theorem 1.14): Note that the sets $A - B$, $A \cap B$, and $B - A$ are disjoint and their union is $A \cup B$ (Fig 1.11).

Therefore,

$$n(A \cup B) = n(A - B) + n(A \cap B) + n(B - A)$$

$$= n(A - B) + n(A \cap B) + n(B - A) + n(A \cap B) - n(A \cap B)$$

(note how we made use of (1.24) and (1.25) to obtain RHS terms)

$= n(A) + n(B) - n(A \cap B)$, from which (1.23) follows.

□

In Theorem 1.14 (b), we used two sets. This result can recursively be extended for union of any finite number of sets. Thus, for three sets, we note the following.

Lemma 1.16: If A, B and C are finite sets, then

$$n(A \cup B \cup C) = n(A) + n(B) + n(C)$$

$$- \; n(A \cap B) - n(B \cap C) - n(A \cap C) + n(A \cap B \cap C) \quad \text{... (1.26)}$$

Proof: We have,

$$n(A \cup B \cup C) = n(A) + n(B \cup C) - n[A \cap (B \cup C)]$$

$$= n(A) + n(B) + n(C) - n(B \cap C) - n[A \cap (B \cup C)] \quad \text{... (1.27)}$$

Since intersection operation distributes over union operation, *i.e.*,

$A \cap (B \cup C) = (A \cap B) \cup (A \cap C)$, we get

$$n[A \cap (B \cup C)] = n[(A \cap B) \cup (A \cap C)]$$

$$= n(A \cap B) + n(A \cap C) - n[(A \cap B) \cap (A \cap C)]$$

$$= n(A \cap B) + n(A \cap C) - n(A \cap B \cap C) \quad \text{... (1.28)}$$

Therefore, for obtaining the expression for $n(A \cup B \cup C)$, we substitute (1.28) in (1.27) and rearrange the terms to get:

$$n(A \cup B \cup C)$$

$$= n(A) + n(B) + n(C) - n(A \cap B) - n(B \cap C) - n(A \cap C) + n(A \cap B \cap C)$$

□

Example 1.17: If X and Y are two sets such that $X \cup Y$ has 50 elements, X has 28 elements and Y has 32 elements, how many elements does $X \cap Y$ have?

Solution: Identifying in (1.23) as $A = X$, $B = Y$, and noting that we are given the following:

$$n(X) = 28, \; n(Y) = 32, \text{ and } n(X \cup Y) = 50$$

Rearranging the terms in (1.23), we get:

$$n(A \cap B) = n(A) + n(B) - n(A \cup B) \quad \text{... (1.29)}$$

Substituting values as given in this example in (1.29), we get:

$$n(X \cap Y) = 28 + 32 - 50$$
$$= 10.$$

1.5 SET EQUIVALENCES AND THEIR PROOFS

Using the set operations in section 1.3, we may generate complicated and big expression for representing a set. To study the simplification of such set expressions, we need the rules for set equivalences. We call these rules as "Set Equivalences". They are given in the tabular fashion below.

Equivalence Laws of Sets

Double Complement	$\overline{(\overline{A})} \equiv A$	Commutative Laws	$A \cap B \equiv B \cap A$ $A \cup B \equiv B \cup A$
De Morgan's Laws	$\overline{(A \cap B)} \equiv \overline{A} \cup \overline{B}$ $\overline{(A \cup B)} \equiv \overline{A} \cap \overline{B}$	Associative Laws	$(A \cap B) \cap C \equiv A \cap (B \cap C)$ $(A \cup B) \cup C \equiv A \cup (B \cup C)$
Idempotent Laws	$A \cap A \equiv A$ $A \cup A \equiv A$	Distributive Laws	$A \cap (B \cup C) \equiv (A \cap B) \cup (A \cap C)$ $A \cup (B \cap C) \equiv (A \cup B) \cap (A \cup C)$
Identity Laws	$A \cap U \equiv A$ $A \cup \Phi \equiv A$	Absorption Laws	$A \cap (A \cup B) \equiv A$ $A \cup (A \cap B) \equiv A$
Inverse Laws	$A \cap \overline{A} \equiv \Phi$ $A \cup \overline{A} \equiv U$	Domination Laws	$A \cap \Phi \equiv \Phi$ $A \cup U \equiv U$
Set Difference	$A - B \equiv A \cap \overline{B}$	Subset not a subset	$S \subseteq T \equiv (\forall x)\ (x \in S \rightarrow x \in T)$ $S \not\subset T \equiv (\exists\ x)\ (x \in S \wedge x \notin T)$

Table 1.2: Equivalence Laws of Sets

We can prove these laws using membership table method.

Example 1.18: Prove, for arbitrary sets A, B, and C:

$$[(\overline{(A \cap B)} \cup C) \cap (\bar{A} \cup B)] \subseteq [(\bar{A} \cup C)]$$

Solution: One approach is to simplify the expression on the left hand side of the "subset of ($\subseteq$)" using Equivalence Laws of Sets.

$[(\overline{(A \cap B)} \cup C) \cap (\bar{A} \cup B)]$

$\equiv [((\bar{A} \cup \bar{B}) \cup C) \cap (\bar{A} \cup B)]$ ... De Morgan's Law (complement of $\cap$)

$\equiv [(\bar{A} \cup (\bar{B} \cup C)) \cap (\bar{A} \cup B)]$ ...Associativity of $\cup$

$\equiv [(\bar{A} \cap (\bar{A} \cup B)) \cup ((\bar{B} \cup C) \cap (\bar{A} \cup B))]$ ... Distribute $\cap$ over $\cup$

$\equiv [(\bar{A}) \cup ((\bar{B} \cup C) \cap (\bar{A} \cup B))]$ ... Absorption of B in $\bar{A}$

$\equiv [(\bar{A}) \cup ((\bar{B} \cap (\bar{A} \cup B)) \cup (C \cap (\bar{A} \cup B))]$ ... Distribute $\cap$ over $\cup$

$\equiv [(\bar{A}) \cup ((\bar{B} \cap \bar{A}) \cup (\bar{B} \cap B)) \cup (C \cap (\bar{A} \cup B))]$ ... Distribute $\cap$ over $\cup$

$\equiv [(\bar{A}) \cup ((\bar{B} \cap \bar{A}) \cup (\Phi)) \cup (C \cap (\bar{A} \cup B))]$ ... Inverse Law for B

$\equiv [((\bar{A}) \cup (\bar{B} \cap \bar{A})) \cup (C \cap (\bar{A} \cup B))]$ ...Identity Law, and Assocativity of $\cup$

$\equiv [\bar{A} \cup (C \cap (\bar{A} \cup B))]$ ... Absorption of $\bar{B}$ in $\bar{A}$

$\equiv [(\bar{A} \cup C) \cap (\bar{A} \cup (\bar{A} \cup B))]$ ... Distribute $\cup$ over $\cap$

$\equiv [(\bar{A} \cup C) \cap (\bar{A} \cup B)]$ ... Associativity of $\cup$, and Simplification

To prove Left Hand Side (LHS) $\subseteq$ Right Hand Side (RHS), we start with arbitrary $x \in$ LHS. We prove that it logically implies that $x \in$ RHS. One possible proof is as follows:

$x \in [(\overline{A} \cup C) \cap (\overline{A} \cup B)] \Rightarrow (x \in \overline{A} \cup C) \wedge (x \in \overline{A} \cup B) \Rightarrow x \in (\overline{A} \cup C)$, *i.e.*, $x \in$ RHS. Hence the result.

□

Alternate approaches and solutions are possible for the above problem. It is possible to try this example with membership table method. Since there are three (set) variables A, B, C, the membership table has 8 rows, which is manageable for membership table construction. Also compare and contrast this problem with Example 2.2 of part 2 of Module 1 dealing with Logic, where we discussed the simplification of a formula in propositional logic.

Example 1.19: Give suitable sets *A*, *B*, (as well as $\overline{A}, \overline{A \cap B}$), and *C* to show that the following is not true:

$$[\overline{A} \cup C] \subseteq [(\overline{(A \cap B)} \cup C) \cap (\overline{A} \cup B)] \quad .$$

Solution: Consider the expression: $[\overline{A} \cup C] \subseteq [(\overline{(A \cap B)} \cup C) \cap (\overline{A} \cup B)]$

To define $\overline{A}$, we need to specify the universal set U. Let U = $\{a, b, c, d, e\}$. Consider the set $A = \{a, b, c, d\}$, $B = \{a, b\}$, $C = \{b, c\}$. Hence, $\overline{A} = \{e\}$.
With the above sets, LHS = $[\overline{A} \cup C] = \{b, c, e\}$.
We note that $[\overline{A} \cup B] = \{a, b, e\}$, and, $[(\overline{A} \cup C) \cap (\overline{A} \cup B)] = \{b, e\}$.
Hence, RHS = $[(\overline{(A \cap B)} \cup C) \cap (\overline{A} \cup B)] \equiv [(\overline{A} \cup C) \cap (\overline{A} \cup B)] = \{b, e\}$.
Thus, LHS $\not\subset$ RHS, as needed.

□

As an exercise, work out the solution of Examples 1.18, 1.19 using the other approach (*i.e.*, and approach that expresses the set operations in terms of operations in propositional logic).

PART 2

Binary Relations

Sentences in a language have a sequential or ordered structure having finite length. Study of structure of "strings of finite length" (*e.g.*, "Jambuwant" is string of length 9) is useful in computer science. In fact, study of restricted versions of such strings led to development of various programming languages in last six decades or so. Such study of structure of "strings" as well as how it leads us to formulate various programming languages is not in our present scope of our present discussion. In this part, we introduce the notion of "ordered pair" and how study of certain subsets of universe of "ordered pairs" leads us to notion of "equivalences" as well as "partial orderings", two main heavily used concepts that are frequently needed in formulating the scenarios in computer science.

2.1. CARTESIAN PRODUCT OF SETS

A "tuple" denotes the ordered pair (*i.e.*, consisting of two) elements. The elements in a tuple are drawn from a set.

We summarize the properties of ordered pair in the following observations.

<u>Observation 2.1</u>: Repeated (Multiple) occurrences of elements are allowed in a tuple. For example, (c,c) has two occurrences of "c".

<u>Observation 2.2</u>: There is an order (or, an arrangement) of elements in a tuple. Hence, we say that tuple (a,b) is difference than the tuple (b,a).

Contrast these observations with the Observations 1.2, and 1.3 for sets.

Definition 2.1: (*Cartesian product*) The Cartesian product of two sets A, and B, is denoted by $A \times B$. The $A \times B$ is a set of all ordered pairs (a, b) such that $a \in A$, and $b \in B$. Thus,

$$A \times B = \{ (a, b) \mid a \in A, b \in B \} \quad \ldots (2.1)$$

Note in the above definition that the elements of the Cartesian product do come from the universal set (say U_A) from which the elements of the set A are drawn; similarly its elements do come from the universal set (say U_B) from which the elements of the set B are drawn. Thus, this notion needs the construction of the universal set for $A \times B$; it can in turn be defined in terms of Cartesian product itself: the universal set for $A \times B$ is the set $U_A \times U_B$.

Example 2.1: Consider the sets $A = (a, b, c\}$ and $B = \{1, 2\}$.

The Cartesian product $A \times B = \{ (a, 1), (a, 2), (b, 1), (b, 2), (c, 1), (c, 2) \}$.

We depict the construction of the above Cartesian product in the figure 2.1 below.

B → / A ↓	1	2
a	$(a, 1)$	$(a, 2)$
b	$(b, 1)$	$(b, 2)$
c	$(c, 1)$	$(c, 2)$

Figure 2.1: Cartesian Product of two sets as two-dimensional array

Example 2.2: The set of all points in two-dimensional plane is represented by Cartesian product $\mathbb{R} \times \mathbb{R}$, and given in Figure 2.2 below.

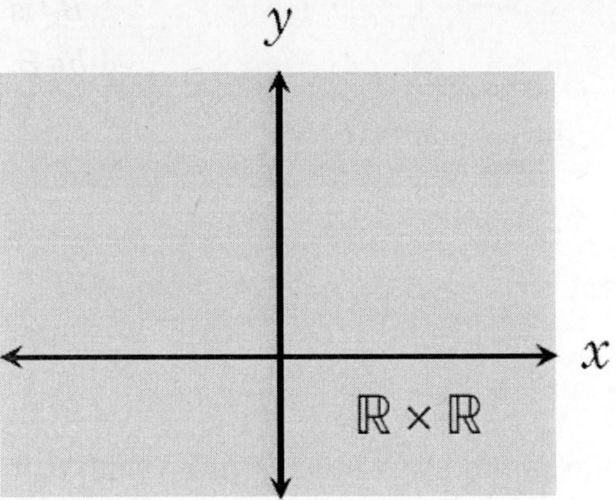

Figure 2.2: Cartesian Product R×R

Example 2.3: The set of all discrete points in two-dimensional plane is represented by Cartesian product N×N, and given in Figure 2.3 below.

Figure 2.3: Cartesian Product N×N

Example 2.4: The Cartesian product R×N

consists of collection of lines of real numbers, indexed by the set of natural number. Thus, for natural number 0, we have one line of reals; for natural number 1, we have other line of reals, … and so on. It is given in Figure 2.4 below.

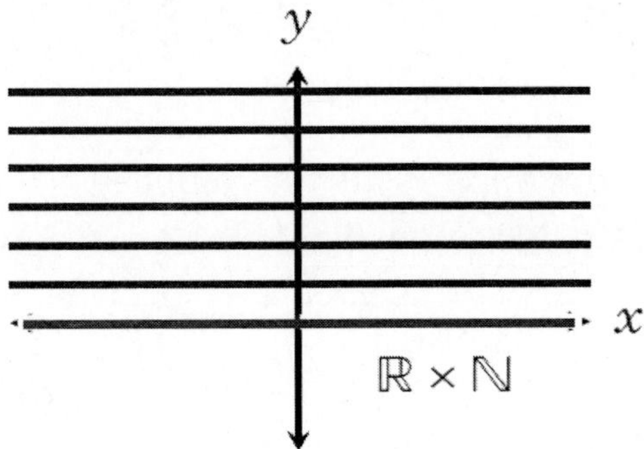

Figure 2.4: Cartesian Product R×N

Example 2.5: Le us assume that we have the sets A, B, C, with $U_A = U_B = U_C$ (say, $= U$); further assume that the set $B \neq \Phi$. If $A \times B \subseteq C \times C$, then prove that $A \subseteq C$.

Solution: Since $B \neq \Phi$, there is at least one element, say $b \in B$. In order to prove $A \subseteq C$, we assume an arbitrary $x \in A$. We need to prove, from the given facts, that $x \in C$. We give the following steps to prove this.

$x \in A \Rightarrow (x, b) \in A \times B$ ... because $\exists\, b \in B$, and cross product "×" would pair x with that b

$\Rightarrow (x, b) \in C \times C$ ... because we are given that $A \times B \subseteq C \times C$

$\Rightarrow x \in C$ ... due to the definition of $C \times C$

Thus, for an arbitrary $x \in A$, we have $x \in A \Rightarrow x \in C$, *i.e.*,

Hence, $A \subseteq C$.

□

2.2. Binary Relations

We frequently come across the statements having the form given below.

$\mathcal{R}(x, y)$: x is related (in some way) to y.

Say $\mathcal{R}(x, y)$ We say that such values x, and y, are $\mathcal{R}$-related by a binary relationship $\mathcal{R}(.,.)$.

Consider a few of such examples, which are given below.

(f) $H(x, y) = x$'s Hostel is the same as y's Hostel.
(g) $T(x, y) = x$'s height is more than (or equal to) y's height.
(h) $B(x, y) = x$'s birthday is within 7 days after y's birthday.
(i) $L(x, y) = x$ likes y.
(j) $R(x, y) = x$ relies on y.

In these examples, we assumed that the above two-place predicates are defined over the same set $\boldsymbol{U}$ = all students in your university/institute.

When both the variables draw values from the same set, say set A, we say that the binary relation is defined on the set A. When this is the case, since all possible pairs of values x, y also forms a set, which we called as the Cartesian product $A \times A$ (introduced in Section 1.6), a specific binary relation is a subset of $A \times A$.

Notation 2.1: A notation of $R(x,y)$, or xRy, (also sometimes, ${}_xR_y$, or, Rx,y, or $R_{x,y}$), or $(x, y) \in R$, are some of the notations used to denote a binary relation R, relating x to y. We also read this as "x is R-related to y".

Observation 2.3: A binary relation R on A is a subset of $A \times A$.

Example 2.6: Consider a binary relation P on the set of all human beings, say **H**, defined as follows.

xPy : x is a parent of y.

The binary relationship P true iff x is a parent (either father or mother) of y. This relationship relates an element of **H** to another element of **H**, and hence it is a subset of **H** × **H**, we may call the first set in this cross-product as a domain, and the second set as a co-domain. Note that, a given x (parent) in the domain set may have many (zero, one, or more) children (elements y in the co-domain set), so this relationship relates one element x in the domain set to multiple elements y in the co-domain set; and hence it is not a function (we also say that it is not a functional relationship). Thus, we have a more general relationship than the functional relationship. Some general properties that some of these relationships possess can fruitfully be used in logical arguments and proofs. In this part, we primarily focus on two important such relationships, which are called as (i) *equivalences*, and (ii) (partial) *orderings*.

Indeed, we expect that, the relationship $H(x, y)$ defined as " x's Hostel is the same as y's Hostel" should have additional properties which should enable us to conclude that, if Ram stays in the same Hostel as that of Gopal, and Gopal stays in the same Hostel as that of Arjun, then Ram also stays in the same Hostel as that of Arjun, and vice versa. Similarly, for the relationship $T(x, y)$ defined as "x's height is more than (or equal to) y's height", we expect that if Uttam's height is more than Raj's height, and Raj's height is more than Ramya's height, we expect that we should logically be able to derive that Uttam's height is more than Ramya's height (but *not vice versa*, unless we have the special case that Uttam, Raj and Ramya all have the same height). In this section, we focus on some additional properties the binary relationships may satisfy so that we can logically conclude such interesting facts.

2.3 BASIC PROPERTIES OF BINARY RELATIONS

We now see three properties that are important for deriving the conclusions as indicated in the previous section. They are (i) Reflexivity, (ii) Symmetry, and (iii) Transitivity. Additionally, we shall also define (iv) Antisymmetry, the property needed for defining the orderings.

2.3.1 Reflexivity

Definition 2.2: (*Reflexivity*) Let R be a binary relation on a set A. We define the relation R to be reflexive if and only if for all elements x of the set A, we have $(x,x) \in R$.

In other words, the relation R is reflexive when every element is related to itself under the relationship R. It is useful to remember the following formulation of the property of reflexivity while solving the problems.

The relation R on A is reflexive $\Leftrightarrow (\forall x \in A)\ (xRx)$ … (2.2)

Example 2.7: Consider the set $A = \{1, 2, a, b\}$. Let the relation R on A be defined as follows:

$$R = \{\ (1,1), (a,a), (b,b), (2,2), (1,2), (a,b)\ \}.$$

Here, we have listed the set of all tuples included in R: this was possible for the here because the set A on which the relation is defined had very few (four) elements and the number of tuples in the relation are also very few (six). This relation R is reflexive, as

$$(\forall x \in A)\ (xRx) \equiv {}_1R_1 \wedge {}_2R_2 \wedge {}_aR_a \wedge {}_bR_b$$

is a "True" proposition.

□

Example 2.8: Consider the set $A = \{1, 2, a, b\}$. Let the relation R on A be defined as follows:

$$R = \{\ (1,1), (a,b), (b,a), (b,b), (2,2)\ \}.$$

This relation R is not reflexive, as

$$(\forall x \in A)\ (xRx) \equiv {}_1R_1 \wedge {}_2R_2 \wedge {}_aR_a \wedge {}_bR_b$$

is a "False" proposition. It is false because ${}_aR_a$ is False.

□

Example 2.9: For $m > 1$, we define the relationship $xRy : x \equiv y \pmod{m}$, also denoted by $\langle x = y \rangle_m$ (read as "Congruent modulo m") in integers. While we presume that you are familiar with this notion earlier in your school mathematics, we would also discuss this notion in more details in Module 4 of our course, dealing with Modular Arithmetic. Specifically, for a given set of integers $\mathbb{Z}$, the relationship $x\mathrm{R}y$ is a binary relationship, and it is defined on the elements of $\mathbb{Z}$, the set of integers. Since for any arbitrary integer, say x, we have $x-x = 0$, and $m|0$, we have $x\mathrm{R}x$, and hence this ("congruent modulo m", for integer $m > 1$) relationship is reflexive.

□

Example 2.10: We defined the relationship $\subseteq$ (read as "is subset of") on sets in Section 1.2 (equation 1.11). Specifically, for a given set S, the relationship $\subseteq$ is a binary relationship, and it is defined on the elements of $\mathbf{P}(S)$, the power set of S. Thus, the relationship $\subseteq$ is defined on the set $A = \mathbf{P}(S)$. Since for any arbitrary set, say C, we have $C \subseteq C$, the relationship $\subseteq$ is reflexive.

□

Example 2.11: Let us consider the relationship $xRy : x \mid y$ (x divides y) defined on the set of positive integers (the set $\mathbb{Z}^+$). Since every positive integer divides itself, this relationship is reflexive.

□

2.3.2 *Symmetry*

Definition 2.3: (*Symmetry*) Let R be a binary relation on a set A. We define the relation R to be symmetric if and only if for all elements x, y of the set A, if $(x,y) \in R$ then $(y, x) \in R$.

It is useful to remember the following formulation of the property of symmetry.

The relation R on A is symmetric $\Leftrightarrow (\forall x, y \in A)\ [\ (x,y) \in R \rightarrow\ (y, x) \in R]$ ... (2.3)

Note that the defining property for symmetry involves conditional, viz., $[((x,y) \in R) \rightarrow ((y, x) \in R)]$. We note here that the conditional $(x,y) \in R \rightarrow\ (y, x) \in R$ is vacuously true when the antecedent is false. Thus, for checking whether the relation R is symmetric or not, when we have $(x,y) \notin R$, we should not check whether $(y, x) \in R$ or $(y, x) \notin R$. Further, we note that the conditional $(x,y) \in R \rightarrow\ (y, x) \in R$ is true when $x = y$. This necessitates us to concentrate on distinct values of x, y while checking for symmetry. When x, y are distinct and $(x,y) \in R$, we should have $(y, x) \in R$ in order that the relation R is symmetric. We illustrate this point in the examples below.

Example 2.12: Consider the set $A = \{1, 2, a, b\}$. Let the relation R on A be defined as follows:

$$R = \{\ (1,1), (a,a), (b,b), (2,2), (1,2), (a,b)\ \}.$$

This relation R is not symmetric, as $\exists x = 1, y = 2$, such that:

$$(\ (1,2) \in R\ ) \wedge (\ (2, 1) \notin R\ ).$$

This invalidates the conditional $(x,y) \in R \rightarrow (y, x) \in R$, which is involved as a defining property of the symmetry of R. In other words,

$$(\forall x, y \in A)\ [\ (x,y) \in R \rightarrow\ (y, x) \in R]$$

is a "False" proposition (it evaluates to "F" for at least one value assignments $x = 1, y = 2$). Hence, R is not symmetric.

□

Example 2.13: Consider the set $A = \{1, 2, a, b\}$. Let the relation R on A be defined as follows:

$$R = \{\ (1,1), (a,b), (b,a), (b,b), (2,2)\ \}.$$

Since we have $(a,b) \in R$, the property of symmetry needs to be checked for the (distinct) values of $x=a$, $y=b$. To check this, we need to find out whether $(b,a) \in R$. Since $(b,a) \in R$, and this is only the distinct pair of values $\in R$, we conclude that this relation R is symmetric.

□

Example 2.14: For $m > 1$, we define the relationship $xRy : x \equiv y \pmod{m}$, also denoted by $\langle x = y \rangle_m$ (read as "Congruent modulo m") on integers. Specifically, for a given set of integers $\mathbb{Z}$, the relationship xRy is a binary relations (discussed in Module 4 of our course, dealing with Modular Arithmetic), and it is defined on the elements of $\mathbb{Z}$, the set of integers. We have, for any arbitrary integers, say x as well as y,

$$\begin{aligned} xRy &\Rightarrow m|(x-y) \\ &\Rightarrow \exists\, k\in \mathbb{Z}, \text{ such that } (x-y)= k\times m \\ &\Rightarrow \exists\, k'\in \mathbb{Z}, \text{ such that } (y-x)= k'\times m \text{ (choose } k' = -k) \\ &\Rightarrow m|(y-x) \\ &\Rightarrow yRx, \end{aligned}$$

and hence this ("congruent modulo m", for integer $m>1$) relationship is symmetric.

□

Example 2.15: We defined the relationship $\subseteq$ (read as "is subset of") on sets in Section 1.2 (equation 1.11). Specifically, for a given set S, the relationship $\subseteq$ is a binary relationship, and it is defined on the elements of **P**(S), the power set of S.

Let us choose $S = \{a, b, c\}$. Further, let us have two sets $S_1= \{a\}$, and $S_2 = \{a, b\}$. Then we have $S_1\subseteq S_2$; however, we also have S_2 is not a subset of S_1. The reason why S_2 is not a subset of S_1 is as follows. Referring to the definition of this relationship of $\subseteq$ in Section 1.2, we note that $(b\in S_2)\wedge(b \notin S_1)$, so the element b falsifies the defining property for $S_2\subseteq S_1$.
Since we gave one example (of the above sets S_1, S_2) such that we have $(S_1\subseteq S_2)\wedge(S_2 \not\subset S_1)$, the relationship $\subseteq$ is not symmetric.

□

Example 2.16: Let us consider the relationship $xRy : x \mid y$ (x divides y) defined on the set of positive integers. Since 2|4, but 4~|2, this relationship is not symmetric.

□

2.3.3 *Antisymmetry*

Definition 2.4: (*Antisymmetry*) Let R be a binary relation on a set A. We define the relation R to be antisymmetric if and only if for all elements x, y of the set A, if $(x,y)\in R$ and $x \neq y$, then $(y, x)\notin R$.

It is useful to remember the following formulation of the property of antisymmetry.

The relation R on A is antisymmetric

$$\Leftrightarrow (\forall x, y \in A) [((x,y)\in R \wedge (x \neq y)) \rightarrow (y, x) \notin R] \quad \ldots (2.4)$$

This necessitates us to concentrate on distinct values of x, y while checking for antisymmetry. When x, y are distinct and $(x,y)\in R$, we should *not* have $(y, x)\in R$ in order that the relation R is antisymmetric.

Note that the defining property for antisymmetry involves conditional, viz., ($(x,y)\in R \wedge (x \neq y)$)$\rightarrow$ $(y, x)\notin R$. We note here that the conditional $(x,y)\in R \wedge (x \neq y) \rightarrow (y, x)\in R$ is vacuously true when the antecedent is false. Thus, for checking whether the relation R is antisymmetric or not, when we have the two cases: either (i) $(x,y)\notin R$, or (ii) $x = y$, we should not check whether $(y, x)\in R$ or $(y, x)\notin R$.
We also note that the defining property of antisymmetry can also be expressed by its logically equivalent form given below.

The relation R on A is antisymmetric

$$\Leftrightarrow (\forall x, y \in A) [((x,y)\in R \wedge (y, x)\in R) \rightarrow (x = y)] \quad \ldots (2.5)$$

We illustrate the above points in the definition of antisymmetry in the examples below.

Example 2.17: Consider the set $A = \{1, 2, a, b\}$. Let the relation R on A be defined as follows:

$$R = \{ (1,1), (a,a), (b,b), (2,2), (1,2), (a,b) \}.$$

Observation: This relation R is antisymmetric. To check the antisymmetry, we note that there are two pairs of distinct values, namely (1,2), and (a,b) which are of interest for checking the defining conditional of antisymmetry. We have:

$((1,2) \in R) \wedge ((2, 1) \notin R)$, and,

$((a,b) \in R) \wedge ((b, a) \notin R)$.

This verifies the conditional $(x,y)\in R \rightarrow (y, x)\notin R$ (for distinct x, y), that is involved as a defining property of the antisymmetry of R. In other words,

$$(\forall x, y \in A) [((x,y)\in R \wedge (x \neq y)) \rightarrow (y, x) \notin R]$$

is a "True" proposition (it evaluates to "T" for all elements in A). Hence, R is antisymmetric.

□

Example 2.18: Consider the set $A = \{1, 2, a, b\}$. Let the relation R on A be defined as follows:

$$R = \{ (1,1), (a,b), (b,a), (b,b), (2,2) \}.$$

Observation: In this relation, we have two distinct elements of A, namely a, and b, such that $(a,b)\in R \wedge (b,a) \in R$, this invalidates the following property:

$$(\forall x, y \in A) [((x,y)\in R\wedge(x\neq y))\rightarrow (y, x)\notin R],$$

which defines the antisymmetry (the antecedent is true for $(a,b)\in R \wedge (a\neq b)$, and the consequent is false due to $(b,a) \in R$). So this relation is not antisymmetric.

□

Example 2.19: For $m > 1$, we defined the relationship $xRy : x \equiv y \pmod{m}$, also denoted by $\langle x = y\rangle_m$ (read as "Congruent modulo m") on integers (also discussed in Module 4 of our course, dealing with Modular Arithmetic). Specifically, for a given set of integers $\mathbb{Z}$, the relationship xRy is a binary relationship, and it is defined on the elements of $\mathbb{Z}$, the set of integers. Choosing $m = 2$, we find that the distinct integers 3 and 1 are related under this relationship as ${}_3R_1$ as well as ${}_1R_3$. Hence, R is not antisymmetric.

□

Example 2.20: We defined the relationship $\subseteq$ (read as "is subset of") on sets in Section 1.2 (equation 1.11). . Specifically, for a given set S, the relationship $\subseteq$ is a binary relationship, and it is defined on the elements of **P**(S), the power set of S.

To prove that the relationship $\subseteq$ is antisymmetric, we make use of the following equivalent definition of antisymmetry. Specifically, we note that,

The relation R on A is antisymmetric

$$\Leftrightarrow (\forall x, y \in A) [((x,y)\in R\wedge(y, x)\in R)\rightarrow (x = y)]$$

From the definition of set equality, we have

$(S_1 \subseteq S_2) \wedge (S_2 \subseteq S_1) \Rightarrow (S_1 = S_2)$ for arbitrary sets S_1, and S_2.

Hence $\subseteq$ is antisymmetric.

□

Example 2.21: Let us consider the relationship $xRy : x \mid y$ (x divides y) defined on the set of positive integers. It is possible to prove that $(x|y) \wedge (y|x) \Rightarrow (x = y)$; hence this relationship is antisymmetric.

We note that, to define the expressions $(x|y)$ as well as $(y|x)$, we need the divisor to be positive nonzero integer. We need this information for the proof of $(x|y) \wedge (y|x) \Rightarrow (x = y)$ (which we have omitted here).

From the above examples, we note that, although both (2.4) as well as (2.5) are logically equivalent formulations for antisymmetry, sometimes (2.4) is useful for proving that the given relationship is not antisymmetric, while (2.5) is many times useful for proving that the given relationship is antisymmetric, and hence you should remember both these equivalent formulations.

2.3.4. *Transitivity*

Definition 2.5: (*Transitivity*) Let R be a binary relation on a set A. We define the relation R to be transitive if and only if for all elements x, y, z of the set A, if $(x,y) \in R$ and $(y,z) \in R$, then $(x, z) \in R$.

The above definition translates to the following formula which defines the transitivity.

The relation R on A is transitive

$$\Leftrightarrow (\forall x, y, z \in A) [((x,y) \in R \wedge (y,z) \in R) \rightarrow (x, z) \in R] \quad \ldots (2.6)$$

Note that the defining property for transitivity involves conditional, viz., $((x,y) \in R \wedge (y,z) \in R) \rightarrow (x,z) \in R$. We note here that the conditional $((x,y) \in R \wedge (y,z) \in R) \rightarrow (x,z) \in R$ is vacuously true when the antecedent $((x,y) \in R \wedge (y,z) \in R)$ is false.

To check the transitivity, it is important to concentrate on two pairs (x,y) and (y,z), each having distinct values (i.e., $x \neq y$, and $y \neq z$). Note that the second component of one pair must be the same as the first component of the other pair (in the pairs (x,y) and (y,z), it is y).

To ensure the transitivity, for any two pairs (x, y), (y, z), having $x \neq y$, and $y \neq z$ such that $(x, y) \in R \wedge (y, z) \in R$, we need to ensure that the pair (x, z) is in R. If there are no two pairs (x, y), (y, z), with $x \neq y$, and $y \neq z$ such that $(x, y) \in R \wedge (y, z) \in R$, then we say that R is trivially transitive. If we succeed in finding out the two pairs with $x \neq y$, and $y \neq z$ such that $(x,y) \in R \wedge (y,z) \in R$, and the pair (x, z) is not in R, this x, y, z serves as a counter-example to establish that the relation R is not transitive. Note that it is needed to give specific (one set of) values of x, y, z for giving such a counter-example.

Sometimes it is useful to use the following logically equivalent formulation of the property of transitivity.

The relation R on A is transitive

$$\Leftrightarrow (\forall x, y, z \in A) \, [\, ((x,y) \in R \wedge (x,z) \notin R \,) \rightarrow \, (y, z) \notin R] \quad \ldots (2.7)$$

We illustrate the above points in the definition of transitivity in the examples below.

<u>Example 2.22</u>: Consider the set $A = \{1, 2, a, b\}$. Let the relation R on A be defined as follows:

$$R = \{ \, (1,1), (a,a), (b,b), (2,2), (1,2), (a,b) \, \}.$$

We note that there are no two pairs (x, y), (y, z), with $x \neq y$, and $y \neq z$ such that $(x, y) \in R \wedge (y, z) \in R$. Hence, R is trivially transitive.

□

<u>Example 2.23</u>: Consider the set $A = \{1, 2, a, b\}$. Let the relation R on A be defined as follows:

$$R = \{ \, (1,1), (a,b), (b,a), (b,b), (2,2) \, \}.$$

We note that there are two pairs $(x=a, y=b)$, $(y=b, z=a)$, with $x \neq y$, and $y \neq z$ such that $(x, y) \in R \wedge (y, z) \in R$, and the pair $(x=a, z=a) \notin R$. Hence, the given relation is not transitive.

□

Example 2.24: For $m > 1$, we defined the relationship $x\mathrm{R}y : x \equiv y \pmod{m}$, also denoted by $\langle x = y \rangle_m$ (read as "Congruent modulo m") on integers (discussed in Module 4 of our course, dealing with Modular Arithmetic). Specifically, for a given set of integers Z, the relationship $x\mathrm{R}y$ is a binary relationship, and it is defined on the elements of Z, the set of integers.

For the relationship xRy to hold, we need to have $m|x-y$. In other words, $x-y = k_1m$, for some integer k_1. For the relationship yRz to hold, we need to have $m|y-z$. In other words, $y-z = k_2m$, for some integer k_2. Consider $x-z = (x-y)+(y-z) = k_1m + k_2m = (k_1+ k_2)m$. Choosing $k =(k_1+ k_2)$, and noting that k is integer, it follows that $m \mid (x-z)$. Hence, this relationship is transitive.

□

Example 2.25: The relationship $\subseteq$ (read as "is subset of") on sets. Specifically, for a given set S, the relationship $\subseteq$ is a binary relationship, and it is defined on the elements of $\mathbf{P}(S)$, the power set of S.

To prove that the relationship $\subseteq$ is transitive, we make use of the following definition of $\subseteq$

$$S_1 \subseteq S_2 \equiv \forall x\,(x\in S_1 \rightarrow x\in S_2)$$
$$S_2 \subseteq S_3 \equiv \forall x\,(x\in S_2 \rightarrow x\in S_3)$$
$$\text{Hence, } (S_1 \subseteq S_2)\wedge(S_2 \subseteq S_3)$$
$$\equiv [\forall x\,(x\in S_1 \rightarrow x\in S_2)]\wedge [\forall x\,(x\in S_2 \rightarrow x\in S_3)]$$
$$\Rightarrow \forall x[\,(x\in S_1 \rightarrow x\in S_2)\wedge(x\in S_2 \rightarrow x\in S_3)\,] \text{ (distributivity of } \forall \text{over } \wedge)$$
$$\Rightarrow\forall x[\,(x\in S_1 \rightarrow x\in S_3)\,] \text{ ...(Law of Syllogism – LS)}$$
$$\Rightarrow S_1 \subseteq S_3$$

We note that, in the above steps, besides the definition of $\subseteq$, the law of syllogism (LS) is used for concluding that $S_1 \subseteq S_3$. Hence, $\subseteq$ is transitive.

□

Example 2.26: Let us consider the relationship $x\mathrm{R}y : x \mid y$ (x divides y) defined on the set of positive integers. Consider the expression $(x|y)\wedge(y|z)$. This means, $\exists$ two integers, say k_1, and k_2, such that $(y = k_1x)\wedge (z = k_2y)$. Hence, we have, $(z = k_2\,k_1x)$. Noting that the product of two integers $k_2\,k_1$ is another integer, say k, we have, $(z = kx)$, which also means that $x|z$ (x divides z). Hence, this relationship is transitive.

□

2.4 REPRESENTATION OF BINARY RELATIONS

There are various ways to represent the binary relations. In this section, we specify a few of them.

2.4.1 *Binary relation as a two-place predicate*

Consider the two place predicate defined on the universe of the set of all students in your institute:

$H(x, y) = x$'s Hostel is the same as y's Hostel.

Indeed, $H(x, y)$ is one way to specify, and hence, represent a binary relation defined on the set A, consisting of the universe of the variables involved on the two-place predicate.

2.4.2 *Binary Relation as a Set*

Consider the relation R on the set $A = \{1, 2, a, b\}$. We can represent that relation as follows:

$$R = \{ (1,1), (a,a), (b,b), (2,2), (1,2), (a,b) \}.$$

Here, we have listed the set of all tuples included in R: this was possible for this example because:

(i) R is a set, and set can be represented by listing all its elements;
(ii) The elements of R are tuples, which belong to the Cartesian product $A \times A$.
(iii) The elements of R are finite, and a small number (here it is 6).

The previous two representations, *viz.*, two-place predicate, and set of tuples in the form of a list, are more useful for specifying the binary relation. To reveal the interesting properties like reflexivity, symmetry, transitivity, etc., there are other representations of binary relations. We shall see two such representations below.

2.4.3 *Binary Relation as a 0-1 Matrix*

In the above, we considered the relation R on the set $A = \{1, 2, a, b\}$. We represented that relation as follows:

$$R = \{ (1,1), (a,a), (b,b), (2,2), (1,2), (a,b) \}.$$

The above list contains the tuples belonging to a relation. Noting that $R \subseteq A \times A$, we may form the (square) matrix whose rows as well as columns are labeled by the elements of A, and choose to fill up the $(i, j)^{th}$ entry to be 1 if the corresponding tuple is in R. If the corresponding tuple is not in R, we choose to fill up the $(i, j)^{th}$ entry by 0. Thus, we get the following matrix, say $\mathbf{M}_R$, for representing the relation R:

$$\mathbf{M}_R = \begin{array}{c} \\ 1 \\ 2 \\ a \\ b \end{array} \begin{array}{c} \begin{array}{cccc} 1 & 2 & a & b \end{array} \\ \begin{bmatrix} 1 & 1 & 0 & 0 \\ 0 & 1 & 0 & 0 \\ 0 & 0 & 1 & 1 \\ 0 & 0 & 0 & 1 \end{bmatrix} \end{array} \qquad \ldots (2.8)$$

As a use of the above representation, we state a few of the properties of the above matrix that useful for discovering the properties relation R Since the above matrix has all 1's in the diagonal, it is reflexive. Since it is not symmetric, the given relation R is not symmetric. You should examine more such connections.

2.4.4 *Binary Relation as a directed Graph (digraph)*

Directed graphs (digraphs) are useful for visual representation and formally we define as well as introduce graphs as well as digraphs in Module 6: Graphs. In digraphs, we use vertices to represent elements, and arrow to represent directed relationship. Thus, in a binary relation, when we have the tuple $(a, b) \in R$, we introduce the directed arrow from the element a in the domain of R, to the element b in the co-domain of R.
When both the domain as well as co-domain are the same set, as is the case when we have a binary relation on the set (say A), we directed arrow for representing the tuple $(a, b) \in R$ no more runs from one set to other, but it runs from one element in the set A to the other element in the same set A.

To be more specific, we choose to represent the elements of set A by dark dots (like •), and the arrow runs from one dark dot to the other dark dot. These dark dots are called as vertices, and the directed arrows are called as arcs. The collection of vertices and all directed arcs representing a binary relation is defined as its directed graph (digraph) representation. If we use the elements of A to label the vertices, we get labeled digraph representation. We note that

Consider the relation R given below on a set $A = \{1, 2, a, b\}$ as given earlier in Example 2.7.

$$R = \{ (1,1), (a,a), (b,b), (2,2), (1,2), (a,b) \}.$$

The labeled digraph representation for the above relation is given below.

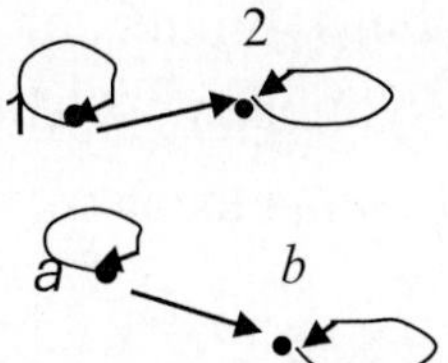

Figure 2.5. Labeled digraph representation of a binary relation.

In section on poset, we make use of labelled digraph representation of a binary relation to develop Hasse diagram of a partially ordered set (poset).

The digraph representation for the above relation is given below.

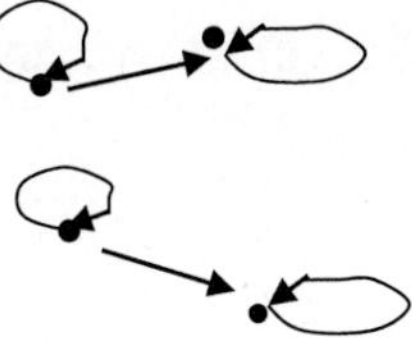

Figure 2.6. Digraph representation of a binary relation.

As a visual digraph representation, possibly the first thing we notice visually is that the above digraph is not connected. Second thing we notice is that there are loops on every vertex (point). Such loops are called as self-loops. Third thig we may notice is that there is a pair of vertices with the directed arrow in one direction, but there is no directed arrow in the reverse direction. Additional analysis of such graphs useful for many problems in graph theory and basic properties are connectivity and regularity. We call such properties as graph-theoretic properties. Additionally, the existence of paths of some special types like Euler paths and Hamilton paths, have important consequences in Computer Science for design and analysis of algorithms as well as theory of computation, and we introduce such paths in module on Graphs.

2.5 PARTIAL ORDERINGS

2.5.1. Definition of Partial Order

Definition 2.6 (*Partial Order Relation*) A binary relation is a partial order relation if and only if it is (i) reflexive, (ii) anti-symmetric, and (iii) transitive.

When we compare the definition of partial order with the definition of equivalence relation, we note that the symmetry is replaced by anti-symmetry. Commonly used symbol to represent the partial order is "≤", which also represents the usual "less than or equal to" relationship on real numbers.

Example 2.27 Consider the two place predicate defined on the universe of the set of all students in your institute/university:

T(x, y) = x's height is greater than or equal to y's height.

We note that the binary relation as defined on the set A of all students in your institute/university by the two-place predicate T(x, y) is reflexive, antisymmetric, and transitive. Hence the relation T(x, y) is a partial order relation.

□

Example 2.28: Consider the set $A = \{1, 2, a, b\}$. Let the relation R on A be defined as follows:

$$R = \{ (1,1), (a,a), (b,b), (2,2), (1,2), (a,b) \}.$$

We have noted that this relation (i) reflexive, (ii) antisymmetric, and (ii) transitive. Hence, it is a partial order relation.

□

Example 2.29: Consider the set $A = \{1, 2, a, b\}$. Let the relation R on A be defined as follows:

$$R = \{ (1,1), (a,b), (b,a), (b,b), (2,2) \}.$$

We have noted earlier that this relation is not antisymmetric, further it is not reflexive, as well as it is not transitive. Hence, it is not a partial order relation.

□

Example 2.30: For $m > 1$, we defined the relationship $xRy : x \equiv y \pmod{m}$, also denoted by $\langle x = y \rangle_m$ (read as "Congruent modulo m") on integers in the module on Modular Arithmetic. Specifically, for a given set of integers Z, the relationship xRy is a binary relationship, and it is defined on the elements of Z, the set of integers.

We saw that this relationship is (i) reflexive, (ii) transitive; but it is not antisymmetric. Hence, it not partial order relation.

□

Example 2.31: We defined the relationship $\subseteq$ (read as "is subset of"). Specifically, for a given set S, the relationship $\subseteq$ is a binary relationship, and it is defined on the elements of **P**(S), the power set of S.

We showed that the relationship $\subseteq$ is (i) reflexive, (ii) antisymmetric, and (iii) transitive. Hence it is a partial order relation.

□

Example 2.32: Let us consider the relationship $xRy : x \mid y$ (x divides y) defined on the set of positive integers. We proved that this relationship is (i) reflexive, (ii) antisymmetric, and (iii) transitive. Hence it is a partial order relation.

□

2.5.2. Hasse Diagrams

Since partial order relations are binary relations in the first place, we may represent them in by a labeled digraph. In computer science, we often come across the hierarchical arrangements which have abstract property of ordering. To highlight and visualize the implicit order, German mathematician Helmut Hasse (1898-1979) has developed a specialized diagram, which is now called Hasse diagram, for representing partial order relations defined on a set with few elements.

In Example 2.31, we saw that relationship $\subseteq$ (read as "is subset of") on sets is partial order. Let us choose the set $S = \{1, 2\}$ to illustrate this partial order relation.

Example 2.33: With $S = \{1, 2\}$ the relationship $\subseteq$ as defined on the elements of **P**(S), the power set of S, is a binary relationship which is also a partial order. The set representation of this binary relation $\subseteq$ is given below.

$$\subseteq = \{ (\varnothing, \varnothing), (\{1\}, \{1\}), (\{2\}, \{2\}), (\{1, 2\}, \{1, 2\}), (\varnothing, \{1\}), (\varnothing, \{2\}), (\varnothing, \{1, 2\}), (\{1\}, \{1, 2\}), (\{2\}, \{1, 2\}) \}.$$

We give the 0-1 matrix representation of the above relation $\subseteq$ below.

$$\begin{array}{c} \\ \Phi \\ \{1\} \\ \{2\} \\ \{1,2\} \end{array} \begin{array}{c} \begin{array}{cccc} \Phi & \{1\} & \{2\} & \{1,2\} \end{array} \\ \begin{bmatrix} 1 & 1 & 1 & 1 \\ 0 & 1 & 0 & 1 \\ 0 & 0 & 1 & 1 \\ 0 & 0 & 0 & 1 \end{bmatrix} \end{array}$$

Figure 2.7: Matrix representation of subset relation

We now give the labeled digraph representation of the above relation below.

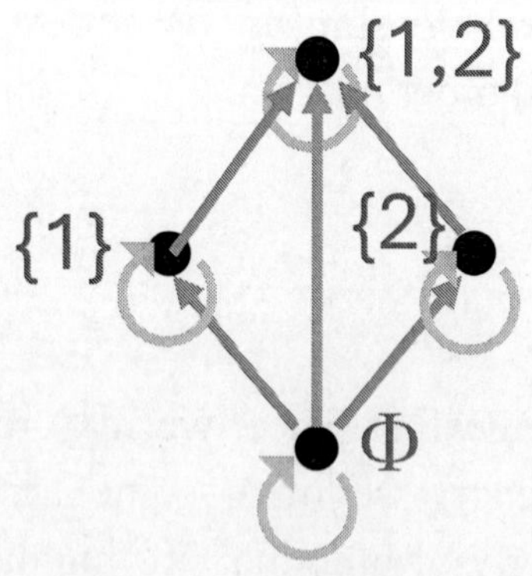

Figure 2.8: Labeled digraph for the relation $\subseteq$.

□

Hasse diagram highlights the "structure of order" in a given partial order relation. For doing so, it uses some conventions to simplify the above digraph representation. Some considerations to achieve the simplification are given below.

(i) The self-loop does not give any additional information about the order (hierarchy).

(ii) The implicit order from bottom to top is utilized for diagrammatic visualization of the partial order relation. Hence, the directions of the arcs are removed, and they are understood to be "usual" (say bottom to top) order in obtaining an Hasse diagram. We call undirected arcs as edges.

(iii) The transitive dependencies which follow from the implicit order from the bottom to top are not shown by edges (undirected arcs).

Using these points, we now give the Hasse diagram for labeled digraph for $\subseteq$ defined on $S = \{1, 2\}$.

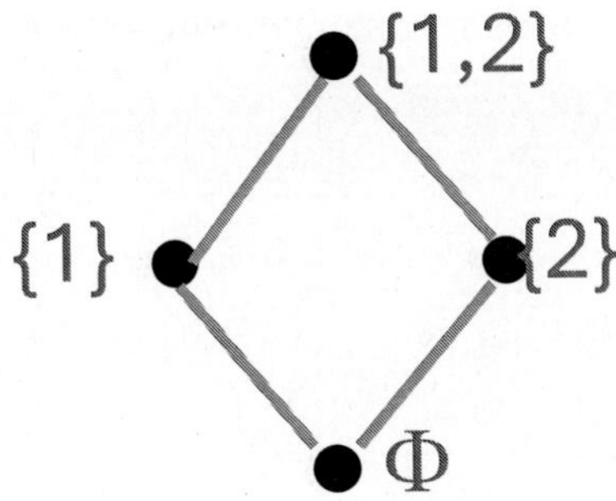

Figure 2.9: Hasse Diagram representation of labeled digraph for the relation $\subseteq$.

2.5.3. *Minimal and Least Elements*

Definition 2.7: (Poset) : Let us assume that we have a partial order (say $\leq$) defined over the set S, with $S \neq \Phi$. We also use the term poset to denote collection $(A, \leq)$.

Definition 2.8: (*Minimal element*) : For a poset $(S, \leq)$, an element $x \in S$ is called as a minimal element if there is no $y \in S$, such that $(y \leq x) \wedge (y \neq x)$.

We note that,

(i) a minimal element exists for a poset $(S, \leq)$ for any partial order $\leq$, and,

(ii) there may be one or more minimal elements in a given poset.

Example 2.34: Consider the following poset $(S, \leq)$ whose Hasse diagram is given in Figure 2.10 below.

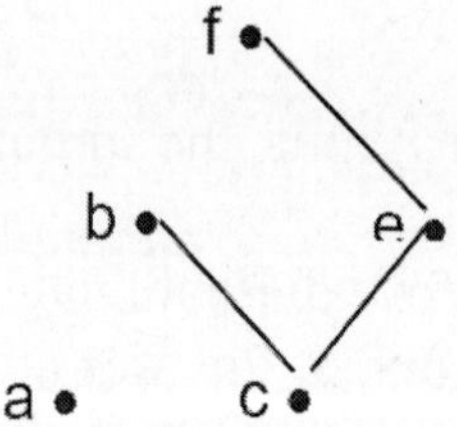

Figure. 2.10: Hasse Diagram for poset in Example 2.34

We note that, for the element a we note that there is no element y, such that $y \leq a$. Also for the element c we note that there is no element y, such that $y \leq c$. Hence, this poset has two minimal elements, viz, a and c. Further, for illustration, we note that b is not a minimal element, as there is another element c, such that $c \leq b$.

□

<u>Definition 2.9</u>: (*Least element*): For a poset $(S, \leq)$, an element $x \in S$ is called as the least element if, for every $y \in S$, we have $(x \leq y)$.
We note that,

(i) the least element may not exist for a poset $(S, \leq)$. and,
(ii) if the least element exists, it is unique (there is only one least element).

<u>Example 2.35</u>: Consider the following poset $(S, \leq)$ whose Hasse diagram is given in Figure 2.4. This poset does not have any least element.

□

<u>Example 2.36</u>: Consider the following poset $(S, \leq)$ whose Hasse diagram is given in Figure 2.5.

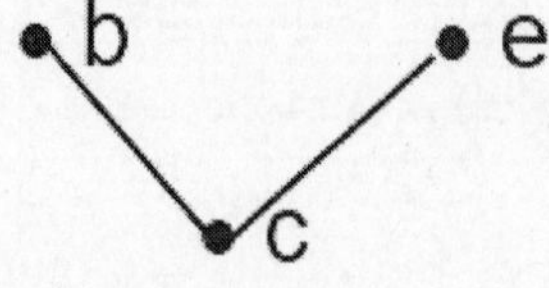

:

Figure. 2.11: Hasse diagram for poset in Example 2.36

This poset has the element c as its least element.

□

2.5.4. *Maximal and Greatest Elements*

Definition 2.10: (*Maximal element*) : For a poset $(S, \leq)$, an element $x \in S$ is called as a maximal element if there is no $y \in S$, such that $(x \leq y) \wedge (y \neq x)$.

We note that,

(i) a maximal element exists for a poset $(S, \leq)$ for any partial order $\leq$, and,
(ii) there may be one or more maximal elements in a given poset.

Example 2.37: Consider the following poset $(S, \leq)$ whose Hasse diagram is given in Figure 2.4.

We note that, for the element a we note that there is no element y, such that $a \leq y$. Also for the element b we note that there is no element y, such that $b \leq y$. Further, for the element f, we note that there is no element y, such that $f \leq y$. Hence, this poset has three maximal elements, viz, a, b, and f. Further, for illustration, we note that c is not a maximal element, as there is another element, say e, such that $c \leq e$.

□

Definition 2.11: (*greatest element*): For a poset $(S, \leq)$, an element $x \in S$ is called as the greatest element if, for every $y \in S$, we have $(y \leq x)$.

We note that,

(i) the greatest element may not exist for a poset $(S, \leq)$. and,
(ii) if the greatest element exists, it is unique (there is only one greatest element).

Example 2.38: Consider the following poset $(S, \leq)$ whose Hasse diagram is given in Figure 2.5.
This poset does not have any greatest element.

□

Example 2.39: Consider the following poset $(S, \leq)$ whose Hasse diagram is given in Figure 2.5.
This poset does not have the greatest element (it has two elements, viz., b, and e, as the maximal elements).

□

Example 2.40: Consider the following poset (S, ≤) whose Hasse diagram is given in Figure 2.6.

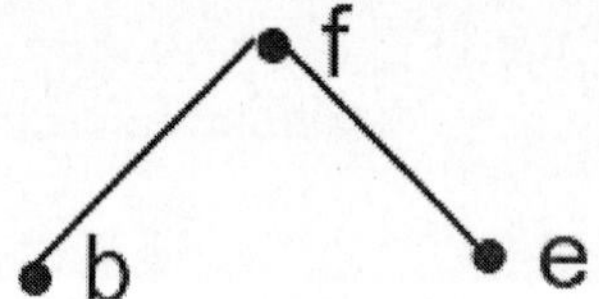

Fig. 2.12: Hasse diagram for poset in Example 2.40

We note that, for the poset in Figure, the element f is the greatest element, as every other element y in S (*i.e*, $y = b$, $y = e$) satisfies the relation $y \leq f$.

□

2.5.5. Poset, Linearly ordered set, and Well ordered set

Definition 2.12 (Partially Ordered Set, also called as *Poset*): A set, say *S*, together with a partially ordered relation, say $\leq_P$ defined on *S*, is a poset and is denoted by a pair (S, $\leq_P$).

On the previous subsections, we noted that in a poset, it is possible that there may be some 2-subsets, say, $\{s_1, s_2\}$ amongst which the partial order relation $\leq_S$ is not defined. In Example 2.24, the elements *a*, and 1 are not related (similarly, the elements *a*, and 2 are not related; can you find any other pairs of elements that are not related?).

Definition 2.13 (Linearly Ordered Set, also called as *Totally ordered set*): When the ordering relation is defined amongst all 2-subsets of given set (say *S*), then such s set, say *S*, together with the concerned partially ordered relation, say $\leq_T$ is a linearly ordered set, or totally ordered set, and is denoted by a pair (S, $\leq_T$).

As an example, the set of integers Z, together with usual ≤ relation defined on it is linearly ordered set.

We noted that the set of integers Z, together with usual ≤ relation is a linearly (also called as totally) ordered set; however, as we observed in Example 3.16 of part 3

(Predicate Logic) in Module 1 dealing with Logic, a while a $\leq$ relation is defined on all its 2-subsets, there is no least element in set. In case we restrict ourselves to a subset N of Z, we also have a least element in N. This structure, having least element deserves special name and mathematicians have proved deeper and interesting theorems for well-ordered sets, and their discussion is beyond our present scope. Here, we only remark that, the point of view of its usefulness, we note that proof by induction are possible when we have starting point as least element.

Definition 2.14 (*Well Ordered Set*): A given set (say *S*), together with the linearly ordered (totally ordered) relation, say $\leq_W$ having a least element, is denoted by a pair (S, $\leq_W$), and is called as well-ordered set.

We note that the set of natural numbers N is a well-ordered set. While we noted that the set of integers Z is not well-ordered with our usual ordering, it is possible to construct other ordering relation on the elements of Z with which the set Z is well ordered. You may like to have a look at part 4, Examples 4.4 to 4.6 in this context. Posets are important in Computer Science and Engineering. Various representations of Posets as needed in various areas like distributed computing, with interest, are (1) Vector-Clock Representation of Poset, and (2) Dimension Representation of Poset. These representations have been introduced in Vijay K. Garg, *Introduction to Lattice Theory with Computer Science Applications*, John Wiley and Sons, Inc., (2015).

2.6. EQUIVALENCES

2.6.1. *Definition of Equivalence Relation*

Definition 2.15 (*Equivalence Relation*) A binary relation is an equivalence relation if and only if it is (i) reflexive, (ii) symmetric, and (iii) transitive.

Example 2.41: Consider two place predicate defined on the universe of the set of all students in your institute/university:

$H(x, y) = x$'s Hostel is the same as y's Hostel.

Consider a binary relation defined on the set A of all students in your institute/university by the two-place predicate $H(x, y)$. We note that, for an arbitrary student, say x, "$H(x, x)$ = x's Hostel is the same as x's Hostel" is true; hence $H(x, y)$ is reflexive. If "$H(x, y)$ = x's Hostel is the same as y's Hostel" is true, then "$H(y, x)$ = y's Hostel is the same as x's Hostel" is also true; hence H(x, y) is symmetric. Further, if "$H(x, y)$ = x's Hostel is the same as y's Hostel" is true, and "$H(y, z)$ = y's Hostel is the same as z's Hostel" is true, then it follows that "$H(x, z)$ = x's Hostel is the same as z's Hostel" is true. Thus, the relation $H(x, y)$ is transitive.

Since the binary relation $H(x, y)$ is (i) reflexive, (ii) symmetric, and (iii) transitive, it is an equivalence relation.

We note that the set of all students in your institute/university gets partitioned into parts, say H_1, H_2, ..., H_k parts (sets), where k denotes the total number of hostels in your institute/university. We further note that the same student cannot stay in two different hostels; so the pairwise intersection of any two parts, say $H_i \cap H_j$ is not a null set. Hence, we say that these parts are mutually exclusive. Further, if all students in your institute/university have some hostel assigned, the union of all these parts is the set of all students in your institute/university. So, we say that the parts are collectively exhaustive.

□

Example 2.42: Consider the set $A = \{1, 2, a, b\}$. Let the relation R on A be defined as follows:

$$R = \{ (1,1), (a,a), (b,b), (2,2), (1,2), (a,b) \}.$$

We have noted that this relation (i) reflexive, and (ii) transitive. However, since it is not symmetric, it is not an equivalence relation.

□

Example 2.43: Consider the set $A = \{1, 2, a, b\}$. Let the relation R on A be defined as follows:

$$R = \{ (1,1), (a,b), (b,a), (b,b), (2,2) \}.$$

We have noted earlier that this relation is symmetric, but it is not reflexive, as well as it is not transitive. Hence, it is not an equivalence relation.

□

Example 2.44: For $m > 1$, we defined the relationship $xRy : x \equiv y \pmod{m}$, also denoted by (read as "Congruent modulo m") on integers in the module dealing with Modular Arithmetic. Specifically, for a given set of integers $\mathbb{Z}$, the relationship xRy is a binary relationship, and it is defined on the elements of $\mathbb{Z}$, the set of integers.

We saw that this relationship is (i) reflexive, (ii) symmetric, and (iii) transitive. Hence this relationship is an equivalence relationship. This equivalence relationship partitions the set of all integers into m classes. These classes are:

(1) the class of all integers congruent to 1 modulo m;
(2) the class of all integers congruent to 2 modulo m;
.. ..
.. ..
(m) the class of all integers congruent to m (also to 0) modulo m.

We note that the (infinite) set $\mathbb{Z}$ of integers gets partitioned into the above m mutually exclusive and collectively exhaustive parts.

□

Example 2.45: We defined the relationship $\subseteq$ (read as "is subset of") on sets in part 1 on Sets. Specifically, for a given set S, the relationship $\subseteq$ is a binary relationship, and it is defined on the elements of **P**(S), the power set of S.

We showed that the relationship $\subseteq$ is (i) reflexive, (ii) non-symmetric, and (iii) transitive. Since the relationship $\subseteq$ is not symmetric, it is not an equivalence relationship.

□

Example 2.46: Let us consider the relationship $xRy : x \mid y$ (x divides y) defined on the set of positive integers. We proved that this relationship is (i) reflexive, (ii) non-symmetric, and (iii) transitive. Since it is not symmetric, it is not an equivalence relationship.

□

2.6.2. *Definition of Partition of a Set*

From the Examples 2.41 and 2.44 above, we observed that the equivalence relationship partitions the underlying set on which the binary relationship is defined into mutually exclusive and collectively exhaustive classes. We now state the notion of a partition of a given set.

Definition 2.16 (*Partition of a Set*) A partition (say Π) of a set S is a collection of nonempty disjoint subsets $\{ S_1, S_2, \ldots, S_n\}$ of S whose union equals S.
In other words, the subsets $\{ S_1, S_2, \ldots, S_n\}$ of S which form the partition of S, have the following two important properties:

(i) $S_1 \cup S_2 \cup \ldots \cup S_n = S$, and, (collectively exhaustive)
(ii) For all $i \neq j$, $(1 \leq i, j \leq n)$, $S_i \cap S_j = \Phi$ (mutually exclusive).

Notation 2.2: We call each of the nonempty subsets $S_1, S_2, \ldots, S_n$ as the *part* (sometimes the *class*, or even as the *cell*) of a partition Π. Further, we denote the partition $\Pi = \{ S_1, S_2, \ldots, S_n \}$.

Example 2.47: Let $S = \{1, 2, a, b\}$. Then,

(i) $\{ \{a\}, \{1\}, \{2\}, \{b\} \}$ is a partition of S.
(ii) $\{ \{a, b\}, \{1, 2\} \}$ is a partition of S.
(iii) $\{ \{a, \text{b}, 1\}, \{2\} \}$ is a partition of S.
(iv) $\{ \Phi, \{a, b\}, \{1, 2\} \}$ is *not* a partition of S.
(v) $\{ \{a, b\}, \{1, 2\}, \{a, 2\} \}$ is *not* a partition of S.

□

2.6.3. *Theorems relating Equivalences and Partitions*

Definition 2.17: (Equivalence Class of an element) Let R be an equivalence relation on the set A. Let an element $x \in A$. We denote the equivalence class of an element x with respect to the relation R by the notation $R[x]$, and we define $R[x]$ as follows.

$$R[x] = \{ y \in A \mid xRy \}$$

Notation 2.3: We also note that, when the context makes the relation R clear, we omit R, and use the notation $[x]$ to denote the equivalence class of an element x with respect to the equivalence relationship R.

We now state the theorem which enables us to obtain the partition for a given an equivalence relation.

Theorem 2.1: An equivalence relation R on the set A determines a partition of A. The partition consists of a set whose elements are $[x]$ where $x \in A$ (we note that the notation $[x]$ is defined above).

We illustrate the use of this theorem in the following example.

Example 2.48: Let $A = \{0, 1, 2, 3, 4, 5\}$ and let us define the relationship R on these six numbers as the congruence modulo 3 operation. Thus, two integers $x, y \in A$ are related by the relation R, if and only if $3 | (x - y)$ (the integer 3 divides $(x - y)$).

	0	1	2	3	4	5
0	1	0	0	1	0	0
1	0	1	0	0	1	0
2	0	0	1	0	0	1
3	1	0	0	1	0	0
4	0	1	0	0	1	0
5	0	0	1	0	0	1

Figure 2.13: 0-1 Matrix representation for relation in Example 2.44

We give the representation of this relation R in the 0-1 matrix form as in Fig. 2.13:

We note that the above 0-1 matrix has all 1's in diagonal (reflexivity), and it is symmetric. Further, R is a transitive relation.

From the above 0-1 matrix, we have the following equivalence classes of the elements:

$[0] = \{0, 3\}$,

$[1] = \{1, 4\}$,

$[2] = \{2, 5\}$,

$[3] = \{0, 3\}$,

$[4] = \{1, 4\}$.

We observe that the collection of all the above equivalence classes of elements is:

$\{ \{0, 3\}, \{1, 4\}, \{2, 5\} \}$.

We further observe that the above collection consists of the sets which are mutually exclusive and collectively exhaustive; hence it is a partition. Note that in the above representation of a set in the list form, we have omitted the duplicate elements, as the multiple occurrences in a set do not matter. Thus, we have demonstrated the method of obtaining the partition of a set for a given equivalence relation.

□

We may rewrite the above 0-1 matrix in Example 2.48 by clubbing the elements in the respective classes together, to get the following matrix.

$$
\begin{array}{c} \\ 0 \\ 3 \\ 1 \\ 4 \\ 2 \\ 5 \end{array}
\begin{array}{c}
\begin{array}{cccccc} 0 & 3 & 1 & 4 & 2 & 5 \end{array} \\
\begin{bmatrix}
1 & 1 & 0 & 0 & 0 & 0 \\
1 & 1 & 0 & 0 & 0 & 0 \\
0 & 0 & 1 & 1 & 0 & 0 \\
0 & 0 & 1 & 1 & 0 & 0 \\
0 & 0 & 0 & 0 & 1 & 1 \\
0 & 0 & 0 & 0 & 1 & 1
\end{bmatrix}
\end{array}
$$

Figure 2.14: Rearranged 0-1 Matrix representation for relation in Example 2.44

We note the nice block structure of this matrix. We further note that is possible to reveal such a nice structure only after we have re-arranged both the rows as well as columns. For certain problems like identifying the structure of graphs (Module dealing with Graph) in the problems like Graph isomorphism, we need to perform similar re-arrangement of both the rows as well as columns.

We now state the theorem which enables us to obtain the equivalence relation from a given partition.

Theorem 2.2: A partition Π of a given set A determines an equivalence relation (say R) on A. To obtain R, we take the Cartesian product of each part (of Π) with itself, and collect all the tuples so formed.

We illustrate the use of this theorem in the following example.

Example 2.49: Let $A = \{0, 1, 2, 3, 4, 5\}$ and let us assume that we have the following partition

$$\Pi = \{ \{0, 5\}, \{1, 2, 3\}, \{4\} \}.$$

To obtain the equivalence relation R corresponding to Π, we take the Cartesian products of each parts in Π with itself. Since Π has three parts, viz., $\{0, 5\}$, $\{1, 2, 3\}$, $\{4\}$, we need to take the Cartesian products $\{0, 5\}\times\{0, 5\}$, $\{1, 2, 3\}\times\{1, 2, 3\}$, $\{4\}\times\{4\}$, and take the union of all the resulting tuples. Thus, we have:

$$\begin{aligned} R &= \{0, 5\}\times\{0, 5\}, \{1, 2, 3\}\times\{1, 2, 3\}, \{4\}\times\{4\} \\ &= \{ (0, 0), (0, 5), (5, 0), (5, 5), \\ &\quad (1, 1), (1, 2), (1, 3), (2, 1), (2, 2), (2, 3), (3, 1), (3, 2), (3, 3), \\ &\quad (4, 4) \}. \end{aligned}$$

You may like to verify that R is reflexive, symmetric and transitive; hence it is an equivalence relation.

□

We have discussed binary relations above. In general, it is possible to study properties of n-ary relations (for arbitrary $n \geq 2$). Indeed, Edger F. Codd studied deployment of n-ary relations (they are also called as Tables, using the terminology of representing the data in the tabular form) for storage of data long back in 1968; he also demonstrated that the retrieval of useful information needed from such stored data (he called them Tables) as answer to practical queries can be expressed as operations on relations (Tables) resulting in smaller Tables. You would revisit Edger F. Codd's Relational Algebra (as well as Relational Calculus) in the course on Database Systems, where efficient ways of implementing Codd's operations on Relations are also of practical importance.

While Edger F. Codd's proposal was not so practical in 1968 due to the state of Computing hardware, conceptual simplicity of Codd's proposal has today, specially due to advances in Computing hardware, made it almost universal form of database in Computer Science and Information Technology. It is popularly called relational database management system (RDBMS). Codd's relational algebra as well as relational calculus have interesting conceptual operations coupled with ideas about their practical implementations, and we refer the interested reader to courses on Database Systems.

PART 3

Functions

3.1 FUNCTIONS

Functions have been used in Science and mathematics for many centuries. We begin with a notion, which is familiar to us in our earlier school studies for subjects like sciences and mathematics. In the schools and Junior College, you have come across functions of a real variable. Denoting the real variable by x, we have studied the functions, such as: $x + 5$, $x^2 + x + 5$, $1/(x+3)^2$, $\sin x$, e^x, $\log x$, etc.

Notation 3.1: A notation of $f(x)$ is also used to denote such functions. We read this notation as "a function f of the variable x".

In such cases, generally we assume that the variable x refers to an arbitrary real number. In this notation, we observe that the name of a function f comes before (*prefixed to*) the variable(s) involved in it. When we are given a value of a variable x, the function $f(x)$ simply produces some (other) value. We may represent this using the following diagram:

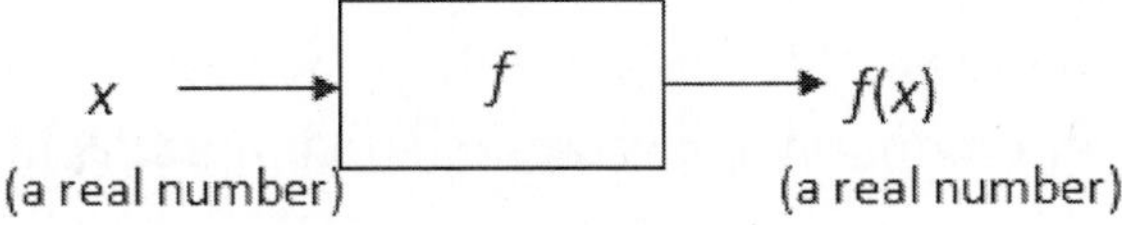

Figure 3.1: Block diagram representation of a (real valued) function of a real variable.

In this section, we informally introduce a structure called as a *function*, in which we attempt to capture the important properties of functions of real variables like the above. Pictorially, we represent such functions by two-dimensional graph, with the x-axis (abscissa, horizontal axis) representing the real values of a (free) variable x, and y-axis (ordinate, vertical axis) representing the corresponding value of the function (in this case, $\sin x$).

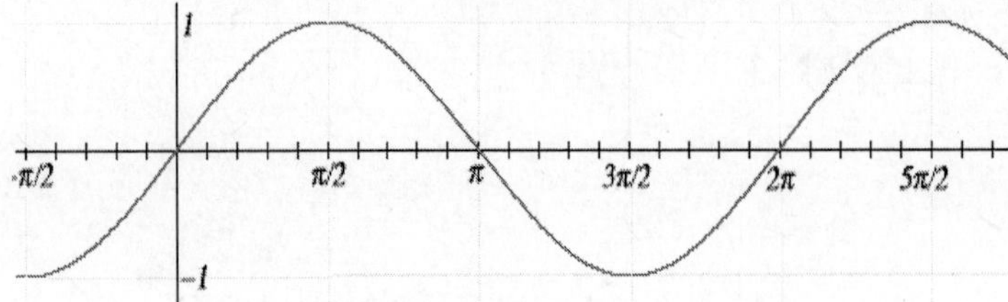

Figure 3.2: A graph of function sin *x*.

Using the above graphical representation of sin *x*, we note the following two properties:

(3) for any (arbitrary) given value of *x*, there is exactly one value of sin *x* ;

(4) however, there may be cases where the value of a function sin *x* is same for two different values of *x*. Indeed, for two (in fact, more) different values of *x*, say $x = \pi/2$, $x = 5\pi/2$, $x = 9\pi/2$, …, the value of sin *x* is same (=1).

3.1.1 *Notion of Abstract Function*

When we use the notion of function for abstractions, we need to generalize the above familiar notion of a real valued function of a real variable to handle situations where the variable may not assume real values, and the function in turn may not result in a real value. In other words, our variable (of a function) may not necessarily be a real number, but it may have its elements from any general (arbitrary) set. Additionally, the function may not result in other real number, but is may result in the values from an arbitrary set. The function represents an association between these two (arbitrary) sets, say from the set *A* to the set *B*. Thus, our diagrammatic representation of a function gets modified as follows:

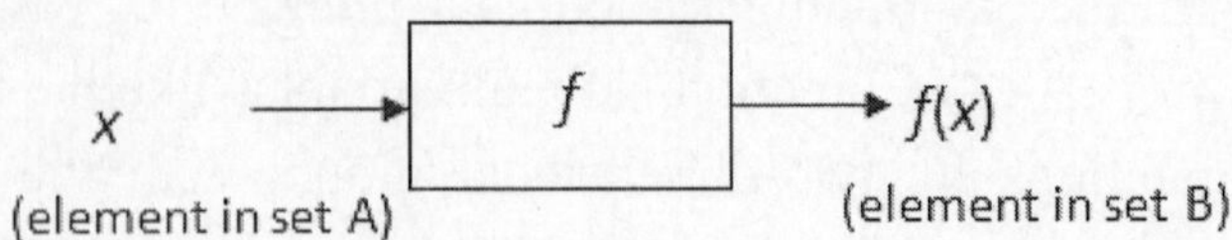

Figure 3.3: Block diagram representation of an arbitrary function.

Let us elaborate this point. Consider the notion of *value* of the goods (say cattle, metal, food, etc.) in early human civilization. With our sensory organs like eye, ear, etc., we do not see any such property like *value* of the physical objects like cattle, metal, food, etc. within these objects. However, even in the early human civilization dating at least 1000 BC, humans (sapiens – wise) have *mentally* been able to create this new concept of value of goods. Using functions, we may associate a purely mental concept like value of goods, or we may use it to represent an association between two existing physical objects.

Let us analyse what is involved in such associations. We need two collections of objects for such an association. The element within the first collection is assigned a *unique* object within the second collection. Let us take an example.

Example 3.1: (*Rank Assignment*) Consider the task of assignment of ranks to the students John, Ankur, Richard, James, Mary, …, in the school. Based on the performance of students, it is quite likely that two students, say Ankur and Mary may have the same rank, say rank 2. However, we do not assign multiple ranks to one single student. For example, Richard cannot be assigned the rank 4 as well as rank 10. In other words, we have:

some rule, which associates a unique rank to a student, and,

every student in the collection of students is assigned a rank, i.e., no student is left out without assigning a rank.

□

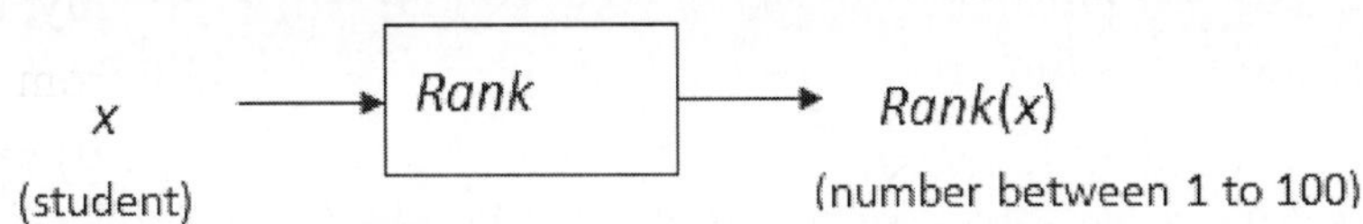

Figure 3.4: Block diagram representation of a *Rank* function.

In the scenario of Example 3.1, we have two sets of objects, the first set is set of students, and the second set of set of possible ranks. Assume that the rank assigned to a student is a positive integer ranging from 1 to 100. Let us denote the set of students by *A*, and set of possible ranks by *B*. In terms of this formalism, we formulate the following as our first definition of function.

Definition 3.1: Given two sets *A* and *B*, we define a function, say *f*, from *A* to *B*, denoted symbolically by $f: A \rightarrow B$, iff *f* satisfies the following properties:

c) *f* is a rule of assigning the value of *B* to an arbitrary (any) value of *A*;

d) f assigns a value of B to <u>every element</u> $a \in A$;
e) f assigns a <u>unique</u> value of B to an arbitrary(any) $a \in A$;

We have split the definition of our abstract notion of function into three parts to highlight three aspects of the definition.

I) The first aspect, by which we state that f is a rule of assignment, is an intuitive part in this definition, and we do not intend to comment on how to formalize this part here. One way to express this formalization is to view the function as a binary relation, satisfying some additional properties. It is possible for us to illustrate important aspects of the concept of function f even when we do not deal with such formalization, and we choose this approach.

II) The second aspect requires that our function be defined for every element in the set A. When this condition is not satisfied, we sometimes say that we have a modified notion function, called a *partial* function.

III) The third aspect allows our function to be visualized as a "function machine", accepting an input, and producing a unique output for a given input. Thus,

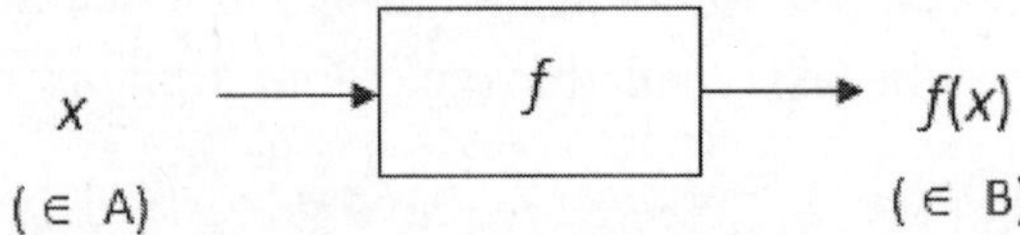

Figure 3.5: Block diagram representation of a function $f: A \to B$.

<u>Definition 3.2</u>: (*Domain and Co-domain*) For the abstract function $f: A \to B$, the set A is called as a *domain* of a function f, and the set B is called as a *co-domain* of a function f.

<u>Notation 3.2</u>: (*Form*, or *type* of a function): For the abstract function f, we say that the abstract function f is of the form $A \to B$, where A is the domain of f, and B is its co-domain. Alternately, it the literature, it is also said that the function f is of the type $A \to B$.

While working with functions, very frequently we are able do represent function by giving some rule; however, identifying the form of a function is needed for defining the function properly; sometimes this identification is not direct or straightforward, and it may even be challenging.

<u>Example 3.2</u>: Let $A = \{a, b, c\}$, and $B = \{1, 2, 3\}$. Then the following assignment is a function: $f(a) = 1, f(b) = 1, f(c) = 2$.

3.2 IMAGE AND RANGE

Definition 3.3: (*Image*) of a domain element x is the (unique) element $f(x)$.

In Example 3.2 above, the image of element a is 1; the image of element b is 1, and the image of element c is 2. We also note that the element 3 in the co-domain is not image of any element in the domain. This observation motivates us the following notion of a range of our abstract function.

Definition 3.4: (*Range*) Let us assume that we have the abstract function $f: A \to B$. In general, the elements in the domain A may not map to all elements of B. Hence, we define the notion of a range. The range of f is the subset of the co-domain, consisting of all elements of B which are images of some element a in the domain A.

$$\text{range}\,(f) = \{\, y \in B \mid \exists x \in A,\ y = f(x) \,\} \qquad \dots (3.1)$$

The range of the abstract function $f: A \to B$ in Example 3.2 is $\{1, 2\}$, which is different from the set $B = \{1, 2, 3\}$.

Definition 3.5: (*image set*) Image of a subset A_{Sub} of a domain is the *set* of all range elements y, such that $y = f(x)$, for $x \in A_{Sub}$.

Thus, $\forall x \in A_{Sub}$, we define

$$\text{Image}\,(A_{Sub}) = \{\, (x \in A_{Sub}) \wedge (y = f(x)) \,\} \qquad \dots (3.2)$$

Example 3.3: Let $A = \{a, b, c\}$, and $B = \{1, 2, 3\}$. Consider a function: $f(a) = 1, f(b) = 1, f(c) = 2$ as given in Example 3.2. The image of the subset $\{a, b\}$ for this function is $\{ f(a), f(b) \} = \{ 1, 1\} = \{1\}$. The image of subset $\{a, c\}$ for this function is $\{ f(a), f(c) \} = \{ 1, 2\}$.

3.3 ARROW DIAGRAM, PRE-IMAGE SET

Definition 3.6: (*Arrow Diagram*) The visual representation of a function $f: A \to B$ can be done by giving two Venn diagrams, one for the domain set A, other for the co-domain set B, and the arrows pointing from the elements in the domain set A to the elements in the co-domain set B. This representation is called as "arrow diagram" of the abstract function f.

The arrow diagram for the function f: $A \rightarrow B$ in Example 3.2 is given below in Figure 3.6 below.

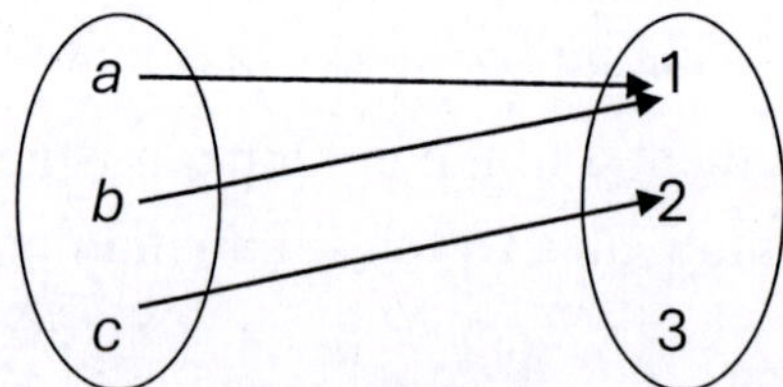

Figure 3.6: Arrow diagram for f: {a, b, c}→{1,2,3} in Example 3.2.

Definition 3.7: (*Pre-image set*) Consider the function f: $A \rightarrow B$. Pre-image of a co-domain element y is the *set* of all domain elements x, such that $y = f(x)$.

In general, $\forall y \in B$, we define

$$\text{pre-image } (y) = \{ x \in A \mid y = f(x) \} \qquad \ldots (3.3)$$

Notation 3.3: (pre-image set of y) To denote the pre-image set of an element y in the co-domain of an abstract function f: A→B, we also use the notation $f^{-1}(y)$.

For the Example 3.2, for which an arrow diagram is given in Figure 3.6 above, we note that the pre-image of 1, i.e., $f^{-1}(1)$, is $\{a, b\}$; the pre-image of 2, i.e., $f^{-1}(2)$, is a singleton set $\{c\}$; the pre-image of 3, i.e., $f^{-1}(3)$, is a null set Φ. We note that pre-image is a *set*, which is a subset of the domain. We contrast this with the image, which is an *element* (in the co-domain).

We defined the concept of *Pre-image set* for an element in the codomain; however, it can be easily generalised to Pre-image set for a "subset of the co-domain".

Definition 3.8: (*Pre-image of subset*) Consider the function f: $A \rightarrow B$. Pre-image of a subset, say B_{sub}, of co-domain B is the union of pre-images of element y in B_{sub}. That is, it is a *set* of all domain elements x, such that $y = f(x)$, for arbitrary element y in B_{sub}.

Notation 3.4: (pre-image of subset B_{sub} of (codomain B)) Given an abstract function f: $A \to B$, pre-image of subset B_{sub} of codomain B is the union of preimages $f^{-1}(y)$, $\forall y \in B_{sub}$. Thus, we have the following.

$$\text{pre-image } (B_{sub}) = \bigcup_{y \in B_{sub}} f^{-1}(y) \quad \ldots (3.4)$$

3.4 Graph Representation of Function

Using the concept like the graph of a real valued function of a real variable, we give another representation of a function, called graphical representation of an abstract function.

Definition 3.9: (*Graph of a function*) In this representation, for the values in domain, we assign the points on x-axis (abscissa), and we assign the values in the co-domain to the y-axis (ordinate). The (x, y) points of the function are shown on two-dimensional plane by dots. This representation is called as graph of a function, or graphical representation of a function.

The graph of a function f: $A \to B$ in Example 3.2 is given below in Figure 3.7.

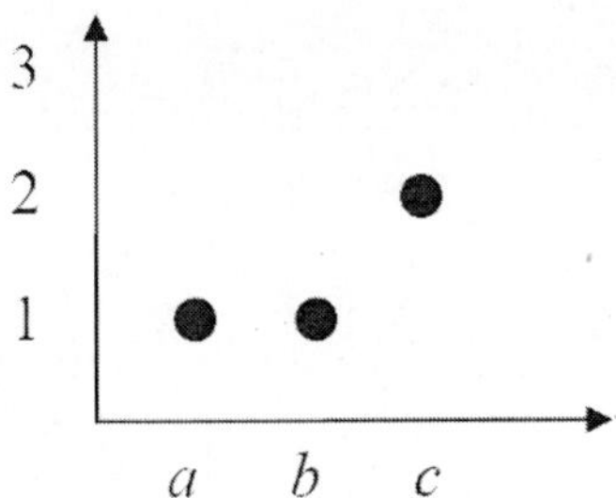

Figure 3.7: Graph of a function f: $\{a, b, c\} \to \{1,2,3\}$ in Example 3.2

3.5 Examples of Non-Functions

We now give the following examples to illustrate the assignments of co-domain values to the domain values which may not be functions.

Example 3.4: Let $A = \{a, b, c\}$, and $B = \{1, 2, 3\}$. Then the following assignment is not a function: $f(a) = 1, f(b) = 1, f(c) = 2, f(c) = 3$.

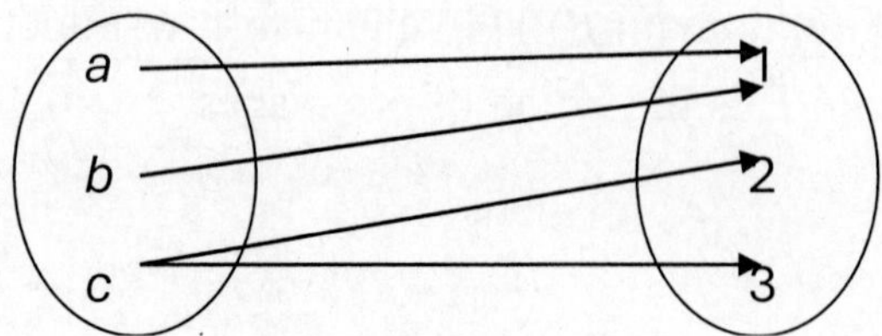

Figure 3.8: Arrow diagram for an *assignment rule* from $\{a, b, c\} \rightarrow \{1,2,3\}$ which is not a function (Example 3.3).

In Figure 3.8, the arrow diagram does not represent a function as the domain element c maps to two elements, *viz*., 2, and 3, in the co-domain.

Example 3.5: Let $A = \{a, b, c\}$, and $B = \{1, 2, 3\}$. Then the following assignment is not a function: $f(a) = 1, f(b) = 1$.

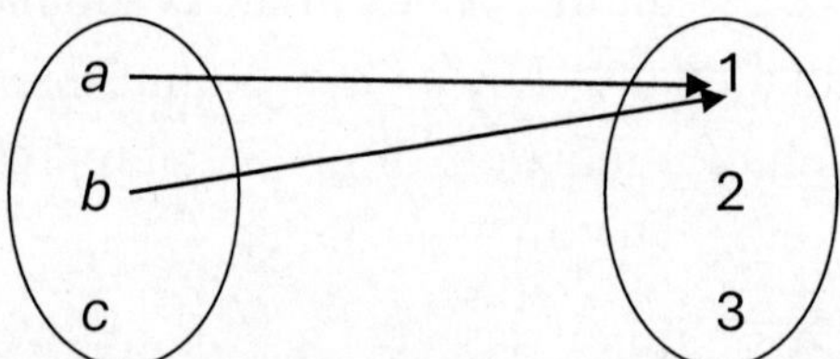

Figure 3.9: Arrow diagram for an *assignment rule* from $\{a, b, c\} \rightarrow \{1,2,3\}$ which is not a function (Example 3.4).

In Figure 3.9, the arrow diagram does not represent a function as the domain element c does not map to any element in the co-domain.

Example 3.6: Let $A = \{a, b, c\}$, and $B = \{1, 2, 3\}$. Then the following assignment is a function: $f(a) = 1$, $f(b) = 3$, $f(c) = 1$.

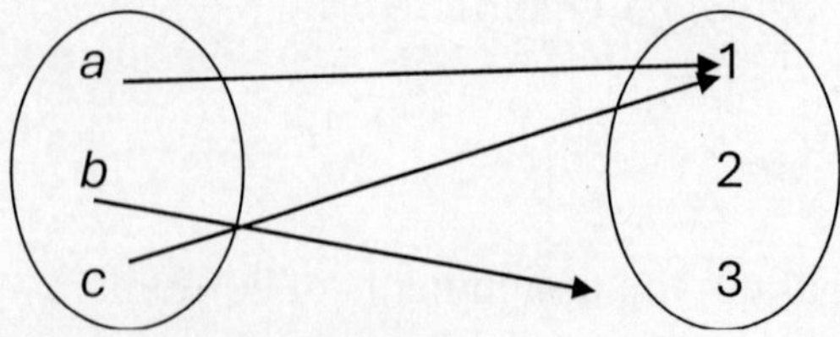

Figure 3.10: Arrow diagram for an *assignment rule* from $\{a, b, c\} \rightarrow \{1,2,3\}$ for Example 3.5

We re-emphasise that, in Figure 3.8, the arrow diagram does not represent a function as the domain element c does not have a single element in codomain as its image. In Figure 3.9, the arrow diagram represents a function on the partial domain $\{a, b\}$, so it is called as a partial function; however, with the domain set $\{a, b, c\}$, the arrow diagram in Figure 3.9 is not a function. The arrow diagram in Figure 3.10 represents a function.

3.6 Some Useful Functions

In representing the data, we need to convert the real (or fractional) values to nearest integer. Two important functions, viz., Floor(x), and Cealing(x), are frequently used to convert real values to integer values.

i. Floor function

Definition 3.10: The Floor function has the form: $\mathbb{R} \rightarrow \mathbf{Z}$, and is defined by assigning the closest integer less than or equal to x to Floor(x).

Notation 3.5: The floor function Floor(x) is also represented as $\lfloor x \rfloor$.

ii. Ceiling function

Definition 3.11: The Ceiling function has the form: $\mathbb{R} \rightarrow \mathbf{Z}$, and is defined by assigning the closest integer greater than or equal to x to Ceiling(x).

Notation 3.6: The ceiling function Ceiling(x) is also represented as $\lceil x \rceil$.

Some useful properties of Floor and Ceiling functions

$\lfloor x + 1 \rfloor = \lfloor x \rfloor + 1$,
$\lceil x - 1 \rceil = \lceil x \rceil - 1$,
$\lceil x \rceil = \lfloor x \rfloor$ if and only if $x \in Z$,
$\lceil x \rceil = \lfloor x \rfloor + 1$ if and only if $x \notin Z$,
$\lfloor x \rfloor = \lceil x - 1 \rceil$ if and only if $x \notin Z$.

i. *Factorial function*

Definition 3.12: The factorial function has the form: N → $\mathbf{Z}^+$. It is denoted by Factorial(n), or by $n!$, and is defined recursively as follows:

$$n! = \begin{cases} (n-1)! \times n, & \text{for } n > 0 \\ 1, & \text{for } n = 0. \end{cases} \quad \ldots (3.5)$$

The topic of recursion would briefly be dealt with in the module on Modular Arithmetic. Here it suffices to give an alternate equivalent definition of factorial as follows:

$$n! = \begin{cases} 1 \times 2 \times \ldots \times n, & \text{for } n > 0 \\ 1, & \text{for } n = 0. \end{cases} \quad \ldots (3.6)$$

ii. *Some well-known functions*

We are familiar with many real valued functions of a real variable x; additionally, we note that some functions use integer values. We frequently need some well-known functions in our study of computer science (*e.g*, in analysis and design of algorithms, databases, knowledge representation and artificial intelligence, etc.). We give a few such functions below.

1) The square function (denoted by square(x), or simply by x^2) is defined as

$$\text{square}(x) = x^2 = x \times x \quad \ldots (3.7)$$

2) Exponentiation (raising x) to the base b function is defined as

$$\exp(x) = b^x \quad \ldots (3.8)$$

3) The log (logarithmic) function measures the size of the exponent to the suitable base b (>0, and $\neq$ 1). In computer science, we frequently take base $b = 2$; this situation arises when we use binary trees as data structures, where we select one of the two choices at a time. If x is a positive real number, then

$$\log_b x = y \text{ means } x = b^y \qquad \text{... (3.9)}$$

We note that the $\log_b$ function has the form: $\mathbb{R}^+ \to \mathbb{R}$. We note that $\log_b$ is inverse of the function exp, on suitably defined domain and range sets.

4) Mod function: for an integer a, and positive integer b (with $b \neq 0$), in terms of the floor function defined Definition 3.10, we have the definition of mod function as follows:

$$a \bmod b = a - b\lfloor a/b \rfloor \qquad \text{... (3.10)}$$

(Note: As per common convention, we have omitted the multiplication sign in $b\times \lfloor a/b \rfloor$ to get the equivalent short-hand notation $b\lfloor a/b \rfloor$ in the above..)

5) Max function: These functions takes two operands, say x_1, and x_2, and it is defined as below.

$$\begin{aligned} \text{Max}(x_1, x_2) &= x_1 \quad \text{if } x_1 \geq x_2, \\ &= x_2 \quad \text{if } x_1 < x_2. \end{aligned} \qquad \text{...(3.11)}$$

3.7 BIJECTIVE FUNCTIONS

3.7.1 One-To-One Functions : Injections

Definition 3.13: A function $f : A \to B$ is called injective (also called as *one-to-one* function, or also called as an *embedding*) if it maps distinct elements of A to distinct elements of B.

Different ways of expressing the property of *one-to-one* functions:

i) No element in the co-domain B is an image of two distinct elements in the domain A;

ii) The set $f^{-1}(y)$ is either a null set, or a singleton set for any arbitrary $y \in B$, the co-domain set;

iii) $\forall x_1, x_2 \in A\ [(x_1 \neq x_2) \rightarrow (f(x_1) \neq f(x_2))]$

iv) $\forall x_1, x_2 \in A\ [(f(x_1) = f(x_2)) \rightarrow (x_1 = x_2)]$

The arrow diagram for a typical one-to-one function is given in the following Figure.

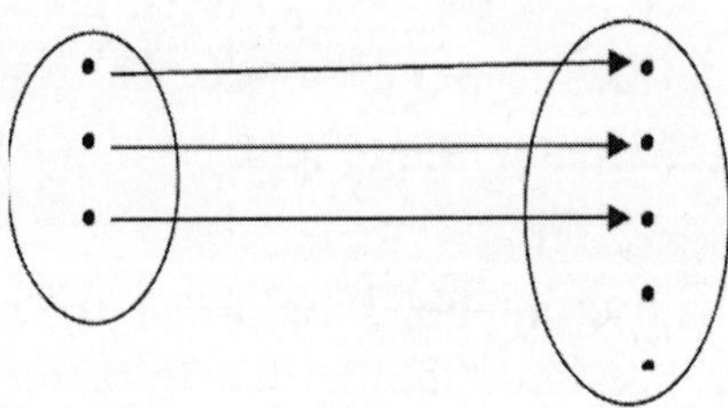

Figure 3.11: Arrow diagram for a typical one-to-one function.

3.7.2 *Onto Functions: Surjections*

We defined range(f) in equation (3.1). The notion of surjection uses range(f).

Definition 3.14: A function $f : A \rightarrow B$ is called surjective (also called as *onto B*) if range(f) = B, the co-domain of the function f.

The arrow diagram for a typical onto function is given in the following Figure.

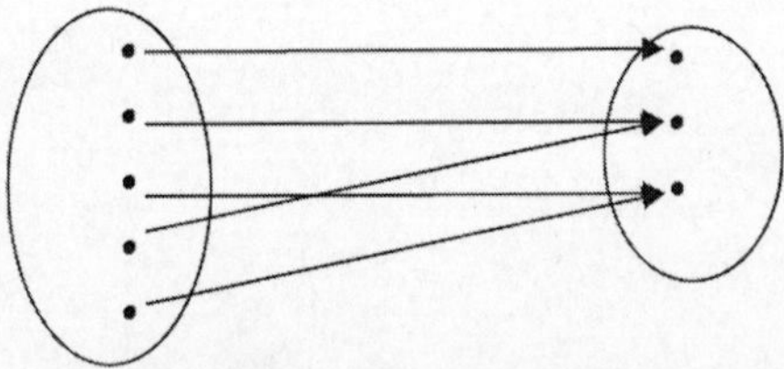

Figure 3.12: Arrow diagram for a typical onto function.

Example 3.7: (*non-one-to-one, but onto* function) Consider the function $f : R \rightarrow Z$, defined by $f(x) = \lceil x+1 \rceil$. This function is not one-to-one because $f(0.3) = 2 = f(0.4) = f(1.0)$. However, this function is onto Z, because, for every $y \in Z$, there exists a number $x = y - 1 \in R$, such that $f(y - 1) = y$.

□

Example 3.8: (*one-to-one, but non-onto* function) Consider the function $f: \mathbb{N} \to \mathbb{N} \times \mathbb{N}$, defined by $f(x) = (x, x)$. This function is one-to-one because if $x, y \in \mathbb{N}$, and $x \neq y$, then $f(x) \neq f(y)$. However, this function is not onto $\mathbb{N} \times \mathbb{N}$, because, for example, the pre-image of the ordered pair (0, 1) is a null set (nothing maps to the ordered pair (0, 1)).

□

Example 3.9: (*non-one-to-one, but onto* function) Consider the function $f: \mathbb{N} \to \mathbb{N} \times \mathbb{N}$, defined by $f(x, y) = 2x + y$. This function is not one-to-one because, for example, $f(0, 2) = f(1, 0)$.

This function is onto $\mathbb{N}$, because, we first note that any $z \in \mathbb{N}$ is either even or odd. If it is even, it is of the form $2x$, where $x \in \mathbb{N}$. Choosing $(x, 0) \in \mathbb{N} \times \mathbb{N}$, we note that there is an element $(x, 0)$ in the domain whose image is z. If it is odd, it is of the form $2x+1$, where $x \in \mathbb{N}$. Hence, choosing $(x, 1) \in \mathbb{N} \times \mathbb{N}$, we note that there is an element $(x, 1)$ in the domain whose image is z.

Thus, in both the cases, there is at least one element in the domain whose image is z, for any arbitrary $z \in \mathbb{N}$. Hence, f is onto $\mathbb{N}$.

□

3.8 INVERSE FUNCTIONS

Definition 3.15: A function $f: A \to B$ is called bijective (also called as *one-to-one onto* function, or also called as an ***invertible***) if it is both injective (one-to-one) and surjective (onto).

The arrow diagram for a typical bijection (one-to-one onto function) is given in the following Figure.

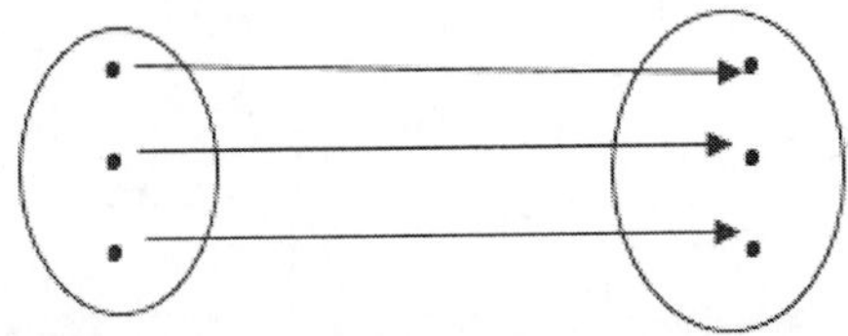

Figure 3.13: Arrow diagram for a typical bijective (one-to-one onto function).

Example 3.10: Let us consider a set A with elements as all real values in an open interval $(0, 1) = \{x \in \mathbb{R} \mid 0 < x < 1\}$, and let the set B be the set of all positive real values, *i.e.*, $\mathbb{R}^+$. Consider the function $f: A \rightarrow B$, defined as follows.

$$f(x) = \frac{x}{1-x} \quad \text{... (3.12)}$$

Prove that the above function f is a bijection.

Solution: We give the solution in two parts. Let us first prove that f is one-to-one.

Part I: (Proof for the function f being *one-to-one*): For proving this, let us assume the contrary, i.e., assume that f is not one-to-one. Hence, if possible, let us assume that there exist two values, say v_1, and v_2, with $v_1 \neq v_2$, $0 < v_1, v_2 < 1$, such that $f(v_1) = f(v_2)$. From (3.12), we have,

$$f(v_1) = \frac{v_1}{1-v_1} = f(v_2) = \frac{v_2}{1-v_2} \quad \text{... (3.13)}$$

Hence,

$$\frac{v_1}{1-v_1} = \frac{v_2}{1-v_2} \quad \text{... (3.14)}$$

Since $1-v_1, 1-v_2 \neq 0$, we can simplify (3.14) to get the following.

$$(v_1)(1-v_2) = (v_2)(1-v_1),$$

i.e., $(v_1 - v_1v_2) = (v_2 - v_2v_1)$, ... (3.15)

Due to commutativity of multiplication of real numbers, we have,

$$v_1v_2 = v_2v_1 \quad \text{... (3.16)}$$

To both sides of (3.15), we add the respective sides in (3.16). Thus, we have,

$$(v_1 - v_1v_2) + v_1v_2 = (v_2 - v_2v_1) + v_2v_1, \quad \text{... (3.17)}$$

Hence, we have,

$$v_1 = v_2, \quad \text{... (3.18)}$$

which contradicts our initial assumption $v_1 \neq v_2$.

Hence the function f is one-to-one.

Now let us prove that the function f is onto.

Part II: To prove that f is onto the co-domain set $\mathbb{R}^+$, we consider any arbitrary number $y \in \mathbb{R}^+$, and try to find out $x \in (0,1)$ such that $y = f(x)$.

From (3.12), we have,

$$y = \frac{x}{1-x},$$

$\Rightarrow$ $(1-x)\,y = x$, (since $x < 1$, we have $x \neq 1$, and we can multiply by $(1-x)$)

$\Rightarrow$ $y - x\,y = x$,

$\Rightarrow$ $y = x + x\,y$,

$\Rightarrow$ $y = x(1+y)$,

$$\Rightarrow x = \frac{y}{1+y} \qquad \text{... (3.19)}$$

We note that (3.19) is always defined as $y > 0$, so the denominator cannot become zero.

Next, we need to prove that $0 < \frac{y}{1+y} < 1$. We do this again in two parts:

part (a): $\frac{y}{1+y} > 0$, and, part (b): $\frac{y}{1+y} < 1$.

Part (a): Since $y > 0$, this implies that $(1 + y) > 0$. Further, $1 + y \neq 0$; so we can divide y by this non-zero number $(1 + y)$. Hence $\frac{y}{1+y} > 0$.

Part (b): Since $y > 0$, this implies that $(1 + y) > y\ (> 0)$. Hence, $\frac{y}{1+y} < 1$.

Thus, $\frac{y}{1+y}$ is a (real number) in the set A = (0,1). Thus, for any arbitrary number $y \in \mathrm{R}^+$, we have found out $x = \frac{y}{1+y} \in (0,1)$, such that $y = f(x)$. Hence, the function f is onto (0,1).

From part (a), and part (b) above, the function f is one-to-one and onto; hence the function f is a bijection.

□

3.9 Composite Functions

We use expressions like $\sin(x^2)$, by which mean sin(square(x)). We note that by the expression $\sin^2(x)$, we mean square($\sin(x)$). These two expressions, namely, $\sin(x^2)$, and

$\sin^2(x)$, define the single (new) function in terms of two functions; in these two examples, the two functions involved are the same (viz., sin, square), but the order of their application is different. Since we know that the two functions $\sin(x^2)$ and $\sin^2(x)$ are different functions, we note that the change in the order results in different resulting functions.

A few more such examples in which we define a new function in terms of known functions are: $\lceil \log_2 x \rceil$, or, $\log_2(x^2)$, $\tan(\sin x)$, etc.; these expressions combine the application of two functions. For example, in the expression $\lceil \log_2 x \rceil$, we first apply the function $\log_2(.)$, which results in some real value; next we apply ceiling function, which integrates the real value. In the expression $\tan(\sin x)$, the operand is x. We apply function sin(.) on it to get the value of $\sin(x)$. Next, we take tan(.) of that resulting value. This is an example of composition of functions tan(.) and sin(.), which can also be written as tan**o**sin (.), to be read as tan–oh–sin. This expression denotes the composition of two functions. Let us now come back to the framework of the abstract functions *f*, and *g*.

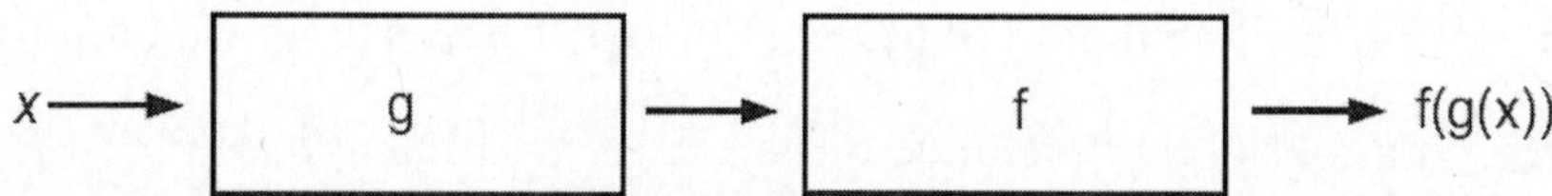

Figure 3.14 Representation of the function composition *f* **o** *g*.

<u>Definition 3.16</u>: (*Composition-compatible functions*) In order that the composition of two abstract functions, say *f* and *g*, is possible, they need to be composition-compatible. The result of applying the first function (say *f*) must be an element in the domain of the second function (say *g*). One way to satisfy this condition is, the co-domain of the first function *f* is the domain of the second function *g*.

We note that the function composition *g* **o** *f* is not defined when the range (and hence, co-domain) of *f* is not the same as the domain of *g*.

<u>Definition 3.17</u>: (Definition of function composition *g* **o** *f*): Let the two functions *f*, and *g*, be composition compatible. To illustrate with the example, let functions *f* and *g* be of the form:

$$f : A \to B, \text{ and } g : B \to C.$$

These functions are *g***o***f* compatible, because we have $(g \circ f)(x) = g(f(x))$ and is read "*g* composed with *f* of *x*" or "*g* of *f* of *x*". The domain of $(g \circ f)$ is *A*, and codomain of (*g* **o** *f*) is *C*. We also note that the function *f* and *g* are, in general, not *fog* compatible (think of special situation, *i.e.* condition(s) on sets *A*, *B*, and *C*, when these functions would be *fog* compatible).

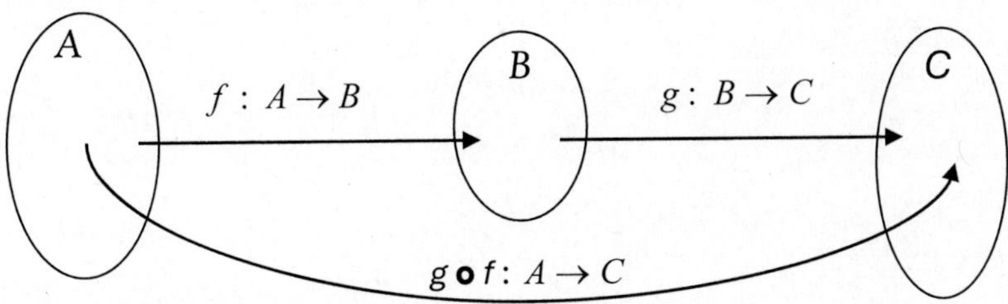

Figure 3.15 Representation of function composition $g \mathbf{o} f$, explicitly showing the domains, codomains of respective functions

One of the programming language paradigms is Functional programming (FP) (incidentally, there used to be, and even sometimes being used as language named FP as well, and it has been one of the earlier Functional programming languages). Today's popular language, namely, Python, is one such language that has constructs for Functional programming. Functional programming has basic construct as un-named functions, also called as lambda expressions. The discipline of Functional programming constructs the complete computer program using composition of various basic functions. You would practice more about such discipline of writing computer programs when you study Python language.

PART 4

Uncountability and Limits to Counting

4.1 COUNTABLE AND UNCOUNTABLE SETS

In notation 1.9, we used the term "cardinality" for set. We defined cardinality of (finite) set to be the (natural) number of elements in that (finite) set. What happens when the set has infinitely many elements? We can count the number of elements in two sets when they are finite, and we define two finite sets to have equal cardinality when they have the same (natural) number of elements.

What happens when a set has infinitely many elements? In particular, is it that all infinite sets have the same size? This question requires us to make our notion of "having same size" more precise. Our modern notion of size of a set is in terms of the notion introduced by George Cantor (1845-1918) (German Mathematician, born in Saint Petersburg, Russia). The attempt for rigorous definition of real numbers in 19th century led to George Cantor to make the notion of infinite sets precise. Cantor discovered and emphasised the importance of one-to-one-correspondence (bijection, that we studied in earlier part 3 about Functions), and established the mathematics of size of sets of different sizes, also termed as transfinite numbers. One interesting definition that Cantor gave for infinite sets is:

Figure 4.1: Bronze monument to Cantor in Halle Neudstadt

Figure 4.2: George Cantor

Definition 4.1 (Cantor's Definition of Infinite set): A set S is infinite iff there exists a bijection from S to its proper subset.

Using the above definition of infinite set, Cantor defined finite set as follows.

Definition 4.2 (Cantor's definition of finite set): A set S is finite iff it is not infinite.

In the first instance, Cantor's definition of infinite set is a bit surprising, and you may ponder why Cantor's definition of infinite set (given in Definition 4.1 above) is in order. Cantor's definition of finite set S implies that there is no bijection from S to its proper subset.

In the above approach, Cantor first defined infinite set and then he defined finite set to be negation of the notion of infinite set. Ever since the dawn of human civilization, we have first recognized and studied finite collections (sets). After understanding finite collections, it follows that infinite collection is the one that is not finite. Since it is intuitive for us to first define finite sets and define infinite sets as negation of our notion of finite sets, we introduce the same below, and we would stick to these definitions as our definitions of finite sets and infinite sets. Our approach (given below) would also allow us to precisely define countable and uncountable sets, the notions that form the basis for today's Computer Science, Artificial Intelligence and Machine Learning.

Let us start with one known infinite set, namely set of natural numbers (by the way, this set can be constructed, starting with null set, set operations and set abstraction mechanism that we introduced earlier).

The Peano axioms, also known as Peano postulates, formulated by Italian mathematician Giuseppe Peano in 1889 to attempt to give rigorous foundation for natural numbers, whose collection (set) is usually represented as a set N. Interestingly, Peano axioms enable us to construct an infinite set using only finite set of symbols and rules (axioms, also known as postulates). These axioms are:

1) Zero is a natural number.
2) Every natural number has a successor that is itself a natural number. (Using a bit of abstract language, we can state it as: set of natural numbers is closed under

successor operation. We would see more mathematical structures, and meaning of what we mean by "closed", in our Module on Algebra, where we would formally define Groups, Rings, Fields, etc.)

3) Zero is not successor of any number.
4) If the successor of two natural numbers is the same, then the original numbers are the same.
5) If a collection contains zero, and successor of every number in the collection, that collection is precisely the collection of natural numbers.

In the above, Zero is assumed as basic undefined notion, and the notion of successor invokes the addition by one, the operation on natural numbers. Based on Peano's axioms (postulates), and using the notion of sets we stated with in this part, it is possible to replace these undefined notions in terms of notions (specifically, Zero in terms of null set Φ; and successor in terms of (i) set as abstraction mechanism, and (ii) set union operation). Taking recourse to this approach, we give the following formulation (definition) of set of Natural numbers.

Definition 4.3 (set of Natural numbers): Using sets and above axioms of Peano, we give the construction for the set of natural numbers $\mathbb{N}$, starting with null set Φ, and using only set operations:

1. $\Phi \in \mathbb{N}$
2. If $n \in \mathbb{N}$, then $n \cup \{n\} \in \mathbb{N}$
3. Nothing else is in $\mathbb{N}$ unless its being so follows from 1 and 2 above.

In the above construction, we note that $\mathbb{N}$ is set of sets. How many elements are there in the set $\mathbb{N}$ constructed using only three – some of you may say, only two – rules above? We illustrate how few elements of $\mathbb{N}$ look like in the following example, where we construct a few elements by starting with rule 1, and by repeated application of rule 2 in Definition 4.3 above.

Example 4.3: Using Definition 4.3, enumerate (*i.e.* list down) all elements of set denoted by $n = 3$.

Solution: Using the step 1 in the definition, we start with Φ (using notation of natural numbers, it is denoted by 0 (Zero)). Next natural number is by one application of step 2, and we get the following:

If $\Phi \in \mathbb{N}$, then $\Phi \cup \{ \Phi \} \in \mathbb{N}$, this gives us the next element in $\mathbb{N}$ to be $\{ \Phi \}$, which we denote as natural number 1 (One).

The next application of step 2 gives us the following:

If $\{ \Phi \} \in \mathbb{N}$, then $\{ \Phi \} \cup \{ \{ \Phi \} \} \in \mathbb{N}$, this gives us the next element in N to be

$\{ \Phi, \{ \Phi \} \}$, which we denote as natural number 2 (Two).

The next application of step 2 gives us the following:

If $\{ \Phi, \{ \Phi \} \} \in \mathbb{N}$, then $\{ \{ \Phi, \{ \Phi \} \} \cup \{ \{ \{ \Phi, \{ \Phi \} \} \} \in \mathbb{N}$, this gives us the next element in $\mathbb{N}$ to be

$\{ \Phi, \{ \Phi \}, \{ \{ \Phi, \{ \Phi \} \} \}$, which we denote as natural number 3 (Three).

□

It should be clear to the reader as simple exercise of the extension of Solution of Example 4.3 as to how other elements of $\mathbb{N}$ are generated (specially by using repeated application of set abstraction and set union operation as used in step two).

We observe that $\mathbb{N}$ is set of sets. The question that you may ponder about is: what is the universal set from which elements of $\mathbb{N}$ are drawn? Is such universal set unique?

In step 1 of the Definition 4.3, we started with null set Φ, and denoted it by symbol Zero. This also results in our set of natural numbers to include (and start with) Zero. Suppose we want to modify Definition 4.3 to exclude Zero from the set of natural numbers. We leave it to you to modify Definition 4.3 to construct the infinite set of numbers starting with 1 (One). Observe that you would start from singleton set in step 1; since you have multiple choices for singleton sets, you would conclude that the representations other numbers (like the one we worked out in Example 4.3) would be unique. This observation justifies why our natural numbers include the number 0 (Zero).

As discussed in our discussion on Sets, we have evidence that ancient wisdom in our country had deeper thoughts about the study of "collections", and it would be interesting to gather evidence about our discovery of "zero" along the line of thought similar to the above.

In the following, we make use of Definition 4.3 for the set of natural numbers.

Definition 4.4: (finite set): We define set (say *S*) to be finite set iff there exists bijection (also called as one-to-one correspondence) from *S* to a set (say *n*) belonging to $\mathbb{N}$.

Definition 4.5: (Countable set): We define set (say *S*) to be countable (also called as Denumerable) set iff one of the following two conditions are satisfied:

1. Set *S* is finite (that is, there exists a bijection from *S* to set n, where $n \in \mathbb{N}$), or,
2. (when set *S* is not finite, i.e. it is infinite), there exists a bijection from *S* to set $\mathbb{N}$.

When the set is countable, you can enumerate, *i.e.* enlist all the elements in the set. In computer science, such ability to enlist all elements (or not being able list) is important for solutions of many problems

Surprising results are: set of Integers $\mathbb{Z}$, even set of rational numbers $\mathbb{Q}$, are countable in the sense that there exists bijection from these sets to set of natural numbers. (Intuitive ideas in proofs are sketched in diagram below; however rigorous proofs are left as exercises).

Example 4.4: Consider the set $\mathbb{N} = \{ 0, 1, 2, 3, 4, 5, \ldots \}$ and the set $\mathbb{Z} = \{ \ldots, -2, -1, 0, 1, 2, \ldots\}$. Prove:

(i) $\mathbb{N}$ is proper subset of $\mathbb{Z}$,
(ii) There is bijection (one-to-one correspondence) from $\mathbb{N}$ to $\mathbb{Z}$.

Solution: (i) In order to establish that $\mathbb{N}$ is proper subset of $\mathbb{Z}$, we observe the following:

(a) All elements of $\mathbb{N}$ are in $\mathbb{Z}$ (i.e. N is subset of $\mathbb{Z}$)

(b) there exists (at least) one element (say -2) that is in $\mathbb{Z}$, that is not in $\mathbb{N}$ (i.e. $\mathbb{Z}$ is not subset of $\mathbb{N}$).

(i) Existence of bijection (one-to-one correspondence) from N to Z also means the set $\mathbb{Z}$ of integers is denumerable, or it is possible to list down all elements of $\mathbb{Z}$ in the form of enumeration (list, that is one way infinite). The following diagrammatic representation would be useful to visualise this construction:

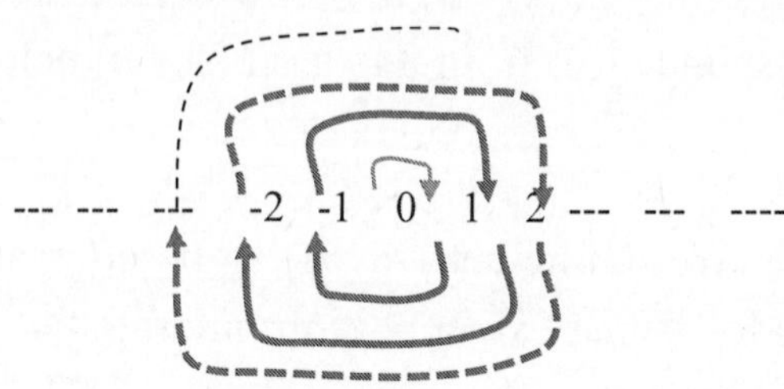

Figure 4.3: Diagrammatic representation to list all integers

Using the above, in the following Example, we give the function in mathematical notation.

Example 4.5: Consider the function f from $\mathbb{Z}$ to $\mathbb{N}$ defined as:

$$f(n) = n \quad \text{when } n = 0$$

$$= 2*n - 1 \quad \text{for positive } n\text{, and } n \geq 1$$

$$= -2*n \quad \text{for negative } n\text{, and } n \leq -1$$

Prove that the above function is:

(a) onto $\mathbb{N}$

(b) one-to-one

Solution:

(a) We observe that $f(n)$ takes value 0 due to first line in its definition. It takes all odd numerical values (including 1) due to its second line, and it takes all even values (including 2) due to its third line in the definition. Odd numbers, even numbers together with 0 are precisely (and the only) members of $\mathbb{N}$. Hence $f(n)$ is onto $\mathbb{N}$.

(b) Intuitively Figure 4.3 helps in visualizing that $f(n)$ is one-to-one. (Formal proof is left as exercise to the reader).

□

Since $f(n)$ as defined in Example 4.5 is one-to-one as well as onto, it is bijection (also called as "one to one correspondence") between its domain set (which is $\mathbb{Z}$) and range set (which is $\mathbb{N}$). Since we demonstrated the existence of bijection from the set of integers to the set of natural numbers, in Cantor's sense of formulation of sizes of infinite sets, these two sets have the same size. Cantor introduced the term "transfinite cardinal number" to denote different sizes (cardinalities) of infinite sets. Amongst such transfinite cardinal numbers, he denoted the smallest one by Hebrew symbol, $\aleph_0$ (pronounced as aleph-null). All infinite sets from which bijection (*i.e.*, one-to-one correspondence) exists to the set of Natural Numbers $\mathbb{N}$ have the cardinality $\aleph_0$.

Using the above terminology, our Example 4.5 has established that set of integers, denoted by $\mathbb{Z}$, have the cardinality $\aleph_0$.

When we discussed functions, we noted that inverse exists for bijective functions. To work out the inverse of the function f given in Example 4.5, we consider the following figure.

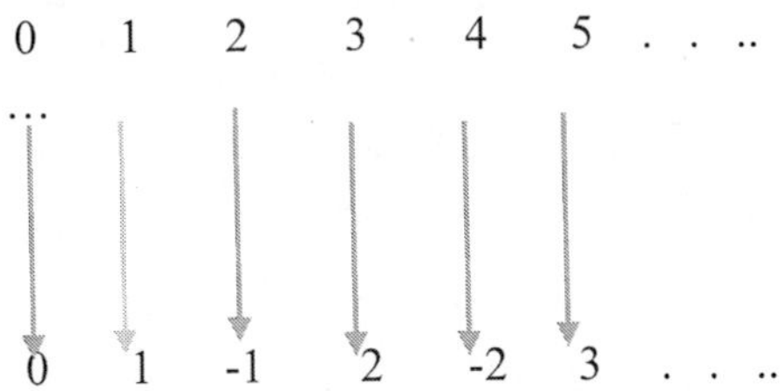

Figure 4.4: Enumeration (one-way infinite list) for all integers

Using the Figure 4.4, we work out the function g, which is inverse of f in the following Example.

Example 4.6: Consider the function g from $\mathbb{N}$ to $\mathbb{Z}$ defined as:

$$
\begin{aligned}
g(n) &= n && \text{when } n = 0 \\
&= -(n/2) && \text{for even values of } n,\ n \geq 2 \\
&= 1 + (n-1)/2 && \text{for odd values of } n \geq 1
\end{aligned}
$$

Prove that the above function g is:

a. onto $\mathbb{Z}$
b. one-to-one
c. inverse of function f defined in Example 4.5.

Solution: Left as exercise.

□

You may think that the infinite sets like $\mathbb{N}$, or $\mathbb{Z}$ are discrete, in the sense that they have gaps and hence we can interleave them and hence we are able to show that their cardinality $\aleph_0$.

Between any to rational numbers (no matter how close they are), there is always other rational numbers (as an example, consider average of two distinct rationals, which is also rational number), and in this sense there are no gaps between two rational numbers (in which sense the rational numbers have "gaps" is other interesting question, resulting in necessity of real numbers; however this is beyond the scope of our present consideration and discussion. You might have had chance to look into the definition of real numbers, and their properties in your Mathematics course on Calculus).

Cantor, long back in 1870's, knew that the set of (positive) rational numbers also has the cardinality $\aleph_0$. This also means, it is possible to enumerate (or list down, as one-way infinite list) all positive rational numbers. One way to consider listing of all positive rational numbers is given below (you are encouraged to find out other ways, especially considering the representation of rational number as p/q, where p and q are positive integers).

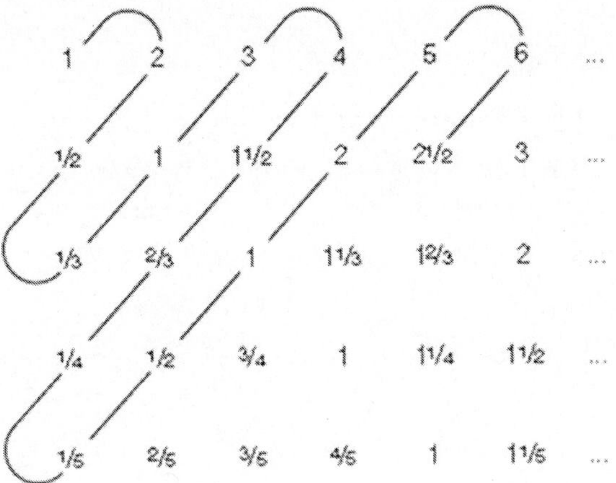

Figure 4.5: One enumeration scheme for rationals

Consider the set of all positive integers in the first line. The second line lists down the halves (i.e. ½) of the first line; the third line lists down one thirds (i.e. 1/3) of the first line, and so on. Next, we give (one) enumeration scheme that would list down all positive rationals as follows. We consider these of rationals as one way infinite list by "snaking around" (refer to Figure 1.33) the diagonals of the two-dimensional arrangement and deleting any rational number that is already encountered before. For Figure 4.5, it results in the following list:

1, 2, 1/2, 1/3, 3, 4, 3/2, 2/3, 1/4, 1/5, 5, 6, 5/2, ...

Figure 4.6: One enumeration (listing) of all positive rational numbers

Since we exhausted all rational numbers, rational numbers are countable.

Example 4.7: Give one-to-one correspondence from the set of all positive rationals to the set N that is intended in the Figure 4.5.

Solution: Left as exercise (routine, albeit not so trivial one).

□

There are many different ways of creating "snaking patterns", and we showed one way of doing it in Figure 4.5. Idea about other possibility is given in Figure 4.7 below:

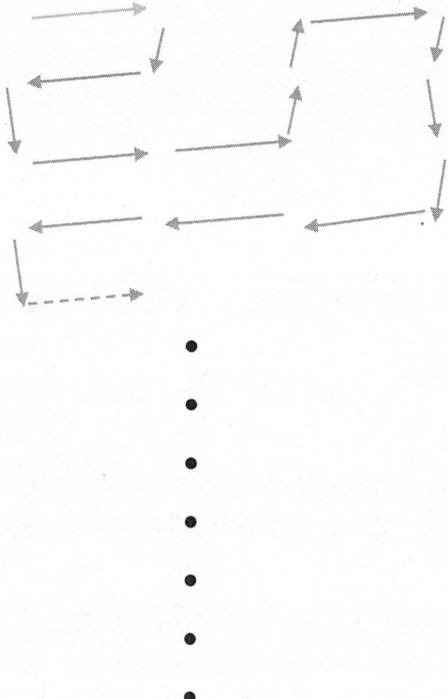

Figure 4.7: Other way of enumeration of points in two-dimensional arrangement

Can you think of other ways?

Using the above ideas, Cantor introduced arithmetic of transfinite numbers. Specifically, he introduced two properties of $\aleph_0$. He stated them as:

i. $\aleph_0 + \aleph_0 = \aleph_0$ (noting that, even when there are infinitely many numbers added to set of natural numbers to get set of integers, the resulting infinite set has the cardinality same as cardinality of set of natural numbers), and,
ii. $\aleph_0 * \aleph_0 = \aleph_0$ (follows intuitively from Figures 4.5, 4.7).

The result (ii) above can be generalized to:

iii. $\aleph_0 * \aleph_0 * \ldots * \aleph_0 = \aleph_0$, where the number of *'s in the left side are finite.

Does the result hold when the number of *'s in the left side of (iii) above are infinite (may be of cardinality $\aleph_0$)? We would examine this question in the next (few) subsections. Before we move to the next subsection, after our detailed understanding of countable set, we give the following definition of uncountable set.

<u>Definition 4.6:</u> (Uncountable set): We define set (say *S*) to be uncountable iff it is not countable.

From the definition 4.6, it follows (using formulation of logic covered in module 1, work out formally and convince yourself) that the set *S* is uncountable iff it is infinite and there is no bijection from *S* to (infinite) set $\mathbb{N}$.

4.2 CANTOR'S DIAGONAL ARGUMENT

There are infinite sets that are not countable. Basic proof technique requires to prove this is "Proof by contradiction" (this is very powerful proof technique, and we shall revisit this proof technique later in our course in the module on Proof Techniques). Cantor used this proof technique to prove that set of real numbers (denoted by $\mathbb{R}$) cannot be put in one-to-one correspondence with the set of natural numbers (denoted by $\mathbb{N}$) . For this purpose, Cantor made use of known result about representing real numbers between the interval from 0 to 1. Any real number in this interval can be expressed as with 0 as integral part, followed by fractional part represented by decimal point (".") followed by a sequence (which could be finite, or infinite) of decimal digits. We shall assume this property of real numbers for our discussion below.

<u>Theorem 4.1:</u> Set of real numbers in interval from 0 upto 1 is not countable.

<u>Proof</u>: By using the proof of contradiction (will be discussed in the module on Proof Technique) it is possible to prove that in the interval from 0 to 1 is uncountable. Assume

that these real numbers (i.e., real numbers in the interval 0 to 1) are countable. Since we know (we assume this) that each such number can be represented by sequence of digits after the decimal point, we can create a list like the one in Figure 4.8 below, *exhausting all such reals in the interval 0 to 1* (x being arbitrary real number in the interval 0 to 1, not denoting the same real number for different occurrences in the following figure),

1← → x| =0.256173...

2← → x| =0.654321...

3← → x| =0.876241...

4← → x| =0.600000...

5← → x| =0.676787...

6← → x| =0.387515...

7← → x| =0.256173...

... ...

... ...

n← → x| =0.a_1 a_2 a_3 a_4 a_5 a_6... a_n...

... ...

Figure 4.8: All real numbers (Fractions) in interval from 0 upto 1 enlisted (as assumed to be possible for our proof by contradiction)

Now, we construct the number *b* as follows:

b =0.b_1 b_2 b_3 b_4 b_5 b_6... b_n...

In order to construct the above b, we make the following choices (making use of information in Figure 4.8 above):

b_1 not equal to 2, say 3

b_2 not equal to 5, say 1

b_3 not equal to 6, say 7

b_4 not equal to 0, say 2

b_5 not equal to 8, say 5

…

b_n not equal to a_n

…

Figure 4.9: Diagonalization technique to construct number *b*.

Then b =0.b_1 b_2 b_3 b_4 b_5 b_6...... = 0.31725… is not in the list, and hence our starting assumption that we had finished all real numbers in the interval 0 to 1 in the listing in Figure 1.36 has to wrong.

Hence, we have come up with contradiction. We trace back why we have such contradictory situation, and we point out that our original assumption that the real numbers in the interval 0 to 1 are countable (that we exhausted them by enlisting as claimed in Figure 4.8) has to be wrong. Hence, by the proof technique we know as "proof by contradiction", we have a "proof" that the real numbers (which incidentally include the real numbers in the interval 0 to 1) are uncountable.

□

The above construction of number *b* is an example of Cantor's famous Diagonal argument. We are taking elements in the diagonal as per our choice (here the choice is to select them as elements different than the one we have at diagonal). This diagonal argument can be generalized to prove Cantor's power set theorem, which we state in the next subsection.

For numbers represented by the sequence of decimal digits in the fractional part, we note that, for rational number, the sequence of digits is either finite, or there is finite sequence that always repeats infinitely many times; hence one can predict the digit in i^{th} position given the position *i* and a rational number. However, for irrational number, there is no rule that would allow us to predict the digit in arbitrary position *i* in the sequence. While we leave the reader to ponder about these properties, more details of these properties is beyond the scope of our discussion.

After establishing that the set of real numbers cannot be put in one-to-one correspondence with the set of natural numbers, Cantor introduced special symbol to denote cardinality of set of real numbers, and it is "*c*" (as abbreviation for "continuum").

Example 4.8: Prove that the **transcendental** numbers (that is, the non-algebraic numbers, like π and e) form an uncountable set—so in fact almost all real numbers are transcendental.

Solution: Requires revision of what algebraic numbers, non-algebraic numbers and transcendental numbers are and it is left as exercise.

□

Cantor's diagonal argument arises in many forms in formal proofs in Computer Science as well as in Artificial intelligence, and it is one of the important techniques extensively put to use in Computer Science.

4.3 POWER SET THEOREM (also known as Cantor's Power Set Theorem)

Theorem 4.2: (Cantor's Power Set Theorem): For any set A and its power set $\mathbf{P}(A)$, there is no one-to-one correspondence from A to $\mathbf{P}(A)$.

Note that the set A in Theorem 4.2 is any arbitrary set; in particular, the theorem holds for all infinite sets, and not just for finite sets, as well as for infinite sets with cardinalities $\aleph_0$ and c that we introduced till now. In fact, this is one theorem, whose proof, based on Cantor's Diagonal Argument, is very general having profound consequences for the foundations of Set Theory.

Proof (of Theorem 4.2): We need to show that, for arbitrary set A, there is no bijection $g : A \rightarrow \mathbf{P}(A)$.

For using the proof by contradiction, let us suppose g is such a bijection. Let

$S = \{ a \in A : a \notin g(a) \} \subseteq A$

Since $S \in \mathbf{P}(A)$, $S = g(x)$, for some $x \in A$, because g is onto (surjective).

There are two possibilities: 1. $x \in S$, and 2. $x \notin S$

1. If $x \in S$ then $x \notin g(x) = S$, *i.e.* $x \notin S$, a contradiction
2. If $x \notin S$ then $x \in g(x) = S$, *i.e.* $x \in S$, a contradiction

Therefore no such bijection is possible.

□

In the above short proof, the construction of set S is based on Cantor's diagonal argument as applied to set A of any arbitrary size (note that the set A need not have cardinality restricted to $\aleph_0$). The above proof used two important proof techniques that we would see in our module on "Proof Structures", namely, (i) Proof by Contradiction, and (ii) Proof by Cases.

In the intellectual pursuit of humans, this short proof is one of the most creative and intellectually satisfying proofs, with profound consequences. It allowed Cantor to construct hierarchy of infinite sets with larger and larger cardinalities. According to this theorem, the power set of set of natural numbers cannot have cardinality $\aleph_0$, and Cantor introduced the notation $\aleph_1$ to denote the cardinality of this (infinite) set. Similarly, by taking power set of power set of set of natural numbers, Cantor introduced the notation $\aleph_2$ to denote this infinite set. This allowed Cantor to formulate infinitely many sizes, namely, $\aleph_0$, $\aleph_1$, $\aleph_2$, $\aleph_3$, $\aleph_4$, … which are infinitely many cardinalities, and they represent the hierarchy of sizes of infinite sets. Thus, by iteratively taking the power set of an infinite set and applying Cantor's theorem, we obtain an endless hierarchy of infinite cardinals, each strictly larger than the one before it. Consequently, the theorem implies that there is no largest cardinal number (colloquially, "there's no largest infinity").

Many questions about the cardinal numbers remain. Since we know that $\mathbb{Z}$ and $\mathbb{Q}$ are the same size, and that $\mathbb{R}$ is larger, one natural question is whether there are any sets `between' $\mathbb{Z}$ and $\mathbb{R}$, that is, strictly bigger than $\mathbb{Z}$ (and $\mathbb{Q}$) but strictly smaller than $\mathbb{R}$. The *continuum hypothesis* is:

There is no set A with $\aleph_0 <$ cardinality(A) $< \mathbf{c}$.

That is, the continuum hypothesis asserts that $\boldsymbol{c}$ (denoting the cardinality of $\mathbb{R}$) is the first cardinal number larger than $\aleph_0$. We note that, the continuum hypothesis *cannot be proved to be true and cannot be proved to be false*. In the 1920's, Kurt Gödel (famous for his Incompleteness Theorem, having profound consequences in defining what Computation is) showed that the continuum hypothesis cannot be *disproved*, and in the early 1960's, Paul Cohen showed that it cannot be *proved* either.

In set theory we introduced till now, the universal set contains all sets. All elements of power set of *U* are sets, and by intuitive definition of universal set, they must be in *U*, allowing us to conclude that cardinality of power set of *U*, *i.e.*, **P**(*U*) cannot be greater than the universal set *U*. However, Cantor's power set theorem states that cardinality of **P**(*U*) is strictly greater than cardinality of *U*. This paradox, known as Cantor's paradox, has questioned the very existence of universal set, and thus has shaken foundations of set theory that we introduced till now (the one that is often referred to as "Intuitive Set Theory"). Logicians and Mathematicians have introduced "Axiomatic Set Theory" in which Cantor's paradox is circumvented. Although this discussion in intellectually interesting, it is beyond the scope of our present discussion, and you may refer to books like Patrick Suppes on this topic.

4.4 LIMITS OF COMPUTING

You are familiar with the programming. Computer programs solve variety of problems. A computer program is a sequence of alphabet symbols. Alphabet symbols are finite. In particular, we note that there are 26 alphabet symbols, added to them punctuation symbols, capital letters, etc., we have less than 100 symbols together to construct the sequence of characters that form our computer program.

The program that is a sequence of finitely many number of characters of alphabet symbols, can be represented in the memory of computer as finite sequence of only two symbols (bits), namely 0 (switch being in off position) and 1 (switch being in on position).

The length of program, as measured by the number of bits it occupies, can be large, but it is finite. It follows that the number computer programs correspond to the number of different finite bit strings that one can form. How many such programs are possible? While some strings of bits may no longer be valid representations of some computer program, we conclude that it is possible to create infinitely many such sequences of bits, or infinitely many strings. How many such bit strings of finite length can be created from two symbols, namely 0 and 1? Using our understanding of Countable sets, we observe that we have countable such different programs possible.

What do we deploy the computer program for? Computer program is written to perform a task, or solve a problem. For simple argument, let us assume that, for a given input, our computer has capability of only two output states, namely "accept" or "reject" (We refer to such problems as "decision problems", and in our course on Theory of Computation, we would study more about such problems, and prove how they are equivalent to all problems that computer can solve.) The input to computer is another finite sequence of bit-strings. When a bit-string is fed to our computer program as input, some of these bit strings would be accepted by the computer program while the others are not accepted. Thus, one computer program characterizes, or represents, a subset of set of possible (countably infinite) strings.

From the above intuitive argument, we conclude the following:

(i) Number of computer programs are countable.

(ii) Number of ("decision") problems that we can create correspond to the number of subsets of strings of 0's and 1's. Since the number of strings of 0's and 1's are countably infinite, the number of subsets of this countably infinite set is uncountably infinite, and this is precisely the number of ("decision") problems that we can formulate.

In other words, we rephrase the above two observations as follows.

(i) Number of computer programs are countably infinite.

(ii) Number of ("decision") problems that we want our computer program to solve are, due to Power set Theorem of Cantor, are uncountably infinite.

Cantor's Power Set Theorem has empowered us to give insights about the above two infinite sets. We note that the number of problems that one can formulate and pose, is uncountably infinite, while the number of distinct computer programs are countably infinite. Hence, the number of distinct problems (uncountably infinite, cardinality $\aleph_1$) is much bigger than the number of computer programs that one can write (countably infinite, cardinality $\aleph_0$). Cantor power set theorem states that infinite set of cardinality $\aleph_1$ cannot be put in one-to-one correspondence with infinite set of cardinality $\aleph_0$ thereby empowering us to conclude that there are many tasks/problems than the number of distinct computer programs. One computer program can solve at most one problem (there is functional relationship between the set of computer programs and the set of problems (*i.e.*, the tasks it solves). So, countably infinite computer programs can solve only countably infinitely many problems. This allows us to conclude that there are uncountably infinitely many problems/tasks that no computer can solve. In this sense, computing capability of any general computer has to be limited, and we refer to this as "limitations of computing".

In this section, we noted one of the interesting consequences of Cantor's Power Set Theorem about the limits of computing. Our approach has necessarily been sketchy and intuitive. Formal and precise approach for our intuitive argument given in this section requires us to carefully study formal models of computing, define in precise details what computation is, as well as what the problem/task is. Such approaches are indeed pursued in other courses in Computer Science, and we refer to courses like Formal Languages and Automata Theory, Theory of Computation, theoretical computer science etc. for readers interested in more rigorous approach about the limitations of computing.

UNIT SUMMARY

This module has enabled us to develop insights about the limitations of "intuitive set theory". Part 4 has been the most important part of this module, and to understand its main contents, namely (i) the limits of computation, and, (ii) structure as well as existence of infinitely many infinite sets, we covered basics about sets, relations, and functions first three parts.

In part 1, we started with intuitive notion of set, and studied how sets are described by listing (enumerating) its elements. We quickly realised the limitations of enumeration approach for representing sets, and we made use of logical machinery of "Predicate logic" to represent sets by the property that all its elements possess. Set has its intrinsic operation as only one operation, namely belonging to, and it is defined from the elements to a given set. This approach however assumes that elements have to be from some "collection", which we conveniently assumed to be coming from some "universal set".

Using the formalism of logic, and the above belonging to operation, we saw that the notions of (i) subset, (ii) set union, (iii) set intersection, and (iv) set difference operations can be defined. These operations have great similarity with operations in logic (mainly propositional logic) and we pointed them out.

We gave Equivalence laws of sets and pointed that they are like Laws of Logic covered in module 1 on logic. What are these similarities? Conceptually, do we have abstract structure that represent common properties of both? The answer is, yes, and we would briefly come back to it when we study Algebraic structures in module 7.

To introduce the notion of ordering for infinite sets, and develop the notion of infinite sets having same size, we needed to formalize the notions of (i) partial orderings, and (ii) equivalence relations. In part 2 of this module, we started with Cartesian Product of two sets, and studied properties of binary relations that formally allow us to develop (i) partial orderings, and (ii) equivalences.

In part 3 of this module, we introduced functions, primarily focusing on clarifying special type of functions called "bijections", as well as high level operation of composition defined over functions. We cursorily pointed out that developing computer software can be considered as function compositions applied repeatedly and recursively, and this observation has led to paradigm of programming languages known as "functional programming" languages, where anonymous functions, also called as lambda expressions are form basic functions that can be repeatedly composed to develop the software program.

Bijections are required in part 4, to express Cantor's insights for infinite sets. The structure of bijections defined over a finite set has interesting algebraic properties, and we shall briefly comment on them in our module on algebraic structures later.

Finally, in part 4, we introduced Cantor's notion of infinite sets, and introduced his "diagonalization argument". While one application of diagonalization argument is to prove that the cardinality of real numbers is more than the cardinality of rational numbers, we also pointed that application of diagonalization technique also leads us to conclude that there are fundamental limitations of any computing system, and we large number of problems that no computer can solve. Diagonalization argument is radical tool extensively used in theoretical computer science to prove interesting properties. In current era of Artificial Intelligence and Machine Learning (AIML), computer software seems to surpass human capabilities; however, diagonalization argument is the essential tool for understanding limitations of the tasks that AIML can do (exercise 19 below aims to illustrate this point).

Exercises:

1. For all the sets A, B, C prove that $\overline{(A-B)-(B-C)} = \bar{A} \cup B$

2. Let P(C) denote the power set of C. Given A={1,2} and B={2,3}, find each of the following:
   P(A∩B) P(A) P(A∪B) P(AxB)

3. Foe all sets A and B prove $(A \cup B) \cap \overline{A \cap B} = (A - B) \cup (B - A)$ by showing each side of the equation is a subset of the other.

4. The symmetric difference of A and B, denoted by $A \oplus B$ is the set containing those elements in either A or B but not in both A and B.
   Draw a Venn diagram for $A \oplus B$
   Prove: $(A \oplus B) \oplus B = A$

5. State whether the following statements are true or false. Explain why? (⊂,⊆, and ⊄)

$1 \in \{1, \{1\}\}$ …..	$N \in \{N\}$ ….
$1 \not\subset \{1, \{1\}\}$ ….	$N \not\subset \{N\}$ …
$\{1\} \in \{1, \{1\}\}$ ….	$\phi \notin \{N\}$
$\{1\} \subseteq \{1, \{1\}\}$ ….	$\phi \subseteq \{N\}$ …
$\{\{1\}\} \notin \{1, \{1\}\}$	$\phi \in \{\phi, N\}$
$\{\{1\}\} \subseteq \{1, \{1\}\}$	$\phi \subseteq \{\phi, N\}$
$N \notin N$	$\{N\} \subseteq \{\phi, N\}$ …
$N \subseteq N$	$\{N\} \not\subset \{\phi, \{N\}\}$ …
$\phi \notin N$	$\{N\} \in \{\phi, \{N\}\}$ …
$\phi \subseteq N$ …	$\{(1,2), (2,2), (7,1)\} \subseteq N \times N$

6. a) Let A, B and C be sets. Prove or disprove
   $$(B - A) \cup (C - A) = A - (B \cup C)$$
   b) Prove or disprove statement " If $A \cup (B - A)$ is not a subset of B, then A cannot be a subset of B"

7. Definition 2.1 about Cartesian product of two sets is as follows. The Cartesian product of two sets *A*, and *B*, is denoted by *A*×*B*. The *A*×*B* is a set of all ordered pairs

(a, b) such that $a \in A$, and $b \in B$. This definition is recursive as it states that $A \times B$ is also a set.

(i) Explain how the recursion allows you to define Cartesian product of finite collection of sets. What is the structure of typical element it generates when you extend it to collection of n sets?

(ii) Does the definition allow you to define ordered n-tuples? In particular, does n-tuple have the same structure as you would get in part (i) above?

(iii) Does the above definition allow you to define Cartesian product of infinite collection of sets? Explain.

8. Let X = {a,b,c}, P(X is the power set of X. Q(X) = P(X) – { {a,b,c}}. Define a binary relation R on Q(X) as follows: for all A,B ϵ Q(X) , A R B ≡ A⊆ B.
   a) Is R a total order? Justify your answer.
   b) Give out all greatest, least, maximal and minimal elements of Q(X) with respect to R.

9. a) Let $R1 \supseteq R2$ be relations on a set A. Which of the following are true?
   $R1$ reflexive (symmetric, transitive, antisymmetric)
   $\Rightarrow R2$ reflexive (symmetric, transitive, antisymmetric)
   b) Let $R1 \subseteq R2$ be relations on a set A. Which of the following are true?
   $R1$ reflexive (symmetric, transitive, antisymmetric)
   $\Rightarrow R2$ reflexive (symmetric, transitive, antisymmetric)

10. Given a set A ={a,b,c,d,e} , the Hasse Diagram for the poset(A,R_1) is shown in figure.

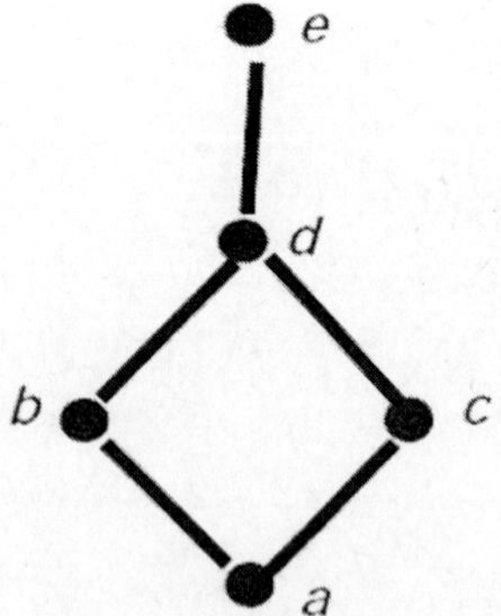

Express the relationship R_1 explicitly as a 0-1 matrix (Relation Matrix). Construct a directed graph on A which represents the relationship R_1

11. Givena set A = {a,b,c,d} and the relationship R_1 = {(a,a) , (a,d),(b,b) (c,a),(c,b),(c,d),(d,d) } , verify that R_1 is partial order. Find its Hasse diagram.

12. Draw the Hasse diagram for the poset $(\prod(A), \subseteq)$ where A = {a,b,c}

13. Given a set A = {a1,a2,….an} ,and the partial ordering relationship R1 on A. Further, suppose M(R1) is a relation matrix. Give suitable condition on the elements of the matrix M(R1) to recognize the maximal, minimal element(s). Further, give the suitable condition(s) on the elements of the matrix M(R1) for the existence of greatest, least element(s).

14. (This is warm-up question reviewing basics of sets and logic).

Faced with engine problems, Captain Shashi Bhushan made an emergency landing on the beach of the island of Knights and Knaves. The island is inhibited by these two distinct groups of people, knights and knaves. Knights always tell the truth and knaves always lie. Shashi Bhushan decided that his best move was to reach the capital of the island.

(a) Walking on the beach, Shashi Bhushan came to an intersection, where he saw two men, *A*, and *B*. After hearing Shashi Bhushan's story, *A* told Shashi Bhushan, "The capital is in the mountains or the road to the right goes to the capital." *B* then said, "The capital is in the mountains and the road to the right goes to the capital." Then *A* looked up and said, "That man is a lier." Shrugging his shoulders, *B* then said, "If the capital is in the mountains, then the road to the right goes to the capital."

Captain Shashi Bhushan then thought for a while, thanked both *A* and *B*, and started walking down the road on the left. Did Captain Shashi Bhushan make correct decision? Explain your reasoning for coming up with the decision (using logic).

(b) Walking up the road to the left, Shashi Bhushan encountered a group of people gathered at what he thought to be a bus stop. He approached three persons, *C*, *D*, and *E*, and asked them whether the road went to the capital and whether the location was indeed a bus stop. He received the following three different responses:

C : "The road goes to the capital, and the bus stop is not here."
D : "The road does not go to the capital, and the bus stop is here."
E : "The road does not go to the capital, and the bus stop is not here."

Confused and somewhat perplexed, Shashi Bhushan asked them whether they are knights or knaves. To this they all answered, "Two of us are knights, and one is knave." Shashi Bhushan concluded that the location was indeed a bus stop, and the road went to the capital. Was Shashi Bhushan's conclusion correct? Explain (using logic).

(c) At the bus stop, Shashi Bhusan noticed signs for three buses, B_1, B_2, and B_3, and approached another trio of persons, F, G, and H. The following conversation took place:

F : "At least one of B_1 and B_2 goes to the capital."
G : "B_1 goes to the capital."
H : "B_2 and B_3 go to the capital."
F : "B_3 goes to the beach."
G : "B_2 and B_3 go to the beach."
H : "B_1 goes to the beach."

Give your advise to Shashi Bhushan (with the explanation of your logical reasoning) about which bus he should take.

(d) After reaching the bus terminal at the capital, Shashi Bhushan saw three Computers. He asked the young man, I, whether the computers had the internet connections. The man I replied, "Computer 1 is not connected to the internet, Ask that man, J; he is a knight." When Shashi Bhushan approached that man, he told Shashi Bhushan, "Computer 2 has internet connection, but Computer 3 does not." Third man, K, overheard the conversation, and he said, "If Computer 2 has internet connection, then so does Computer 1. Computer 3 is not connected to the internet."

Is it possible for Shashi Bhushan to conclude which computer had the internet connection? Explain your logical reasoning.

(e) At the bus terminal, Shashi Bhushan overheard the following conversation between two persons, L and M.

L : "I like oranges."

M : "You do not like oranges. You like mangoes."

L : "We both like mangoes."

Is it possible for Shashi Bhushan to draw the conclusions for the following:

(i) Does L like oranges? (ii) Who likes mangoes?

Explain your answer(s) as logically as possible.

15. A survey by XYZ Economist indicated that, of the 700 families they surveyed in rural part of India, 220 own a television set but not refrigerator, 200 own refrigerator but no cooking gas stove, 170 own cooking gas stove but no television set, 80 own television set and refrigerator but no cooking gas stove, 80 own refrigerator and cooking gas stove but no television set, 70 own cooking gas stove and a television set but no refrigerator, and 50 do not have any of these. Find the number of families (in the survey) with:

(i) exactly one of these items (television set, refrigerator, and cooking gas stove),

(ii) exactly two of these items,

(iii) all of the items,

(iv) at least one of the items, and,

(v) having a refrigerator.

whenever it is possible. Explain your answer(s).

16. In Lemma 1.16, we extended the Theorem 1.14 (b) for counting the number of elements in union of three sets.

In this exercise, you need to extend Theorem 1.14(b) for union of countable sets. What difficulty you encounter, and how would you circumvent them?

17. For the following multiple-choice questions, state whether the choice is correct or wrong (zero, one or more choices can be correct).

(a) Let R, S, T be binary relations on a set A. Which of the following is/are true?

a. If R and S are transitive, $R \cup S$ is transitive.
b. If R and S are anti-symmetric, $R \cup S$ is anti-symmetric.
c. If R and S are reflexive, $R \cap S$ is reflexive.
d. If R and S are transitive, $R \cap S$ is transitive.
e. If R and S are anti-symmetric, $R \cap S$ is anti-symmetric.

(b) Let sets R, S, T be defined as follows (N denote set of natural numbers):

$R = \{ x \in \mathrm{N} \mid x \text{ is divisible by } 6 \}$,
$S = \{ x \in \mathrm{N} \mid x \text{ is divisible by } 15 \}$,
$T = \{ x \in \mathrm{N} \mid x \text{ is divisible by } 18 \}$.

Which of the following is true?

a. $R \subseteq T$
b. $R - S \subseteq T$
c. $T \subseteq R - S$
d. $R \cap S \subseteq T$
e. $R \cap S \supseteq T$

(c) Let R be relation on $\{ a,b,c,d \}$ and $R = \{ (a,a), (b,b), (a,b), (b,c), (c,c), (d,d), (c,d), (a,c), (b,d), (a,d) \}$. Which of the following is/are true?

a. R is symmetric relation
b. R is anti-symmetric relation
c. R is an equivalence relation
d. R is an ordered set
e. R is a poset

(d) Let P(X) denote the power set of X, where $X = \{ a, b, c, d, e, f \}$. Let R be a binary relation on P(X), such that ARB if and only if $A \cap B = B$. Which of the following is/are true?

a. R is symmetric relation
b. R is anti-symmetric relation
c. R is an equivalence relation

d. R is an ordered set

e. R is a poset

18. Let M be a Boolean (0-1) matrix representing a binary relation R on a finite set. We define the Boolean matrix product of a Boolean matrix by replacing usual addition by Boolean operator $\vee$, and by replacing the usual multiplication by Boolean operator $\wedge$. Let M^2 denote the Boolean matrix product of M taken with the same matrix M. Further, we define the ordering over the truth values 0 and 1 as $0 \leq 1$. Further, we define the matrix ordering as $M^2 \leq M$ when, $\forall\ i, j \in A$, we have, $M^2[i, j] \leq M[i, j]$.

    Prove or disprove that a binary relation R on a finite set is transitive, if and only if the Boolean matrix product $M^2 \leq M$, where M is a Boolean matrix representation of a binary relation R.

19. (a) A function $f: \mathbb{R} \rightarrow \mathbb{R}$ is defined as follows:

$$f(x) = \begin{cases} x^2 & \text{if } x \geq 0 \\ 2x & \text{if } x < 0 \end{cases}$$

(i) Is f one-to-one? Prove or give a counterexample.

(ii) Is f onto? Prove or give a counterexample.

20. Consider a bus with infinitely many seats. Let us call such bus as "Super-bus". In a typical such Superbus, no two passengers can occupy the same seat.
    a) For this situation, are the following statements equivalent?
        i. "Every seat in the bus is occupied by a passenger.", and,
        ii. "No more guests can be accommodated."

    b) Assume that infinitely many Superbuses, each bus being full of passengers, arrive at some intermediate bus stop, and exhaust their fuel, so that they cannot proceed further. In this bus stop, there is only one single Superbus, completely empty, having fuel in it. Is it possible to accommodate all passengers in Superbuses with empty fuel to this single Superpbus fuel? If yes, give method to do the same.

21. There is a relation known as " has color" which goes from the set F = { orange, cherry, pumpkin, banana} to the set C = { orange, red, green, yellow}. What pairs are in "has color"?

22. The domain of a function (or binary relation) is the set of numbers appearing in the first coordinate. The range of a function(or binary relation) is the set of numbers appearing in the second coordinate. Consider the set {0,1,2,3,4,5,6} and the function $f(x) = x^2 \bmod 7$. Express this function as a relation by explicitly writing out the set of ordered pairs it contains. What is the range of this function?

23. Sketch the graph of the relation $\{ (x.y) \mid x,y \in R \text{ and } y > x^2 \}$

24. Consider the numbers from 1 to 10. Give the set of pairs of these numbers that corresponds to the divisibility relation.

25. Draw a five- pointed star, label all 10 points. There are 40 triples of these labels that satisfy the betweenness relation. List them.

26. What relation on the numbers from 1 to 10 does the following set of ordered pairs represent?
{ (1,1),(1,2),(1,3),(1,4),(1,5),1,6),(1,7),(1,8),(1,9),(1,10),
(2,2), (2,3),(2,4),(2,5),2,6),(2,7),(2,8),(2,9),(2,10),
(3,3),(3,4),(3,5),3,6),(3,7),(3,8),(3,9),(3,10),
(4,4), (4,5),4,6),(4,7),(4,8),(4,9),(4,10),
(5,5), (5,6),(5,7),(5,8),(5,9),(5,10),
(6,6), (6,7),(6,8),(6,9),(6,10),
(7,7), (7,8),(7,9),(7,10),
(8,8) , (8,9),(8,10),
(9,9),(9,10),
(10,10) }

27. Computer programming is one of the essential skills that Computer Science and Engineering student need to acquire, specially in their first year of study itself. Educational institutes offering Computer Science and Engineering program has, as mandatory requirement, the laboratories fully equipped with computers, networked with each-other, and the lab sessions have lab instructors who guide the students in these programming classes. With rapid and exceptional developments in Artificial Intelligence and Machine Learning techniques, AI programs passing famous "Turing Test", reality of autonomous driverless vehicles moving from one part of country to other, and many such seemingly unbelievable wonders by computer software programs, a SuperBrilliant Innovative Software Company claims to have developed "Super lab-instructor", which itself is a computer program, and the Sales Manager of this company

proposes to the Board of one of the Educational institutes that it is economical and timely to remove all lab instructors in these programming classes and replace them by installing their "Super lab-instructor" program in all computers in the lab.

Should the Board of this Educational institute accept the proposal of sales manager of SuperBrilliant Innovative Software Company? Clearly explain.

28. In our discussion of Cantor's Power set Theorem, we stated: "...This allowed Cantor to formulate infinitely many sizes, namely, $\aleph_0$, $\aleph_1$, $\aleph_2$, $\aleph_3$, $\aleph_4$, ... which are infinitely many cardinalities, and they represent the hierarchy of sizes of infinite sets." Does it also follow that you can formulate infinitely many sizes of nature $\aleph_s$, where s is an element an infinite set having size $\aleph_r$? (Note that r need not be restricted to the set of Natural numbers, and it could also be an element of some infinite set of arbitrarily size). Investigate nontrivial properties of such construction.

29. Assuming that the set of natural numbers is well-ordered with usual "≥" ordering, prove the following.
    a. If A is non-null subset of the set of natural numbers, then set A is well-ordered with usual ordering as defined on the set of natural numbers.
    b. Given integers a and b with $b > 0$ there exist integers q and r for which $a = qb + r$ and $0 \leq r < b$.

30. (a) In section 2.5.5, we defined "well-ordered set". We also noted that the set of integers, Z, as well as the set of rational numbers, Q, are not well-ordered with usual "≤" operation as defined on these numbers. In the light of discussion in part four (Examples 4.4 to 4.7), however, it is possible to introduce new orderings on these numbers (in fact, many – are there infinitely many such orderings?) with which these numbers are well-ordered. Construct at least one such ordering for Z, as well as for Q.

(b) Are the sets of (i) real numbers, and (ii) complex numbers, well-ordered? If no, give a proof for the same. If yes, give an ordering (separately, on each of these sets) with which these sets are well-ordered.

LABORATORY WORK

There is a programming paradigm called "*functional programming*". As a computer science student, it is important to know what this domain of programming is.

Functional programming (also called FP) is a way of thinking about software construction by creating pure functions. It avoids concepts of shared state, mutable data observed in Object Oriented Programming. Functional languages emphasize on expressions and declarations rather than execution of statements. Therefore, unlike other procedures which depend on a local or global state, value output in FP depends only on the arguments passed to the function.

Characteristics of Functional Programming

- Functional programming method focuses on results, not the process
- Emphasis is on what is to be computed
- Data is immutable
- Functional programming decomposes the problem into 'functions'
- It is built on the concept of mathematical functions which uses conditional expressions and recursion to do perform the calculation
- It does not support iteration like loop statements and conditional statements like If-Else

While functional programming can be done in Python, to emphasize the features of functional programming (even in Python), you should develop familiarity with Erlang programming language.

Erlang is a functional programming language which also has a runtime environment. It was built in such a way that it had integrated support for concurrency, distribution and fault tolerance. Erlang was originally developed to be used in several large telecommunication systems from Ericsson. Erlang is old and has proven track records. Erlang is 33 years old, it was invented by physicist, who believed processor speeds would get saturated before 30 years, they wanted such a system which is horizontally scalable which is called distributed computing. Not only that, they wanted a system that would sustain failures based on systems will fail for any reason. Adding to this, they wanted a mechanism to deploy updates when the system is running which is called *hot code reloading*. The threading are also lightweight.

Erlang is a general-purpose concurrent, garbage-collected programming language and runtime system. It stays strong while building concurrency programs. Erlang provides language-level features for creating and managing processes with the aim of simplifying concurrent programming. The Erlang runtime system is designed for systems with these traits: Hot swapping, where code can be changed without stopping a system. The Erlang programming language has immutable data, pattern matching, and functional programming. The sequential subset of the Erlang language supports eager evaluation, single assignment, and dynamic typing.

Erlang is part of what makes Whatsapp able to operate on such a large scale. It was designed to natively support concurrency, it employs a ***process-based model*** where we have small isolated processes that can communicate with each other through messages. These processes can also communicate with processes that are outside of the core it runs on. WhatsApp has chosen Erlang a language built for writing scalable applications that are designed to withstand errors. Erlang uses an abstraction called the Actor model for it's concurrency Instead of the more traditional shared memory approach, actors communicate by sending each other messages. Actors unlike threads are designed to be lightweight.

KNOW MORE

Please go through an interesting (online) book: Learn You Some Erlang for Great Good! (A beginner's Guide). Learn You Some Erlang for Great Good! https://learnyousomeerlang.com/ . This book is like earlier book on Haskell, that is another functional programming language: Learn You a Haskell for Great Good! http://www.learnyouahaskell.com/ .

A few chapters in the above books (similar chapters for Haskell) of interest are:

Recursion | Learn You Some Erlang for Great Good!
Higher Order Functions | Learn You Some Erlang for Great Good!
Functionally Solving Problems | Learn You Some Erlang for Great Good!

In module 1, you have familiarized yourself with Ideone.com. Ideone is an online compiler and debugging tool which allows you to compile source code and execute it online in more than 60 programming languages.

https://ideone.com/l/erlang is one website for Online Erlang compiler and IDE - API provided by Sphere Engine - Ideone.com

Familiarize yourself with Erlang's as well as Haskell's functional programming part.

REFERENCES AND SUGGESTED READINGS

1. N. Ya.Vilenkin, *Stories About Sets*, Academic Press, New York (1968) (Original In Russian, 1963).
2. Paul R. Halmos, *Naïve Set Theory*, originally published by Van Nostrand, Princeton, N.J., in series: The University series in undergraduate mathematics; Reprinted: Springer Science+Business Media, LLC, New York. (1974).
3. George Gamow, *One two three ... infinity & Speculations of Science*, Part 1: Playing with numbers (pages 1 to 40), The Viking Press, New York 1947 (1961 Edition). (downloading link: https://www.pdfdrive.com/one-two-three-infinty-facts-speculations-in-science-d60737079.html)
4. Patrick Suppes, *Axiomatic Set Theory*, D Van Nostrand Company, Princeton, New Jersey, (1960).
5. Keith Delvin, *Sets, Functions, and Logic: An Introduction to Abstract Mathematics* (Third Edition), Chapman & Hall/CRC Mathematics series, Taylor & Francis e-Library, (2005).

Additional Reading (Functional Programming books):

1) Miran Lipovaca, Learn You a *Haskell* for Great Good! A Beginner's guide. No Scratch Press, San Francisco (2011).
2) Fred Hebert, Learn You Some *Erlang* for Great Good! A Beginner's guide. No Scratch Press, San Francisco (2013).

Additional Reading (Poset Representations, Algorithms):

1. Vijay K. Garg, *Introduction to Lattice Theory with Computer Science Applications*, John Wiley and Sons, Inc., (2015).

Dynamic QR Code for Further Reading

3 PROOF STRATEGIES

UNIT SPECIFICS

(Module on Proof Strategies)

We cover the following proof strategies in this module:

- *Introduction to Proof methods and strategies*
- *Direct Proof (also called as Forward Proof)*
- *Indirect Proof (also called as Proof by Contraposition)*
- *Proof by Contradiction*
- *Proof by Necessity and Sufficiency*
- *Proof by Induction*

RATIONALE

Why Proof Strategies important to Computer Science?

Learning proof strategies in discrete mathematical structures serves several important purposes:

1. *To build the theoretical foundation of computer science to understand the fundamental principles that underlie algorithms, data structures, and computational complexity theory.*
2. *for analyzing algorithms and their efficiency, to rigorously prove properties of algorithms, such as correctness and runtime complexity.*
3. *In safety-critical systems, such as those used in aerospace or medical devices, formal verification is essential to ensure correctness and reliability. Proof strategies provide the theoretical framework for formal verification techniques.*
4. *Logic, propositional calculus, and predicate logic help to understand and apply logical reasoning, which is fundamental in designing algorithms, writing correct programs, and solving problems in computer science.*
5. *Learning proof strategies in graph theory enables students to prove theorems about connectivity, paths, cycles, and other graph properties.*

6. *In networking and communication systems. Proof strategies are used to analyze and prove properties of protocols, routing algorithms, network topologies, and communication protocols.*
7. *Proof strategies are essential for proving the security properties of cryptographic protocols, such as confidentiality, integrity, and authenticity.*

PRE-REQUISITES

Mathematics at school level (till Class X)

UNIT OUTCOMES

List of outcomes of this unit is as follows:

U3-O1: Understand Proof Strategies.

U3-O2: Apply direct proof and simplify expressions.

U3-O3: Apply indirect proof and simplify expressions.

U3-O4: Apply proof by Contradiction.

U3-O5: Apply proof by necessity and sufficiency.

U3-O6: Apply proof by induction.

Unit-3 Outcomes	EXPECTED MAPPING WITH COURSE OUTCOMES (1- Weak Correlation; 2- Medium correlation; 3- Strong Correlation)								
	CO-1	CO-2	CO-3	CO-4	CO-5	CO-6	CO-7	CO-8	CO-9
U3-O1	3	-	-	2	1	1	-	-	-
U3-O2	2	-	2	-	-	2	-	-	-
U3-O3	1	2	3	-	1	-	-	-	-
U3-O4	-	-	2	-	-	-	-	-	-
U3-O5	3	-	-	2	1	3	-	-	1
U3-O6	-	-	2	-	-	2	-	-	2

PROOF STRATEGIES

3.1 INTRODUCTION TO PROOF METHODS AND STRATEGIES

To justify that the computer program works properly, you might have run it on a few sample data sets and checked whether the output is as expected. As an example, consider writing a program for computing factorial of a positive integer. A typical approach is to give small positive numbers such as 3, 4, 5, 6, 7 as input to your factorial program, and run your program to verify that your program gives the expected output (in this case, the expected output is: 6, 24, 120, 720, 5040). Even professional software developers rely on such "verification" and claim that they have "proved" that their program is "correct". However, this approach does not guarantee that the program would work correctly for all possible data sets (for factorial program, for inputs such as ninety seven, five lakh sixty-seven thousand two hundred nineteen, eighty two lakhs thirty seven thousand four hundred and seventy two, and even larger values). Infinitely many input data sets are possible for many programs software developer writes. Additionally, his/her programs run on a machine having limitations with finitely many resources (finite memory, finite time to run the programs, concurrent sharing of resources), and they run in software environment that manages resources.

As a slight digression, let us consider the following propositions:

Question 3.1.1: Given any two real values a, and b, (that is, for a, and $b \in \mathbf{R}$), does there exist (at least one) other real number, say c, such that the following equation is satisfied:

$$a^2 + b^2 = c^2 \quad (\text{for } a, b, \text{ and } c \in \mathbf{R}) \qquad \ldots \qquad (1.1)$$

Have you come across the above proposition in your school mathematics (geometry) book(s)? Is the above proposition obvious? Which type(s) of proof would you use to prove the same?

Question 3.1.2: Let us modify the above proposition to restrict all values of a, b, and c to rational numbers. (that is, for a, b, $c \in \mathbf{Q}$). Given a, and b both (arbitrary) rational numbers, does there exist (at least one) other rational number, say c, such that the following equation is satisfied:

$$a^2 + b^2 = c^2 \quad (\text{for } a, b, \text{ and } c \in \mathbf{Q}) \qquad \ldots (1.2)$$

Have you come across the above proposition in your school algebra book(s)? Is the above proposition obvious? Which proof would you use to provc the same? In case the above (1.2) does not hold for any arbitrary a, and b as rational numbers, can you state the restrictions on a, and b as rational numbers, so that the above (1.2) would hold? You may note that, this question essentially involves the characterization of the property, expressed in the form of (i) if and only if statement, or as (ii) necessity and sufficiency. At this stage, you are encouraged to review the meaning of the words "necessity" and "sufficiency" from Module on Logic, as included in its part I on Propositional Logic, when we discussed Conditionals.

In the context of Question 1.2 above, consider the value of $a = 1$, and value of $b = 1$. Now this question reduces to the following question.

Question 3.1.3: Does there exist a rational number, say c, such that the following equation is satisfied:

$$2 = c^2 \quad (\text{for } c \in \mathbf{Q}) \qquad \ldots (1.3)$$

This question essentially is the famous proposition, namely, "square root of two is irrational", whose proof is given in school level mathematics books. You are encouraged to review the same, specially in the light of earlier questions (together with your attempts for answering them), and fix your conceptual understanding about the issues involved. You may also note that we have briefly touched upon about the (need for the existence of) irrational numbers in part 4 of the Module on Sets, Relations, and Functions. When we revisit the section on Proof by Contradiction (PC), we shall sketch very briefly this proof of the fact that square root of two is irrational.

Let us now modify the Question 1.2 to restrict the values a, b, c to positive integers.

Question 3.1.4: Let us modify the above proposition to restrict all values of a, b, and c to positive integer numbers. (that is, for $a, b, c \in \mathbb{Z}^{+}$). Given a, and b both (arbitrary) positive integer numbers, does there exist (at least one) other positive integer number, say c , such that the following equation is satisfied:

$$a^2 + b^2 = c^2 \quad (\text{for } a, b, \text{ and } c \in \mathbb{Z}^{+}) \qquad \ldots (1.4)$$

For arbitrary positive integer numbers a, and b, other positive integer c, such that the equation (1.4) is satisfied may not exist. For example, taking $a = 1$, and $b = 1$, there is no positive integer c, such that (3.4) is satisfied. However, by taking $a = 3$, and $b = 4$, we have c = 5 so that (1.4) is satisfied. Such triples (*e.g.* (3,4,5)) of positive integers are called as **Pythagorean triples**. Passingly, we note the geometrical interpretation of the Pythagorean triple (3,4,5) as right angled triangle on Euclidean (flat) surface with base of 3 units, and height as 4 units have the diagonal measuring 5 units. There exist infinitely many Pythagorean triples. in fact, you may observe that it is quick to construct, from the base Pythagorean triple (3,4,5), other Pythagorean triple (6,8,10), just by doubling the values of a, b, c each. You may choose to triple them to get other Pythagorean triple (9,12,15), and so on by multiplying a, b, c any positive integer.

However, you may also note that, there is other Pythagorean triple, say (5, 12, 13) that cannot be derived from the base triple (3,4,5). We observe that, in the Pythagorean triples (3,4,5) as well as(5, 12, 13), there is exactly one even number and two odd numbers. Constructivists are interested in characterizing such nontrivial Pythagorean base triples.

Can Pythagorean triples with two even numbers and exactly one odd number exist? Can Pythagorean triples with all three odd numbers exist?

Pierre J. Fermat posed slightly different version of our Question 1.4, by modifying it as the following.

(source: Image taken from https://www.bbvaopenmind.com/en/science/leading-figures/fermat-and-the-greatest-problem-in-the-history-of-mathematics/)

Question 3.1.5: Let a, b, and c be positive integer numbers, (that is, for $a, b, c \in \mathbb{Z}^+$). Does there exist a **Fermat triple (*a*, *b*, *c*)** of **positive integers**, such that the following equation is satisfied:

$$a^n + b^n = c^n \quad (\text{for } a, b, \text{ and } c \in \mathbb{Z}^+, n \geq 3) \qquad \text{... (1.5)}$$

While he scribbled in his note that he had worked out an elegantly short proof about the non-existence of **Fermat triple (*a*, *b*, *c*)** of **positive integers**, no one could decipher his proof till date. The non-existence of Fermat Triples as stated by Fermat came to be known as Fermat's Last Theorem. The 1670 edition of Diophantus's *Arithmetica* includes Fermat's commentary, referred to as his "Last Theorem" (*Observatio Domini Petri de Fermat*), posthumously published by his son (its exact version is available on the website https://en.wikipedia.org/wiki/Fermat%27s_Last_Theorem#/media/File:Diophantus-II-8-Fermat.jpg).

Mathematicians did not accept it as theorem, but at "Conjecture" till 1994. This is because, no one could give its acceptable proof till 1994. The question eluded the greatest minds for centuries, with many attempts for the same.

The complete and celebrated proof of Fermat's Last Theorem as we accept it now was first given by the British mathematician Andrew Wiles in 1994, and it is published in 1995.

(source: Image taken from https://en.wikipedia.org/wiki/Andrew_Wiles)

The above discussion emphasizes the nontrivial creative and innovative energy needed in proof techniques.

Let us come back to our discussion about computer science, and importance of proofs in it.

To get some insight about proving the correctness of such a computer program, we need to rely on some well-known proof strategies. Software developers constantly develop new programs, and they must "prove" the correctness of their programs. Many professional software developers only verify the behaviour of their software for few cases (like the toy example for factorial, where you might verified that it worked "correctly" for 3, 4, 5, 6, 7 as input) consider such verification as a "proof" to claim that their program/software has been "proven" to work "correctly" for all situations! Sadly, the mistakes/slips in their software remain very common and they cost us dearly (not just in terms of money, but their potential for resulting in disasters like widespread power failure, accidents in nuclear reactors, aeroplanes, bullet trains, automated plants, drug design, and even for their impact on disturbing balance in nature resulting in increased pollution, melting of glaciers, impact on agriculture, etc). These observations have resulted in the accumulated body of knowledge in terms of art and craft of software development, and last six decades have resulted in constant updates in this area; some of them are covered in subsequent courses in Computer Science and Engineering (CSE). In this module, we review known proof strategies for proving mathematical theorems. These strategies are important as they form a convenient toolbox for CSE professional in his/her professional career.

What are proof strategies? In our study of Module on Logic, we have already stated inference rules and how to write down "proofs" using these inference rules. We also observed that construction of "short" (and what we refer to as "elegant") proof requires practice about deciding which inference rule(s) are to be applied, and it is like a jigsaw puzzle. The same analogy gets carried over for proof strategies. The proofs are like jigsaw puzzles. In jigsaw puzzles, we need to put in all pieces together so that all of them fit properly to create the end-result (final picture in puzzle). We do not have a recipe to solve such puzzles; however, with some experience for solving such puzzles, we know that there are some strategies that work better. In this module, we study a few of such strategies. In fact, in modules on Logic, as well as on Sets, Relations and Functions, we have already made use of some proof strategies in order to prove some interesting theorems/properties. In this module, we re-state them so that we have these strategies are available to us at one place. It would be convenient for us to recollect them when we need to deploy them for new proof.

3.2 TERMINOLOGY

The *definition* is logical, precise, unambiguous explanation of the (special, sometimes also called as 'technical') meaning of the term. Some knowledge about the topic(s) for which we are discussing is needed, and we state the definitions with this assumption. In the absence of such definitions, it would have been a very confusing and difficult task to even start clear and (somewhat) unambiguous discussion that we are engaged (e.g., in module one, concerning Logic, and module two, concerning Sets, Relations and Functions) with.

Mathematics (and indeed any theory of knowledge, *e.g.*, Psychology, Physics, Chemistry, Biology, *etc.*), starts with assuming/defining terms that seem to be 'obvious'. Our understanding of mathematics/body of knowledge grows when we engage in deriving logical consequences of our assumptions/definitions. The process results in accumulation of such logical consequences that are of enough interest (from the point of view of using them; these uses may not be restricted to practical situations) from intellectual/conceptual point of view.

Once we have recognised such a logical consequence to be of great interest, we call it as a *theorem*. Since theorem is a logical consequence of some other already known fact(s) and/or definition(s) in the area/domain of our exploration, it is typically an "if .. then .." statement ('conditional'), and it is a *true* statement (in given theory/ body of knowledge we deal with). In the parlance of proofs, to distinguish, a statement that is not (at least independently) of great interest, and hence not significant, is called as *proposition*. A proposition, whose main purpose is to lead us to a theorem, is called as a *lemma*. Thus, a *lemma* helps us to prove a theorem. After a theorem is established/ proposition is stated, its obvious/quick consequence is called as *corollary*.

A *proof* of a theorem is a revelation about the process (*i.e.*, a sequence, or trail) of logical consequence(s) to the extent that we, having some knowledge in the relevant domain, accept it with 'conviction'. Logicians, mathematicians, (and sometimes scientists) however, been painfully been aware of the western world's slippery convictions (*e.g.* prosecution of Galileo for his support of his theory of heliocentrism, which upholds that Earth and planets revolve around Sun).

Indeed, in modules one (dealing with Logic) and in Module two (dealing with Sets, Relations, and Functions), we attempted to make precise such *convincing revelation*(s), that we called as '*proof*'(s), and we have already introduced construction of proofs for (logical) arguments. We saw that the (logical) arguments have premises as well as a conclusion. Premises have a role of either earlier proven (assumed to be true) theorems, or definitions (assumptions, axioms, which we assume to be true). To reach to the conclusion logically, we saw the discipline of applying only one logical equivalence / logical implication at a time (using suitable substitution rule), sequentially numbering all steps one-by-one, and reaching to the conclusion in finitely many steps. While writing down such a proof consists of finitely many steps, these steps may become too many to be unwieldy, thereby we are having a fear of getting lost in the details. Such an approach is not desirable because it would not emphasize on the explicit insight of main part of proof. However, we note that, such a 'high level' details of the proof need to be written in such a way that it is revealing to the reader. For this purpose, it is assumed that the reader of the proof has some domain knowledge that forms understanding of words, symbols, and their meanings that the author of proof wants to convey. The author of the proof as well as the reader need to have precise and exact understanding of these meanings, so that the essence of proof in unambiguously conveyable and legible.

In this module, we restate some main strategies in construction the proofs. While we cannot cover all proofs and we do claim to be exhaustive, we review some main proof strategies in this module. These proof strategies would form a repository of techniques for construction of proof(s).

3.3 Direct Proof (also called as Forward Proof)

To prove the statements which are in the form of conditionals (*i.e.* of the form $P \rightarrow Q$), we suppose that P is true (we assume that it is true), and using known facts, and inference rules in logic, we prove that Q is true.

The theorem is typically a *conditional* statement; hence it involves two parts: the *hypothesis* and the *conclusion*. To prove the theorem, we first need to clearly identify all hypotheses.

With your earlier exposure to integers, we assume what is an even integer and what is odd integer. (We would give little more format treatment about these concepts in the next section; however, as an illustration, we state the following proposition.

Proposition 3.3.1: If i is even integer, then $(i+1)$ is odd integer.

Proof: As an illustration of the Direct Proof (also called as Forward Proof), the reader is encouraged to assume that " i is even integer." Using the (intuitive, or formal, depending on the reader's current background), the reader is encouraged to construct, as illustrative exercise, the direct proof to conclude that "($i+1$) is odd integer."

□

In the module on Sets, Relations and Functions, we came across many examples of this proof techniques. At this stage, the reader is encouraged to review how we used direct proof technique in Theorems 1.14 (concerning the number of elements in the union of two sets in the module on Sets, Relations and Functions), Example 1.18 (where we established, *i.e.* proved, the subset relationship in two set expressions in the module on Sets, Relations and Functions), Example 2.5 (again, where we established, *i.e.* proved, the subset relationship in other two set expressions, involving Cartesian Product, in the module on Sets, Relations and Functions), and many more proofs that we already covered in earlier modules (You are encouraged to revisit the earlier modules to check which ones are examples of Direct Proof strategy).

3.4 RECASTING THE STATEMENTS AS CONDITIONS FOR PROOF

Consider the following statement:

Proposition 3.4.1: The cube of every negative real number is negative.

The statement is not stated as conditional (*i.e.*, "if … then …") statement. However, with our familiarity of Predicate logic, we realise that this statement is universally quantified. When we consider the domain of discourse to be the set of negative real numbers, denoted by $\mathbf{R}^-$, we have the following formulation.

$$\forall x \in \mathbf{R}^- \, ((x^3 < 0)) \quad \ldots (4.1)$$

To illustrate the point that conditional can be used as a re-statement of universally quantified formula, let us consider the domain of discourse to be the set of real numbers. In this domain of discourse, this statement is a theorem. We may formulate the above as universally quantified formula given below.

We note that all variables in the above are bound, and hence its truth value is either true or false.

Thus, the statement:

The cube of every negative real number is negative.

can be is either true or false.

To prove this proposition (as true), we may like to re-state the above statement as follows.

$$\forall x\ [x \in \mathbf{R} \mid (x < 0) \rightarrow (x^3 < 0)] \qquad \ldots (4.2)$$

The antecedent part of conditional allows us to start the forward (also called as "direct") proof by assuming the antecedent as one of the premises. This would allow us to use 'direct proof' as strategy. Sometimes, we may not succeed in working out the direct proof.

3.5 Indirect Proof (Also Called as Contrapositive Proof)

Suppose i is an integer. Consider the following proposition.

Proposition 3.5.1: If ($121*i + (679*i+986)^{1357} + 54343$) is even integer, then i is odd integer.

The forward (i.e., direct proof) for this proposition requires you to assume the proposition "($121*i + (679*i+986)^{1357} + 54343$) is even integer". This allows you to write down the following:

Proposition 3.5.2:

"there exists some integer, say, j, such that $121*i + (679*i+986)^{1357} + 54343 = 2 * j$.

This "*defining property*" of even integer (refer to however has resulted in introduction of new integer j (which is, however, dependent on i, as per the above relationship. Is it functional relationship?). Direct proof (or, forward proof) requires you to assume proposition 5.2 and proceed in step-by-step fashion, by applying inference rules that we studied in the module in logic, to prove that i is odd integer.

While it is not very difficult to work out the forward proof as well for the above proposition (the reader is encouraged to do the same), recasting the above proposition in its contrapositive equivalent is more clean and systematic way of expressing the main argument in your forward proof (if you succeeded in working out the same).

Hence, let us state the contrapositive of Proposition 5.1 as follows.

Proposition 3.5.3: If i is even integer, the $(121*i + (679*i+986)^{1357} + 54343)$ is odd integer.

Proof: As an illustration of the Direct Proof (also called as Forward Proof), the reader is encouraged to assume that "i is even integer." Using the (intuitive, or formal, depending on the reader's current background), the reader is encouraged to construct, as illustrative exercise, the direct proof to conclude that "$(121*i + (679*i+986)^{1357} + 54343)$ is odd integer."

□

3.6 PROOF BY CONTRADICTION (PC)

In the module on Sets, Relations, and Functions, we came across some of the excellent examples of proof by contradiction. Once such examples that we considered is the Theorem 4.1 of the module on Sets, Relations, and Functions. A few are as follows:

(i) Let us recall that theorem; it states: "The set of real numbers from 0 upto 1 is not countable". To convince yourself about this proof technique, you are encouraged to revisit its proof as given in Module on Sets, relations, and Functions (Part 4).

(ii) Let us recall the proof of Theorem 4.2: (Cantor's) Power set Theorem of the Module on Sets, Relations, and Functions. This theorem essentially states that any set and its power set cannot be put in one-to-one correspondence. This implied to us that we are allowed to construct "hierarchy" of infinite sets, none of which can be put in one-to-one correspondence. The proof that we gave in that we gave for Power Set Theorem in Module on Sets, Relations and Functions is one of the excellent examples of Proof by Contradiction.

Is it possible for you construct Direct proof for these two examples? You may note that such questions, as investigated by mathematicians and logicians, have led to interesting developments.

There are infinitely many tasks that we may want computing devises to preform, but none of computing devises would ever be able to perform them. In fact, the arguments in the above two examples are extensively applied in Computer Science using famous "Diagonalization" argument. This "Diagonalization argument" essentially relies on this proof technique, namely Proof by Contradiction.

In the remaining part of this section, primarily for strengthening conceptual understanding, let us continue our exposition of Proof by Contradiction in layman's language.

Let us revisit Proposition 4.1. When we are at loss about working out the direct proof of this proposition, we may raise the following question.

(i) Is it false? If it is false, what is strategy to prove that it is false?

For this purpose, we note the negation of (4.1), which is given below.

$$\exists x\ [x \in \mathbf{R} \mid (x < 0) \wedge \sim (x^3 < 0)] \qquad \ldots (6.1)$$

The expression in (3.3) is equivalent to the following.

$$\exists x\ [x \in \mathbf{R} \mid (x < 0) \wedge (x^3 \geq 0)] \qquad \ldots (6.2)$$

When we try to disprove it, and we do not seem to make progress about it, we may come back to the earlier case, as given below.

(ii) Is it true? What should be our strategy to prove that it is true?

The reader is encouraged to explore deployment of appropriate proof techniques to questions like these.

Theorem 3.6.1 (Question 1.3 revisited): Square root of two (denoted as $\sqrt{2}$) irrational.

Sketch of Proof: (Proof by contradiction). Suppose the contrary. Thus, we are allowed to assume that square root of two is rational. By the definition of rational number that we know, we may write,

$\sqrt{2} = \frac{p}{q}$, with p integer, q positive integer (not equal to zero),

and no common factor between p and q, *i.e.* (GCD(p,q) = 1) (such numbers are also called as relatively prime, *i.e.*, p and q are relatively prime.

... (6.3)

Squaring both sides of (x.x), and multiplying both sides by q^2, we obtain,

$$p^2 = 2*q^2 \quad \text{... (6.4)}$$

Hence, by the definition of the even number, p^2 must be even. This implies that p must be even. Hence, we can write,

$$p = 2*s \quad \text{for some positive integer } s \quad \text{... (6.5)}$$

Squaring both sides of (6.5), we get,

$$p^2 = 4*s^2 \quad \text{for some positive integer } s \qquad \ldots (6.6)$$

Substituting (6.6) into (6.4), we get,

$$4*s^2 = 2*q^2 \qquad \ldots (6.7)$$

Dividing both Left Hand Side (LHS) and Right Hand Side (RHS) of (6.7), we get,

$$2*s^2 = q^2 \qquad \ldots (6.8)$$

This implies that q is even. However, with the assumption that $\sqrt{2}$ is rational, p is also even. Thus, p, and q both are forced to be even, thereby implying that $(GCD(p,q) \geq 2)$, and hence p, and q have common factor greater than or equal to two, *i.e.*, p and q are not relatively prime. This however, contradicts our assumed representation of any rational number to be represented in the form $\frac{p}{q}$, with p and q are relatively prime.

We may like to note that the source of this contradiction is our assumption that $\sqrt{2}$ is rational. Hence, using the proof by contradiction technique, we have proved that $\sqrt{2}$ is not rational. Hence, we proved that $\sqrt{2}$ is irrational.

□

Example 3.6.1: Prove that, there are no positive integer solutions for the equation:

$x^2 - y^2 = 6.$

Solution: Let us assume that there are positive integer solutions for variables x, as well as y. With the integer solutions for x, as well as y, we note that $(x+y)$ is integer, as well as $(x-y)$ is integer. Since $x^2 - y^2 = (x+y)\times(x-y)$, two distinct factors of 6 must be either $(x+y)$, or $(x-y)$.

Let us now examine two positive integer factors of 6. Let us call them say p, q. Thus, $6 = p\times q$. We know that $6 = 2\times3$, or 1×6.

Equating the two factors to $(x+y)$, $(x-y)$, we note that the following four cases arise.

Case I: $(x+y) = 2$, $(x-y) = 3$. This gives, $x = 5/2$, $y = -1/2$, both are non-integers.

Case II: $(x+y) = 3$, $(x-y) = 2$. This gives, $x = 5/2$, $y = 1/2$, both are non-integers.

Case III: $(x+y) = 1$, $(x-y) = 6$. This gives, $x = 7/2$, $y = -5/2$, both are non-integers.

Case IV: $(x+y) = 6$, $(x-y) = 1$. This gives, $x = 7/2$, $y = 5/2$, both are non-integers.

Let us now examine the other possibility of negative integer factors of 6. Let us call them say p, q. Thus, $6 = p\times q$. We know that $6 = (-2)\times(-3)$, or $(-1)\times(-6)$.

Equating the two factors to $(x+y)$, $(x-y)$, we note that the following additional four cases arise.

Case V: $(x+y) = -2$, $(x-y) = -3$. This gives, $x = -5/2$, $y = 1/2$, both are non-integers.

Case VI: $(x+y) = -3$, $(x-y) = -2$. This gives, $x = -5/2$, $y = -1/2$, both are non-integers.

Case VII: $(x+y) = -1$, $(x-y) = -6$. This gives, $x = -7/2$, $y = 5/2$, both are non-integers.

Case VIII: $(x+y) = -6$, $(x-y) = -1$. This gives, $x = -7/2$, $y = -5/2$, both are non-integers.

These are the only possible cases, and contradiction arises in all cases. Hence, due to the proof by contradiction, the original statement follows.

In your school mathematics, you have already read about the following interesting theorem about primes.

Theorem 3.6.2. There are infinitely many primes.

Hint for sketch of Proof: Proof by contradiction is used to prove the existence of infinitely primes.

Additional exercises (for practice)

Exercise 6.1: Prove that there are no integer solutions for the equation $y^2 = 4x + 3$

Exercise 3.6.2: Prove that $\log_2 7$ is irrational.

We note that somewhat formal treatment is needed to establish the context to precisely communicate the notions involved in the proof strategies. Hence, in the next subsection, we briefly review formal concepts involved in numbers.

3.7 NUMBERS: SOME DEFINITIONS

In module on Sets, we have encountered sets of numbers: (i) $\mathbb{N}$: Natural numbers, (ii) $\mathbb{Z}$: Integers, (iii) **Q** : Rationals, and (iv) **R** : Reals. We assume some familiarity with these numbers, especially usual ordering relationship, operations like addition, subtraction, multiplication, division and exponentiation and their closure (as well as non-closure) properties as defined on these sets.

Number theory mainly deals with the set of integers. To set our notations and ensure common understanding, we give several definitions below.

Notation 3.7.1: (*divides*) We use the notation $a \mid b$ to denote " a divides b". In the expression $a \mid b$, we call the first number, *i.e.* number a as *divisor*, and the second number *i.e.* number b as *dividend.*

Notation 3.7.2: (*is integer multiple of*) We use the notation $d \mid c$ to denote "c is integer multiple of d". (also "d divides c").

Definition 3.7.1: (*divides*) Given two integers a and b, we define $a \mid b$ (to be read as "a divides b") when there is an integer, say q, such that $b = qa$, *i.e.*, b is some *integer multiple* of a.
In other words,

$$a \mid b \equiv (\exists q \in \mathbb{Z})[b = qa] \quad \ldots (7.1)$$

Example 3.7.1: We say that:

(i) $7 \mid 42$ (7 divides 42) because 42 is six times 7, *i.e.*, 42 is integer multiple of 7.
(ii) $7 \mid -35$ (7 divides -35) because -35 is -5 times 7, *i.e.*, -35 is integer (here, -5) multiple of 7.
(iii) $-7 \mid 21$ (-7 divides 21) because 21 is -3 times 7, (and -3 is integer).
(iv) $-7 \mid -56$ (-7 divides -56) because -56 is 8 times 7 (and 8 is integer).
(v) 7 does not divide 45, and we denote it by $7 \sim\mid 45$, or by $\sim(7 \mid 45)$.
(vi) 2 does not divide 1, and we denote it by $\sim(2 \mid 1)$.
(vii) 3 does not divide 1, and we denote it by $\sim(3 \mid 1)$.

□

There is difference in the notation $a \mid b$ that we have stated above and a / b (read as "a divided by b", and sometimes in short as, "a by b"). Some differences are as follows.

- The expression $a \mid b$ is a proposition (in the sense that we introduced in the module on logic, refer to equation (3.5) above for our formulation), and hence its value is either true or false (and not any number).
- The expression a / b is a number (it is integer if $b \mid a$, *i.e.*, b divides a; when b does not divide a, the expression a / b is not closed over the set of integers. As an example, we saw in Example 3.1 (v) that $7 \sim\mid 45$ (also sometimes denoted by $7 \nmid 45$), and hence the expression 45/7 dose not result in integer value. When restricted to set of integers, the operation a / b needs to be given some specific meaning. We shall discuss the same below.
- In the expression $a \mid b$, the first operand is *divisor*, and the second operand is *dividend.*
- In the expression a / b, the first operand is *dividend*, and the second operand is *divisor*.

Definition 3.7.2: (*even integer*) Given an integer a, we define a to be "*even*" integer when $2 \mid a$, *i.e.*, there is some integer, say q, such that $a = 2q$, *i.e.*, a is some *integer multiple* of 2.

Although the above definition seems to be stated as a (one way) conditional statement, definitions are essentially biconditional. Thus, it is more precise to state the above definition as follows.

Definition 3.7.3: (*even integer -definition restated as biconditional*) Given an integer a, we define a to be "*even*" integer when and only when $2 \mid a$, *i.e.*, there is some integer, say q, such that $a = 2q$, *i.e.*, a is some *integer multiple* of 2.

Note that the meaning of the propositional connective when and only when is that it is biconditional. As a common convention, and for the purpose of economy of words, we would not use such a language (as used in Definition 7.3, with biconditional connective), for definitions. It would however, be understood as common convention that a conditional in definition essentially denotes a biconditional.

Notation 3.7.3: (Predicate $Even(a)$) Using the definition 7.2 above, we introduce the notation for predicate $Even(a)$ with the domain of discourse being $\mathbb{Z}$, the set of Integers, as follows.

$$Even(a) \equiv 2 \mid a \equiv (\exists q \in \mathbb{Z})[a = 2q] \qquad \ldots (7.2)$$

Example 3.7.2:

(i) $Even(24) \equiv (\exists q \in \mathbb{Z})[24 = 2q]$,

… the RHS predicate logic expression has truth value T (with satisfying value of q being equal to 12, and hence Even(24) is T(rue). We express this fact as: 24 is an even number,

$$Even(24) \equiv \text{T(rue)}.$$

(ii) $Even(19) \equiv (\exists q \in \mathbb{Z})[19 = 2q]$,

… the RHS predicate logic expression has truth value F .. how do you prove this?

… there is no integer q satisfying the property $19 = 2q$). In other words, the following predicate logic expression evaluates to true.

$$\sim \{(\exists q \in \mathbb{Z})[19 = 2q]\} \equiv (\forall q \in \mathbb{Z})[19 \neq 2q], \qquad \ldots (7.3)$$

… how would you prove the RHS of equation (7.3) above?

… would principle of mathematical induction help you to prove the universal quantification $\forall q \in \mathbb{Z}$ in equation (7.3)?

… which proof strategy would work to prove that 19 is not even?

We express this fact as: 19 is not even number, *i.e.,*

$Even(19) \equiv$ F(alse).

(iii) $Even(0) \equiv (\exists q \in \mathbb{Z})[0 = 2q]$,

… the RHS predicate logic expression has truth value T (with satisfying value of q being equal to 0, and hence Even(0) is T(rue). In ordinary language, 0 is an even number. (This may not match with your 'belief'; we have logical explanation why we call 0 an even number),

$Even(0\equiv$ T(rue).

□

We noted the proof strategy for proving the property *Evan*(a) requires us to guess one value, namely $q \in \mathbb{Z}$, satisfying the equation $a = 2q$. It turned out that our *knowledge base* enabled us to "solve" equation $a = 2q$ with known value of a and unknown variable value of $q \in \mathbb{Z}$. While it worked for this specific example, would such "solving" work when we have other properties? In order to enable us to do such "solving", which additional properties we assumed? Recognizing such questions are interesting, investigations about their characteristics, and related aspects, is an interesting part that we would touch upon in our topic in Modular Arithmetic, Algebra and to some extent in other modules of our course. Raising such questions and obtaining their algorithmic answers is basic conceptualization in courses like AI, ML, Security, and other advanced courses in Computer Science and Engineering

Definition 3.7.4: (*odd integer*) Given an integer a, we define a to be "*odd*" integer when $\sim(2 \mid a)$, *i.e.*, when a is not even,
i.e., a is not *integer multiple* of 2,
i.e., there is no integer, say q, such that $a = 2q$.

□

Notation 3.7.4: (Predicate *Odd*(a)) Using the definition 7.3 above, we introduce the notation for predicate *Odd*(a) with the domain of discourse being $\mathbb{Z}$, the set of Integers, as follows.

$$Odd(a) \equiv \sim(2 \mid a) \equiv (\forall q \in \mathbb{Z})[a \neq 2q] \quad \ldots (3.8)$$

Example 3.7.3:

(i) $Odd(24) \equiv (\forall q \in \mathbb{Z})[24 \neq 2q] \equiv \sim \{(\exists q \in \mathbb{Z})[24 = 2q]\}$,

… the last RHS predicate logic expression has truth value F (because, it is in negated form of existentially quantified formula, and existentially quantified part has satisfying value for predicate expression in curly braces for value of q being equal to 12, and hence *Odd*(24) is F(alse). We express this fact as: 24 is not odd number,

$Odd(24) \equiv F$.

(ii) $Odd(19) \equiv (\forall q \in \mathbb{Z})[19 \neq 2q]$,

… the RHS predicate logic expression has truth value T (Refer to notes and questions raised for Example 7.2(ii)). We express this fact as: 19 is odd number,

$Odd(19) \equiv T$.

(iii) $Odd(0) \equiv (\forall q \in \mathbb{Z})[0 \neq 2q] \equiv \sim\{ (\exists q \in \mathbb{Z})[0 = 2q]\}$,

… the last RHS predicate logic expression has truth value F (because, it is in negated form of existentially quantified formula, and existentially quantified part has satisfying value for predicate expression in curly braces for value of q being equal to 0, and hence $Odd(0)$ is F(alse). We express this fact as: 0 is not odd number,

$$Odd(0) \equiv F.$$

□

In Part 4 of Module 2 dealing with Sets, Relations, and Functions, we defined the set of natural numbers using Peano's axioms. The second Peano's axiom states that If $n \in \mathbb{N}$, then $n \cup \{ n \} \in \mathbb{N}$; in simplified and well-known form, we restate it as follows:

$$(\forall n \in \mathbb{N}) [\{ (n \in \mathbb{N}) \rightarrow ((n + 1) \in \mathbb{N})) \} \qquad \ldots (7.9)$$

From (7.9) and the definition of the set of integers $\mathbb{Z}$ (we assume the reader's familiarity with the definition of integers as extension of natural numbers), we have the following proposition.

<u>Proposition 3.7.1</u>: Successor of every integer is an integer; in other words,

$$(\forall i \in \mathbb{Z}) [\{ (i \in \mathbb{Z}) \rightarrow ((i + 1) \in \mathbb{Z})) \} \qquad \ldots (7.10)$$

<u>Theorem 3.7.1</u>: If i is an even integer, then $(i+1)$ is not even integer. In other words, if $2|i$, then $\sim(2|(i+1))$.

Symbolically, we write the above theorem as follows.

$$(\forall i \in \mathbb{Z}) [(2|i) \rightarrow (\sim (2|(i+1))] \qquad \ldots (7.11)$$

At this stage, we request you to re-construct the proof of the above theorem yourself. With our earlier discussion of proof techniques, and your earlier familiarity with proofs, we ask the question for you to think: Which proof strategy is most appropriate prove the above theorem? Are there alternate proof strategies to prove the above theorem that would result in more "elegant" proof?

□

Based on the above theorem, we have the following theorem.

Theorem 3.7.2: (Structure of odd integers): The integer i is odd integer if and only if (*iff*) there is some integer, say q, such that $i = 2q + 1$, *i.e.*, the remainder of integer division $i/2$ is 1.

We omit the proof of this theorem with the remark that it follows from Theorem 3.7.1. In some books, the above theorem is taken as "definition of odd integers"; with that approach, however, you need to "prove" that odd integers have the property that they are not even, *i.e.*, $\sim(2 \mid a)$.

□

In Definition 3.7.1, we introduced the notion of "*divides*", and noted that "*divides*" is binary relationship defined on the set of integers. In terms of this relationship, for every integer $b \in \mathbb{Z}$, we define the set of all divisors of b as follows.

Definition 3.7.5: (*All Divisors*) Given an integer b, we define the set

$$\textit{All-Divisors}(b) = \{ a \in \mathbb{Z} \mid a \mid b \} \qquad \ldots (7.12)$$

That is, the set of all divisors of an integer b is collection (*i.e.* set) of all integers that divide b.

Example 3.7.4:

(i) $\textit{All-Divisors}(24) = \{-24, -12, -8, -6, -3, -2, -1, 1, 2, 3, 6, 8, 12, 24\}$.
We omit the proof as it is straightforward to verify that these fourteen integers are divisors of 24, and there are no more other integers which are divisors of 24.

(ii) $\textit{All-Divisors}(19) = \{-19, -1, 1, 19\}$.

We omit the proof as it is straightforward to verify that these four integers are divisors of 19, and there are no more other integers which are divisors of 19.

(iii) $All\text{-}Divisors(0) = \mathbb{Z}$.

We note that, for any integer a, we have, $0 = 0 \times a$, and hence we have the result that $All\text{-}Divisors(0) = \mathbb{Z}$.

□

In Computer Science and Cryptography, it is common convention to restrict our discussion to positive integers $\mathbb{Z}^+$, and hence we consider only *positive divisors*. With this modification, we restate the definition of set of *positive divisors* (sometimes also called as *Divisors*) as follows.

Definition 3.7.6: (*Positive-Divisors*) Given an integer b, we define the set

$$Positive\text{-}Divisors(b) = \{ a \in \mathbb{Z}^+ \mid a \mid b \} \quad \ldots (7.13)$$

That is, the set of positive divisors of an integer b is collection (*i.e.* set) of all positive integers that divide b.

Example 3.7.5:

(i) $Positive\text{-}Divisors(24) = Positive\text{-}Divisors(-24) = \{1, 2, 3, 6, 8, 12, 24\}$.

We omit the proof as it is straightforward to verify that these seven positive integers are divisors of 24, and there are no more other positive integers which are divisors of 24.

(ii) $Positive\text{-}Divisors(19) = Positive\text{-}Divisors(-19) = \{1, 19\}$.

We omit the proof as it is straightforward to verify that these two positive integers are divisors of 19, and there are no more other positive integers which are divisors of 19.

(iii) $Positive\text{-}Divisors(0) = \mathbb{Z}^+$.

We note that, for any integer a, we have, $0 = 0 \times a$, and hence we have the result that $Positive\text{-}Divisors(0) = \mathbb{Z}^+$.

□

In the discussions in Computer Science, especially in Cryptography and Security, we restrict the domain of discourse to the set of natural numbers ℕ. From the above discussion, and Example 3.5, we have the following lemma.

Proposition 7.2: (*Trivial Divisors*) Given a natural number $n \in \mathbb{N}$, we have,

(i) 1 divides *n*, and,
(ii) *n* divides *n*.

Proof of the lemma follows from the definition of divides relationship, and sketch is briefly stated below.

(i) Consider the proposition : $1 \mid n \;\equiv\; (\exists q \in \mathbb{Z})[n = q \times 1]$
... the RHS predicate evaluates to True when we choose $q = n$.
Hence, the result that 1 divides *n*.

(ii) Consider the proposition : $n \mid n \;\equiv\; (\exists q \in \mathbb{Z})[n = q \times n]$
... the RHS predicate evaluates to True when we choose q = 1 (the multiplicative identity).
Hence, the result that 1 divides *n*.

□

Do we have two distinct trivial divisors or 1? Do we have any other number having such a property?

Example 3.7.6:

(i) *Trivial-Divisors*(24) = {1, 24}.
(ii) *Trivial-Divisors*(19) = {1, 19}.
(iii) *Trivial-Divisors*(0) = {1, 0}.
(iv) *Trivial-Divisors*(2) = {1, 2}.
(v) *Trivial-Divisors*(1) = {1}.

□

Definition 3.7.7: (*Nontrivial-Divisors*) For a given natural number $n \in \mathbb{N}$, Lemma 3.1 gives us its trivial divisors as 1, and *n* itself. All other positive divisors of *n* are defined as nontrivial divisors of n. Thus, we define the set of non-trivial divisors as a set difference below.

For $n \in \mathbb{N}$, *we have,*
Nontrivial-Divisors(n) = *Positive-Divisors*(n) – *Trivial-Divisors*(n) ... (7.14)

Example 3.7.7:

(i) *Nontrivial-Divisors*(24) = {2, 3, 6, 8, 12}.
(ii) *Nontrivial-Divisors*(19) = Φ.
(iii) *Nontrivial-Divisors*(2) = Φ.
(iv) *Nontrivial-Divisors*(0) = $\mathbb{N} - \{1, 0\}$,
(v) *Nontrivial-Divisors*(1) = Φ, so 1 has empty set of non-trivial divisors.

□

Definition 3.7.7: (*absence of nontrivial divisors*) Given a natural number $n \in \mathbb{N}$, we define n to have absence of nontrivial divisors when its set of nontrivial divisors is a null set.

□

With the absence of nontrivial divisors, we have made our progress about developing some understanding of prime numbers; however, we are still missing some aspect of prime numbers. Fundamental theorem of arithmetic states that any natural number greater than 1 can be expressed as unique product of primes. This property would not hold when we allow 1 to have the status of prime (because 1 raised to any number, say 1^{26543} remains 1, so it would not allow unique product for numbers). This is one reason why the number 1is not regarded as prime. Hence, we refine the approach as below.

Definition 7.8: (*Prime numbers*): A given natural number $n \geq 2$ is prime when its set of positive divisors has two *distinct* and no more elements. These only two *distinct* divisors are the trivial divisors. We also noted that the two trivial divisors are: (i) multiplicative identity, *i.e.* 1, and, (ii) the number n itself.

Since 1 does not have two distinct divisors, it is excluded to be prime in the above definition.

<u>Theorem 3.7.1:</u> Prime numbers are infinitely many.

(**<u>Sketch of</u>**) **<u>Proof</u>**: The proof strategy is to use Proof by Contradiction (PC).

To start the argument in Proof by Contradiction, we assume that Prime numbers are not infinitely many; *i.e.*, we assume that Prime numbers are finitely many.

Let us consider the set of all these prime numbers, and denote the set by some symbol, say $\mathbb{P}$. By our assumption, the set $\mathbb{P}$ is finite, and it contains all prime numbers. Thus, in case we come across any prime number, we expect it to be a member of the set $\mathbb{P}$.

Now let us rethink about whether all primes would be member of the set $\mathbb{P}$. For this investigation, let us consider an arbitrary element p that is in $\mathbb{P}$. Let us multiply all elements in $\mathbb{P}$, and add one to the product obtained. This means, we construct, from elements of $\mathbb{P}$, a new number, say q, by the following operation:

$$q = \{\prod_{p \in P} p + 1\} \qquad \dots (7.15)$$

We note that $q > p$, for every $p \in \boldsymbol{P}$. Additionally, when we observe that q is not divisible by any $p \in \boldsymbol{P}$. Thus, we constructed a new number that is greater than all primes (that we collected in the set $\mathbb{P}$, and this new number is not divisible by any prime (because of our assumption, we had all primes already included in $\mathbb{P}$). Hence q qualifies to be prime, and thus, it should have been an element of $\mathbb{P}$. Thus, we reached the contradiction.
Hence we have proved that prime numbers are infinitely many.

□

<u>Definition 3.7.9</u>: (*Composite numbers*): A given natural number $n \geq 2$ is composite when we can express n as being equal to $a \times b$, with $a, b \geq 2$, and $a \in \mathbb{Z}^+ \wedge a \geq 2$, $b \in \mathbb{Z}^+ \wedge b \geq 2$.

We did not define a number to be composite if it is not prime. We note that the number 1 has unique properties: it is neither *prime* nor *composite*. Hence, composite number cannot be defined to be a number that is not prime.

Proposition 3.7.3 (some Closure properties of Integers): For integers a, b, c, we have:

(i) $a + b \in \mathbb{Z}$

(ii) $a - b \in \mathbb{Z}$

(iii) $a.b$ (also written as: $a \times b$, or simply ab when there is no ambiguity) $\in \mathbb{Z}$

□

The set of integers is not closed under division operation, However, when we have two integers a, b, satisfying the property that a divides b (we introduced the notation 3.1 to denote it as $a \mid b$), the division operation on the set of integers is closed.

Definition 3.7.8 (quotient): When a divides b, the result is an integer, which is also called as *quotient*, and it is normally denoted by the symbol q.

We allowed the numbers a as well as b to be negative integers. When both numbers a as well as b are negative, we choose to drop the negative signs of both integers, thereby considering the *divisor* (*i.e.* number a) as well as *dividend* (*i.e.* number b) to be positive integers. When one of these two numbers is negative, the quotient is negative integer. In such a case, without loss of generality, we assign the negative sign to *dividend* (*i.e.* number b). This convention allows us to consider the *divisor* to be always a positive integer. We note that the divisor is positive integer, and thus we have avoided division by zero (*i.e.*, we excluded the case of *divisor* (*i.e.* number a) being zero (additive identity)).

We already made use of the proposition 7.3 as well as the above closure of division operation when we defined $a \mid b$ in Definition 1.1 and expressed the proposition $a \mid b$ as quantified formula $(\exists q \in \mathbb{Z})\ [b = qa]$ in equation (4.4) earlier. What happens when the proposition $a \mid b$ is false?

We have already seen that the set of natural numbers, denoted by $\mathbb{N}$, includes the number zero, and zero is the least element in $\mathbb{N}$. For the following discussion, we find it convenient to introduce a notation for a finite set consisting of first n natural numbers.

Notation 3.7.5: We introduce the notation $[n]$ to represent the set of first n natural numbers (starting with and including 0). Thus,

$$[n] = \{ 0, 1, \ldots, n-1\} \qquad \ldots (7.16)$$

When we have two integers such that a does not divide b, the result of division b/a does not result in an integer, and hence the division operation b/a is not closed for the set of integers $\mathbb{Z}$. We also noted that we do not allow division by zero by restricting our divisor to be a positive integer. In this setting, we are now ready to state the following proposition, also known as division algorithm.

Proposition 7.4: (Division Algorithm). Given a pair of two numbers a and b such that $a \in \mathbb{Z}^+$ and $b \in \mathbb{Z}$ (*i.e.*, given $(a, b) \in \mathbb{Z}^+ \times \mathbb{Z}$), there exists a *unique* pair (q, r) where q is positive integer and r is natural number with the property that $0 \leq r < q$, (*i.e.*, $\exists\ (q, r) \in \mathbb{Z} \times [a]$), such that the following holds:

$$b = q\,a + r \qquad \ldots (7.17)$$

The proposition 7.4 is also called as Euclid's Division Lemma.

This proposition is very interesting as it guarantees us the existence of *functional* mapping from the set $\mathbb{Z}^+ \times \mathbb{Z}$ to the set $\mathbb{Z} \times [a]$, where a is the first element of the corresponding tuple in the domain set $\mathbb{Z}^+ \times \mathbb{Z}$ in a functional map.

In the above, we observe that the description of the functional mapping required us to define the codomain set as $\mathbb{Z} \times [a]$, where a is the first element of a tuple in the domain set $\mathbb{Z}^+ \times \mathbb{Z}$ in a functional map.

To avoid this reference to the first element of a tuple in the domain set in a functional map, we could have allowed more (than required) elements in the codomain set, by stating the structure of codomain set as $\mathbb{Z} \times \mathbb{N}$.

To restrict the codomain set from this more general structure $\mathbb{Z} \times \mathbb{N}$ to $\mathbb{Z} \times [a]$, we needed to "extract" the first component value of tuple in the domain set $\mathbb{Z}^{+} \times \mathbb{Z}$ in a functional map. While this violates the principle of working at abstract high level of sets, it allowed us to restrict our codomain set by making use of the value of the element being mapped.

Can you observe the usefulness of such formulation(s) for the purpose of efficiency in Relational Databases? Do Edger F. Codd's conceptual proposal for relational databases have a place for such formulations?

We note that the uniqueness of pair (q, r) in equation (7.16) above follows because of well-ordering property of the set of natural numbers. We encourage the reader to convince himself about the same.

In modular arithmetic, we care only about the remainders. Some interesting properties of this modular arithmetic is at youtube video https://www.youtube.com/watch?v=6ZrO90AI0c8

3.8 Proof by Necessity and Sufficiency

3.8.1 Necessity

In the module on Logic, we saw that P is necessary (condition) for Q is logically equivalent, in our formal logic notations, as $\sim P \rightarrow \sim Q$, which is logically equivalent to its contrapositive as $Q \rightarrow P$. Hence to prove that P is necessary for Q, the Direct Proof (Forward Proof) would start with assuming Q, and then using application of inference rules at each step, prove P.

3.8.2 *Sufficiency*

In the module on Logic, we saw that P is sufficient (condition) for Q is logically equivalent, in our formal logic notations, as $P \rightarrow Q$. Hence to prove that P is sufficient for Q, the Direct Proof (Forward Proof) would start with assuming P, and then using application of inference rules at each step, prove Q.

3.8.3 *Necessary and Sufficiency*

To prove P is necessary and sufficient (condition) for Q, we prove $(Q \rightarrow P) \wedge (P \rightarrow Q)$. In other words, it is modelled using biconditional logical operation. Thus, P is necessary and sufficient (condition) for Q, means $(P \leftrightarrow Q)$.

3.8.4 *Examples for Necessary and Sufficiency*

Many examples of necessary and sufficiency were already discussed in the module on Sets, Relations and Functions. One type of examples is when we proved logical equivalences as well as set equivalences. Other important use of necessity and sufficiency is to prove the equivalence of apparently different approaches to define the same mathematical (structural) notion. One such example that we considered in the module on Sets, Relations and Functions is the notion of Equivalence Relations and Partitions. In the areas of Computer Science (and in various branches of Engineering as well), we shall encounter many statements involving "necessary and sufficient" conditions.

(i) When we define structure called tree (in module on Graph Theory), we would see its various necessary and sufficient conditions, as defined in terms of various properties of graphs, such as: (i) a connected graph without cycles, (ii) minimally connected graph, etc.

(ii) Some interesting characterizations (necessary and sufficient conditions) that we would cover in the module on Graph Theory are conditions for existence of Planar Graphs, and Eular Graphs. In fact, these necessary and sufficient conditions for trees, Eular Graphs, and Planar Graphs have.

(iii) Abstract Algebra (and Graph Theory) has conceptually deep and interesting applications for design of algorithms in computer science, because it is possible to (re-)formulate interesting tasks in the design of algorithms in terms of special structures as necessary and sufficient conditions.

With this note, we postpone the discussion of such concepts to be covered in various courses in computer science, such as Databases (*e.g.*, characterizing the algorithms for handling concurrent transactions, Computer Networks (*e.g.*, characterization of communication protocols), Cloud Computing and Block Chain (*e.g*, characterization of scheduling of various resources), etc.

3.9 DISPROOF BY A COUNTER-EXAMPLE

Consider the following example.

Example 3.9.1: Consider statement "For every positive integer n, Factorial(n) = $n! \leq 2^n$ ".

We try first few positive integer values for n and find out whether the inequality holds.

For $n = 1$, we have $1! = 1$, and $2^1 = 2$. So, the inequality $1! \leq 2^1$ holds.

For $n = 2$, we have $2!\ 2\times1! = 2$, and $2^1 = 2$. So, the inequality $2! \leq 2^1$ holds.

For $n = 3$, we have $3! = 3\times2! = 6$, and $2^3 = 8$. So, the inequality $3! \leq 2^3$ holds.

For $n = 4$, we have $4! = 4\times3! = 24$, and $2^4 = 16$. So, the inequality $4! \leq 2^4$ does not hold.

Hence, the inequality "$n! \leq 2^n$" does not hold for all positive integers.

□

You may now like to verify how we have used disproof by a counterexample in Examples 3.4, 3.5 in the part 3, dealing with Functions of Module 2: Sets, Relations and Functions.

We now illustrate why disproof by a counter-example is an important proof strategy.

Example 3.9.2: Prove or disprove: All positive integers of the form $2^{2^n}+1$ (with n being positive integer) are prime numbers.

We note that French mathematician Pierre de Fermat (1607-1665) once stated (we call that he conjectured, as he did not give "convincing" proof) that all positive integers of the form $2^{2^n}+1$ (with n being positive integer) are prime numbers.

We note a few values of positive integers of the form $2^{2^n}+1$ in the following.

$2^{2^1}+1 = 4+1 = 5$, known prime number
$2^{2^2}+1 = 16+1 = 17$, known prime number
$2^{2^3}+1 = 256+1 = 257$, known prime number
$2^{2^4}+1 = 65356+1 = 65357$, known prime number
$2^{2^5}+1 = 4,294,967,296 + 1 = 4,294,967,297$

Is the positive integer $2^{2^5}+1 = 4,294,967,297$ prime? Pierre de Fermat thought that it is prime.

In 1729, Swiss mathematician Leonhard Euler (1707-1783) solved this problem in 1729 and he proved that = 4,294,967,297 is not as it be written as the product of 641 and 6,700,417.

□

Example 3.9.3: Prove or disprove: All positive integers of the form $n^2 - n + 41$ (with n being positive integer) are prime numbers.

Solution: For various values of n, we tabulate the values of the expression $n^2 - n + 41$ below.

Number	$n^2 - n + 41$
1	41
2	43
3	47
4	53
5	61
6	71
7	83
8	97
9	113
10	131
11	151
12	173
13	197

After calculating these values for $n = 1$ to 13, we verified in the above table that the values of the expression $n^2 - n + 41$ are prime numbers. Does it guarantee that the values of expression $n^2 - n + 41$ are prime numbers for all values of n ?

Consider the value of expression $n^2 - n + 41$ for value of $n = 41$. The expression evaluates to 41×41, which is clearly non-prime (*i.e.*, composite) number. Thus, value of $n = 41$ is counterexample, and hence we proved that the expression $n^2 - n + 41$ is not prime for all values of n.

□

3.10 PROOF BY EXHAUSTIVE CASES

When the statement says that each of the finite number of distinct cases satisfy some property, it may be possible to prove the statement by considering each of these finite number of cases, and prove that the property holds for each individual case.

Example 3.10.1: You come across the statement, "The number 4 does not divide (n^2+2) for $2 \leq n \leq 6$, n being an integer". We also represent it symbolically as: " $4\sim|(n^2+2)$ for $2 \leq n \leq 6$, n being an integer". Can we prove this statement? Yes, and simple proof is given below.

Proof: The above statement has five distinct cases, viz., $n=2$, $n=3$, $n=4$, $n=5$, $n=6$.

(i) For the case $n=2$, $(n^2+2) = 6$, and since $4\sim|6$, the statement holds.
(ii) For the case $n=3$, $(n^2+2) = 11$, and since $4\sim|11$, the statement holds.
(iii) For the case $n=4$, $(n^2+2) = 18$, and since $4\sim|18$, the statement holds.
(iv) For the case $n=5$, $(n^2+2) = 27$, and since $4\sim|27$, the statement holds.
(v) For the case $n=6$, $(n^2+2) = 38$, and since $4\sim|38$, the statement holds.

Thus, the statement " $4\sim|(n^2+2)$ for $2 \leq n \leq 6$, n being an integer" is true.

□

The above "proof", although acceptable as being correct, it does not allow is to conclude more general (and modified) result "The number 4 does not divide (n^2+2) for n being a positive integer" (How would you prove it? Which proof strategy do you need to prove this?)

Example 3.10.2: Consider the values of Factorial for $n = 2,3$. Suppose we want to establish Factorial(n) $\leq 2^n$, for $n = 2,3$.

Proof: This statement has two distinct cases, viz., $n=2$, $n=3$.

(i) For the case n=2, Factorial(2) = 2, and this value is $\leq 2^2 = 4$, and the statement holds.

(ii) For the case n=3, Factorial(3) = 6, and this value is $\leq 2^3 = 8$, and the statement holds.

Thus, the statement "Factorial(n) $\leq 2^n$, for $n = 2,3$" is true.

□

The above "proof" is acceptable as being correct. Should we hasten to generalize it to "Factorial(n) $\leq 2^n$, for n being a positive integer ≥ 2" ? How would you prove it? Which proof strategy do you need to prove this?

3.11 More Terminology

In Example 9.1, we discovered that the inequality "$n! \leq 2^n$" does not hold for all positive integers. For $n = 4$, we observed that, the inequality "$n! > 2^n$" holds. This leads us to an interesting question: whether "$n! > 2^n$" holds for $n \geq 4$. To investigate this question, we may try a few more values of n, and observe the following.

For $n = 5$, we have $5! = 5\times4! = 120$, and $2^5 = 32$. So, the inequality $5! > 2^5$ holds.

For $n = 6$, we have $6! = 6\times5! = 720$, and $2^6 = 64$. So, the inequality $6! > 2^6$ holds.

For $n = 7$, we have $7! = 7\times6! = 5040$, and $2^7 = 128$. So, the inequality $7! > 2^7$ holds.

We now start suspecting that "the inequality $n! > 2^n$ holds for all $n \geq 4$" might be a true statement. However, note that, with the above numerical verification for a few values of n, we cannot be sure that it would hold for all values of $n \geq 4$. Since we do not yet have a proof for the statement "the inequality $n! > 2^n$ holds for all $n \geq 4$", at this stage, with this state of our knowledge, it is not correct to call it as a theorem. Such interesting statements, which have neither been proven to be true nor have been proven to be false, are called as *conjectures*. Historically, conjectures have played very important role for advancing the state of our knowledge.

The proof needs to be based on inference rules. The statement "the inequality $n!>2^n$ holds for all $n \geq 4$" is in fact a collection of infinitely many statements, and the claim requires us to guarantee that infinitely many statements must be proven to be true. We need to make use of the construction of natural numbers to guarantee that such infinitely many statements can be proven to be true. While it is possible to formally take recourse to Peamo's axioms for Natural numbers to do the same, in an elementary way, we state the *principle of mathematical induction*, using which we can work out proofs for such statements.

3.12 PRINCIPLE OF MATHEMATICAL INDUCTION

In section 9, we came across the statement "the inequality $n! > 2^n$ holds for all $n \geq 4$". We note that this statement involves the parameter n, the natural number. We denote such statement by P(n), which is in fact a one-place predicate involving n as a variable. Suppose that we wish to prove P(n). The principle of mathematical induction allows us to give the proof of such predicates. We state the principle below.

Theorem 3.12.1: (Principle of Mathematical Induction) Let P(n) be the predicate involving n, an arbitrary natural number as a variable. Suppose that the following statements are true:

(1) Basis step : the statement P(a) is true for some $a \in$N,
(2) Inductive step : assuming P(k) ($k \geq a$, and k is arbitrary) is true, we are able to prove that P(k+1) is true.

Then, principle of Mathematical Induction allows us to conclude that P(n) is true for all $n \geq a$.

Example 3.12.1: The inequality $2^n < n!$ holds for all $n \geq 4$, n a natural number.

Proof: We first identify the one-place predicate :

P(n) = $n! < 2^n$ holds for all $n \geq 4$, n a natural number.

We now use principle of Mathematical Induction.

Basis step: For $n = 4$, we verified earlier in section 8.3, that $2^4 < 4!$.

Inductive step: We assume $P(k) \equiv 2^k < k!$ holds for all $k \geq 4$. Assuming this, we now consider 2^{k+1}.

We note that, $2^{k+1} = (2)\times(2^k)$

$$< (2)\times k! \quad \text{(for arbitrary } k \geq 4)$$

$$< (k+1)\times k! \quad \text{(since } k > 2)$$

$$< (k+1)!$$

Hence, we proved that $P(k+1) \equiv 2^{k+1} < (k+1)!$ Holds.

Thus, assuming $P(k)$, we proved $P(k+1)$, for arbitrary $k \geq 4$. Hence, by principle of mathematical induction, it follows that the inequality $2^n < n!$ holds for all $n \geq 4$, n a natural number.

□

For solving some problems, sometimes we need additional assumptions during the inductive step. The following version of the principle of mathematical induction, called as "Strong principle" is sometimes used.

Theorem 3.12.2: (Strong principle of Mathematical Induction) Let $P(n)$ be the predicate involving n, an arbitrary natural number as a variable. Suppose that the following statements are true:

(1) Basis step : the statement $P(a)$ is true for some $a \in N$,
(2) Inductive step : assuming $P(a) \wedge P(a+1) \wedge \ldots \wedge P(k)$ ($k \geq a$, and k is arbitrary) is true, we are able to prove that $P(k+1)$ is true.

Then, the strong principle of Mathematical Induction allows us to conclude that $P(n)$ is true for all $n \geq a$.

Example 3.12.2 (as open exercise): By applying strong principle of Mathematical Induction, modify the argument in the sketch for proof of Theorem 7.1 to prove that primes are infinitely many.

□

UNIT SUMMARY

This unit provides an overview of different proof techniques essential in discrete mathematics, emphasizing the importance of rigorously proving statements and theorems. Terminology section introduces fundamental terminology related to proofs, including propositions, predicates, and logical connectives, laying the groundwork for understanding formal mathematical arguments. Direct Proof explains the direct proof method, where a proposition is proved true by directly establishing the truth of its implications using logical reasoning and previously established facts. Recasting the statements as conditions for Proofs, describes the process of reformulating statements into equivalent forms that are easier to prove, often by breaking down complex statements into simpler ones or utilizing logical equivalences. Indirect Proof introduces the concept of indirect proof, also known as proof by contrapositive, where a proposition is proved true by showing that its contrapositive statement is true. Proof by Contradiction explains proof by contradiction, a technique where a proposition is proved true by assuming its negation and deriving a contradiction, thus establishing the original proposition's truth. Numbers Some Definitions section provides definitions of fundamental concepts related to numbers, such as natural numbers, integers, rational numbers, and irrational numbers, essential for understanding mathematical proofs involving numerical properties. Proof by Necessity and Sufficiency section explores the concepts of necessity and sufficiency in mathematical proofs, clarifying the conditions under which a proposition is necessary or sufficient for another proposition to be true. Disproof by a Counter Example, Illustrates the use of counterexamples to disprove propositions, demonstrating how a single example that violates a statement's conditions can invalidate its universality. Proof by Exhaustive Cases introduces proof by exhaustive cases, a technique where all possible cases or scenarios are considered and proven individually to establish the truth of a proposition. More Terminology section expands on terminology used in mathematical proofs, including quantifiers, predicates, and universal and existential statements, providing a deeper understanding of logical reasoning in proofs. Principle of Mathematical Induction, discusses the principle of mathematical induction, a powerful proof technique used to establish the truth of statements involving natural numbers by proving a base case and demonstrating that if the statement holds for one case, it holds for the next, thereby proving its truth for all natural numbers.

EXERCISE

1. Explain the difference between a direct proof and an indirect proof, providing an example of each.
2. Define the term "contrapositive" and explain how it is used in proof methods.
3. Prove that if a and b are odd integers, then a+b is even using direct proof.
4. Identify the necessity and sufficiency conditions in the statement: "A number is divisible by 6 if and only if it is divisible by both 2 and 3."
5. Give an example of a statement that is necessary but not sufficient for another statement, and vice versa.
6. Disprove the statement "All prime numbers are odd" by providing a counterexample.
7. Prove that the sum of the first n positive odd integers is n^2 using proof by exhaustion.
8. Explain the principle of mathematical induction and how it is used to prove statements about natural numbers.
9. Prove by contradiction that there are infinitely many prime numbers.
10. Define the terms "base case" and "inductive step" in the context of mathematical induction, and explain their importance in constructing a valid proof.
11. Prove that the square of any even integer is also even using direct proof.
12. Define the term "lemma" in the context of mathematical proofs and provide an example of its usage.
13. Prove that the sum of two rational numbers is rational using direct proof.
14. Using the principle of mathematical induction, prove that 1+2+3+…+n=n(n+1)/2 for all positive integers n.
15. Show by counterexample that the statement "If a and b are irrational numbers, then a+b is irrational" is false.
16. Given the statement "For all real numbers x, if x^2 is irrational, then x is irrational," prove it using proof by contrapositive.
17. Prove that if n is an integer and n^2 is even, then n is even using proof by contradiction.
18. Using proof by exhaustion, determine whether the following statement is true or false: "For all positive integers n, 3n+2 is odd."
19. Prove that if aa and bb are rational numbers and $a \neq 0$, then ab is rational using proof by cases.
20. Given the statement "If x is a real number such that x^3 is irrational, then x is irrational," prove it using proof by contrapositive.

Supplementary Reading and Additional Exercises:

Richard Hammark, *Book of Proof*, Creative Commons Attribution-No Derivative Works 3.0 License. Virginia Commonwealth University, Weblink: https://www.people.vcu.edu/~rhammack/BookOfProof/
The following chapters in this book (involving about 70 pages, including exercises):

Chapter 4 (Direct Proof): pages 113 to 127,

Chapter 5 (Contrapositive Proof): pages 128 to 136,

Chapter 6 (Proof by Contradiction) : pages 137 to 146,

Chapter 7 (Proving non-conditionals) : pages 147 to 156,

Chapter 9 (Disproof) : pages 172 to 179

Chapter 10 (Mathematical Induction) : pages 180 to 200

together with the exercises given in the above chapters.

KNOW MORE

Alfred North Whitehead, Bertrand Russell, *Principia Mathematica: Volume 1* and *Volume 2*, Second Edition, The Syndics of the Cambridge University Press 1927 Bentley House, London, U.K. (reprinted 1963). Volume 1: 671 pages; Volume 2: 742 pages. (downloading links: https://www.uhu.es/francisco.moreno/gii_mac/docs/Principia_Mathematica_vol1.pdf, https://www.uhu.es/francisco.moreno/gii_mac/docs/Principia_Mathematica_vol2.pdf)

REFERENCES AND SUGGESTED READINGS

1. Ronald S. Calinger. *Leonhard Euler: Mathematical Genius in the Enlightenment*, Princeton University Press, 2015.
2. William Dunham. *Journey Through Genius: The Great Theorems of Mathematics*, Penguin Books, 1991.
3. David S. Gunderson. *Handbook of Mathematical Induction. Discrete Mathematics and its Applications*, CRC Press, 2011.
4. Steven Strogatz — the acclaimed mathematician and author — hosts the new Quanta Magazine podcast "The Joy of Why.", Youtube video link https://www.youtube.com/watch?v=-v78qiTrnkQ (March 18, 2022).
5. 2021's biggest Breakthroughs in Math and Computer Science, Youtube Video: https://www.youtube.com/watch?v=9uASADiYe_8&t=302s

6. Srivathsa Joshi , Mathematics is queen of sciences: An exploration of mathematics, Youtube Video link https://www.youtube.com/watch?v=8mve0UoSxTo (2015).
7. Tesla's 3-6-9 and Vortex Math: Is this really the key to the universe? Youtube Video: https://www.youtube.com/watch?v=6ZrO90AI0c8 (19 Feb. 2022).
8. Martin Aigner and G¨unter M. Ziegler. *Proofs from The Book*, Springer, sixth edition, 2018

Martin Aigner, left, and Günter Ziegler at the Freie Universiat, Berlin. (The first author of this book, Narendra, together with his doctoral student, was on DAAD Fellowship at Freie Universitat, Berlin)

Dynamic QR Code for Further Reading

4 Modular Arithmetic

UNIT SPECIFICS

Through this unit we have discussed the following aspects:

- *Modular Arithmetic and Divisibility;*
- *Theory of Congruences*
- *Primality and Fundamental Theorem of arithmetic*
- *Coprimality and Euler's Totient Function*
- *GCD and Extended GCD*
- *Chinese Reminder Theorem*

In this chapter, we covered the above mentioned concepts.

Introduction:

This Unit is devoted to understand the properties of numbers. Some important concepts that are useful in the field of computer science are introduced.

The notion of divisibility of integers is introduced in the beginning. Whenever an integer is divided by another integer we get a remainder, modular arithmetic operates with such remainders is called modulus.

We introduce concept of primality, where positive numbers will have only one and themselves as positive divisors. After understanding fundamental theorem of arithmetic which infers every positive integer has a unique factorization of prime numbers. We will also introduce the concept of Greatest Common Divisor (GCD) and understand Extended Euclidean algorithm for computing it. We will explain how to solve linear congruences as well as systems of linear congruences. Which can be applied on Chinese remainder theorem. The notion of pseudo primes, coprimes and relative primes are also important to understand most of the applications in computer science especially in the field of cryptography, for developing various cryptographic protocols. Number theory is one of the purest subjects and an essential tool for providing security in various applications.

RATIONALE

Why do you learn Number Theory?

Number theory is a highly specialized field of advanced mathematics that is used in various scientific fields such as physics, cryptography, and computer science. Therefore, gaining expertise in number theory is crucial for researchers working in these areas. Number theory is a complex and highly challenging field of mathematics that requires precise thinking and deep logical reasoning. People who enjoy a good intellectual challenge may find this subject fascinating and exciting.

Why is study of Modular Arithmetic to computer science?

Modular arithmetic is a system of arithmetic for integers that involves performing arithmetic operations with respect to a fixed modulus, or a number which is used as a basis for calculating remainders. In modular arithmetic, the remainder is always taken with respect to the modulus value, meaning that when two numbers are congruent modulo a given modulus value, they have the same remainder when divided by that modulus value. It is often used in cryptography, computer science, and number theory.

PRE-REQUISITES

Mathematics at school level(till Class X)

UNIT OUTCOMES

List of outcomes of this unit is as follows:

U4-O1: Understand properties of divisibility and modular arithmetic.

U4-O2: Apply Theory of Congruences and simplify expressions.

U4-O3: Understand Primality and Fundamental Theorem of arithmetic.

U4-O4: Apply Coprimality and Euler's Totient Function.

U4-O5: Apply GCD and Extended GCD to solve problems.

U4-O6: Apply Chinese Reminder Theorem to solve problems.

Unit-4 Outcomes	EXPECTED MAPPING WITH COURSE OUTCOMES (1- Weak Correlation; 2- Medium correlation; 3- Strong Correlation)								
	CO-1	CO-2	CO-3	CO-4	CO-5	CO-6	CO-7	CO-8	CO-9
U4-O1	2	2	2	2	3	3	1	-	3
U4-O2	3	1	1	1	3	3	2	-	3
U4-O3	2	2	2	3	3	3	2	-	3
U4-O4	3	2	2	2	3	3	1	-	3
U4-O5	3	2	2	3	3	3	1	-	3
U4-O6	3	2	2	3	2	3	1	-	3

Modular Arithmetic

Number Theory being a branch of mathematics, explores conceptual theory behind numbers, and their properties especially integers. It is one of the interesting field for a mathematician and has profound applications in the field of computer science. Some of the applications include storage and organization of data, cryptographic encryption and decryption, error correcting and detecting codes in networking, random number generators which are useful in generating public and private keys in various cryptographic algorithms. Below mentioned are some of the major applications of number theory in Computer Science.

1. Cryptography: Number theory is widely used in the field of cryptography to create secure communication channels. By applying number theory, we can generate public and private keys that make it difficult for hackers to access the sensitive information transmitted over the internet.
2. Coding Theory: Number theory is also used in coding theory for correcting errors that occur during the transmission of data over noisy channels. This is accomplished through algebraic structures like cyclic codes, Hamming codes, and Reed-Solomon codes.
3. Gaming: Number theory is useful in developing algorithms and statistical models used in gaming. For example, analyzing the distribution of prime numbers allows for the creation of pseudorandom number generators that are difficult to predict.
4. Genetics: Number theory has applications in genetics by predicting the probability of getting a specific genetic trait or the likelihood of two individuals having the same DNA sequence.
5. Finance: Number theory has also been used in finance to develop statistical models for risk assessment, predicting stock prices, and modeling option prices.
6. Physics: Number theory has been extensively used in physics, especially in the study of quantum mechanics and particle physics. For example, prime numbers theory can aid in understanding the distribution of energy levels of atoms.
7. Image Processing: Number theory is used in image processing to encrypt images and to separate composite images into their individual components. It is also applied in image compression algorithms that enable the storage of vast amounts of visual data.
8. Cryptocurrency: Number theory is the foundation of cryptocurrency systems like Bitcoin, which is based on the concept of the Elliptic Curve Digital Signature Algorithm (ECDSA). Using number theory, Bitcoin transactions can be securely verified and authenticated.

4.1 MODULAR ARITHMETIC

Definition 4.1: Suppose a positive integer number say a is divided by another number n, we write the remainder obtained as a mod n, and the integer obtained with this division is referred as modulus. This approach can be mathematically represented as $a = qn + r$; $0 \leq r < n$; $q = \lfloor a/n \rfloor$

Example 4.1: 13 mod 7 = 6; - 13 mod 7 = 6

Now let us define congruent modulo n.

Definition 4.2: Two integers a and b are said to be congruent modulo n, if n is an integer such that n>1 and n is a divisor of their difference such that there exists an integer k where a-b=kn. If k mod n exists then we can write $a \equiv k \pmod{n}$.

Example 4.2: In modulus 12, $38 \equiv 14 \pmod{12}$; 38-14=24 which is a multiple of 12; in other way 38 and 14 have same remainder 2 when divided by 12.

4.1.1 Properties of Congruences

Let us now discuss some important properties of congruences:

1. If n is a number that divides difference of two numbers p and q then $p \equiv q \pmod{n}$
2. If $p \equiv q \pmod{n}$ is true this implies that $q \equiv p \pmod{n}$
3. If $p \equiv q \pmod{n}$ is true and $q \equiv r \pmod{n}$ is also true this implies that $p \equiv r \pmod{n}$

As a proof of the first property, if $n \mid (p-q)$, then $(p-q) = kn$ for some k. now we can write p as p=q+kn. Now the fact is that, (p mod n) is equivalent to the remainder when q+kn is divided by n) which is equivalent to the remainder when q is divided by n which is same as *q* mod *n*. Thus we can write,

(p mod n) => (q+kn) mod n => (*q* mod *n*).

Example 4.3: $21 \equiv 1 \pmod{5}$ because 21 - 1 = 20 = 5 x 4

$17 \equiv 2 \pmod{3}$ because 17 - 2 = 15 = 3 x 5

$89 \equiv 9 \pmod{10}$ because 89 - 0 = 80 = 10 x 8

Similarly proof of the remaining properties is left as an exercise to the reader.

4.1.2 Modular Arithmetic Operations

Modular arithmetic operation is a mathematical operation used to perform arithmetic operations in a fixed range or modulus. It involves finding the remainder after division of one number by another, and the remainder is restricted to a fixed range or modulus.

Note that, by definition the mod operator maps all integers into the set of integers {0, 1, …. , $(n - 1)$}.This should provoke you to question: Can we perform arithmetic operations within the confines of this set? Definitely it turns out to be "we can"; this technique is known as **modular arithmetic**.

For example, in the arithmetic modulo 7, 5 + 4 in modulo 7 would be expressed as (5+4) mod 7 = 2 this implies, arithmetic operation is performed and remainder is obtained after divisibility.

Let us now discuss some important properties of Modular arithmetic:

Assume p and q be any integer and n to be a natural number then

1. [(p mod n) + (q mod n)] mod n = (p + q) mod n
2. [(p mod n) - (q mod n)] mod n = (p - q) mod n
3. [(p mod n) * (q mod n)] mod n = (p * q) mod n

Let us verify the first property. Defining (p mod n) as r_p and (q mod n) as r_q Then, as per the definition of congruent modulo, we can write, $p = r_p + jn$ and $q = r_q + kn$ for some integer j and k respectively. Then,

$$\begin{aligned}(p + q) \bmod n &= (r_p + jn + r_q + kn) \bmod n \\ &= (r_p + r_q + (k+j)n) \bmod n \\ &= (r_p + r_q) \bmod n \\ &= [(p \bmod n) + (q \bmod n)] \bmod n\end{aligned}$$

Similarly proving remaining properties can be ease and is left as an exercise to the reader.

Let us now proceed to work out some examples of the above discussed three properties:

Example 4.4:

17 mod 3 =2 and 10 mod 3 = 1 ; then [(17 mod 3)+ (10 mod 3)] mod 3 = (17+10) mod 3 = 0
17 mod 3 =2 and 10 mod 3 = 1 ; then [(17 mod 3) -(10 mod 3)] mod 3 = (17-10) mod 3 = 7 mod 3 =1
17 mod 3 =2 and 10 mod 3 = 1 ; then [(17 mod 3) x (10 mod 3)] mod 3 = (17x10) mod 3 = 170 mod 3 =2

Exponentiation can also be performed by repeated multiplication, as in ordinary arithmetic.

To find 11^7 mod 13, we can proceed as follows:

11^2 mod 13 = 121 ≡ 4 (mod 13)
11^4 mod 13 = (11^2) x (11^2) ≡ 4^2 ≡ 3 (mod 13)
11^7 mod 13 =11 mod 13 x 11^2 mod 13 x 11^4 mod 13 ≡ 11 mod 13 x 4 mod 13 x 3 mod 13 ≡ 132 mod 13 ≡ 2 (mod 13)

From this it is inferred that, the rules for ordinary arithmetic involving addition, subtraction, and multiplication can carry over into modular arithmetic.

Consider modular addition and multiplication modulo 8 as shown in figure below. It is observed that the results are straightforward, observe the pattern in the matrix, aren't they symmetric on the principal diagonal, this is also in conformance to the commutative property of addition and multiplication. There can be additive inverse to each integer. The additive inverse can be extracted from the left hand column, when you scan the corresponding row of the matrix to find 0, so integer that is on top of that column is additive inverse. This is also applicable for modular multiplication table to find multiplicative identity and multiplicative inverse. As shown in table -w is additive inverse and w^{-1} is multiplicative inverse.

+	0	1	2	3	4	5	6	7
0	0	1	2	3	4	5	6	7
1	1	2	3	4	5	6	7	0
2	2	3	4	5	6	7	0	1
3	3	4	5	6	7	0	1	2
4	4	5	6	7	0	1	2	3
5	5	6	7	0	1	2	3	4
6	6	7	0	1	2	3	4	5
7	7	0	1	2	3	4	5	6

Addition Modulo 8

x	0	1	2	3	4	5	6	7
0	0	0	0	0	0	0	0	0
1	0	1	2	3	4	5	6	7
2	0	2	4	6	0	2	4	6
3	0	3	6	1	4	7	2	5
4	0	4	0	4	0	4	0	4
5	0	5	2	7	4	1	6	3
6	0	6	4	2	0	6	4	2
7	0	7	6	5	4	3	2	1

Multiplication Modulo 8

w	-w	w^{-1}
0	0	-
1	7	1
2	6	-
3	5	3
4	4	-
5	3	5
6	2	-
7	1	7

Additive and Multiplicative inverses modulo 8

4.1.3 Properties of Modular Arithmetic

Consider a set of nonnegative integers less than n, Z_n = { 0,1, 2,…….(n-1)}. Now we define **set of residues**, or **residue classes mod n**. Each integer in Z_n represents a residue class. We can label the residue classes (mod n) as [0],[1],[2],…..[n-1] where, $[r] = \{a: a$ is an integer, $a \equiv r \pmod{n}\}$

For example, The residue classes (mod 4) are as shown in table below.

[0]	{ …, -16,-12,-8,-4,0,4,8,12,16,….}
[1]	{ …, -15, -11,-7,-3,1,5,9,13,17,….}
[2]	{ …, -14,-10,-6, -2, 2,6,10,14,18,…}
[3]	{ …, -13,-9,-5,-1,3,7,11,15,19,…}

The smallest non negative integer used to represent the residue class among all the integers in a residue class. The process of finding this smallest non negative integer for the congruent modulo is called reducing k modulo n. If modular arithmetic is performed within Z_n that holds the properties given in table below, that implies Z_n is a commutative with a multiplicative identity element. The peculiar feature of modular arithmetic, that distinguishes itself from ordinary arithmetic is as explained herewith.

It can be deduced from the properties of congruences that
if $(a + b) \equiv (a + c)$ (mod n) **then** $b \equiv c$ (mod n) ......(4)

This Equation (4) proves to be consistent with the existence of an additive inverse. Because if additive inverse of a is added to both sides of eq.4 adding the additive inverse of a to both sides of Equation (4.4), we have ((-a) +a+b) ≡ ((-a) + a+ c) mod n so, b ≡ c(mod n). However, the following statement is true only with the constraint: If (a x b) ≡ (a x c) (mod n) then b ≡ c(mod n) if a is relatively prime to n ....(5)

But what do you mean by relatively prime, two integers are said to be relatively prime if both of them have a common positive factor as 1. Now we can say eq. 5 is consistent if a multiplicative inverse exists, so when we apply multiplicative inverse on bothe sides of eq. 5 with the similar approach we have $((a^{-1})ab) \equiv ((a^{-1})ac)$ (mod n) so, $b \equiv c$ (mod n)

Property	Expression
Commutative Laws	(w+x) mod n = (x+w) mod n (w x x) mod n = (x+w) mod n
Associative Laws	[(w+x) + y] mod n = [w+ (x+y)] mod n [(w x x) x y] mod n = [w x (x x y)] mod n
Distributive Laws	[w x (x+y)] mod n = [(w x x)+ (w x y)] mod n
Identities	(0 +w) mod n = w mod n (1 x w) mod n = w mod n
Additive Inverse(-w)	For each w belong to Z there exits a a z such that w + z = 0 mod n

Think, what is the reason for this behaviour of any general modulus n. Definitely the multiplier *a* fail to produce a full set of residues when it is run through 0 to n-1 if a and n have any factors in common.

Example 4.5: With a=6 and n = 8

Z8	0	1	2	3	4	5	6	7
Multiply by 6	0	6	12	18	24	30	36	42
Residues	0	6	4	2	0	6	4	2

When multiplied by 6, we do not have a complete set of residues so that there is more than one integer to to the same residue. For instance, 6 x 0 mod 8 = 6 x 4 mod 8 ; 6 x 1 mod 8 = 6 x 5 mod 8 ; and so on. As this is a many to one mapping, there can be no unique multiplicative inverse be found.

Example 4.6: With a = 5 and n = 8 , whose only common factor is 1,

Z8	0	1	2	3	4	5	6	7
Multiply by 5	0	5	10	15	20	25	30	35
Residues	0	5	2	7	4	1	6	3

Observe that all the integers are present in the line of residues, although in a different order. It can be generalized that in Z_n an integer has a multiplicative inverse if it is relatively prime to n. You can observe that the integers 1, 3,5,7 have their inverses, what we call as multiplicative inverse, but remaining integers do not possess them.

4.2 DIVISIBILITY

Divisibility is the property of being able to divide one number by another without leaving a remainder. In other words, a number is divisible by another if it can be evenly divided by that number, such that the result of division, quotient is an integer. For example, 10 is divisiblc by 2 because when 10 is divided by 2, the result is 5, with no remainder. Conversely, 10 is not divisible by 3 because when 10 is divided by 3, the result is 3 with a remainder of 1. Formally defined as below.

Definition 4.3: If there are two integers say p and q such that $p \neq 0$ then we can say that p divides q if there is an integer k for q=kp. In mathematical representation we write p divides q as $p|q$. also we can say that p is a factor of q and q is a multiple of p.

If $p|q$ then $q|p$ is an integer say it is k, if p does not divides q, then we write this as $p \nmid q$.

Some important properties:

Consider any integers x, y, z such that $x \neq 0$, then the following properties holds

1 If $x|y$ and $x|z$, then $x|(y + z)$.

2 If $x|y$, then $x|yz$ for all integers z.

3 If $x|y$ and $y|z$, then $x|z$.

A factor of a number is a whole number that divides evenly into the given number without leaving a remainder. For example, factors of 12 are 1, 2, 3, 4, 6, and 12 because they can all be divided without leaving a remainder. Factors can be positive or negative. Now we define it formally.

Definition 4.4: For two integers p and q such that $p \neq 0$, we can say that p divides q if there is an integer k for q=pk. If p divides q then we say that p is a factor of q and q is called as a multiple of p. **Ex.** 3 | 21 True or False ? **True because it signifies 3 divides 24 which is true.** So, 3 is a factor of 21 and 21 is a multiple of 3. But if we take 3 | 5 True or False ? Now the answer is definitely "**False**"

4.2.1 Division Algorithm

The division algorithm is a mathematical procedure to find the quotient and remainder of a division. Given two integers, a dividend (a number being divided) and a divisor (a number dividing the dividend), the algorithm produces two integers, the quotient and the remainder, where the quotient is the number of times the divisor divides into the dividend, and the remainder is the amount left over after the division is complete.

The division algorithm states that for any two integers a and b, with b not equal to 0, there exist unique integers q and r such that $a = bq + r$, where $0 \leq r < |b|$.

<u>Example 4.7</u>: when dividing 17 by 5, the quotient is 3 and the remainder is 2. In mathematical notation, $17 \div 5 = 3$ with a remainder of 2, which can be represented as $17 = 5 \times 3 + 2$.

The division algorithm is used in many areas of mathematics, including number theory, algebra, and calculus. It is also used in computer science and programming to perform division and find remainders. Formal representation is as shown below.

Theorem:
For any integer a where exists another positive integer d, there will be two integers q and r such that r lies between 0 and d (0 <= r < d) and a = dq + r, where q = a / d, r =a%d with a and d are dividend and divisor respectively,

4.2.2 Primes

A positive integer greater than 1 that has no positive integer divisors other than 1 and itself is termed as prime number. For example, considering the range of numbers from 1 to 30, 2, 3, 5, 7, 11, 13, 17, 19, 23, and 29 are found to be prime.

Prime numbers are important in mathematics because of their unique properties and their role in number theory. Here are some of the reasons why prime numbers are important:

1. Building blocks of numbers: Prime numbers cannot be divided by any other number except for 1 and itself. This property makes them the building blocks of all other numbers. Every positive integer greater than 1 can be expressed as a product of prime numbers.
2. Cryptography: Prime numbers are used in cryptography to maintain the security of data. The security of encryption algorithms such as RSA and Diffie-Hellman relies on the difficulty of factoring large composite numbers into their prime factors.
3. Patterns and structures: Prime numbers have unique patterns and structures that are of interest to mathematicians. For example, the distribution of primes is not regular, and the gaps between consecutive primes become larger as we move along the number line.

4. Applications in various fields: Prime numbers have applications in fields such as physics, biology, computer science, and economics. For example, the properties of prime numbers are useful in the study of quantum mechanics and in the design of communication protocols.
5. Challenges and puzzles: Prime numbers have always been a source of fascination for mathematicians. There are many unsolved problems related to prime numbers, such as the twin prime conjecture, which states that there are infinitely many pairs of primes that differ by 2. The study of prime numbers continues to be a rich and active area of research in mathematics.

Definition 4.5: Any positive integer p that is greater than 1 and that is divisible only by 1 and by itself (p) is termed as **a prime** number

Example 4.8: 13, 31, 59, 71, ...

$1 \mid 13$ and $13 \mid 13$, $1 \mid 31$ and $31 \mid 31$, etc. you cannot find any other factors for a prime number.

Another important ones are coprime and relatively prime and composite numbers. They have huge significance in the number theory.

Two numbers are said to be coprime if they have no common divisors other than 1. This means that they have the greatest common divisor (GCD) as 1.

Relatively prime is a term used interchangeably with coprime. It means the same thing – two numbers have no common divisors other than 1. However, relatively prime is a term that is usually used for a set of more than two numbers. For example, if three numbers have no common divisors other than 1, they are said to be relatively prime.

A composite number is a positive integer that has at least one factor other than 1 and itself. In other words, it is a number that can be divided evenly by at least two positive integers other than 1 and itself. For example, 4 is a composite number because it can be divided evenly by 2, whereas 3 is a prime number because it can only be divided evenly by 1 and 3.

Now just think how do you determine whether the given number is a prime or a composite number. Look at the approaches followed.

Let n be the given number. Then in order to determine whether it is a prime we can test:

• Method-1: if any number $x < n$ divides the given number exists then it is a composite. If you test for all numbers $x < n$ and do not find the proper divisor then n is a prime.

• Method-2: if any prime number x < n divides the given number exists then it is a composite. If you test all primes $x < n$ and do not find a proper divisor then also we say n is a prime.

• Method-3: if any prime number x < divides the given number exists then it is a composite. If we test all primes $x < n$ and do not find a proper divisor now we say n is a prime.

Now you can think solution for the question in various other dimensions.

4.2.3 Fundamental theorem of Arithmetic:

Every positive integer greater than 1 can be expressed uniquely (excluding the order of the factors) as a product of primes. This means that any composite number can be factored into a unique set of prime numbers, and that the product of two or more prime numbers cannot be factored again. This is called Fundamental Theorem of Arithmetic.

For example, the number 60 can be factored into 2 x 2 x 3 x 5, and this is the unique prime factorization of 60. The Fundamental Theorem of Arithmetic is a key concept in number theory and forms the basis of many mathematical proofs and applications. Few other e**xamples can be** 12 = 2*2*3 and 21 = 3*7. And this Process of finding out factors of the product term is called **factorization**.

4.2.4 Congruence Relation

Congruence relation refers to the relationship between two integers or sets of integers, where the remainders of both integers when divided by a fixed integer are the same. The congruence relation is denoted by the symbol "≡", and it is read as "is congruent to."

For example, if $a \equiv b \bmod 7$, it means that a and b have the same remainder when divided by 7. This can also be written as: a mod 7 = b mod 7.

Congruence relation is used in many areas of discrete mathematics, including number theory, cryptography, and computer science, among others. It is an important concept in modular arithmetic, which is the study of operations on remainders. Formal definition is given below.

Definition 4.6: For any two integers p and q there exists a positive integer m, if $m|(p-q)$ then we say p is congruent to q modulo m representing it with notation $p \equiv q \pmod{m}$, it is a congruence and m is its modulus.

If p is not congruent to q modulo m, we write $p \not\equiv q \pmod{m}$. So two integers are congruent mod m if and only if they have the same remainder when divided by m.

4.2.5 Theorem on Congruences

Theorem: for any positive integer m the two integers a and b are congruent modulo m iff there is a positive integer satisfying the relation $a = b + km$

Proof:

If $a \equiv b(\bmod m)$, then (by the definition of congruence) $m|(a - b)$. Hence, there is an integer k such that $a - b = km$ and equivalently $a = b + km$. Conversely, if there is an integer k such that $a = b + km$, then $km = a - b$. Hence, $m|(a - b)$ and $a \equiv b(\bmod m)$.

Congruence: Examples

<u>Example 4.9:</u> Determine Whether 17 is congruent to 5 modulo 6, and Whether 24 and 14 are congruent modulo 6.

Solution: $17 \equiv 5(\bmod 6)$ because 6 divides $17 - 5 = 12$.

$24 \not\equiv 14(\bmod 6)$ since $24 - 14 = 10$ is not divisible by 6.

Note: The uses of "mod" are different in the following expressions.

$a \equiv b(\bmod m)$, and $a \bmod m = b$

$a \equiv b(\bmod m)$ describes a binary relation on the set of integers. But $a \bmod m = b$, the notation mod denotes a function (from integers to integers). For two integers a and b there is a positive integer m iff $a \bmod m = b \bmod m$

4.2.6 Congruences of Sums and Products

Theorem:

Let m be a positive integer. If $a \equiv b(\bmod m)$ and $c \equiv d(\bmod m)$, then $a + c \equiv b + d(\bmod m)$ and $ac \equiv bd(\bmod m)$.

Proof:

Since $a \equiv b(\bmod m)$ and $c \equiv d(\bmod m)$, by the Theorem above there are integers s and t with $b = a + sm$ and $d = c + tm$. Therefore, $b + d = (a + sm) + (c + tm) = (a + c) + m(s + t)$, and $bd = (a + sm)(c + tm) = ac + m(at + cs + stm)$. Hence, $a + c \equiv b + d(\bmod m)$ and $ac \equiv bd(\bmod m)$.

Corollary:

Let m be a positive integer and let a and b be integers. Then $(a + b) \bmod m = ((a \bmod m) + (b \bmod m)) \bmod m$, $ab \bmod m = ((a \bmod m)(b \bmod m)) \bmod m$.

4.2.7 Arithmetic modulo m

Arithmetic modulo m is a type of arithmetic that involves performing operations (addition, subtraction, multiplication, and division) on integers with the result being the remainder when divided by a specified integer m, called the modulus. For example, in arithmetic modulo 7, 9 + 4 = 2 (since 9 + 4 = 13, which has a remainder of 2 when divided by 7), and 5 x 3 = 1 (since 5 x 3 = 15, which has a remainder of 1 when divided by 7).

Let $Z_m = \{0, 1, \ldots, m - 1\}$. The operation $+_m$ is defined as $a +_m b = (a + b) \bmod m$. This is addition modulo m. The operation x_m is defined as $a \, x_m \, b = (a \times b) \bmod m$. This is multiplication modulo m.

Using these operations is said to be doing arithmetic modulo m.

Example 4.10: Find $7 +_{11} 9$ and $7 \, x_{11} \, 9$.

Solution: Using the definitions above:

$7 +_{11} 9 = (7 + 9) \bmod 11 = 16 \bmod 11 = 5$

$7 \, x_{11} \, 9 = (7 \times 9) \bmod 11 = 63 \bmod 11 = 8$

The following are the list of properties of Arithmetic modulo m:

Closure property: If a, b $\in Z_m$, then $a +_m b$ and $a \, x_m \, b$ belong to Z_m.

Commutativity: If a, b $\in Z_m$, then $a +_m b = b +_m a$ and $a \, x_m \, b = b \, x_m \, a$.

Associativity: If a, b, c $\in Z_m$, then $(a +_m b) +_m c = a +_m (b +_m c)$ and $(a \, x_m \, b) \, x_m \, c = a \, x_m \, (b \, x_m \, c)$.

Distributivity: If a, b, c $\in Z_m$, then $a \, x_m \, (b +_m c) = (a \, x_m \, b) +_m (a \, x_m \, c)$ and $(a +_m b) \, x_m \, c = (a \, x_m \, c) +_m (b \, x_m \, c)$.

Identity elements: If a $\in Z_m$ then $a +_m 0 = a$ and $a \, -_m \, 1 = a$. Here the elements 0 and 1 are identity elements for addition and multiplication modulo m, respectively.

Additive inverses: If $0 \neq a \in Z_m$, then m - a is the additive inverse of a modulo m. Moreover, 0 is its own additive inverse so, $a +_m (m - a) = 0$ and $0 +_m 0 = 0$.

4.3 COPRIMALITY AND EULER'S TOTIENT FUNCTION

Two numbers are coprime if their greatest common divisor equals 1(1 is considered to be co-prime to any number) as already discussed in previous section.

Euler's totient function has many applications in number theory, cryptography, and other areas of mathematics. It is named after the Swiss mathematician Leonhard Euler, who introduced the function in the 18th century. Euler's totient function, denoted as Φ (n), is a number theory function that counts the number of positive integers less than or equal to n that are relatively prime to n (i.e., have no common factors other than 1). In other words, it gives the number of integers k such that gcd(k,n)=1 where gcd denotes the greatest common divisor.

For example, Φ (6) is equal to 2, since the only positive integers less than or equal to 6 that are relatively prime to 6 are 1 and 5. Similarly, Φ(10) is equal to 4, since the positive integers less than or equal to 10 that are relatively prime to 10 are 1, 3, 7, and 9as represented in the tables below.

Here are values of Φ (n) for the first few positive integers:

n	1	2	3	4	5	6	7	8	9	10	11	12	13	14	15	16	17	18
Φ (n)	1	1	2	2	4	2	6	4	6	4	10	4	12	6	8	8	16	6

The list of co-primes is as shown for n=15 in the table below.

n	φ(n)	numbers coprime to n
1	1	1
2	1	1
3	2	1, 2
4	2	1,3
5	4	1,2,3,4
6	2	1,5
7	6	1,2,3,4,5,6
8	4	1,3,5,7
9	6	1,2,4,5,7,8
10	4	1,3,7,9
11	10	1,2,3,4,5,6,7,8,9,10
12	4	1,5,7,11
13	12	1,2,3,4,5,6,7,8,9,10,11,12
14	6	1,3,5,9,11,13
15	8	1,2,4,7,8,11,13,14

4.3.1 Properties of Euler's Totient Function:

The following properties of Euler totient function are sufficient to calculate it for any number:

- If p is a prime number, then gcd(p, q) = 1 for all 1 <= q < p. Therefore we have: Φ (n) = n-1
- If p is a prime number and k >= 1, then there are exactly p^k / p numbers between 1 and p^k that are divisible by p. Which gives us: Φ (p^k) = p^k - p^{k-1}
- If a and b are relatively prime, then: Φ (ab) = Φ (a) x Φ (b)

It follows from the Chinese remainder theorem which is discussed in section 4.5. The Chinese remainder theorem guarantees, that for each $0 <= x < a$ and each $0 <= y < b$, there exists a unique $0 <= z < a\,b$ with $z \equiv x \bmod(a)$ and $z \equiv y \bmod(b)$. It's not hard to show that z is coprime to $a\,b$ if and only if x is coprime to a and y is coprime to b. Therefore the amount of integers coprime to $a\,b$ is equal to product of the amounts of a and b.

In general for not coprime a and b, the equation $\Phi(ab) = \Phi(a) \cdot \Phi(b) \cdot \frac{d}{\Phi(d)}$ where, $d = \gcd(a,b)$ holds

4.3.2 Application in Euler's theorem

Cryptography: The function φ(n) is used in RSA public-key cryptography, where it plays a crucial role in the encryption and decryption of messages. The security of the RSA cryptosystem is based on the fact that it is difficult to factor large numbers into their prime factors, and the totient function helps to ensure that the encryption and decryption process is secure.

Modular arithmetic: The totient function is used in modular arithmetic to find the multiplicative inverse of an integer modulo n. Specifically, if a and n are relatively prime, then there exists an integer b such that ab ≡ 1 (mod n), and b is given by b ≡ a^(φ(n)-1) (mod n).

Euler's theorem: Euler's theorem, which states that a^φ(n) ≡ 1 (mod n) if a and n are relatively prime, is a powerful tool in number theory and has many applications. For example, it can be used to prove Fermat's little theorem and to compute discrete logarithms.

Primitive roots: A primitive root of a prime p is an integer g such that every integer relatively prime to p can be expressed as a power of g modulo p. The existence of primitive roots is related to the value of φ(p), and the totient function is used to determine the number of primitive roots modulo a prime.

Number theory: The totient function has many applications in number theory, including the study of prime numbers, Diophantine equations, and the distribution of prime numbers. For example, it can be used to prove that there are infinitely many primes, and to derive estimates for the size of the prime factors of an integer.

The most famous and important property of Euler's totient function is expressed in Euler's theorem:

$a^{\Phi(n)} \equiv 1 \bmod m$ if a and m are relatively prime.

In the particular case when m is prime, Euler's theorem turns into Fermat's little theorem:

$a^{m-1} \equiv 1 \bmod m$

Euler's theorem and Euler's totient function occur quite often in practical applications, for example both are used to compute the modular multiplicative inverse. As immediate consequence we also get the equivalence:

$a^n \equiv a^{n \bmod \Phi(m)} \bmod m$

This allows computing x^n mod m for very big n, especially if n is the result of another computation, as it allows to compute n under a modulo.

Example 4.11:

a) Find φ(n) for the following: i) 165 ii) 1716 iii) 13 iv) 9 v) 4 vi)15

Solution:

i. 165 = 15*11, φ(165) = φ(15)*φ(11) = 80. $8^{80} \equiv 1$ mod 165

ii. 1716 = 11*12*13, φ(1716) = φ(11)*φ(12)*φ(13) = 480. $7^{480} \equiv 1$ mod 1716

iii. φ(13) = 12, $9^{12} \equiv 1$ mod 13

iv. $9 = 3^2$, φ(9) = 9* (1-1/3) = 6

v. $4 = 2^2$, φ(4) = 4* (1-1/2) = 2

vi. 15 = 3*5, φ(15) = 15* (1-1/3)*(1-1/5) = 15*(2/3)*(4/5) =8

Example 4.11:

b)How many numbers in {1,2,…,200}{1,2,…,200} are coprime to 100?

There are ϕ(100)=(4−2)(25−5)=40

40 coprime numbers to 100 in {1,2,…,100}.{1,2,…,100}.

Since gcd(a,b)=gcd(a−b,b),gcd(a,b)=gcd(a−b,b),

gcd(101,100)=gcd(1,100),

gcd(102,100)=gcd(2,100),

⋮

gcd(200,100)=gcd(100,100).

So there are ϕ(100)=40 coprime numbers to 100 in {101,102,…,200}.{101,102,…,200}.

So the answer is 40+40=80.40+40=80.

Example 4.12:

Find the number of positive integers n ≤ 168n ≤168 such that gcd(n,168)=8

These are the positive integers of the form 8m, where m≤21 and gcd(m,21)=1.

So the answer is ϕ(21)=(3−1)(7−1)=12.

4.4. GCD AND EXTENDED EUCLIDEAN ALGORITHM

4.4.1 GCD

The **greatest common divisor (GCD),** also called the **greatest common factor,** of two numbers is the largest number that divides them both. For instance, the greatest common factor of 20 and 15 is 5, since 5 divides both 20 and 15 and no larger number has this property. The concept is easily extended to sets of more than two numbers: the GCD of a set of numbers is the largest number dividing each of them.

The GCD is used for a variety of applications in number theory, particularly in modular arithmetic and thus encryption algorithms such as RSA. It is also used for simpler applications, such as simplifying fractions. This makes the GCD a rather fundamental concept to number theory, and as such a number of algorithms have been discovered to efficiently compute it.

The GCD of several numbers may be computed by simply listing the factors of each number and determining the largest common one. While in practice this is terribly inefficient, for particularly small cases it is doable by hand. The process may be split up using the method of factor pairs: once one determines a factor aa of a number nn, the quotient naan is necessarily a factor as well. For instance, since 2 is a factor of 24, 242=12224=12 is a factor as well.

Euclid's GCD algorithm:
Euclid's GCD algorithm is one of the earliest, most elementary and most important algorithm in the world
of mathematics. It gives a recursive way to calculate the GCD.
Suppose we are given two numbers a, b, s.t., $a \geq b$. The algorithm gcd(a, b) is given below.

If $b = 0$ then Output a
end
if $b = 1$ then Output 1
end
Say $a = qb + r$, then find gcd(b, r)

Example 4.13:
Find the greatest common divisor of 30,36,30,36, and 24.24.
The divisors of each number are given by can be written as
30:1,2,3,5,6,10,15,30
36:1,2,3,4,6,9,12,18,36
24:1,2,4,6,12,24

The largest number that appears on every list is 6,6, so this is the greatest common divisor:
gcd(30,36,24)=6

Example 4.14:
Compute gcd(4200,3780,3528)
We have,
$4200=2^3\cdot 3\cdot 5^2\cdot 7^3$
$780=2^2\cdot 3^3\cdot 5\cdot 7$
$3528=2^3\cdot 3^2\cdot 7^2$.
Since 2 appears in each of these factorizations, it will appear in the GCD as well. It is taken to the smallest power seen in the factorizations, which in this case is 2. So the GCD will contain 2222 in its factorization. Continuing along these lines, we obtain a GCD of
$2^2\cdot 3\cdot 7=84$.

Solve it:

Three gold coins of weight 780 g, 840 g, and 960 g are cut into small pieces of equal weight. If it takes 2 people to transport one piece of gold, what is the fewest number of people that are needed to transport all these pieces?

4.4.2 Applications of the GCD :

The greatest common divisor (GCD) of two or more integers is a fundamental concept in number theory with many applications in various fields of mathematics, computer science, and engineering. Some of the main applications of GCD are:

- Simplifying fractions: The GCD can be used to simplify fractions by dividing both the numerator and the denominator by their GCD. For example, the fraction 12/18 can be simplified to 2/3 by dividing both 12 and 18 by their GCD, which is 6.
- Euclid's algorithm: Euclid's algorithm is a method for finding the GCD of two integers that is based on the observation that the GCD of two numbers is the same as the GCD of the smaller number and the difference between the two numbers. Euclid's algorithm has many applications in cryptography, error correction, and other areas of computer science and engineering.
- Diophantine equations: Diophantine equations are equations that involve integer solutions only. The GCD is often used to solve Diophantine equations, since it can help to determine whether a solution exists, and if so, what form it must take.
- Modular arithmetic: The GCD is used in modular arithmetic to find modular inverses, which are essential for performing division and other arithmetic operations in modular arithmetic.

- Primality testing: The GCD is used in some primality testing algorithms to test whether a given integer is prime or composite.
- Public-key cryptography: Public-key cryptography is a cryptographic system that uses two keys, one public and one private, for secure communication. The security of the system is based on the fact that it is computationally difficult to factor the product of two large prime numbers. The GCD is used in some algorithms for generating large prime numbers for use in public-key cryptography.

Overall, the GCD is a fundamental concept in number theory with many important applications in mathematics, computer science, and engineering.

4.4.3 Extended Euclidean algorithm

Theorem:Given integers a, b $\geq$ 0, there exist two integers k, l, such that, gcd(a, b) = ka + lb. It is clear from the argument before that these coefficients can be obtained by keeping track of coefficients in Euclid's algorithm. This is called the extended Euclidean algorithm.

We can formally describe the process we used above. This process is called the *extended Euclidean algorithm*. It is used for finding the greatest common divisor of two positive integers a and b and writing this greatest common divisor as an integer linear combination of a and b. The steps of this algorithm are given below.

1. Set the value of the variable c to the larger of the two values a and b, and set d to the smaller of a and b.
2. Find the quotient and the remainder when c is divided by d. Call the quotient q and the remainder r. Use the division algorithm and expressions for previous remainders to write an expression for r in terms of a and b.
3. If $r = 0$, then gcd(a, b) = d. The expression for the previous value of r gives an expression for gcd(a, b) in terms of a and b. Stop.
4. Otherwise, use the current values of d and r as the new values of c and d, respectively, and go back to step 2.

4.4.4 Solving Linear Diophantine Equations

This is one of the applications of extended Euclidean algorithm. Diophantine equation is of the form ax+by =c where x and y are variables and a, b, and c are constants, solving such an equation is equivalent to computing extended Euclidean algorithm with the numbers a and b. after this next simple step is to solve Diophantine equation.

Depending on the relationship between c and gcd(a,b) we can deduce 3 cases.

<u>Case (i):</u> When c = gcd(a,b)

Consider a = 1398 and b = 324 and c= 6, then the equation becomes $1398x + 324y = 6$, computing the gcd of a and b we get 6, expressing in terms of 1398 and 324 we get $6 = -19(1398) + 82(324)$. Now the solution of the Diophantine equation is $x = -19$, $y = 82$. So the observation here is $c = \gcd(a, b)$, the extended Euclidean algorithm will give us a solution for x and y directly.

<u>Case (ii):</u> When c is a multiple of gcd(a,b)
Consider $c = k \cdot \gcd(a, b)$, k is an integer, we can find solution by writing gcd(a,b) in terms of a, b the with the coefficient k. $1398x + 324y = 60$ is the Diophantine equation, as $\gcd(1398, 324) = 6$, using extended Euclidean algorithm we can write $6 = -19(1398) + 82(324)$. RHS of equation is multiple of 6 ie 10(6)
So 60 =10(6)

$= \quad 10[-19(1398) + 82(324)]$

$= \quad -190(1398) + 820(324)$.So $x = -190$, $y = 820$ is a solution to this Diophantine equation

<u>Case (iii):</u> When c is not a multiple of gcd(a,b)
As seen with two cases with extended Euclidean algorithm we can write any multiple of gcd(a,b) in terms of integer multiples of a and b thus solving Diophantine equation, but when c is not a multiple of gcd(a,b), how to perform this is challenging, but possible. If c is not a multiple of $\gcd(a, b)$, then there are *no* integer solutions to the equation $ax + by = c$. So the extended Euclidean algorithm is all we need—it will give us all integer solutions if any exist, and otherwise there are no integer solutions to the Diophantine equation at all. Consider Diophantine equation $4x + 6y = 1$. The greatest common divisor of 4 and 6 is 2, and 1 is not a multiple of 2. So this Diophantine equation has no solutions. After some thought, it should be clear why this is so: Whatever integers we choose for x and y, the value of the left-hand side $4x + 6y$ must be even, but the right-hand side is 1, which is odd.

<u>Example 4.13:</u>
Find the distance d between each pair of integers:
(*a*) 3 and –7; (*b*) –4 and 2; (*c*) 1 and 9; (*d*) –8 and –3; (*e*) –5 and –8.
The distance d between a and b is given by $d = |a - b| = |b - a|$.
$d = |a| + |b|$ when a and b have different signs, and $d = |a| - |b|$ when a and b have the same sign and $|a| > |b|$.

Thus: *(a)* $d = 3 + 7 = 10$; *(b)* $d = 4 + 2 = 6$; *(c)* $d = 9 - 1 = 8$; *(d)* $d = 8 - 3 = 5$; *(e)* $d = 8 - 5 = 3$.

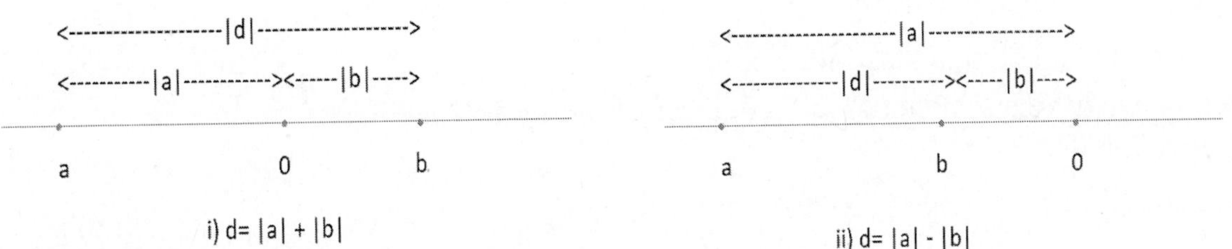

i) d= |a| + |b|

ii) d= |a| - |b|

4.5 CHINESE REMAINDER THEOREM

The Chinese Remainder Theorem is a theorem in number theory that provides a way to find a unique solution to a system of simultaneous congruences. The theorem is named after the Chinese mathematician Sun Tzu, who is said to have discovered it in the 3rd century AD.

The Chinese Remainder Theorem (CRT) was motivated by a practical problem in ancient Chinese mathematics, namely the problem of finding solutions to a system of linear congruences with pairwise relatively prime moduli.

The original problem was to determine the date of a Chinese festival, which was celebrated every 15 days, and was determined by a complex system of lunar and solar cycles. The problem was to find the date of the festival given various astronomical observations, each of which corresponded to a linear congruence with a different modulus. The Chinese mathematicians solved this problem using the CRT, which enabled them to find a unique solution that satisfied all the congruences simultaneously.

The CRT was later generalized by European mathematicians in the 18th and 19th centuries, and has since become a fundamental theorem in number theory and algebra. The theorem provides a powerful tool for solving systems of linear congruences, which arise in many areas of mathematics, computer science, and engineering. It also has applications in coding theory, cryptography, and error correction, among other areas. The CRT is motivated by the observation that if we have two integers a and b that are relatively prime, then any integer x can be expressed in the form $x = ay + bz$, where y and z are integers. This follows from Bézout's identity, which states that there exist integers u and v such that $au + bv = 1$, and hence $x = a*(ux) + b(v*x)$.The CRT generalizes this idea to systems of linear congruences with pairwise relatively prime moduli, and provides a way to find a unique solution that satisfies all the congruences simultaneously. The motivation for the theorem is therefore to solve a fundamental problem in number theory and algebra, and to provide a tool for solving many other problems that arise in mathematics and engineering.

Theorem:

The theorem can be stated as follows:

Suppose we have a system of k congruences of the form:

$x \equiv a_1 \pmod{m_1}$

$x \equiv a2 \pmod{m_2}$

...

$x \equiv a_k \pmod{m_k}$

where the moduli $m_1, m_2, ..., m_k$ are pairwise relatively prime (i.e., $\gcd(m_i, m_j) = 1$ for all $i \neq j$). Then there exists a unique solution x modulo the product of the moduli $M = m_1 * m_2 * ... * m_k$, and the solution can be expressed in the form:

$x \equiv a_1 M_1 y_1 + a_2 M_2 y_2 + ... + a_k M_k y_k \pmod{M}$

where $M_1, M_2, ..., M_k$ are the "partial moduli" defined by $M_i = M/m_i$, and $y_1, y_2, ..., y_k$ are integers satisfying the congruences:

$M_1 y_1 \equiv 1 \pmod{m_1}$

$M_2 y_2 \equiv 1 \pmod{m_2}$

...

$M_k * y_k \equiv 1 \pmod{m_k}$

The Chinese Remainder Theorem has many applications in number theory, algebra, and computer science, including:

- Solving systems of linear congruences: The theorem provides a systematic method for finding the unique solution to a system of linear congruences.
- Error correction in coding theory: The theorem is used in coding theory to correct errors in data transmission by encoding the original message using a product of pairwise relatively prime moduli, and then decoding it using the Chinese Remainder Theorem.
- Computation in finite fields: The theorem is used in finite field arithmetic to compute modular inverses and to perform other arithmetic operations efficiently.
- Chinese remainder hashing: The theorem is used in computer science to construct hash functions that can be evaluated efficiently using the Chinese Remainder Theorem.

Chinese riddle: Is there a positive integer p such that when p is divided by 3 it yields a remainder 2, when p is divided by 5 it yields a remainder 4, and when *p* is divided by 7 it yields a remainder 6. In other words, we seek a common solution of the following three congruence equations:

$x \equiv 2 \pmod 3,\ x \equiv 4 \pmod 5,\ x \equiv 6 \pmod 7$

The 10 integers in Z_{10}, that is the integers 0 through 9, can be reconstructed from their two residues modulo 2 and 5 (the relatively prime factors of 10). Say the known residues of a decimal digit x and $r_2 = 0$ and $r_5 = 3$; that is, x mod 2 =0 and x mod 5 =3 . Therefore, x is an even integer in Z_{10} whose remainder, on division by 5, is 3.The unique solution is x = 8.

<u>Example 4.13</u>: The system of congruences a ≡ 2 mod 3, a ≡ 3 mod 5, …a ≡ 2 mod 7 has the solution 23 modulo 105, because 23 mod 3 = 2, 23 mod 5 = 3, and 23 mod 7 = 2. We can write down every solution as 23 + 105 x k for k ∈Z.

The following mathematical formulation of CRT is most useful.

$$M = \prod_{i=1}^{k} m_i$$

Where, m_i the are pairwise relatively prime; that is $\gcd(m_i, m_j) = 1$, for $1 \le i, j \le k$, and $i \neq j$. We can represent any integer A in Z_m by a k-tuple whose elements are in Zm_i using the following correspondence:

$A \Leftrightarrow (a_1, a_2, \ldots, a_k)$ ….(7)

where $A \in Z_M$, $a_i \in Z_{mi}$ and $a_i = A \bmod m_i$ for $1 \le i \le k$. The CRT makes two assertions.

1. The mapping of Equation (7) is a one-to-one correspondence (called a **bijection**) between and the Cartesian product $Z_{m1} \times Z_{m2} \times Z_{m3} \ldots \times Z_{mk}$. That is, for every integer A such that $0 \le A \le M$, there is a unique k-tuple $(a_1, a_2, \ldots, a_k)$ with $0 \le a_i \le m_i$ that represents it, and for every such k-tuple $(a_1, a_2, \ldots, a_k)$, there is a unique integer A in Z_M .

2. Operations performed on the elements of Z_M can be equivalently performed on the corresponding k-tuples by performing the operation independently in each coordinate position in the appropriate system.

Let us demonstrate the **first assertion**. The transformation from A to $(a_1, a_2, \ldots, a_k)$, is obviously unique; that is, each a_i is uniquely calculated as $a_i = A \bmod m_i$

Computing A from $(a_1, a_2, \ldots, a_k)$ can be done as follows. Let $M_i = M/m_i$ for $1 \le i \le k$. Note that $M_i = m_1 \times m_2 \times \ldots m_{i-1} \times m_{i+1} \times \ldots m_k$ so that $M_i = 0 \pmod{m_j}$ for all j not equal to I

Then let $ci = Mi \times Mi^{-11} \bmod mi$ for $1 \le i \le k$ ….8

By the definition of *Mi*, it is relatively prime to *mi* and therefore has a unique multiplicative inverse mod *mi*. So Equation (8.8) is well defined and produces a unique value c_i .We can now compute

$$A \equiv \sum_{i-1}^{k} a_i c_i \quad mod\ M \qquad ....9$$

UNIT SUMMARY

In this unit Modular Arithmetic, Divisibility, Coprimality and Euler's Totient Function, GCD and Extended Euclidean Algorithm, Chinese Remainder Theorem are discussed in brief. Modular arithmetic deals with numbers "wrapping around" after reaching a certain value called the modulus. It is used in various areas of mathematics and computer science. Divisibility concerns the relationship between two integers where one divides the other without leaving a remainder. Division Algorithm, Primes, Fundamental Theorem of Arithmetic, Congruence Relation are the major subtopics covered. Coprimality refers to numbers that have no common factors other than 1. Euler's Totient function calculates the number of positive integers less than n that are coprime to n. Properties of Euler's Totient Function and Application in Euler's Theorem are dealt here. The greatest common divisor (GCD) of two integers is the largest integer that divides both of them without leaving a remainder. Applications of GCD, Extended Euclidean Algorithm, Solving Linear Diophantine Equations are discussed in brief. The Chinese Remainder Theorem provides a solution to systems of congruences with pairwise coprime moduli. It states for pairwise coprime integers, there exists a unique integer satisfying properties of congruences.

Exercises

1. What is 2008^{2008} mod 3?
2. Suppose we want to factor a number X with 220 digits, how long does it takes?
3. Find the largest possible value of the greatest common divisor of the numbers 5^n+65^n+6 and 8^n+78^n+7, where n^n is an arbitrary positive integer.
4. How many ordered pairs of integers (a,b)(a,b) are there, such that $100 \le a \le 1000, 100 \le b \le 1000$ and a/b=12/21 ? Assume:For an ordered pair of integers (a,b)(a,b), the order of the integers matter. The ordered pair (1,2)(1,2) is different from the ordered pair (2,1)(2,1).
5. If n = $p_1^{k1}\ p_2^{k2}\ p_3^{k3}\ ......\ p_l^{kl}$ is a natural number. Then φ(n) = n $(1-\frac{1}{p_1})\ (1-\frac{1}{p_2}).... (1-\frac{1}{p_k})$

6. Solve $x^2 = 10 \mod 13$ by trial and error. There are two solutions.
7. Suppose $x^2 = a \mod p$ where p is a prime. Show that for any $0 < a < p$, there are exactly two solutions or none.
8. Solve the quadratic equation $x^2 + 3x + 11 = 0 \mod 11$
9. Show that a number n is prime iff, $1.2. \cdot \cdot \cdot (p - 1) = -1 \mod n$. This is known as Wilson's theorem.
10. Solve the equation $x^2 + 5x + 8 = 0 \mod 11$.

REFERENCES AND SUGGESTED READINGS

1. Rosen, K. H. (2019). Discrete Mathematics and Its Applications. (8th Edition) ISBN10: 125967651X ISBN13: 9781259676512.
2. Niven, I., Zuckerman, H. S., & Montgomery, H. L. (1991). An introduction to the theory of numbers. John Wiley & Sons.
3. Norman L. Biggs, Discrete Mathematics, (2nd ed. 2002), Oxford University Press.
4. Shoup, V. (2009). A computational introduction to number theory and algebra, Cambridge University Press.
5. Stallings, William. "The principles and practice of cryptography and network security 7th edition, isbn-10: 0134444280." *Pearson Education* 20.1 (2017): 7.

Dynamic QR Code for Further Reading

5 Combinatorics

UNIT SPECIFICS

Through this unit we have discussed the following aspects:

- *Permutations*
- *Combinations*
- *Principle of Inclusion and exclusion*
- *Pigeonhole principal*
- *Generating Functions*
- *Recurrence Relations*

In this chapter, we covered the above-mentioned concepts.

Introduction:

This Unit is devoted to understand the principles of counting. Some important concepts that are useful in the field of computer science are introduced. Here the reader is introduced the basic principles of counting with permutation and combination exercises, then understanding pigeonhole and Inclusion exclusion principles, you will see Generating Functions and Recurrence Relations.

RATIONALE

Why do you learn basics of counting?

Ability to count or to enumerate objects is on of the important problem solving skill. It is possible to determine enough number of telephone numbers, or IP addresses. When probability of events need to be computed then counting is extensively used, counting also play a key role in mathematical biology for instance DNA sequencing. counting is used to determine the complexity of algorithms. One has to learn basic techniques of counting, analyse the problem and perfrom combinatorial analysis to solve simple to complex problems.

PRE-REQUISITES

Mathematics at school level(till Class X)

UNIT OUTCOMES

List of outcomes of this unit is as follows:

U5-O1: Understand basic principles of counting.

U5-O2: Apply Theory of permutations to solve counting problems.

U5-O3: Apply Theory of combinations to solve counting problems.

U5-O4: Understand the principles of Inclusion-Exclusion and Pigeon hole.

U5-O5: Apply concepts of Generating functions to solve problems.

U5-O6: Apply Recurrence relations to solve recursive problems.

Unit-5 Outcomes	EXPECTED MAPPING WITH COURSE OUTCOMES (1- Weak Correlation; 2- Medium correlation; 3- Strong Correlation)								
	CO-1	CO-2	CO-3	CO-4	CO-5	CO-6	CO-7	CO-8	CO-9
U5-O1	2	2	2	2	1	3	1	1	3
U5-O2	2	1	1	1	2	3	-	1	3
U5-O3	2	2	2	2	1	3	-	1	3
U5-O4	2	2	2	2	2	3	-	1	3
U5-O5	2	2	2	2	2	3	2	1	3
U5-O6	2	2	2	2	3	3	2	1	3

Combinatorics

The counting problem in discrete mathematics refers to the task of determining the number of possible outcomes or arrangements in a given scenario. This involves applying mathematical principles to count the number of ways that an event or object can occur. The counting problem can range from simple tasks such as counting the number of ways to arrange a set of objects to more complex problems such as determining the number of possible outcomes in a game of chance or the number of permutations in a cryptographic system.

We can solve some counting problems by finding ways to arrange distinct elements belonging to a set where order cannot be a matter. We can solve some counting problems by finding ways to select a specific element where order can be a concern.

5.1 PERMUTATIONS

An ordered arrangement of a set of discrete and distinct objects is termed as Permutation. If the number of elements are r then it is a r permutation.

For example, there is a box containing chocolates you need to select 3 chocolates from it, then what are the number of ways to do this? There is a group of 10 Australian girls then what is the number of different committees of 5 girls that can be formed from it?

In this unit you will find methods to solve such problems.

Example 5.1: Let us consider above said problem, There is a group of 7 Australian girls then what is the number of different committees of 5 girls that can be formed from it?

First thing is the order in which a girl is selected matters, There are seven ways to select the first girl to stand at the start of the line. Once this girl has been selected, there are six ways to select the second student in the line. After the first and second girls have been selected, there are five ways to select the girl. By the product rule, there are $7 \cdot 6 \cdot 5 = 210$ ways to select five girls from a group of seven Australian girls.

Theorem: If n is a positive integer and r is an integer with $1 \leq r \leq n$, then there are r-permutations of a set with n distinct elements
$P(n, r) = n(n-1)(n-2) \cdots (n-r+1)$.

The first element can be chosen in n ways, then remaining are n-1 so n-1 ways to choose next element, following the same process subsequently until there are n-(r-1) elements, then rth element can be chosen in n-r+1 ways. Now applying the product rule we get $n(n-1)(n-2) \cdots (n-r+1)$ as r permutations .

Note that $P(n, 0) = 1$ whenever n is a nonnegative integer because there is exactly one way to order zero elements. That is, there is exactly one list with no elements in it, namely the empty list

Lemma: If n and r are integers with $0 \leq r \leq n$, then $P(n, r) = \frac{n!}{(n-r)!}$

Proving this is left as an exercise for the reader as this is studied in lower classes.

5.2 COMBINATIONS

Now, let us think about another counting problem mentioned earlier.

selection of objects from unordered set is termed as combinations. If there are r elements of an unordered set then it is a r combination.

Example 5.2: There is a set having {R,G,B,W} then {R,B,W} becomes a three combination from the color set, {W,R,B} is same as the previous one as the order does not matter with combinations.

The number of r-combinations of a set with n distinct elements is denoted by C(n, r). Note that C(n, r) is also denoted by $\binom{n}{r}$ and is called a binomial coefficient.

Theorem: when n , non-negative integer, number of elements and r, an integer, ranging from $0 \leq r \leq n$ then r combinations of a set of n elements is given by

$$C(n, r) = \frac{n!}{r!\,(n-r)!}$$

Proof: The r-permutations of the set which is P (n, r) can be obtained by forming the r-combinations of the set which is C(n, r). Now, ordering the elements in each r-combination, can be done in P (r, r) ways. by the product rule,

$$P(n, r) = C(n, r) \cdot P(r, r).$$

Solving for C(n, r) we get ,

$C(n, r) = \frac{P(n,r)}{P(r,r)}$ Sibstituting from the previous results,

We get, $C(n, r) = \frac{\frac{n!}{(n-r)!}}{\frac{r!}{(r-r)!}} = \frac{n!}{r!(n-r)!}$

Cancelling out (n-r)! from numerator and denominator we can write it as

$$C(n, r) = \frac{n!}{r!(n-r)!} = \frac{n(n-1)....(n-r+1)}{r!}$$

Lemma: Let n and r be nonnegative integers with r ≤ n. Then C(n, r) = C(n, n − r).

$$C(n, r) = \frac{n!}{r!(n-r)!}$$

As proved by theorem

$$C(n, n-r) = \frac{n!}{(n-r)![n-(n-r)]!} = \frac{n!}{r!(n-r)!}$$

From this we infer C(n, r) = C(n, n − r)

Example: A group of 30 people have been trained as astronauts to go on the first mission to Mars. How many ways are there to select a crew of six people to go on this mission (assuming that all crew members have the same job)?

The number of ways to select a crew of six from the pool of 30 people is the number of 6-combinations of a set with 30 elements, because the order in which these people are chosen does not matter. By Theorem 2, the number of such combinations is C(30, 6) = 30! / 6! 24! = 30 · 29 · 28 · 27 · 26 · 25 / 6 · 5 · 4 · 3 · 2 · 1 = 593,775.

Permutations and Combinations

	Order significant	Order not significant
Repetitions allowed	n^k	$\binom{n+k-1}{k}$
Repetitions not allowed	n(n-1)….(n-k+1)	$\binom{n}{k}$

5.3 INCLUSION EXCLUSION PRINCIPLE

The inclusion-exclusion principle is a mathematical principle that allows one to calculate the size of a union of several sets in terms of the sizes of their intersections. It is a counting technique used to count the number of elements that belong to at least one of two or more sets, given the size of each set and the size of their intersections.

The principle states that the size of the union of two or more sets is equal to the sum of the sizes of each set minus the sum of the sizes of their pairwise intersections, plus the size of the intersection of all sets. The formula for the inclusion-exclusion principle is:

$|A \cup B \cup ...| = |A| + |B| + ... - |A \cap B| - |A \cap ...| - |B \cap ...| + |A \cap B \cap ...|$

Where A, B, ... are sets and | | represents the size or cardinality of the set.

The inclusion-exclusion principle is used in combinatorics and probability theory to calculate probabilities, in graph theory to calculate the number of paths or cycles in a graph, and in other fields of mathematics to count objects or arrangements. It is a useful tool for solving complex counting problems and has many applications in real-world situations.

Consider the problem of finding the number of elements in the union of two finite sets.

Now it can be computed using the relation $|A \cup B| = |A| + |B| - |A \cap B|$. Inference is that the number of elements in the union of the two sets A and B is the sum of the numbers of elements in the sets and the difference of the number of elements in their intersection which is:

$|A \cup B| = |A| + |B| - |A \cap B|$.

Theorem: For finite sets $X_1,X_2,X_3,\ldots X_n$, union of all the sets can be deduced by the following relation

$$|X1 \cup X2 \cup X3 \cup \ldots \cup Xn| = \sum_{1 \le i \le n} |X_i| - \sum_{1 \le i < j \le n} |X_i \cap X_j|$$

$$+ \sum_{1 \le i < j < k \le n} |X_i \cap X_j \cap X_k| - \cdots + (-1)^{n+1} |X_i \cap X_j \cap \ldots \cap X_k|$$

Proof:

Assume $X_1,X_2,X_3,\ldots X_n$ be finite sets with x as a member of exactly r of such sets where r >=1 and r <=n. then this element is counted by that a is a member of exactly r of the sets A1, A2, . . . , An where $1 \le r \le n$. This element is counted C(r, 1) times by |Xi |.

It is counted C(r, 2) times by $|X_i \cap X_j|$. In general, it is counted C(r, m) times by the summation involving m of the sets X_i. Thus, this element is counted exactly

$C(r, 1) - C(r, 2) + C(r, 3) - \cdots + (-1)^{r+1}C(r, r)$ times by the expression on the right-hand side of this equation. Our goal is to evaluate this quantity.

By Corollary 2 of Section 6.4, we have
$C(r, 0) - C(r, 1) + C(r, 2) - \cdots + (-1)^r C(r, r) = 0.$
Hence,
$1 = C(r, 0) = C(r, 1) - C(r, 2) + \cdots + (-1)^{r+1}C(r, r).$

We will prove the formula by showing that an element in the union is counted exactly once by the right-hand side of the equation. Suppose that a is a member of exactly r of the sets $A_1, A_2, \ldots, A_n$ where $1 \leq r \leq n$. This element is counted C(r, 1) times by $|A_i|$. It is counted C(r, 2) times by $|A_i \cap A_j|$. In general, it is counted C(r, m) times by the summation involving m of the sets A_i. Thus, this element is counted exactly

$C(r, 1) - C(r, 2) + C(r, 3) - \cdots + (-1)^{r+1}C(r, r)$
times by the expression on the right-hand side of this equation. Our goal is to evaluate this quantity. By Lemma 2 of previous section, we have,
$C(r, 0) - C(r, 1) + C(r, 2) - \cdots + (-1)^r C(r, r) = 0.$
Hence,
$1 = C(r, 0) = C(r, 1) - C(r, 2) + \cdots + (-1)^{r+1}C(r, r)$

Therefore, each element in the union is counted exactly once by the expression on the right-hand side of the equation. This proves the principle of inclusion–exclusion. The inclusion–exclusion principle gives a formula for the number of elements in the union of n sets for every positive integer n. There are terms in this formula for the number of elements in the intersection of every nonempty subset of the collection of the n sets. Hence, there are $2^n - 1$ terms in this formula.

Example: Derive a formula for the number of elements in the union of four sets.
Solution: The inclusion–exclusion principle shows that
$|A_1 \cup A_2 \cup A_3 \cup A_4| = |A_1| + |A_2| + |A_3| + |A_4|$
$- |A_1 \cap A_2| - |A_1 \cap A_3| - |A_1 \cap A_4| - |A_2 \cap A_3| - |A_2 \cap A_4|$
$- |A_3 \cap A_4| + |A_1 \cap A_2 \cap A_3| + |A_1 \cap A_2 \cap A_4| + |A_1 \cap A_3 \cap A_4|$
$+ |A_2 \cap A_3 \cap A_4| - |A_1 \cap A_2 \cap A_3 \cap A_4|.$
Note that this formula contains 15 different terms, one for each nonempty subset of $\{A_1, A_2, A_3, A_4\}$.

Example:

A total of 1232 students have taken a course in Spanish, 879 have taken a course in French, and 114 have taken a course in Russian. Further, 103 have taken courses in both Spanish and French, 23 have taken courses in both Spanish and Russian, and 14 have taken courses in both French and Russian. If 2092 students have taken at least one of Spanish, French, and Russian, how many students have taken a course in all three languages?

Solution: Let S be the set of students who have taken a course in Spanish, F the set of students who have taken a course in French, and R the set of students who have taken a course in Russian. Then,

$|S| = 1232, |F| = 879, |R| = 114,$

$|S \cap F| = 103, |S \cap R| = 23, |F \cap R| = 14,$

and

$|S \cup F \cup R| = 2092.$

When we insert these quantities into the equation

$|S \cup F \cup R| = |S| + |F| + |R| - |S \cap F| - |S \cap R| - |F \cap R| + |S \cap F \cap R|$

we obtain,

$2092 = 1232 + 879 + 114 - 103 - 23 - 14 + |S \cap F \cap R|.$

We now solve for $|S \cap F \cap R|$. We find that $|S \cap F \cap R| = 7$. Therefore, there are seven students who have taken courses in Spanish, French, and Russian. This is illustrated in Figure below.

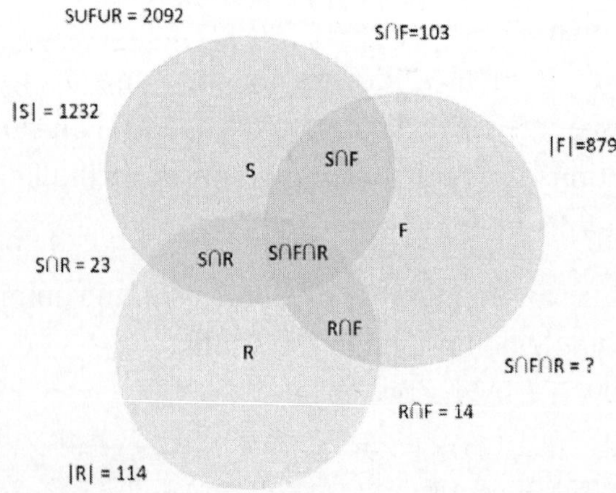

Figure 5.1 : Set of students who have taken Spanish, French and Russian

5.4 PIGEON HOLE PRINCIPLE

The pigeonhole principle is a mathematical principle that states that if there are more pigeons (or any other objects) than pigeonholes (or any other compartments), then at least one pigeonhole must contain two or more pigeons. In other words, if you have n objects distributed into (n-1) compartments, then at least one compartment must contain more than one object.

Consider a flock of birds, especially pigeons in this context, which are 10 in number. All these birds flies into 9 pigoenholes, as there are 10 in number, atleast one of these pigeonholes must have two pigeons in it and atmost one in each pigeon in each hole means atmost nine pigeons could be accommodated. This illustrates the general principle called pigeon hole principle, which states that " If there are more pigeons than the pigeonholes then there must be atleast one pigeonhole with at least two pigeons I n it". This principles in realtime scenario can be applied to any objects instead of pigeons.

Figure 5.2: pigeons in 9 pigeonholes

Statement : If there a positive integer k and there are k+1 or more objects are placed in k boxes, then there is atleast one box containing two or more of the objects.

This can be proved with Proof by contraposition, suppose when none of the k boxes contain more than one object, then total number of objects would be at most k, because there are atleast k+1 objects, this is a contradiction.

Proof: We prove the pigeonhole principle using a proof by contraposition. Suppose that none of the k boxes contains more than one object. Then the total number of objects would be at most k. This is a contradiction, because there are at least k + 1 objects.

The pigeonhole principle, also known as the Dirichlet drawer principle or the box principle, stating that if n objects are placed into m boxes (n > m), then at least one of the boxes must contain more than one object.

This principle is illustrated by imagining a scenario where you have more socks than there are drawers, and you randomly put each sock into a drawer. It's almost certain that at least one drawer will have more than one sock in it. German Mathematician G. Lejeune Dirichlet, often used this principle in his work. Dirichlet was not the first person to use this principle; a demonstration that there were at least two Parisians with the same number of hairs on their head dates to the 17th century.

The Dirichlet drawer principle is a fundamental concept in combinatorics and is used in many fields, including computer science, cryptography, and probability theory. It helps to understand the importance of recognizing patterns and repetitions in various mathematical situations.

The pigeonhole principle is often used in combinatorics, probability, and computer science to prove the existence of certain patterns or structures. It can also be used in day-to-day life to make predictions and estimate the likelihood of certain events. For example, if there are 30 students in a classroom and only 29 seats, then at least one student will have to stand. This is because there are more students than seats, and the pigeonhole principle guarantees that at least one student will not have a seat.

Example: There is a group of 369 people, there must be atleast four people with their birthday on same day because there are only 365 possible birthdays.

Example: Some exam to be graded from 0 to 50 points, If in a class atleast two of them receive same score then how many students must have been there in the class.

As exam to be graded from 0 to 50 points, possible scores are 51, then there must be atleast two students with same score, according to pigeonhole principle.

In a more generalized way, If N objects are placed into k number of boxes, then there is atleast one box containing atleast $\lceil N/k \rceil$ objects.

Some graceful applications of pigeonhole principle

- Birthday problem: In a group of 23 people, there is at least a 50% chance that two people have the same birthday.
- Dirichlet's theorem: If there are n objects distributed among k containers ($n > k$), then at least one container must contain more than $\lfloor n/k \rfloor$ objects.

- Subset sum: Given a set of n integers, there are 2^{n-1} non-empty subsets. If we choose n+1 subsets, at least two of them have the same sum.
- Ramsey's theorem: In any complete graph with six nodes, either there are three nodes that form a triangle or there are three nodes that form an independent set.
- Schur's theorem: For any integer k, there exist integers x, y, and z such that $x + y = z$ and all three are divisible by k.
- Pigeonhole sorting: A sorting algorithm that uses the pigeonhole principle to sort a sequence of integers efficiently.
- Chessboard problem: If two corners of a standard 8x8 chessboard are removed, the remaining board cannot be covered by 31 dominos, each of which covers exactly two adjacent squares.

5.5 GENERATING FUNCTIONS

This is an extremely powerful tool in discrete mathematics. This is used to manipulate sequences. We look at a single function to encode a given sequence instead of an infinite sequence.

Generating functions are a powerful tool in discrete mathematics that allow us to study sequences and combinatorial problems. A generating function is essentially a function that encodes information about a sequence or a set of combinatorial objects in a formal power series.

For example, consider the sequence of natural numbers {1, 2, 3, ...}. The generating function for this sequence is simply:

$f(x) = 1 + x + x^2 + x^3 + ...$ which is an infinite series. The coefficient of x^n in this series is the nth term of the sequence.

Generating functions are beneficial to solve a variety of problems in combinatorics, such as counting the number of ways to arrange objects or count the number of partitions of an integer. The power of generating functions lies in their ability to convert complicated combinatorial problems into simple algebraic manipulations of power series.

There are many techniques for manipulating generating functions, including differentiation, integration, and multiplication. These techniques allow us to transform a generating function for one sequence into a generating function for another sequence, or to extract information about the underlying combinatorial problem from the generating function.

So a generating function allowing us to manipulate the sequence as a single entity, by providing a formal structure that is intimately related to numerical sequence. The goal of understanding the sequence is better with a generating function.

<u>Definition:</u>

Consider a sequence having the entities p_0, p_1, p_2....p_n,.... Then f(x) is the corresponding generating function of the series

$F(x)= p_0+ p_1x+ p_2x^2....p_nx^n +.... =\sum_{i=0}^{\infty} p_i x^i$

Here p_n is the coefficient of x^n in f(x) also, n^{th} term of the sequence in f(x).

<u>Example:</u>

Derive generating function of the series 1,1,1,1,......

$F(x)= 1 + x + x^2+ x^3+... =\sum_{i=0}^{\infty} x^i$

<u>Example:</u>

Derive generating function of the series 1,1,1,1,1,1,0,0,0...

$F(x)= 1 + x + x^2+ x^3+ x^4 + x^5$

<u>Example:</u>

Derive generating function of the series 1,4,6,4,1,0,0,0,....

$F(x)= 1 + 4x + 6x^2+ 4x^3+ x^4 = (1+x)^4$

<u>Example:</u>

A series is represented by $3 + 8x^2+ x^3+ \frac{x^5}{7} +100x^6 +$ ... represent it as a sequence.

P0 = 3, coefficient of x_0 is 3

P1 = 0, coefficient of x_1

P2 =8, coefficient of x_2

P3= 1

And so on, so we have the sequence as 3,0,8,1,1/7, 100,...

Applications of generating functions:

- Combinatorics and probability theory: Generating functions can be used to count the number of ways to select or arrange objects, or to calculate the probabilities of certain events occurring. For example, the coefficient of a term in a generating function can represent the number of ways to choose a certain number of elements from a set.

- Graph theory: Generating functions can be used to study properties of graphs, such as the number of paths between two nodes or the number of ways to color the vertices of a graph.
- Number theory: Generating functions can be used to study the properties of integers and prime numbers. For example, the generating function for the prime numbers can be used to study their distribution and properties.
- Computation: Generating functions can be used to simplify complex calculations by transforming a complicated summation or sequence into a simple algebraic expression.
- Physics: Generating functions can be used to solve problems in physics, such as the calculation of the partition function in statistical mechanics or the correlation functions in quantum field theory.

Counting things using generating functions:

Generating functions are beneficial in solving problems about counting.

In Binomial Theorem, for the term in $(1+x)^n$, the $\binom{n}{r}$ is the coefficient of x^r . The generating function for the binomial coefficient is $(1+x)^n$. The number of ways of choosing x from r of the n factors, while choosing 1 from the other factors is given by the coefficient of x^r.

Example:

There is a shop which sells some item I in packages of 1,5,20 or 75. In how many ways can Sheela buy 95 item of I.

Modeling this with a generating function, exponent of x represent number of items in x and coefficient of x will be number of ways person can buy n items. As he could buy 0 to any number of items, we can represent it as

$F(x)= 1 + x + x^2+ x^3+\ldots =\sum_{i=0}^{\infty} x^i = \frac{1}{(1-x)}$ There is exactly one way of choosing, Assuming items are unique, When a person buy items in a package of 5, here i represents package,

$F(x)= 1 + x^5 + x^{10}+ x^{15}+\ldots =\sum_{i=0}^{\infty} x^{5i} = \frac{1}{(1-x^5)}$

5.6 RECURRENCE RELATION

A recurrence relation is a mathematical equation that describes a sequence of numbers in terms of its previous terms. The relation usually states that the nth term of the sequence is a function of one or more of the preceding terms. Recurrence relations can be used to model a wide variety of phenomena, including population growth, the dynamics of physical systems, and the behaviour of artificial intelligence algorithms. Recurrence relations are often used in the mathematical fields of combinatorics, number theory, and graph theory. They can be represented using various notations, including subscript notation, functional notation, and Sigma notation.

In this course, primary focus is on the class of finite order linear recurrence relations with constant coefficients. Examining closed form expressions from which recurrence relations arise. We will elucidate on methods for solving them.

If n is the size of a problem, then T(n) denotes the time required to solve a problem of size n, Recurrence relations are used to determine the running time of recursive programs, thus recurrence relations are themselves recursive in nature.

Consider a sequence of numbers represented by S, a finite number of terms of S are rlated to previous terms of S when S is a recurrence relation. $k \geq k_0$ where k_0 is in the domain of S then S(k) can obviously expressed in terms of some and/or all of the preceding terms of S(k). for domain of S given by {0,1,2,…} then the terms S0, S1 … cannot be easily defined by rhe recurrence relation. Only initial and boundary conditions forms the actual definition of S.

$\forall n \in N$ setting an = f(n) where f is defined by f: N→R the a_n is called as a **sequence**

For $a_n = f(a_{n-1} \dots a_{n-k})$ where f is defined by f: R^k→R and $a_1 \dots a_k$ are known then a_n is called as a **recursively defined sequence**. I is given by the recurrence relation $a_n = f(a_{n-1} \dots a_{n-k})$

A recurrence relation is called as a linear function, the following case gives an instance. $a_n = f(a_{n-1} \dots a_{n-k}) = s_1 a_{n-1} + \dots + s_k a_{n-k} + f(n)$ where s_i, f(n) are real numbers. When f(n)= 0 then linear recurrence relation is homogeneous. The term k determines the order of the recurrence relation.

In this unit we an approach to solve linear recurrence relations with k, 1 and 2.

Homogeneous linear recurrence relations:

Let $a_n = s_1a_{n-1}$ be a first order linear recurrence relation with $a_1 = k$. Notice, $a_2 = s_1k$, $a_3 = s_1$, $a_2 = s_2^1k$, $a_4 = s_1a_3 = s_1^3 k$, and in general $a_n = ks_1^{\ n-1}$

Nonomogeneous linear recurrence relations:

When f (n) = 0, we will search for a particular solution a_pn which is similar to f(n). We will still solve the homogeneous recurrence relation setting f (n) temporarily to 0 and the solution of this homogeneous recurrence relation will be ah n and $a_n = a_p\, n + a_h\, n$

Linear recurrence relation with constant coefficients:

A linear recurrence relation containing constant coefficients is a mathematical relationship between the terms of a sequence, where each term is a linear combination of the previous terms, and the coefficients in the relationship are constant. In other words, it is a recursive formula that expresses each term of a sequence as a linear combination of a fixed number of previous terms.

A linear recurrence relation with constant coefficients can be written in the form:

$a_n = c_1a_{\ n-1} + c_2a_{n-2} + ... + c_ka_{nk}$

where a_1, a_2, ..., a_k are given initial values, and c_1, c_2, ..., c_k are constants. This formula tells us that the n-th term of the sequence (an) can be calculated by using a linear combination of the previous k terms (a_{n-1}, a_{n-2}, ..., a_{n-k}).

The simplest example of a linear recurrence relation with constant coefficients is the Fibonacci sequence:

$a_1 = 1$, $a_2 = 1$, $a_n = a_{n-1} + a_{n-2}$ for $n > 2$

Here, the recurrence relation tells us that each subsequent term is the sum of the two previous terms. This relationship has constant coefficients ($c_1 = 1$, $c_2 = 1$) and defines the Fibonacci sequence.

Linear recurrence relations with constant coefficients are important in many areas of mathematics and physics, as they arise naturally in the analysis of a wide range of phenomena. They can be used to model growth and decay processes, population dynamics, financial systems, and many other real-world phenomena.

Second order homogenous linear recurrence relations:

A second order homogeneous linear recurrence relation is of the form:

$a_n = c_1a_{n-1} + c_2a_{n-2}$

where c1 and c2 are constants and no term in the recurrence relation depends on a non-homogeneous solution. Now we have to find a solution to this. The characteristic equation for this recurrence relation is: $r_2 - c_1r - c_2 = 0$

Solution to the recurrence relation can be obtained by solving the characteristic equation to acquiring the roots r1 and r2:

$r_{1,2} = (c_1 \pm \sqrt{(c_{12} + 4c_2)})/2$

There can be 3 types of solutions based on the nature of the roots of the characteristic equation.

i) roots are distinct ($r1 \neq r2$), the general solution is:

$a_n = A(r_1)n + B(r_2)n$

ii) roots are repeated ($r1 = r2$), the general solution is:

$a_n = (A + B_n)r_1n$

iii) roots are complex conjugates ($r_{1,2} = \alpha \pm \beta i$), the general solution is:

$an = (A \cos \beta n + B \sin \beta n)\alpha n$

in all the above cases, A and B are constants concluded by using the initial conditions.

$a_0 = A + B = c$

$a_1 = Ar_1 + Br_2 = d$

obviously, c and d are constants. Solving for A and B yields:

$A = \frac{(d-cr_{2})}{r_1r_2-r_{12}}$ $B = \frac{(cr_1-d)}{r_1r_2-r_{12}}$

So, the general solution for the recurrence relation can be found by substituting these values of A and B into the appropriate expression for the general solution.

UNIT SUMMARY

This unit provides a brief introduction on permutations, Combinations, Inclusion-Exclusion Principle, Pigeonhole principle, Generating Functions, and Recurrence relation.

Permutations refer to arrangements of objects in a specific order. The number of permutations of n distinct objects taken r at a time is given by P(n,r). Combinations are selections of objects without considering the order. The number of combinations of n distinct objects taken r at a time is denoted by C(n,r). The Inclusion-Exclusion Principle is a counting technique used to calculate the size of the union of multiple sets. It states that to find the size of the union of nn sets, one must include the sizes of each individual set, subtract the sizes of all pairwise intersections, add back the sizes of all triple intersections, and continue this process until all possible intersections have been considered. The Pigeonhole Principle states that if nn items are placed into mm containers and n>mn>m, then at least one container must contain more than one item. It's a simple yet powerful principle often used in combinatorics and probability. Generating functions are used to represent sequences of numbers as power series. They provide a systematic way to encode information about a sequence, allowing for various operations such as addition, multiplication, and differentiation to be performed on the sequence. A recurrence relation is an equation that defines a sequence recursively in terms of its previous terms. It expresses the nn-th term of a sequence as a function of earlier terms. Solving recurrence relations often involves finding a closed-form solution for the sequence.

EXERCISE:

1. Prove that

   $\binom{n}{k}\binom{k}{l}=\binom{n}{l}\binom{n-l}{k-l}$

2. A sum of n terms need to be bracketed so that the sum can be calculated by adding two terms at a time. In how many ways it can be bracketed? Modify your solution to bracket such that sum can be calculated by adding three terms at a time. Generalize your solution to bracket m terms out of n terms.

3. In between integers 1 and 50 find the number of integers which are multiples of 3 or 4 but not both. Verify the same.
4. There is a group of newly graduated undergrads, who are 50 in number. 36 of them like maaza, 24 of them like coke, and each of them like to have atleast one of the drinks. Find out how many of them like both the drinks.
5. Find Generating function for the following sequences:

a) 1, 3, 5, 0, 0, 0, . . .

b) 1, 2, 22, 23, 24, . . .

c) 1, 5, 10, 15, 10, 5, 1, 0, 0, 0, . . .

d) 1, 5, 10, 10, 5, 1, 0, 0, 0, .

6. Suppose that 101 positive integers are arranged in a circle. The sum of all the numbers is 300. Prove that you can always choose a consecutive sequence of numbers which sum to 200.
7. There are 2504 computer science students at a school. Of these, 1876 have taken a course in Java, 999 have taken a course in Linux, and 345 have taken a course in C. Further, 876 have taken courses in both Java and Linux, 231 have taken courses in both Linux and C, and 290 have taken courses in both Java and C. If 189 of these students have taken courses in Linux, Java, and C, how many of these 2504 students have not taken a course in any of these three programming languages?

a. How many elements are in the union of five sets if the sets contain 10,000 elements each, each pair of sets has 1000 common elements, each triple of sets has 100 common elements, every four of the sets have 10 common elements, and there is 1 element in all five sets?

b. Determine which of these are linear homogeneous recurrence relations with constant coefficients. Also, find the degree of those that are.

a) $a_n = 3a_{n-1} + 4a_{n-2} + 5a_{n-3}$

b) $a_n = 2na_{n-1} + a_{n-2}$

c) $a_n = a_{n-1} + a_{n-4}$

d) $a_n = a_{n-1} + 2$

e) $a_n = a^2_{n-1} + a_{n-2}$

f) $a_n = a_{n-2}$

g) $a_n = a_{n-1} + n$

PRACTICAL

1. The series 1,2,5,14,42... is termed as Catalan numbers and 1,2,5,15,52,.... Is termed as Bell numbers. Analyse the series, Define a recurrent relation and Implement a function in C language to print n numbers of the series.
2. Derive a divide-and-conquer recurrence relation for the number of comparisons used to find a number in a list using a binary search.

KNOW MORE

Stirling Number:

First kind of Sterling number is defined by the rule $(-1)^{n-k}$ s(n,k) is the number of permutations of {1,….,n} with k cycles.

Second kind of Stirling number S(n,k) is the number of partitions of {1,….,n} with k non empty parts. The definitions can be extended to all n and k by defining the Sterling numbers to be 0 unless $1 \leq k \leq n$

REFERENCES AND SUGGESTED READINGS

a. Liu, C. L., & Mohapatra, D. P. (2008). Elements of Discrete Mathematics. Tata McGraw-Hill.

b. Rosen, K. H. (2019). Discrete Mathematics and Its Applications. (8th Edition) ISBN10: 125967651X ISBN13: 9781259676512.

c. Cohen, D. I. A. (1978). Basic techniques of combinatorial theory. John Wiley.

d. Norman L. Biggs, Discrete Mathematics, (2nd ed. 2002), Oxford University Press.

e. Smullyan, R. M. (1995). First-order logic. Courier Corporation.

f. Bóna, M. (2006). A walk through combinatorics: an introduction to enumeration and graph theory.

g. Cameron, P. J. (1994). Combinatorics: topics, techniques, algorithms. Cambridge University Press.

h. Herstein, I. N. (2006). Topics in algebra. John Wiley & Sons.

Dynamic QR Code for Further Reading

6 Some Algebraic Structures

UNIT SPECIFICS

Through this unit we have discussed the following algebraic structures:

- *Semigroups*
- *Monoids*
- *Homomorphism*
- *Isomorphism*
- *Group*
- *Abelian Group*
- *Permutation Group and Cayley Theorem*
- *Cosets*
- *Finite fields*
- *Fermat's Little Theorem*

After completion of this module, you should be able to recognize and apply basic concepts involvingabove algebraic structures for variety of simple applications.

The important applications of group theory are: Since group theory is the study of symmetry, whenever an object or a system property is invariant under the transformation, the object can be analysed using group theory. The algorithm to solve Rubik's cube works based on group theory. This Unit is devoted to understand the basic terms and terminology related to Graph Theory

RATIONALE

Why do you learn basics of Group Theory?

Groups play a fundamental role in Abstract Algebra: many algebraic structures, including rings, fields, and modules, can be seen as formed by adding new operations and axioms based on groups. Researchersoften use group theory to explain many kinds of phenomena. In recent years, group theory has been introduced into crystallography to further explore the macroscopic symmetry of crystals from a mathematical point of view.

In the 19th century, Galois founded group theory and used it to solve the problem of the quintic equation. In the past two hundred years, group theory has penetrated geometry, algebraic topology, function theory, functional analysis, and many other branches of mathematics. It has important applications in theoretical physics, quantum chemistry, algebraic coding, automata theory, and so on. Particularly, crystallography needs to figure out the mathematical model of crystal structure by group theory. An ordered group has at least one generator, and it is viable that a group has more identified elements than the amounts of generators for everyday applications.

PRE-REQUISITES

Mathematics at school level (till Class X)

UNIT OUTCOMES

List of outcomes of this unit is as follows:

U6-O1: Understand the concepts of groups.

U6-O2: Apply the properties of cosets.

U6-O3: Prove Homomorphism and isomorphism.

U6-O4: Apply properties of groups to solve numeric problems.

U6-O5: Apply finite fields to analyze and solve real-time problems.

U6-O6: Apply Fermat's little theorem to solve problems.

Unit-6 Outcomes	EXPECTED MAPPING WITH COURSE OUTCOMES (1- Weak Correlation; 2- Medium correlation; 3- Strong Correlation)								
	CO-1	CO-2	CO-3	CO-4	CO-5	CO-6	CO-7	CO-8	CO-9
U6-O1	2	2	2	2	1	3	3	-	2
U6-O2	1	1	1	-	-	1	3	-	1
U6-O3	2	2	1	1	1	2	3	-	2
U6-O4	1	1	1	2	2	2	3	-	2
U6-O5	2	1	1	1	1	1	3	-	1
U6-O6	2	1	1	2	2	2	3	-	2

Some Algebraic Structures

6.1 Semigroup

In Computer Science and Cryptography, the topics that were considered earlier to be part of pure mathematics, have found important applications and we rapidly review the related concepts of some algebraic structures that have found such applications in last few decades.

Many properties of structures that we study in this module have been introduced as part of traditional higher algebra in old classic books like Hall and Knight's Higher algebra (Chapter XXX: Theory of Numbers).

However, the nomenclature and terminology of structures is new, and is attributed to the French mathematician Evariste Galois, who is considered father of the algebraic structures that we study in this module.

Finite fields have been named as Galios fields.

E. Galios had a tragic untimely death in a duel at the age of twenty but had in his all to brief life made a revolutionary contribution, namely the founding of group theory.

source: Wikipedia

Definition 6.1: **Semigroup**: A finite or infinite set S with a binary operation 'θ' (θ: composition) is called semigroup following two conditions simultaneously hold:

1. Closure: $\forall (a, b) \in S \times S, (a\,\theta\, b) \in S$
2. Associative: $\forall a, b, c \in S, (a\,\theta\, b)\,\theta\, c = a\,\theta\,(b\,\theta\, c)$

Example 6.1: The set of positive integers (excluding zero) with addition operation is a semigroup.

Thus, $\mathbb{Z}^+ = \{1, 2, 3, \ldots\}$, with operation addition, denoted by "+", as defined over the set of positive integers $\mathbb{Z}^+$ is a semigroup. For the sake of illustrating the definition 6.1, t we shall denote the set of positive integers $\mathbb{Z}^+$ by S.

We verify that the closure property holds as for every pair $(a, b) \in S \times S$, we have $(a+b) \in S$, *i.e.*, $(a+b)$ belongs to the set S. For example, $7+29 = 36 \in S$,

Associative property also holds for every element $a, b, c \in S$, $(a+b) + c = a + (b+c)$. For example, $(29+57) + 91 = 29 + (57+91)$, which is equal to 177.

□

Having noted that the two expressions as stated in Example 6.1 evaluate to the same value, we may prefer to write the concerned expression as 29+57+91. We note that, when such an expression is to be evaluated by applying only one the binary operation at a time, we have two choices:

i) First, we evaluate the expression 29+57, to get the intermediate result as 86. Using the concept of expression evaluation tree, we may diagrammatically show this sequence of operations as follows:

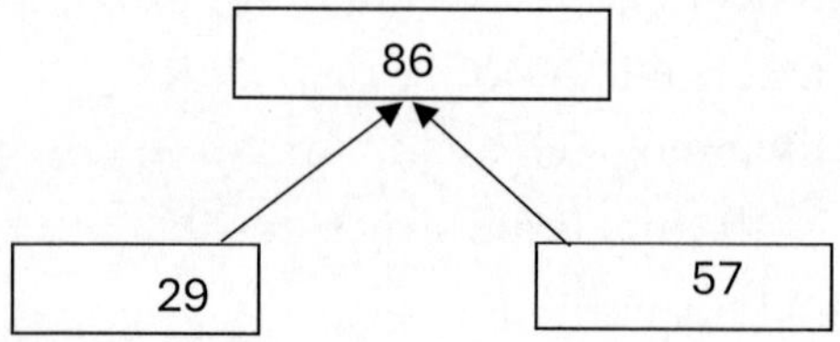

Figure 6.1: Evaluation tree for 29+57

Next, the number 91 is added to the intermediate result 86, to get the final result as

177.

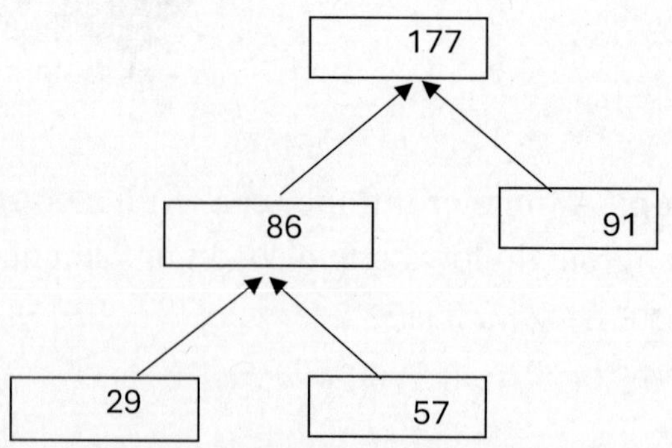

Figure 6.2: Evaluation tree for (29+57)+91

ii) In the second approach, we first evaluate the expression 57+91, to get the intermediate result as 148.

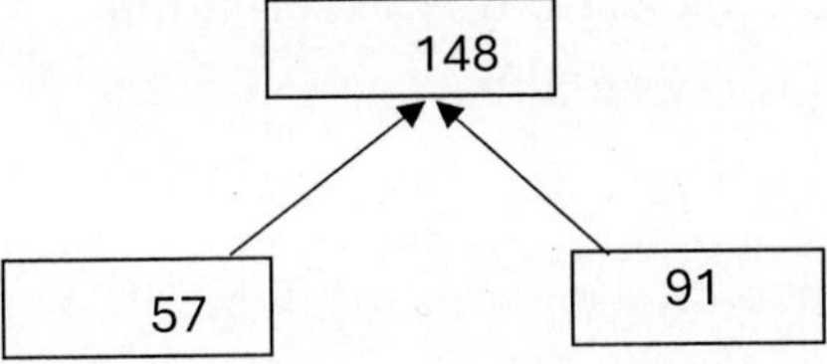

Figure 6.3: Evaluation tree for 57+91.

Next, the number 29 is (pre-)added to the intermediate result 148, to get the final result as 177. Note that, in the following tree, we showed the number 29 to the left side of the intermediate result 148, to diagrammatically depict that is it pre-added.

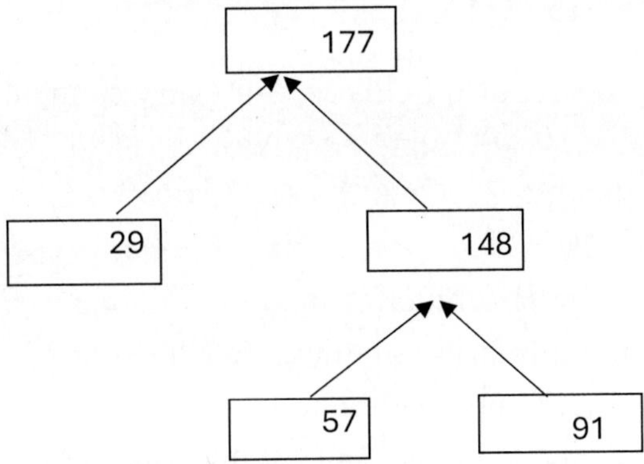

Figure 6.4: Evaluation tree for 29+(57+91).

We note that, the two expression (evaluation) trees as given in Figure 6.2, and figure 6.4 are different (note that the intermediate evaluated values are different); however the result is the same for these two expression trees. This result is same due to associativity property.

□

Question 6.1: Is the set of positive integers (excluding zero) with multiplication operation a semigroup? Thus, this question asks you to find out whether $\mathbb{Z}^+ = \{1, 2, 3, \ldots\}$, with operation multiplication, denoted by "×", as defined over the set of positive integers $\mathbb{Z}^+$ is a semigroup?

You may like to verify that, the answer to this question is yes. Thus, the set of positive integers $\mathbb{Z}^+$ together with multiplication operation, denoted by "×", as defined over the set of positive integers, is a semigroup. We state this observation in Example 6.2 below, together with sketch of the proof of this claim.

Example 6.2: The set of positive integers (excluding zero) with multiplication operation is a semigroup.

For $\mathbb{Z}^+ = \{1, 2, 3, \dots\}$, with operation multiplication, denoted by "×":

1. Closure property holds as, for every pair $(a, b) \in \mathbb{Z}^+$, $(a \times b) \in \mathbb{Z}^+$, *i.e.*, $(a \times b)$ is positive integer, and hence it is in the set $\mathbb{Z}^+$. For example, $3 \times 5 = 15 \in \mathbb{Z}^+$

2. Associative property also holds as, for every element $a, b, c \in \mathbb{Z}^+$, $(a \times b) \times c = a \times (b \times c)$, For example, $(3 \times 2) \times 5 = 3 \times (2 \times 5) = 30 \in \mathbb{Z}^+$.

Natural question that arises in our mind is, having seen two different semigroups, the first one being the one in Example 6.1, and second one in Example 6.2, can we say something about the similarity of these two different structures? We shall investigate this question in the next subsection(s) in this module, where we would introduce homomorphism and isomorphism (of different structures).

□

Question 6.2: Is the set of positive integers, excluding zero, and one, *i.e.*, the set $\{2, 3, 4, 5, \dots\}$, with:

(i) addition operation a semigroup?
(ii) multiplication operation a semigroup?

Question 6.3: Is the set of positive integers, excluding zero, one, two, and three *i.e.*, the set $\{4, 5, 6, \dots\}$, with:

(i) addition operation a semigroup?
(ii) multiplication operation a semigroup?

Question 6.4: Is the set $\{7^3, 7^4, 7^6, \dots\}$, with:

(iii) addition operation a semigroup?
(iv) multiplication operation a semigroup?

Question 6.5: Is the set of positive integers (excluding zero) with exponentiation operation a semigroup? Thus, this question asks you to find out whether $\mathbb{Z}^+ = \{1, 2, 3, \ldots\}$, with operation exponentiation, (sometimes also denoted by "↑"), as defined over the set of positive integers $\mathbb{Z}^+$ is a semigroup?

Note that this question asks you to investigate whether the expressions like

$(2^3)^5$ and $(2^{(3^5)})$ are equal?

You may like to note that $(2^3)^5 = 2^3 . 2^3 . 2^3 . 2^3 . 2^3 = 2^{3+3+3+3+3} = 2^{3*5} = 2^{15}$,

whereas $(2^{(3^5)}) = 2^{243}$.

From the above brief discussion, we conclude that the set of positive integers with exponentiation operation is not a semigroup. The following expression evaluation trees illustrates this point.

i) First, we evaluate the expression 2^3, to get the intermediate result as 8. Using the concept of expression evaluation tree, we may diagrammatically show this sequence of operations as follows:

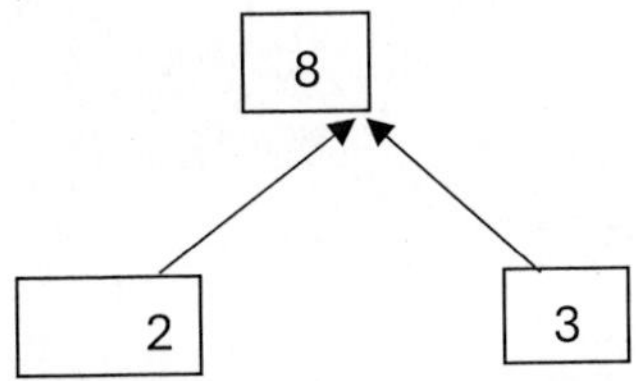

Figure 6.5: Evaluation tree for 2^3.

Next, the exponentiation operation is applied to the intermediate result 8 toraise it to 5, to get the final result as 32768.

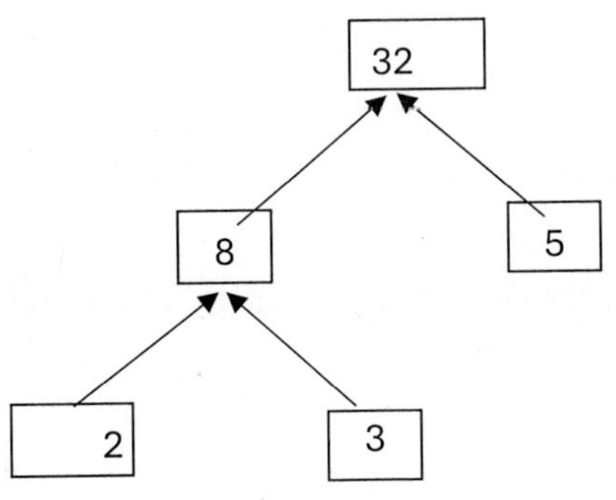

Figure 6.6: Evaluation tree for $(2^3)^5$.

ii) In the second approach, we first evaluate the expression 3^5, to get the intermediate result as 243.

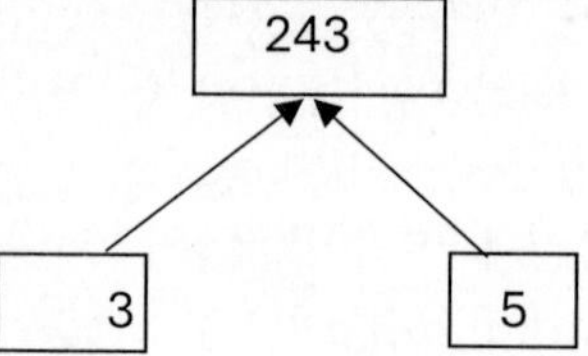

Figure 6.7: Evaluation tree for 3^5.

Next, we raise the base 2 to this intermediate result 243, to get the final result as 2^{243}.

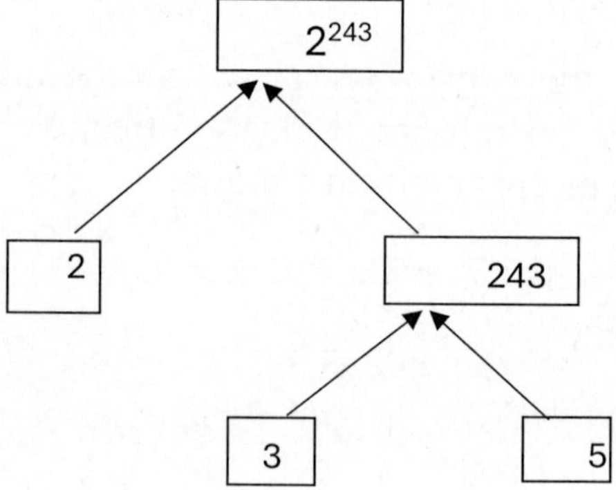

Figure 6.8: Evaluation tree for $(2^{(3^5)})$.

Since the exponentiation operation does not satisfy the associativity property, we observe that the values of the expressions as shown in Figure 6.6 and Figure 6.8 are different.

Example 6.3: ((Ɍ, º)): □

In the module on Sets, Relations and Functions, we studied the notion Composite Functions. As an extension of this notion, consider a collection of binary relations, say Ɍ = { R_1, R_2, … R_n} defined on a set S (*i.e.* each of R_i is subset of the Cartesian product $S \times S$). Given two such binary relations, say R_i, and R_j, define the notion of Composite Relation $R_i \circ R_j$. We note that the relation $R_i \circ R_j$ is also a relation on the set S. As an easy exercise, prove that the operation composition (*i.e.*, "º") defined on the collection of binary relations Ɽ (*i.e.*, the structure (Ɽ, $^{\circ}$)) , is associative. This proves that we have discovered yet another semigroup, whose objects are binary relations, say { R_1, R_2, … R_n} defined on a set *S*, and it forms a semigroup together with the composition (*i.e.*, "o") operation defined on the binary relations.

□

Example 6.4: ((Ꟶ, $^{\circ}$)):

In the module on Sets, Relations and Functions, we studied the notion Composite Functions. Consider a collection of binary functions, say Ꟶ = { $f_1, f_2, \ldots f_n$} defined on a set *S* (*i.e.* each of f_i is a function with domain as *S* and range as *S*). Given two such binary functions, say f_i, and f_j, define the notion of Composite function $f_i \circ f_j$. We note that the function $f_i \circ f_j$ is also a function on the set *S*. As an easy exercise, prove that the operation composition (*i.e.*, "o") defined on the collection of functions Ꟶ (*i.e.*, the structure (Ꟶ, $^{\circ}$)) , is associative. This proves that we have discovered yet another semigroup, whose objects are binary relations, say { $f_1, f_2, \ldots f_n$} defined on a set *S*, and it forms a semigroup together with the composition (*i.e.*, "o") operation defined on the binary functions.

□

6.2 Homomorphism

Definition 6.2: **Semigroup Homomorphism**: A semigroup homomorphism is a (functional) map between semigroups that preserves the respective semigroup operations.

Given semigroups $G \equiv (D,*)$, and $H \equiv (R,+)$, and a function $f: D \rightarrow R$, then f is semigroup homomorphism from structure *G* to structure *H* if and only if,

$$f(x) + f(y) = f(x * y), \qquad \ldots(6.1)$$

(with + is operation in range set R, * is operation in domain set D).

Definition 6.3: **Monoid**: Monoid is semigroup with the "identity element" (with respect to) binary operation 'θ' : composition or "multiplication", or sometimes "addition")), say e (also denoted by 1 (for "*"), or 0 (for "+")): *i.e.*, the following additional property holds:

3. Identity: $\exists\, e \in S$, such that $\forall\, a \in S\, (\, a\, \theta\, e) = a$

Question 6.6: In a finite monoid, is it possible to have two distinct identity elements?

Question 6.7: Is the set of positive integers (excluding zero) (*i.e.*, set $\mathbb{Z}^+$) with addition operation is a monoid?

The answer is no, because there is no identity element with respect to addition operation in the set $\mathbb{Z}^+$. However, when we expand this set to include the number zero, we get the set $\mathbb{N} = \{\, 0, 1, 2, 3, 4, \ldots \}$ and the set $\mathbb{N}$ together with (usual addition operation (denoted by +) is a monoid.

□

Question 6.8: Is the set of positive integers (excluding zero) (*i.e.*, set $\mathbb{Z}^+$) with multiplication operation (denoted by $\times$) is a monoid?

(Refer to our earlier Example 6.2, where we stated that set $\mathbb{Z}^+$ with multiplication operation (denoted by $\times$) is a semigroup. Hence, for settling this question, we need to verify whether the third property, as stated in Definition 6.3 above is satisfied, which asks us to find out whether there exists an identity element with respect to the multiplication operation. The answer is yes, because the number "1" acts as identity element with respect to addition operation in the set $\mathbb{Z}^+$.

□

An interesting question now is, whether the monoid structures $(\, \mathbb{N}\, , +\,)$ and $(\, \mathbb{Z}^+, \times\,)$ are similar (in some sense)? Stating their respective identity elements, we may like to denote these structures as $(\, \mathbb{N}\, , +, 0\,)$ and $(\, \mathbb{Z}^+, \times\, , 1\,)$.

The notion of homomorphism allows us to investigate the answer to such as question. For this purpose, we closely re-examine the definition of homomorphism, and recognize that our main task is to construct homomorphic function connecting the two sets (here the two sets under consideration are: ℕ and $\mathbb{Z}^+$), so that the structural property of underlying operations (here the operations are +, and ×) are persevered (in the sense that they satisfy the condition in (6.1) above. This construction requires us to identify suitable homeomorphism function. To facilitate this, we have already introduced the operation of exponentiation in Question 6.5 above, and now we use the same in the example below.

Example 6.5: The function 2^n : ℕ → $\mathbb{Z}^+$ (Exponentiation with base 2) serving as Monoid Homomorphism from (ℕ, +, 0) to ($\mathbb{Z}^+$, ×, 1) illustrated in diagrammatic fashion.

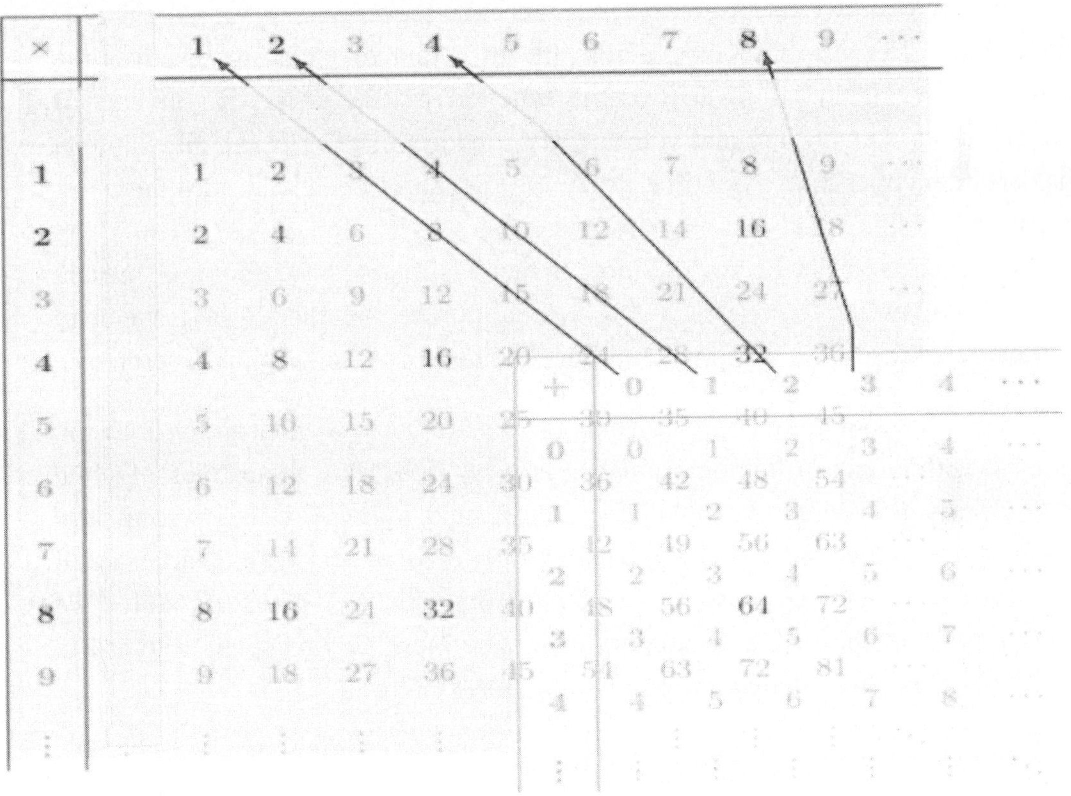

Figure 6.9: The function 2^n : ℕ → $\mathbb{Z}^+$ (Exponentiation with base 2) as Monoid Homomorphism from (ℕ, +, 0) to ($\mathbb{Z}^+$, ×, 1), illustrated in diagrammatic fashion

Note that the homomorphism from (ℕ, +, 0) to ($\mathbb{Z}^+$, ×, 1), that we gave above happens to be one-to-one, but it is not onto. Hence, it is not bijective.

Question 6.9: Can you construct a homomorphism from ($\mathbb{N}$, +, 0) to ($\mathbb{Z}^+$, ×, 1), that is not one-to-one, and also not onto?

Question 6.10: Can you give an example of (some other) monoid structures, where you have homomorphism from first monoid structure to second monoid structure that is both not one-to-one and also not onto?

Question 6.11: Does there exist a function serving as monoid homomorphism from from ($\mathbb{Z}^+$, ×, 1) to ($\mathbb{N}$, +, 0) ?

In Question 6.11, you may come across the difficulty of trying to discover the function $\mathbb{Z}^+ \rightarrow \mathbb{N}$, that is inverse of the function 2^n. We know that inverse of exponentiation is logarithm, and you may try function like $log_2()$. As an example, consider the number 3 in $\mathbb{Z}^+$, and let us try $log_2(3)$; unfortunately, it does not work because this value is not in $\mathbb{N}$. However, this observation gives rise to why mathematicians see the beauty in more general structures (within this present context, you may like to consider the set of real numbers, $\mathbb{R}$ than $\mathbb{Z}^+$, $\mathbb{N}$). We shall illustrate this point below when we introduce the notion of isomorphic structures.

While our discussion above is elementary, we state here (without going into the details) that the topic of homomorphisms is very rich, and in abstract algebra, the *fundamental theorem on homomorphisms*, also known as the *fundamental homomorphism theorem*, or the *first isomorphism theorem*, relates the structure of two objects between which a homomorphism is given, and of the kernel and image of the homomorphism. The motivated reader is referred to rich literature on abstract algebra for pursuing these interests.

Let us now revisit our examples Example 6.3, Example 6.4 discussed earlier involving composite relations and composite functions (on a set *S*) and investigate them when structures in Example 6.3 and Example 6.4 can be called as Monoid.

Example 6.5: (Monoid ($\mathcal{R}$, ^{o})): □

Suppose that, in a collection of binary relations, say $\mathcal{R} = \{ R_1, R_2, \ldots R_n\}$ defined on a set S (*i.e.* each of R_i is subset of the Cartesian product $S \times S$), we have one relation, called identity relation R_I, which is defined as:

R_I includes (s, s), for all s in S, and it does not have any other pair. ...(6.1)

Then, $(\mathbf{R} = \{R_1, R_2, \ldots R_n\}, \circ)$
where one of R_i is the identity relation R_I with the property in (6.1 above,
is monoid.

□

Example 6.6: (Monoid $(\mathbf{F}, \circ)$):

Suppose that, in a collection of of binary functions, say $\mathbf{F} = \{f_1, f_2, \ldots f_n\}$ defined on a set S (*i.e.* each of f_i is a function with domain as S and range as S), we have one function, called identity function f_I, which is defined as:

f_I includes $f_I(s) = s$ for all s in S, and it does not have any other pair. ...(6.2)

Then, $(\mathbf{F} = \{f_1, f_2, \ldots f_n\}, \circ)$
where one of f_i is the identity relation f_I with the property in (6.2) above,
is monoid.

□

In fact, Examples 6.5, 6.6 form one basis of study of framework of modern Algebraic Structures with finitely many elements. While further study of the structure (Monoid $(\mathbf{R}, \circ)$) (Examples 6.3, 6.5 above) does not seem to be illustrative for this purpose, we shall investigate the structure (Monoid $(\mathbf{F}, \circ)$) further in next few section(s), and it would be one of the motivating factors for us to introduce our next Algebraic Structure, namely Group.

6.3 Isomorphism

We continue our discussion about similarity of structures. In Example 6.3 above, we used $2^n : \mathbb{N} \rightarrow \mathbb{Z}^+$ (Exponentiation with base 2) as monoid Homomorphism from $(\mathbb{N}, +, 0)$ to $(\mathbb{Z}^+, \times, 1)$.

While we note that the above function serves the purpose of preserving the operations + and × between the concerned monoids, this function is not onto $\mathbb{Z}^+$, and hence it is not bijection. Sometimes, however, we may be able to construct a bijective that preserves the structures (*i.e.*, operations, in the sense as given in the definition of semigroup isomorphism below).

Definition 6.4: **Semigroup Isomorphism**: A semigroup isomorphism is a bijective map between semigroups that preserves the respective semigroup operations.

Given semigroups $G \equiv (D,*)$, and $H \equiv (R,+)$, and a function $f: D \rightarrow R$, then

f is semigroup isomorphism from structure G to structure H if and only if,

(i) f is bijective, (so f^{-1} exists, and $f^{-1}: R \rightarrow D$ ...(6.3)

(ii) $f(x) + f(y) = f(x * y)$ ...(6.4)

(iii) $f^{-1}(x) * f^{-1}(y) = f^{-1}(x + y)$, ...(6,5)

(with + is operation in range set R, * is operation in domain set D).

In other words, an isomorphism is a homomorphism that is both one-to-one and onto.

Example 6.7: Consider the following two monoids:

(i) $G \equiv (\mathbb{R}^+, \times)$, the set of positive real numbers with multiplication,

(ii) $H \equiv (\mathbb{R}, +)$, the set of real numbers with addition.

Please verify that the above do indeed satisfy the properties of monoids.

Using your knowledge of real numbers, logarithms (and exponential function), it is easy to verify homomorphism from G to H, is logarithmic function from $\mathbb{R}^+$ to $\mathbb{R}$.

$$log: G \rightarrow H \quad ...(6.6)$$

To verify that it is indeed homomorphism from G to H, we recall the following property of logarithms:

$$log\, x + log\, y = log\,(x \times y) \quad \ldots(6.7)$$

To verify that it is an isomorphism, we have to check whether the inverse of the log function, as defined from $\mathbb{R}^+ \rightarrow \mathbb{R}$, is bijection.

Let us first check that this function is one-to-one. Suppose that

$$log\, x = log\, y \quad \ldots(6.8)$$

Since the logarithmic values (*log*s)are equal in (6.8) above, raising both sides to the power of *e*, we get,

$$e^{\log x} = e^{\log y} \quad \ldots(6.9)$$

However, with our knowledge of exponents and logarithms, (6.9) simplifies to

$$x = y \quad \ldots(6.10)$$

Thus, for all values x, y in the set $\mathbb{R}^+$, we proved that,

($log\, x = log\, y$) implies ($x = y$), that is, *log* function is one-to-one.

We also note that the *log* function assumes a very large negative value when its argument x is very small positive value; *log* function is zero when x is 1, and it takes large positive value when x is sufficiently large. We depict this in the following figure:

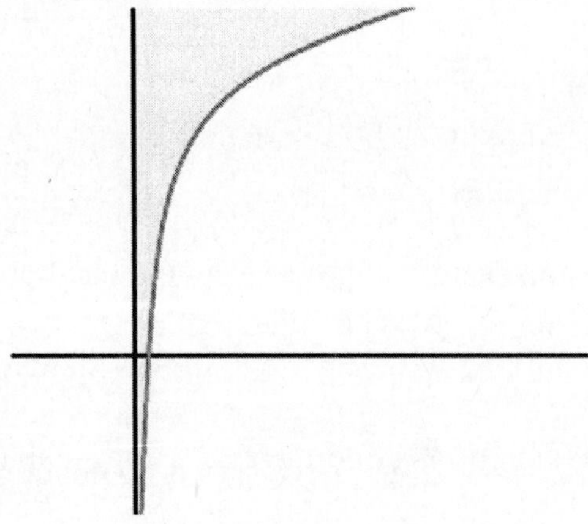

$Range = (-\infty, +\infty)$

Figure 6.10: Behaviour of log function (as its argument takes positive real values)

Thus, the log function is onto the range set $\mathbb{R}$, which is set for our second monoid H ≡ ($\mathbb{R}$, +), the set of real numbers with addition.

Due to above homomorphism that is also a bijection. Hence, we call it as isomorphism.

So, the two monoid structures

(i) G ≡ ($\mathbb{R}^+$, ×), the set of positive real numbers with multiplication,
(ii) H ≡ ($\mathbb{R}$, +), the set of real numbers with addition,

are isomorphic.

□

Questiom 6.12 Consider the homomorphism that we established in Example 6.3 from ($\mathbb{N}$, +, 0) to ($\mathbb{Z}^+$, ×, 1). After solving Example 6.4, is the solution to Example 6.3 obvious? Can you construct homomorphisms from ($\mathbb{N}$, +, 0) to ($\mathbb{Z}^+$, ×, 1), other than the one we gave in Example 6.3?

Question 6.13: Can you construct other (i.e., besides exponentiation/logarithm) isomorphism for the monoid structures $(\mathbb{R}^+, \times)$ and $(\mathbb{R}, +)$?

Question 6.14: How many distinct monoid isomorphisms exist between the pair of monoids $(\mathbb{R}^+, \times)$ and $(\mathbb{R}, +)$? Does there exist an algorithm to generate (systematically) all such distinct monoid isomorphisms between this pair of monoids?

Example 6.8:

Consider the following two monoids:

(i) $\mathbb{C}^\times \equiv$ set of nonzero complex numbers with multiplication $\times$

(ii) $S^1 \equiv$ set of complex numbers with absolute value 1 (*i.e.*, $|z| = 1$, where z is complex number) with multiplication $\times$)

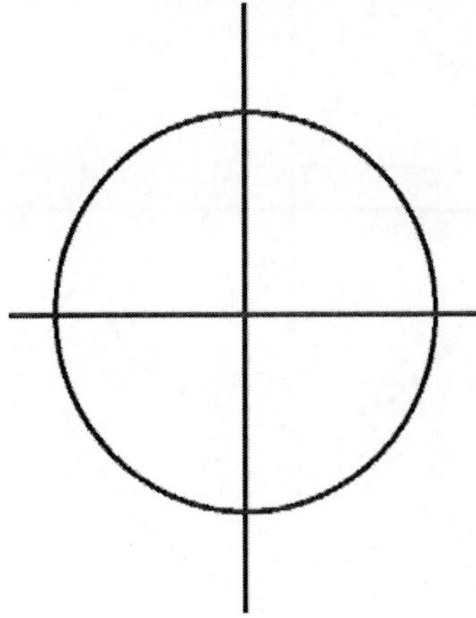

Figure 6.11: $S^1 \equiv$ set of complex numbers with absolute value 1

Please verify that the above do indeed satisfy the properties of monoids. Now, the question that we want to investigate is: does there exist a homomorphism from $\mathbb{C}^\times$ to S^1.

Every complex number can be written in in the form of its polar co-ordinates (r, θ).This means, every complex number can also be written in the form $z = r \times e^{i\theta}$, where r is the distance of a complex number to the complex point (0,0) (also called the origin of the complex plane) and the angle θ is the angle how much in anticlockwise direction we need to rotate from the positive x-axis to reach the point.

We now give one homomorphism between these two monoids $\mathbb{C}^{\times}$, and S^1 as follows:

$$f: \mathbb{C}^{\times} \rightarrow S^1, \text{ with}$$

$$f(r \times e^{i\theta}) = e^{i\theta} \qquad \dots (6.11)$$

we can depict the definition of the above function pictorially in the figure below.

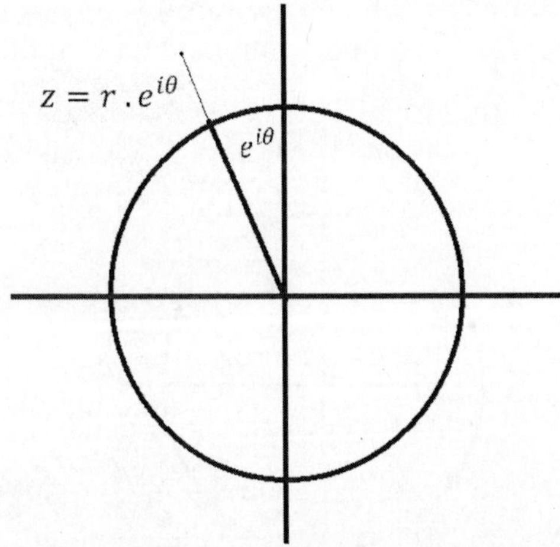

Figure 6.12: pictorial illustration of the function $f(r \times e^{i\theta}) = e^{i\theta}$

To check whether the function f given above is indeed homomorphism, let us consider two complex numbers, $z = r \times e^{i\theta}$, and $w = s \times e^{i\alpha}$. By the definition of f, wehave,

$$f(z) = e^{i\theta}, \quad \text{and} \quad f(w) = e^{i\alpha} \qquad \dots (6.12)$$

To check whether the homomorphic property is satisfied, we need to check

$f(z) \times f(w)$ is indeed equal to $f(z \times w)$

Let us first consider the expression $f(z \times w)$ of above, *i.e.*, $f(z \times w) = f(r \times e^{i\theta} \times s \times e^{i\alpha})$

$$= f(r \times s \times e^{i\theta} \times e^{i\alpha})$$

$$= (e^{i\theta} \times e^{i\alpha}) \qquad \text{, using (6.11).} \qquad \ldots (6.13)$$

Now, let us consider the expression $f(z) \times f(w)$, which by substituting the values from (6.11), we get

$$f(z) \times f(w) = (e^{i\theta} \times e^{i\alpha}) \qquad \text{, using (6.12).} \qquad \ldots (6.14)$$

Thus, using (6.13) and (6.14), we established that the function f is indeed homomorphism. We, however, observe that the function f is not isomorphism.

□

Question 6.15: Is it possible to construct isomorphism for two structures:

(i) $\mathbb{C}^{\times} \equiv$ set of nonzero complex numbers with multiplication $\times$

(ii) $S^1 \equiv$ set of complex numbers with absolute value 1 (*i.e.*, $|z| = 1$, where z is complex number, with multiplication $\times$)

□

6.4 Group

In the last two sections, we introduced two very important concepts for (algebraic) structures, namely,

(i) Homomorphism, and,

(ii) Isomorphism.

When two (algebraic) structures are isomorphic, structurally as well as mathematically, one may concentrate only on one of these (isomorphic) structures.

After few sections, we shall give characterization of finite groups as being isomorphic to another structure that is defined as permutation group. This characterization requires us to deploy the notion of isomorphism of these two structures. In fact, one of the important theorems for finite groups is "isomorphism theorem(s)" that we shall introduce in the next few sections (section 6.7).

The structures in Discrete mathematics have finite number of elements, and the structures like semigroups as well as monoids of interest in Discrete mathematics have finitely many elements. To study our similarity (in the sense of being isomorphic) of such structures having finitely many elements, we require additional property in monoids to be satisfied. We noted that monoids have an identity element. To study the finite structures further as being isomorphic, we require additional property in finite monoids. That property requires existence of inverse for every element. Monoid satisfying this property is called as special (algebraic) structure, called Group. Formally, we state the definition of structure group below.

Definition 6.5: **Group**: Group is monoid with the "inverse element" for every element (for, say $a \in S$, its inverse for the binary operation 'θ' is denoted by, say, $a^{-1} \in S$ with following additional property:

4. Inverse: $\forall a \in S \exists a^{-1} \in S$, such that $\forall a \in S\ (a\ \theta\ a^{-1}) = e$.

We may like to restate the above definition of Group by spelling out all properties that the structure needs to satisfy in the following properties of group.

Definition 6.5a (alternate definition): **Group**: Group (G) is denoted by (G, θ). It is a group of elements with a binary operation 'θ' that satisfies four properties. These properties are:

1. **Closure** – If a and b are elements of G, therefore $c = a\ \theta\ b$ is also an element of set G. This can define that the result of using the operations on any two elements in the set is another element in the set.
2. **Associativity** – If a, b, and c are element of G, therefore $(a\ \theta\ b)\ \theta\ c =$ a $\theta(b\ \theta\ c)$, means it does not substance in which order it can use the operations on higher than two elements.
3. **Identity** – For all a in G, there occur an element e in G including $e\ \theta$

$a = a$
$a\,\theta\, e = a.$

4. **Inverse** – For each a in G, there occur an element a^{-1} known as the inverse of a such that, $a\,\theta\, a^{-1} = a^{-1}\,\theta\, a = e.$

Notation: When the context makes it clear, it is conventional to use "." for the operation θ. Thus, $c = a\,\theta\, b$ can also be written as $c = a.b$ and still further, we may even omit "." to write $c = ab$. Literature sometimes refers to such operation as multiplicative operation of the group, and allow us to talk of "powers" of an element for denoting repeated application of group operation on the same element. Thus, $a^3 = aaa$, which can also be written as $a.a.a$, or by showing the abstract group operation θ explicitly as $(a\,\theta\, a\,\theta\, a)$.

Example 6.9: The set of $(n\times n)$ non singular matrices form a group with matrix multiplication operation. We also note that, in general, matrix multiplication operation (θ) is non-commutative, i.e., for two matrices A, B (as far as the above example is concerned, we would take them to be $(n\times n)$ non singular matrices), $A\,\theta\, B \neq B\,\theta\, A$.

□

Example 6.7: The set of all (3×3) matrices with the entries of the (upper triangular)form:

$$\begin{bmatrix} 1 & a & b \\ 0 & 1 & c \\ 0 & 0 & 1 \end{bmatrix}$$

Figure 6.13: pictorial illustration of upper triangular matrix.

forms a group with matrix multiplication operation.

□

Example 6.10: The set of six transformations $f_1, f_2, f_3, f_4, f_5, f_6$ on the set of complex numbers defined by:

$$f_1(z) = z, \quad f_2(z) = \frac{1}{z}, \qquad f_3(z) = 1 - z\,,$$

$$f_4(z) = \frac{z}{z-1}, \quad f_5(z) = \frac{1}{1-z}, \qquad f_6(z) = \frac{z-1}{z}$$

These transformations form an abelian group of order six with respect to the composition. (To verify this claim, you need to establish that that all five properties are satisfied.) Recall that, we have defined composition of the two functions or product of two functions in Module 2 on Sets, Relations and Functions.

□

Example 6.11: (Group **(ꟻ, ⁰)**):

Let us revisit Example 6.6, with each function f_i in the set **ꟻ** = $\{f_1, f_2, \ldots f_n\}$ is also required be bijection on a finite set *S*. We, of course also include a trivial bijection, which we may call as identity bijection (as defined in (6.2) in the previous subsection). To recall, we have one function, called identity function f_I, which is defined as:

f_I includes $f_I(s) = s$ for all s in *S*, and it does not have any other pair. …(6.2)

Then, we know (from Module 2 on Sets, Relations and Functions) that bijective maps (functions) are invertible.

Hence, the above structure **(ꟻ, ⁰)** is a group.

□

Suttle point to ponder about in the above example is: the set **ꟻ** = $\{f_1, f_2, \ldots f_n\}$ has each function f_i to be bijection on a finite set *S*. While considering the structure Group **(ꟻ, ⁰)**, we never stated (and not required) that the collection **ꟻ** needs to have *all bijections* defined on *S*. In fact, *the (proper) subset* of set of all possible *bijections* that is closed with composition operation "o" (and satisfies the four properties of Group (with respect to the composition operation that we denoted by "o") suffices for the purpose of Example 6.11.

Example 6.12:

Not every set with a binary operation is a group. For example, if we let modular multiplication be the binary operation on $\mathbb{Z}_n$, then $\mathbb{Z}_n$ fails to be a group. The element 1 acts as a group identity since $1 \cdot k = k \cdot 1$ for any $k \in \mathbb{Z}_n$; however a multiplicative inverse for 0 does not exist since $0 \cdot k = k \cdot 0 = 0$ for every k in $\mathbb{Z}_n$. Even if we exclude the number 0 to consider the set $\mathbb{Z}_n \setminus \{0\}$, we still may not have a group. For instance, let $2 \in \mathbb{Z}_6$. Then 2 has no multiplicative inverse since, the row in the multiplication table of $\mathbb{Z}_6$ works out as follows:

$$0 \cdot 2 = 0 \quad 1 \cdot 2 = 2 \quad 2 \cdot 2 = 4 \quad 3 \cdot 2 = 0 \quad 4 \cdot 2 = 2 \quad 5 \cdot 2 = 4$$

Thus, we do not have any number in $k \in \mathbb{Z}_6$ such that

$k \,.\, 2 = 1$;

hence the (multiplicative) inverse of 2 does not exist in $\mathbb{Z}_6$.

□

Definition 6.6 (order of group *G*):

For a finite group *G*, the number of elements in *G* is defined to be the order of *G*. When no confusion arises, we use the notation $|G|$ to denote the order of *G*.

Definition 6.7 (order of an element in group *G*):

Given an arbitrary element *a* of a (finite) group *G*, since we defined (in notation the operation a^p as applying the group operation (p-1) times to *a*. The least positive integer p, such that $a^p = e$, is defined to be an order of an element in a group *G*.

We shall re-visit the concept of order, together with illustrative example(s), when we discuss permutations and permutation groups.

6.5 Abelian Group

A group in which the result of applying the group operation to two group elements does not depend on the order in which they are written is called an Abelian group.

Niels Henrik Abel

source: Wikipedia

Abelian groups are named after early 19th century mathematician Niels Henrik Abel.

Abelian groups are generally simpler to analyze than nonabelian groups are, as many objects of interest for a given group simplify to special cases when the group is abelian.

The simplest examples of abelian groups are **cyclic groups**, which are groups generated by a single element and thus isomorphic to $\mathbb{Z}_n$;

We recall that, $\mathbb{Z}_n$ is the set of integers {0, 1, ,... , $n-1$}, with group operation of addition modulo n.

Definition 6.8: (**Abelian Group**): Group (G) is called as Abelian Group, if it satisfies the following four properties more one additional property of commutativity.

5. **Commutativity** – For all a and b in G, we have $a \theta b = b \theta a$

Example 6.13: The integers $\mathbb{Z}$ = { .... , -1, 0,1, 2, ...} form a group under the operation of addition. The binary operation on two integers m, $n \in$ Z is just their addition "+". Since the integers under addition already have a well-established notation "+", we will use the operator + instead of θ ; that is , we shall write $m+n$ instead of $m \theta n$. The identity is 0, and the inverse of $n \in \mathbb{Z}$ is written as $-n$ instead of n^{-1}. Notice that the set of integers under addition have the additional property that $m + n = n + m$ and therefore form an abelian group.

Question 6.16: As seen in the above example, the set of integers forms abelian group with addition ("+") operation, but it is infinite. Can you construct an abelian group on finite set of numbers? (see discussion after two more examples).

Example 6.14:

Consider $\mathbb{Z}_n$ = { 0, 1, 2, …, n-1 } with symbols 0, 1, 2, … , n-1 as the representative elements of congruence classes modulo n (Please review definition of Congruence Classes from the topic on Modular Arithmetic, and on the topic of Sets, Relations and Functions, in case you desire so). These elements form abelian group with "+"under modulo n operation.

Question 6.17:

What about modulo "*" (multiplication) operation over the set $\mathbb{Z}_n$ = { 0, 1, 2, …, n- 1 } with symbols 0, 1, 2, … , n-1 as the representative elements of congruence classes modulo n ?

Example 6.15:

Consider the multiplication table for the set $\mathbb{Z}_8$ = { 0, 1, 2, …, 7 } with symbols 0, 1, 2, … , 7 as the representative elements. The table is given below.

.	0	1	2	3	4	5	6	7
0	0	0	0	0	0	0	0	0
1	0	1	2	3	4	5	6	7
2	0	2	4	6	0	2	4	6
3	0	3	6	1	4	7	3	5
4	0	4	0	4	0	4	0	4
5	0	5	2	7	4	1	6	3
6	0	6	4	2	0	6	4	2
7	0	7	6	5	4	3	2	1

Figure 6.14: Multiplication table for the set $\mathbb{Z}_8$ = { 0, 1, 2, …, 7 }.

From the above table, we note that elements 2, 4, 6 do not have multiplicative inverse.

□

6.6 Permutation Group and Cayley Theorem

In the module on Combinatorics, we studied how n objects can be arranged when taken r at a time; we denoted such an arrangement by a *Permutation of n objects taken r at a time.* The number of ways in which n objects can be arranged when taken r at a time is denoted by an expression $^{n}P_{r}$ (or, P^{n}_{r}).

In this section, we study special type of permutations, which are *Permutation of n objects taken n at a time.* In other words, we study the arrangements of n objects at n distinct places, without allowing the repetition of any objects. Thus, suppose we have n objects $\{ a_1, a_2, \dots a_n\}$.

One way to arrange these n objects is as an ordered n-tuple $(a_1, a_2, a_3, \dots a_n)$. (Kindly refer to the notion of ordered n-tuple from the module on Sets, Relations, and Functions, where we introduced n-tuple as generalization of the ordered pair; and this was done when we were discussing the Cartesian Product of the sets.)
Second way to arrange (or, as we call it, permute) these n objects is as an ordered n-tuple $(a_2, a_1, a_3, \dots a_n)$.

Third way to arrange these n objects is as an ordered n-tuple $(a_2, a_3, a_1, \dots a_n)$.
You may observe that we are maintaining some order of the indices while generating these arrangements. Specially,

In the first arrangement, the order of indices is $(1, 2, 3, \dots, n)$
In the second arrangement, the order of indices is $(2, 1, 3, \dots, n)$
In the third arrangement, the order of indices is $(2, 3, 1, \dots, n)$

.

.

In the last (*i.e.*, factorial$(n)^{\text{th}}$) arrangement),
the order of indices is $(n, n\text{-}1, n\text{-}2, \dots, 1)$

Can you now see the pattern in which these arrangements of these indices are enumerated (*i.e.* listed) above? Consider the arrangement of these indices as a string with n places (characters, where each character is distinct). Then the next listed arrangement is precisely in the lexicographic order. (More discussion about the algorithm to list down such arrangements exhaustively is given in reference books like C.L. Liu, etc., and such algorithms are computationally interesting.)

When we consider the topic of permutation groups, the objects are all permutations (of n objects, taken n at a time). This also means, in a permutation group, the number of elements in the set are always factorial(n), for some natural number n. Pay attention to what we are doing here: although we start with a set with n objects, for defining the permutation group, we do not consider the set of n objects, but first we generate all possible permutations (arrangements) of these n objects. (There are factorial(n) such arrangements that we get). These factorial(n) arrangements form the set of elements of permutation group. In other words, the objects of permutation groups are permutations (of some n objects). Thus, wen note that the permutation groups are always defined over the sets having factorial(n) objects.

The above discussion indicates that we should crystallize the concept of permutation by giving its definition. We find it convenient to refer back to our discussion of bijective functions (given in the Module on Sets, Relations and Functions) for this purpose. For finite sets, the concepts of (i) permutation, and (ii) bijection are identical.

Hence, we give one definition of permutation below.

Definition 6.9: **Permutation:**

Let S be a non-empty finite set, then a one-one onto mapping to itself that is as shown below is called a permutation, denoted by P.

$$P: \; S \xrightarrow[\;]{\substack{1-1,\\ onto}} S$$

(i) The number of elements in finite set S is called the degree of Permutation, often denoted by symbol n.
(ii) We use the notation Π_n to denote the set of factorial(n) permutations Π_n that are obtained from the finite set having n elements. is called a set of all permutations of degree n.

Definition 6.10: **Finite Symmetric Group** (also denoted by ***Sym*(*n*)**) **:**

□

Finite Symmetric Group is defined as group with its objects as *all* bijections Π_n (permutations) defined on a non-empty finite set (say, S, with $|S| = n$), and with the group operation being the *composition of functions* (often denoted by "o", to be read as "oh"). When no ambiguity arises, we prefer to denote such a group by the symbol S_n.

□

Question 6.18: Verify that the symmetric group $S_n = (\Pi_n , o)$ indeed satisfies all four group properties (axioms).

Question 6.19: Consider the mathematical structure with its objects being set of all one-to-one functions defined over the finite S, together with function composition operation o. Is such a structure a (i) semigroup, (ii) monoid, (iiii) group?

Question 6.20: Consider the mathematical structure with its objects being set of all onto functions defined over the finite S, together with function composition operation o. Is such a structure a (i) semigroup, (ii) monoid, (iiii) group?

We recall the French mathematician Evariste Galois, whose contributions are related to this concept of symmetric group.

(source: Wikipedia)

For the interested reader, we state (without proof, as we have not defined concepts involved in fully appreciating the following statement) that the symmetric group defined on finite S (with $|S| = n$), is a Galios Group (note that we have not defined this concept yet) of the general polynomial of degree n, and it plays important role in the Galios Theory.

We note that, in combinatorics, the symmetric groups, their elements (permutations), and their representations provide a rich source of problems involving Young tableaux, plactic monoids, and the Bruhat order. However, this discussion is beyond our scope of present discussion, and interested reader is encouraged to pursue his interests, which are very useful for construction of algorithms.

6.6.1: *Cauchy notation for representing Permutation*

Augustin-Louis Cauchy has introduced two-line notation for representing the arrangements. This notation lists all elements in the first row, and for each element, its image with this bijection (permutation).

source: Wikipedia

$$\sigma = \begin{pmatrix} x_1 & x_2 & x_3 & \cdots & x_n \\ \sigma(x_1) & \sigma(x_2) & \sigma(x_3) & \cdots & \sigma(x_n) \end{pmatrix}$$

One arrangement (permutation, or bijection) of {1, 2, 3, 4, 5}, say, σ, can be shown in the above notation as:

$$\sigma = \begin{pmatrix} 1 & 2 & 3 & 4 & 5 \\ 2 & 4 & 5 & 1 & 3 \end{pmatrix};$$

We may also represent σ in terms of cycle notation as: ((1, 2, 4), (3, 5)) because you can verify that there are two cycles that can be seen from the above Cauchy's two-line notation.

6.6.2: *Cycle notation for representing Permutation*

Let us further illustrate the cycle notation with respect to the above bijection

$$\sigma = \begin{pmatrix} 1 & 2 & 3 & 4 & 5 \\ 2 & 4 & 5 & 1 & 3 \end{pmatrix};$$

We note that the arrangement (or, bijection σ) satisfies

$\sigma(1) = 2$; $\sigma(2) = 4$; $\sigma(4) = 1$; thereby forming a cycle (1, 2, 4).

We note that the elements 1, 2, 4 need not appear in any special order for this cycle representation.

Similarly, the arrangement (or, bijection σ) satisfies

$\sigma(3) = 5$; $\sigma(5) = 3$; thereby forming a cycle (3, 5).

Again, we note that the elements 3, 5 need not appear in any special order for this cycle representation.

Combining both the cycles, we may also represent a given permutation in terms of cycle notation as ((1,2,4), (3,5)), or even 1,2,4)(3,5) which is quite compact notation.

When the objects are denoted by single letters or digits, commas and spaces can also be dispensed with, and we have a notation such as (124) (35).

□

Notation: When no confusion arises, in the cycle notation, we omit 1-cycles (or cycles of length 1). To illustrate this point, let us consider the following example.

Example 6.12: Consider the permutation $\sigma = \begin{pmatrix} 1 & 2 & 3 & 4 & 5 & 6 & 7 & 8 \\ 2 & 8 & 3 & 4 & 5 & 7 & 6 & 1 \end{pmatrix}$;

We may omit 1-cycles (3 3) (4 4) (5 5) as they are obvious when we use the numbers from 1,2 till numbers 6,7,8 in the following cycle notation of the above permutation as (1 2 8) (6 7).

□

Example 6.13: Let G={ 1 } element then permutation are S_n or $P_n = \binom{1}{1}$

Example 6.14: Let G= { 1, 2 } elements then permutations are

$$\begin{pmatrix} 1 & 2 \\ 1 & 2 \end{pmatrix}, \begin{pmatrix} 1 & 2 \\ 2 & 1 \end{pmatrix}$$

We note that, when we read the sequence of digits in the second row of the above list, we obtain: (1,2), (2,1), which is dictionary (lexicographic) order of the arrangements.

Example 6.15: *Let G={ 1, 2, 3 } elements then permutation are **3!=6**. These are,*

$$\begin{pmatrix} 1\,2\,3 \\ 1\,2\,3 \end{pmatrix}, \begin{pmatrix} 1\,2\,3 \\ 1\,3\,2 \end{pmatrix}, \begin{pmatrix} 1\,2\,3 \\ 2\,1\,3 \end{pmatrix}, \begin{pmatrix} 1\,2\,3 \\ 2\,3\,1 \end{pmatrix}, \begin{pmatrix} 1\,2\,3 \\ 3\,1\,2 \end{pmatrix}, \begin{pmatrix} 1\,2\,3 \\ 3\,2\,1 \end{pmatrix}.$$

We note that, when we read the sequence of digits in the second row of the above list, we obtain: (1,2, 3), (1, 3, 2), (2, 1, 3), (2, 3, 1), (3, 1, 2), (3, 2,1), which is dictionary (lexicographic) order of the arrangements.

□

6.6.3: Reading the Symbol of Permutation

Suppose that a permutation is $\begin{pmatrix} 1\,2\,3\,4\,5\,6 \\ 2\,3\,1\,4\,6\,5 \end{pmatrix}$

- First, we see that in a small bracket there are two rows written, these two rows have numbers. The smallest number is 1 and the largest number is 6.

- Starting from the left side of the first row we read as:
  - an image of 1 is 2, anImage of 2 is 3,
  - an image of 3 is 1,
  - an image of 4 is 4 **(**Self image = identical = identity**)**,
  - an image of 5 is 6 and image of 6 is 5.

- The above thing can be also read as: Starting from the left side of the first row 1 goes to 2, 2 goes to 3, 3 goes to 1, 4 goes to 4,5 goes to 5, and 6 goes to 6.

Definition 6.11: Multiplication (**Composition**) of Permutation:

We note that we treat the composition operation as being similar to the composition operation of functions that we saw in the module on Sets, Relations, and Functions. Thus, the permutation A is treated as function, say f, taking the values in domain $[n] = \{1, 2, \ldots, n\}$ to the range $[n] = \{1, 2, \ldots, n\}$. Similarly, other permutation, say B, is treated as other function, say g, taking the values in domain $[n] = \{1, 2, \ldots, n\}$ to the range $[n] = \{1, 2, \ldots, n\}$.
Next, we define the composition of such functions, say $f \circ g$, as the multiplication, or composition of the permutations, and it is denoted symbolically as AoB, or $A.B$, or simply as AB, when the context makes it clear.

Example 6.16:

If $A = \begin{pmatrix} 1\,2\,3\,4\,5 \\ 2\,3\,1\,4\,5 \end{pmatrix}$ $B = \begin{pmatrix} 1\,2\,3\,4\,5 \\ 1\,3\,4\,5\,2 \end{pmatrix}$ find the product AB and BA

Solution:

Given,

$$A = \begin{pmatrix} 1\,2\,3\,4\,5 \\ 2\,3\,1\,4\,5 \end{pmatrix}, \text{ and } B = \begin{pmatrix} 1\,2\,3\,4\,5 \\ 1\,3\,4\,5\,2 \end{pmatrix}$$

$$A.B = \begin{pmatrix} 1\,2\,3\,4\,5 \\ 2\,3\,1\,4\,5 \end{pmatrix} \cdot \begin{pmatrix} 1\,2\,3\,4\,5 \\ 1\,3\,4\,5\,2 \end{pmatrix}$$

To obtain *A.B*, we first start writing by the first row as: (1 2 3 4 5) in the permutation *B*. (These numbers can be visualized as the place-holders of the resulting arrangement, or permutation).

Here we can see that in first bracket 1 goes to 1 *i.e.* image of 1 is 1, and in the permutation *A*, 1 goes to 2 *i.e.* image of 1 is 2. Hence we will write 2 under 1 in the bracket shown below, to get

$$A.B \text{ as} = \begin{pmatrix} 1 & 2 & 3 & 4 & 5 \\ 2 & 1 & 4 & 5 & 3 \end{pmatrix}$$

Similarly, we obtain,

$$B.A = \begin{pmatrix} 1 & 2 & 3 & 4 & 5 \\ 1 & 3 & 4 & 5 & 2 \end{pmatrix} \begin{pmatrix} 1 & 2 & 3 & 4 & 5 \\ 2 & 3 & 1 & 4 & 5 \end{pmatrix}$$

$$= \begin{pmatrix} 1 & 2 & 3 & 4 & 5 \\ 3 & 4 & 1 & 5 & 2 \end{pmatrix}$$

□

Just as *A.B* denotes the product of two permutations, we use convenient notation A^2 to denote the product *A.A*. In terms of such a notation, we now define the order of the permutation.

Notation (Permutation Matrix Representation): We also introduce the 0-1 ($n \times n$) matrix representation of the permutation on n numbers $[n] = \{1, 2, \ldots, n\}$. Consider the permutation $A = \begin{pmatrix} 1\,2\,3\,4\,5 \\ 2\,3\,1\,4\,5 \end{pmatrix}$. For representing this permutation as 0-1 ($n \times n$) matrix, we first construct the ($n \times n$) matrix with its columns labeled as $\{1, 2, \ldots, n\}$, and its rows also labeled as $\{1, 2, \ldots, n\}$, in that order. Reading each vertical pair, say $\begin{pmatrix} cj \\ ri \end{pmatrix}$ of *A*, pair as available the above permutation representation of *A*, we put the entry 1 in the matrix representation at the place (row i, column j). Thus we get the following structure for our permutation A on [5]:

$$\begin{array}{c} \\ 1 \\ 2 \\ 3 \\ 4 \\ 5 \end{array} \begin{array}{c} \begin{array}{ccccc} 1 & 2 & 3 & 4 & 5 \end{array} \\ \begin{bmatrix} & & 1 & & \\ 1 & & & & \\ & 1 & & & \\ & & & 1 & \\ & & & & 1 \end{bmatrix} \end{array} \qquad \ldots (6.15)$$

In the above matrix, we put zeroes in the blank places. Thus, for permutation A, we get its $(n\times n)$ matrix representation, that we call as permutation matrix P_A, as follows:

$$P_A = \begin{bmatrix} 0 & 0 & 1 & 0 & 0 \\ 1 & 0 & 0 & 0 & 0 \\ 0 & 1 & 0 & 0 & 0 \\ 0 & 0 & 0 & 1 & 0 \\ 0 & 0 & 0 & 0 & 1 \end{bmatrix} \qquad \ldots. (6.16)$$

Similarly, for the permutation B, its permutation matrix representation (with the notation that we introduced above), is:

$$P_B = \begin{bmatrix} 1 & 0 & 0 & 0 & 0 \\ 0 & 0 & 0 & 0 & 1 \\ 0 & 1 & 0 & 0 & 0 \\ 0 & 0 & 1 & 0 & 0 \\ 0 & 0 & 0 & 1 & 0 \end{bmatrix} \qquad \ldots. (6.17)$$

Theorem 6.1: The permutation matrix representation of the composition AoB (also denoted by $A.B$, or simply as AB) of permutations A, and B (as defined in Definition 6.8), when represented by the permutation matrices P_A and P_B (with the notations introduced above), is simply the matrix Product ($P_A \times P_B$).

The proof of this theorem is left to the reader as revision of elementary row operations, elementary column operations on matrices, and their relationship for matrix multiplication.

As an illustrative example, let us obtain the matrix Product ($P_A \times P_B$) for the matrices given in (6.16) and (6.17) above, to obtain the following:

$$\begin{bmatrix} 0 & 0 & 1 & 0 & 0 \\ 1 & 0 & 0 & 0 & 0 \\ 0 & 1 & 0 & 0 & 0 \\ 0 & 0 & 0 & 1 & 0 \\ 0 & 0 & 0 & 0 & 1 \end{bmatrix} \times \begin{bmatrix} 1 & 0 & 0 & 0 & 0 \\ 0 & 0 & 0 & 0 & 1 \\ 0 & 1 & 0 & 0 & 0 \\ 0 & 0 & 1 & 0 & 0 \\ 0 & 0 & 0 & 1 & 0 \end{bmatrix} = \begin{bmatrix} 0 & 1 & 0 & 0 & 0 \\ 1 & 0 & 0 & 0 & 0 \\ 0 & 0 & 0 & 0 & 1 \\ 0 & 0 & 1 & 0 & 0 \\ 0 & 0 & 0 & 1 & 0 \end{bmatrix} \quad \ldots (6.18)$$

From the above, we obtain $A.B$ as $= \begin{pmatrix} 1 & 2 & 3 & 4 & 5 \\ 2 & 1 & 4 & 5 & 3 \end{pmatrix}$.

Similarly, you may like to obtain $B.A$ by the matrix product ($P_B \times P_A$):

$$\begin{bmatrix} 1 & 0 & 0 & 0 & 0 \\ 0 & 0 & 0 & 0 & 1 \\ 0 & 1 & 0 & 0 & 0 \\ 0 & 0 & 1 & 0 & 0 \\ 0 & 0 & 0 & 1 & 0 \end{bmatrix} \times \begin{bmatrix} 0 & 0 & 1 & 0 & 0 \\ 1 & 0 & 0 & 0 & 0 \\ 0 & 1 & 0 & 0 & 0 \\ 0 & 0 & 0 & 1 & 0 \\ 0 & 0 & 0 & 0 & 1 \end{bmatrix} = \begin{bmatrix} 0 & 0 & 1 & 0 & 0 \\ 0 & 0 & 0 & 0 & 1 \\ 1 & 0 & 0 & 0 & 0 \\ 0 & 1 & 0 & 0 & 0 \\ 0 & 0 & 0 & 1 & 0 \end{bmatrix} \quad \ldots (6.19)$$

From the above, we obtain $B.A$ as $= \begin{pmatrix} 1 & 2 & 3 & 4 & 5 \\ 3 & 4 & 1 & 5 & 2 \end{pmatrix}$.

□

Definition 6.12: **Order of Permutation**

For a given permutation P if $P^n = I$ where I is Identity Permutation, then n is the order of permutation.

Example 6.17: Let a permutation be $P = \begin{pmatrix} a & b & c \\ b & c & a \end{pmatrix}$.

Consider $P^2 = \begin{pmatrix} a & b & c \\ b & c & a \end{pmatrix} . \begin{pmatrix} a & b & c \\ b & c & a \end{pmatrix} = \begin{pmatrix} a & b & c \\ c & a & b \end{pmatrix}$,

which is not identity permutation, I.

However, now consider $P^3 = P^2.P$

$$= \begin{pmatrix} a & b & c \\ c & a & b \end{pmatrix} . \begin{pmatrix} a & b & c \\ b & c & a \end{pmatrix}$$

$$= \begin{pmatrix} a & b & c \\ a & b & c \end{pmatrix},$$

which is an identity permutation, I.

Hence, the order of permutation $P = \begin{pmatrix} a & b & c \\ b & c & a \end{pmatrix}$ is 3.

□

We observe that, in cycle notation, the above permutation can be written as only one cycle as $(a\ b\ c)$.

Question 6.21: Consider the permutation whose representation in cycle notation is ($(a\ c)$, (b)). What is the order of this permutation?

Example 6.18: How many times $\begin{pmatrix} 1 & 2 & 3 & 4 \\ 3 & 1 & 4 & 2 \end{pmatrix}$ be multiplied to itself to produce times $\begin{pmatrix} 1 & 2 & 3 & 4 \\ 1 & 2 & 3 & 4 \end{pmatrix}$?

Consider $P^2 = \begin{pmatrix} 1 & 2 & 3 & 4 \\ 3 & 1 & 4 & 2 \end{pmatrix} . \begin{pmatrix} 1 & 2 & 3 & 4 \\ 3 & 1 & 4 & 2 \end{pmatrix} = \begin{pmatrix} 1 & 2 & 3 & 4 \\ 4 & 3 & 2 & 1 \end{pmatrix}$

which is not identity permutation, I.

Now consider $P^3 = P^2.P$

$$= \begin{pmatrix} 1 & 2 & 3 & 4 \\ 4 & 3 & 2 & 1 \end{pmatrix} . \begin{pmatrix} 1 & 2 & 3 & 4 \\ 3 & 1 & 4 & 2 \end{pmatrix}$$

$$= \begin{pmatrix} 1 & 2 & 3 & 4 \\ 2 & 4 & 1 & 3 \end{pmatrix}$$

which is not identity permutation, I.

However, now consider $P^4 = P^3.P$

$$= \begin{pmatrix} 1 & 2 & 3 & 4 \\ 2 & 4 & 1 & 3 \end{pmatrix} . \begin{pmatrix} 1 & 2 & 3 & 4 \\ 3 & 1 & 4 & 2 \end{pmatrix}$$

$$= \begin{pmatrix} 1 & 2 & 3 & 4 \\ 1 & 2 & 3 & 4 \end{pmatrix} .$$

which is an identity permutation, I.

Hence, the order of permutation $P - \begin{pmatrix} 1 & 2 & 3 & 4 \\ 3 & 1 & 4 & 2 \end{pmatrix}$ is 4.

¬

We observe that, in cycle notation, the above permutation can be written as only one cycle as (1 2 3 4).

Question 6.22: Consider the permutation whose representation in cycle notation is ((1 4 3), (2)). What is the order of this permutation?

Example 6.19: How many times $\begin{pmatrix} 1 & 2 & 3 & 4 \\ 1 & 3 & 4 & 2 \end{pmatrix}$ be multiplied to itself to produce times $\begin{pmatrix} 1 & 2 & 3 & 4 \\ 1 & 2 & 3 & 4 \end{pmatrix}$?

Consider $P^2 = \begin{pmatrix} 1 & 2 & 3 & 4 \\ 1 & 3 & 4 & 2 \end{pmatrix} . \begin{pmatrix} 1 & 2 & 3 & 4 \\ 1 & 1 & 4 & 2 \end{pmatrix} = \begin{pmatrix} 1 & 2 & 3 & 4 \\ 1 & 4 & 2 & 3 \end{pmatrix}$

which is not identity permutation, I.

Now consider $P^3 = P^2.P$

$$= \begin{pmatrix} 1 & 2 & 3 & 4 \\ 1 & 4 & 2 & 3 \end{pmatrix} . \begin{pmatrix} 1 & 2 & 3 & 4 \\ 1 & 3 & 4 & 2 \end{pmatrix}$$

$$= \begin{pmatrix} 1 & 2 & 3 & 4 \\ 1 & 2 & 3 & 4 \end{pmatrix}$$

which is identity permutation, I.

Hence, the order of permutation $P = \begin{pmatrix} 1 & 2 & 3 & 4 \\ 1 & 3 & 4 & 2 \end{pmatrix}$ is 3.

□

We observe that, in cycle notation, the above permutation can be written as only one cycle as (1) (2 3 4).

Question 6.22: Consider the permutation whose representation in cycle notation is (1 4 3) (2) . What is the order of this permutation?

Question 6.23: What is the order of permutation $\begin{pmatrix} 1 & 2 & 3 & 4 & 5 \\ 3 & 4 & 1 & 2 & 5 \end{pmatrix}$?

Example 6.20: What is the order of the permutation ((1 4 2 8)) ? Note that, in the cycle notation, recognizing that we omitted one-cycles for the other numbers occurring in-between 1 to 9 in the above cycle notation, the complete permutation in expanded cycle notation is ((1 4 2 8) (3 3) (5 5) (6 6) (7 7)). Hence the above cycle notation denotes the permutation

$$\sigma = \begin{pmatrix} 1 & 4 & 2 & 8 & 3 & 5 & 6 & 7 \\ 4 & 2 & 8 & 1 & 3 & 5 & 6 & 7 \end{pmatrix},$$

which we may also write as

$$\sigma = \begin{pmatrix} 1 & 2 & 3 & 4 & 5 & 6 & 7 & 8 \\ 4 & 8 & 3 & 2 & 5 & 6 & 7 & 1 \end{pmatrix},$$

By now it should be obvious to you that the order of the above permutation is 4.

□

From the above examples, you may have noted that any permutation can be written as decomposed into disjoint cycles. The decomposition into disjoint cycles allows us to conclude about how many times the permutation must be multiplied by itself so that it results in an identity permutation (which represents the order of the permutation). We summarize the observations regarding cycles of permutations in the following theorem.

Theorem 6.2: (i) The order of k-cycle is k.

(ii) The order of permutation that is represented by the product of disjoint cycles is the Least Common Multiple (LCM) of the lengths of all its disjoint cycles.

The proof is left as simple exercise to the reader.

□

In the Definition 6.10 of **Finite Symmetric Group** (also denoted by ***Sym*(*n*)), we included** *all* bijections Π_n (permutations) defined on a non-empty finite set (say, S, with $|S| = n$), and with the group operation being the *composition of functions* (often denoted by "o", to be read as "oh").

The question arises whether we can consider the subset of the set of all permutations (bijections) and still have a group? To settle down this question, we need to revisit the properties (also called as axioms) of group structure.

Group axioms require us the existence of identity permutation to be included in the subset, and closeness of the subset (of the permutations, or bijections that we are considering) with respect to the composition operation of permutations. Indeed, such subsets of permutations exist, and we distinguish them by giving the name as "*Permutation Group*" . Hence, we state that the Subgroups of symmetric groups are called permutation groups

Note that we have not yet defined the concept of subgroup, and we shall refer the reader to the next subsection to refresh this concept. To capture this notion of permutation group, we now define it in the following.

Definition 6.13: **Permutation Group:**

A **permutation group** is a group G whose elements are permutations of a given finite set S, together with whose group operation is the composition of permutations in G

(which are thought of as bijective functions from the set S to itself), and the elements of such a collection satisfy the properties (axioms) of the group.

As we noted earlier, the permutation group may not have all permutations included in it. But we have special permutation group, that we denoted by Sym(S). The purpose of defining the permutation Group (that is different than Sym(S)) is the following important theorem in finite (discrete) group theory.

Arthur Cayley, (born August 16, 1821, Richmond, Surrey, England—died January 26, 1895, Cambridge, Cambridgeshire), **English mathematician and leader of the British school of pure mathematics** that emerged in the 19th century

(source: wikipedia)

Theorem 6.3 (Cayley's theorem): Every finite group is *isomorphic* to some permutation group.

As a general observation, you may have noted that the number of elements in group Sym(S) is factorial($|S|$), *i.e.*, $n!$ for some finite n. To appreciate the proof of Cayley's Theorem, we first need to develop the concepts of (i) subgroup, and (ii) Isomorphic structures. We shall do the same in the next few sections.

Since the set of elements in permutation group is subset of set of elements in Sym(S), we can say that the number of elements in permutation group is less than or equal to the number of elements in Sym(S). In fact, in the next few sections, we shall investigate this relation in much more general way, in the context of Group theory, when we study the size of subgroup(s), with respect to size of group in which this subgroup is defined.

Note: The way in which the elements of a permutation group permute the elements of the set is called its group action. Group actions have applications in the study of symmetries, combinatorics and many other branches of mathematics, physics and chemistry.

As stated above we jumped to use the concepts like:

(i) subgroup, and,
(ii) isomorphic algebraic structures.

In the next few sections, we shall now define and clarify these notions.

6.7 Subgroup

Definition 6.14:

A structure (H, θ) that is derived from a group (G, θ), with the property that:

H is subset of G (not necessarily proper subset)

is said to be subgroup of (G, θ).

When context makes is clear, we also call the structure (G, θ), it G. Similarly, the structure (H, θ) is referred to as H. For example, consider two groups [{1,-1}, .] and [{1,-1,i,-i}, .], We say that {1,-1} is subgroup of {1,-1,i,-i} when the context makes it clear that we are referring to the group operation "." In both the groups.

Criteria for a subset to be a subgroup:

A non empty subset H of G is a subgroup of G if and only if:

i) $a, b \in H \Rightarrow a \theta b \in H$, and,

ii) $a \in H \Rightarrow a^{-1} \in H$ where a^{-1} is inverse of a which $\in G$

In other words, subgroup H is a subset of a group G if it satisfies all the four properties possessed by the group structure simultaneously, namely,

1. Closure,
2. Associative,
3. (Existence of) Identity element, and,
4. (Existence of) Inverse for every element.

Subgroup H of a group G is also denoted by $H \leq G$. A subgroup H that has property that $H \subset G$ (H is proper subset of G), is also called as proper subgroup, and we denote the same by $H < G$.

Example 6.21:

Specify a proper subgroup of the additive group $\mathbb{Z}_6$. The Cayley table of $\mathbb{Z}_6$ is provided below.

+	$[0]_6$	$[1]_6$	$[2]_6$	$[3]_6$	$[4]_6$	$[5]_6$
$[0]_6$	$[0]_6$	$[1]_6$	$[2]_6$	$[3]_6$	$[4]_6$	$[5]_6$
$[1]_6$	$[1]_6$	$[2]_6$	$[3]_6$	$[4]_6$	$[5]_6$	$[0]_6$
$[2]_6$	$[2]_6$	$[3]_6$	$[4]_6$	$[5]_6$	$[0]_6$	$[1]_6$
$[3]_6$	$[3]_6$	$[4]_6$	$[5]_6$	$[0]_6$	$[1]_6$	$[2]_6$
$[4]_6$	$[4]_6$	$[5]_6$	$[0]_6$	$[1]_6$	$[2]_6$	$[3]_6$
$[5]_6$	$[5]_6$	$[0]_6$	$[1]_6$	$[2]_6$	$[3]_6$	$[4]_6$

One nontrivial subgroup is $\{0,3\}$;

+	$[0]_6$	$[1]_6$	$[2]_6$	$[3]_6$	$[4]_6$	$[5]_6$
$[0]_6$	$[0]_6$	$[1]_6$	$[2]_6$	$[3]_6$	$[4]_6$	$[5]_6$
$[1]_6$	$[1]_6$	$[2]_6$	$[3]_6$	$[4]_6$	$[5]_6$	$[0]_6$
$[2]_6$	$[2]_6$	$[3]_6$	$[4]_6$	$[5]_6$	$[0]_6$	$[1]_6$
$[3]_6$	$[3]_6$	$[4]_6$	$[5]_6$	$[0]_6$	$[1]_6$	$[2]_6$
$[4]_6$	$[4]_6$	$[5]_6$	$[0]_6$	$[1]_6$	$[2]_6$	$[3]_6$
$[5]_6$	$[5]_6$	$[0]_6$	$[1]_6$	$[2]_6$	$[3]_6$	$[4]_6$

Another subgroup $\{0,2,4\}$

+	$[0]_6$	$[1]_6$	$[2]_6$	$[3]_6$	$[4]_6$	$[5]_6$
$[0]_6$	$[0]_6$	$[1]_6$	$[2]_6$	$[3]_6$	$[4]_6$	$[5]_6$
$[1]_6$	$[1]_6$	$[2]_6$	$[3]_6$	$[4]_6$	$[5]_6$	$[0]_6$
$[2]_6$	$[2]_6$	$[3]_6$	$[4]_6$	$[5]_6$	$[0]_6$	$[1]_6$
$[3]_6$	$[3]_6$	$[4]_6$	$[5]_6$	$[0]_6$	$[1]_6$	$[2]_6$
$[4]_6$	$[4]_6$	$[5]_6$	$[0]_6$	$[1]_6$	$[2]_6$	$[3]_6$
$[5]_6$	$[5]_6$	$[0]_6$	$[1]_6$	$[2]_6$	$[3]_6$	$[4]_6$

6.8 Isomorphic Structures

6.8.1 Revisit to Homomorphic Structures

Considering the concept of homomorphism introduced in the context of monoid structures, let us now generalize the same for structures with single operation as follows.

Definition 6.15: Homomorphic Structures

Given two structures (with single operation) $G \equiv (D,*)$, and $H \equiv (R,+)$, and a function $f: D \rightarrow R$, then

f is structural homomorphism from structure G to structure H if and only if,

$$f(x) + f(y) = f(x * y), \qquad \ldots(6.20)$$

(with + is operation in range set R, * is operation in domain set D).

6.8.2 Definition of Isomorphic Structures

Definition 6.16: Isomorphic Structures

Given two structures (with single operation) $G \equiv (D,*)$, and $H \equiv (R,+)$, and a *bijective* function $f: D \rightarrow R$, then

f is structural isomorphism from structure G to structure H if and only if,

$$f(x) + f(y) = f(x * y), \qquad \ldots(6.21)$$

(with + is operation in range set R, * is operation in domain set D).

We note that isomorphism means homomorphism, together with the restriction that the homomorphic function needs to be restricted to bijection (1-1 onto map).

Question 6.24: Is every finite semigroup is isomorphic to the semigroup of binary relations (on some set S) (($\mathbf{R}$, ^{o})) that we introduced in Example 6.3?
Solution is left for the readers.

6.9 Sketch of the Proof of Cayley's Theorem

Cayley theorem states that every finite group is isomorphic to some permutation group. This also essentially means, the study of finite groups as structures can be restricted to study of permutation groups. This statement has profound consequences in computer science, specially for design of algorithms (however, such discussion is outside the scope of present context, and we leave it for other courses in Computer Science).

We have already prepared some ground for Cayley's theorem when we defined permutation group. With the notations introduced in the previous section, we have already stated that a permutation group is a subgroup of ***Sym*(*n*)**.

Let G be a finite group (G, θ), and let some element $a \in G$. Then, (due to closure property of group), for every $x \in G$, we have, $(a \; \theta \; x) \in G$.
Now, let us define a function f_a: $G \rightarrow G$ by the following:

$$f_a(x) = a \; \theta \; x \quad (\text{note } x, a \text{ both} \in G) \qquad \ldots(6.22)$$

We now give sketch of the proof of Cayley's theorem.

The initial part of proof of Cayley's theorem investigates the properties of the function $f_a(x)$ that we defined in (6.17) and they are given in the following three parts.

Part I: To prove that the function $f_a(x)$ is well-defined, we need to prove that,

$$(x = y) \Rightarrow f_a(x) = f_a(y)$$

Given, $(x = y)$, and from (6.17),

we have, $a \; \theta \; x = a \; \theta \; y \Rightarrow f_a(x) = f_a(y)$

□

We claim that the function $f_a(x)$ is a bijection (permutation) of G in the following two parts.

Part II: To prove that $f_a(x)$ is one-to-one, we need to prove that $f_a(x) = f_a(y) \Rightarrow (x = y)$

Given, $f_a(x) = f_a(y)$, we have,

$$a \; \theta \; x = a \; \theta \; y, \quad \text{...(6.24)}$$

and we know that a^{-1} exists in Group, so by pre-multiplying (in the sense of doing the following operation) a^{-1} in (6.24) (6.23),

$$a^{-1} \; \theta \; (a \; \theta \; x) = a^{-1} \; \theta \; (a \; \theta \; y), \quad \text{...(6.25)}$$

$$(a^{-1} \; \theta a) \; \theta \; x = (a^{-1} \; \theta \; a) \; \theta \; y, \quad \text{...(6.26)}$$

$$==> (x = y)$$

□

Part III: To prove that $f_a(x)$ is onto, for every y in the codomain G, we need to prove that there exists some x in the domain (*i.e.*, again in G, as domain and codomain is same in our case). For a given y, let us consider

$$x = a^{-1} \; \theta \; y$$

Then, $f_a(a^{-1} \; \theta \; y) = a \; \theta \; (a^{-1} \; \theta \; y) = (a \; \theta \; a^{-1}) \; \theta \; y = y.$

□

Let us now consider other set G' consisting of the set of (bijective) functions (or permutations)

$$G' = \{f_a : a \text{ in } G\}, \qquad \ldots(6.27)$$

We note that the number of elements in G and G' are same. We also note that the elements of G' are permutations f_a (as defined in (6.22) above). Now, we claim that G' as defined in (6.27) above is group; *i.e.*, it satisfies the four group axioms, namely, closure, associativity, existence of identity, and existence of inverse. This part of the proof is rather straightforward, and we leave the reader to complete the same.

With the above, we have claimed that there is a homomorphic mapping from G to G' which is also bijective. Hence, the two structures are isomorphic.

Question 6.25: Which proof technique(s) (from the proof techniques discussed in the module on Proof Techniques) we used when we claim to have given the "proof" of Cayley's theorem?

Solution is left for the readers.

6.10 Cosets and Normal Subgroups

Definition 6.17: **Coset (or translate)**

In group theory, a subgroup H of a group G may be used to decompose the underlying set of G into disjoint equal-size subsets called cosets.

Cosets (both left and right) have the same number of elements (cardinality) as does H. Furthermore, H itself is both a left coset (left translate) and a right coset (right translate).

Definition 6.18; (**left coset**, or left translate; **right coset,** or right translate) :

Let $H \leq G$ and let a in G.

The left coset of H containing a is the set: $a\theta H = \{ a\theta h \mid h \text{ in } H\}$.

The right coset of H containing a is the set $H\theta a = \{h\theta a \mid h \text{ in } H\}$.

When the group operation is "+" (denoted by "addition"), we use the notation for left coset (also called as left translate of H with a) as: $a{+}H$; and for right coset (right translate of H with a) as : $H + a$. a is called the coset representative of $a{+}H$.

When the context makes clear about the group operation θ, it is customary in the literature to omit the symbol θ (to read it as multiplication operation of a group), and we have the following symbolism for left coset and right coset.

Let $H \leq G$ and let a in G.

The left coset of H containing a is the set: $aH = \{ ah \mid h \text{ in } H\}$.

The right coset of H containing a is the set $Ha = \{ha \mid h \text{ in } H\}$.

Similarly, we introduce the notation : $aHa^{-1} = \{ aha^{-1} \mid h \text{ in } H\}$

Properties of Cosets (translates):

Let H be a subgroup of G and a, b in G.

1. a belongs to aH
2. $aH = H$ iff a belongs to H
3. $aH = bH$ iff a belongs to bH
4. aH and bH are either equal or disjoint
5. $aH = bH$ iff $a^{-1}b$ belongs to H
6. $|aH| = |bH|$
7. $aH = Ha$ iff $H = aHa^{-1}$
8. $aH \leq G$ iff a belongs to H

Proof of these properties is left as an exercise to the reader.

□

Definition 6.19: *Index of a subgroup*: Let G be a group and H be a subgroup of G. We define index of H in G, denoted by $[G : H]$ to be the number of left cosets (left translates) of H in G.

When the group G is Abelian group (*i.e.*, the group operation is commutative), with H being a subgroup of G, for every $a \in G$, whenever aH is left coset in G, Ha is right coset in G.

It turns out that, even when G is not Abelian group, there may exist a subgroup H of G, with the property that for every $a \in G$, whenever aH is left coset in G, Ha is right coset in G.

Definition 6.20: **Index of subgroup**:

The number of distinct left and right cosets of the subgroup is also called the index of the subgroup.

A subgroup of index 2 in G is sometimes of interest in group theory.

Definition 6.21: **Normal Subgroup**

Let G be a group and H be its subgroup. Thus $H \leq G$. If the following condition is satisfied:
$\forall (a, b) \in G \times H, \ [(ab = ba)]$
Then the subgroup H is defined to be normal subgroup of G.

Alternately, the main condition for normal subgroup can be re-phrased as:

$$\forall a \in G \ [(aba^{-1} \in H) \ \forall b \in H]$$

Notation: For a given group G, and its subgroup H, we define the notation:

$$aHa^{-1} = \{\forall b \in H \mid aba^{-1} \}$$

Definition 6.22: Alternate definition of Normal Subgroup

With the above notation, we say that the subgroup H of the group G is *normal* if and only if,

$$\forall a \in G \ [aHa^{-1} \subseteq H \ \}.$$

Due to the above definition, normal subgroups also called as self-conjugates.

We now note some properties of normal subgroups.

(i) We note that, every group has two trivial normal subgroups, namely, the group consisting of the identity element $\{e\}$ of the group, and the whole group G itself. The normal subgroups if G, other than trivial subgroups are non-trivial normal subgroups.
(ii) If a subgroup H is of index 2 in G, then H is normal subgroup of G.
(iii) Every subgroup of cyclic group is normal subgroup.
(iv) Every Abelian Group has nontrivial normal subgroup.
(v) The intersection of two normal subgroups is a normal subgroup.

6.11 Lagrange's Theorem

Lagrange's theorem is the most important single theorem in group theory. It helps answer many interesting questions like:

- How large is the symmetry group of a volleyball? A soccer ball?
- How many groups of order $2 \times p$ where p is prime? (*i.e.*, of the order like: 4, 6, 10, 14, 22, 26, …)
- Is 2^{257}-1 prime? – Is computer security possible?
- etc.

Theorem 6.4: Lagrange's Theorem

If G is finite group and H is subgroup of G. Then,

(i) $|H|$ divides $|G|$.

(ii) The number of distinct left (right) cosets of H in G is $|G|/|H|$

Joseph Lagrange

Let us state the following two lemmas that help us prove the Lagrange theorem.

Lemma 1: If G is a finite group and H is its subgroup, then there is a one to one onto relationship (*i.e.*, a bijection) between H and *any* coset (any translate) of H. Thus, there is bijection between H and aH. Also there is bijection between H and Ha.

The proof of this lemma can be worked out from the arguments similar to the proof of Cayley's theorem that we discussed earlier.

Lemma 2: If G is a finite group and H is its subgroup. Let us define a relation $\sim$ on the elements of G as follows:

$$g_1 \sim g_2 \quad \equiv \quad \{(g_1, g_2) \in G \times G \mid g_1H = g_2H\}$$

Then, the relation $\sim$ is an equivalence relation.

The proof of this lemma follows from the eight properties of cosets (translates) that we have included section on Cosets, and is left to the reader.

□

Sketch of Proof of Lagrange's Theorem:

With the help of the above lemmas, we give, in the following, the sketch of the proof of the Lagrange's theorem.

Let H be any subgroup of a finite group G, *i.e.*, $H \leq G$. Let $|H| = m$, and $|G| = n$. Because of the property 4 of Cosets, we note that the cosets aH and bH are either equal or disjoint. Hence, the cosets partition the set G.

Since G is a finite group, the number of discrete left cosets are also finite, say p. Let $H = \{h_1, h_2, \ldots, h_m\}$, then:

(i) $ah_1, ah_2, \ldots, ah_m$ are the m distinct members of aH.

(ii) $bh_1, bh_2, \ldots, bh_m$ are the m distinct members of bH.

We prove that $ah_1, ah_2, \ldots, ah_m$ are the m distinct members as follows. Suppose, $ah_i = ah_j$. Since, in G, the inverse of a exists (let it be denoted by a^{-1}), premultiplying by a^{-1} both the sides, we have,

$$ah_i = ah_j \Rightarrow a^{-1}ah_i = a^{-1}ah_j \Rightarrow h_i = h_j$$

Hence, by contrapositive of $ah_i = ah_j \Rightarrow h_i = h_j$, we get, $h_i \neq h_j \Rightarrow ah_i \neq ah_j$; this proves that aH has m distinct members.

Similarly, bH has m distinct members.

We have assumed that $|G| = n$. Since different cosets (say, aH, bH) each have m distinct elements, and by Lemma 2, it follows that collection of elements of all these distinct cosets (each coset for each element in G) (we already assumed that there are p such distinct left cosets), would give us all elements of G. Thus,

$$m \times p = n \text{, or in other words, } |H| \times p = |G|, \qquad \ldots(6.28)$$

In other words, m divides n, which means, $|H|$ divides $|G|$, which proves the first part of the Lagrange's theorem.

From (6.28), and the above arguments, it follows that the number of distinct left (right) cosets of H in G is $|G|/|H|$, which proves the second part of the Lagrange's theorem.

□

6.12 Corollaries (and Consequences) of Lagrange's Theorem

For practical applications of Lagrange's theorem, the following corollaries, that immediately follow from Lagrange's theorem, are useful.

Corollary 6.1: If G is a finite group with $|G| = m$, then the order of any $a \in G$ divides the order of G, and we also have (additionally) $a^{m} = e$.

Proof: Let the order of a be p. By definition (refer to notation about the order of element in group in the section on Group), we have, $a^p = e$, where p is such least positive integer. Hence, we can say, $a, a^2, a^3, \ldots, a^{p-1}, a^p = e$, are the elements in group G such that they are all different and they form a subgroup. Since the subgroup has order p, and also p the order of a. By Lagrange's theorem, since a, $a^2, a^3, \ldots, a^{p-1}, a^p = e$, form a subgroup, p divides $|G|$. So, we can write, $m = ip$, where i is a positive integer.

So, $a^m = a^{pi} = (a^p)^i = (e)^i = e$.

□

Corollary 6.2: A finite group G with $|G|$ as prime, does not have proper subgroups.

Proof: Given that $|G|$ is prime. By definition of prime, $|G|$ has two divisors, namely one (*i.e.* number 1) and $|G|$. By Lagrange's Theorem, the only subgroups of G that are possible are $\{e\}$ and G itself. So, there are no proper subgroups of G.

□

Corollary 6.3: A group with $|G|$ being prime, is a cyclic (group).

Proof: Suppose, $|G|$ (≥ 2) is prime. Consider $a \neq e \in G$.

Due to Corollary 6.1, the order of a divides $|G|$ ($= m$, say). Hence, the order of a is either 1 or m. But the order of a is not equal to1, since $a \neq e$. Therefore, the order of a is $= |G|$ (which is a prime number). Hence, G is generated by (all $|G|$ powers of) a. We also observe that all $|G|$ powers of a distinct (elements of G). Hence, G is cyclic.

□

Consequences: Next, we find it convenient to reiterate and summarize important consequences of the Lagrange's theorems in the following seven facts as applicable for finite groups. In particular, the Lagrange's theorem states the following:

If G is finite group and H is subgroup of G. Then,

(i) $|H|$ divides $|G|$.

(ii) The number of distinct left (right) cosets of H in G is $|G|/|H|$. Hence, index (defined as the number of left cosets (left translates)) of H in G, that we denoted by $[G : H]$ is $|G|/|H|$.

(iii) The powers of any $a \in G$ would generate possible subgroup of G. Hence, due to (i) above, the order of $a \in G$ divides $|G|$.

(iv) Due to Corollary 6.1, the order of any $a \in G$ divides $|G|$.

(v) Due to Corollary 6.1, for any $a \in G,\ a^{|G|}$ is an identity element (denoted by e) in G.

(vi) Due to Corollary 6.2, when $|G|$ is prime, it does not have any proper subgroups.

(vii) When $|G|$ is prime, it is cyclic.

Theorem 6.5: Let p be prime. A positive integer i is its own inverse modulo p iff p divides $(i+1)$ or p divides $(i-1)$ (symbolically, $p \mid (i-1) \ \vee\ p \mid (i-1)$).

Proof: Let i be its own inverse modulo p. Then, by definition,

$$i \times i \equiv 1 \pmod{p} \qquad \ldots (6.31)$$

Hence, $p \mid i^2 -1$. Thus,

$$p \mid (i-1) \ \vee\ p \mid (i-1) \qquad \ldots (6.32)$$

Hence, we get, $i \equiv 1 \pmod{p} \ \vee\ i \equiv -1 \pmod{p}$

Conversely, suppose that $i \equiv 1 \pmod{p} \ \vee\ i \equiv -1 \pmod{p}$ ... (6.33)

Then, $i^2 \equiv 1 \pmod{p}$ ... (6.34)

□

6.13 Euler Theorem

In the module on Modular Arithmetic, we defined Euler Totient function $\varphi(n)$ as the cardinality of the set of positive integers (less than n) mod n, which are relatively prime to n. Euler's theorem is stated in terms of $\varphi(n)$. We have also defined and explained below the meaning of $\varphi(n)$. Thus, we note that $\varphi(n) = |$ [Coprime n] $|$; (we have defined what [Coprime n] stands for in the discussion below).

Theorem 6.5: **Euler's Theorem** (also called as **Fermat Euler Theorem**, or **Euler's Totient Theorem)**

Let n be a positive integer. For every positive integer g that is relatively prime to n, we have, in the modulo n arithmetic:

$$g^{\varphi(n)} = 1 \text{ (modulo } n).$$

Note about the value of g: In Euler Theorem as stated above, we considered every positive integer g that is relatively prime to n. Suppose that g is not relatively prime to n, and assume that g is bigger than n. Then the claim 1 is, remainder of g when divided by n (*i.e.*, (g modulo n)) is also not relatively prime to n.

We now give the proof of our claim 1 that, when g is bigger than n, and g is not relatively prime to n, the representative of g in modulo n as represented by remainder (that is, (g modulo n)) is also not relatively prime to n.

Proof of Claim 1: Since g and n have common factor, say h, (since h is factor of n, *i.e.* $h \mid n$, so we have, h is less than n, and in modulo n arithmetic, its representative remainder value in modulo n operation does not change) we have

$$h \mid g \Rightarrow g = k_1 \times h$$
$$h \mid n \Rightarrow n = k_2 \times h$$

g modulo n is remainder of g when g is divided by n, that is:

$$g = k_3 \times n + (g \text{ modulo } n),$$

Substituting $g = k_1 \times h$, $n = k_2 \times h$, we get,

$$k_1 \times h = k_3 \times k_2 \times h + (g \text{ modulo } n),$$

Hence, (g modulo n) = $(k_1 - k_3 \times k_2) \times h$

Thus, (g modulo n) and n has common factor, namely h. Hence they are not relatively prime (that is, (g modulo n) and n are not coprime.

□

We now give the proof of our claim 2 that, when g is bigger than n, and g is relatively prime to n, the representative of g in modulo n as represented by remainder (that is, (g modulo n)) is also relatively prime to n.

Proof of Claim 2: It is given that g and n do not have common factor. We use the technique of proof by contrapositive.

Hence, we assume the contrary; that is, assume that (g modulo n) is not relatively prime to n. Thus, (g modulo n) and n have common factor, say h. We have (since h is factor of n, *i.e.* $h \mid n$, so we have, h is less than n, and in modulo n arithmetic, its representative remainder value in modulo n operation does not change).

$$h \mid (g \text{ modulo } n) \Rightarrow (g \text{ modulo } n) = k_1 \times h$$
$$h \mid n \Rightarrow n = k_2 \times h$$

(g modulo n) is remainder of g when g is divided by n, that is:

$$g = k_3 \times n + (g \text{ modulo } n),$$

Substituting (g modulo n) = $k_1 \times h$, and $n = k_2 \times h$, in the above, we get,

$$g = k_3 \times n + (g \text{ modulo } n) = k_3 \times k_2 \times h + (g \text{ modulo } n)$$
$$= k_3 \times k_2 \times h + k_1 \times h = (k_3 \times k_2 + k_1) \times h$$

This means, g and n have common factor h, and hence they are not relatively prime.

Hence the proof of the claim.

□

We now state our claim 3. Suppose that g is relatively prime to n, and assume that g is bigger than n. Then the claim 2 is, remainder of g^i when divided by n (*i.e.*, (g^i modulo n)) is also relatively prime to n.

Sketch for Proof of Claim 3: Follows from arguments on similar lines for the proofs of claims 1, 2.

□

Now we concentrate of the sketch of the proof of our Euler theorem. We note that, from the above claims, since we are considering modulo n operations (that we introduced in the module on Modular Arithmetic), without loss of generality, we can take the value of g to be remainder of division by n, which is guaranteed to be less than n in modulo n arithmetic.

Sketch of Proof:

For the positive integer g greater than n which is relatively prime to n, we note that Consider the set of positive integers (less than n) mod n, which are relatively prime to n. In the module on Modular Arithmetic, while studying Euler Totient function $\varphi(n)$, we stated that, $\varphi(6)$ is equal to 2, since the only positive integers less than or equal to 6 that are relatively prime to 6 are 1 and 5. Similarly, $\varphi(10)$ is equal to 4, since the positive integers less than or equal to 10 that are relatively prime to 10 are 1, 3, 7, and 9. In that module, we also stated the following:

n	φ(n)	[Coprime n]: numbers coprime to n
1	1	1
2	1	1
3	2	1, 2
4	2	1,3
5	4	1,2,3,4
6	2	1,5
7	6	1,2,3,4,5,6
8	4	1,3,5,7
9	6	1,2,4,5,7,8
10	4	1,3,7,9
11	10	1,2,3,4,5,6,7,8,9,10
12	4	1,5,7,11
13	12	1,2,3,4,5,6,7,8,9,10,11,12
14	6	1,3,5,9,11,13
15	8	1,2,4,7,8,11,13,14

The set of integers mod n, that are relatively prime (*i.e.* coprime) to n, are given in the last column in the above table. Since the number in the last column, say m (modulo n), is relatively prime to n, we have:

(1) its first power, i.e. m (modulo n) is relatively prime to n (see last column)
(2) its second power m^2 (modulo n) , would also remain relatively prime to n
(3) its third power, say m^3 (modulo n) would also remain relatively prime to n
(4) Its fourth power, say m^4 (modulo n) would also remain relatively prime to n
(5) Its fifth power, say m^5 (modulo n) would also remain relatively prime to n

.

.

and so on.

The question now arises is, can the process of these powers of m go on to generate distinct numbers that are relatively prime to n forever, or when it would stop? For this purpose, we make two observations.

1. First, since we are considering congruent modulo operations, and m is representative element in the modulo n, it cannot be bigger than n; hence the process must give rise to a number less than n.
2. Second, and more important observation follows from the listing above, which says that these powers are all relatively prime to n; because of this property, these powers generated must be one of the numbers in the last column (of the nth row).

From the theory that we covered earlier, it follows that these distinct powers of m that is relatively prime to n, after sufficiently raising (to say p), generate the multiplicative identity 1 in the group of congruent modulo n operations. Since we are talking about the powers, it is easy to also see that the (multiplicative) inverse exists, and hence such distinct powers of m form a (sub-)group. Since the numbers (less than n) that are relatively prime to n are $\varphi(n)$, in the worst case, these powers would generate all $\varphi(n)$ numbers (listed in the last column of the above table.

As an illustrative example, you may like to verify that, for $n = 9$, choosing one number, say 4, its powers:

(i) $4^2 \bmod 9 = 16 \bmod 9 = 7$, (note 7 is also present in the last column);

(ii) $4^3 \bmod 9 = 64 \bmod 9 = 1$, (we got 1 here; so next power would be repetition: let us verity by continuing the process

(iii) $4^4 \bmod 9 = 256 \bmod 9 = 4$ (we got repetition)

(iv) $4^5 \bmod 9 = 1024 \bmod 9 = 7$ (observe how value at (i) is repeating!)

(v) $4^6 \bmod 9 = 4096 \bmod 9 = 1$ (observe how value at (ii) is repeating!)

We use the notation $[n]$ to denote the set of positive integers $\{1, 2, \ldots, n\}$. Amongst $[n]$, the numbers coprime to n are collected and let us call that set as [Coprime n].

With this notation, we note that:

$\varphi(n) = |\,[\text{Coprime } n]\,|$

(*i.e.*, size of the set [Coprime n],

which also means number of elements in the set [Coprime n]).

Earlier, while looking at examples of Groups, we noted that, for any positive integer n, while considering the modular multiplication as the binary operation on $\mathbb{Z}_n$, we noted that the structure ($\mathbb{Z}_n$, $\times_{(\text{mod } n)}$) fails to be a group. Hence, we consider the set of all numbers less than n that are relatively prime to n, *i.e.*, the set [Coprime n] (as we defined above), the structure ([Coprime n], $\times_{(\text{mod } n)}$) and want to investigate whether it is a group. We note that, in $\mathbb{Z}_n$, the set of elements that have multiplicative inverses with respect to $\times_{(\text{mod } n)}$ operation are precisely the numbers ($< n$) that are coprime to n. (While we omit the proof of this fact, we encourage the reader to convince himself/herself about the same.) Thus, the structure ([Coprime n], $\times_{(\text{mod } n)}$) is a group. We explain this fact in the paragraph below.

In the modulo n arithmetic, for $g \in$ [Coprime n], let us consider the powers of g. We had already defined the concept of order of g to be that number, say q, such that $g^q = 1$ (identity element). We state (proof omitted, and left to the reader to convince himself by working out that all group properties, specially existence of multiplicative inverse) that, the set [Coprime n] forms a group with multiplication operation modulo n (note that this group may have subgroups).

Suppose g $\in$ [Coprime n]. Consider distinct powers of g (modulo n). We get at most q distinct numbers from these distinct powers. These powers of q (as distinct numbers) (modulo n) form a (sub-)group structure.

We note that [Coprime n] also forms a group structure, with the same multiplication operation (modulo n). Thus, [Coprime n] is (possibly) a bigger group, and it contains the (possible) subgroups as distinct powers of g, g $\in$ [Coprime n].

The relationship between the group [Coprime n] and the (sub-) group consisting of distinct powers of g, g ∈ [Coprime n] has to obey the Lagrange's theorem (particularly, Corollaries 6.1 to 6.3).

Specially from Corollary 6.1, it follows that, for any g ∈ [Coprime n], $g^{|[\text{Coprime } n]|} = 1$, which is (the famous) Euler's Theorem.

□

6.14 Fermat's Little Theorem

Theorem 6.6: **Fermat's Little Theorem**

For every positive integer a and every prime p, $a^p \bmod p = a \bmod p$.

Sketch of Proof 1 (Inductive Proof):

First we note that this is a statement for every positive integer a. The Principle of Mathematical Induction requires us to verify the statement for base case. Let $a = 1$ be the base case. We have $1^p \bmod p$, $= 1 \bmod p$, which establishes that the statement is true for the base case. Next, let us assume that it is true for arbitrary positive integer, say k (we may symbolically denote this by H(k). Thus we are allowed to assume (using principle of mathematical induction) that H(k) is true. That is,

$$\text{H}(k): \ k^p \bmod p = k \bmod p.$$

Using the above, we need to prove H(k+1). That is, we need to prove that.

$$\text{H}(k{+}1): \ (k+1)^p \bmod p = (k+1) \bmod p$$

Now we realize that the left side expression $(k + 1)^p$ can be expanded, using binomial theorem of positive integral index, we have,

$$(k+1)^p = \sum_{i=0}^{p} \binom{p}{i} k^i 1^{p-i}$$

generating the terms with powers as k^p, k^{p-1}, k^{p-2}, … , with their coefficients as $\binom{p}{i}$. While the coefficient of the term k^p is 1 (as $\binom{p}{p}$ is 1), and H(k) allows us to have the result as $k^p \bmod p = k \bmod p$. What about the other coefficients $\binom{p}{i}$, for $(p\text{-}1) \geq i \geq 1$, we note that each such coefficient $\binom{p}{i}$ has one factor as integer p, and hence, their remainder is zero when (mod p) is applied. What about the last term with $\binom{p}{0}$ and it is multiplied with $k^0 1^p = 1$? Since we know that that $\binom{p}{0} = 1$, it contributes to addition of 1. Hence,

$$(k + 1)^p \bmod p = k \bmod p + 1 = (k + 1) \bmod p$$

Hence H(k+1) is proved.

Hence, for a given arbitrary p, the result follows for every positive integer a.

We note that the above proof is elementary, and we were ready to give such a proof in Module on Modular Arithmetic itself, as in the above proof, we did not use any result from abstract algebra, *i.e.*, we did not use any results of groups, subgroups, cosets, etc.

Since we have already covered Euler's Theorem in the previous section, we can make use of Euler Theorem to prove Fermat Little Theorem. This forms our second approach for the proof, which is briefly outlined below.

Sketch of Proof 2 (As special case of Euler Theorem):

We revisit the statement of Euler Theorem as follows:

(Euler Theorem):

Let n be a positive integer. For every positive integer g that is relatively prime to n, we have, in the modulo n arithmetic:

$$g^{\varphi(n)} = 1 \text{ (modulo } n).$$

Let n be a prime number p in the above.

Since the Fermat Little Theorem is a statement for every positive integer a, we need to consider two disjoint cases, as given in the following.

Case 1: Suppose positive integer a ($> p$) has, as a factor, the prime p, that is, a =

$k_1 \times p$. Then,

$a^p \pmod p = (k_1 \times p)^p \pmod p = (k_1 \times p)^{p-1} \times (k_1 \times p) \pmod p$

$= [(k_1 \times p)^{p-1} \times k_1] \times p \pmod p = 0.$

Also, in such a case, $a = k_1 \times p \pmod p = 0$.

Hence, the Fermat Little theorem holds.

Case 2: Suppose positive integer a ($> p$) does not have, as factor, the given prime p. Thus, a and p are relatively prime in this case, and the condition in Euler theorem is satisfied; so we can now apply Euler Theorem. (Also may like to additionally note that prime number is always prime to all positive integers $< p$).

In this case, the above Euler Theorem reduces to:

Let p be prime. For every positive integer a that is relatively prime to n, we have, in the modulo n arithmetic:

$$a^{\varphi(n)} = 1 \text{ (modulo } n).$$

For every prime p, in the (modulo p) arithmetic, we note that (all congruent class representative numbers less than p) are relatively prime to p. Thus, the numbers:

$$1, 2, 3, \ldots, (p-1)$$

are all relatively prime to p. They are $(p - 1)$ in number. This also means, for prime number p, the Euler totient function,

$\varphi(p) = |\text{[Coprime } p]| = (p-1)$

Thus, we get, $a^{\varphi(p)} = 1 \text{ (modulo } p),$

that is, $a^{(p-1)} = 1 \text{ (modulo } p),$

Multiplying both sides by a, we get,

$$a^p = a \text{ (modulo } p),$$

which is what is needed to be proved for Fermat Little Theorem.

□

Sketch of Proof 3 (Group theory based):

In modular arithmetic, we also know that, for any positive integer a, when we consider it modulo p, we get its representative (class number value as) remainder between 0 to ($p - 1$).

We want to treat the case when remainder is 0 separately, as in Case 1 below. Thus, consider two cases.

Case 1: Suppose positive integer a ($> p$) has, as a factor, the prime p, that is, $a = k_1 \times p$. Then,

$a^p \pmod{p} = (k_1 \times p)^p \pmod{p} = (k_1 \times p)^{p-1} \times (k_1 \times p) \pmod{p}$
$= [(k_1 \times p)^{p-1} \times k_1] \times p \pmod{p} = 0.$

Also, in such a case, $a = k_1 \times p \pmod{p} = 0$.

Hence, the Fermat Little theorem holds.

Case 2: Suppose positive integer a ($> p$) does not have, as factor, the given prime p. Thus, a and p are relatively prime.

In the modulo p results, we consider the numbers upto (p -1) (because, in this case, we are assuming numbers that are necessarily relatively prime to p, so it is not divisible by p, so remainder 0 cannot arise, the value p is out of question when we consider modulo p values) , when we want apply Group theory based approach. Thus, we consider the positive numbers (p -1) as

$$\{ 1, 2, 3, \ldots, (p-1) \}$$

being the elements of our group under consideration. With modulo p operation, and usual multiplication of positive integers, the group:

$$(\{ 1, 2, 3, \ldots, (p-1) \}, \times_{(\text{modulo p})})$$

is a group (please verify that, it is indeed a group, *i.e.* existence of inverse for every element). We note that it is cyclic, (please verify that it is cyclic, *i.e.* there exists (at least one element in this group) which acts as generator, whose all p powers are distinct elements in this group).

For a given a and p that are relatively prime,

$a \pmod{p}$ is one of the elements in $\{ 1, 2, 3, \ldots, (p-1) \}$,

Further, a^2 and p that are relatively prime, so,

a^2 (mod p) is one of the elements in { 1, 2, 3, … , (p -1) },

Further, a^3 and p that are relatively prime, so,

a^3 (mod p) is one of the elements in { 1, 2, 3, … , (p -1) },

.

.

.

Hence in the group ({ 1, 2, 3, … , (p -1) }, $\times_{(\text{modulo } p)}$), from Corollary 1 of Lagrange's theorem, we have,

$$a^{(p-1)} = 1 \text{ (modulo } p\text{)},$$

Multiplying both sides by a, we get,

$$a^p = a \text{ (modulo } p\text{)},$$

which is what is needed to be proved for Fermat Little Theorem.

□

Example 6.19: Find 50^{11} mod 11.

Due to Fermat's little theorem, 50^{11} mod 11 = 50 mod 11 = 6Note:
You may like to check it as per the calculations:

50^{11} = 4,882,812,500,000,000,000 = 11*443,892,045,454,454,454 + 6

So, 50^{11} mod 11 = 6

Example 6.20: Prove that 2^{257}-1 is not prime.

(Proof by contradiction): Assume the contrary, i.e., $p = 2^{257}$-1 is prime.

Using Python script below, we get p = 231584178474632390847141970017375815706539969331281128078915168015826 259279871

It is easy to calculate p, but factoring is hard!

However 10^p mod p is equal to, by Fermat's little theorem, = (10 mod p) = 10. So 10^{p+1} mod p should be 100.

To calculate 10^{p+1}, note that

$$10^{2^a} . 10^{2^a} = 10^{2^a + 2^a} = 10^{2 \cdot 2^a} = 10^{2^{a+1}}$$

Execute the following short script In Python shell and observe:

```
p = 2**257-1
t = 10
for n in range(257):
    t = (t*t)%p
print t
```

Now verify that t is:
18516485248061877085646028981954059300764404592819021566648
9016000575884803793

- Since this number is not 100, p is not prime.

□

Example 6.21: Thru this example, we illustrate that the converse of Fermat Little Theorem is not true. Consider $3^{90} = 1 \pmod{91}$; however, we know that 91 is not prime, as $91 = 13 \times 7$.

□

We are familiar with various numbers such as: Real numbers $\mathbb{R}$, Rational numbers $\mathbb{Q}$, Complex numbers $\mathbb{C}$. We are familiar with two operations on numbers, namely addition and multiplication. The abstract properties of these two operations are studied in the abstract structures namely rings, and fields. In the next few sections, we shall discuss these structures.

6.15 Rings, Fields and Finite Fields

Definition 6.23: Ring: A ring R is a structure (R, +, ×). It has two binary operations +, ×. These binary operations have the following properties:

Part A: (properties of +): The structure (R, +) is Abelian Group. Let the identity of this group be denoted by 0.

Part B: (properties of ×): The structure (R, ×) is a semigroup.

Part C: (Distributivity of × over +): The following distributive laws hold for all a, b, c in R:

(i) $a \times (b + c) = (a \times b) + (a \times c)$
(ii) $(a + b) \times c = (a \times c) + (b \times c)$

Example 3.22: The structure $(\mathbb{Z}_n, +_n, \times_n)$, that is, the set $\mathbb{Z}_n$ (for $n \geq 2$) of residue (modulo) representatives, together with modulo n addition operation $(+_n)$ and modulo n multiplication operation $(\times_n)$ is a ring. We note that, when n is not prime, the structure $(\mathbb{Z}_n, \times_n)$ is not a group, the multiplicative inverse may not exist. However, this structure obeys the Ring properties.

Example 3.23: The set of polynomials together with polynomial addition and polynomial multiplication is a ring.

Example 3.24: The set of square matrices with usual matrix addition operation as well as with usual matrix multiplication is a ring. In fact, it is ring with identity matrix as identity of multiplication. Such ring is called as ring with multiplicative identity. However, the matrix multiplication is not commutative, so, we also sometimes call such a structure as, non-commutative structure, to distinguish it from Commutative ring.

Notations:

(i) In the Ring, the identity element with respect to + operation always exists, and such identity element is conventionally called as "*zero*" element, and often denoted by 0, when no confusion arises.
(ii) in case the left as well as right identity element exists with respect to the × operation, such identity element is conventionally called as "*unity*" element, and often denoted by 1, when no confusion arises.
(iii) Ring is called "*commutative* ring" if the × operation is commutative.

Definition 6.24**:** Integral Domain: Commutative ring with unity (*i.e.* with identity of ×) that is not zero (*i.e.* identity of +), together with the additional property that:

$$\forall (a, b) \in R \times R, \ [(a \times b = 0) \rightarrow ((a = 0) \vee (b = 0))]$$

is defined to be an integral domain.

Question 3.26: Does the structure $(\mathbb{Z}_n, +_n, \times_n)$, that is, the set $\mathbb{Z}_n$ (for $n > 2$, n not prime) of residue (modulo) representatives, together with modulo n addition operation $(+_n)$ and modulo n multiplication operation $(\times_n)$ is an integral domain?

Example 3.25: The set of 2×2 matrices (together with matrix addition, and matrix multiplication operation) is not a integral domain. The reason is as follows.

Consider the matrix product of two non-zero matrices $\begin{bmatrix} 1 & 0 \\ 0 & 0 \end{bmatrix}$ and $\begin{bmatrix} 0 & 0 \\ 1 & 1 \end{bmatrix}$. We have,

$$\begin{bmatrix} 1 & 0 \\ 0 & 0 \end{bmatrix} \times \begin{bmatrix} 0 & 0 \\ 1 & 1 \end{bmatrix} = \begin{bmatrix} 0 & 0 \\ 0 & 0 \end{bmatrix}.$$

Definition 6.25: Ring Homomorphism

Suppose that we have two rings R and R', and a function $f: R \rightarrow R'$. For clarity, let us denote addition in ring R by $+_R$ and multiplication in ring R by $\times_R$. Similarly, let us denote addition in ring R' by $+_{R'}$ and multiplication in ring R' by $\times_{R'}$

The function $f: R \rightarrow R'$ is defined to be ring homomorphism, if and only if,

$\forall (a, b) \in R \times R$, (i) $f(a +_R b) = f(a) +_{R'} f(b)$, and,

(ii) $f(a \times_R b) = f(a) \times_{R'} f(b)$,

We note that, when n is not prime, the structure $(\mathbb{Z}_n, \times_n)$ is not a group, the multiplicative inverse may not exist. However, this structure obeys the Ring properties.

Notations:

(i) When the ring homomorphism is one-to-one, it is also called as *monomorphism*.

(ii) When the ring homomorphism is onto R', it is also called as *epimorphism*

Definition 6.26: Ring Isomorphism

Suppose that we have two rings R and R', and a ring homomorphism function $f: R \rightarrow R'$, that is monomorphism as well as epimorphism. Then such a homomorphism is called ring isomorphism,

In other words, ring homomorphism that is both monomorphism as well as epimorphism is defined to be ring isomorphism.

Question 6.27: Suppose we have two rings R, R' both with unity. Does there exist a ring homomorphism that does not map the unity of R to the unity of R'?

Definition 6.27: Field

A commutative ring with unity not equal to zero, such that every nonzero element in the ring has multiplicative inverse is called a Field.

In other words, for the ring structure R to be qualified as being called as a field, we have (R, +, ×), we have:

> Part A: (properties of +): The structure (R, +) is Abelian Group. Let the identity of this group be denoted by 0.
> Part B: (properties of ×): The structure (R, ×) is a semigroup.
> Part C: (Distributivity of × over +): The following distributive laws hold for all a, b, c in R:
> i) $a \times (b + c) = (a \times b) + (a \times c)$
> ii) $(a + b) \times c = (a \times c) + (b \times c)$
>
> (Field Properties):
> i) $1 \neq 0$
> ii) (properties of ×) : The structure (R-{0}, ×) is Abelian Group.

Notation: We call Field to be a *finite Field*, when the number of elements in the Field are finite. In discrete mathematics, we are interested only in finite Fields.

Question 6.27: Can we define the *finite Field* to be the structure with the following properties?

> Consider the structure (F, +, ×), with two binary operations +, × satisfying the following:
> Part A: (properties of +): The structure (F, +) is Abelian Group. Let the identity of this group be denoted by 0.
> Part B: (properties of ×): The structure (F, ×) is Abelian group.
> Part C: (unity being different than zero): The identity element of the structure (F, +) is different than the identity element of the structure (F, ×).

Part D: (Distributivity of × over +): The following distributive laws hold for all a, b, c in R:

i) $a \times (b + c) = (a \times b) + (a \times c)$

ii) $(a + b) \times c = (a \times c) + (b \times c)$

Example 6.26: In Example 3.22, we noted that the structure ($\mathbb{Z}_n$, $+_n$, $\times_n$), that is, the set $\mathbb{Z}_n$ (for $n \geq 2$) of residue (modulo) representatives, together with modulo n addition operation ($+_n$) and modulo n multiplication operation ($\times_n$) is a ring. We also noted that, when n is not prime, the structure ($\mathbb{Z}_n$, $\times_n$) is not a group, the multiplicative inverse may not exist. However, this structure obeys the Ring properties. Hence such a structure is also not a (finite) Field.

Example 6.27: To continue with Example 3.22, and Example 3.36, now assume that n is not prime, say it is denoted by p. The structure ($\mathbb{Z}_p$, $+_p$, $\times_p$), that is, the set $\mathbb{Z}_p$ (for $p \geq 2$) of residue (modulo) representatives, together with modulo p addition operation ($+_p$) and modulo p multiplication operation ($\times_n$) is a ring. We also noted that, when n is not prime, the structure ($\mathbb{Z}_p$, $\times_p$) is a group, as we know that the multiplicative inverse exists. It is easy to verify that such a structure is also a (finite) Field.

Question 6.28:

(a) For positive integer n ≥ 4, consider the structure ([Coprime(n)] , $+_n$, $\times_n$), is it a Field? What are the non-trivial relationships of this structure with ($\mathbb{Z}_n$, $+_n$, $\times_n$) ?

(b) In the part (a), for positive integer n ≥ 4, we considered the structure

([Coprime(n)] , $+_n$, $\times_n$).

In this structure, we know that the part ([Coprime(n)] , $\times_n$) is Abelian Group. This question how asks you to construct $+_{Rn}$ so that the structure

([Coprime(n)] , $+_{Rn}$, $\times_n$)

Is a field? Is it possible to construct such a field for all non-prime n values? If know, can you characterize (at least state a few non-trivial properties) of such non-prime n numbers?

UNIT SUMMARY

- Discussed the primary concepts of groups and semi groups, evaluation is represented with tree graphically also shown how binary relations form a semi group with composition operation on binary functions.

- Semigroup homomorphism is a map between semigroups to preserve respective semigroup operations.
- Monoid is a semigroup with identity element, we saw how notion of homomorphism connect structural property of operations.
- Group is a monoid with inverse element of every element, also satisfies closure, associativity identity, inverse and commutativity properties.
- Notations for representing permutations like Cauchy and cycle notations are introduced.
- Cosets have the same cardinality as its subgroup, index and alternate definition of normal subgroups are discussed.
- Lagrange's theorem and its following corollaries are discussed for the practical applications.

Why do we need Abstract Algebraic Structures?

Let us examine a question: Why do we consider groups? This added abstraction makes problems easier. By reducing to a generic object defined by axioms, we can see a clearer picture of what's going on (that is, what depends on what) and why. For example, working on arithmetic problems mod 11 all the time, you might be able to prove many things, and even guess a general picture, so working out these specific examples is a good idea to understand the properties. However, you'll never see how far your theory extends unless you think about what makes the proof work and what axioms are essential to demonstrating its truth. The next paragraph is one example of the above.

We noted that the structure ($\mathbb{Z}_n$,, $\times_{(\text{mod } n)}$) fails to be a group. However, the structure ([Coprime n],, $\times_{(\text{mod } n)}$) is a group. Since [Coprime p] = {1, 2, 3, … (p-1) }, and the structure ([Coprime p] , $\times_{(\text{mod } p)}$) is a group, from Corollary 1 of Lagrange's theorem, it quickly follows the Fermat's Little Theorem, namely, for every positive integer a and every prime p, $a^p \bmod p = a \bmod p$. Similarly, the usefulness of Euler Totitent function, as well as the Euler theorem, namely the following,

> Let n be a positive integer. For every positive integer g that is relatively prime to n, we have, in the modulo n arithmetic:
>
> $g^{\varphi(n)} = 1$ (modulo n).

is clear when we have (Corollary 1 of) Lagrange Theorem.

We also note that, given p being a prime number, the structure ($\mathbb{Z}_p$,, $+_{(\text{mod } p)}$, $\times_{(\text{mod } p)}$) is a field (because, ($\mathbb{Z}_p - \{0\}$, $\times_{(\text{mod } p)}$), *i.e.*, ([Coprime p] , $\times_{(\text{mod } p)}$), is a group, in fact an

Abelian Group, and it follows easily that $\times_{(\text{mod } p)}$ distributes over $+_{(\text{mod } p)}$. We denote this field by the symbol $\mathscr{F}_p$. Such fields are also called as Galios Fields.

We note that the Field $\mathscr{F}_2$ has lot of similarities with Set Theory (with $+_{(\text{mod } 2)}$ being considered as having properties similar to set union operation $\cup$, and , $\times_{(\text{mod } 2)}$ being considered as having properties similar to set intersection operation $\cap$, null set being special element as identity with respect to set union operation).

The Field $\mathscr{F}_2$ has lot of similarities with Propositional Logic (with $+_{(\text{mod } 2)}$ being considered as having properties similar to logical or operation $\vee$, and, $\times_{(\text{mod } 2)}$ being considered as having properties similar to logical and operation $\wedge$, null set Φ being special element as identity with respect to set union operation).

The above shows the usefulness of abstract concepts for studying the unification of concepts that have been widely useful in apparently non-related domains like, logical thinking, set theory, and modulo arithmetic, physical symmetry, etc.

Exercises:

1. Show that the following forms a commutative group with respect to multiplication of integers. a. $G=\{3^n : n \in Z\}$ b. $G= \{2^{n+1} : n \in Z\}$
2. Assume $G = \{ (x,y) : x,y \in R$ and not both zero$\}$ and * be binary operation defined by $(x,y) * (p,q) = (xp-yq,xq+yq)$ Show that (G,*) is an abelian group.
3. Consider M as a set of all matrices of size 2x2, inverse symmetric matrix where $m\neq0$. Show that (M,*) forms an abelian group under matrix multiplication.
4. The center of a group G is defined by $C(G) = \{ x \in G : xb = bx$ for every $x \in G \}$ ie. The set of all elements in G that commute with every element of G. Show that C(G) is a subgroup of G.
5. If $x \in G$ define $N(a) = \{ x \in G : xb = bx\}$ ie. the set of all elements in G that commute with a. Show that N(a) is a subgroup of G. Here N(a) is usually termed as normalizer or centraliser of $x \in G$.
6. Let *H* be a subgroup of *G*, show that,
   i. $Ha = H$ iff $a \in H$
   ii. $Hh = H$ iff $h \in H$
   iii. $b \in H$ iff $Ha = Hb$
   iv. $Ha = Hb$ iff $ab^{-1} \in H$; $aH = bH$ iff $a^{-1}b \in H$

7. If p and q are two elements of a group, then
   i) $o(a) = o(xax^{-1}) = o(x^{-1}ax)$ for all $x \in G$
   ii) $o(ab) = o(ba)$
   iii) if $a^m = e$ then $o(a)$ divides m

8. Find the smallest subgroup of Z containing 18, 30 and 40

9. Prove that every group of order less than 6 is abelian.

10. How many generators does the following have:
   i) a cyclic group of order n
   ii) an infinite cyclic group

11. Let H be a subgroup of index 2 in G. Show that H is normal subgroup of G

12. If H is the only subgroup of finite order m in the group G then show that H isa normal subgroup of G.

13. Show that any infinite cyclic group is isomorphic to the group (Z,+).

14. Show that any two cyclic group of the same order are isomorphic.

15. Prove or disprove the following:
   i. If G and G' are two groups of order 6 then they are isomorphic.
   ii. If G and G' are two groups of order 31 then they are isomorphic.

16. Prove that a group of order p^2, where p is a prime number must have a normalsubgroup of order p.

17. Determine which of the following are even permutations.
   i) (1 2 3 4 5) (1 4 5) (2 3)
   ii) (1 3 2) (1 4 5 6)

18. Determine the order of each element in A_4. Also show that A_4 has no subgroupof order 6.

19. Show that 10!+1 is divisible by 11

20. What is the remainder when 5!25! is divided by 31!

21. What is the remainder when 5^{100} is divided by 7?

22. Show that if p is an odd prime then 2(p-3)! ≡ -1(mod p)

23. Find a reduced residue system modulo 2m , where m is a positive integer.

24. Show that if $a_1, a_2, \ldots a_{\Phi(m)}$ is a reduced residue system modulo m, where m is a positive integer with m≠2, then $a_1 + a_2 + \ldots + a_{\Phi(m)} \equiv 0 (\text{mod } m)$

25. Show that if a is an integer such that a is not divisible by 3 or such that a is divisible by 9 then $a^7 \equiv a \bmod 63$

26. Show that a finite cyclic group of order n is isomorphic to Zn

27. Let M and N be normal subgroups of G then prove that

$$\frac{NM}{M} \approx \frac{N}{N \cap M}$$

KNOW MORE

Wikipedia and various educational resources:

- Akos Seress. *Permutation group algorithms*. Cambridge Tracts in Mathematics, 152. Cambridge University Press, Cambridge, 2003.
- Meenaxi Bhattacharjee, Dugald Macpherson, Rögnvaldur G. Möller and Peter M. Neumann. *Notes on Infinite Permutation Groups*. Number 1698 in Lecture Notes in Mathematics. Springer-Verlag, 1998.
- Peter J. Cameron. *Permutation Groups*. LMS Student Text 45. Cambridge University Press, Cambridge, 1999.
- Peter J. Cameron. *Oligomorphic Permutation Groups*. Cambridge University Press, Cambridge, 1990.

REFERENCES AND SUGGESTED READINGS

1. Thomas W. Judson, Robert A. Beezer, Abstract Algebra: Theory and Applications, (from Website: abstract.pugetsound.edu on 09 Aug 2021) (358 pages; 23 Chapters, of which we are interested in first 7 chapters – page nos 1 to 90 of the book; Chapter 9: Isomorphism - page nos 114-125, and Chapter 11: Homomorphism – Page numbers: 134-141.

2. Liu, C. L., & Mohapatra, D. P. (2008). Elements of Discrete Mathematics. TataMcGraw-Hill.

3. Rosen, K. H. (2019). Discrete Mathematics and Its Applications. (8th Edition)ISBN10:125967651X ISBN13: 9781259676512.

4. Wielandt, H. (1964). Finite Permutation Groups. Academic Press. Henry Sinclair Hall and Samuel Ratcliffe Knight, Higher Algebra: A Sequel to Elementary Algebra for Schools, (Fourth Edition), MacMillan, London, 1896.

5. Herstein, I. N. (2006). Topics in algebra. John Wiley & Sons.

6. Norman L. Biggs, Discrete Mathematics, (2nd ed. 2002), Oxford University Press.

7. Shoup, V. (2009). A computational introduction to number theory and algebra, Cambridge University Press.

8. NOTES: Group Theory Notes by Donald L. Kreher, (18th March 2020): 135pages; website: https://pages.mtu.edu/~kreher/

9. "Permutation group", Encyclopedia of Mathematics, EMS Press, 2001

10. Alexander Hulpke. GAP Data Library .

Dynamic QR Code for Further Reading

7 Graphs

UNIT SPECIFICS

Through this unit we have discussed the following aspects:

- *Graphs Basics*
- *Connected Components*
- *Paths, Cycles and Trees*
- *Hamiltonian and Eulerian Walks*
- *Coloring*
- *Planarity*
- *Matching*

In this chapter, we covered the above-mentioned concepts.

This Unit is devoted to understand the basic terms and terminology related to Graph Theory

RATIONALE

Why do you learn basics of Graph Theory?

Graph theory is important for the following reasons:

1. Solving problems: Graph theory provides a structured way to model problems and find solutions. It is extensively used in computer science, operations research, optimization, and artificial intelligence.

2. Network analysis: Graph theory provides a set of tools and techniques to analyze and understand complex networks and their properties. This is crucial in fields such as transportation, telecommunications, social networks, and epidemiology.

3. Design of algorithms: Graph theory is fundamental in designing algorithms for tasks such as network flow, path-finding, and matching problems.

4. Optimization: Graph theory provides a framework for optimization problems such as minimizing distances, maximizing coverage, and minimizing costs. These are important in logistics, scheduling, and resource allocation.

5. Cryptography: Graph theory is used to develop secure, efficient cryptographic algorithms.

6. Social choice theory: Graph theory is used to study the preference structures of society in areas such as voting theory and fair division.

Overall, Graph theory has numerous practical applications in a wide range of fields, making it a crucial discipline in modern science and technology.

Graph Theory has found a humungous number of applications in engineering. Understanding Graph Theory is very useful for those who are into Language Processing or Computer Networks, physical sciences and numerous other fields.

PRE-REQUISITES

Mathematics at school level (till Class X) Graphs Basics

UNIT OUTCOMES

List of outcomes of this unit is as follows:

U7-O1: Understand basic concepts of Graph Theory.

U7-O2: Apply Theory of connected components to solve problems.

U7-O3: Apply concepts Paths, Cycles and Trees to solve real-time problems.

U7-O4: Understand the principles of Hamiltonian and Eulerian walks.

U7-O5: Apply concepts of graph coloring and planarity to solve problems.

U7-O6: Apply concept of matching to solve problems.

Unit-1 Outcomes	EXPECTED MAPPING WITH COURSE OUTCOMES (1- Weak Correlation; 2- Medium correlation; 3- Strong Correlation)								
	CO-1	CO-2	CO-3	CO-4	CO-5	CO-6	CO-7	CO-8	CO-9
U7-O1	2	2	1	1	1	1	-	-	2
U7-O2	1	1	1	2	2	2	-	-	2
U7-O3	2	1	-	1	1	2	-	-	1
U7-O4	1	1	2	2	2	2	-	-	2
U7-O5	2	2	2	2	2	2	-	-	2
U7-O6	1	2	1	1	1	1	-	-	1

Graphs

7.1 FUNDAMENTALS OF GRAPHS

7.1.1 What is a Graph?

In real time often we see objects are interconnected with each other, if such interconnected objects represented as points, we call them as vertices, A pair of these objects are connected by links, call them as edges that connect the vertices. To represent such an arrangement of objects, which is a collection of vertices and edges we use a pictorial representation called Graph, represented as G={V,E}. Formally, a graph is a pair of sets **(V, E)**, where **V** forms the set of vertices and E forms the set of edges, connecting the pairs of vertices. Observe the figure below which is a graph.

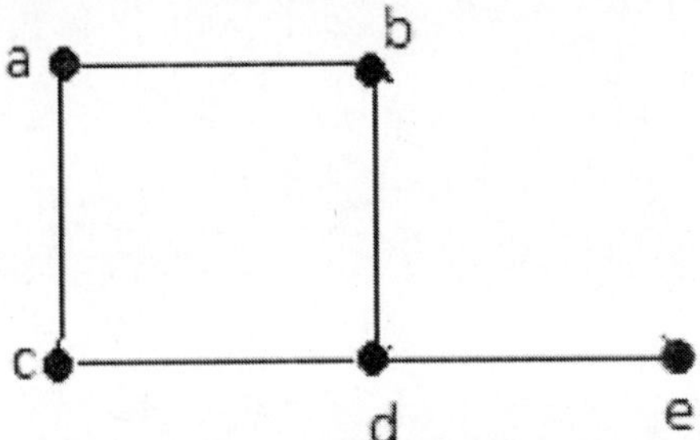

In the this figure, it is composed of two sets; V = {a, b, c, d, e} and E = {ab, ac, bd, cd, de}

A graph is a pictorial representation of points and lines connected to the points. It has at least one line joining a set of two vertices with no vertex connecting itself. Let us now look into some fundamental terms and terminology of graphs.

7.1.2 Graphs Terminology

i) A point is a particular position in a 1D, 2D or 3D space. Here D is used to signify the term dimension. A point is represented with a dot and denoted by an alphabet as shown below.

• a

Fig: Point by named as 'a'.

ii) <u>Line</u>: Any two points have a connection between them, and the connection is formed by a solid link (geometrically which is a collection of several points) forms a **Line**, represented as shown below.

Fig: a line ab connects the points 'a' and 'b'.

iii) <u>Vertex</u>:

In a graph we often see a special type of point, where multiple links meet, thus forming a Vertex of a Graph, also referred as a **node**. In Similarity to points, a letter is used to denote a vertex.

• a

Here, the vertex is named with an alphabet 'a'.

iv) Edge

in the context of graph a line that links two vertices can be mathematically termed as an edge. Edge will have a vertex in the starting point as well as at the ending point. Edge cannot exist without a vertex, there can be multiple edges arising from a single vertex.

a •———• b

Here, 'a' and 'b' form two vertices of a graph and the link between them is called an edge.

Now let us combine all these terms to get a clear picture about graph. As we mentioned earlier that, a graph 'G' as G = (V, E) Where V is a set of formed by all its vertices and E is a set formed by all edges in the graph. Observe the graph I , having a, b, c, and d as the vertices and ab, ac, cd, and bd as the edges. Also

Observe the following graph II having a, b, c, and d as the vertices and ab, ac, ad, and cd as four edges.

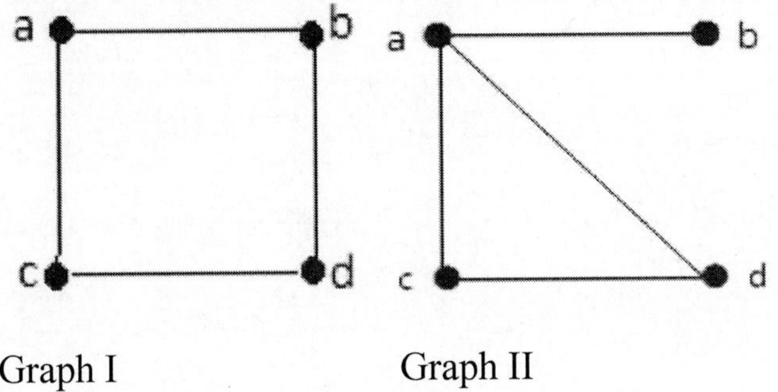

Graph I Graph II

v)Loop

In a graph, often we see an edge is arise from one vertex is intersected to the same vertex itself, forms a loop.

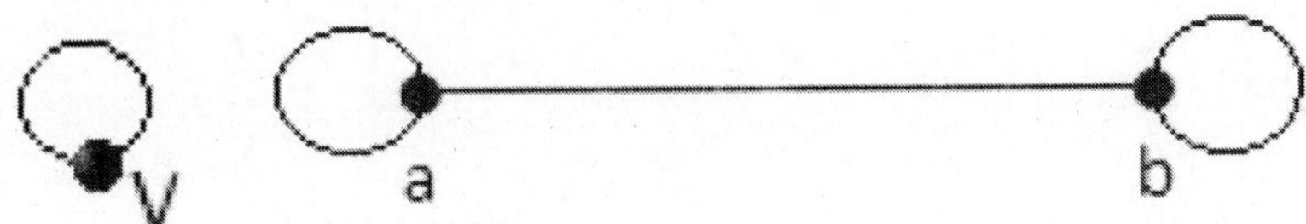

Here is a graph with single vertex V having a edge arising and ending at V itself thus forms a loop. In the next figure you can see a graph with vertices a and b having two loops. So in a graph with n vertices there can be 0 or n loops.

vi) Degree

The number of vertices adjacent to another vertex V or in simple terms number edges intersecting a vertex is called **degree** of a vertex, denoted by deg(V).

When a graph has n vertices, the following relation must be satisfied by the degree of any vertex.

$\deg(V) \leq n - 1 \ \forall \ V \in G$

This is applicable only for simple graph ie. a graph with no loops in it.

vii) Directed and undirected graphs:

Graph can be formed by marking direction on the edges, due to which a graph can be **directed** or **undirected**. The degree parameter varies based on whether a graph is directed or undirected.

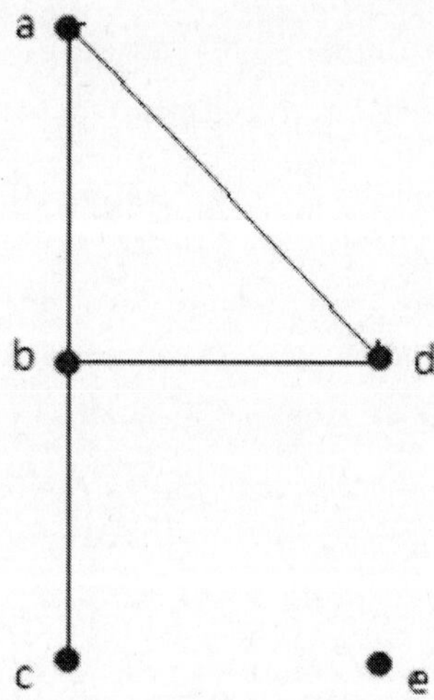

This is an Undirected Graph,

Degree of vertex a = 2

Degree of vertex b = 3

Degree of vertex c = 1 this is special and termed as **pendent vertex**

Degree of vertex d = 2

Degree of vertex e = 0 this is also special and termed as **isolated vertex**

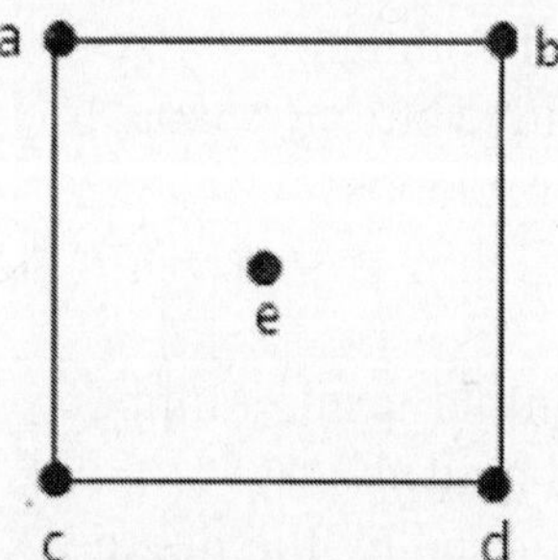

In this graph,

Degree of vertex a = 2

Degree of vertex b = 2

Degree of vertex c = 2

Degree of vertex d = 2

Degree of vertex e = 0

It is clear that there is no pendent vertex in this graph.

viii) Indegree and outdegree:

Now, let us consider a directed graph, where, each vertex will have both **indegree** and **outdegree**. The number of edges which are intersecting into a vertex V, is called as Indegree of vertex V **denoted by** minus followed by deg, like this, deg−(V). the number of edges which are arising out from the vertex V, called as Outdegree of vertex V **denoted by** plus followed by deg, like this, deg+(V).

Consider the directed graph given below. At vertex 'a', 'ad' and 'ab' are two edges, are moving outwards as seen by the direction head. Hence its outdegree is of vertex 'a' is 2. Similarly, observe that, there is an edge 'ga', originating towards vertex 'a'. Hence the indegree of vertex 'a' is 1. Analogously the indegree and outdegrees of all vertices are as shown in the table below.

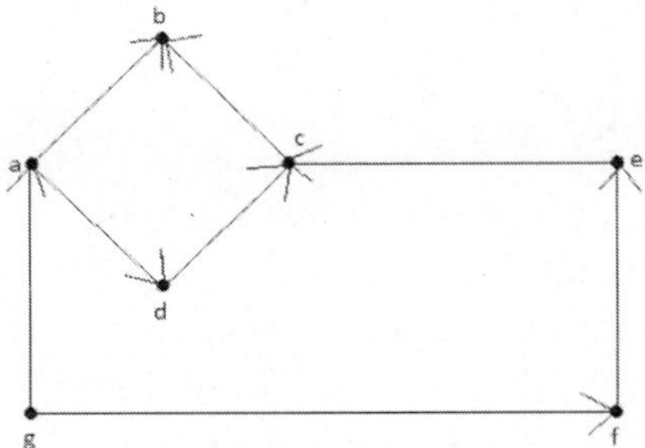

Vertex	Indegree	Outdegree
a	1	2
b	2	0
c	2	1
d	1	1
e	1	1
f	1	1
g	0	2

Consider another directed graph given below. At Vertex 'a' an edge 'ae' is moving outwards from it. Hence outdegree of this vertex is 1. Similarly, the graph also has an edge 'ba' moving towards vertex 'a'. Hence the indegree of this vertex 'a' is 1.

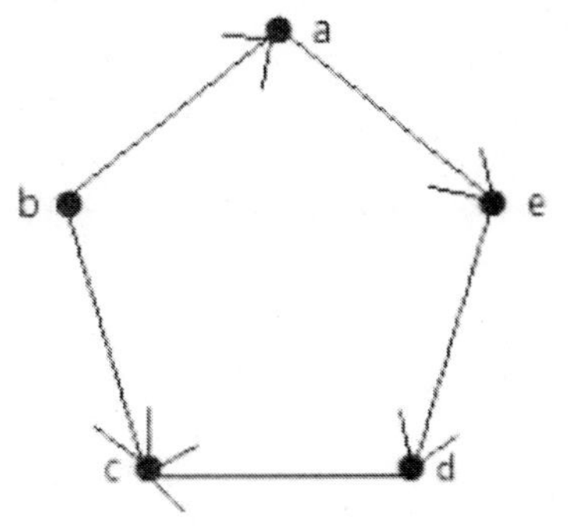

Vertex	Indegree	Outdegree
a	1	1
b	0	2
c	2	0
d	1	1
e	1	1

Now we revisit the terms pendent and isolated vertex which were termed as special earlier. A vertex with single degree is called a pendent vertex. A vertex with zero degree is called an isolated vertex.

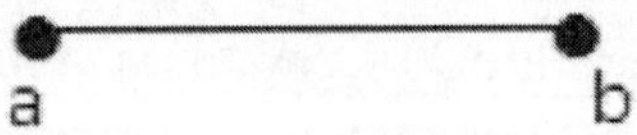

I II

Here in I, both vertices a and b are pendent vertices as they have degree of 1. Whereas, in II

the vertices 'a' and 'b' are isolated vertices as they have no connectivity between each other, the degree of both of them is zero.

ix) Adjacency

In a graph, if there is an edge between the two vertices, then two vertices are said to be **adjacent** to each other. The adjacency of vertices is maintained by the single edge connects those two vertices. Analogously, in a graph, two edges are also said to be adjacent if there is a shared vertex between the two edges. Here, the adjacency of edges is maintained by the single vertex that connects two edges.

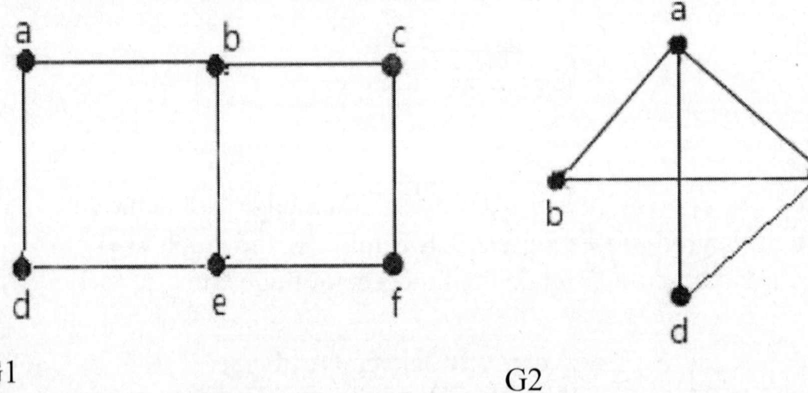

G1 G2

In the above graph G1 –

- 'a' and 'd' are the adjacent vertices, because of the common edge 'ad'
- 'a' and 'b' are the adjacent vertices, because of the common edge 'ab'
- be' and 'de' are the adjacent edges, because of the common vertex 'e'
- ab' and 'be' are the adjacent edges, because of the common vertex 'b'

Similarly In the graph G2 –

- 'c' and 'b' are the adjacent vertices, because of the common edge 'cb'.
- 'a' and 'd' are the adjacent vertices, because of the common edge 'ad'.
- 'ac' and 'cd' are the adjacent edges, because of the common vertex 'c'.
- 'ad' and 'cd' are the adjacent edges, because of the common vertex 'd'.

x) Parallel Edges

In a graph, often there are instances when a pair of vertices are connected by multiple edges, then such edges are named as parallel edges.

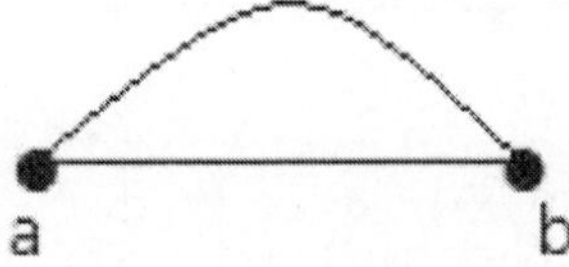

In the above graph, vertices 'a' and 'b' are connected by two edges 'ab' and 'ba' between them. So there is a parallel edge seen here.

xi) Multi Graph

A graph consisting of atleast one pair of parallel edges is said to be a Multigraph.

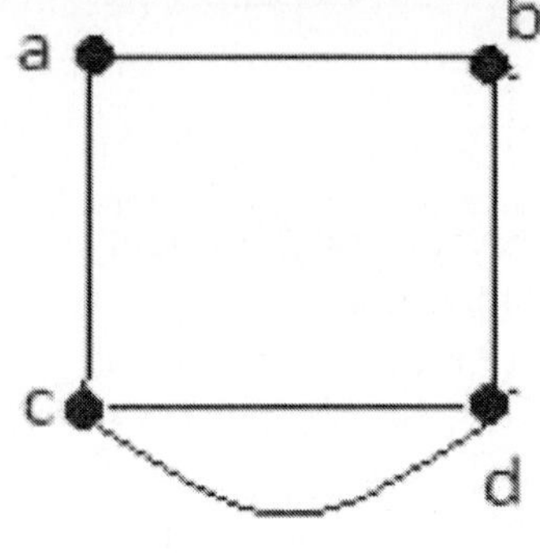

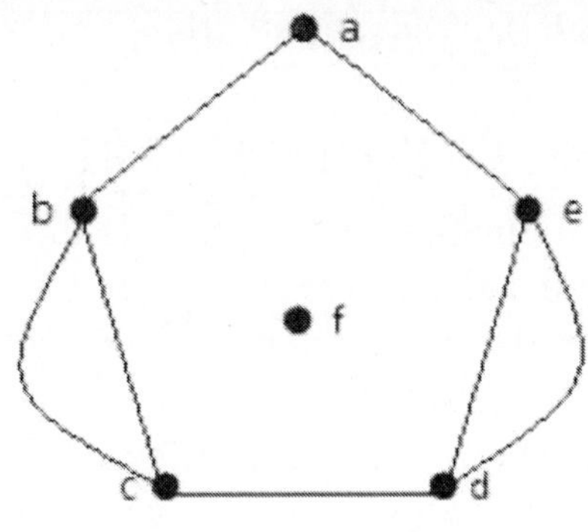

G2

G1 is a Multigraph, among the five edges 'ab', 'ac', 'cd', 'dc', and 'bd'. Since 'c' and 'd' have two parallel edges between them. Similarly, in G2, the vertices 'b' and 'c' have double edges. The vertices 'e' and 'd' also have double edges between them. Hence it is also a Multigraph.

xii) Degree Sequence of a Graph

The sequence obtained by ordering the degrees of all vertices in ascending or descending order,
is termed as the degree sequence of the graph.

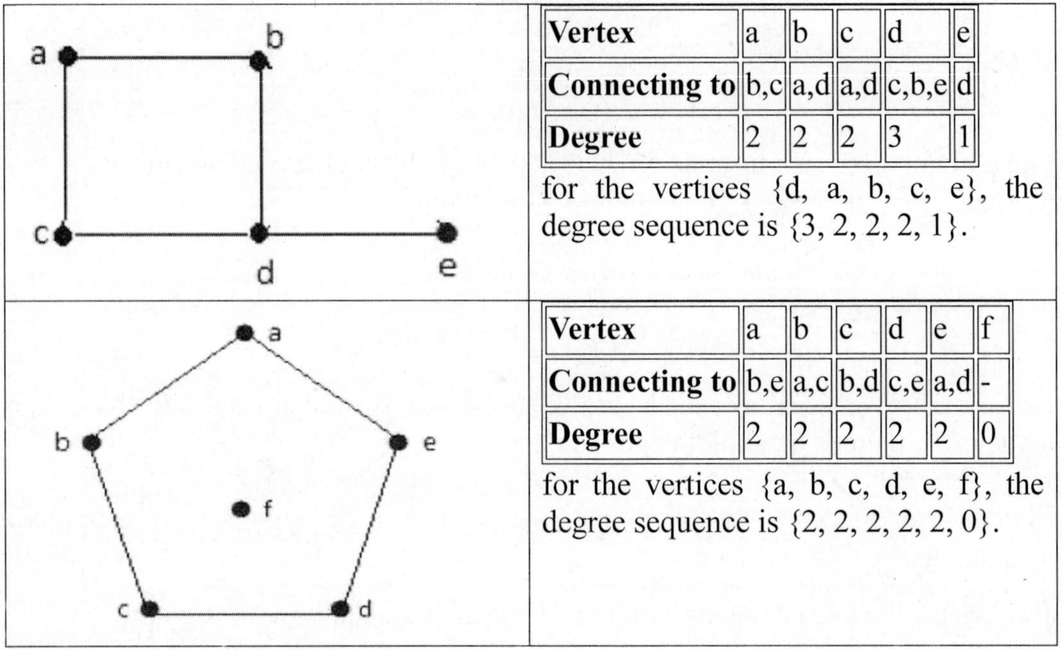

Vertex	a	b	c	d	e
Connecting to	b,c	a,d	a,d	c,b,e	d
Degree	2	2	2	3	1

for the vertices {d, a, b, c, e}, the degree sequence is {3, 2, 2, 2, 1}.

Vertex	a	b	c	d	e	f
Connecting to	b,e	a,c	b,d	c,e	a,d	-
Degree	2	2	2	2	2	0

for the vertices {a, b, c, d, e, f}, the degree sequence is {2, 2, 2, 2, 2, 0}.

7.2 CONNECTED COMPONENTS

One of the main application of graph is to find the reachability of nodes in many real time problems. This is possible when nodes are connected and there comes a concept of connected components. A connected component of an undirected graph is a graph or a subgraph where each pair of vertices(normally called as nodes in this scenario) is coupled with each other via a pathway of a set of vertices.
If any node from the set of vertices can reach any other vertex by traversing edges, forms a set of nodes which are constituents of connected component in an undirected graph. Testing for the connectedness of vertices are suffice to examine **reachability in a graph. So the conclusion is** in connected components, all the nodes are always reachable from each other. Some graphs have a single connected component and some will have multiple. We shall see them in subsequent sections.

7.2.1 One Connected Component

Undirected graph having single connected component, observe the same in the example given below:

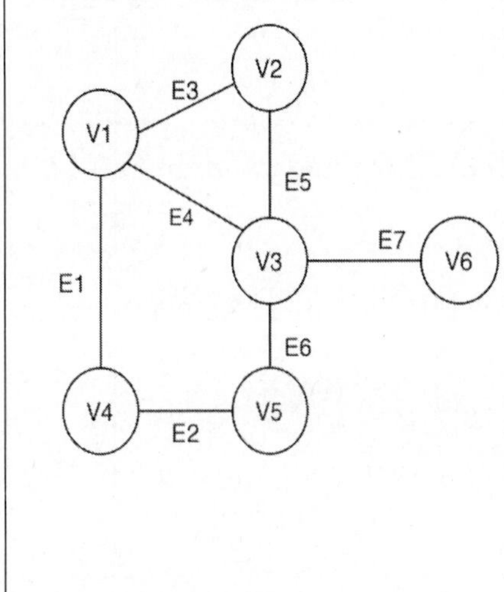

G(V,E) graph.
edge set E = {E1,E2,E3,E4,E5,E6,E7}.
vertex set V = { V1, V2, V3, V4, V5, V6} and
C1be the has one connected component of the graph G
C1 contains all the nodes of G.
To check whether C1 satisfy the condition:
Choose any two random vertices V1 and V6: It has been observed that V1 is reachable via V6 and vice versa is also true. V6 is reachable to V1 via: E4, E7 or E3,E5,E7 or E1, E2,E6,E7 also V1 is reachable to V6 via: E7,E4 or E7,E5,E3 or E7,E6,E2,E1. Repeating the same with other pairs in C1, it is found that graph has a connected component.

7.2.2 More Than One Connected Component

Let us consider another undirected graph having three connected components:

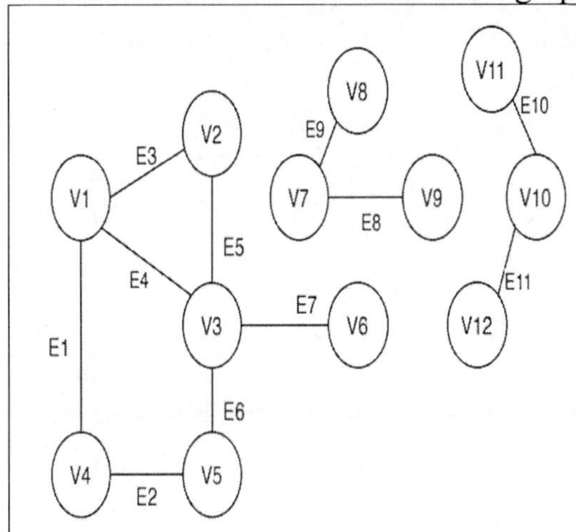

G2(V,E),
E = {E1,E2,E3,E4,E5,E6,E7,E8,E9,E10,E11}
V =
{V1,V2.V3,V4,V5,V6,V7,V8,V9,V10,V11,V12}
G2 has three connected components call them as C1, C2 and C3.
Where C1 = {V1,V2,V3,V4,V5,V6}
C2 = { V7,V8,V9} and
C3 = {V10,V11,V12} .
To check whether C1, C2, C3 satisfy the condition:
Pick a pair of vertex from each set and repeat the process as shown in previous example.

C1: pick vertices V4 and V6

- V6 is reachable to V4 via E2,E6,E7 or E1,E4,E7 or E1,E3,E5,E7
- V4 is reachable to V6 via E7,E6,E2 or E7,E4,E1 or E7,E5,E3,E1

C2: pick vertices V8 and V9

- V9 is reachable to V8 via E9, E8
- V8 is reachable to V9 via E8, E9

C3: pick the vertices V11 and V12

- V11 is reachable to V12 via: E11,E10
- V12 is reachable to V11 via: E10,E11

Thus, we can conclude that C1, C2 and C3 follow the connected component definition.

The connected components always holds some important properties. They are as mentioned here:

1. **The connected component set is always non-empty.**
2. **The connected component sets are pairwise disjoint.**

the union of connected components will give the set of all vertices of the given graph when there are more than one connected components in a given graph.
For example in Graph G2:

C1 U C2 U C3 = {V1, V2, V3, V4, V5, V6} U {V7, V8, V9} U {V10, V11, V12}
= {V1, V2, V3, V4, V5, V6, V7, V8, V9, V10, V11, V12}

The intersection between two different connected component sets will be a *null* set or an empty set.
Let's consider the connected components of graph G2 again. In G2, let's check this property:

C1 ∩ C2 ∩ C3 = {V1,V2,V3,V4,V5,V6} ∩{ V7,V8,V9} ∩ {V10,V11,V12} = Φ

7.3 PATH, CYCLE AND TREES

To reach a particular node or an intended node there are some mechanisms to trace a graph, called graph traversals. Here we mention some of such methods.

7.3.1 Walk

When we traverse a graph, we encounter a sequence of vertices and edges where no edge appear more than once however a vertex may appear more than once, such a sequence of nodes form a walk in the graph.

Open walk- if starting and ending vertices of a walk are different, such a walk is called as open walk. i.e. the origin vertex and terminal vertex are different.

Closed walk- if starting and ending vertices of a walk are same or identical, such a walk is called as closed walk. i.e. the origin vertex and terminal vertex are same and walk starts and ends at same vertex.

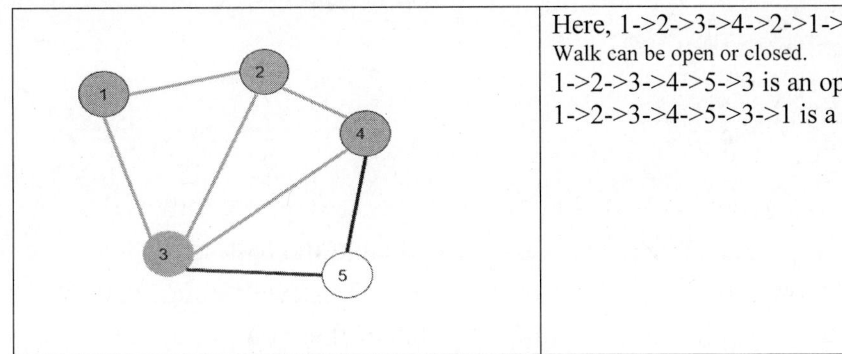

Here, 1->2->3->4->2->1->3 is a walk.
Walk can be open or closed.
1->2->3->4->5->3 is an open walk.
1->2->3->4->5->3->1 is a closed walk.

7.3.2. Trail – Trail is a sort of open walk in which vertex can be repeated but no edge is repeated. For the graph given below, 1->3->8->6->3->2 forms a trail, 1->3->8->6->3->2->1 will form a closed trail.

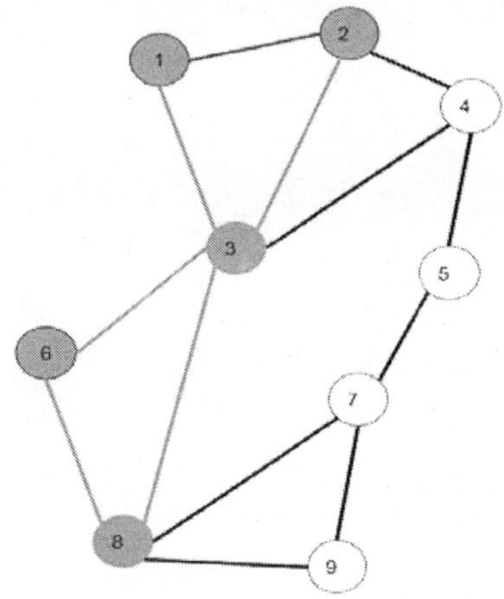

7.3.3. Circuit

Traversing a graph such that edge cannot be repeated but vertex can be repeated as a closed trail is called as circuit. For the graph below Here 1->2->4->3->6->8->3->1 is a circuit. Circuit can have repeated vertices only; thus it is a closed trail.

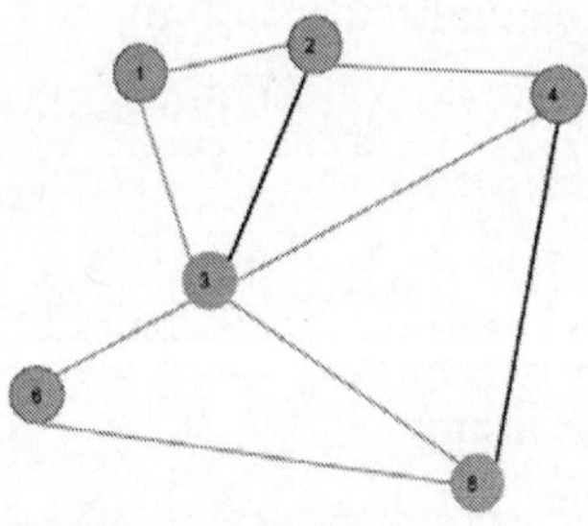

7.3.4. *Path*

If we traverse a graph such that neither vertex nor edge is repeated during traversal. As path is also a trail, thus it is also an open walk. In other words, path is a walk with no repeated vertices. This directly implies that no edges will ever be repeated and hence is redundant to write in the definition of path. In the example below, Here 6->8->3->1->2->4 is a Path, observe that neither vertex nor edge is repeated here.

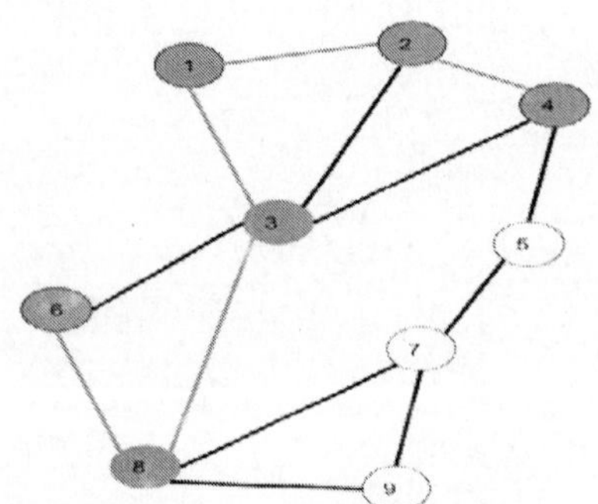

7.3.5. *Cycle*

During graph traversal, when vertex is not repeated but edge can be with a liability that same starting and ending vertex, thus forming a cycle in the path. Traversing a graph such that we do not repeat a vertex nor we repeat a edge but with same starting and ending vertex, then we get a cycle. In the example below, Here 1->2->4->3->1 is a cycle. observe that, Cycle is a closed path, neither edges nor vertices are repeated. But to form a closed sequence start and end vertices remains same

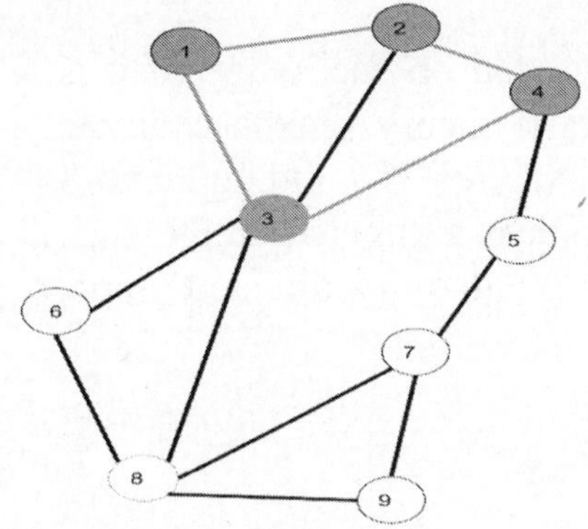

7.3.6 Types of graphs

Subjected to the number of edges, number of vertices, interconnectivity, and the overall structure of a graph there are various types of graphs, among them few important ones are listed and described here.

i) Trivial Graph

A graph having only one vertex is called a Trivial Graph. In following graph example, there is only one vertex 'a' with no edges. Thus forming a Trivial graph

Example

a

ii) Null Graph

A graph having no edges is called a Null Graph. In the following graph example, three vertices a, b, and c, are found but there are no edges connected among them. Thus, forming a Null Graph

a

b c

iii) Directed Graph

A graph that possess a direction marked by an arrow head on each edge of it is directed graph and has greater significance in the graph theory. In the example graph given below, there are 7 vertices ‘a’, ‘b’, ‘c’, ‘d’, ‘e’, ‘f’, and ‘g’, and 8 edges ‘ab’, ‘cb’, ‘dc’, ‘ad’, ‘ec’, ‘fe’, ‘gf’, and ‘ga’. As it is a directed graph, each edge exhibits an arrow mark that shows its direction. Note that in a directed graph, ‘fe is different from ‘ef

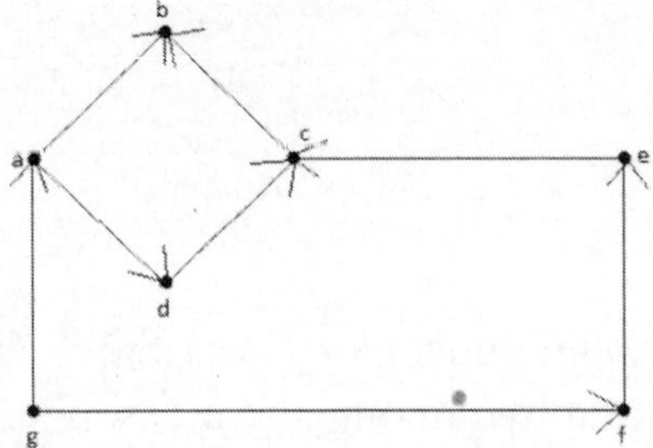

iv) Non-Directed Graph

A graph that do not possess any direction marked by an arrow head on the edge of it is undirected graph and also has greater significance in the graph theory. In the example graph given below, a’, ‘b’, ‘c’, ‘d’, ‘e’, ‘f’, ‘g’ are the vertices, and ‘ab’, ‘bc’, ‘cd’, ‘da’, ‘ag’, ‘gf’, ‘ef’ are the edges. Since it is a non-directed graph, the edges ‘ab’ and ‘ba’ are same. Similarly other edges also considered in the same way. A non-directed graph contains edges but the edges are not directed ones.

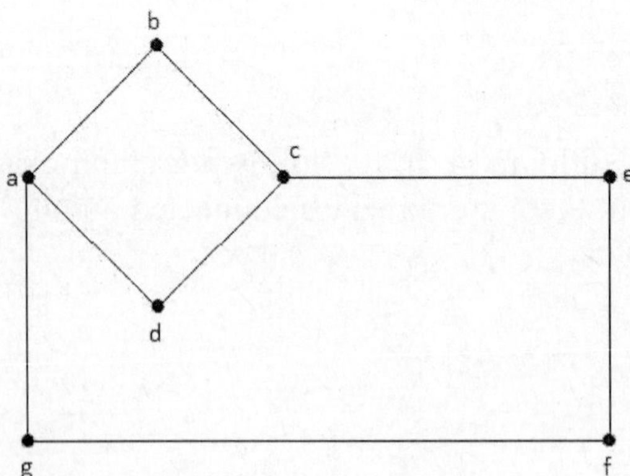

v) Simple Graph

A graph having no **parallel edges nor contain any loops** is said to be a simple graph. When there is a graph of n vertices then 2^{nC2} number of simple graphs are possible, which is $2^{n(n-1)/2}$.

A simple graph with 'n' vertices can have a maximum of $^{n}C_2$ number of edges where, $^{n}C_2 = n(n - 1)/2$. In the following graph, there are three vertices and edges. This can be proved by using the above formulae.

The maximum number of edges possible with n=3 = $^{n}C_2 = n(n-1)/2 = 3(3-1)/2 = 6/2 = 3$ edges

The maximum number of simple graphs with n=3 = $2^{nC2} = 2^{n(n-1)/2} = 2^{3(3-1)/2} = 2^3 = 8$

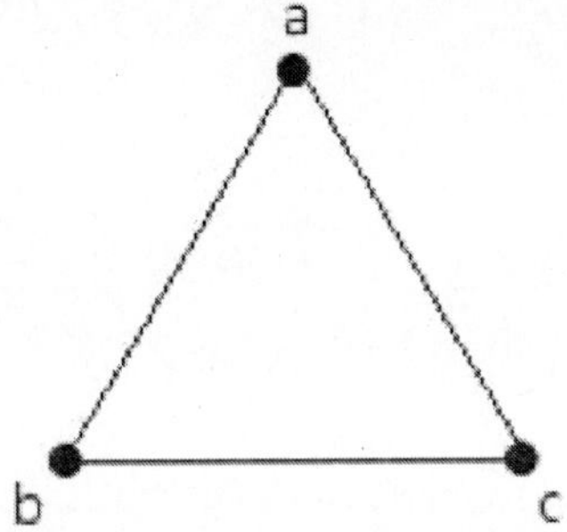

The possible eight graphs are as shown here.

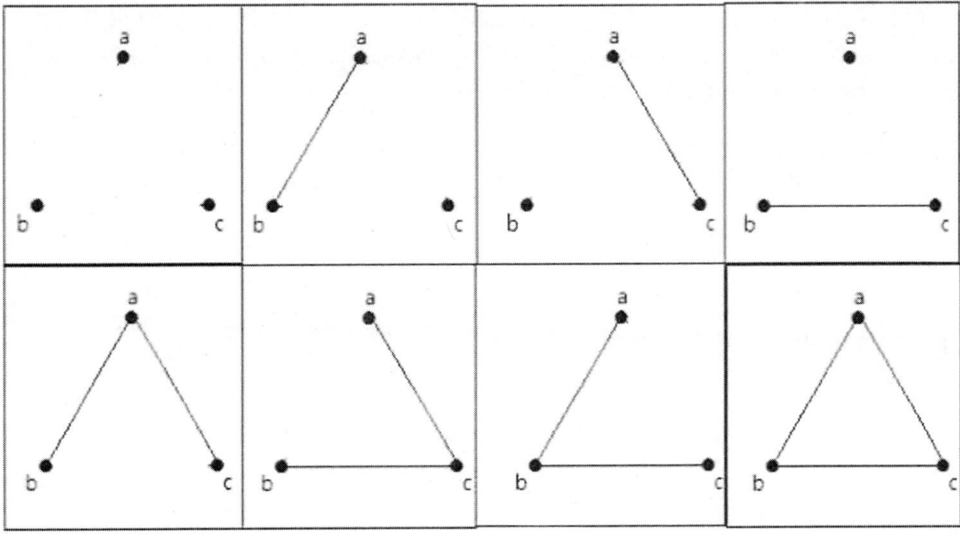

vi)Connected Graph

If there exists a path between every pair of vertices in a graph G then the graph G is said to be connected. For every vertex in the graph, there should be at least one edge. In the following graph, each vertex has its own edge connected to other edge. Hence it is a connected graph. Accordingly we can say that it is connected to some other vertex at the other side of the edge.

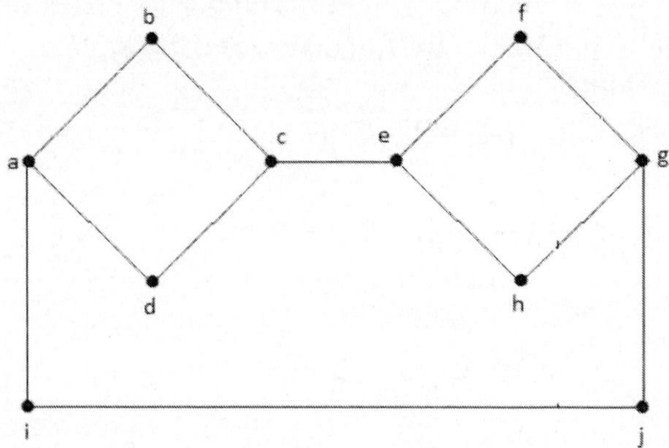

vii) Disconnected Graph

A graph G is disconnected, if it does not contain at least two connected vertices. The following graph is an example of a Disconnected Graph, where there are two components, one with 'a', 'b', 'c', 'd' vertices and another with 'e', 'f', 'g', 'h' vertices. The two components are independent of each other and not connected. Hence it is called disconnected graph. Similarly In this example graph G2, there are two independent components, a-b-f-e and c-d, which are not connected to each other. Thus forming a disconnected graph as well.

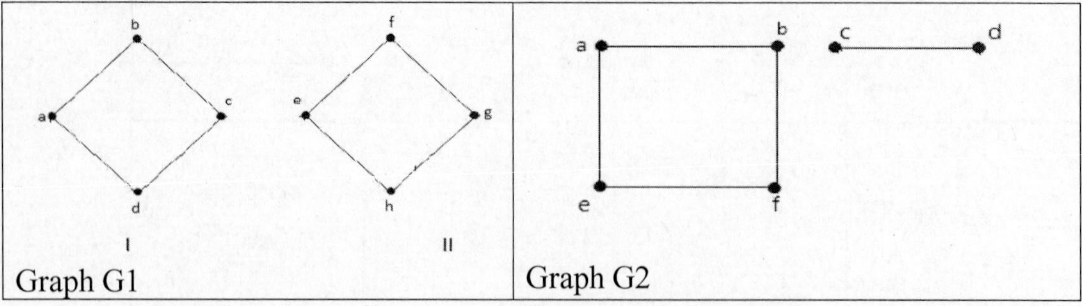

Graph G1 | Graph G2

viii) Regular Graph

If degree of all vertices is same in a given graph then such a graph G is said to be regular graph and a regular graph of degree k is termed as a 'k-regular graph'. In the following example graphs, all the vertices have the same degree. So these graphs are called regular graphs. Also, all the vertices have degree 2. Thus, they form 2-Regular Graphs.

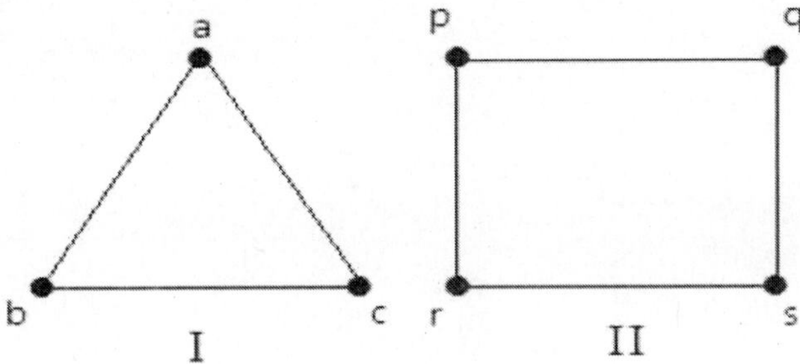

ix) Complete Graph

A simple graph in which each vertex is connected to every other vertex is called a complete graph, it is **denoted by 'K_n'**. In such a graph, a vertex will have edges with all other vertices, to form a complete graph. In other words, if a graph has n mutual vertices, then it is called a complete graph.
In the following graphs, each vertex in the graph is connected with all the remaining vertices in the graph except by itself.

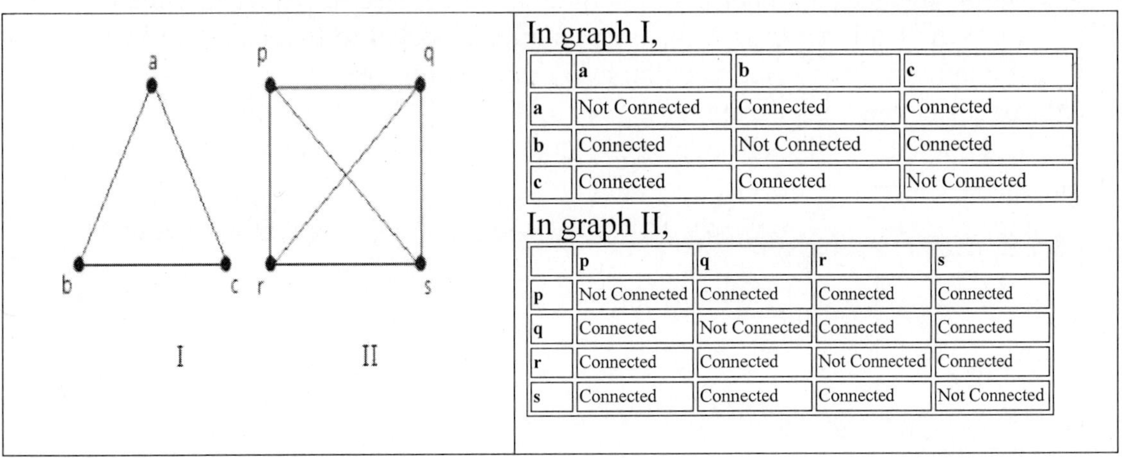

In graph I,

	a	b	c
a	Not Connected	Connected	Connected
b	Connected	Not Connected	Connected
c	Connected	Connected	Not Connected

In graph II,

	p	q	r	s
p	Not Connected	Connected	Connected	Connected
q	Connected	Not Connected	Connected	Connected
r	Connected	Connected	Not Connected	Connected
s	Connected	Connected	Connected	Not Connected

x) Cycle Graph

In a simple graph of n vertices and n edges, provided n is greater then or equal to 3, having a cycle of length n formed by all its edges is said to be Cycle graph. The degree of each vertex in such a graph is two. Cycle graph is represented by C_n . In the examples below you can see 3 cycle graphs where n is 3, 4 and 5 respectively. Graph I has cycle 'ab-bc-ca' formed by 3 vertices and edges respectively. Graph II has cycle 'pq-qs-sr-rp' formed by 4 vertices and edges respectively. Graph III has cycle 'ik-km-ml-lj-ji' formed by 5 vertices and edges respectively. They arc all cycle graphs.

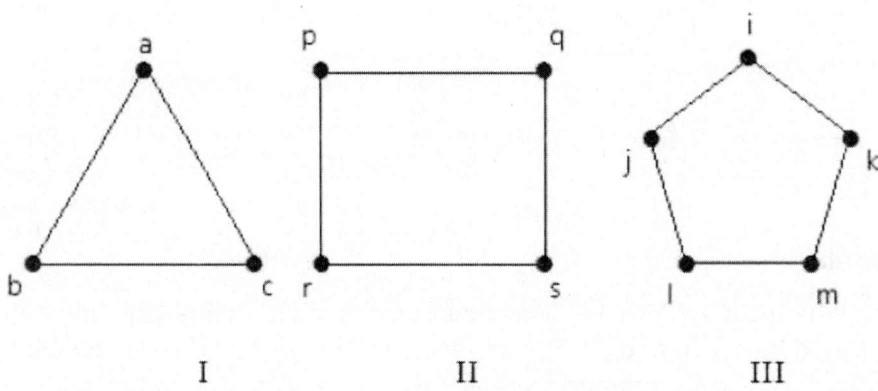

xi) Wheel Graph

A cycle graph becomes a wheel graph with an addition of a new vertex, which is called hub. Where all vertices of cycle graph are connected to this hub. Unlike C_n for Cycle graph and K_n for regular graph W_n is used to represent a wheel graph. Number of edges in a wheel graph is sum of number of edges from hub to all other vertices and number of edges from all other nodes in cycle graph excluding a hub.

No. of edges in W_n = No. of edges from hub to all other vertices + No. of edges from all other nodes in cycle graph without a hub.

$= (n-1) + (n-1)$

$= 2(n-1)$

Example

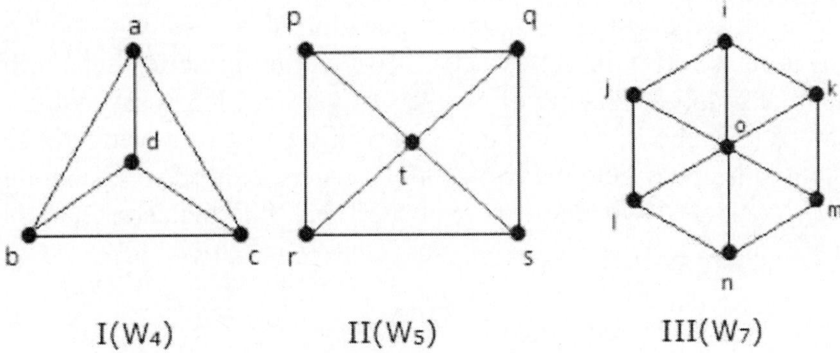

Consider the wheel graphs W4, W5 and W6.
W4 is obtained by C3, cycle graph of 3 vertices, by addition of vertex at the mid point called 'd', so the number of edges in this graph is 2(n-1) = 2(3) = 6
W5 is obtained by C5, cycle graph of 4 vertices, by addition of vertex at the mid point called 't', so the number of edges in this graph is 2(n-1) = 2(4) = 8
W6 is obtained by C6, cycle graph of 5 vertices, by addition of vertex at the mid point called 'o', so the number of edges in this graph is 2(n-1) = 2(5) = 10

xii) Cyclic Graph and Acyclic Graph

A graph **with at least one** cycle is called a cyclic graph. A graph **with no cycles** is called an acyclic graph. In the example graphs given below, G1 Cyclic graph with two cycles a-b-c-d-a and c-f-g-e-c in it and G2 is acyclic graph.

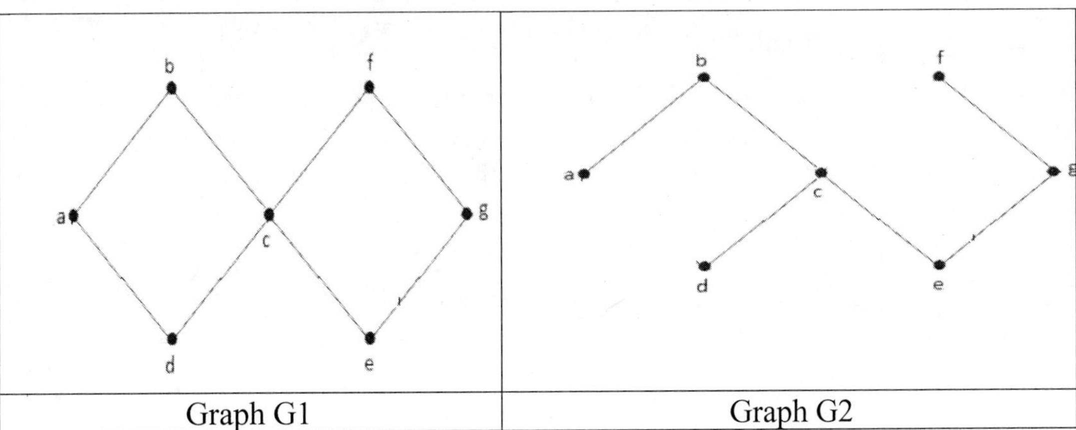

Graph G1	Graph G2

xiii) Bipartite Graph

It is a special graph with huge significance in Graph Theory. A simple graph G = (V, E) is said to be a bipartite graph with vertex partition V = {V_1, V_2} if every edge of Edge set E joins a vertex in vertex set V1 to a vertex in vertex set V_2. In other words, a Bipartite graph consisting of two sets of vertices, let us say, V1 and V2, and drawing an edge, it should connect any vertex in set V_1 to any vertex in set V_2. In the example graph given below, two sets of vertices can be seen, naming them as V_1 and V_2. consider, two edges named 'ae' and 'bd' that connects the vertices of two sets V_1 and V_2.

Example

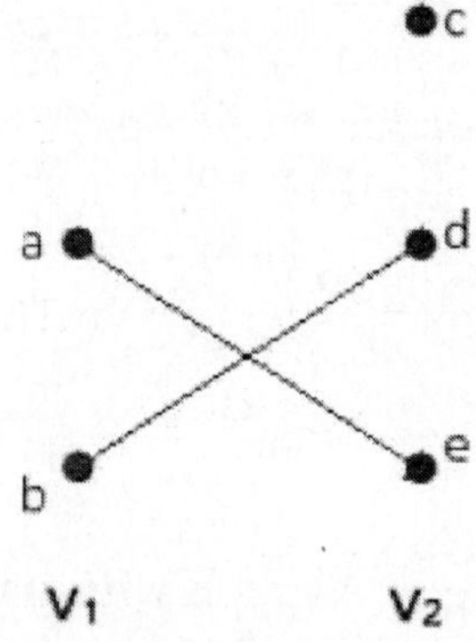

xiv) Complete Bipartite Graph

It is a special type of Bipartite graph, in which from the vertex partition V = {V_1, V_2} every vertex in V_1 is connected to every vertex of V_2. In other words, a complete bipartite graph connects each vertex from set V_1 to each vertex from set V_2. The following example graph is a complete bipartite graph because it has edges connecting each vertex from set V_1 to each vertex from set V_2.

Example

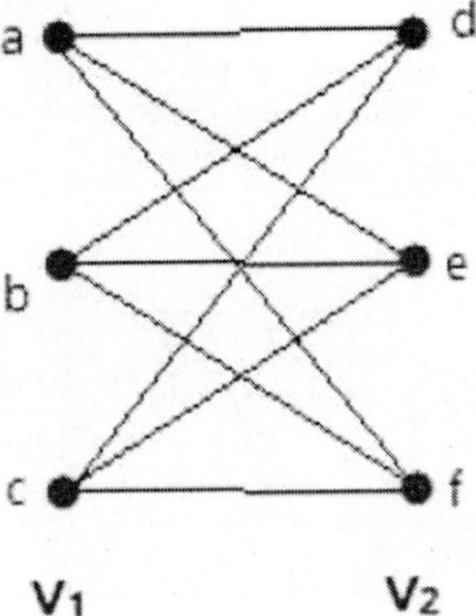

If $|V_1|$ is number of vertices in set V1 be m and $|V_2|$ is number of vertices in set V2 be n, then the complete bipartite graph is represented by $K_{m,n}$ that comply with the following conditions.

- $K_{m,n}$ has mn edges and m+n vertices and.
- $K_{m,n}$ is a regular graph if m=n.

xv) Star Graph

A star graph is a complete bipartite graph if a single vertex belongs to one set and all the remaining vertices belong to the other set. A complete bipartite graph of the form $K_{1,\ n-1}$ is a star graph with n-vertices. In the example graphs, out of 'n' vertices, all the 'n–1' vertices are connected to a single vertex. Hence it is in the form of $K_{1,\ n-1}$ which are star graphs.

Example

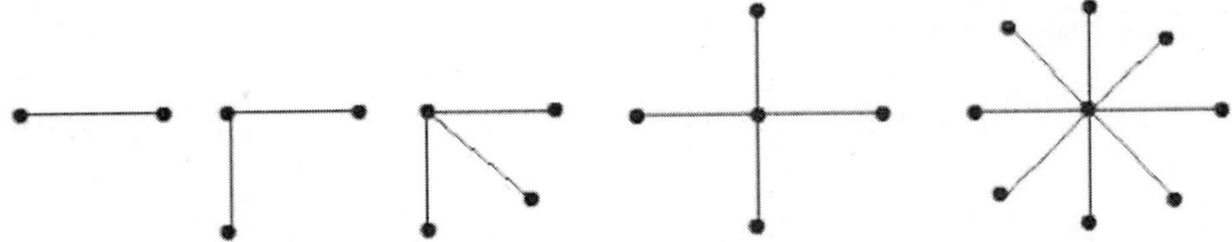

xvi) Complement of a Graph

Let 'G^c' be a simple graph with some vertices as that of 'G' and an edge {U, V} is present in 'G^c', if the edge is not present in G. It means, two vertices are adjacent in 'G^c' if the two vertices are not adjacent in G.

If the edges that exist in graph I are not present in another graph II, and if both graph I and graph II are combined together to form a complete graph, then graph I and graph II are called complements of each other.

Example

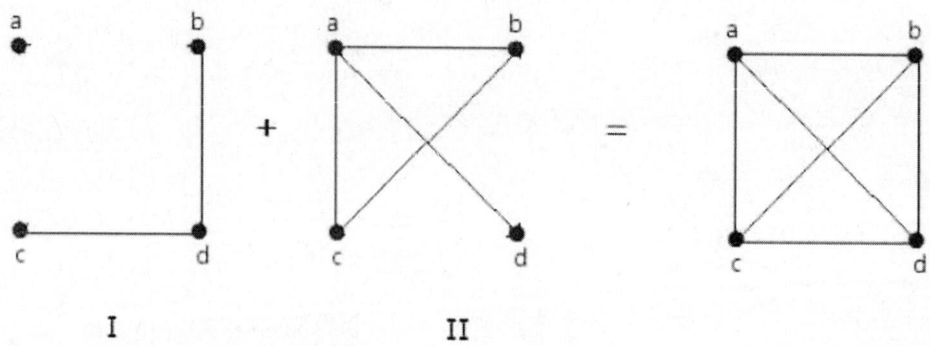

In the following example, graph-I has two edges 'cd' and 'bd'. Its complement graph-II has four edges.

Note that the edges in graph-I are not present in graph-II and vice versa. Hence, the combination of both the graphs gives a complete graph of 'n' vertices.

Note – A combination of two complementary graphs gives a complete graph.

If 'G' is any simple graph, then,

$|E(G)| + |E('G^{c}')| = |E(K_n)|$, where n = number of vertices in the graph.

Example

Let 'G' be a simple graph with nine vertices and twelve edges, find the number of edges in G^c.

You have, $|E(G)| + |E(G^c)| = |E(K_n)|$

$12 + |E(G^c)| = 9(9-1) / 2 = {}^9C_2$

$12 + |E(G^c)| = 36$

$|E(G^c)| = 24$

'G' is a simple graph with 40 edges and its complement G^c has 38 edges. Find the number of vertices in the graph G or G^c.

Let the number of vertices in the graph be 'n'.

We have, $|E(G)| + |E(G^c)| = |E(K_n)|$

$40 + 38 = n(n-1)/2$

$156 = n(n-1)$

$13(12) = n(n-1)$

$n = 13$

7.3.7 Trees

Tree is an interesting special type of graph without cycles in it. In simple words a connected acyclic graph is called a tree. Different terms are used to represent its edges and vertices. Edges of a tree are called branches, vertices which contain elements or values are called as nodes. A node can be an internal node or a leaf node. If it is present in the last level, they are leaf nodes. Every node will have an ascendent and descendant node. Leaf nodes do not possess any ascendants. Ascendant node can be called as parent and descendant node can be called as child node. There will be a single parent for the entire graph called as root node.

Trees are graphs that do not contain even a single cycle. They represent hierarchical structure in a graphical form. Trees belong to the simplest class of graphs. Despite their simplicity, they have a rich structure. Trees provide a range of useful applications as simple as a family tree to as complex as trees in data structures of computer science.

A tree with 'n' vertices has 'n-1' edges. If it has one more edge extra than 'n-1', then the extra edge should obviously has to pair up with two vertices which leads to form a cycle. Then, it becomes a cyclic graph which is a violation for the tree graph.

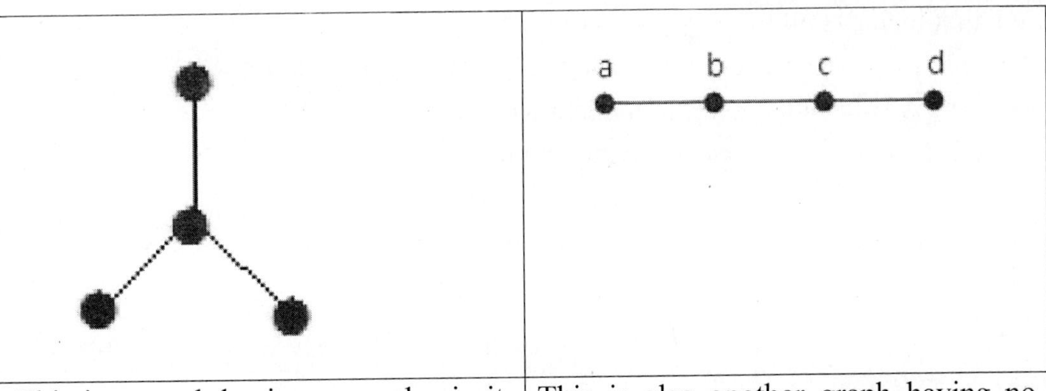

This is a graph having no cycles in it, thus it can be called as a tree because it is connected with four vertices and three edges comply with rule n vertices and n-1 edges. Also observe every tree	This is also another graph having no cycles in it, and thus it is a tree as well with 4 vertices and three edges. the vertices 'a' and 'd' have degree one. And the other two vertices 'b' and 'c'

has two vertices of single degree.	has degree two forming no cycle. Observe, there should be at least two single edges anywhere in the graph. It is nothing but two edges with a degree of one.

A tree can be often disconnected. A **disconnected acyclic graph** is called a forest. In other words, a disjoint collection of trees is called a forest. In the cxample below you can find two sub graphs, although, it is a single disconnected graph. as no cycles found in this graph, obviously it is a forest.

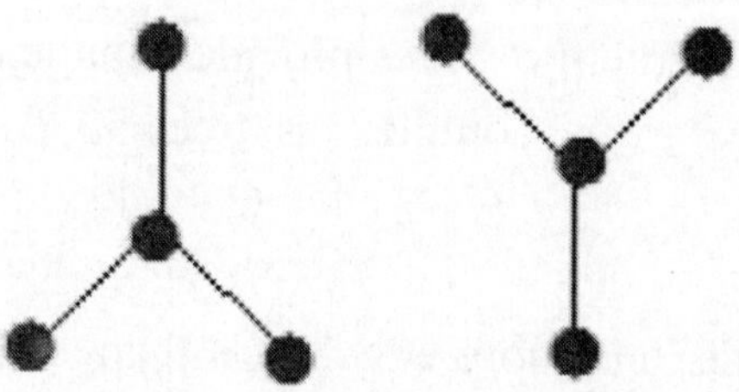

Another kind of tree which is often interesting is a spanning tree. Let G be a connected graph, then the sub-graph H of G is called a spanning tree of G if H is a tree also H contains all vertices of G. A spanning tree T of an undirected graph G is a subgraph that includes all of the vertices of G.

In the example given below, G is a connected graph and H is a sub-graph of G. Clearly, the graph H has no cycles, it is a tree with six edges which is one less than the total number of vertices. Hence H is the Spanning tree of G.

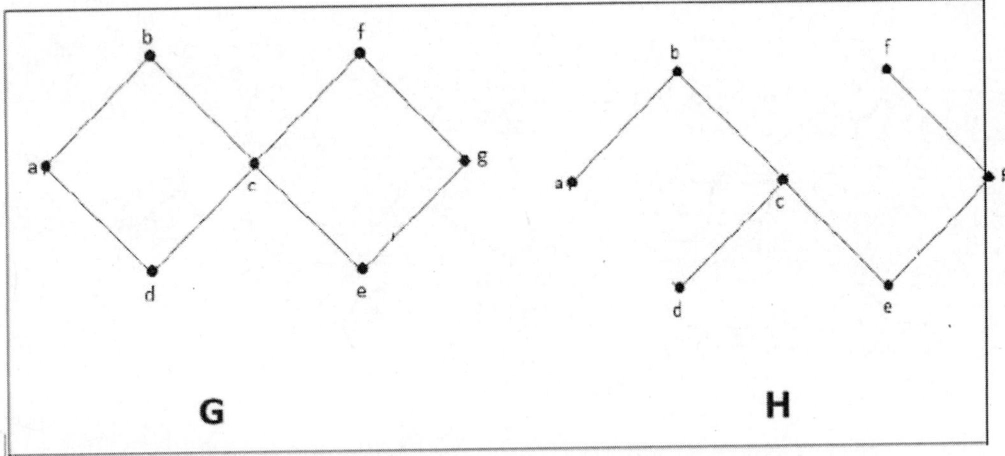

In the above example, G is a connected graph and H is a sub-graph of G. Clearly, the graph H has no cycles, it is a tree with six edges which is one less than the total number of vertices. Hence H is the Spanning tree of G.

7.4 EULER AND HAMILTON PATHS

In graph theory often we encounter problems when traversal begins and ends at same vertex or passing over the edge sometimes. These paths are of special interest while solving realtime problems. A path that passes through every edge exactly once is called as Euler path. Whenever such a path begins and ends at the same vertex from where it started is called as Euler Cycle. Similarly when a path that passes through every vertex exactly once but not every edge is called as Hamiltonian path. If such a path starts and ends at same vertex from where it started then it is called a Hamiltonian cycle.

7.4.1 Euler Paths

A path that passes through every edge exactly once is called as Euler path. Consider path d→c→a→b→d→e in the graph G1 given below, Each edge of the Graph appears exactly once, and each vertex of 'G' appears at least once along an entire route. This is a Euler Path. Any graph is said to be traversable if it includes a Euler's route or path in it. If in an Euler's path if the beginning and ending vertices are the same, the path is termed an Euler's circuit. Consider path a→b→c→d→a→g→f→e→c→a in the graph G2 given below since the starting and ending vertex is found to be same in this path, thus the graph has a euler's circuit.

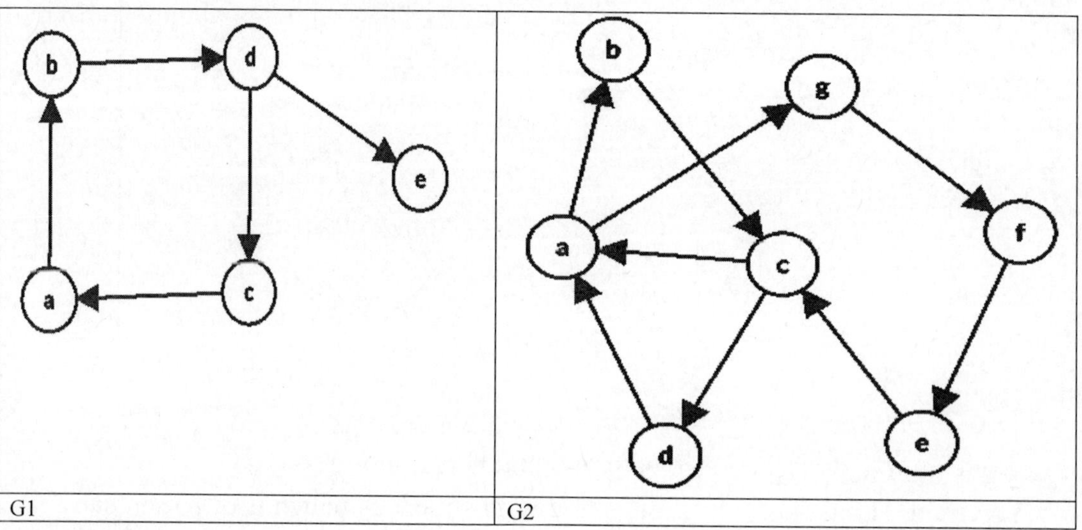

G1 G2

7.4.2 Euler Circuit Theorem

According to Euler's Circuit Theorem any graph G is traversable if there are two or no vertices are there whose degree is odd in a linked or connected graph. If the graph has exactly two vertices with odd degree then such a graph may consist of a Euler path but not Euler Circuit. Such Euler path starts with an odd degree vertex but ends with another odd degree vertex.

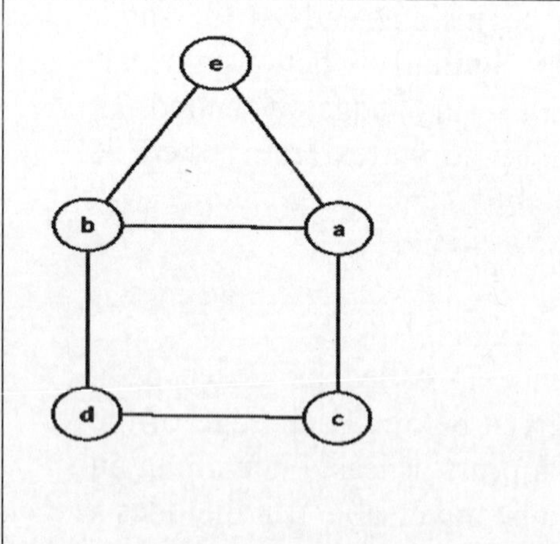

Consider path b→e→a→b→d→c→a in the given graph. this is a Euler path but not a Euler Circuit. This graph has Euler path but not Euler Circuit. It is also clear that vertices b and a have odd degree and they are odd degree vertices.

Thus in a connected graph if there are no vertices having odd degree , then Euler's circuit exists for sure in such a graph.

7.4.3 Hamilton Path

In a graph G if there is a simple path that travels through each and every vertex exactly once such a path is called as Hamilton path.

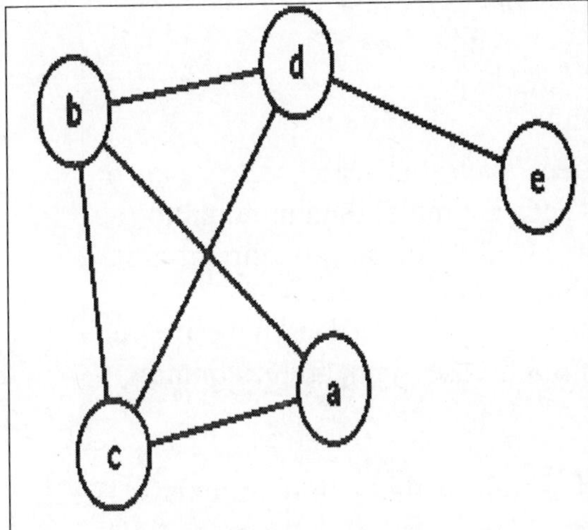

In this graph consider a path e→d→b→a→c this path travels across all the vertices exactly once, thus it is a Hamilton path.

Important point to be noted is each graph edge appears exactly once in Euler's circuit whereas in Hamilton cycle some graph edges may be skipped.

There are very important applications of Hamilton path. Some of which are listed here.

A toy example of Hamilton path is preparing a bus route map to pick up passengers by a package tour organizer. For example, node representing passengers, road representing the edges, bus path represents a Hamilton path. In numerous fields like operation research, electronic circuit design, computer graphics, genomes mapping, and many areas also use Hamilton path in one way or the other way. Many small fragments of genetic code are combined by genome mapping.

7.4.4 Hamilton Circuit

A circuit in a graph that runs across every vertex exactly once forms a Hamiltonian circuit. There are no easy ways to detect a Hamilton path or circuit as similar to Euler path and circuit. This is a NP hard problem. But some conditions like existence of a vertex of single degree in the graph and several other requirements rule out the presence of Hamilton course in the graph. here we present certain theorems that provide such conditions for testing the existence of Hamilton paths in a graph thus classifying it as Hamilton graph.

7.4.5 Dirac's Theorem

For a simple graph G having n number of vertices such that n is greater than or equal to 3 and the degree of each vertex of graph G is also greater than n/2 then the graph is Hamilton Circuit.

7.4.6 Ore's Theorem

For a simple graph G having n number of vertices such that n is greater than or equal to 3 and sum of the degrees of any two vertices is greater than or equal to the number of vertices in the graph, then such a graph also has a Hamilton circuit in it.

Note: A connected graph is a Euler graph, when all of its vertices have a even degree and any two nodes have odd degree, in such case such graph contains a Euler path but not a Euler circuit.

Example: Examine the following graph and find which of the following exists. i) Euler path or circuit, ii) Hamilton path or circuit?

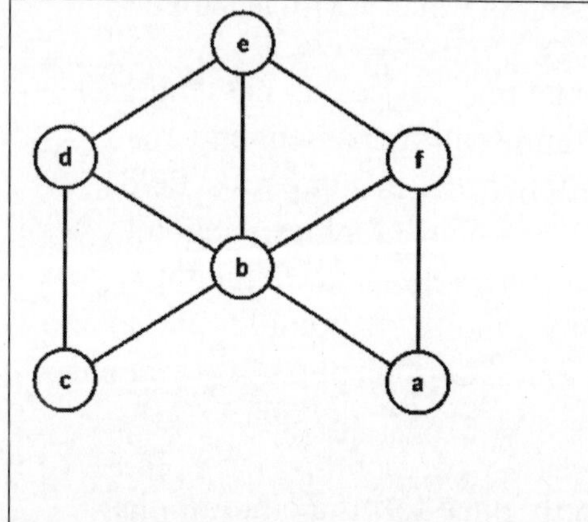

Examining the graph carefully we find that there exists a Hamilton path and circuit but not Euler path and circuit.

As the graph contains four vertices of odd degree the graph is not traversable. Also there exists a Hamiltonian cycle in the graph, that routes over all vertices by skirting around the internal edges.

Example: Examine the following graph and find whether Hamilton path or circuit exists.

<table>
<tr>
<td>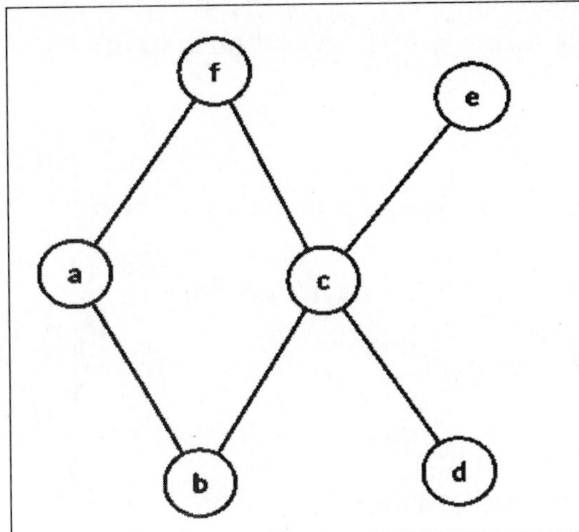
</td>
<td>No, the preceding graph does not include a Hamiltonian circuit since it has two vertices of degree one.</td>
</tr>
</table>

Example: In a undirected complete graph having atleast more than two vertices say n where n>2, then what is the number of different Hamilton cycles seen in the graph.

So far what we understood is a Hamiltonian circuit flows via individual vertex right once. A Hamiltonian circuit with identical starting and ending vertices is known as a Hamiltonian cycle. in a complete undirected graph having n vertices, n permutations are possible to visit each vertex. There are also n possible vertices from where to start and two possible different directions to move, whether clockwise or anticlockwise. From this total n! cycles any of the will belong to a group of 2n cycles with the same edges, thus there are n! over 2n which is half of the (n-1)! number of distinct cycles in the graph.

7.5 GRAPH COLORING

Important components of a graph are vertices, edges and regions. Labelling of these components under some constraints is always essential in solving real-time problems. Graph coloring is a naïve method for labelling such components. In a graph there should be no same color for two adjacent vertices or edges or regions. Any graph that is colored satisfying these criteria and with minimum number of colors is said to be **properly colored graph**. and the minimum number of colors used to color the graph is said to be the **chromatic number** of the graph. Constraints set on graph coloring are number of colors, order of colors, assignment method of colors and many. The component to color whether vertex or edge or region. Components that get the same colors form independent sets. Graph coloring is one of the most important concepts in graph theory. It is used in many real-time applications of computer science such as, Data mining, Networking,

Image capturing and segmentation, Process scheduling and resource allocation, clustering and many.

7.5.1 Vertex Coloring

The process of assigning colors to the vertices of a graph seeing that none of the adjacent vertices get a similar color. Here adjacent means the vertices sharing a common edge. This is a simple concept that no two vertices will get identical colors.

7.5.3 Region Coloring

Similar to vertex coloring region coloring is a process of assigning colors to the regions of a planar graph seeing that none of the adjacent regions get a same color. Here adjacent means the regions possessing a common edge.

7.5.3 Edge Coloring

Similar to vertex coloring and region coloring, edge coloring is a process of assigning colors to the edges of a planar graph seeing that none of the adjacent edges get a same color. Here adjacent means the edges having a common vertex between them.

Example

Take a look at the following graph. The regions 'aeb' and 'befc' are adjacent, as there is a common edge 'be' between those two regions.

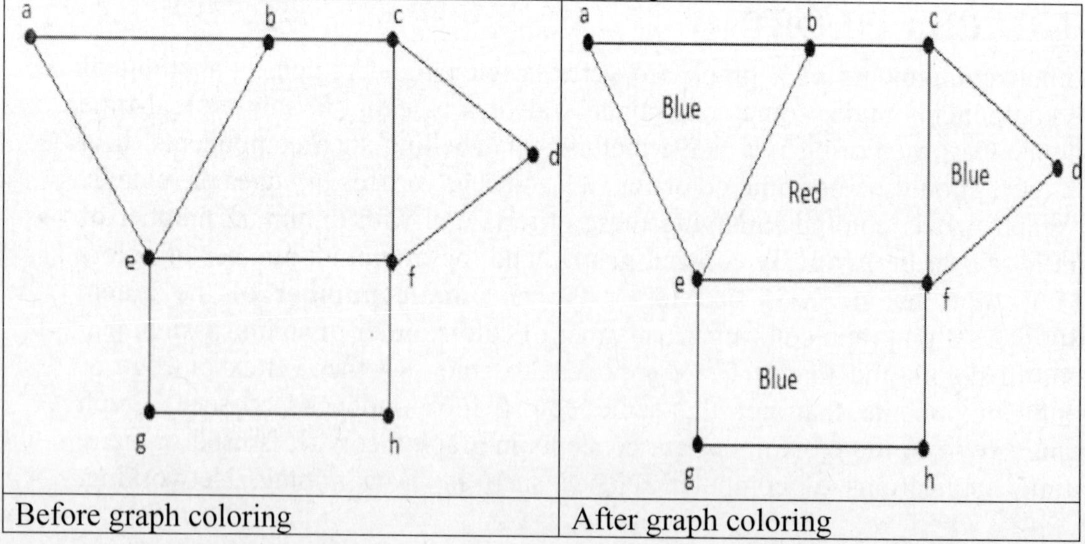

Before graph coloring	After graph coloring

7.5.4 Chromatic Number

In all the three methods of graph coloring you can observe one thing that there arises a situation when we can color the graph with minimum number of colors. Finding the least minimum number of colors is very interesting problem. So the minimum number of colors required for coloring vertices of a graph is said to be called as chromatic number associated with that graph, here chroma means color. Chromatic number is denoted by $\chi(G)$. when $\chi(G) = 1$ means the graph can be colored with a single color, this obviously means that the graph is a null graph. So the inference is $\chi(G)$ must be always greater than or equal to 2. Sometimes the graph can be colored with chromatic number that is equal to the number of vertices in a graph, such a graph is said to be n-coverable. Thus when $\chi(G) = n$ then the graph is n coverable.

Example

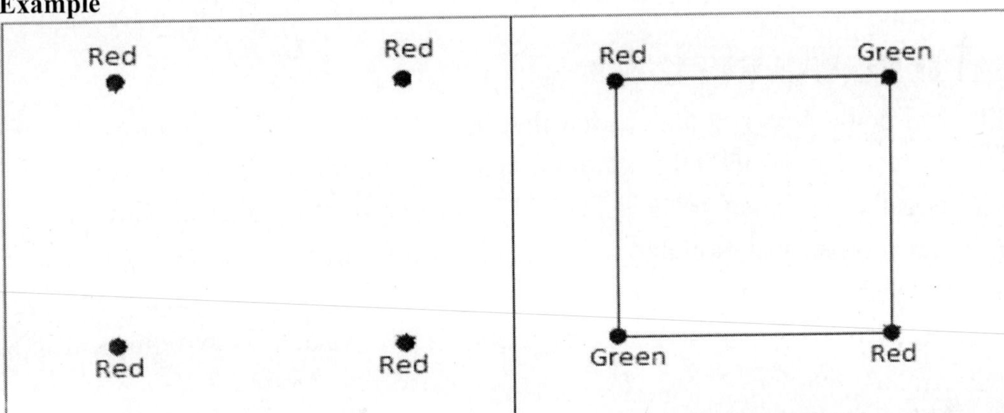

Note –

Similarly, the other regions are also coloured based on the adjacency. This graph is coloured as follows –

Example

The chromatic number of Kn is

- n
- n–1
- [n/2]
- [n/2]

Consider this example with K_4.

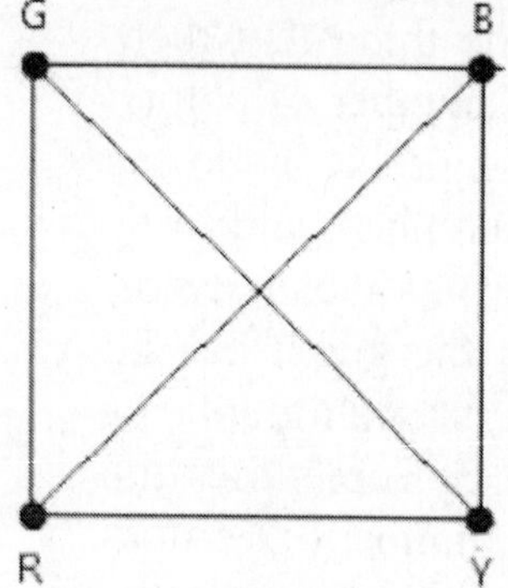

In the complete graph, each vertex is adjacent to remaining (n – 1) vertices. Hence, each vertex requires a new color. Hence the chromatic number of $K_n = n$.

7.6 GRAPH PLANARITY

A graph that can be drawn on a plane such that no two edges cross each other or meet each other at any point which is a non-vertex omitting that a vertex on which it is incident is called a planar graph. Usually planar graph is a plane drawing. A graph that violates otherwise is called a non planar graph. In the example below, Graph G2 is a planar graph whereas graph G1 is a non planar graph, as you can see edges ac and be are overlapping on each other. But G2 is rewritten by avoiding the overlap.

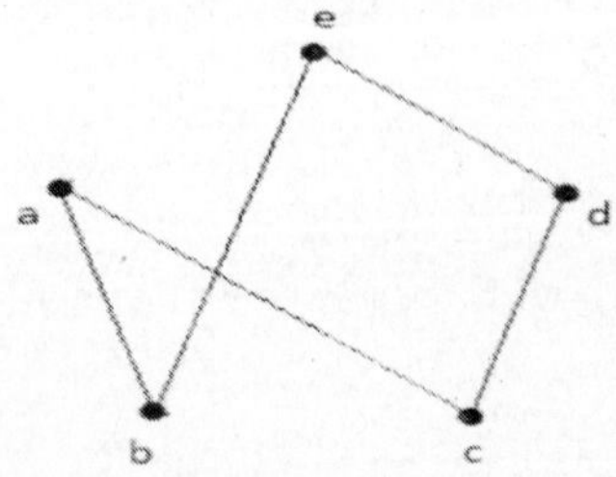

Fig: G1 – Non Planar Graph

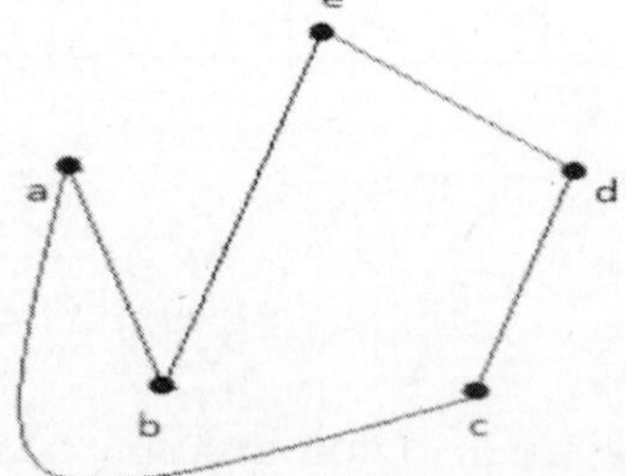

Fig: G2 – Planar Graph

Consider the graph K4, having four vertices and five edges, this can be drawn in the plane without overlapping or crossing edges, thus the graph K_4 is planar. The plane drawings of this K4 can be obtained in three ways, that are as mentioned in subsequent figure.

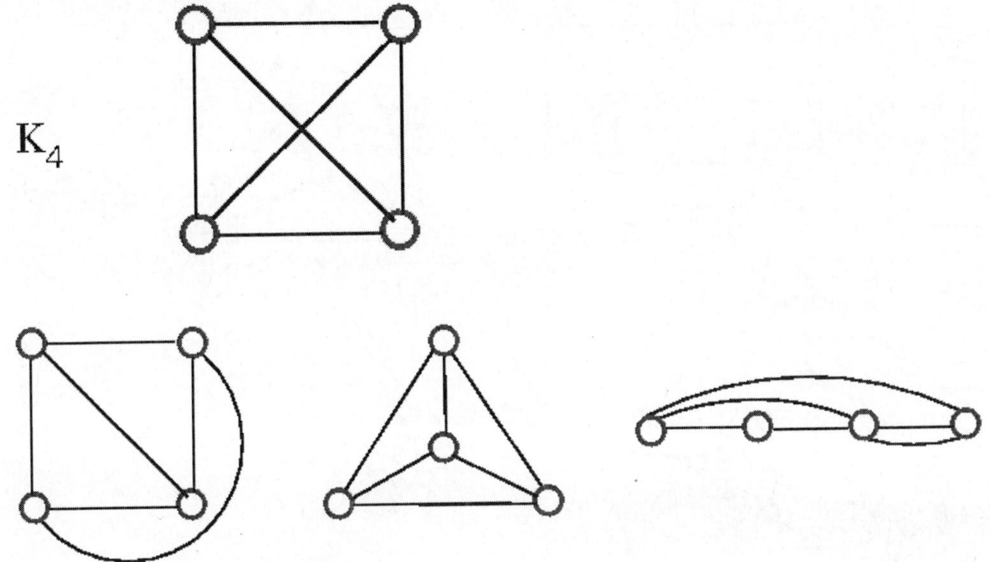

Convex and regular polyhedron in 3D space are platonic in geometry. The five Platonic graphs are all planar. Same number of faces which are regular and congruent meet at each vertex. Five such platonic graphs are tetrahedron (with four faces), cube (six faces), octahedron (eight faces), dodecahedron (twelve faces) and icosahedron (twenty faces). As these solids were hypothesized by Plato, ancient Greek philosopher, they are named so. All these platonic graphs are planar in nature. Assume the complete bipartite graph K3,3, is it planar? The answer is no. as K3,3 has at least one crossing in it in every version of its drawing and it has a cycle that must be shown in its drawing.

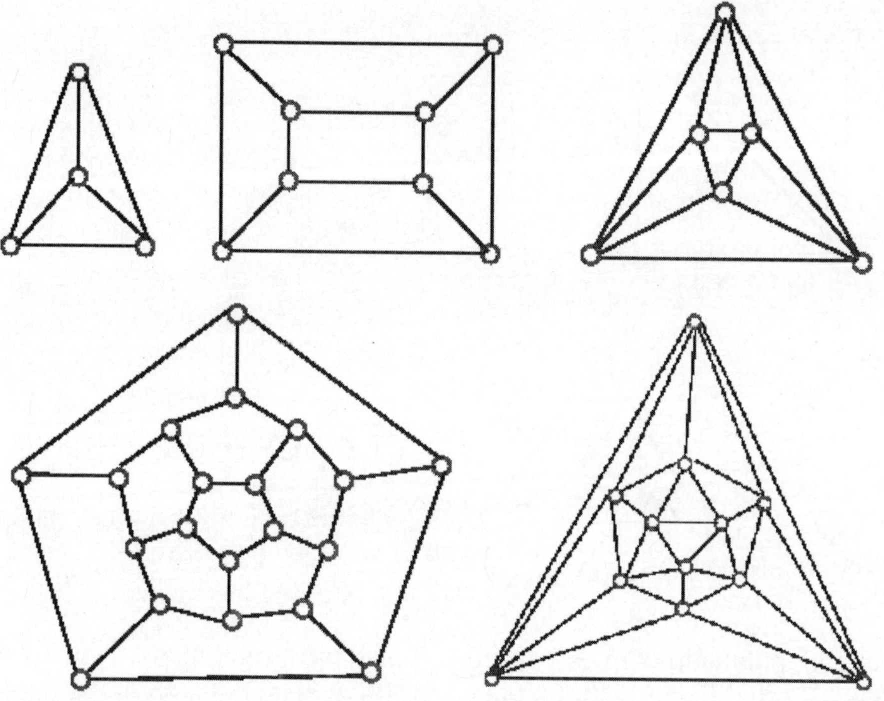

If you closely observe, then you can find that the plane is divided by the planar graph into some are that is connected, such an area is called a region. Consider any planar graph you can find that regions. In the graph G1, there are 5 regions marked from 1 to 5. The number of edges that enclose the regions r is called degree of a bounded region represented by deg(r). Similarly for graph G2 the regions are marked by R1 and R2 also deg(r) is shown for both the graphs.

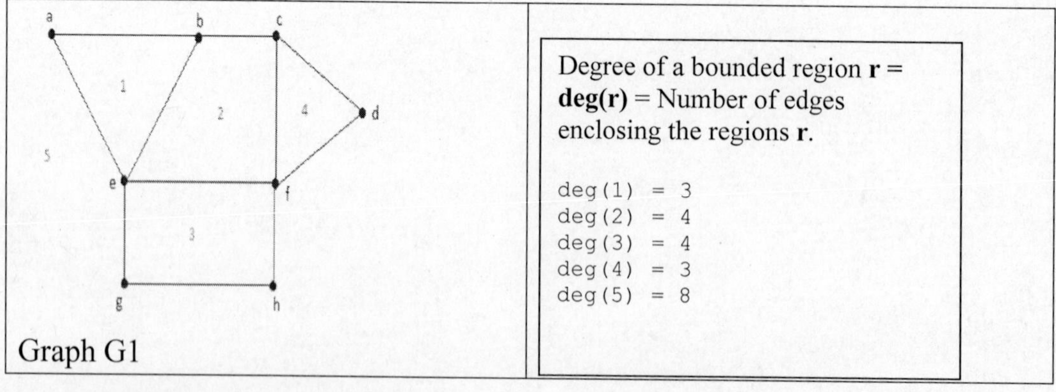

Graph G1

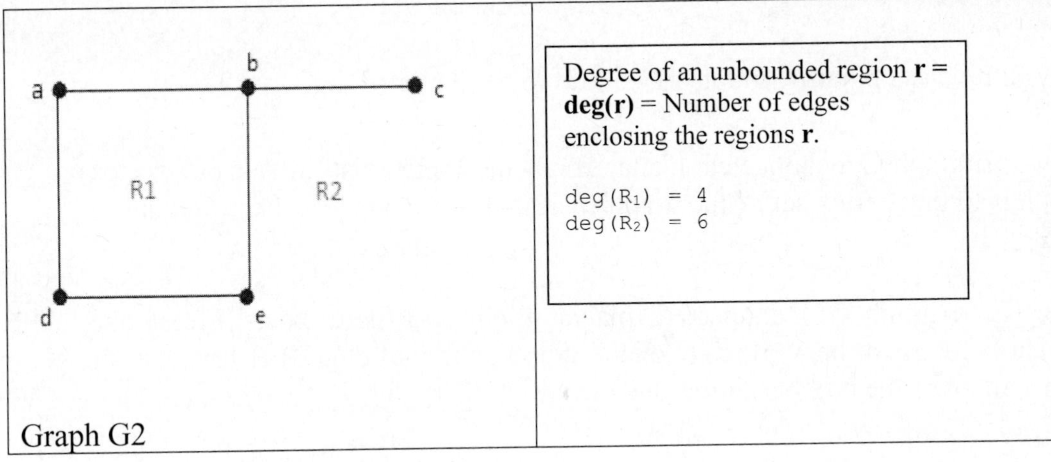

Graph G2

Properties of a planar Graph:

<u>Property-1</u>: For a planar graph of n vertices, sum of the degrees of all the vertices is twice the number of edges. This can be written in mathematical notation as $\sum_{i=1}^{n} \deg(V_i) = 2|E|$

<u>Property-2</u>: For a planar graph of n regions, sum of the degrees of all the regions is twice the number of edges. This can be written in mathematical notation as $\sum_{i=1}^{n} \deg(r_i) = 2|E|$

<u>Property-3</u>: If graph G is connected and planar, with respect to Euler Formula sum of the number of vertices and the number of regions is 2 added to the number of edges. $|V| + |R| = |E| + 2$

<u>Property-4</u>: If graph G is connected, planar and have K components in it, then sum of the number of vertices and the number of regions is sum of the number of edges and K+1. $|V| + |R| = |E| + (K+1)$

<u>Property-5</u>: If graph G a connected, planar graph then the difference between three times the number of vertices and the number of edges is always greater than or equal to 6 ie. $3|V| - |E| \geq 6$

<u>Property-6</u>: If graph G a connected, planar graph then the number of regions is always less than or equal to 2/3 times the number of edges. $|r| \leq \frac{2}{3}|E|$

<u>Property-7</u>: K_n is a complete graph, and is said to be planar iff $n<5$

Property-8: $K_{m,n}$ is a bipartite graph and is said to be planar iff $m<3$ or $n>3$

Property-9: If graph G a connected, planar graph and there exists atleast one vertex that belongs to the Vertex set of the graph such that deg(V) is less than or equal to 5 then $|E| \leq 3|V| - 6$

|

Property-10: If graph G a connected, planar graph and there exists atleast one vertex that belongs to the Vertex set of the graph such that deg(V) is less than or equal to 5 and R is the number of regions then $|R| \leq 2|V| - 4$

Euler's Formula

For a planar graph G is drawn on a plane, it partitions the plane into several regions as mentioned earlier, only one of these regions is infinite called as infinite region. If R is any region then degree of R is number of edges in a walk around the boundary of that region R. (if all regions have same degree then G is Face-Regular of degree G)

For example, the following graph G has four regions or faces, f_4 being the infinite region/face.

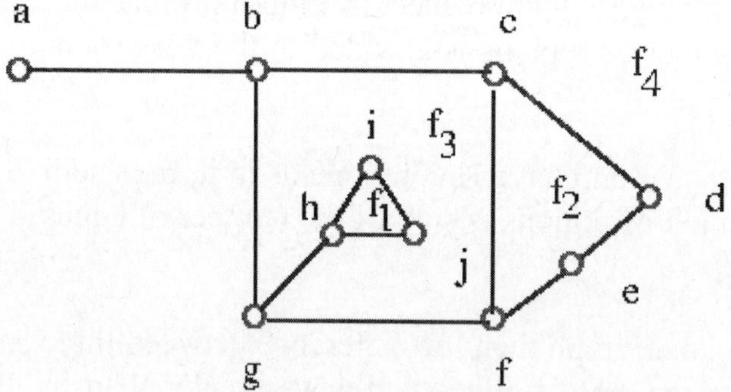

It is easy to see from above graph that deg f_1=3, deg f_2=4, deg f_3=9, deg f_4=8.

According to Euler, If V, E, and R denote the number of vertices, edges, and regions respectively of a connected planar graph, then we get V-E+R = 2

Note that the sum of all the degrees of the regions is equal to twice the number of edges in the the graph , since each edge either borders two different faces (such as bg, cd, and cf) or occurs twice when walk around a single region (such as ab and gh). The Euler's formula relates the number of vertices, edges and regions of a planar graph.

The Euler formula tells us that all plane drawings of a connected planar graph have the same number of faces namely, $2+E-V$.

Theorem (Euler's Formula) *Let G be a connected planar graph, and let V, **E** and **R** denote, respectively, the numbers of vertices, edges, and faces in a plane drawing of G. Then **V - E + R** = 2*

Proof We employ mathematical induction on edges, E. The induction is obvious for E=0 since in this case V=1 and R=1. Assume that the result is true for all connected plane graphs with fewer than E edges, where E is greater than or equal to 1, and suppose that G has E edges. If G is a tree, then V=E+1 and R=1 so the desired formula follows. On the other hand, if G is not a tree, let C be a cycle edge of G and consider G-C. The connected plane graph G-C has V vertices, E-1 edges, and R-1 regions so that by the inductive hypothesis,

$V - (E - 1) + (R - 1) = 2$

which implies that, $V - E + R = 2$.

We can obtain a number of useful results using Euler's formula.

7.7 MATCHING

In real time we encounter several instances where we need to test the similarity between graphs. In many fields like computer vision and pattern recognition, graphs encode a lot of structural information. Important tool will be graph matching for comparing data graph and model graph.

The exact graph matching is called graph isomorphism problem, exact matching of a graph to another graph is subgraph isomorphism problem. When exact matching is impossible the it is inexact graph matching problem.

For an undirected graph, when no two edges share the same vertex, then there is a matching in set of edges. Matching of a graph is a subgraph where each node of the subgraph has either zero or one edge incident on it. More formally, let 'G' = (V, E) be a graph. A subgraph is called a matching M(G), **if each vertex of G is incident with at most one edge in M**, i.e., deg(V) $\leq$ 1 $\forall$ V $\in$ G which means in the matching graph M(G), the vertices should have a degree of 1 or 0, where the edges should be incident from the graph G. Matching graph is denoted as M(G).

Example

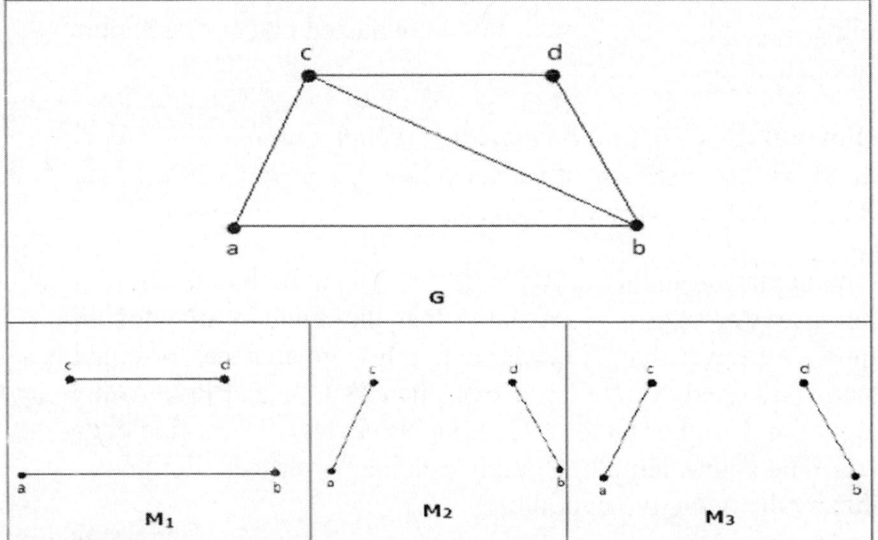

In a matching, if degree of vertex in vertex set V is 1 then vertex V is said to be matched, else if it is 0 then vertex V is not matched. No two edges are adjacent in a matching, because if so then degree of the vertex which is joining them will have degree of 2 but this disregards the matching rule.

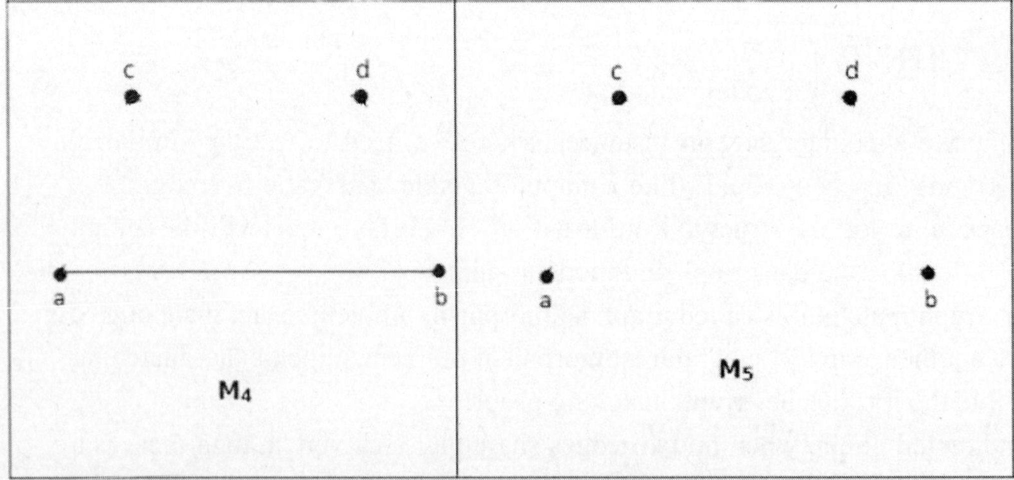

7.7.1 Maximal Matching

A matching M of graph 'G' is said to maximal **if no other edges of 'G' can be added to M**. adding of an edge which is in G but not in M makes an unmatch. In more simpler words, maximal matching M is not a proper subset of any other matching of G. M1, M2, M3 from the above graph are the maximal matching of G. Adding any edge would result in no longer graph matching.

Example

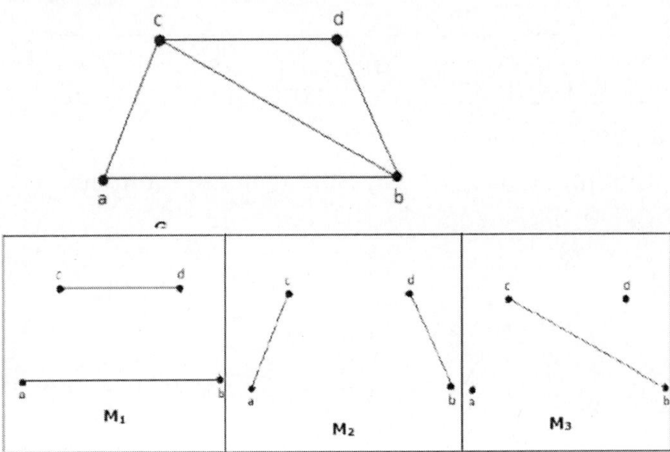

7.7.2 Maximum Matching

Maximum matching is defined as the maximal matching with maximum number of edges. Matching is said to be maximal and has maximum number of edges. Many maximum matchings of a graph are possible . every maximum matching is a maximal matching but vice versa is not true. In the figure g2 and g3 are maximum matching whereas in next fig g3 is maximum matching. The number of edges in the maximum matching of 'G' is called its **matching number**.

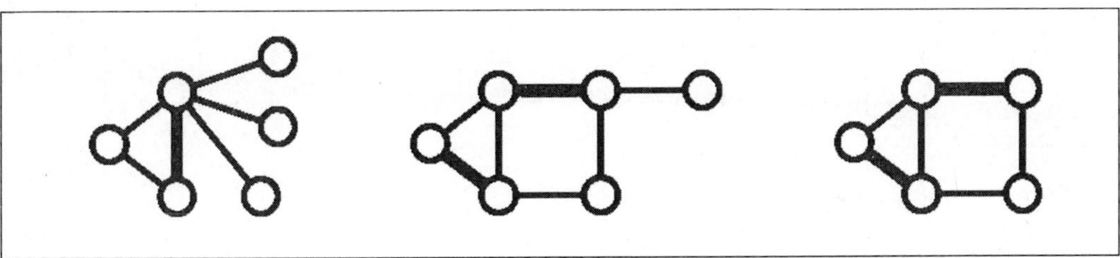

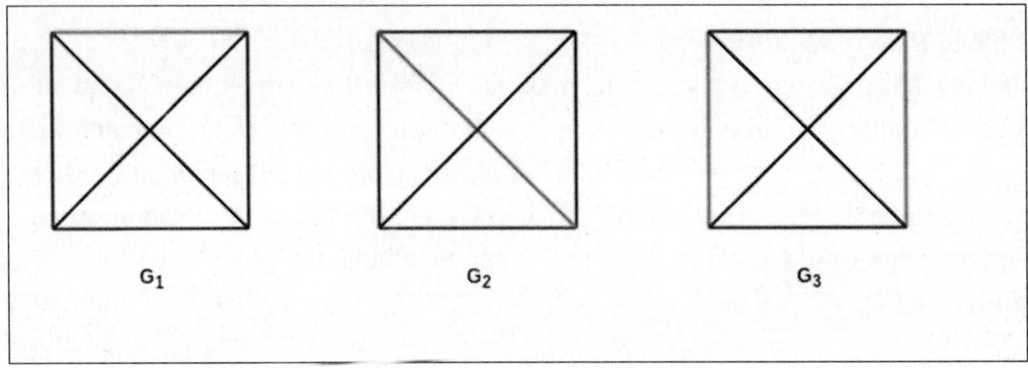

For a graph given in the above example, M1 and M2 are the maximum matching of 'G' and its matching number is 2. Hence by using the graph G, we can form only the subgraphs with only 2 edges maximum. Hence, we have the matching number as two.

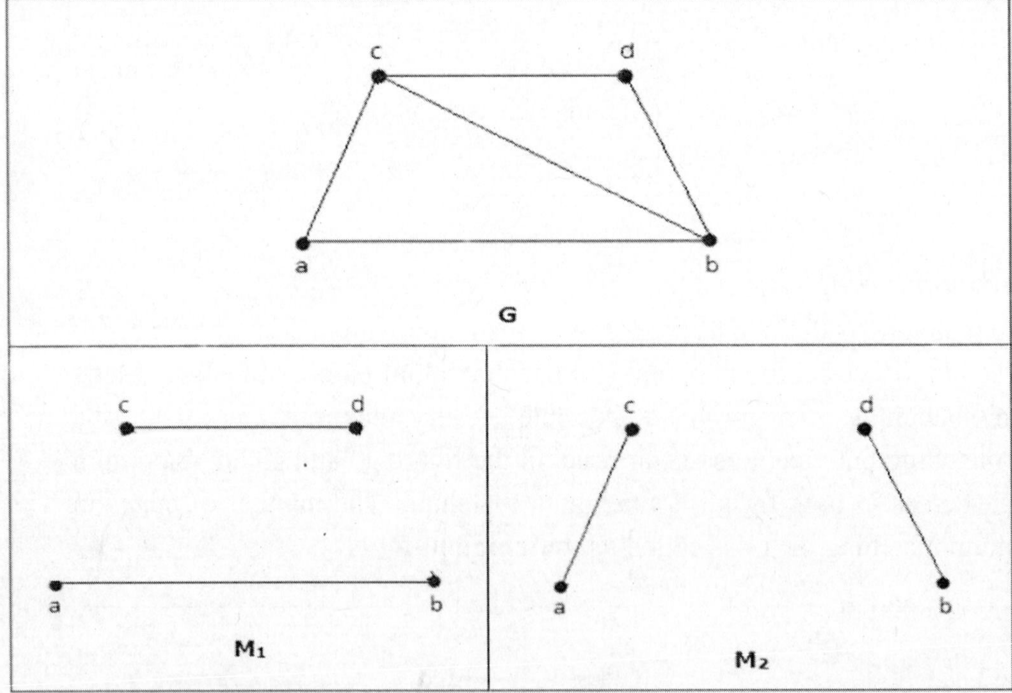

7.7.3 Perfect Matching

A matching (M) of graph (G) is said to be a perfect match, if every vertex of graph g (G) is incident to exactly one edge of the matching (M), i.e., if every vertex is connected to exactly one edge. The degree of each and every vertex in the subgraph should have a degree of 1. deg(V) = 1 ∀ V. Every perfect matching is a maximum matching, but vice versa is not true.

Since every vertex has to be included in a perfect matching, the number of edges in the matching must be |V|/2 where V is the number of vertices. Therefore, a perfect matching only exists if the number of vertices is even.
For example in the first figure, G_3 is a perfect matching.
A matching is said to be near perfect if the number of vertices in the original graph is odd, it is a maximum matching and it leaves out only one vertex. For example, in the second figure, the third graph is a near perfect matching.

Example
In the following graphs, M1 and M2 are examples of perfect matching of G.

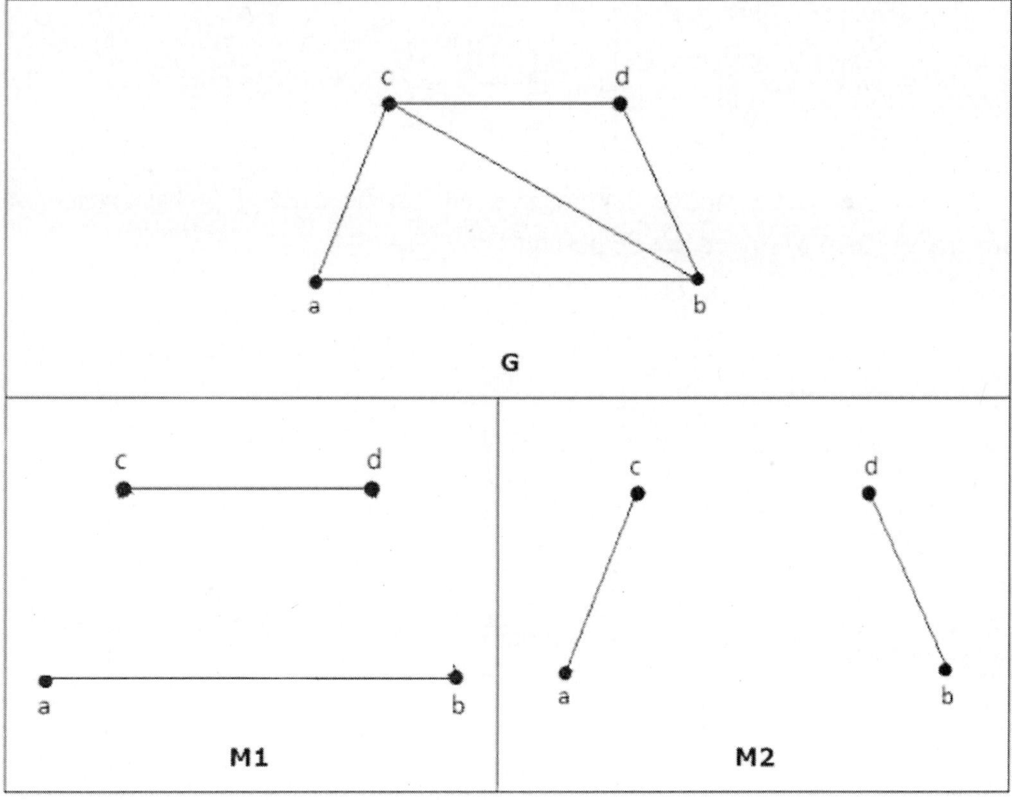

Note – Every perfect matching of graph is also a maximum matching of graph, because there is no chance of adding one more edge in a perfect matching graph. A maximum matching of graph need not be perfect. If a graph 'G' has a perfect match, then the number of vertices |V(G)| is even. If it is odd, then the last vertex pairs with the other vertex, and finally there remains a single vertex which cannot be paired with any other vertex for which the degree is zero. It clearly violates the perfect matching principle.

Example

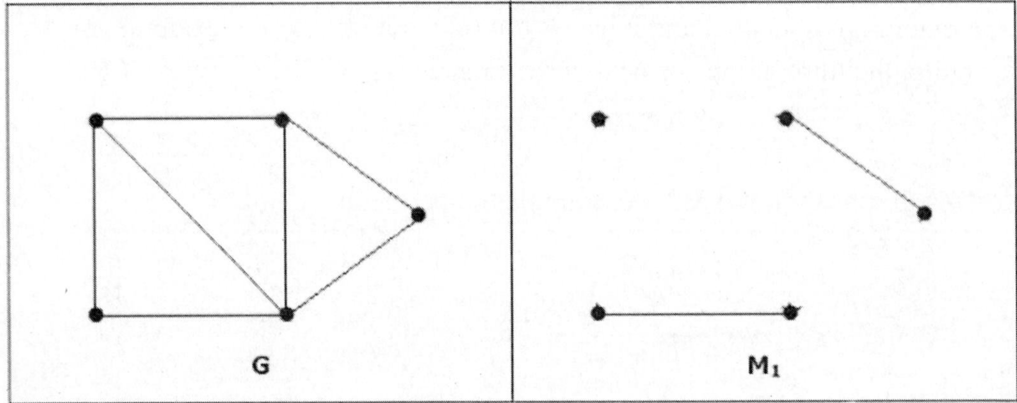

Note – The converse of the above statement need not be true. If G has even number of vertices, then M1 need not be perfect.

Example

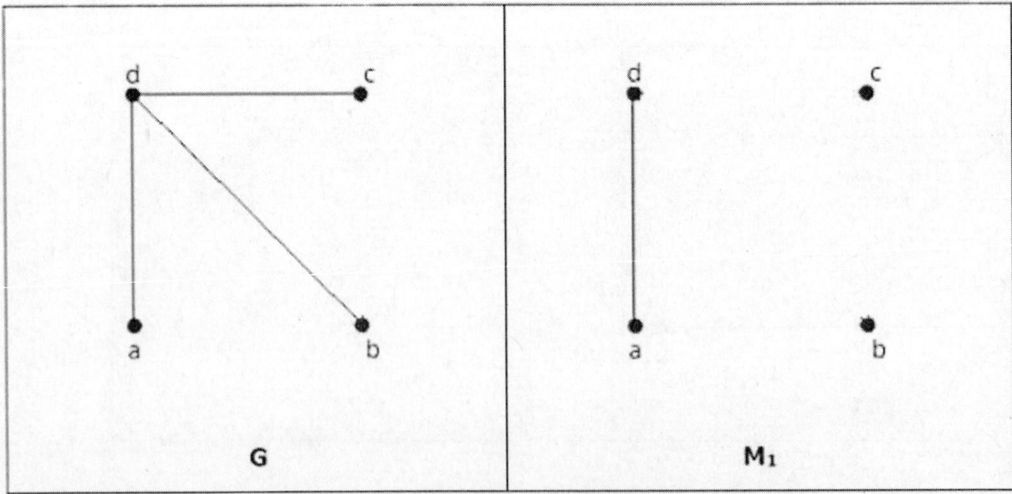

It is matching, but it is not a perfect match, even though it has even number of vertices.

7.6.4 Bipartite matching

Matching has many applications in flow networks, scheduling, and planning, graph coloring, neural networks etc. The most common of these is the scheduling problem where there are m tasks which may be completed by n workers. The tasks and workers represent the two sets of vertices in a bipartite graph, where a task is connected to a worker if the worker can complete it. The problem therefore is to find a maximum matching.

UNIT SUMMARY

This unit introduces the concept of a graph as a mathematical structure consisting of vertices/nodes connected by edges/arcs. We cover basic terms and definitions related to graphs. Highlighted basic terms and definitions related to graphs. Definitions of walk, trail, circuit, path, cycle, trees are illustrated with examples. An outline of types of graphs including directed, undirected, simple, and multigraphs is provided. Euler path, Hamilton paths, Euler Circuit and Hamilton Circuit are explained along with theorems providing conditions for the existence of Hamiltonian paths or cycles in graphs. Graph coloring problem is addressed with Vertex Coloring, Region Coloring, Edge Coloring, and Chromatic Number. Graph Planarity section examines graphs that can be drawn without any edges crossing. An outline of Maximal Matching, Maximum Matching, Perfect Matching, Bipartite Matching is discussed in brief.

Excercises:

1. The sequence of degrees of all vertices of a given graph is written in descending order is termed as degree sequence of a graph. For example, for the Graph G1 given below the degree sequence is 4, 4, 4, 3, 2, 1, 0. Similarly Find the degree sequence of the following graphs G2 to G6

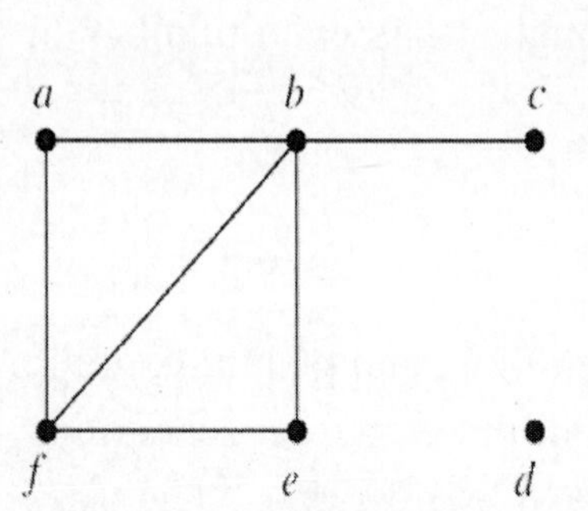

a b c f e d	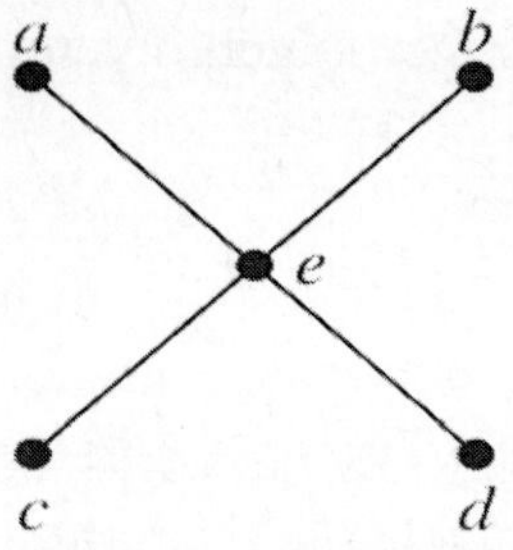 a b e c d	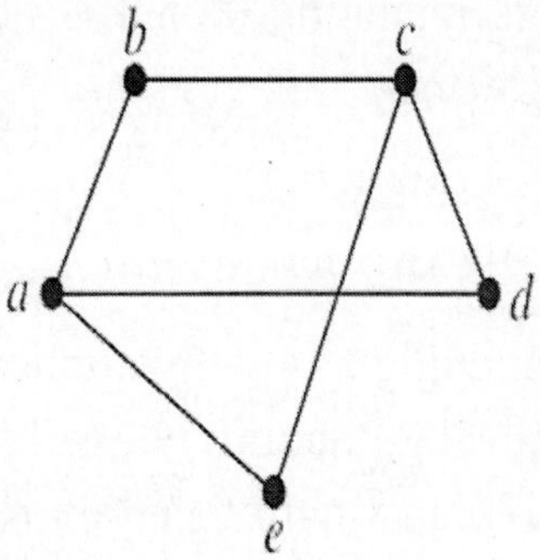 b c a d e
G1	G2	G3
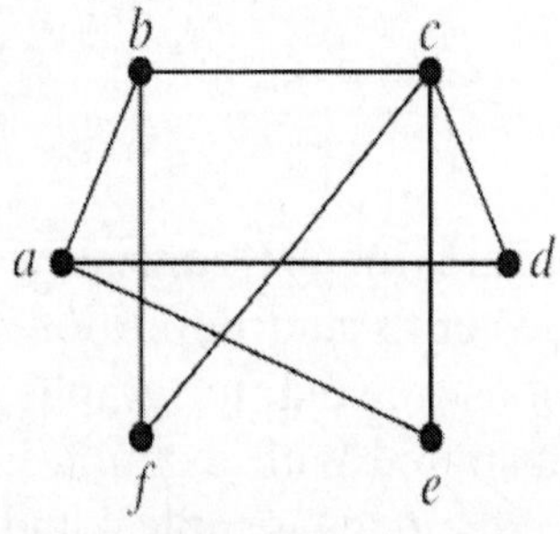 b c a d f e	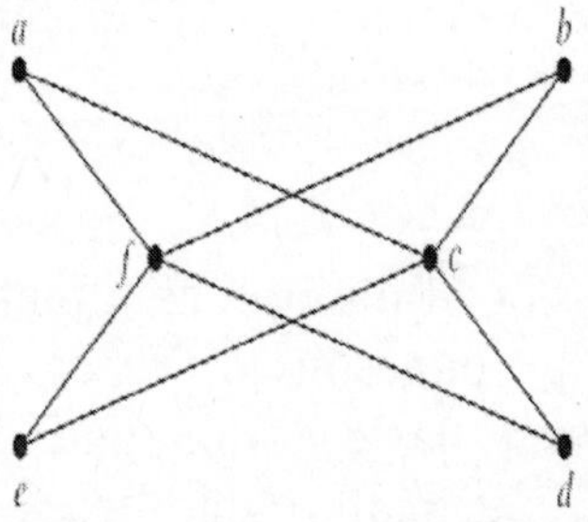 a b f c e d	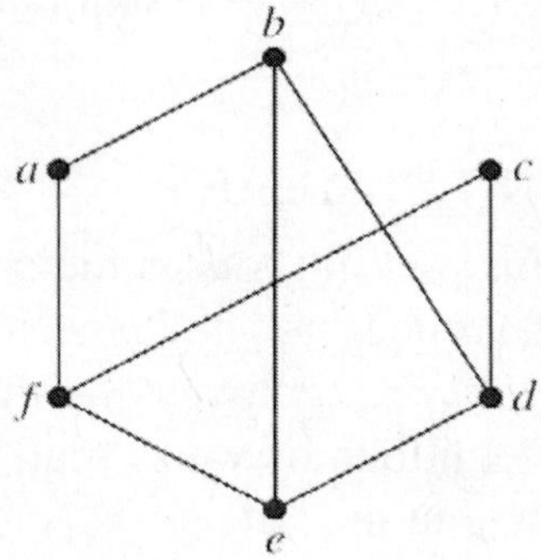 b a c f d e
G4	G5	G6

2. Identify the isolated and pendent vertices in the graphs G1 to G8.

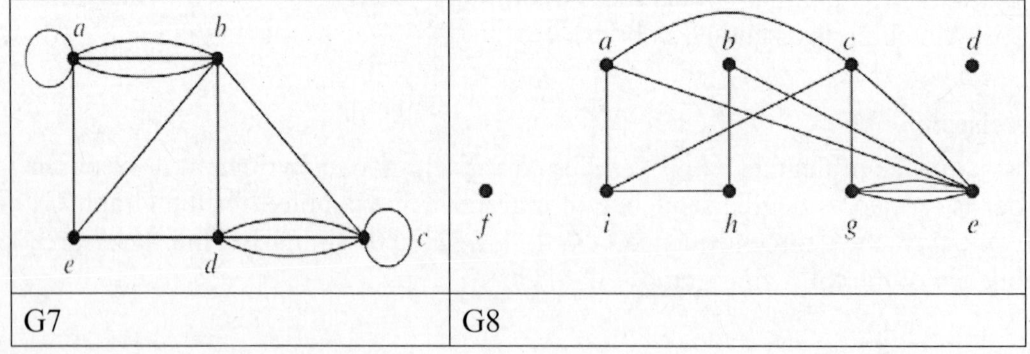

3. Find the indegree and outdegree of all the graphs given below.

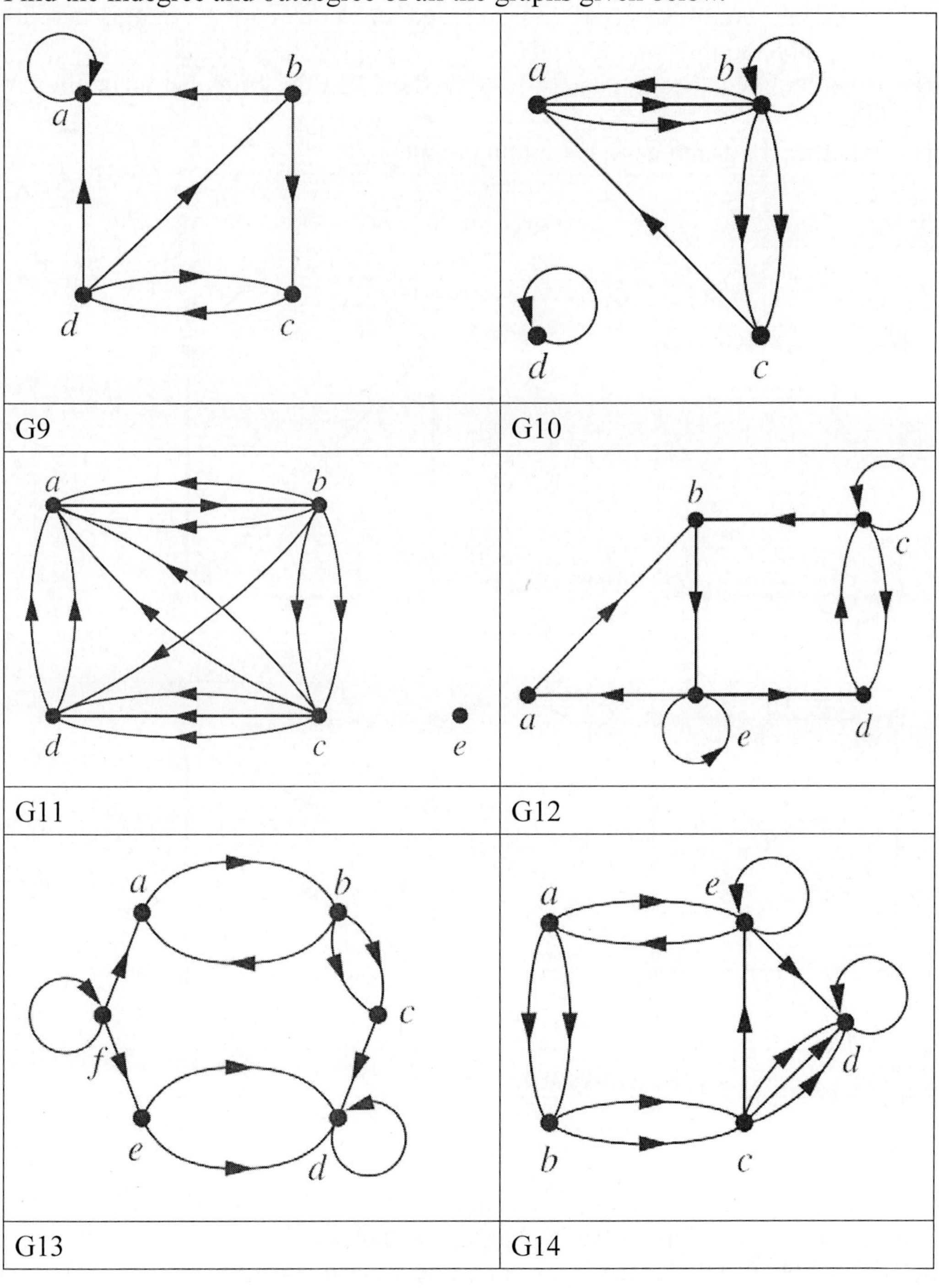

4. For each of these graphs, determine
   (i) whether Dirac's theorem can be used to show that the graph has a Hamilton circuit,
   (ii) whether Ore's theorem can be used to show that the graph has a Hamilton circuit,
   (iii) whether the graph has a Hamilton circuit.

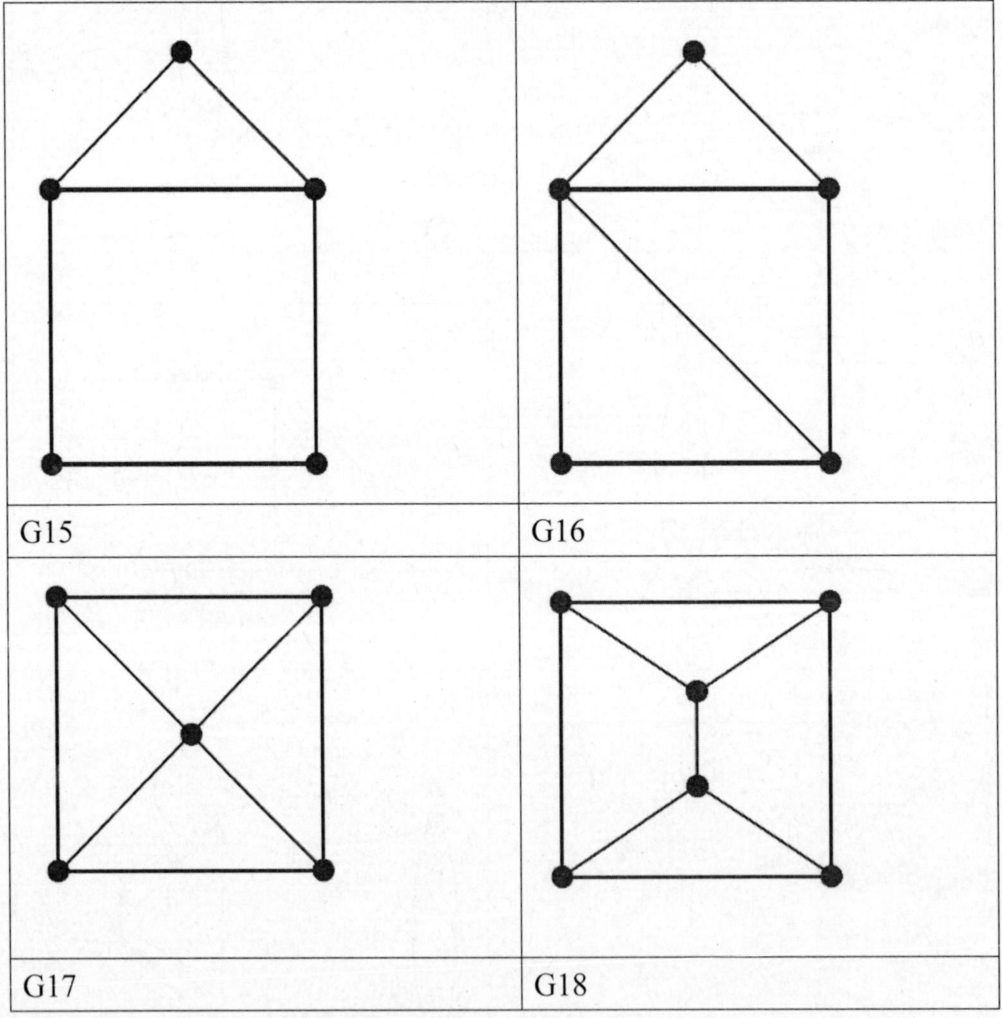

5. How do you prove that the graph given below which is called Peterson Graph, does not have a Hamilton circuit? Also show that a subgraph is obtained after deleting vertex v and all edges incident with v have a Hamilton circuit.

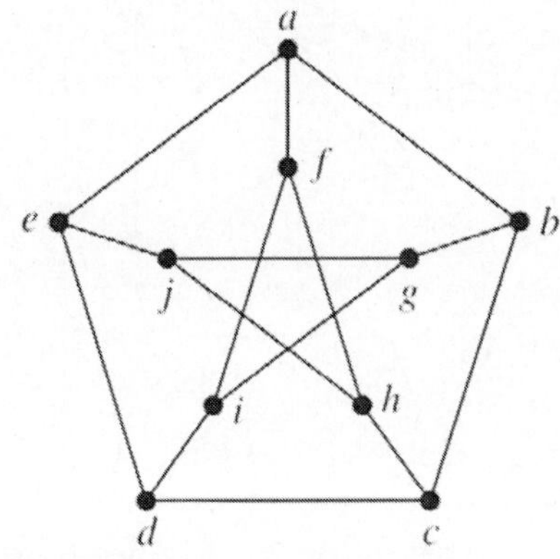

6. Which of these nonplanar graphs have the property that the removal of any vertex and all edges incident with that vertex produces a planar graph?

   a) K_5 b) K_6 c) $K_{3,3}$ d) $K_{3,4}$

7. Redraw the following graphs without any edge crossing.

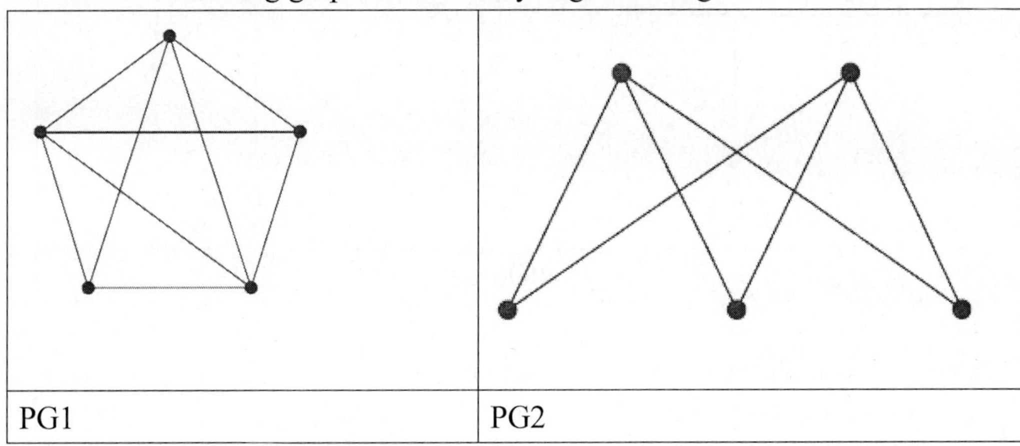

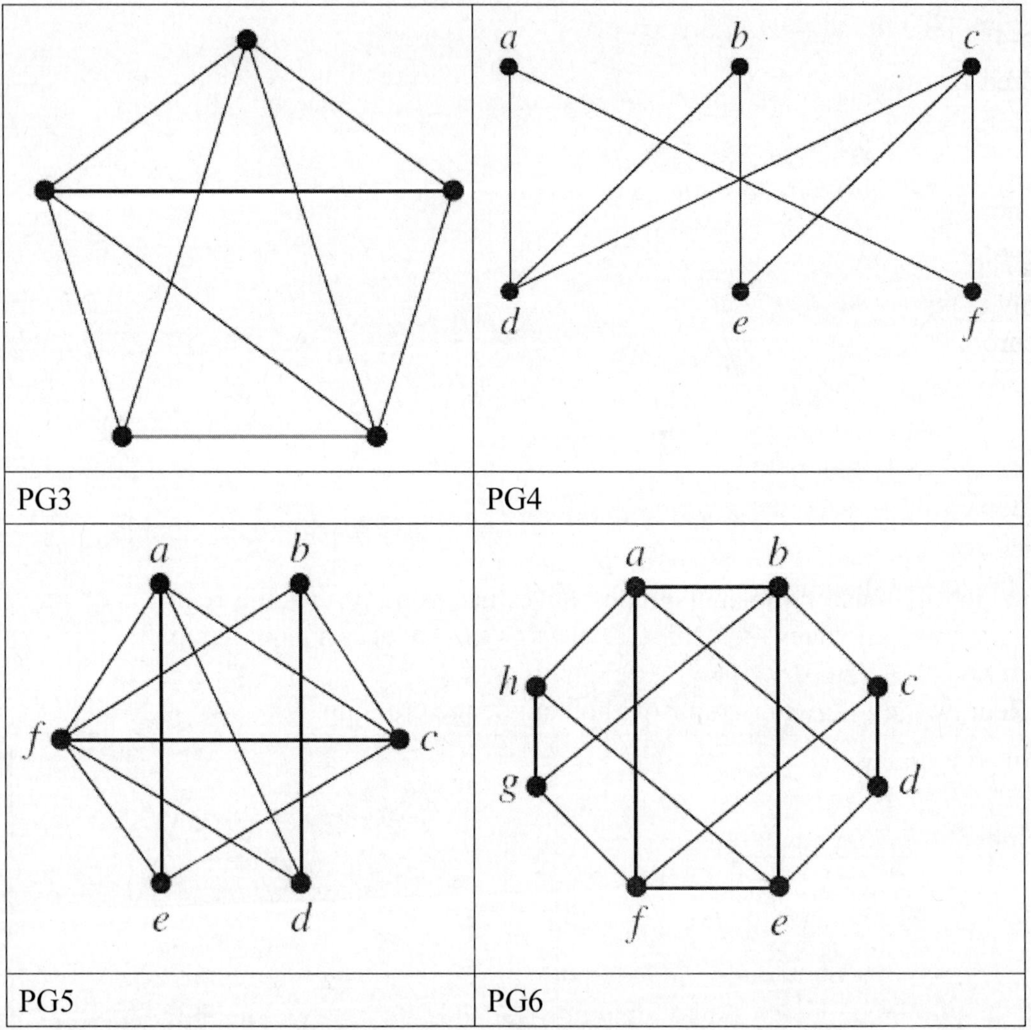

8. This algorithm can be used to color a simple graph:
Step-1: list the vertices $v_1, v_2, v_3, \ldots, v_n$ in order of decreasing degree so that,

$\deg(v_1) \geq \deg(v_2) \geq \cdot \cdot \cdot \geq \deg(v_n)$.

Step-2: Assign color 1 to v_1 and to the next vertex in the list not adjacent to v_1 (if one exists),
and successively to each vertex in the list not adjacent to a vertex already assigned color 1.

Step-3: Then assign color 2 to the first vertex in the list not already colored.

Step-4: Successively assign color 2 to vertices in the list that have not already been colored and are not adjacent to vertices assigned color 2.

Step-5: If uncolored vertices remain, assign color 3 to the first vertex in the list not yet colored, and use color 3 to successively color those vertices not already colored and not adjacent to vertices assigned color 3.

Step-6: Continue this process until all vertices are colored.

Apply this algorithm and show the colored version of the graph given below . Find its chromatic number.

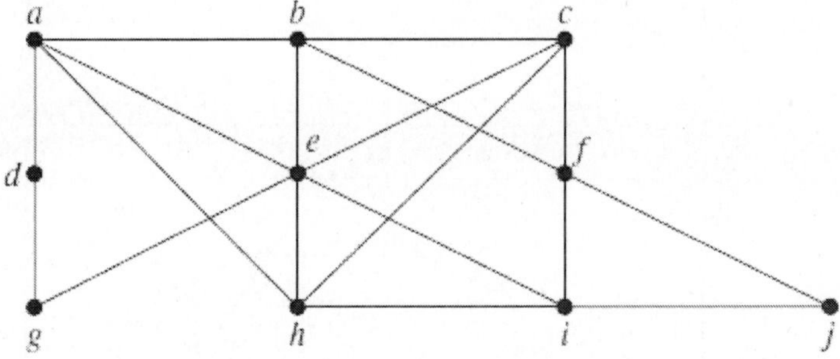

9. Find the chromatic number of the given graph.

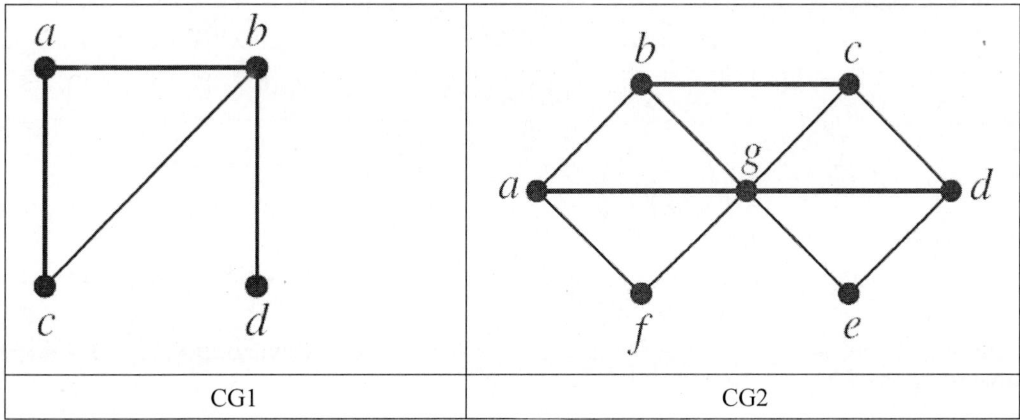

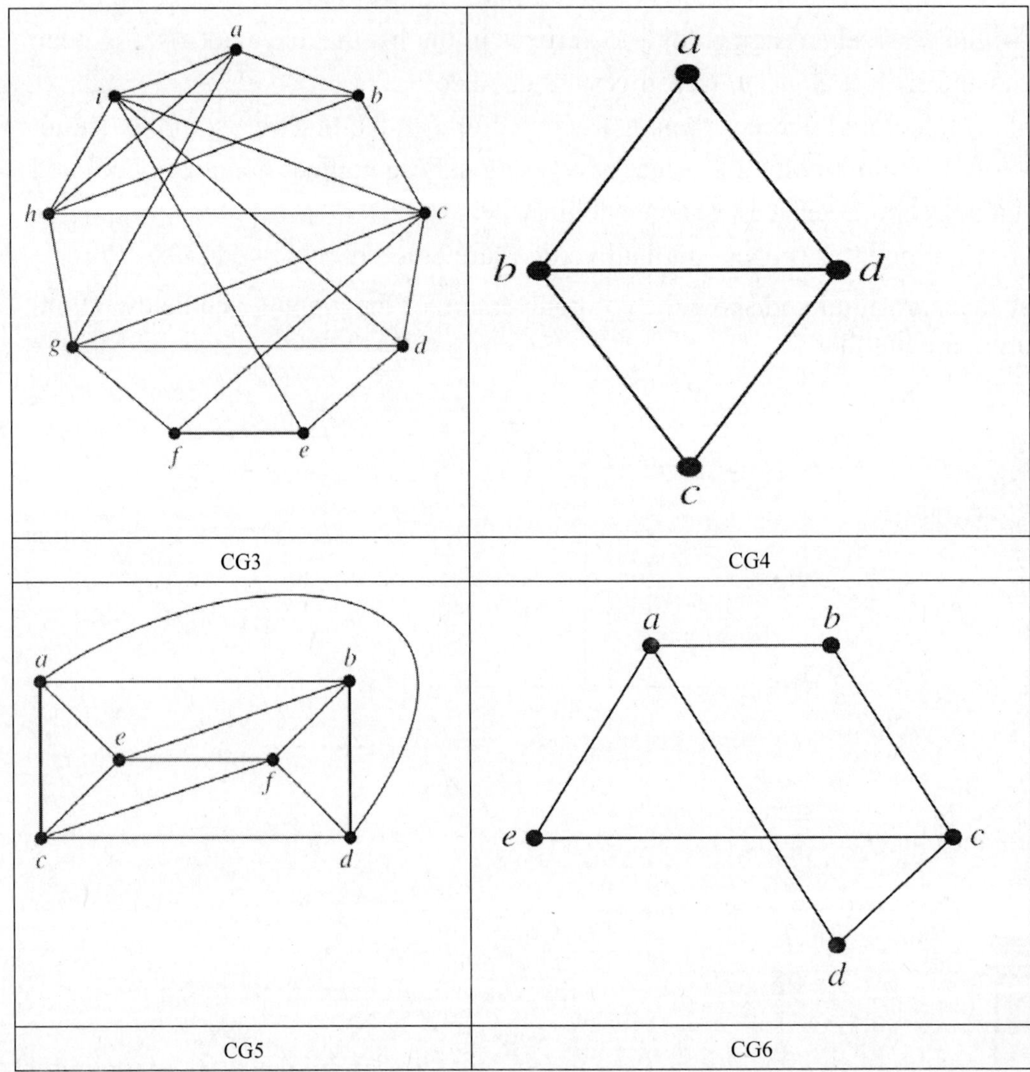

KNOW MORE

- Khan Academy provides comprehensive tutorials on various topics in graph theory, covering basics to advanced concepts.

https://www.khanacademy.org/computing/computer-science/algorithms/graph-representation/a/representing-graphs)

- Brilliant offers interactive courses on graph theory fundamentals, including graph representation, traversal, and algorithms.

(https://brilliant.org/courses/graph-theory-fundamentals/)

- MIT OCW offers a course on Mathematics for Computer Science, including lectures and materials on graph theory.

(https://ocw.mit.edu/courses/electrical-engineering-and-computer-science/6-042j-mathematics-for-computer-science-fall-2005/)

- Coursera offers a specialization in Discrete Mathematics, which covers graph theory along with other topics.

(https://www.coursera.org/specializations/discrete-mathematics)

- Wolfram MathWorld provides a comprehensive encyclopedia entry on graph theory, covering definitions, theorems, and algorithms.

(https://mathworld.wolfram.com/topics/GraphTheory.html)

REFERENCES AND SUGGESTED READINGS

1. Norman L. Biggs, Discrete Mathematics, (2nd ed. 2002), Oxford University Press.
2. Rosen, K. H. (2019). Discrete Mathematics and Its Applications. (8th Edition) ISBN10: 125967651X ISBN13: 9781259676512.
3. Bóna, M. (2006). A walk through combinatorics: an introduction to enumeration and graph theory.

Dynamic QR Code for Further Reading

8 Discrete Probability

UNIT SPECIFICS

Through this unit we have discussed the following aspects:

- *Discrete Sample Space*
- *Probability Distribution*
- *Random Variables*
- *Expectation*
- *Variance*
- *Bernoulli Trials*
- *Conditional Probability and Dependence*

In this chapter, we covered the above-mentioned concepts.

Introduction:

This Unit is devoted to understand the principles of Discrete Sample Space. Some important probability distributions that are useful in the field of computer science are introduced. Then the reader is introduced the Random Variables and it significance. Then We introduce Expectation and variance. The reader will understand Bernoulli Trials and its significance. Finally, we conclude with Conditional Probability and dependence.

RATIONALE

Why do you learn basics of Probability?

Ability to count or to enumerate objects is on of the important problem solving skill. It is possible to determine enough number of telephone numbers, or IP addresses. When probability of events need to be computed then counting is extensively used, counting also play a key role in mathematical biology for instance DNA sequencing. counting is used to determine the complexity of algorithms. One has to learn basic techniques of counting, analyse the problem and perform combinatorial analysis to solve simple to complex problems.

Why do you learn basics of Probability?

PRE-REQUISITES

Mathematics at school level (till Class X)

UNIT OUTCOMES

List of outcomes of this unit is as follows:

U8-O1: Understand basic principles of Discrete Sample Space.

U8-O2: Apply Theory of probability to solve counting problems on Probability distributions.

U8-O3: Apply Theory of random Variables to solve counting problems.

U8-O4: Understand the principles of Expectation and Variance.

U8-O5: Apply concepts of Bernoulli Trials to solve problems.

U8-O6: Apply the concept of condition probability to solve problems on dependence.

Unit-1 Outcomes	EXPECTED MAPPING WITH COURSE OUTCOMES (1- Weak Correlation; 2- Medium correlation; 3- Strong Correlation)								
	CO-1	CO-2	CO-3	CO-4	CO-5	CO-6	CO-7	CO-8	CO-9
U8-O1	2	1	3	2	2	2	-	3	2
U8-O2	2	2	1	2	2	2	-	3	2
U8-O3	2	1	1	2	2	2	-	3	2
U8-O4	2	1	1	2	1	2	-	3	2
U8-O5	2	2	2	2	2	3	-	3	3
U8-O6	2	2	2	2	2	3	-	3	-

Discrete Probability

8.1 DISCRETE SAMPLE SPACE

A discrete sample space is a type of sample space in probability theory where each possible outcome is a distinct and individual event. In other words, a discrete sample space has a finite or countable set of possible outcomes. For example, when rolling a single six-sided die, the possible outcomes are discrete and finite: 1, 2, 3, 4, 5, or 6. Another example would be flipping a coin, as there are only two distinct, discrete outcomes: heads or tails.

In contrast, a continuous sample space has an infinite set of possible outcomes, such as the possible values of a random variable on a continuum, such as the distribution of heights or weights in a population.

Discrete sample spaces are important in probability theory because they allow us to calculate the probability of an event by dividing the number of favorable outcomes by the total number of possible outcomes. This can be represented using mathematical formulas, and allows us to analyze the probability of complex events through the use of combinations and permutations.

8.1.1 Terminology

Sample Space: The sample space, S, for a random phenomenon is the set of all possible outcomes.

Examples:

1. Tossing a coin – outcomes $S = \{$**Head, Tail**$\}$
2. Rolling a die – outcomes
   $S = \{\ \}$
   $= \{1, 2, 3, 4, 5, 6\}$

Event: The **event**, *E*, is any subset of the **sample space**, *S*. i.e. any set of outcomes (not necessarily all outcomes) of the random phenomena

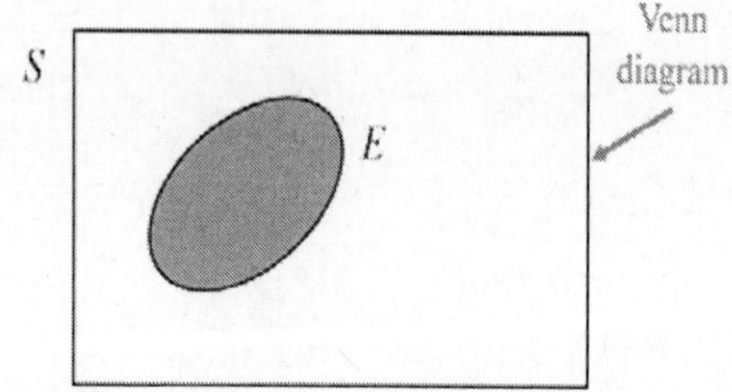

The **event**, E, is said to **have occurred** if after the outcome has been observed the outcome lies in E.

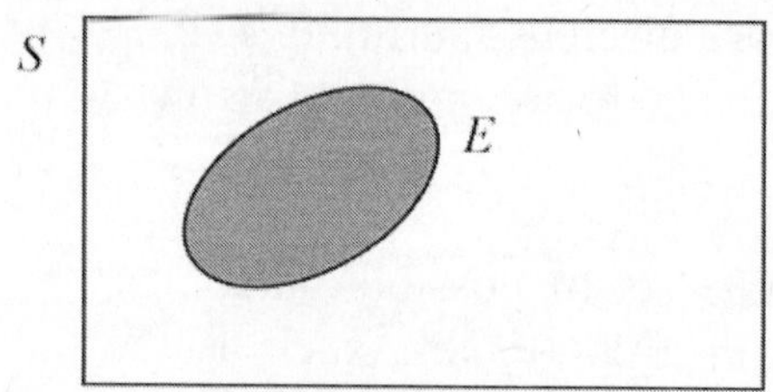

Examples

1. Rolling a die – outcomes
   $S = \{1, 2, 3, 4, 5, 6\}$

E = the event that an even number is rolled
$= \{2, 4, 6\}$

Special Events:

The Null Event, The empty event - f

$f = \{ \Phi \}$ = the event that contains no outcomes

The Entire Event, The Sample Space - S

The empty event, f, never occurs.

The entire event, S, always ⚀,⚁,⚂,⚃,⚄,⚅ occurs.

8.1.2 Set operations on Events:

Union

Let A and B be two events, then the **union** of A and B is the event (denoted by $A \cup B$) defined by:

$A \cup B = \{e \mid e$ belongs to A **or** e belongs to $B\}$

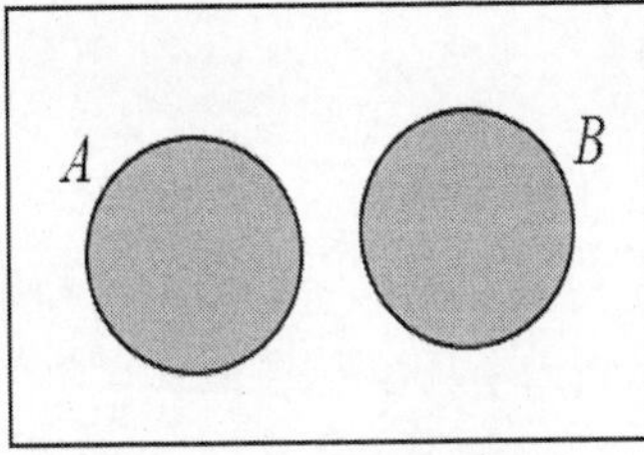

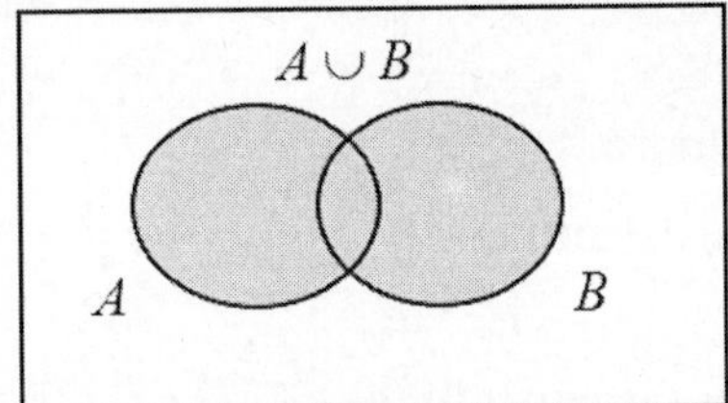

The event $A \cup B$ **occurs** if the event A **occurs or** the event and B **occurs** .

Intersection

Let A and B be two events, then the **intersection** of A and B is the event (denoted by $A \cap B$) defined

$A \cap B = \{e|\ e$ belongs to A **and** e belongs to $B\}$

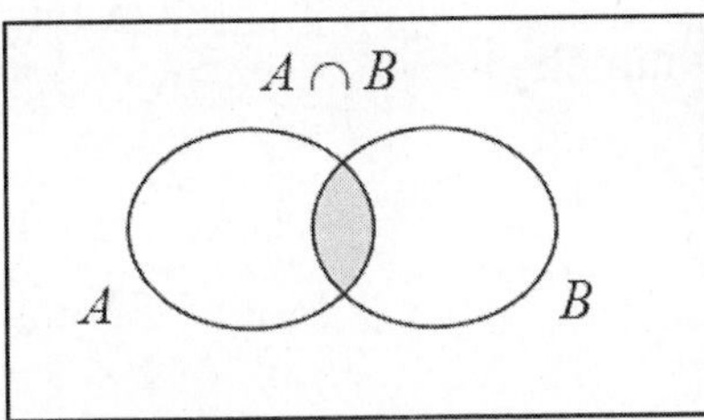

The event $A \cap B$ **occurs** if the event A **occurs and** the event and B **occurs** .

Complement

Let A be any event, then the **complement** of A (denoted by $\bar{A}$) defined by:

$= \{e|\ e$ **does not** belongs to $A\}$

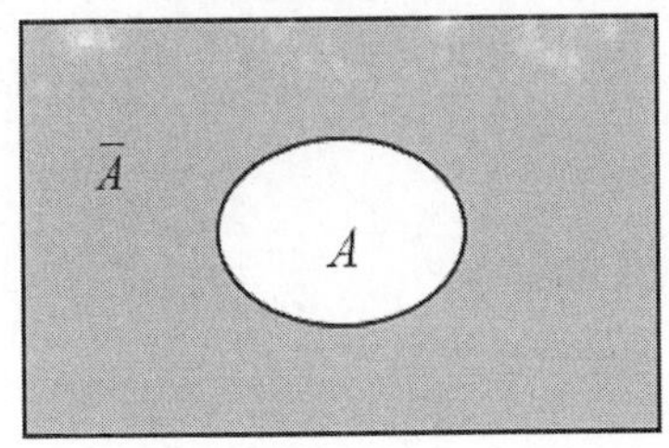

$\bar{A}$

The event **occurs** if the event A **does not occur**

In problems you will recognize that you are working with:

1. **Union** if you see the word **or**,
2. **Intersection** if you see the word **and**,
3. **Complement** if you see the word **not**.

8.1.3 Types of events

Definition: Mutually exclusive events

Two events A and B are called **mutually exclusive** if:

$A \cap B = \Phi$

If two events A and B are are **mutually exclusive** then:

1. They have no outcomes in common.
2. They can't occur at the same time. The outcome of the random experiment can not belong to both A and B.

Definition: Probability of an Event E.

Suppose that the sample space $S = \{o_1, o_2, o_3, \ldots o_N\}$ has a finite number, N, of oucomes.

Also each of the outcomes is equally likely (because of symmetry).

Then for any event E

$$P[E] = \frac{n(E)}{n(S)} = \frac{n(E)}{N} = \frac{\text{Number of outcomes in the event } E}{\text{Total number of outcomes}}$$

n(A) → Number of elements of Event E

Thus this definition of $P[E]$, i.e.

$$P[E] = \frac{\text{Number of outcomes in the event } E}{\text{Total number of outcomes}}$$

Applies only to the special case when

1. The sample space has a finite no.of outcomes, and
2. Each outcome is equiprobable

   If this is not true a more general definition of probability is required.

8.1.4 Rules of Probability

Rule1: The additive rule (Mutually exclusive events)

$P[A \cup B] = P[A] + P[B]$

$P[A \text{ or } B] = P[A] + P[B]$

if $A \cap B = \Phi$ (A and B mutually exclusive)

If two events A and B are **mutually exclusive** then:

1. They have no outcomes in common.
2. They can't occur at the same time. The outcome of the random experiment can not belong to both A and B.

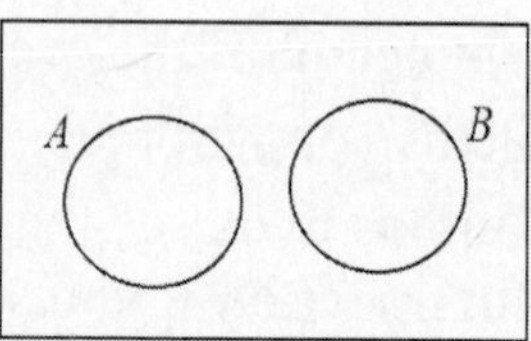

Rule2: The additive rule

$P[A \cup B] = P[A] + P[B] - P[A \cap B]$

$P[A \text{ or } B] = P[A] + P[B] - P[A \text{ and } B]$

When $P[A]$ is added to $P[B]$ the outcome in $A \cap B$ are counted twice hence

$P[A \cup B] = P[A] + P[B] - P[A \cap B]$

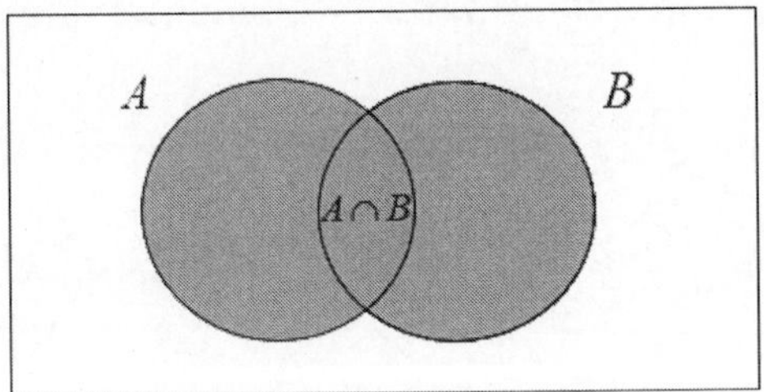

Example:

Saskatoon and Moncton are two of the cities competing for the World university games. (There are also many others). The organizers are narrowing the competition to the **final 5 cities.**

There is a 20% chance that Saskatoon will be amongst the **final 5**. There is a 35% chance that Moncton will be amongst the **final 5** and an 8% chance that both Saskatoon and Moncton will be amongst the **final 5**. What is the probability that Saskatoon or Moncton will be amongst the **final 5.**

Solution:

Let A = the event that Saskatoon is amongst the **final 5**.

Let B = the event that Moncton is amongst the **final 5**.

Given $P[A] = 0.20$, $P[B] = 0.35$, and $P[A \cap B] = 0.08$

What is $P[A \cup B]$?

Note: "and" $\equiv \cap$, "or" $\equiv \cup$.

$P[A \cup B] = P[A] + P[B] - P[A \cap B]$

$=0.20 + 0.35 - 0.08 = 0.47$

Rule3: Rule for complements:

$\mathbf{P[\bar{A}] = 1 - P[A]}$

Complement:

Let A be any event, then the **complement** of A (denoted by $\bar{A}$) defined by:
$\{e|\ e$ **does not** belongs to $A\}$

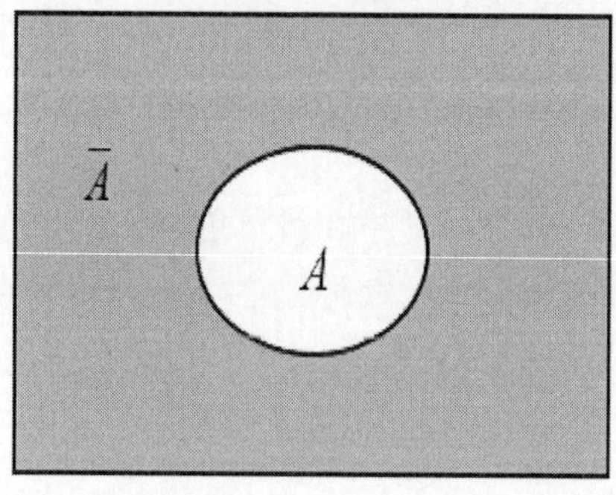

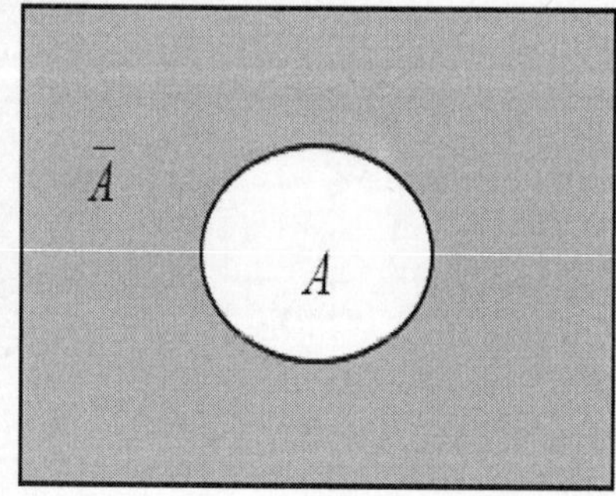

The event **occurs** if the event A **does not occur** $\bar{A}$ and A are mutually Exclusive

S = A U $\bar{A}$

Thus 1 = P[S] = P [A] + P [$\bar{A}$]

P[$\bar{A}$] = 1 – P [A]

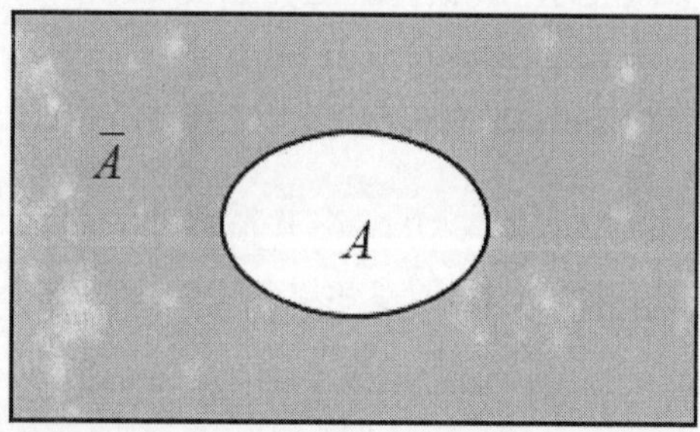

8.1.5 Conditional Probability

- Frequently before observing the outcome of a random experiment you are given information regarding the outcome
- How should this information be used in prediction of the outcome.
- Namely, how should probabilities be adjusted to take into account this information
- Usually the information is given in the following form: You are told that the outcome belongs to a given event. (i.e. you are told that a certain event has occurred)

Definition

- Suppose that we are interested in computing the probability of event A and we have been told event B has occurred.
- Then the conditional probability of A given B is defined to be:

$$P[A|B] = \frac{P[A \cap B]}{P[B]} \text{ if } P[B] \neq 0$$

Rationale:

- If we're told that event B has occurred then the sample space is restricted to B.
- The probability within B has to be normalized, This is achieved by dividing by $P[B]$
- The event A can now only occur if the outcome is in of $A \cap B$. Hence the new probability of A is:

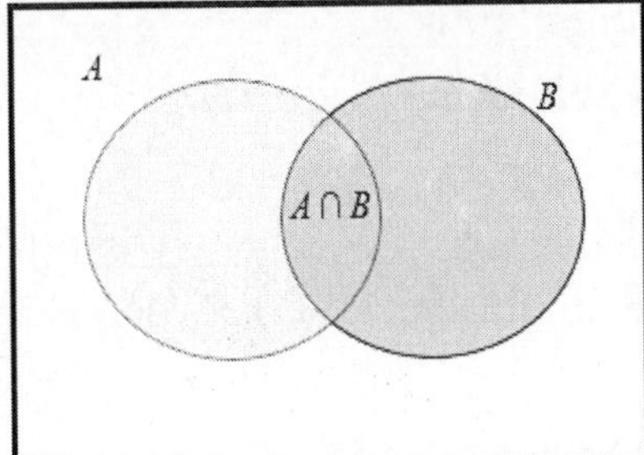

Example:

The academy awards is soon to be shown.

For a specific married couple the probability that the husband watches the show is 80%, the probability that his wife watches the show is 65%, while the probability that they both watch the show is 60%.

If the husband is watching the show, what is the probability that his wife is also watching the show

Solution: The academy awards is soon to be shown.

Let B = the event that the husband watches the show

$P[B]$= 0.80

Let A = the event that his wife watches the show

$P[A]$= 0.65 and $P[A \cap B]$= 0.60

$$P[A|B] = \frac{P[A \cap B]}{P[B]} = \frac{0.60}{0.80} = 0.75$$

Independence

Definition

Two events A and B are called **independent** if $P[A \cap B]$ **= P[A] P[B]**

If P[A] $\neq$ 0 and P[B] $\neq$ 0 then $P[A|B] = \frac{P[A \cap B]}{P[B]} = \frac{P[A]P[B]}{P[B]} = P[A]$

and

$$P[B|A] = \frac{P[A \cap B]}{P[A]} = \frac{P[A]P[B]}{P[A]} = P[B]$$

Thus, in the case of independence the conditional probability of an event is not affected by the
knowledge of the other event

Difference between independence and mutually exclusive:

Mutually exclusive

Two mutually exclusive events are independent only in the special case where,
P[A] =0 and P[B] =0 also $P[A \cap B] = 0$
Mutually exclusive events are highly dependent otherwise.
A and B **cannot** occur simultaneously. If one event occurs the other event does not occur.

Independent events:

$P[A \cap B]$ **= P[A] P[B] or**

$$\frac{P[A \cap B]}{P[A]} = P[A] = \frac{P[A]}{P[S]}$$

The ratio of the probability of the set A within B is the same as the ratio of the probability of the set A within the entire sample S.

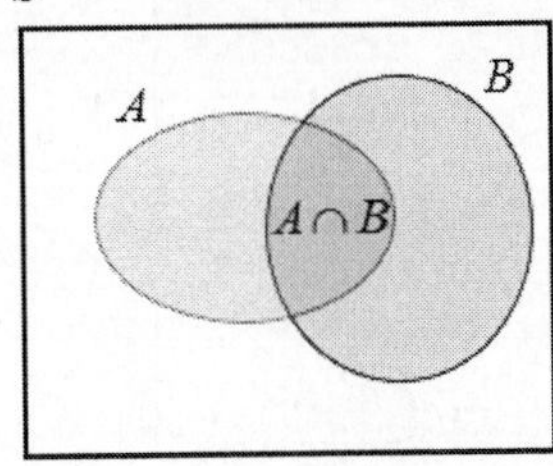

Rule4: The multiplicative rule of probability

$$P[A \cap B] = \begin{cases} P[A]P[B|A] & if\ P[A] \neq 0 \\ P[B]P[A|B] & if\ P[B] \neq 0 \end{cases}$$

$P[A \cap B]$= P[A] P[B]
if A and B are **independent**.

8.2 RANDOM VARIABLES AND PROBABILITY DISTRIBUTIONS

One of the key concepts in Probability is Random variables and probability distributions. The value of a random variable depends on the outcome of a random event. If the event is flipping a coin, then the number of heads appear can be 0 or 1 or 2. The outcome of this event will be the value of the random variable. So, the the random variable depends on the outcome of the random event. How to describe the likelihood of each possible value of a random variable? The solution is with probability distributions. This can take two forms. 1. Discrete Probability distribution 2. Continuous probability distribution.

When the random variable takes countably finite number of possible values, then it is a discrete probability distribution. Similarly when the random variable takes continuous possible range of values, then it is a continuous probability distribution. Definition: *A random variable X on a sample space S is a real-valued (measurable) function on S; that is,* $X : S \to \mathbb{R}$. *A discrete random variable is a random variable that takes on only a finite or countably infinite number of values.*

Discrete probability distributions	Continuous probability distributions
binomial distribution: describing the number of successes in a fixed number of independent trials	normal distribution: which describes many natural phenomena such as heights and weights
Poisson distribution: number of events that occur in a fixed interval of time.	exponential distribution: often used to model waiting times

When an experiment is repeated to a fixed number of times, The value of the random variable differs and varies from trial to trial. Though we intend to represent the outcome of an experiment as a number, but the actual outcome need not be a number. Let S be the sample space, R be the a function to associate real value with every basic event in the sample space S, R represent a random variable.

Nature of R	Termed as	Corresponding Probability distribution	Represented as
R is finite	Discrete Random Variable	**probability mass function**	**pmf**
R is infinite	continuous random variable	**probability density function**	**pdf**

Example:
Event: coin flipping measuring lifetime of an object
How many times: 10 when used for several days
Random variable be : X Y is positive real
X is discrete takes values from 0 to 10 Y can take continuous random value.
Some other Examples: Strength of the class on Friday, Number of defective bolts in a box of 20, number of patients to consult a particular doctor tonight.

Example:
Event: measuring lifetime of an object
How many times: when used for several days
Random variable be :Y is positive real
Y can take continuous random value.
Some other examples include: the amount of sugar content present in a fruit, height and weight of a set of students.

For a discrete random variable X and a real value a, the event "X = a" includes all the basic events of the sample space in which the random variable X assumes the value a. That is, "X = a" represents the set $\{s \in S \mid X(s) = a\}$.We denote the probability of that event by

$$Pr(X = a) = \sum_{s \in S: X(s)=a} Pr(S)$$

Example:
Event: throwing a dice
How many times: two
Random variable be :X is positive whole number taking value 4
Set of basic events = {(1, 3), (2, 2), (3, 1)}. $Pr(X = 4) = \frac{3}{36} = \frac{1}{12}$

The definition of independence that we developed for events extends to random variables.

Definition: Two random variables X and Y are independent if and only if
$Pr((X = x) \cap (Y = y)) = Pr(X = x) \cdot Pr(Y = y)$
for all values x and y. Similarly, random variables $X_1, X_2, \ldots, X_k$ are mutually independent
if and only if, for any subset $I \subseteq [1, k]$ and any values x_i, $i \in I$,

$$Pr(\bigcup_{i \in I} X_i = x_i) = \prod_{i \in I} Pr(X_i = x_i)$$

8.2.1 PMF and PDF

Probability Mass Function (PMF): A list of probabilities that is associated with each of the possible values of a random variable which is also the probability distribution of a discrete random variable is termed as the probability function or the probability mass function.
More formally written as, the probability distribution of a discrete random variable X is a function which gives the probability $p(x_i)$ that the random variable equals x_i, for each value x_i:
$p(x_i) = P(X=x_i)$
It satisfies the following conditions:

- $0 <= p(x_i) <= 1$
- sum of all $p(x_i)$ is 1 $\sum_{i=1}^{N} p(x_i)=1$

Example Tossing a fair coin

Tossing once	Tossing twice
Outcomes: H -- P(H) = 0.5 T -- P(T) = 0.5	Outcomes: HH -- P(HH) = 0.25 HT -- P(HT) = 0.25 TH -- P(TH) = 0.25 TT -- P(TT) = 0.25

So, sum of probability of all outcomes add up to 1 so, it is called probability mass function or p.m.f.

Cumulative distribution function: All random variables (discrete and continuous) have a cumulative distribution function. It is a function giving the probability that the random variable X is less than or equal to x, for every value x.

Formally, the cumulative distribution function F(x) is defined to be:
F(x) = P(X<=x) for -infinity < x < infinity

For a discrete random variable, the cumulative distribution function is found by summing up the probabilities as in the example below.

For a continuous random variable, the cumulative distribution function is the integral of its probability density function.

Probability Density Function (PDF): A list of probabilities that is associated with each of the possible values of a random variable which is also the probability distribution of a continuous random variable is termed as the probability Density function.

More formally, the probability density function, f(x), of a continuous random variable X is the derivative of the cumulative distribution function F(x):

$$f(x) = \frac{d}{dx}F(x)$$

Since F(x) = P(X ≤ x) it follows that

$$\int f(x)dx = F(b) - F(a) = P(a < X < b)$$

Since F(x) = P(X<=x) If f(x) is a probability density function then it must obey two conditions:

- that the total probability for all possible values of the continuous random variable X is 1:
  $\int f(x)dx = 1)$
- that the probability density function can never be negative: f(x) > 0 for all x.

Example

Discrete case: Suppose a random variable X has the following probability distribution p(xi):

X_i	0	1	2	3	4	5
$P(X_i)$	1/32	5/32	10/32	10/32	5/32	1/32

This is actually a binomial distribution: Bi(5, 0.5) or B(5, 0.5).
The cumulative distribution function F(x) is then:

X_i	0	1	2	3	4	5
$P(X_i)$	1/32	6/32	16/32	26/32	31/32	32/32

F(x) does not change at intermediate values.
For example:
F(1.3) = F(1) = 6/32
F(2.86) = F(2) = 16/32

Based on a probability distribution we can easily calculate probabilities for values that are less than or equal to a given value. The probability of X is less than or 1 is 0.1. Similarly, probability of X is less than or equal to 2 is (0.1+0.3) =0.4 and so on.

8.3 MEAN OF A RANDOM VARIABLE

The mean of a random variable indicates its average or central value. It is a useful summary value of the variable's distribution. As it is the expected average outcome from many observation so we can tell it as Expected value also.
Stating the expected value gives a general impression of the behavior of some random variable without giving full details of its probability distribution (if it is discrete) or its probability density function (if it is continuous).

- The mean of a discrete random variable is the probability-weighted average of all possible values that the random variable can take. Check the below formula for mean of discrete random variable.
- The mean of a continuous random variable is the average of all possible values that the random variable can take. We can represent that as integral and function of X. Check the formula for mean of a continuous random variable.

Example:

- For Discrete Case: When a die is thrown, each of the possible faces 1, 2, 3, 4, 5, 6 (the xi's) has a probability of 1/6 (the p(xi)'s) of showing. The expected value of the face showing is therefore:
- $\mu = E(X) = (1 \times 1/6) + (2 \times 1/6) + (3 \times 1/6) + (4 \times 1/6) + (5 \times 1/6) + (6 \times 1/6) = 3.5$
- Notice that, in this case, E(X) is 3.5, which is not a possible value of X.

The expected value of a random variable X is symbolized by E(X) or μ.

If X is a discrete random variable with possible values x1, x2, x3, …, xn, and p(xi) denotes P(X = xi), then the expected value of X is defined by:

$\mu = E(X) = \sum xi \,.\, p\,(xi)$

where the elements are summed over all values of the random variable X.

If X is a continuous random variable with probability density function f(x), then the expected value of X is defined by:

$\mu = E(X) = \int x \;\; f(x)dx$

8.4 VARIANCE OF A RANDOM VARIABLE

The variance of a random variable is a non-negative number which gives an idea of how widely spread the values of the random variable are likely to be; the larger the variance, the more scattered the observations on average.

Stating the variance gives an impression of how closely concentrated round the expected value the distribution is; it is a measure of the 'spread' of a distribution about its average value.

Variance is symbolized by V(X) or Var(X) or σ^2

The variance of the random variable X is defined to be:

$V(X) = \sigma^2 = E(X - E(X))^2 = E(X^2) - E(X)^2$

where E(X) is the expected value or mean of the random variable X.

- The larger the variance, the further that individual values of the random variable (observations) tend to be from the mean, on average;
- the smaller the variance, the closer that individual values of the random variable (observations) tend to be to the mean, on average;
- taking the square root of the variance gives the standard deviation, i.e.:
  $\sqrt{V(X)} = \sqrt{\sigma^2} = \sigma = s$
- The variance and standard deviation of a random variable are always non-negative.

Take the following example where a distribution has been shown for a person to get involved in a traffic accident. The mean risk is 1/25 accident/ year

To calculate the variance follow the steps given in diagram.

So far, variance of random variable has been discussed in terms of discrete variable only.

Some examples of random variables and probability distributions

Coin flip: The random variable is the number of heads that come up in a single flip of a fair coin. The probability distribution is a discrete uniform distribution with two possible outcomes – heads or tails, each with a probability of 0.5.

Roll of a die: The random variable is the number that comes up when rolling a fair six-sided die. The probability distribution is a discrete uniform distribution with six possible outcomes, each with a probability of 1/6.

Number of customers in a store: The random variable is the number of customers who visit a store in a given day. The probability distribution could be a Poisson distribution, which would describe the probability of a certain number of customers arriving based on the average number of customers per day.

Height of people in a population: The random variable is the height of an individual in a population. The probability distribution could be a normal distribution, which describes the distribution of many natural phenomena including heights and weights.

Time between customer arrivals: The random variable is the time between when one customer leaves and the next customer arrives at a store. The probability distribution could be an exponential distribution, which is often used to model waiting times.

Understanding random variables and probability distributions is essential for a wide range of applications, from finance and economics to engineering and data science.

8.5 BERNOULLI TRIALS

Bernoulli Experiments, Binomial Distribution

Consider an event of answering a multiple choice question, then the common questions to be answered are i) with what probability all questions are guessed right. ii) with what probability none of them are right. iii) with what probability atleast three are right iv) on an average how many are right.

Such an experiment lead to Bernoulli Experiment and it is in Binomial distribution. So by definition a Bernoulli experiment involves repeated independent trials of an experiment that has two outcomes success or failure. In the above case the experiment is to be repeated for more number of questions, and the answer for the question may be correct or wrong.

So in general Bernoulli experiment with n trials will have the following set of rules Among them the first rule is that the experiment has to be repeated a fixed number of times say n. next the experiment has two outcomes for each trial. Then the probability of success is same for each trial, if p represents probability of success then 1-p represents probability of failure. Another rule is that the trials are independent that is outcome of one trial has no influence on the other trial. So X is a random variable for number of success then all possible values of X range from 1 to n

Example: Event: Flip a coin for 15 times to count the number of heads, here trial means each independent flip, that has two outcomes head or tail, where probability of both success and failure on each trial is ½ thus some random variable X is chosen for counting the number of success and failures in 15 trials. This is just an example of Bernoulli experiment with 15 trials.

Example: Event: Drawing a marbel from the bag without replacement.

A bag has 6 red and 4 blues marbles. Assume if five marbles are drawnfrom the bag without replacement then what is the number of observing a red marble. Here the trial is drawing a marble from bag, if the marbel is red that is a success event. But do you think this is a Bernoulli Experiment? Definitely not because the trials are not independent. The probability of success and failure is going to vary from trial to trial, and the the number red and blue is also changing as the marbels are not replaced for every trial. In order to convert it into a Bernoulli experiment we shall now repeat drawing marbles with replacement. Drawing a marbel from bag each time is a trial and now the trials are independent of each other as the marbels are replaced after every draw and also probability of success will be same on each trial.

Let us now consider another Bernoulli experiment with n trials. A Basket ball player takes n number of independent free throws. The probability of him taking six such throws is 0.7 where he gets a basket for each shot. The basket made is recorded for every throw. In this experiment we consider each free throw as a independent trial with the outcome success or failure that is basket or no basket. Here probability of success and failures are in 0:7 ratio. For such a sort of experiments a random variable x decides the number of successes for n number of trial, For the above said example X is counted as six trials.

Once after deciding the random variable, we need to calculate the probability distribution for the random variable X. As described previously in all examples, X defines the number of successes in the Bernoulli experiment with n trials. Here we illustrate it for a small example and deduce a tree diagram for the specific case. Lets continue with the previous example of basket ball player. As he take six independent throw with 0.7 probability to hit a basket on each shot. If we assume X as the number of basket he gets which is a Bernoulli experiment of n trials where n=six with probability p=0.7. this can be represented with tree diagram to find the probability that the player gets exactly 2 baskets or P(X=2). In this diagram B represent hitting the basket and M represents missing the basket.

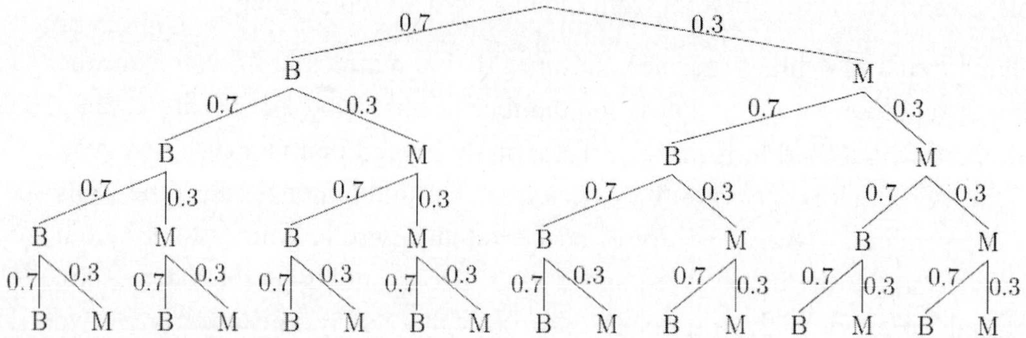

Fig. Tree diagram for n = 4 trials, M is missed the basket, B is hitting the basket. For simplicity 4 trials are shown in the figure.

Therefore, for 6 trials $P(X=2) = C(6,2)\ (0.7)^2\ (0.3)^2$

For 4 trials $P(X=2) = C(4,2)\ (0.7)^2\ (0.3)^2$

To generalize the above discussion if X is assumed to be a random variable to represent the number of successes in a Bernoulli experiment with independent trials represented by n. p and q representing the probability of success and failures respectively (holding the fact q=1-p) then,
P(X=k) is given by the following relation.

$P(X=k) = C(n,k)\ p^k\ q^{n-k}$ here k ranges from 0 to n.

If you visualize the tree diagram for n independent trials, the number of paths with exactly k success among n trials is given by C(n,k), the probability of every such path equals $p^k\ q^{n-k}$
Some event where X=k is a result of any one of these outcomes, here outcome is represented by a path so P(X=k) is taken by sum of probabilities of all paths with exactly k number of successes which is equal to $C(n,k)\ p^k\ q^{n-k}$ This is how we arrived at the above relation.

Example:

Solve for the complete probability distribution of X for the event in which a basket ball player plays four independent free throws with 0:7 ratio of probability for hitting a basket on each shot.

X	P(X)	
0	$C(4,0)\ (0.7^0)(0.3^4)$	0.0081
1	$C(4,1)\ (0.7^1)(0.3^3)$	0.0756
2	$C(4,2)\ (0.7^2)(0.3^2)$	0.2646
3	$C(4,3)\ (0.7^3)(0.3^1)$	0.4116
4	$C(4,4)\ (0.7^4)(0.3^0)$	0.2401
		Sum = 1.0

Thus when X reperesent the number of success in n trials with probability p success in each trial, then distribution of X is a binomial distribution with n and p. Then Expected Value of X can be computed by a product of n and p. Standard Deviation can be computed by product of n, p and 1-p under the square root.

Similarly we can compute expected number of baskets that he gets for 8 independent free throws for 0:7. as $C(8,6)\ (0.7)^6\ (0.3)^2 \approx 0.296$ is the probability the player gets for 6 baskets, then obviously expected number of baskets is $np = 8(0.7) = 5.6$

8.6 CONDITIONAL PROBABILITY AND DEPENDENCE

Dependent Events:

If the occurrence of event A affects the occurrence or non-occurrence of event B, the events are termed as dependent events.

For example: A coloured ball is drawn from a bag. If another ball is drawn from the bag before replacing the first ball, the probability of drawing the second ball will be affected by the probability of drawing the first ball. If the first ball was replaced, the events would have been independent. To find the probability of two dependent events occurring simultaneously, conditional probability is used. If one is altered, it will definitely affect the probability of the other event.

Conditional Probability:

The probability of an event given that another event has occurred is termed as conditional probability. If A and B are two events, then the conditional probability of A given that event B has occurred is given by, $P(A/B) = P(A \cap B)P(B)$

Similarly, if A and B are two events, then the conditional probability of B given that event A has occurred is given by, $P(B/A) = P(A \cap B)P(A)$

Theorem

Assuming A and B to be two dependent events then,

$P(A \cap B) = P(A).P(B/A)$

The probability of simultaneous happening of two events A and B is equal to the probability of A multiplied by the conditional probability of B with respect to A.

Similarly, $P(A \cap B) = P(B).P(A/B)$

The probability of simultaneous happening of two events A and B is equal to the probability of B multiplied by the conditional probability of A with respect to B.

Example 1:

There are 3 red, 6 white and 7 blue balls in a bag. If two balls are drawn one by one, find the probability that the first ball is white and the second ball is blue when the first ball drawn is not replaced.

Solution: Let A be the event of drawing a white ball and B be the event of drawing second a blue ball. Since, the first ball is not replaced before drawing the second ball, the two events are dependent.

Total number of balls = 3 + 6 + 7 = 16

Number of white balls = 6

Therefore, Probability of drawing a white ball, P(A) = 6/16

The number of balls in the bag is now 16 - 1 = 15

Number of blue balls = 7

A blue ball is drawn given that a white ball is drawn. Therefore, conditional probability of B given that A has occurred is,P(B/A) = 7/15

Now, the probability that events A and B occur simultaneously is given by,

$P(A \cap B) = P(A).P(B/A)$
Substituting the respective values,
$P(A \cap B) = 6/16 \times 7/15 = 7/40$
Therefore, the probability that the first ball is white and the second ball is blue when the first ball drawn is not replaced is 7/40.

Example 2:
Two cards are drawn one by one from a pack of 52 cards without replacement. What is the probability that the first card drawn is a king and second is queen?
Solution: Let A be the event of drawing a king and B be the event of drawing a queen. Since, the first card, that is, king is not replaced before drawing the second card, that is queen, the two events are dependent. Total number of balls = 52 Number of kings = 4 Therefore, Probability of drawing a king, P(A) = 4/52
The number of cards in the deck now is 52 - 1 = 51
Number of queen = 4
A queen is drawn given that a king is drawn.
Therefore, conditional probability of B given that A has occurred is, P(B/A) = 4/51
Now, the probability that events A and B occur simultaneously is given by,
$P(A \cap B) = P(A).P(B/A)$
Substituting the respective values, $P(A \cap B) = 4/52 \times 4/51 = 4/663$
Therefore, the probability that the first card drawn is a king and second is queen is 4/663.

Example 3:
There are 19 tickets in a bag numbered from 1 to 19. One ticket is drawn and then a second ticket is drawn without replacement. What is the probability that both the tickets will show even number?

Solution: Let A be the event of getting an even number in the first draw and B be the event of getting an even number in the second draw. Since, the second ticket is drawn without replacing the first ticket, the events are dependent.
Total number of tickets = 19
Even numbered tickets = 9
Therefore, Probability of getting an even number in the first draw = 9/19

Number of tickets left = 18
Number of even numbered tickets left = 8
An even numbered card is drawn given that an even numbered card is drawn before.
Therefore, conditional probability of B given that A has occurred is, $P(B|A) = 8/18$
Now, the probability that events A and B occur simultaneously is given by,
$P(A \cap B) = P(A).P(B|A)$
Substituting the respective values, $P(A \cap B) = 9/19 \times 8/18 = 4/19$
Therefore, the probability that both the tickets will show even number is 4/663.

UNIT SUMMARY

This unit started with basic introduction of terms and concepts related to probability and discrete sample spaces. Set operations on events, types of events are discussed with an outline of fundamental rules of probability and conditional probability. Random variables and probability distribution section introduces probability mass function and probability density function. Calculation of mean of a random variable representing the average outcome over many trials. Variance of a Random Variable measures the spread or variability of a random variable around its mean. Bernoulli Trials examines a sequence of independent experiments with two possible outcomes, typically labeled as success and failure. In Conditional Probability and Dependence section explores conditional probability and the concept of dependence between events, where the occurrence of one event affects the probability of another.

Exercises:

1. A skybag carried by a burglar contains 10 red diamonds, 20 blue diamonds and 30 green diamonds. 5 diamonds are drawn from the bag at Hotel Taj,

Find the probability that i) all diamonds drawn will be blue? (ii) atleast one diamond drawn will be green?

2. Assume that there are three blind persons but they can listen and write well. Three letters are dictated to them and an envelope is addressed to each of them, the letters are inserted into the envelopes at random so that each envelope contains exactly one letter. Find the probability that at least one letter is in its proper envelope.

3. There is a skybag suitcase having 4 wheels in the number lock. Each wheel has 0 to 9 labels so ten digit. With a sequence of four digits the lock opens but there shouldn't be any repeats. Find the probability of getting the right sequence to open the lock of the suitcase.

4. The five teams by name alpha, beta, gama, delta and eta went on a relay race. a) with what probability alpha, beta and gama can finish first, second and third respectively. b) with what probability alpha, beta and gama are first three to finish may be in any order, it does not matters, but all finishing orders are equally likely.

5. There are four cities for which shruthi wish to travel for her vacations in random. If the four cities are named as P, Q, R and S then find the probability that she visits (i) P before Q? (ii) P before Q and Q before R? (iii) P first and Q last? (iv) P either first or second? (v) P just before Q?

6. The result of a qualifying exam is based on the result of two other exams. If a student is chosen at random, the probability that he pass the first exam is 0.8 and passing the second exam is 0.7. i) find the probability of passing atleast one of the exams. ii) Find the probability of passing both the exams.

7. A student will be eligible for the certificate if he qualifies both ML and AI courses. The probability that he pass both courses is 0.5, and passing neither of them is 0.1. If probability of passing ML is 0.75 then find the probability of passing AI course.

8. Two students Neetu and Nivedita appeared for the courses described in question number 7. Neetu will qualify courses with probability 0.05 and Nivedita will qualify with 0.10. the probability that both will qualify the courses is 0.02. then find the probability of the following. i) both Neetu and

Nivedita will not qualify the courses and won't be eligible for certification
ii) Atleast one of them will not qualify the examination.

KNOW MORE

- Khan Academy offers a comprehensive set of tutorials covering probability concepts, including basic probability, permutations, combinations, conditional probability, and more. https://www.khanacademy.org/math/probability
- Coursera offers a specialization in Probability and Statistics, which covers probability theory along with statistical methods. https://www.coursera.org/specializations/probability-statistics
- Wolfram MathWorld provides an extensive encyclopedia entry on probability theory, covering definitions, formulas, theorems, and applications. https://mathworld.wolfram.com/topics/ Probability.html
- The Probability Web is a collection of resources for probability theory and stochastic processes, including textbooks, lecture notes, and online courses. http://www.probabilityweb.org/

REFERENCES AND SUGGESTED READINGS

a. Liu, C. L., & Mohapatra, D. P. (2008). Elements of Discrete Mathematics. Tata McGraw-Hill.
b. Rosen, K. H. (2019). Discrete Mathematics and Its Applications. (8th Edition) ISBN10: 125967651X ISBN13: 9781259676512.
c. Cohen, D. I. A. (1978). Basic techniques of combinatorial theory. John Wiley.
d. Norman L. Biggs, Discrete Mathematics, (2nd ed. 2002), Oxford University Press.
e. Smullyan, R. M. (1995). First-order logic. Courier Corporation.
f. Bóna, M. (2006). A walk through combinatorics: an introduction to enumeration and graph theory.
g. Cameron, P. J. (1994). Combinatorics: topics, techniques, algorithms. Cambridge University Press.
h. Herstein, I. N. (2006). Topics in algebra. John Wiley & Sons.

Dynamic QR Code for Further Reading

CO AND PO ATTAINMENT TABLE

Course outcomes (COs) for this course can be mapped with the programme outcomes (POs) after the completion of the course and a correlation can be made for the attainment of POs to analyze the gap. After proper analysis of the gap in the attainment of POs necessary measures can be taken to overcome the gaps.

Course Outcomes	Expected Mapping with Programme Outcomes (1- Weak Correlation; 2- Medium correlation; 3- Strong Correlation)											
	PO1	PO2	PO3	PO4	PO5	PO6	PO7	PO8	PO9	PO10	PO11	PO12
CO1												
CO2												
CO3												
CO4												
CO5												
CO6												
CO7												
CO8												
CO9												

INDEX

A

Abelian Group,374
Antisymmetry,185
Application in Euler's Theorem,319
Applications of GCD,322
Arguments and Argument forms,38
Arithmetic modulo m,316
Arrow Diagram, Pre-Image set,213

B

Basic Properties of Binary Relations,182
Bernoulli Trials,492
Biconditional and Equivalence,26
Bijective Functions,219
Binary Relation as a 0-1 Matrix,192
Binary Relation as a directed Graph,192
Binary Relation as a set,191
Binary relation as a two-place predicate,191
Binary Relations,180
Bipartite Matching,467

C

Cantor's Diagonal Argument,237
Cartesian Product of Sets,177
Cauchy notation for representing Permutation,379
Chinese Remainder Theorem,325
Chromatic Number,455
Circuit,435
Combinations,334
Complement of a set,168
Composite Functions,223
Compound Predicates,90
Compound Propositions,7
Conditional and Common Phrases,22
Conditional in terms of Disjunction,19
Conditional Probability and Dependence,494
Conditional Probability,482
Congruence Relation,315
Congruences of Sums and Products,316
Conjunction,10
Conjunctive Simplification,65
Contrapositive of Conditional,20
Coprimality and Euler's Totient Function,317
Corollaries of Lagrange's Theorem,400
Cosets and Normal Subgroups,395
Countable and Uncountable Sets,227
Connected Components,432

D

Definition of Isomorphic Structures,392
Definition of Partial Order,194
Describing sets as a list,144
Describing sets by properties,149
Dirac's Theorem,452
Direct Proof (Forward Proof),270
Discrete Sample Space,479
Disjunction,9
Disjunctive Amplification,66
Disjunctive Syllogism,64
Disproof by a Counter Example,293
Divisibility,312
Division Algorithm,312

E

Edge Coloring,454
Equality of sets ,147
Equivalence Relation,201
Equivalence,12
Equivalences from Equivalent Propositions,114
Equivalences,201
Euler and Hamilton Paths,449
Euler Circuit Theorem,450
Euler Paths,449
Euler Theorem,402
Examples of Non-Functions,215
Existential Generalization ,120
Existential Instantiation,120
Extended Euclidean Algorithm,323

F
Fermat's Little Theorem,407
Functions,209
Fundamental Theorem of Arithmetic,315
Fundamentals of Graphs,425

G
GCD and Extended Euclidean Algorithm,321
GCD,321
Generating Functions,341
Graph Coloring,453
Graph Planarity ,456
Graph Representation of Function,215
Graph Terminology,425
Group,369

H
Hamilton Circuit,451
Hamilton Path,451
Hasse Diagrams,195
Homomorphism,359

I
Implication,46
Inclusion Exclusion Principle,336
Indirect Proof (Contrapositive Proof),272
Inference Rules,50
Instantiation,88
Interchanging Quantifiers of different types,108
Interchanging Quantifiers of the same type,104
Intersection of two sets,166
Inverse Functions,221
Inverse of Conditional and Inverse Error,21
Isomorphic Structures,392
Isomorphism,363

L
Lagrange's Theorem,398
Law of Syllogism,55
Laws of Logic,14
Limits of Computing,242

M
Matching,461
Maximal and Greatest Elements,199
Maximal Matching,463
Maximum Matching,463
Mean of a Random Variable,489
Membership Table,156
Minimal and Least Elements,197
Modeling using one-place Predicates,96
Modeling Using the Quantifiers ,105
Modeling using two placc predicates,104
Modular Arithmetic Operations,308
Modular Arithmetic,307
Modus Ponens,51
Modus Tollens,59
More than One Connected Component,433

N
Necessity and Sufficiency,292
Necessity,291
Negated Quantifiers,101
Negation,8
Non-commutativity of Conditional,18
Non-commutativity of Converse Error,18
Notion of Abstract Function,210

O
One Connected Component,433
One-to-one Functions: Injections,219
Onto Functions: Surjections,220
Ore's Theorem,452

P
Partial Orderings,194
Partition of a set,204
Path, Cycle and Trees,434
Path,436
Perfect Matching,464
Permutation Group and Cayley Theorem,376
Permutations,333
Pigeon hole Principle,339
PMF and PDF,487
Poset, Linearly ordered set and Wellordered set,200
Power set Theorem,240
Power Set,158

Pragmatics and Semantics ,125
Predicate Logic,90
Predicates,85
Primes,313
Principle of Mathematical Induction,298
Proof by Contradiction,273
Proof by Contradiction,68
Proof by Exhaustive Cases,296
Proof by Necessity and Sufficiency,291
Proof Methods and Strategies ,263
Proofs using Inference Rules,77
Properties of Congruences,308
Properties of Euler's Totient Function,318
Properties of Modular Arithmetic ,310
Propositional Expressions and their Evaluation,34
Propositional Expressions,37
Propositions,6

Q

Quantification,92

R

Random Variables and Probability Distribution,484
Reading the symbol of permutation,381
Recasting the statements,271
Recurrence Relation,344
Reflexivity,182
Region Coloring,454
Replacement Rule,31
Representation of Binary Relations,191
Review of Arithmetic Expressions,34
Revisit to Homomorphic Structures,392
Rings, Fields and Finite Fields,412
Rule of Conjunction,63
Rules of Probability,482

S

Semigroup,353
Set Difference,169
Soundness, Consistency and Completeness,130
Subgroup,390
Subset as a relationship amongst two sets,153
Subset Relationship,153
Sufficiency,292
Symmetry,183

T

Tautology Generation Rule (TGR) ,33
Tautology, Contradiction and Contingency,14
Theorem on Congruences,316
Theorems relating Equivalences and Partitions,204
Trail,435
Transitivity,188
Trees,447
Truth table for Compound Proposition,11
Types of Events,482
Types of graphs,437
Theorem on Congruences,303
Theorems relating Equivalences and Partitions,
Trail,418
Transitivity,182
Trees,432
Truth table for Compound Proposition,11
Two useful rules,31
Types of Events,470
Types of graphs,431

U

Union of two sets,163
Universal Generalization,119
Universal Instantiation ,118
Universal Set and Definition of set,144
Unless, Else, Otherwise,25

V

Valid and Invalid Argument forms,39
Variance of a Random Variable,491
Venn Diagram for subset relation,154
Vertex Coloring,454

W

Walk,434
Well Formed Formulae(WFF) in Predicate Logic,127
WFF in Predicate Logic,129